SPECIAL EDITION

USING

Macromedia®

Flash™ MX

Michael Hurwicz, Laura McCabe, et al.

201 W. 103rd Street
Indianapolis, Indiana 46290

SPECIAL EDITION USING MACROMEDIA FLASH MX

International Standard Book Number: 0-7897-2762-5

Library of Congress Catalog Card Number: 2002105210

Printed in the United States of America

First Printing: August 2002

05   04   03   02   4   3   2   1

Trademarks

Warning and Disclaimer

Associate Publisher
David Culverwell

Executive Editor
Candace Hall

Acquisitions Editor
Kate Small

Development Editor
Susan Hobbs

Managing Editor
Thomas F. Hayes

Project Editor
Carol L. Bowers

Copy Editor
Chuck Hutchinson

Indexer
Mandie Frank

Proofreader
Jessica McCarty

Technical Editor
Lynn Baus

Team Coordinator
Cindy Teeters

Multimedia Developer
Michael Hunter

Interior Designer
Anne Jones

Cover Designer
Anne Jones

Page Layout
Cheryl Lynch

Graphics
Stephen Adams
Tammy Graham
Oliver L. Jackson, Jr.
Laura Robbins

Contents at a Glance

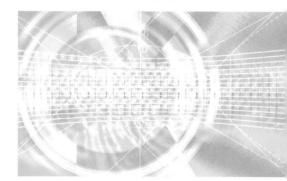

CONTENTS

ABOUT THE AUTHORS

Michael Hurwicz is the Flash Guy at Late Night Design, located at the intersection of art, design, and technology. He has been writing about technical topics for the computer trade press since 1985. Michael is president of Irthlingz, a nonprofit organization dedicated to environmental education and entertainment. You can e-mail Michael at `michael@hurwicz.com` as well as visit his Web site at `http://www.latenightdesign.com`, `http://www.hurwicz.com`, and `http://www.irthlingz.com`.

Laura McCabe is a freelance designer and developer currently living in Baltimore, Maryland. Her eclectic interests have led her through an undergraduate degree in psychology, graduate studies in art and design, and, ultimately, to Flash. In six years of Internet experience, she's honed her skills in design, development, information architecture, and Web production while working with clients such as AARP. Her Flash designs have been featured at the collaborative site Poems That Go, and her personal playground is `http://www.stolenglance.com`. In her spare time, she is a photographer, writer, trainer, editor, sporadic sea kayaker, and recovering book junkie.

Contributors

Lon Coley (`LonColey@ariadne-webdesign.co.uk`) is an IT professional, specializing in Office and Internet applications. Her company site at `http://www.ariadne-webdesign.co.uk` holds far more information than we could put here and is updated as often as time allows. Her experience and expertise means that as well as designing sites for clients, she now acts as a consultant and troubleshooter to companies of all sizes that are looking to improve and develop their Internet presence or that have sites they feel don't do their organization justice. A firm believer that anyone can build a Web site with the right tools and training, Lon often works with companies that want to develop their own Web sites but feel they need an expert "to call on" when they are struggling, or need professional guidance about new technologies when developing their existing sites. An experienced teacher and trainer, Lon writes and develops dedicated customized training courses for business and education. These courses cover the whole spectrum of her expertise and are always prepared with the individual client in mind, thus guaranteeing that the needs of the client are addressed and met in full.

Gary Rosenzweig is the chief engineer, founder, and owner of CleverMedia, a game and multimedia development company in Denver, Colorado. He has written titles on Macromedia Director and Macromedia Flash. Several years ago, Gary started his own company, CleverMedia. Today, CleverMedia owns four of the largest Shockwave and Flash game sites on the Web and creates games for many of the others. Gary lives in Denver, Colorado, with wife Debby, a cat named Lucy, and a dog named Natasha. Other than computers and the Internet, he also enjoys film, camping, classic science fiction books, and writing.

DEDICATION

To Mom and Dad, for always being there.

—Michael Hurwicz

This book is dedicated to Mom and Dad, for their constant encouragement and enthusiasm.

—Laura McCabe

ACKNOWLEDGMENTS

Michael's Acknowledgments

Thank you, thank you, thank you, thank you to:

Kate Small, Susan Hobbs, Carol Bowers, Chuck Hutchinson, and Lynn Baus for editing, shepherding, and tirelessly finding and correcting my mistakes, blunders, and omissions. Chuck went well beyond copyediting, catching a number of substantive errors.

My most excellent agent, David Fugate at Waterside Productions, for making and fostering the connection with Que.

Ralf Bokelberg (`http://www.QLOD.com`) for oxo.fla (Chapter 13), also used as a basis for tictactoe_lc.fla and player_lc.fla in Chapter 20.

Adam Holden-Bache and Mark Lewis, CEO and CTO, respectively, of Mass Transmit (`http://www.masstransmit.com`), for dropdownmenu.fla in the "At Work" section in Chapter 14.

Robin Debreuil (`http://www.debreuil.com`) for MovieClass.fla (Chapter 16), the "double pane" analogy in Chapter 15, and helping me understand OOP.

Gary Grossman, principal engineer, Macromedia Flash team, for the `makeHandler()` function in Chapter 15.

Helen Triolo (`http://i-Technica.com`) for dynamicButtonMovie.fla in Chapter 16 and trigdemo.fla in Chapter 19.

Peter Hall (`http://www.peterjoel.com`) for scratch.fla in Chapter 17 and saveDrawing.fla in Chapter 18.

Andy Hall (`ahall@panache.co.uk`) for spacelisten.fla in Chapter 17 and `curveTo()` in Chapter 18.

Ric Ewing (`rewing@riverdeep.net`) for drawmethods.fla and 4SegCircle.fla in Chapter 18, and for general support and assistance on the drawing API.

Keith Peters (`kp@bit-101.com`, `www.bit-101.com`) for 3Dcube.fla and test5.fla in Chapter 18.

Millie Maruani (`millie@noos.fr`, `http://millie.free.fr`) for api_flower.fla and api_cube.fla in Chapter 18.

Fotios Bassayiannis (`http://fotios.cc`) for amazingArrays.fla in the "At Work" section in Chapter 19.

Robert Penner (`robertpenner@yahoo.com`, `www.robertpenner.com`) for superCon() (same as mySuper()) in Chapter 21.

Laura's Acknowledgments

Many thanks to everyone who helped make my part in this book possible: Tracy Kelly and Chrissy Rey; Sigrid Trumpy for the video clip included in Chapter 10; the online Flash community for constant inspiration and support; Fran and Bob Knisley for their support and fine accommodations; Mom and Charlotte McEnhill for always being there; Horatio at MacWarehouse for exceptional service when my hard disk died; and, most importantly, Kate Small, Lynn Baus, and the fantastic team at Que that includes Susan Hobbs, Carol Bowers, and Chuck Hutchinson.

WE WANT TO HEAR FROM YOU!

As the reader of this book, *you* are our most important critic and commentator. We value your opinion and want to know what we're doing right, what we could do better, what areas you'd like to see us publish in, and any other words of wisdom you're willing to pass our way.

As an associate publisher for Que Publishing, I welcome your comments. You can e-mail or write me directly to let me know what you did or didn't like about this book—as well as what we can do to make our books better.

Please note that I cannot help you with technical problems related to the *topic* of this book. We do have a User Services group, however, where I will forward specific technical questions related to the book.

When you write, please be sure to include this book's title and author as well as your name, e-mail address, and phone number. I will carefully review your comments and share them with the author and editors who worked on the book.

E-mail: feedback@quepublishing.com
Mail: David Culverwell
              Associate Publisher
              Que Publishing
              201 West 103rd Street
              Indianapolis, IN 46290 USA

For more information about this book or another Que title, visit our Web site at www.quepublishing.com. Type the ISBN (excluding hyphens) or the title of a book in the Search field to find the page you're looking for.

INTRODUCTION

Macromedia Flash MX is the latest version of the dominant authoring tool for the Flash Player plug-in, which has become the most widely installed browser plug-in, available in one version or another to 98% of Web users.

Flash started, in 1996, as a tool for creating interactive vector-based animation for the Web. The ability to create vector-based animations that load quickly and still provide sophisticated interactivity is still a core strength of Flash.

At the same time, over the years, and especially with Flash MX, Flash has become a broad-ranging tool that offers database access, XML support, integrated video and audio, prebuilt templates, drag-and-drop components, and access to application servers and real-time communication servers—all under the control of Flash's powerful JavaScript-like scripting language, ActionScript.

Most Flash development teams are now divided into people dedicated to ActionScript and people dedicated to graphical content. Database access/dynamic content is a specialty in itself, as is Flash development for PDAs. Flash has become such a rich environment that it is a rare individual indeed who can even begin to embrace all its possibilities.

At the same time, Macromedia is creating a whole family of MX-branded products under the "Macromedia Studio MX" umbrella. This includes long-standing products that have been rebranded as Dreamweaver MX, Fireworks MX, and ColdFusion MX. It also includes the brand-new streaming video and audio server, Flash Communication Server. Macromedia wants to provide both the tools and platforms to build the next generation of media-rich applications based on Web services.

SO, WHAT ELSE IS NEW?

In addition to its increased breadth, Flash MX offers increased depth with features that enhance existing capabilities. Important enhancements include the following:

- Folders for organizing timeline layers
- New controls above the Stage that make it easier to edit symbols in place
- Shared Library assets
- Color Mixer improvements
- Pixel-level editing
- A "distribute to layers" command that enables you to automatically distribute any number of selected objects to their own layers
- Animated masks
- Enhanced sound controls
- A Free Transform tool that allows you to perform multiple transformations such as moving, rotating, scaling, skewing, and envelope distortion without changing tools

The GUI for the authoring environment has also been radically redesigned, with collapsible, dockable panels that conserve screen real estate, as well as a new Property Inspector that eliminates the need to access many other windows, panels, and dialog boxes.

ActionScript enhancements include the following:

- The ability to dynamically load JPEG and MP3 files
- Anchor points that enable users to use the Forward and Back buttons in their browsers to jump from anchor to anchor
- Code hints that provide command syntax at appropriate times
- Reusable drag-and-drop interface components
- Live preview for components
- An improved debugger
- A more complete object model and event model
- Enhanced support for text boxes and text formatting
- A drawing API that offers all the functionality of the Flash drawing tools
- Faster XML functionality

WHO SHOULD READ THIS BOOK?

Part I, "Flash Environment and Tools," assumes that you are a total beginner who has never used Flash before. Throughout, this book explains concepts and techniques completely, never assuming that you know something about Flash before it is covered in the book.

At the same time, this book assumes that your goal is to become a highly proficient, professional Flash practitioner. It does not hesitate to cover intermediate and advanced topics in depth.

Starting at the beginning, not skipping anything, and still getting deeply into advanced topics means packing as much useful information into each page as possible. Therefore, this book often does not walk you step-by-step through basic tasks. It assumes you are a motivated learner, willing to jump in and experiment.

HOW TO USE THIS BOOK

You can read this book from cover to cover or use it as a random-access reference. Later chapters may assume familiarity with earlier chapters, however. First-time users will probably do well to dive into Flash and play a little bit before starting the book. Realistically, you will probably use this book largely as a reference, to help you solve problems as they arise. On the other hand, Flash MX has so many new features that even experienced Flash users should consider at least skimming the book from beginning to end, looking for the "New in Flash MX" icon.

Where there are sample files on the CD to accompany the text, be sure to look at them, and try playing with them and modifying them. The hands-on experience will prove invaluable, and you may even be able to use a file as a partial basis for your own project.

Also, be sure to check out the many excellent Web resources for Flash developers. If you need a jumping-off place, you can try Michael Hurwicz's site, `http://www.flashoop.com`. Also listed there are several Flash mailing lists, where you can get expert help on any Flash-related topic.

This book is divided into six parts:

   I. Flash Environment and Tools

  II. Animation and Sound

 III. Adding Advanced Interactivity with ActionScript

 IV. Advanced ActionScripting

  V. External Communication with Flash

 VI. Output Options for Flash

Part I (Chapters 1–5) and Part II (Chapters 6–10) focus on using the authoring environment's GUI and on design-oriented functions that require little or no ActionScript.

Part III (Chapters 11–18), Part IV (Chapters 19–25), and Part V (Chapters 26–28) constitute a complete ActionScript user's guide. Part III, "Adding Advanced Interactivity with ActionScript," takes you from the elementary concepts of ActionScript into a number of core features including functions, events, and the drawing API. Part IV, "Advanced ActionScripting," is a guide to working with built-in and custom objects, as well as components, learning interactions, Shared Libraries, and the Flash debugger. Chapter 20, "Using the Built-In Movie Objects," contains some material relating to the Flash Communication Server, as well as the Video, Microphone, and Camera objects. Part V, "External Communication with Flash," covers both communication with the client computer and with servers, including XML-based interaction.

Finally, Part VI (Chapters 29 and 30), "Output Options for Flash," covers output options such as printing, publishing, and exporting Flash files.

CONVENTIONS USED IN THIS BOOK

A monospace font is used to differentiate ActionScript keywords from any other text with special emphasis. For example, you will see the gotoAndPlay() method and the #initclip compiler directive.

In ActionScript code, italicized words are not literal ActionScript but placeholders for actual ActionScript that you will substitute. For example, in Key.isDown(*charCode*), *charCode* is a place-holder for a character code that you will substitute. Key.isDown(Key.UP) is actual ActionScript, in which Key.UP represents the actual character code.

A common ActionScript convention, often used in this book, is to start object names with my when they represent new instances created by the programmer. For instance, TextField represents the built-in class of text fields, not created by the programmer. On the other hand, myTextField is a new text field instance created by the programmer.

At the end of most chapters, you'll find two sections: "Troubleshooting" and "Flash at Work." If you run into problems, don't forget to check out the "Troubleshooting" section, where some of the most common problems are addressed.

Pay particular attention to the examples in the "Flash at Work" sections. These sections include examples, often based on real-world projects, and frequently provide line-by-line explanations of how the program works. There's nothing like seeing a feature at work in a real-world application to give you a feeling for what the feature is really all about.

FLASH ENVIRONMENT AND TOOLS

IN THIS PART

WHAT'S NEW IN FLASH MX

IN THIS CHAPTER

INTERFACE IMPROVEMENTS

Macromedia Flash MX is an impressive leap beyond Flash 5. Improvements and refinements have been made in nearly every area of MX. Plus, you'll find exciting new features such as video support, User Interface (UI) Components, programmatic drawing, and scriptable masks.

From the moment you launch MX, you'll know things have changed. The interface has been streamlined and refined, making it much more usable and intuitive.

Panel Sets

The new MX panel sets work in tandem to save space and organize your workspace. You can collapse the new panels and dock and arrange them to your liking. This capability allows for a tremendous degree of customization. You can even keep most panels at the ready on the desktop, collapsed until you need them. Even the Library and Movie Explorer can be combined with other panels.

The Property Inspector

The most obvious and efficient new interface feature is the Property Inspector. Borrowed from Dreamweaver, this feature consolidates object properties in a central location. Select an object or tool, and the Property Inspector displays the pertinent properties and settings, as shown in Figure 1.1. The Property Inspector has replaced the Flash 5 Stroke, Fill, Text, Paragraph, Character, Instance, Frame, Effect, and Sound panels. Select a movie clip on the Stage, for example, and instance naming, symbol behaviors, coordinates, dimensions, color effects, and the capability to swap symbols are all available in the Property Inspector. It's nearly one-stop shopping, especially when compared to Flash 5, and it allows you to work much more quickly and efficiently.

Figure 1.1
The new Property Inspector is context sensitive and displays settings that are pertinent to selected objects or tools.

New Tools and Menu Items

Flash MX also features new tools and menu items to facilitate design and animation. New design tools include the Free Transform tool in the Toolbox, Break Apart and Distribute to Layers commands in the Modify menu, and Pixel Snapping in the View menu. Layer folders, which function like Library folders, are available help to organize the Timeline and conserve screen real estate. Prebuilt templates provide content creation guidelines for broadcast ads, presentations, quizzes, slide shows, and even content for portable devices.

The Free Transform Tool

The new Free Transform tool offers more control over selections. The Edit Envelope and Distort modifiers make much more complex transformation effects possible, including skewing, perspective, and distortion.

Break Apart and Distribute to Layers

In Flash 5, the Break Apart command automatically converted text blocks into shapes. In MX, Break Apart—accessed by choosing Modify, Break Apart —now offers a much-needed intermediate step and first breaks up a text block into separate letters, as shown in Figure 1.2. You can still use Break Apart to convert text blocks to shapes, but must select it twice—once to convert to letters and again to convert to shapes.

WE THE PEOPLE, IN ORDER TO FORM

Figure 1.2
Break Apart now breaks up a text block into separate letters.

Objects must be on separate layers to be individually animated. The Distribute to Layers command takes multiple objects on a layer and distributes them to separate layers. As an added bonus, new layers are automatically named for any symbols that are selected and distributed. Simply select multiple objects on the Stage and choose Modify, Distribute to Layers. Combine the Break Apart and Distribute to Layers commands and, in two steps, you can break text blocks into letters and distribute them to their own layers that can be animated separately. These features take much of the grunt work out of animation.

Snap to Pixels

Snap to Pixels provides pixel-level control of object placement, and is a long overdue positioning option in Flash. A bane of any Flash designer's life has been the way Flash places objects, and text in particular, not only on whole pixels, or integers, but also on floating points, or pixel fractions. Flash utilizes floating points to ensure smooth rendering of vector graphics, which are mathematically derived and not pixel-based. Floating points, however, work too well and can smooth thin lines, such as text, until they appear blurry. Bitmaps and bitmap fonts, which are mapped to whole pixels, also display incorrectly when placed on floating points. In Flash 5, you had to constantly ensure that objects were placed squarely on integers. The Snap to Pixels option finally allows precise integer alignment, as shown in Figure 1.3. Simply choose View, Snap to Pixels to enable pixel snapping.

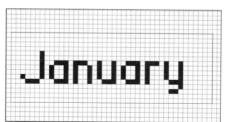

Figure 1.3
Snap to Pixel ensures that objects are precisely aligned to exact pixel coordinates.

⇨ *For more information about Flash's vector format, see Chapter 3, "Drawing and Painting in Flash," page 37. To learn more about bitmaps, see Chapter 4, "Using Bitmaps in Flash," page 55, and Chapter 5, "Working with Text," page 69, for more information about bitmap fonts.*

Layer Folders

The new Timeline folders are another space-saver and a boon to organization and workflow as well. Layers multiply dramatically over the course of a project. There is nothing like trying to scroll through 50 layers in search of a movie clip. Now you can group layers into folders and minimize or expand them as needed. This capability results in tremendous savings in screen real estate, enabling you to maximize the stage, and allows for greater organization of projects than was previously possible. Layers with buttons, for example, can be grouped in a "Buttons" folder. Workflow can be streamlined because it is much easier, even for someone unfamiliar with a project, to locate objects and code on the Timeline.

Templates

MX ships with several predefined templates for specialized content, such as mobile devices, broadcast ads, and presentations, as shown in Figure 1.4. Just add your own text and graphics, and the functionality is taken care of for you.

Figure 1.4
MX features predefined templates for specialized content as well as common navigation elements.

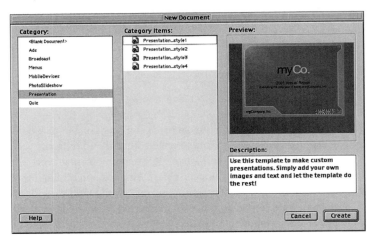

The ad templates come with a guide layer and usage guidelines, as shown in Figure 1.5. You can also create templates with locked content for clients so that they can make minor updates and changes. To access the templates, choose File, New from Template.

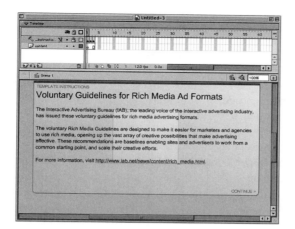

Figure 1.5
The ad templates include usage guidelines for commonly used ad formats.

COMPONENTS

Flash 5 introduced the concept of Smart Clips, reusable movie clips with prebuilt functionality and customizable parameters. Smart Clip functionality has been enhanced and fully integrated into MX, and is now known as *components*. The Components panel, as shown in Figure 1.6, is a library of commonly used interface elements, such as scrollbars and check boxes. With these elements at your fingertips, you can drag and drop functionality, such as a scrollbar onto a text field, as shown in Figure 1.6. After you add a component to a movie, you can easily customize the preset scripting parameters. Macromedia has already released two new component sets since MX was released; they feature interface elements such as tree menus, progress bars, and calendars. Many more components currently being developed promise to make advanced authoring even easier.

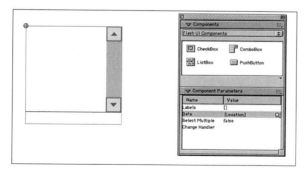

Figure 1.6
UI Components allow you to drag and drop functional, common interface elements.

To learn how to use components, see Chapter 9, "Buttons, Menus, and User Input," page 143. To learn how to create custom components, see Chapter 22, "Components," page 511.

VIDEO SUPPORT

Flash 5 did not offer true video support; video could only be imported as a series of static images or exported to QuickTime. MX fully supports embedded video, creating a seamless experience that does not require external players. You can import video in multiple formats and, with the inclusion of the Sorenson Spark codec (video encoder and decoder), shown in Figure 1.7, you can embed video directly into SWF files. Imported video can be manipulated—rotated, scaled, skewed, masked, and animated—much like other assets, and can also be controlled with ActionScript. Sorenson Spark provides truly impressive compression of large video files. To import video files and access Sorenson Spark, choose File, Import and navigate to a video file on your computer. Compression is applied when your Flash movie is exported.

Figure 1.7
The new Sorenson Spark codec produces higher quality video at smaller sizes and allows you to embed video directly in SWFs.

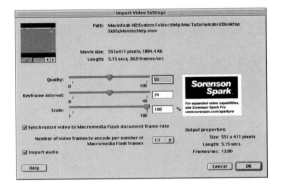

SCRIPTING IMPROVEMENTS

In MX, ActionScript has come into its own as an object-oriented language. The improved object model integrates movie clips, buttons, and text fields, and the event model has been extended, allowing for much more advanced user interaction. These improvements translate into custom movie clip subclasses, clip event handlers with callback functions, and text field control. With MX advancements, Flash is a viable environment for serious application development.

Improved Object and Event Models

Objects within MX have been more tightly integrated. Buttons are now true objects whose properties can be manipulated with ActionScript, and movie clips can receive button events.

As an event-based program, Flash executes code in response to events. In Flash 5 ActionScript, the event handlers that signal code execution remained outside the symbol instances they were accessing and could not be directly changed or disabled during playback. In MX, event handlers are properties of symbols and can even be placed inside symbols so that you can change event handlers at any time.

▷ *For more information about the object and event models, see Chapter 11, "Getting Started with ActionScript," page 169, Chapter 16, "Interaction, Events, and Sequencing," page 303, and Chapter 17, "Unlocking the Power of Movie Clips," page 331.*

Scriptable Masking

In Flash 5, masks could not be modified. Now in MX, movie clips can be masks, which means that masks can be scripted and can even respond to user interaction. This capability opens up a new world of design possibilities. A mask can respond to the user's mouse movements, revealing content as the user moves the mouse pointer over it.

▷ *For more information about scripting masks, see Chapter 17, "Unlocking the Power of Movie Clips," page 331.*

Programmatic Drawing

The new drawing API provides new shape-drawing capabilities via the movie clip object. You can create new movie clips on the fly and use ActionScript to draw shapes from scratch, without graphic assets. That means that an entire graphical interface could be drawn with ActionScript, requiring no premade graphics.

▷ *For more information about programmatic drawing, see Chapter 18, "Drawing with ActionScript," page 367.*

Loading External Images and Sound

Prior to MX, you could not load external images and sounds dynamically. The new MX `loadMovie()` and `loadSound()` functions load JPEG and MP3 files dynamically at runtime via a URL. This means that Flash movies can be much leaner with assets loaded during runtime. Content can also be updated without editing the Flash source files.

▷ *For more information about loading external images and sounds, see Chapter 20, "Using the Built-In Movie Objects," page 443.*

Improved ActionScript Editor

MX interface improvements extend to the ActionScript Editor. Code hints can be displayed while typing, color coding can be customized, and line numbers have been added, as shown in Figure 1.8. The ActionScript Reference panel is bundled with the editor for quick reference. Nonprogrammers will find it much easier to write code.

▷ *For more information about using the ActionScript Editor, see Chapter 11, "Getting Started with ActionScript," page 169.*

Figure 1.8
The improved ActionScript Editor features line numbers and code hints.

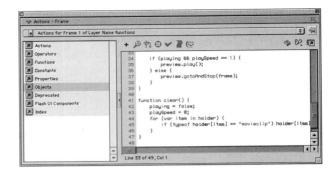

FLASH 5 COMPATIBILITY

Previous versions of Flash have lacked backward compatibility. With MX, you can save your .fla files as Flash 5 documents, as shown in Figure 1.9, and anyone with Flash 5 or MX can open them. This allows you to provide content for users with previous versions of the Flash Player. As you save to Flash 5, you will be warned of any MX-specific content that will be omitted from the saved file.

Figure 1.9
You can save Flash files to Flash 5 format as well as Flash MX.

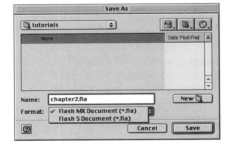

ACCESSIBLE CONTENT

Flash content has been notoriously inaccessible to screen readers used by people with disabilities. MX features a new Accessibility panel, as shown in Figure 1.10, that allows you to add labels and descriptions, much like Alt tags in HTML, to your Flash content so that screen readers and other assistive technologies can convey Flash content.

Figure 1.10
The Accessibility dialog allows you to provide labels and descriptions, making content accessible to screen readers.

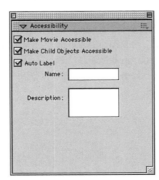

For more information about Flash's accessibility options, see Appendix A, "Making Flash Accessible," page 663.

TROUBLESHOOTING

What happened to Generator?

Flash MX marks a transition away from Generator. Much of Generator's functionality, such as communication with databases via XML, has been incorporated directly into MX. Also, look for upcoming integration with ColdFusion MX and other development platforms.

What happened to the Flash 5 Arrow tool options to rotate and scale?

All the transformation options, including rotate and scale, are now included in the Free Transform tool. Select the Free Transform tool and click an object. You can click and drag a corner point to scale an object or hold the mouse just outside the object until a circle with an arrow appears—the rotate icon—and then click and drag to rotate the object.

THE FLASH INTERFACE

IN THIS CHAPTER

PANEL SETS

The first time you launch Flash MX, you'll notice significant interface improvements. Designers and developers have much more power to customize their working environment and streamline their workflow.

The Flash interface consists of the Stage, the Toolbox, and numerous panels. The placement of these interface elements can be customized to create an individualized working space.

The MX user interface has been greatly streamlined. You can never have too much monitor space when working in Flash (and the minimum resolution has grown from 800×600 to 1024×768), so the new panel sets and Property Inspector have been designed to maximize screen real estate. All the panels can be docked, minimized, or expanded, with the exception of the Timeline and Stage, and the Property Inspector on the Macintosh. If you're on a Mac, you cannot dock any panels to the Timeline and Stage, and the Property Inspector floats on its own. You can dock other panels to the Actions panel, but it also floats on Macs. You can also quickly hide all panels by pressing the Tab key. Press it a second time to restore the panels. Ultimately, the panel sets have the greatest single impact on the overall usability of the MX interface.

The MX panels are

Toolbox	Timeline
Stage	Property Inspector
Align	Color Mixer
Color Swatches	Info
Transform	Actions
Debugger	Movie Explorer
Reference	Output
Accessibility	Components
Component Parameters	Library
Answers	

The Property Inspector

The Property Inspector provides contextual editing options based on the type of object selected, often providing one-stop shopping for object editing. The Flash 5 Stroke, Fill, Text, Paragraph, Character, Instance, Frame, Effect, and Sound panels are completely replaced by the Property Inspector, as shown in Figure 2.1. Unfortunately, the dream is not fully realized. Some attributes still are accessible only in the Options section of the Toolbox, such as Round Rectangle Radius (which draws rectangles with rounded corners), or in other panels. There is also repetition across some panels, such as the fill and stroke settings in the Toolbox, Property Inspector, and Color Mixer. However, the Property Inspector is a great improvement and has helped to nearly eliminate pop-up dialog boxes.

Figure 2.1

The new Property Inspector provides contextual editing options.

Customizing the Panel Layout

To dock panels, drag them by the left corner (below the Close button and beside the title bar; the hand icon appears when you are over the correct spot, as seen in Figure 2.2) onto other panels. To hide a docked panel, drag it by the left corner when the hand icon appears, away from the panels it's docked with; click its close button in the upper-left corner. When several panels are docked, only the top-most panel has a close button, and clicking that close button hides *all* those docked panels.

MX comes with default panel sets, which you can access by choosing Window, Panel Sets. There is a generic Default set, plus Designer and Developer sets in a range of resolutions. Most importantly, you can save your own panel sets. Just create your desired sets and then choose Window, Save Panel Layout.

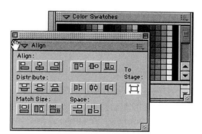

Figure 2.2

To dock a panel, click beside the panel title, and a hand icon will appear. Drag and release on top of another panel.

SETTING DOCUMENT ATTRIBUTES

You can now access document attributes, formerly known as movie properties, from the Property Inspector or by choosing Modify, Document. The Property Inspector shows the Document attributes by default when a new movie is created, or you can access them by clicking on the Stage with no other object selected. The Size button launches a mostly redundant Document Attributes pop-up dialog box, where you can specify the Stage dimensions, match settings, background color, frame rate, and ruler units. The Publish button launches the Publish Settings dialog box. The Background color box provides drop-down color swatches to specify the background color of the Stage. The frames per second (fps) specify the speed at which the movie plays; you can enter the speed directly into the Frame Rate field.

THE TIMELINE

As with traditional film, Flash movies unfold over time. The Timeline is mission control for your movie's content, allowing you to organize and control content that is displayed over time in frames and keyframes. The Timeline, shown in Figure 2.3, houses the frames and layers that comprise a movie as well as the playhead that indicates the current frame.

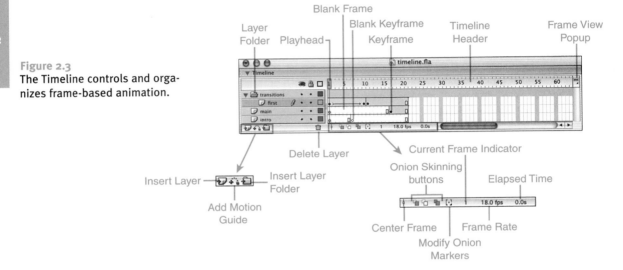

Figure 2.3
The Timeline controls and organizes frame-based animation.

Frames

Frames are discrete, static slices or moments in time that are combined to create movement. Think of old-school flip-book animation. Each page is a static drawing, but when flipped through quickly in a series, the pages create the illusion of movement. Frames allow you to control the sequencing and pace of your movie, and define the overall length. As with film, animations that take place over fewer frames will appear faster in the final movie than those that occur over many frames. To insert frames, choose Insert, Frame or press the keyboard shortcut F5.

Keyframes

Keyframes indicate changes in an animation. Frames store the content of the keyframe that precedes them. It is only when a new keyframe is encountered that the contents of the Stage within a single layer will change.

To insert a keyframe, choose Insert, Keyframe or press keyboard shortcut F6. Any keyframe that follows another keyframe displays the content of the first keyframe, allowing you to make changes to that original content. To add a keyframe that provides you with a blank slate, you must choose Insert, Blank Keyframe or press F7. Keyframes are indicated by filled dots on the Timeline, whereas blank keyframes appear as empty dots.

➡️ *The Timeline, frames, and keyframes are covered in greater depth in Chapter 7, "Animating in Flash," page 109.*

Layers and Layer Folders

Layers enable you to stack content. Think of each layer as an individual strip of film on a piece of clear acetate. Anywhere there is no content within a layer, you can see through that layer to the ones below it. Where there is content, it will obscure the layers below it.

Layers allow you to organize and separate content. You can more easily control content if it is separated into layers. A quirk of Flash is that it merges simple, nongrouped shapes that coexist on a single layer if they intersect. For example, if two red balls on the same layer touch, they become a single object, as shown in Figure 2.4. Separating content into layers also allows you to animate objects individually, creating complex effects. Adding layers does not increase the file size for your published movie, so you can use them as needed to organize your content.

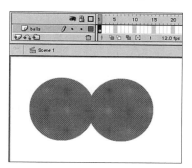

Figure 2.4
Simple, nongrouped shapes on the same layer will merge, forming a single shape, if they intersect.

Flash automatically names layers as they are created and numbers them according to the order in which they are created. Double-click on a layer name, such as Layer 1, on the left side of the Timeline to rename it. Take the time to name your layers well, keeping the names short and descriptive. Well-named layers are signposts that indicate where objects are housed. Large projects can quickly turn into bad road trips as layers multiply, but if you name your layers well, you need never get lost.

The icons to the right of each layer allow you to hide, lock, and show layers as outlines, as shown in Figure 2.5. It's a good idea to lock any layer you aren't currently working with so that you don't inadvertently move content. Option-click (Mac) or Alt+click (Windows) the dot on your layer that's under the lock icon to lock all other layers, or individually click the dots in the lock column to lock and unlock layers. Locked layers display the lock icon. You can also hide layers, using the dots under the eye icon, to see content that is obscured by upper layers. Again, Option-click or Alt+click the visibility dot on any layer to hide all other layers. Hidden layers are represented by red Xs in the left column under the eye icon. You can also display layer content as outlines, which can be helpful when you have many overlapping elements on different layers. The solid square in the right column changes to a square with no fill when a layer is displayed as outlines.

2

Figure 2.5

Layer icons allow you to hide, lock, or show layers as outlines.

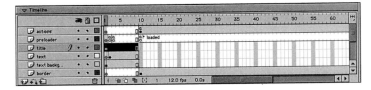

A pencil icon between the layer name and icon columns indicates which layer is currently selected and being edited. Keep in mind that you cannot edit a layer that has been hidden. If you try to edit a hidden layer, the pencil icon appears crossed out, as shown in Figure 2.6.

Figure 2.6

You cannot edit a hidden layer, as shown by the crossed-out current layer icon.

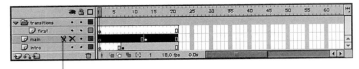

pencil icon crossed out

To rearrange layers, click and drag on a layer name and release it into a new position. You can also Shift+click layers to select more than one layer at a time.

The icons at the bottom of the layers area of the Timeline window enable you to add a new layer, add a guide layer, or insert a layer folder. Guide layers help you to align objects. They can be used for static alignment of elements, such as aligning objects on other layers to objects or custom grids created on guide layers, or can be used as motion guides to align objects along a path as they are moved. You can turn any layer into a guide layer by clicking the Motion Guide Layer icon. Guide layers do not appear in published Flash movies.

Layer folders are a fantastic new MX feature. Now you can group and organize layers into folders. Not only can you more easily find elements in your movies, but you also can save a lot of screen real estate by expanding just the folders containing layers you're currently working with. To place layers in folders, simply drag layers onto folder layers. Click the arrow to the left of folder names to expand and contract layer folders.

Onion Skinning and Multiple Frame Editing

Flash shows only one frame at a time on the Stage. To facilitate alignment, particularly in frame-by-frame animation, you can use onion skinning to display a series of frames simultaneously on the Stage. The onion-skinning buttons are located at the bottom of the Stage and appear as three sets of overlapping squares. The Onion Skin button, as shown in Figure 2.7, displays frames concurrently.

The current frame (beneath the playhead) appears in full color, while the surrounding frames are dimmed and cannot be edited. You can change the number of frames that are visible by dragging the Start Onion Skin and End Onion Skin markers. Moving the playhead changes the current frame and the place where the range of onion-skinned frames begins and ends.

Edit Multiple Frames button

Onion Skin button

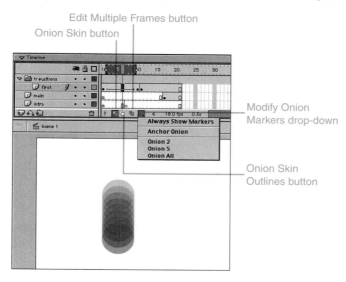

Modify Onion
Markers drop-down

Onion Skin
Outlines button

Figure 2.7
Drag the onion skin markers to display several frames simultaneously.

The Onion Skin Outlines button displays the objects within the range of onion-skinned frames as outlines. To edit all the frames that are onion skinned, select the Edit Multiple Frames button. Finally, there is a Modify Onion Markers button. It is a drop-down with options to anchor markers so that they don't move as the current frame changes. You can also specify a range of frames to onion skin: Onion 2, Onion 5, or Onion All.

THE TOOLBOX

The Toolbox, shown in Figure 2.8, is the home for your Flash power tools. The drawers in this Toolbox are divided into Tools, View, Colors, and Options. Some tools have modifiers, which are displayed in the Options area at the bottom of the Toolbox when those tools are selected.

Tools Section

Selection, drawing, painting, and modifying tools are housed in the Tools section at the top of the Toolbox.

Figure 2.8
The Flash MX Toolbox.

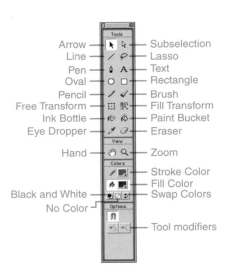

Arrow — Subselection
Line — Lasso
Pen — Text
Oval — Rectangle
Pencil — Brush
Free Transform — Fill Transform
Ink Bottle — Paint Bucket
Eye Dropper — Eraser

Hand — Zoom

Stroke Color
Fill Color
Black and White — Swap Colors
No Color

Tool modifiers

Arrow Tool

You use the Arrow tool to select entire objects in the work area. You can click with the Arrow tool to select an object, draw a marquee to select multiple objects, or double-click to select both the fill and stroke of an object. That's right, clicking a shape that consists of both a stroke and a fill only selects either the stroke or the fill, depending on which is clicked. You will use the Arrow tool more than any other tool, so be sure to memorize its keyboard shortcut, V.

When the Arrow tool is selected, you'll notice that three modifiers are displayed in the Options section at the bottom of the Toolbox. The first, which looks like a magnet, is the Snap to Objects modifier. When it is selected, as it is by default, a black ring appears at the tip of the mouse pointer; this ring gets larger as an object is dragged close enough to another object to snap to it. When all or part of an object is selected on the Stage, the other modifiers, Smooth and Straighten, can be activated. Select a line or part of a shape outline and then click these modifiers to either add points to smooth a shape or remove points to straighten.

Subselection Tool

The Subselection tool selects segments of lines or shape outlines. You also can use it to reveal points on lines and outlines, and then click and drag those points to modify shapes.

Line Tool

Click and drag with the Line tool to draw straight lines. Shift+click to draw perfectly vertical, horizontal, or diagonal lines.

Lasso Tool

Using the Lasso tool, you can make irregularly shaped selections. Think of this tool as corralling awkward areas. Click and drag to draw a freeform selection marquee. The lasso sticks to your mouse until you click again, creating an endpoint.

The Lasso tool has three modifiers. The top two are the Magic Wand and Magic Wand Settings. They allow you to select portions of bitmaps that have been broken apart. Clicking on a bitmap selects pixels according to color range. Continue clicking to add to the selection. The settings include threshold, which determines how sensitive the wand is to color differences in adjacent pixels. Lower numbers result in more precise selections, whereas higher numbers include a broader range of colors. Smoothing determines how much the borders of selections will be smoothed. The last modifier is Polygon mode, which draws lasso selections with straight edges.

Pen Tool

The Pen tool is the most powerful drawing tool. You can harness its power to draw precise paths, with straight or curved segments. Click with the Pen tool to draw straight line segments, or click and drag to draw curved segments.

Text Tool

Clicking with the Text tool creates an insertion point for entering text. Text attributes are assigned in the Property Inspector.

Oval Tool

The Oval tool draws ovals and precise circles. Click and drag to draw an oval, or Shift+drag to draw a perfect circle.

Rectangle Tool

The Rectangle tool draws rectangles and squares. Click and drag to draw a rectangle, or Shift+drag to draw a perfect square. The Round Rectangle Radius modifier for the Rectangle tool allows you to specify a corner radius for rounded corners.

Pencil Tool

Use the Pencil tool to draw rough lines. Unlike the Pen or Line tools, which draw from point to point, the Pencil tool follows the path of the mouse and is the digital equivalent of sketching with a pencil. The Pencil Mode modifier allows you to straighten or smooth paths as you draw.

Brush Tool

The Brush tool simulates brush strokes as you draw. It's the closest to a painting tool in Flash. Its modifiers allow you to select a brush mode, size, and shape and to lock a fill color. The Brush Mode modifier allows you to paint normally over strokes and fills or to protect parts of objects, much like using a stencil. The Paint Fills modifier paints fills and empty sections of the Stage, leaving strokes unchanged. Paint Behind protects objects and paints only empty parts of the Stage. Paint Selection paints just the fill of an object that has been selected on the Stage. Using this approach is an unnecessarily complex way to change a fill, and I strongly suggest that you simply select an object and apply a new fill by using the Fill box in the Property Inspector or in the Color section of the Toolbox. The final Brush Mode modifier is Paint Inside, which allows you to paint roughly over an object and apply the color just to the object's fill, not to the stroke or the Stage.

If you have a pressure-sensitive tablet, the Pressure modifier allows you to vary your brush stroke according to differences in how hard you press as you draw. The harder you press, the wider the stroke.

Free Transform Tool

The Free Transform tool is new in Flash MX. It allows you to apply transformations individually or in combination to objects, groups, instances, and text blocks. Just select an object on the Stage and click the Free Transform tool. A bounding box appears around your selected object and, as you move your mouse around, the various transform methods are indicated by changes in the pointer.

The modifiers include Rotate and Skew, Scale, and two that are new to MX: Distort and Envelope. Distort simulates perspective by allowing you to click and drag the corner or edge handles on the bounding box, realigning the adjoining edges, as shown in Figure 2.9.

Figure 2.9
The Distort modifier reshapes and realigns shapes, simulating perspective.

As you can see in Figure 2.10, Envelope lets you warp and distort selected objects. Selections are contained within a so-called envelope, and you can pull or push Bezier handles to warp the envelope contents. You can even convert the warping into individual keyframes so that it occurs incrementally over time.

Figure 2. 10
The Envelope modifier warps and distorts objects.

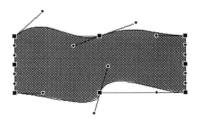

Fill Transform Tool

In addition to solid colors, gradients and even bitmaps can be used as fills. The Fill Transform tool allows you to adjust gradient and bitmap fills. When you click on a gradient or bitmap fill, the bounding box and center of the fill are indicated by circles and boxes that can be dragged. If you hold the pointer over one of these handles, the pointer changes to indicate your editing options. You can reshape, rotate, scale, and skew bitmaps and gradients. You can even tile a bitmap fill.

Ink Bottle Tool

You use the Ink Bottle tool to modify an existing stroke. When you use this tool in conjunction with the Property Inspector, you can edit stroke color, thickness, and style. You also can change any of these settings and click an existing stroke to implement changes.

Paint Bucket Tool

The Paint Bucket tool modifies existing fills. Like you do with the Ink Bottle, you can use the Paint Bucket in conjunction with Property Inspector to edit fills. You can change the fill in either the Property Inspector or the Fill Color box within the Toolbox and click with the Paint Bucket tool to implement changes.

Eyedropper Tool

The Eyedropper tool allows you to copy stroke or fill attributes from one object and immediately apply them to another object. You can also use it to select a bitmap to be used as a fill. Click with the Eyedropper on a stroke or fill that you want to copy. The Eyedropper immediately changes to the Ink Bottle or Paint Bucket, depending on whether a stroke or fill has been selected. If you click on another object, its fill or stroke will be transformed to that of the first object.

Eraser Tool

Using the Eraser tool, you can erase objects in whole or part on the Stage. Simply dragging the Eraser tool erases everything along its path. The Eraser Mode modifiers allow you to specify parameters, such as strokes and fills on the same layer (Erase Normal), fills only (Erase Fills), strokes only (Erase Strokes), only fills that have been selected (Erase Selected Fills), or only fills that you have begun to erase (Erase Inside). The Faucet modifier removes strokes or fills in their entirety with a single click. The Eraser Shape modifier specifies a shape and size for the Eraser.

View Section

You can view and navigate the Stage area by using the viewing tools: the Hand tool and the Zoom tool. The actual size of your movie comprises a small portion of the work area canvas. The Zoom tool allows you to zoom in or out of parts of the Stage. Click on the Zoom tool, or use the keyboard shortcut M or Z, and then click on the Stage or drag a selection box around portions you want to magnify. To zoom out, Option-click (Mac) or Alt+click (Windows) with the Zoom tool.

The Hand tool allows you to navigate the work area. Click on the Hand tool or press the spacebar to use the Hand tool temporarily while using another tool. Typically, when you zoom in on an object, you'll find it necessary to recenter the stage over that object. With the Zoom tool still selected, simply press the spacebar and drag to recenter the Stage. The cursor changes to a hand shape, and you can click and drag the Stage within the work area. Stop pressing the spacebar, and you'll return to the previously selected tool.

> **Caution**
>
> The Faucet modifier has an irregular shape. The drop of water, *not* the faucet itself, makes selections. When you're working with small objects, position the drop of water over what you want to select.

Colors Section

Using the Colors section of the Toolbar, you can set stroke and fill colors. If nothing is selected on the Stage, clicking in the Stroke or Fill boxes defines colors for shapes that will be drawn. If any objects are selected, changing the fill and stroke colors in the Toolbox will change the attributes of those objects.

Just below the Fill and Stroke boxes are three buttons. The Black and White button changes the color settings to the default black stroke and white fill. The No Color button applies either no stroke or no fill, depending on which box is selected. The Swap Colors button swaps the selected stroke and fill colors.

KEYBOARD SHORTCUTS

MX provides keyboard shortcuts for many panel and menu commands. They can save you a lot of time, so you should take the time to memorize the most frequently used shortcuts.

Table 2.1 lists the keyboard shortcuts for the tools. They are so frequently used that they consist of a single key.

Table 2.1   Toolbox Shortcuts

Tool	Keyboard Shortcut
Arrow tool	V
Subselection tool	A
Line tool	N
Lasso tool	L
Pen tool	P
Text tool	T

Tool	Keyboard Shortcut
Free Transform tool	Q
Fill Transform tool	F
Ink Bottle tool	S
Paint Bucket tool	K
Eyedropper tool	I
Eraser tool	E
Hand tool	H
Zoom tool	M, Z

Shortcuts to access the panels are shown in Table 2.2. These shortcuts act as toggles, so you use the shortcuts once to launch a panel and a second time to hide the panel.

Table 2.2   Panel Shortcuts

Panel	Mac	Windows
Tools	Cmd-F2	Ctrl+F2
Timeline	Option-Cmd-T	Alt+Ctrl+F2
Property Inspector	Cmd-F3	Ctrl+F3
Answers	Option-F1	Alt+F1
Align	Cmd-K	Ctrl+K
Color Mixer	Shift-F9	Shift+F9
Color Swatches	Cmd-F9	Ctrl+F9
Info	Cmd-I	Ctrl+I
Scene	Shift-F2	Shift+F2
Transform	Cmd-T	Ctrl+T
Actions	F9	F9
Debugger	Shift-F4	Shift+F4
Movie Explorer	Option-F3	Alt+F3
Reference	Shift-F1	Shift+F1
Output	F2	F2
Accessibility	Option-F2	Alt+F2
Components	Cmd-F7	Ctrl+F7
Component Parameters	Option-F7	Alt+F7
Library	F11	F11

Customizing Keyboard Shortcuts

Flash comes with predefined keyboard shortcuts, but you can also customize the shortcuts. MX ships with several shortcut sets that match those in other popular applications, as shown in Figure 2.11. You can access these sets or create a new set by choosing Edit, Keyboard Shortcuts.

Figure 2.11

MX provides sets of keyboard shortcuts, or you can create your own.

The predefined sets are Macromedia Default, Fireworks 3, Fireworks 4, Flash 5, FreeHand 10, FreeHand 9, Illustrator 10, Illustrator 9, Photoshop 5, and Photoshop 6. If you're new to Flash MX and experienced with any of these other applications, you may prefer to switch to the shortcuts with which you are most familiar.

To create a new set, select the existing set that is most similar to the new set you want to make. Then click the Duplicate Set button to the right of the Current Set drop-down and give your new set a unique name. Then choose one of the commands sets from the Commands drop-down. Choosing from this drop-down displays commands individually so that they can be selected. Click to select a command to change, and the current shortcut and keypress are displayed. You can add additional shortcuts to the original ones or replace them. Click the Change button after you add a shortcut or keypress. When you have completely configured your new set, click OK.

THE LIBRARY

The Library provides a home for your movie's symbols and imported assets. The Library displays a list of its contents, with each item preceded by an icon that indicates the type of content. Items can be grouped into folders, which can be selectively expanded to limit the amount of scrolling required to view the Library contents. Like layers, Library items rapidly multiply over the development of a project and can become a bane of a project if not carefully organized.

Try to anticipate the kinds of assets and symbols that a project will require. Create folders and designate naming conventions before you begin to import assets.

Creating Common Libraries

Flash offers the capability to store permanent Library collections, known as Common Libraries. You can create your own, project-specific Common Libraries to ensure that team members are using the same assets.

MX also comes with some Common Libraries containing sample buttons, sounds, and learning interactions, which you can access by choosing Window, Common Libraries.

THE MOVIE EXPLORER

The Movie Explorer offers the ultimate hierarchical view of every element in your Flash movies. It allows you to display the entire contents of your movie by frame, layer, or scene, as shown in Figure 2.12. That's every symbol, instance name, and line of code and text used, and you can search and replace it all. If you've lost something, you can find it here. You can even print it and have a complete map of your movie's structure and elements.

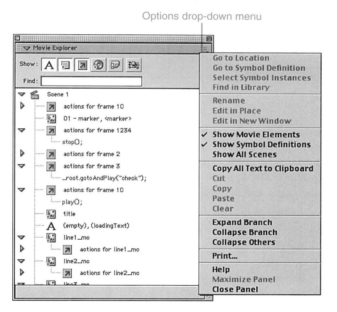

Options drop-down menu

Figure 2.12
The Movie Explorer displays the complete contents of your movie.

To access the Movie Explorer, choose Window, Movie Explorer. You can filter what's displayed by using the buttons at the top of the window. The first shows text, the next shows symbols, then scripts, video/sounds/bitmaps, frames, and the last button allows you to customize what is shown. Just below the icons is the search field.

Navigate through movie elements by using the filter buttons; then double-click to select individual elements in the list. If you double-click text, you can edit it within the Movie Explorer. The options menu (the drop-down list on the upper right) allows you to rename instances and symbols; to edit symbols in place on the Stage or in a new window; or to go to the frame, layer, or scene where a selected element is located. Double-clicking a line of code takes you to that code in the ActionScript Editor.

SETTING FLASH PREFERENCES

Preferences allow you to customize global aspects of the working environment. You access them by choosing Edit, Preferences (see Figure 2.13). Most preferences are simply that—a matter of personal preference. You will find the styles you like and are accustomed to, perhaps that mirror other applications with which you are more familiar, and can set your preferences accordingly. Adjusting the preferences is all about creating your preferred working environment.

Figure 2.13

Preferences allow you to customize global aspects of the MX working environment.

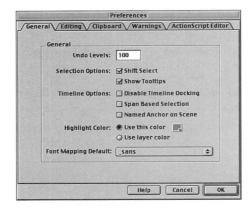

General Preferences

On the first tab, General Preferences as shown in Figure 2.13, the first preference is Undo Levels, which determines the number of undo and redo levels that are kept in memory for each work session. The range is 0 to 200, with a default of 100. The higher the number, the more memory will be required to store the information necessary to achieve the undos and redos. It's best to strike a balance between the number of undos and the memory you have available on your system.

For Windows users, the next preference is Printing Options, with the option Disable PostScript, which is turned off by default. If you have problems printing to a PostScript printer, select this option but be aware that your printing will be slower. The Printing Options are not available on Macintosh.

Next are the Selection Options: Shift Select and Show Tooltips. Both of these options are turned on by default. Enabling Shift Select allows for a single selection only when clicking on the Stage. To select additional objects, you must Shift-select them. If Shift Select is disabled, any objects clicked on the Stage are automatically added to the selection.

Show Tooltips provides contextual information about tools, including keyboard shortcuts, if there are any, when you mouse over tools. This feature is especially helpful when you're first using Flash MX.

You can choose from three Timeline Options. Disable Timeline Docking prevents the Timeline from docking with the Stage so that it floats freely. This feature can be useful for maximizing the Stage if screen real estate is limited. Disable Timeline Docking is turned off by default.

Select Span Based Selection is a new MX Timeline selection style, as shown in Figure 2.14. When this option is enabled, clicking a frame in the Timeline selects the entire span of frames, either between keyframes or from beginning to end if there are no keyframes. In the case of consecutive keyframes, clicking selects an individual keyframe. To select a single non-keyframe, you must Cmd-click (Mac) or Ctrl+click (Windows) or right-click the frame. With Select Span Based Selection disabled, which is the default, clicking a frame selects just that frame. This is the Flash 5 Timeline selection style.

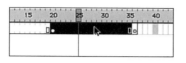

Figure 2.14

MX span-based selection selects spans of frames with a single click.

 Select Named Anchor on Scenes is also new to Flash MX. You now can add named anchors so that the Forward and Back browser buttons jump between scenes in a movie. You also can place anchors to jump from frame to frame, but you must set them manually. When Select Named Anchor on Scenes is enabled, MX automatically places a named anchor on the first frame of each scene in a movie. I believe this preference has limited value because many designers and developers don't use scenes and those who do use them merely as an organizational aid.

The Highlight Color Options determine the color of the bounding box that appears around items as they are selected. Use This Color allows you to select any Web-safe color from a swatches palette. Use Layer Color assigns the color that is assigned to the layer on which the object is located. Each layer, as it is created, is assigned a color code, which is represented by a colored square to the right of the layer name. Choosing Use Layer Color allows you to quickly determine which layer an object is on.

 A new feature in MX is an automatic prompt to replace missing fonts when you're opening a movie that contains fonts not installed on your system. The Font Mapping Default preference allows you to select a default font to use when substituting missing fonts.

Editing Preferences

The Editing Preferences encompass pen and drawing settings as well as vertical text options. All the Editing Preferences are disabled by default.

The Pen Tool options include Show Pen Preview, which previews line segments as you draw before an endpoint is created. The segments appear to stick to the Pen tool until you click to add an endpoint. Otherwise, segments are not shown until an endpoint is created.

Show Solid Points makes unselected anchor points appear solid and selected anchor points appear hollow. When this option is not selected, which is the default, selected anchor points appear solid and unselected points are hollow.

> **Caution**
>
> For named anchors to work, you must select the Flash with Named Anchors option from the Template drop-down menu within the HTML portion of the Publish Settings dialog box.

Show Precise Cursors displays the Pen tool as a cross-hair pointer on the Stage, which makes it easier to place anchor points precisely. The default displays the Pen tool icon. You can also use the Caps Lock key to toggle between these settings while drawing.

In MX, you can now create text that is oriented horizontally or vertically with the click of a single button (the Text Direction button) in the Property Inspector. Anyone who works with Asian languages will breathe a sigh of relief. The Vertical Text options allow you to make vertical text the default by using the Default Text Orientation option. Additionally, you can choose a Right to Left Text Flow option and a No Kerning option. If the No Kerning preference is enabled, you can still kern horizontal text by using the Property Inspector.

The Drawing Settings allow you to customize tolerances and specify snapping, smoothing, and straightening of objects. All the defaults are set to Normal.

Connect Lines determines how close an endpoint being drawn can be to another line without snapping to it. Additionally, it determines the sensitivity of horizontal and vertical line recognition, or how near to horizontal or vertical a line must be drawn to snap to precise horizontal or vertical alignment. When Snap to Objects is turned on, this preference also determines how close two objects must be to snap to each other. The options are Must Be Close, Normal, and Can Be Distant.

When you're drawing in Straighten or Smooth mode, Smooth Curves specifies how much smoothing or straightening is applied to curves or lines. Smoothing removes points from curves, creating gentler arcs, whereas Straighten flattens curved lines. The options are Off, Rough, Normal, and Smooth.

Recognize Lines determines Flash's threshold for recognizing rough Pencil-drawn line segments as lines, which it then makes perfectly straight. The options are Off, Strict, Normal, and Tolerant.

Recognize Shapes determines how precisely shapes must be drawn to be recognized as geometric shapes. They include circles, ovals, squares, rectangles, and arcs. The options are Off, Strict, Normal, and Tolerant.

Click Accuracy sets a threshold for how close the mouse must be to an object to select it. The options are Strict, Normal, and Tolerant.

Clipboard Preferences

The Clipboard Preferences affect how objects are copied to the Clipboard and are platform-specific, with the exception of the FreeHand Text option.

For Windows, the settings are for Bitmaps and Gradients. With Bitmaps, you can specify Color Depth and Resolution parameters, apply antialiasing by selecting Smooth, and set a Size Limit for the amount of RAM used when bitmaps are copied to the Clipboard. A Size Limit of None can be used if memory is limited.

The Gradients setting allows you to specify the quality of gradients copied to the Clipboard and pasted into other applications. This setting does not affect the quality of gradients pasted within Flash, which is always full quality.

The Macintosh has PICT Settings for Type, Resolution, and Gradients. Type specifies the format that is preserved for copied artwork: Objects for vector art or Bitmaps with a range of bit-depth settings. Resolution specifies the dots per inch (dpi) of copied images, and there is a check box option to include PostScript data. Gradients specifies gradient quality in PICTs copied and pasted outside Flash. The default is Normal, and the options are None, Fast, Normal, and Best. The higher the quality setting, the longer it takes to copy artwork. As with the Gradients setting on the Windows platform, this setting does not affect the quality of gradients pasted with Flash, where the full gradient quality will be maintained.

There is a single FreeHand Text option: Maintain Text as Blocks. Selecting this check box allows you to paste text from FreeHand and preserve it as editable text.

Warning Preferences

The Warning Preferences allow you to customize when you will receive warnings. All the warnings are enabled by default.

- **Warn on Save for Macromedia Flash 5 Compatibility** alerts you if you try to save files with MX content in Flash 5 format.

- **Warn on Missing Fonts** gives an alert if you try to open a file containing fonts that are not installed on your system.

- **Warn on Loss of Expert Mode Formatting** alerts you if you attempt to switch from Expert to Normal mode in the Actions panel and will lose formatting applied while in Expert mode.

- **Warn on Reading Generator Content** displays a red "X" over any Generator content. Note that Generator objects are no longer supported.

- **Warn on Inserting Frames When Importing Content** notifies you when the Timeline must be extended to accommodate content you are attempting to import.

ActionScript Editor Preferences

You also can access the ActionScript Editor Preferences from the Actions panel by choosing Preferences from the pop-up menu.

Editing Options allow you to customize formatting within the Actions panel. When you're working in Expert mode, Automatic Indentation indents code, and you can enter a number (up to 4, which is the default) in the Tab Size field to determine the tab amounts. Code Hints will display coding hints as you type in both Normal and Expert modes. The Delay slider allows you to specify a time delay before hints appear; the default is 0.

Text allows you to specify a font and size to display in the Actions panel.

Syntax Coloring allows you to customize text color for syntax elements such as foreground, background, keywords, identifiers, comments, and strings.

All the ActionScript Editor Preferences have default settings, and you can return to the defaults by selecting the Reset to Defaults button at the bottom of the Preferences window.

TROUBLESHOOTING

As I was experimenting with panel sets and layouts, I inadvertently hid a panel. Help!

Don't panic. You can easily restore panels. Here are several options:

- Manually go to the Windows drop-down menu and select a panel you want to display.
- Use the appropriate keyboard shortcut to display a given panel.
- If all panels suddenly disappear, you've probably accidentally pressed the Tab key. Press it again, and your panels should reappear.
- You can always restore the default panel set by choosing Window, Panel Sets, Default Layout.

FLASH AT WORK: CREATING YOUR IDEAL MX INTERFACE

After you've worked in Flash awhile, you will discover the panel sets that work most efficiently for you. Note the panel combinations you use for different tasks and save them as separate sets. If you invest the small amount of time required to create custom panel sets, your productivity will increase.

I use custom drawing and scripting sets. My drawing set includes the Timeline, Property Inspector, Info, Align, Color Mixer, Color Swatches, Components, and Library panels, as shown in Figure 2.15. Note that you can maximize the Stage and collapse docked panels, expanding them as needed, to maximize the work area.

Figure 2.15
A custom drawing panel set.

My scripting set consists of the Timeline, ActionScript Editor, Property Inspector, Components, Component Parameters, and the Movie Explorer.

DRAWING AND PAINTING IN FLASH

UNDERSTANDING VECTOR GRAPHICS

Flash was originally designed as an animation application to translate old-style, incremental animation to the Web. Given its roots in early cel animation, drawing has always been at the core of Flash. Although perhaps not as sexy as the scripting and complex interaction now possible in MX, drawing is still essential to getting the most out of Flash.

Computers display graphics in two formats: vector and bitmap. Bitmaps are made up of discrete units called *pixels*. Each pixel contains a single color. When combined, the variations in pixel color create the patterns that make up an image. Bitmaps contain color information for each pixel in an image plus the dimensions for the image, and transmit images pixel by pixel. Bitmaps are great for displaying subtle variations in color, such as photographic images. But what if you want to change the size of a bitmap image? Well, you either have to re-create the image at the desired dimensions or stretch the image, usually with undesirable results.

By comparison, vector graphics store a series of commands necessary to create an image using lines and curves. The commands, called *vectors*, dictate attributes of lines and curves such as thickness, direction, color, and position, which are then calculated by your computer. Vector graphics allow for much finer detail and can easily be resized without losing definition. When you edit a vector graphic, you simply change the attributes of your lines and curves. Vector graphics are best for displaying simple shapes with flat areas of color, such as icons, logos, and cartoon-style drawings. Both vector and bitmap graphics are drawn on request, but vectors have much smaller file sizes and can be drawn much more quickly. Bitmaps have to be transmitted pixel by pixel, so file size and download time are directly tied to an image's dimensions. Vector graphics transmit instructions, which are then carried out by your processor, so that file size and rendering speed are determined by the complexity of the instructions, not the size of the graphic.

Given its history as an animation program, it's not surprising that Flash is vector-based. Flash can display bitmaps as well but is designed to take advantage of vectors.

USING THE DRAWING TOOLS

There are a few key concepts to grasp about how Flash creates artwork. Shapes drawn in Flash consist of strokes, fills, or both. Strokes are outlines, and fills are interiors. Even in shapes containing both, strokes and fills are independent of each other. That allows you to set their attributes separately, and even to move them independently to create unusual shapes.

Overlapping shapes drawn on the same layer interact. One shape drawn on top of another replaces any portions of the original shape that it obscures. Shapes of the same color merge where they touch, while shapes of different colors remain distinct although overlapped portions are replaced. Lines drawn by the Pencil, Line, Brush, Oval, or Rectangle tools are broken into segments where they intersect other shapes and bisect shapes beneath them.

⇨ *To learn more details about tools in the Toolbox, see Chapter 2, "The Flash Interface," page 17.*

You can take advantage of these unusual behaviors to create interesting negative shapes. To prevent shapes from interacting, group them by selecting them and choosing Modify, Group, or place them on separate layers.

When you draw, Flash sets the stroke color, fill color, or both according to the colors that have been selected in the Stroke and Fill boxes in the Toolbox, in the Property Inspector as you select a tool, or in the Color Mixer panel. Colors set in any of these locations are reflected in the others. Any shape drawn can have a stroke, but only shapes with interiors have fills.

The Line Tool

The Line tool is the most basic of the drawing tools. It draws straight lines or, given what you know about how Flash creates artwork, strokes. Simply select the Line tool; then click and drag to create straight lines. Shift+dragging draws lines that are vertical, horizontal, or diagonal.

You can, of course, use the Line tool to draw closed shapes such as squares or rectangles that can have fills applied to them. However, you must manually add a fill, using the Paint Bucket tool, after you have closed a shape.

The Pencil Tool

The Pencil tool enables you to draw freeform lines and shapes. Select the Pencil tool and then select a pencil mode in the Options section of the Toolbox to straighten, smooth, or maintain rough shapes (using the Ink setting) as you draw. Click and drag to sketch lines that mirror your mouse movements. Shift+drag to draw horizontal or vertical lines. As with the Line tool, you can use the Pencil tool to draw closed shapes but must use the Paint Bucket tool to manually add fills to them.

The Oval and Rectangle Tools

The Oval and Rectangle tools allow you to draw simple shapes quite easily. Click and drag with either tool to draw ovals and rectangles. Shift+drag to draw perfect circles or squares.

You have the option to draw rectangles with rounded corners. It's an imprecise task, but if you have the patience, you can produce good results. When using the Rectangle tool, select the Round Rectangle Radius modifier at the bottom of the Toolbox. Enter a number in the corner radius field. Zero results in straight corners. Finding the best radius for a rounded corner is a matter of trial and error.

The Pen Tool

The Pen tool is the most powerful drawing tool. If you haven't used an illustration program before, the Pen tool will take some getting used to, particularly the way it draws curves. All that power comes with a learning curve, but you'll be rewarded with precisely drawn curves and irregular shapes that cannot be achieved with any other tool.

The Pen tool draws by establishing anchor points that it then connects. Select the Pen tool and move your mouse pointer onto the Stage. Notice that a small x appears to the right of the pen, as shown in Figure 3.1. This icon indicates that you are placing the first anchor.

Figure 3.1
The Pen tool displays a small x as
you place the first anchor point of
a shape.

Drawing Line Segments

To draw line segments, click to place anchor points as you draw. The first anchor point appears as a small hollow dot, which changes to a blue square as you draw additional anchors. Shift+clicking draws vertical, horizontal, or diagonal (45 degree) lines. You must end the anchoring process, indicating to Flash that you've completed a path, whether you draw an open or closed shape. To end an open path, either double-click the final anchor point, Cmd-click (Mac) or Ctrl+click (Windows) away from the path, or click the Pen tool in the Toolbox. To end a closed path, hold the Pen over the first anchor point. A small dot will appear to the right of the Pen, indicating that you can close the path, as shown in Figure 3.2.

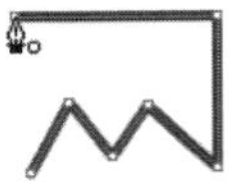

Figure 3.2
The Pen tool displays a small circle if you are correctly positioned
to close a path.

Drawing Curved Segments

The true power of the Pen tool lies in its capability to draw mathematically precise curved segments. These curves are known as *Bezier curves*. To calculate arcs precisely, curves are defined by four elements: two anchor points and two control handles, as shown in Figure 3.3. To draw curves with the Pen tool, click and drag anchor points. Drag in the direction you want your curve to be drawn. The first time you click and drag, you'll see that your anchor point has a control handle. Click to create a second anchor point and drag in the opposite direction—away from the curve—to draw an arc.

Figure 3.3
The anatomy of a curve: two
anchor points and two control
handles.

If you drag the second anchor in the same direction as the first, you'll draw an S-curve, as shown in Figure 3.4.

Figure 3.4
Dragging both anchor points in
the same direction results in an S-
curve.

The length and angle of the control handles determine the shape of the curve. It's best to complete a path before you adjust your curves. It can take quite a while to become proficient with Bezier curves, and only the most experienced computer artists can create them precisely as they draw. It's much more efficient, and less aggravating if you are less experienced, to quickly draw an approximation of your desired shape and then adjust the curves. To close a curved path, click on the initial anchor point and drag away from the curve, as shown in Figure 3.5.

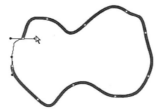

Figure 3.5
Click on the initial anchor point and drag away from the curve to close a curved path.

Adjusting Anchor Points

The fastest way to draw with the Pen tool is to complete a path and then adjust the anchor points. Anchor points in curved paths have control handles, and the anchor points of line segments are corner points. After you draw a shape, you can add or delete anchor and corner points, convert anchor points to corner points and vice versa, or move any existing points.

To adjust anchor points, you must first select them. The placement of anchor points may not be obvious in curved and nonuniform paths. Use the Subselection tool and click on a path to reveal your anchor points, as shown in Figure 3.6.

Figure 3.6
Click on a path with the Subselection tool to reveal anchor points.

If you click directly on an anchor, you both select that point and reveal all others in the path. If you click on a path but not directly on an anchor point, you simply reveal the anchor points in the path and must then click directly on one to select it. Shift+click additional anchor points to add them to the selection. You can then click directly on an anchor to reveal any control handles. Click and drag anchor points to move them, as shown in Figure 3.7. You can also select an anchor point and use the arrow keys to nudge it.

Figure 3.7
Click and drag a control handle to alter the shape of a curve.

As you edit shapes, you may want to change a corner point to a curve point to be able to add curves, or vice versa to straighten a shape. To convert a corner point to a curve point, Option-drag (Mac) or Alt+drag (Windows) to create a control handle. Drag the new control handle in the direction of the curve you want to draw. To convert a curve point to a corner point, select your path with the Subselection tool to reveal your anchor points. Then select the Pen tool and click a curve point to convert it.

You may also find that you need to either add detail to or simplify shapes as you edit them. Adding points allows you to refine a shape by adding detail, either additional curves or corners. To add an anchor point, click on an existing path with the Pen tool. To simplify a shape, you can delete anchor points. The simplest way to delete an anchor point is to click on it with the Subselection tool and press Delete. Or, choose the Pen tool and click once to delete a corner point or twice to delete a curve point.

Adjusting Segments

Segments of paths can also be adjusted, independently of their anchor points. You may find that you need to refine a small portion of a curve. To adjust the size and angles of curves, click and drag their control handles. Where two curved segments intersect, two control handles extend away from a common anchor point. Each handle controls a curve on either side of a common anchor point. Dragging one end of a double-control handle changes both curves on either side of the anchor point, which stays in place, as shown in Figure 3.8.

Figure 3.8
Dragging one end of a double-control handle changes curves on both sides of the shared anchor point.

To adjust the arc of the curved segment between anchor points only, Option-drag (Mac) or Alt+drag (Windows) the one end of a double-control handle.

If a curve segment intersects a straight segment, you'll see a control handle just on the curve side of the anchor. Click and drag this handle with the Subselection tool to change the arc, or click and drag the anchor point to move the curve.

You can also use the Arrow tool to move segments. As the Arrow tool is positioned over a path, a small corner or curve appears to the right of the arrow, indicating which kind of segment can be selected. When you select a curved segment, a small curve appears to the right of the arrow, as shown in Figure 3.9.

Figure 3.9
When the Arrow tool is positioned over a curved segment, a small arc appears beside the pointer.

A right angle appears when you select a straight segment, as shown in Figure 3.10. Click and drag with the Arrow tool to move segments, leaving the anchor points in place.

Figure 3.10
When the Arrow tool is positioned over a straight segment, a small corner shape appears beside the pointer.

The Brush Tool

The Brush tool is the lone Flash painting tool, and the only tool that allows you to mimic brush strokes, as shown in Figure 3.11. You really need a pressure-sensitive tablet, one that allows you to use a stylus instead of a mouse, to get the most realistic brush strokes. Trying to paint with a mouse is like trying to sign a check with a bar of soap. Tablets are sensitive to changes in pressure as you paint and adjust the weight of your strokes accordingly.

Figure 3.11
The Brush tool draws freeform, paintbrush-like strokes.

Choose brush modifiers in the Options section of the Toolbox to adjust the size and shape of your brush. You can also choose among Brush modes that allow you to paint normally, fills only, behind objects, inside objects, or in selections. Combine brush strokes with more precisely drawn shapes to create interesting textures.

EDITING AND ADJUSTING SHAPES

As you've seen, drawing shapes, especially using a mouse, can be far from exact. The best strategy, especially if you are new to the Flash drawing environment, is to draw quick approximations of shapes and then perfect them through editing. Editing an existing shape is far easier than drawing it perfectly from scratch.

Using the Arrow and Subselection Tools

The Arrow and Subselection tools can be used to adjust shapes, as you've seen when working with paths. Simply click segments or points, and drag. Dragging an anchor point changes the anchor position and the size and shape of the adjoining segments. Dragging a segment changes the shape of the segment, while the anchor points on either side of it remain in place.

Straightening and Smoothing

You can also smooth and straighten irregular shapes and paths. For example, you may have drawn freeform curves with the Pencil tool, but some of your curves may appear straighter or flattened. To correct this, select a path or shape with the Arrow tool; then click either the Straighten or Smooth modifiers in the Toolbox. You can repeatedly click either modifier to produce greater changes. Not surprisingly, straight lines or shapes with straight sides are unaffected by the Straighten modifier. Ovals and perfect circles are likewise unaffected by the Smooth modifier, although curved paths can be changed somewhat.

Optimizing Curves

The more anchor points used in drawing curves, the greater the number of calculations that must be made to draw them. In extreme cases this can result in larger file sizes as well as slower rendering. Curves can be optimized to reduce the number of anchor points used to create them. This results in smoother, more refined curves. The goal is to use just as many anchor points as needed to create your desired shape, and no more.

To optimize your curves, select a shape and choose Modify, Optimize. The Optimize Curves dialog box, shown in Figure 3.12, contains a smoothing slider and options to use multiple passes and to show a totals message. Make your selections and click OK. Smoothing reduces the number of points that are used in a given shape. To dramatically reduce the number of points, choose the Multiple Passes option. This results in several smoothing passes being made, with points removed and the shape further refined in each pass until no further optimization is possible. The totals message compares the original number of curves with the optimized number of curves, detailing the extent of the optimization.

Figure 3.12
Using the Optimize Curves dialog box, you can smooth curves.

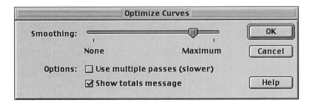

Working with Strokes

A stroke refers to a line, or an outline of a shape. Strokes have three attributes: color, weight, and style. Stroke color can be set in three places: the Stroke box in the Toolbox, the Property Inspector, or in the Color Mixer. Stroke height and style can be set only in the Property Inspector. I typically use the Property Inspector so that I can set all the attributes at once; however, the Property Inspector allows you to choose only Web-safe colors.

A Web-safe color palette was developed four or five years ago in an attempt to ensure that color was displayed uniformly on computer displays. One of the many inconsistencies in Web-delivered content is that different operating systems and browsers display finite sets of colors. The kicker is that browsers and operating systems each have slightly different color palettes to work with. So, a Web-safe palette was developed to use just the 216 generic colors common to the two major browsers, Netscape and Internet Explorer, and the two major operating systems, Macintosh and Windows. These colors are available in the color swatches provided in Flash. However, computer displays have improved at displaying color, so the general consensus is that it is safe to venture beyond the Web-safe 216. After all, 216 colors make a very limited palette with which to design. The Color Mixer allows you to mix your own custom colors and change the alpha, or transparency, of colors.

The Property Inspector is used to assign and edit stroke attributes, including color. Follow these steps to create a stroke:

1. Select the drawing tool of your choice.

   The context-sensitive Property Inspector displays the appropriate attributes—in this case, the stroke attributes, as shown in Figure 3.13.

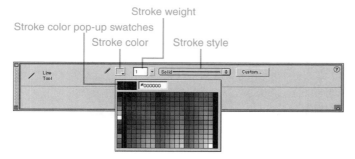

Figure 3.13
The Stroke attributes in the Property Inspector.

2. Click on the color swatch, and select a color from the pop-up swatches.

3. To set the stroke weight, either type a number in the stroke weight field or use the slider to select a number.

   Stroke weights are multiples of .25, ranging from .25 to 10. The higher the number, the thicker the stroke.

4. Finally, set the stroke style. Next to the stroke weight field is a pop-up of common stroke styles, as shown in Figure 3.14. Hairline draws the thinnest stroke at .25 weight, regardless of any weight you may have specified. The other stroke styles can be any weight.

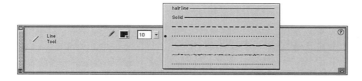

Figure 3.14
You can use the Property Inspector to specify a stroke style.

You can also click the Custom button to create your own stroke style, as shown in Figure 3.15. As with broken-line styles, use custom strokes sparingly. Complicated lines, especially irregular ones, require complicated vector instructions and calculations, which will negatively impact file size and rendering.

Caution

Using any of the broken-line stroke styles will noticeably affect file size and rendering time. Use them sparingly.

Figure 3.15
Using the custom Stroke Style dialog box, you can create your own stroke styles.

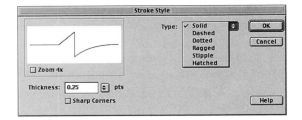

To edit an existing stroke, first make sure nothing is selected on the Stage. The Ink Bottle tool, shown in Figure 3.16, allows you to edit strokes.

Figure 3.16
Use the Ink Bottle tool to edit strokes.

Use the Property Inspector to specify stroke attributes, and then click with the Ink Bottle on a stroke to apply those attributes, as shown in Figure 3.17.

Figure 3.17
To edit a stroke, change the stroke attributes in the Property Inspector and click a stroke with the Ink Bottle.

WORKING WITH FILLS

Fills are interiors of shapes, and can be solid colors, gradients, or even bitmaps. Any closed shape can have a fill, and any shape drawn with the Oval or Rectangle tools will have a fill unless you change the fill box to the No Color option, as shown in Figure 3.18.

Figure 3.18
To draw a closed shape without a fill, click the Fill box in the Toolbox and select the No Color option.

To edit a fill, change the fill settings in the Color Mixer, Property Inspector, or Toolbox and click fills with the Paint Bucket tool, as shown in Figure 3.19.

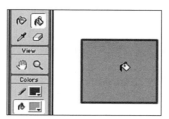

Figure 3.19
To edit a fill, change the fill attributes and click an existing fill with the Paint Bucket.

Solid

As with strokes, fill color can be selected in three places: the Fill box in the Toolbox, the Property Inspector, or in the Color Mixer. To specify a solid fill, simply select a color in one of those locations. To use a non–Web-safe color, you must use the Color Mixer (see Figure 3.20).

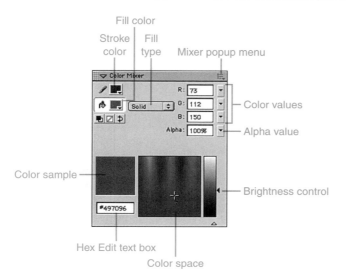

Figure 3.20
The Color Mixer allows you to select custom, non–Web-safe colors as well as gradients to use as fills.

The Color Mixer allows you to choose between two color modes, RGB and HSB. Click on the upper-right corner of the Color Mixer panel, as shown in Figure 3.20, to display the Mixer pop-up menu. Then you can select a color mode. RGB and HSB are two different color models. RGB stands for Red, Green, and Blue, and is the standard additive color model created for graphics viewed on computer monitors. RGB creates colors by mixing the primary computer colors: red, green and blue. RGB is the default color mode. HSB stands for Hue, Saturation, and Brightness, and this color model defines color according to these three values. Unless you are accustomed to using HSB color, leave the mode set to the RGB default.

> **Caution**
>
> When using the Color Mixer, be sure to click on the Stroke or Fill icons, and not the color boxes, to access the Mixer controls. Clicking the color boxes will simply open the swatch pop-ups.

Then click the Fill icon and check that Solid is selected in the Fill pop-up menu. Click in the Color space to select a color. Adjust the brightness slider to further refine your color. You can also adjust the Alpha percentage to make your color partially transparent.

Gradients: Linear and Radial

Gradients can also be used as fills. A gradient creates a gradual blend between two or more colors, progressing gradually from one to the other. Linear gradients display a range between two colors in a continuous gradient. Radial gradients display a color range in a circular pattern from the center outward. Radial gradient fills add depth to circular objects, making them appear three-dimensional. If you click in the Fill color box in the Toolbox, Property Inspector, or Color Mixer, you'll notice sample gradients at the bottom of the Fill color pop-ups, as shown in Figure 3.21.

Figure 3.21
Sample gradients are at the bottom left of the color pop-up windows.

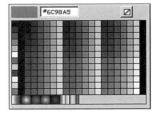

You can also create custom gradients that allow you to specify the colors that are used. To create a custom gradient, you must use the Color Mixer. Click the Fill icon and then select either Linear or Radial from the Fill type drop-down menu. When you select a gradient style, the Gradient definition bar appears in the middle of the Color Mixer pane along with gradient pointers, as shown in Figure 3.22.

To change the color of a gradient, click on one of the Gradient pointers at the ends of the Gradient definition bar to indicate which color you want to change. Then click the color box at the top left of the Color Mixer to select a Web-safe color or in the Color space to choose a custom color. The end of the gradient by the pointer you selected changes to reflect the new color. You can also add additional pointers to further customize the gradient by clicking just below the definition bar, between the two original pointers. Click and drag a pointer to reposition it. To save a custom gradient, click in the upper right of the Color Mixer, as shown in Figure 3.20, to access the Mixer pop-up menu and select Save Swatch. The new gradient is added to the Swatches panel in the current document.

Gradient pointers

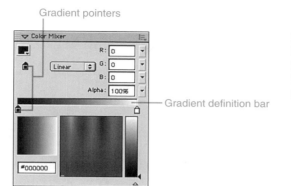

Gradient definition bar

Figure 3.22
In the Color Mixer, you can customize gradients by using the
Gradient definition bar and gradient pointers.

Bitmap

The Color Mixer also allows you to use a bitmap as a fill. Bitmaps are an alternative to traditional
solid or gradient fills. Any bitmap can be assigned as a fill, and it will tile if needed to cover the
entire fill area of an object. Because they will tile, bitmaps produce unusual fills and are typically
used infrequently. To create a bitmap fill, click the Fill icon at the top of the Color Mixer. Then select
Bitmap from the Fill type drop-down menu. The Import to Library dialog box appears, as shown in
Figure 3.23, prompting you to select a bitmap to use.

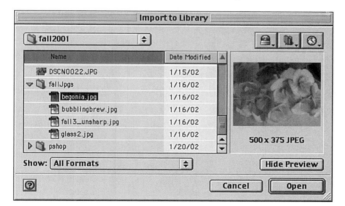

Figure 3.23
The Import to Library dialog box
appears when you select Bitmap
as the Fill type.

The bitmap is displayed as your current color in the box at the top left of the Color Mixer and is
applied as a fill to selected shapes (see Figure 3.24) .

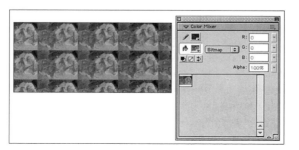

Figure 3.24
Bitmaps are applied as fills using
the Color Mixer.

ERASING

The Eraser tool allows you to selectively or collectively delete strokes and fills on the Stage.

▷ *The Eraser tool and its modifiers are discussed in "Eraser Tool" section, page 27 (Chapter 2, "The Flash Interface").*

To quickly delete the contents of the Stage, double-click the Eraser tool. Choose among the Eraser modifiers and drag to selectively erase fills, lines, selected fills, or inside fills. Click with the Faucet modifier to erase stroke segments or filled areas.

You can also delete items by selecting them with the Arrow tool and pressing Delete.

USING LAYOUT AIDS

Flash provides several aids to help you draw with precision and create unified layouts. Grids, guides, and guide layers help you to align elements within your layouts, helping to create an overall sense of order and intention. If elements are placed randomly, with no relation to other elements within a layout, a design will seem haphazard and will lack a sense of unity.

Grids, Guides, and Guide Layers

Grids, guides, and guide layers help you to place objects precisely on the Stage. Grids and guides provide vertical and horizontal guidelines that objects can be aligned or snapped against. The grid option displays a series of uniformly placed horizontal and vertical lines that cover the Stage, appearing behind any artwork. Guides are individual horizontal and vertical lines that are manually placed on the Stage. Guide layers allow you to create your own visual alignment aids.

Grids provide a visual framework for alignment as you draw or place elements in a layout. Grids are not exported, so they will not be visible in your final movie. To show the grid, choose View, Grid, Show Grid. To edit the grid, choose View, Grid, Edit Grid, and the Grid dialog box will appear, as shown in Figure 3.25. You can specify the spacing of the grid lines in pixels, from 7 to 288.

Figure 3.25
You can change the size, color, and snapping settings of grids in the Grid dialog box.

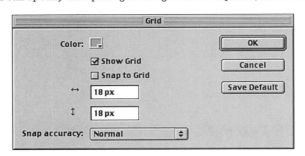

You can also enable snapping so that objects align exactly along the grid.

Whereas grids automatically place guidelines over the entire Stage, guides allow you to place vertical and horizontal guidelines at random intervals on the Stage. Guides are most useful for marking the alignment of recurring elements that give structure to your layout, such as menu bars or columns of text.

To use the guides, you must show the rulers by choosing View, Rulers. Rulers then appear along the top and left side of the Stage. To add a guide, click on the horizontal ruler at the top of the Stage and drag down from it to create horizontal guides, or click and drag across from the vertical ruler on the left to create vertical guides. To move a guide, click and drag it with the Arrow tool. You can also choose View, Guides, Snap to Guides to snap objects to your guides. To remove a guide from the Stage, drag it with the Arrow tool back to its originating ruler.

To edit guides, choose View, Guides, Edit Guides to launch the Guides dialog box, as shown in Figure 3.26. Guide options are almost identical to Grid options, with an additional option named Clear All, which deletes all of your guides.

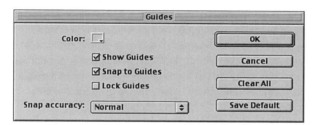

Figure 3.26
You can change the color and snapping settings of guides in the Guides dialog box.

Guide layers allow you to create irregular guides. Grids and guides produce guidelines that are horizontal and vertical and that extend from one end of the Stage to the other. What's special about guide layers is that they allow you to use any of the drawing tools to create your guides. With guide layers, you are not limited to perpendicular guidelines, or even to lines at all. In a guide layer, you could draw a diagonal line, or hexagonal shapes, to use for alignment. Click the Guide icon below the layers to create a guide layer. Draw your guide shapes and then use the Align panel to position elements on other layers to elements on your guide layers.

The Align Panel

Using the Align panel, you can align objects to each other or to the Stage. To align objects to the Stage, select the To Stage button on the right of the panel, as shown in Figure 3.27. Use To Stage to align objects relative to the Stage—for example, to center them or to align them to the left side of the Stage. To align objects to each other, deselect the To Stage button. Select two or more objects, and use the Align buttons to align the right or left edges or to center, or to align the tops or bottoms of objects, or to center them vertically. The Distribute buttons will distribute a series of objects evenly, by their top or bottom edges or by their centers, by their left or right edges, or by their vertical centers.

When Flash aligns objects to each other, it notes which edge you want to align and then uses whichever object's edge is furthest in that direction to align the others.

Figure 3.27
The Align panel aligns objects to
each other or to the Stage.

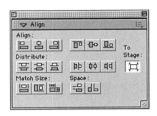

Snapping

Another way to align elements is to use snapping. One of the simplest yet most needed new features in MX is pixel snapping. Because Flash is vector based, you can easily and inadvertently place objects in between whole pixels. These seemingly insignificant pixel fractions can throw off alignment and create problems. Pixel snapping has finally arrived in MX. Pixel snapping works by creating a grid with one pixel spacing between guidelines, and then snaps objects on the Stage to those guidelines. To enable pixel snapping, choose View, Snap to Pixels. Voila! Any object you create or place on the Stage will snap to a whole pixel coordinate. The vast majority of alignment problems are solved. I always turn on pixel snapping as I work to help avoid sub-pixel alignment issues. Unfortunately, MX will turn off pixel snapping whenever you open a new Flash document or launch Flash, so you have to keep turning it on.

You can temporarily disable pixel snapping as you work. Press C to turn it off. It will reactivate as soon as you release C.

CREATING A MASK

Masks are like stencils: They reveal parts of images that are below. Use them to reveal portions of layers in your movies. For example, you can use text as a mask to reveal parts of an image within the shapes of the letters, as shown in Figure 3.28. Creating a mask is easy. Draw simple shapes on a separate layer that is above the layers you want to mask. Contrary to expectations, masks in Flash reveal rather than hide. So, remember to draw your mask in the shapes you want to reveal contents below them. When your mask shape is in place, Ctrl+click or right-click the layer and then select Mask from the context menu. This applies the mask and locks the mask layer and any layers below it that are masked.

 For more details on using masks, see "Working with Dynamic Masks," page 362 (Chapter 17, "Unlocking the Power of Movie Clips").

At 400% magnification, pixel snapping displays its grid. If you zoom in, it will appear. To hide the grid, press and hold X. The grid will reappear when you let go.

Figure 3.28
Text can be used as a mask.

TROUBLESHOOTING

When I click and drag a shape, why does the stroke get left behind?

Clicking to select a shape that has both a stroke and a fill selects only the stroke or the fill, depending on which has been clicked. You must double-click a shape to select both. Alternatively, you can click and drag with the Arrow tool to drag a selection marquee around both.

Can I import vector graphics created in other applications?

Yes, choose File, Import and you can import Illustrator files, in .ai or .eps format, but only in version 8 format or before, unfortunately. You can also import FreeHand files, version 7 through 10 format. You can preserve FreeHand text blocks, layers, library symbols, and pages when importing into Flash. FreeHand is a Macromedia product, so it's not surprising that Flash offers better support for it.

FLASH AT WORK: HOW BIG IS MY SHAPE?

Despite all the precise drawing capabilities Flash has to offer, you have no way of knowing how large a shape is as you draw it. You'd think there would be a way to specify that you want to draw a square that is 15 pixels by 15 pixels, but there isn't. Here are your options:

- Draw a shape, approximating the desired size as best you can; then select and resize it by entering the correct width and height in the Property Inspector or the Info panel. This approach is tiresome but workable with squares, rectangles, and circles. However, if you try it with ovals or rectangles with rounded edges, your curves will become distorted.

■ Create guides at the desired dimensions of your drawn objects. Then draw with guide snapping turned on. As you draw, your shape should snap to the guides, allowing you to draw to your desired size. This approach works passably with squares and rectangles, but it can be difficult to draw circles, ovals, and rectangles with rounded edges so that they align with a rectangular grid.

■ For rectangles with rounded corners, start by perfecting your rounded corners while approximating your desired size. Then select the anchor points around two adjacent corners, as shown in Figure 3.29, and nudge them with the arrow keys until the rectangle is the correct size. This approach can be tedious, but it will preserve the corner radius of your rounded corners as you resize.

Figure 3.29
You can use the Subselection tool to resize rectangles with rounded corners without distorting the corner radius.

USING BITMAPS IN FLASH

IN THIS CHAPTER

IMPORTING BITMAPS

Macromedia Flash may be vector-based, but that doesn't mean your movie content is limited to objects you have drawn in Flash. You can easily import other file formats, including bitmaps. Vector graphics cannot compete with the photorealism of bitmaps. Although you must edit your bitmaps in other programs, Flash allows you to import and transform them.

Flash can import bitmaps in a variety of formats. Many depend on your having QuickTime 4 or higher installed. Table 4.1 lists the file formats that you can import into Flash MX without having QuickTime installed.

Table 4.1   Flash MX Import File Formats for Bitmaps Without QuickTime Installed

Format	File Extension	Platform
Bitmap	.bmp	Windows
Enhanced Windows Metafile	.emf	Windows
FutureSplash Player	.spl	Both
GIF, animated GIF	.gif	Both
JPEG	.jpg	Both
PICT	.pct, .pic	Macintosh
PNG	.png	Both
Flash Player 6	.swf	Both
Windows Metafile	.wmf	Windows

QuickTime extends support for some file formats and is particularly helpful when you're sharing files across Mac and Windows platforms. Table 4.2 lists the import file formats that are available when QuickTime is installed on your system.

Table 4.2   Flash MX Import File Formats with QuickTime Installed

Format	File Extension	Platform
Photoshop	.psd	Both
PICT	.pct, .pic	Both
QuickTime Image	.ptif	Both
Silicon Graphics Image	.sgi	Both
TGA	.tga	Both
TIFF	.tif	Both

Although you can import Photoshop files via QuickTime, the layers are flattened upon import.

In most cases, the format of imported bitmaps is dictated by the application used to edit the bitmap.

The steps to import a bitmap are simple. Imported assets are stored in the Library, so you can import to the Library. This approach is useful when you're importing a series of files. You can import multiple assets and then place them individually on the Stage. Alternatively, you can import directly to the Stage. This approach places an instance on the Stage and the imported file in the Library.

Choose File, Import, as shown in Figure 4.1 to import directly to the Stage, or choose File, Import to Library to import into the Library.

Figure 4.1
You can import files directly to the Stage by choosing Import, or you can import them into the Library.

The Import dialog box opens, as shown in Figure 4.2. This dialog box allows you to navigate to the file that you want to import. From the Show (Macintosh) or Type of File (Windows) drop-down menu, you can choose the type of file you want to import, or you can set it to All Formats. A preview is shown, and when you locate the file you want to import, click Open.

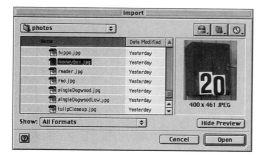

Figure 4.2
The Import dialog box allows you to preview and select files to import.

If you have chosen to import, your selected file will open on the Stage and also be placed in the Library, as shown in Figure 4.3.

Figure 4.3
Choosing Import places an imported file in the Library and an instance on the Stage.

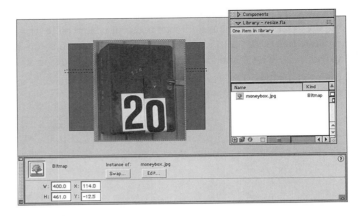

Preparing Bitmaps for Import

Although importing is straightforward, Flash cannot edit bitmaps the way it can edit vector graphics. Therefore, bitmaps must be prepared prior to import to ensure that any editing Flash cannot accomplish has been completed. Most importantly, bitmaps should be cropped and resized to the dimensions that will be used within your Flash movie before they are imported.

It is important to understand how Flash's native vector format influences the way it works with bitmaps. Vector graphics store instructions to create graphics, whereas bitmaps store information to reproduce images pixel by pixel. Although Flash can import bitmaps, you don't have all the vector transformation capabilities at your disposal, and some of the capabilities you do have come at a cost in file size. A dramatic example is resizing bitmaps.

The bitmap that was imported in Figure 4.3 is much too large. If I test the movie (by choosing Control, Test Movie and then View, Bandwidth Profiler in Test mode) with the bitmap at its current size, I can see that the current size of my movie is 60KB, as shown in Figure 4.4.

Figure 4.4
With the overly large imported bitmap, the current file size of the movie is 60KB.

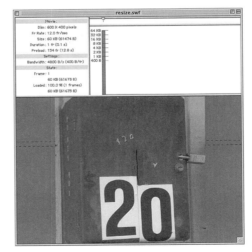

I can resize the bitmap on the Stage by using the Transform tool, holding down the Shift key as I resize to keep the bitmap in proportion. If I test my movie again, even though the dimensions of the bitmap have dropped by 50%, my movie's file size remains at 60KB, as shown in Figure 4.5.

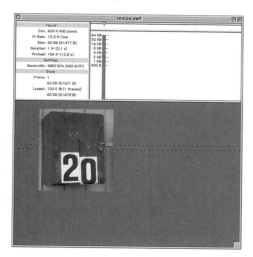

Figure 4.5

Even after the bitmap is shrunk by 50%, the total file size remains at 60KB.

How can this be? With bitmaps, file size is directly affected by image dimensions: The larger the image, the more pixels there are to map. But in Flash, you encounter the limitations of the vector-based approach. Flash is unable to realize the file savings represented by making the image smaller. In addition, file quality decreases if you resize bitmaps, especially if you attempt to enlarge them. Bitmaps contain a finite number of pixels. When you enlarge them, they lack the color information necessary to fill the added pixels, so new pixels are created in tones that are halfway between existing pixels. This results in the strange artifacts that appear in many poorly created bitmaps on the Web.

The moral is: Plan for the inclusion of bitmaps in your movies, and import them at the size they will be used. Resizing the bitmap in Photoshop in the example and importing it at 50% of its original size results in a 40% savings in file size when compared with resizing within Flash, as shown in Figure 4.6.

Figure 4.6

Importing the bitmap at the reduced size brings the movie down to 36KB.

Flash MX provides an Edit button in the Property Inspector, as shown beneath the bitmap instance name in Figure 4.3, that allows you to launch an external image-editing program to edit your imported bitmap. With an imported bitmap selected, click the Edit button to open the bitmap in the application that edited it. You can then edit the bitmap and save it, and your image in Flash is updated. However, when resizing, I've found that using this approach yields a larger file size than simply resizing before importing—48KB as opposed to 36KB in the example using moneybox.jpg. It pays to do your homework and plan your bitmap usage before importing. If you need to resize after importing to Flash, delete the bitmap from the Stage and the Library, go back to your original image and image-editing program, and start over by importing the bitmap from scratch at the desired dimensions.

You can also decrease the file size impact of imported bitmaps by taking advantage of alpha channels. Alpha channels are layers that are added to bitmaps to create transparency. Working with the same imported bitmap example, I created a version in Photoshop using an alpha channel to crop out the background. As you can see in Figure 4.7, this results in a silhouetted version that drops the size of my movie to a mere 6KB.

Figure 4.7
Importing the same bitmap with an added alpha channel to crop out the background results in a 6KB movie.

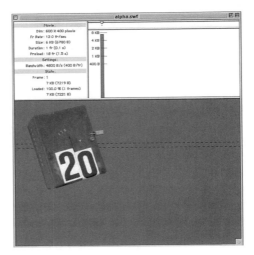

In short, the more thoroughly you know an image-editing program, the better your results will be using bitmaps in Flash. But even if you don't know an image-editing program well, you can take advantage of the file savings resulting from planning, cropping, and resizing your bitmaps before importing.

TRACING BITMAPS

Bitmaps are typically larger in file size than most vector graphics, and can noticeably affect the file size of your movie. Comparing bitmaps and vector graphics is a bit like comparing apples and elephants, though. Bitmap and vector graphic formats have different intended uses. Bitmaps are best for photographic images, and vector graphics work best with drawn art that contains solid areas of color.

⮕ *For more information about vector graphics, see "Understanding Vector Graphics," page 38 (Chapter 3, "Drawing and Painting in Flash").*

Flash offers the option to convert your bitmaps to vector graphics, which reduces file size when you perform this conversion on suitable bitmaps. The process is known as tracing a bitmap.

Not all bitmaps are good candidates for tracing. Tracing any highly detailed photographic image results in a vector graphic with a larger file size than the original bitmap. Remember, vectors work best with simple graphics containing flat colors that are easy to describe with few rendering instructions. Imagine trying to give instructions to draw a representation of a typical, cluttered dorm room. Complicated rendering instructions negate any file savings associated with tracing a bitmap.

Bitmap Versus Vector: The Cost of Graphics

Bitmap and vector graphics both carry a price tag when it comes to content delivery. The cost is different for each format and is determined by the method used to convey graphic information. Because bitmaps map images pixel by pixel, the cost is seen in download speed. Large bitmaps, slow user connection speeds, competition among downloading movie elements for scarce bandwidth, and general Internet congestion can all result in slow loading of bitmaps and, therefore, content that comes at a high cost. Vectors, however, deliver a series of instructions necessary to create graphics that are carried out by the user's computer. These instructions typically take less time to download and usually render quickly, but can stress the user's processor. Users on slower, older computers may have to wait for complex vector graphics to be drawn. Vector graphics can even cost twice as much as bitmaps: Complicated instructions can produce large file sizes that are slow to download; plus those instructions must then be implemented by the user's computer. In extreme cases—such as infinite, random, scripted vectors seen on sites such as www.praystation.com—slower computers may choke on complex calculations and crash if the instructions are too complicated and are allowed to continue executing.

Figure 4.8 offers an example of a good candidate for tracing. The best candidates are simple shapes with large blocks of color.

Images with complicated patterns, such as the one in Figure 4.9, or many color gradations are best left as bitmaps.

Although simple shapes are most easily converted to vectors, you can simplify complex bitmaps and create abstract, stylized vector graphics by using less precise tracing settings.

Figure 4.8
The simple shape of this flower
and its few color gradations make
it a good candidate to trace.

Figure 4.9
This image, with its complex patterns and shadows, is best left as
a bitmap.

To trace a bitmap, select the bitmap instance on the Stage and then choose Modify, Trace Bitmap.
The Trace Bitmap dialog box opens, as shown in Figure 4.10.

Figure 4.10
The Trace Bitmap dialog box
offers control over how a bitmap
is traced.

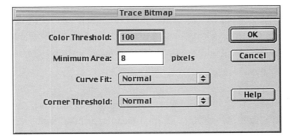

There are four settings for tracing. The Color Threshold option determines how much color detail
will be preserved in the traced bitmap. The lower the number in a range from 1 to 500, the more gra-
dation will be preserved and the more intricate the tracing. The Minimum Area option specifies the
number of surrounding pixels, from 1 to 1000, that will be considered when assigning color to an
individual pixel.

The Curve Fit option determines how closely arcs in curves are adhered to during tracing. The options range from Pixels, the tightest and most intricate tracing, to Very Smooth, the least detailed, as shown in Figure 4.11.

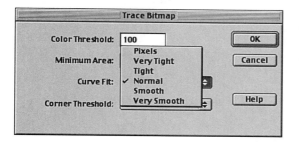

Figure 4.11
The Curve Fit options range from Pixels to Very Smooth when you're tracing a bitmap.

The Corner Threshold option similarly determines how precisely corners are traced—Many Corners, Normal, or Few Corners. Start with the default settings and click OK to get a baseline for your bitmap. Your bitmap is then traced, and you'll notice that more intricate tracings take longer. If you want to adjust the results, choose Edit, Undo or press Cmd-Z (Mac) or Ctrl+Z (Windows). Trace the bitmap again and experiment with the different settings.

Results vary widely, so be open to experimentation. Also, keep an eye on your file size. Less precise settings produce smaller file sizes and more impressionistic images, as shown in Figure 4.12.

Figure 4.12
Traced bitmaps can produce impressionistic effects.

4

More precise settings create vectors that appear very similar to the original bitmaps, as shown in Figure 4.13. However, the more intricate the tracing, the larger the file size.

Figure 4.13
Lower tolerance settings produce more detailed tracings that more closely resemble the original bitmaps.

Optimizing Traced Bitmaps

More intricate tracings can produce Flash movie files that are larger than the original bitmaps. If you must wait more than a couple of seconds while a bitmap is being traced—and you're not on a slow computer—check your file size. Most likely your settings are too precise.

To see how complicated a tracing is, select a traced bitmap and choose View, Outlines to display the tracing outlines. (See Figure 4.14.) To return to Normal view, choose View, Fast.

Figure 4.14
You can view tracing outlines to evaluate the complexity of a traced bitmap.

The extreme detail of the tracing on the right is probably too much to deliver over the Internet. One way to reduce the detail in a tracing is to optimize curves. To do so, choose Modify, Optimize to access the Optimize Curves dialog box, as shown in Figure 4.15.

Drag the Smoothing slider and experiment with different settings. Select Show Totals Message to monitor the number of curves that are removed and click OK. The Totals message appears, as shown in Figure 4.16.

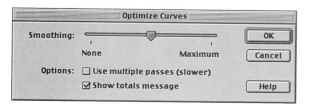

Figure 4.15
By adjusting the settings in the Optimize Curve dialog box, you can simplify a traced bitmap.

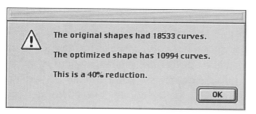

Figure 4.16
The Totals message details the overall reduction in curves.

The Optimize Curves command is powerful, but it cannot bring the most intricate traced bitmaps back from the brink. The maximum improvement is generally in the neighborhood of 40% to 50%. For anything more, undo your tracing and trace the bitmap again.

BREAKING APART BITMAPS

Breaking apart a bitmap separates a bitmap into its component pixels, which can then be selected and modified individually. Unless a bitmap is broken apart, it can only be selected and manipulated globally, as a whole. After a bitmap is broken apart, you can use the drawing and painting tools to edit individual pixels.

To break apart a bitmap, select a bitmap on the Stage and choose Modify, Break Apart. Then you can use the Lasso tool with the Magic Wand modifier to select portions of a bitmap. Clicking a bitmap with the Magic Wand selects pixels according to color range, as shown in Figure 4.17.

Figure 4.17
The Magic Wand modifier of the Lasso tool enables you to select parts of bitmaps, as indicated by the dots.

To access the Magic Wand, select the Lasso tool within the Toolbox. Then click the Magic Wand Properties button from the Lasso options, as shown in Figure 4.18, to refine how selections are made.

Figure 4.18
Select the Lasso tool and then click the **Magic Wand Properties** button to access the settings.

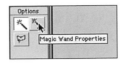

The Threshold option in the Magic Wand Settings dialog box, as shown in Figure 4.19, determines how closely a color must match the pixel that is clicked to be included in the selection. The range is from 0 to 200. The higher the number, the greater the range of colors that are included in selections. Entering **0** selects only pixels that are exactly the same color as the pixel that is clicked. The Smoothing option determines how accurate the edges of selections are; your choices are Pixels, Rough, Normal, and Smooth. Clicking repeatedly with the Magic Wand adds to the selection. When a selection has been made, you can use the Fill controls to change fill colors.

Figure 4.19
The Magic Wand Settings dialog box allows you to refine the way selections are made.

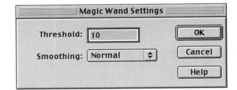

COMPRESSING BITMAPS

Because bitmaps can significantly increase the file size of a movie, it's vital to compress them to minimize file size as much as possible. By default, the original compression settings of a bitmap are used when a movie is published. However, you may be able to improve upon the original compression by tweaking a bitmap's properties, especially if a bitmap has been traced. To access the Bitmap Properties dialog box, select a bitmap in the Library and either click the Properties button, as shown in Figure 4.20, or Ctrl-click (Mac) or right-click (Windows).

Figure 4.20
Click the **Properties** button at the bottom of the Library panel to access the Properties dialog box.

The Bitmap Properties dialog box appears, as shown in Figure 4.21. Choose Photo (JPEG) in the Compression drop-down menu to compress the bitmap in the JPEG format, which will discard pixel information during compression. To maintain the original compression settings of the imported bitmap, check Use Imported JPEG Data. Each time a JPEG is compressed, data is discarded, so image quality becomes progressively worse. Typically, it is best to use the imported JPEG data to prevent image deterioration. You can specify a new JPEG quality setting, but you cannot increase the quality of an imported JPEG and will instead reduce the quality further. To specify a new JPEG quality setting, uncheck Use Imported JPEG Data and enter a number between 1 and 100 in the Quality field. If you specify a new JPEG setting, be sure to check the image quality to ensure that it does not noticeably degrade. Use JPEG with bitmaps that have photographic detail and wide tonal variations.

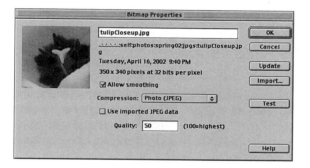

Figure 4.21

In the Bitmap Properties dialog box, you can specify compression settings for imported bitmaps.

To compress without discarding pixel information, choose Lossless (PNG/GIF) in the Compression drop-down menu. Use Lossless with traced bitmaps with simple shapes and fewer colors.

Click Test to compare the file size using your compression settings to the original, as shown in Figure 4.22. Then click the Update button to preview the effects of your settings on the image preview in the upper left of the dialog box. Take the time to experiment with different settings to find the best compromise between image quality and file size. When you're satisfied with your compression settings, click OK.

Bitmaps can greatly enhance Flash movies. When used in combination with native vector art, bitmaps help to create textured, engaging designs and are indispensable for conveying photographic detail. Use bitmaps carefully to manage file size, but by all means incorporate them into your movies.

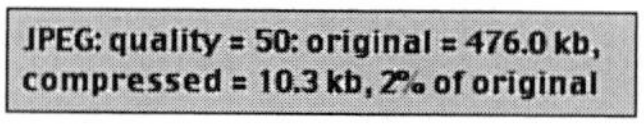

JPEG: quality = 50: original = 476.0 kb, compressed = 10.3 kb, 2% of original

Figure 4.22

Clicking Test compares the resulting file size after compression with the original.

TROUBLESHOOTING

Why do bitmaps appear blurry in my published movie?

Check the Bitmap Properties of bitmaps that appear blurry. Make sure that the Allow Smoothing option is unchecked. Smoothing antialiases a bitmap by smoothing the edges, which can make images appear blurry or out of focus. Also, in the Publish Settings, select the HTML tab and set the quality to Best.

> *For more information about publishing options, see "Specifying Publish Settings," page 647 (Chapter 30, "Optimizing, Publishing, and Exporting Movies").*

Is there any way to trace a bitmap so that it is more detailed in some areas of an image and less so in others?

The trace settings only work globally, producing a standard level of detail throughout an image. However, it is possible to trace the same image twice, with differing amounts of detail, and combine the two by aligning the images on top of each other and erasing the unwanted portions. In this way, you can create a simple tracing for the majority of an image and include more detail in selected areas. This method will increase file size, so use it sparingly.

FLASH AT WORK: ANIMATING BITMAPS

Flash's vector bias is most evident when bitmaps are animated. Flash does not interpolate bitmap information as easily or as well as it does vector information. Remember, bitmaps map each pixel in an image, so there is much more information to interpolate. Bitmap tweens can dramatically increase file size and can produce unwanted effects such as slight stuttering during playback.

Use bitmap animation sparingly and keep the animation simple for best results. Faster, shorter bitmap tweens such as quick zooms are best, and can disguise stuttering that can be apparent in slower tweens. Smaller bitmaps will affect file size less, as will confining animation to as small an area of the Stage as possible. Also, try to confine file-size–intensive effects such as bitmap animation to frames where there are few other effects, or users will have to wait even longer for content to download as movie elements compete for scarce bandwidth. If bitmap animation is crucial, you can experiment with setting a higher frame rate for better quality, but this also increases file size. As always, test several frame rates to make the best compromise between image quality and file size.

WORKING WITH TEXT

WORKING WITH TEXT

Macromedia Flash MX offers a tremendous range of options for manipulating text—from simple static text to highly stylized and animated text. Text can even be pulled in dynamically from external sources at runtime. To make the most of Flash MX's robust text capabilities, you need a firm grasp of how Flash handles text, as well as some of its quirks.

All text displayed on computers is displayed in pixels. How's that, you ask, especially as this book has emphasized Flash's native vector format? Well, computer screens display pixels, period, independently of any application's native format. That's right, chunky squares containing color information. This shape is especially unfortunate for displaying letters. Most letters are not blocky but are instead composed of graceful curves. But the only way computers can transmit the letterforms is to convert curves into pixels, and much is lost in that translation.

Before you decide to throw in the towel and avoid using text, there are ways to overcome—or at least mitigate—blocky monitor pixel display. Antialiasing is an attempt to regain some of the subtlety of curves in a pixel environment. With antialiasing, transitional pixels that are intermediate in color and tone are added between the type and the background, which results in smoother, although potentially fuzzy, letterforms. Say you have black text on a white background. Antialiasing adds some gray pixels around curved areas in the black letters, as shown in Figure 5.1.

Figure 5.1
The letter on the right is antialiased, with gray pixels added on the curves to display smoother letters.

Unfortunately, antialiasing can make text look fuzzy, particularly at small sizes, as you can see in Figure 5.2.

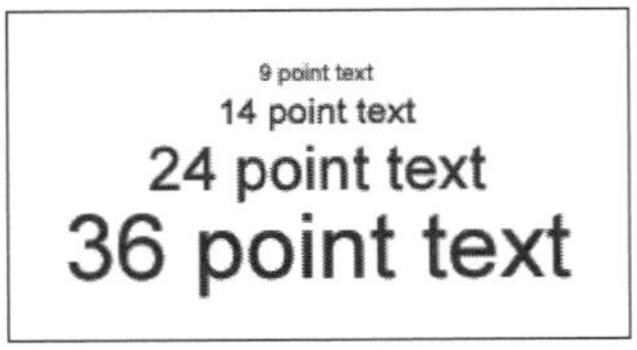

Figure 5.2
Antialiasing works best with relatively large type sizes; otherwise, it makes text appear fuzzy.

9 point text
14 point text
24 point text
36 point text

Enter bitmap fonts. These fonts are designed without curves, specifically for computer display. Because they lack curves, there is no need to antialias. However, because these fonts are designed to the pixel, they must be used at the specific sizes for which they were designed and must be positioned precisely on whole pixels. They are best used at small sizes.

Quality bitmap fonts are becoming more widely available, thanks in large part to the growing popularity of Flash. One of the best sources is www.miniml.com, which features a wide variety of bitmap typefaces, including fonts designed specifically for body text (copy) and headers, plus a serif font.

Bitmap Font Resources

Bitmap fonts are increasingly popular, and new ones are being introduced all the time. Here are some good sources:

`http://cgm.cs.mcgill.ca/~luc/pixel.html` provides an exhaustive list of links to fonts—a fantastic resource.

`http://www.miniml.com` offers a large range of quality styles in multiple sizes. A few free fonts are available, or a 2002 Access Pass provides unlimited access to and use of fonts created in the calendar year for $100.

`http://www.fontsforflash.com/` offers a variety of fonts for sale. Unfortunately, they are offered only in PC format at this time. A few free fonts are offered; you can purchase the rest individually.

The following sites offer free pixel fonts:

- `http://www.dsg4.com/04/extra/bitmap/index.html`
- `http://www.with-m.com/` (select Item and then Font to access the bitmap fonts)
- `http://www.orgdot.com/aliasfonts/`

THE TEXT TOOL

You need to start with the basics. Before you even begin to type, make sure that Snap to Pixels is turned on (View, Snap to Pixels). This setting ensures that bitmap fonts align exactly to whole pixels and, when text is placed directly on the Main Timeline, prevents fuzziness. However, when text is embedded within symbols and then placed on the Main Timeline, pixel snapping does not guarantee against blurry fonts.

> *To learn more information about preventing blurry fonts, see the "Troubleshooting" section at the end of this chapter, page 84.*

To add text to your movies, simply follow these steps:

1. Select the Text tool.

2. Click on the Stage to create an insertion point.

3. Start typing.

That's all there is to it. Alternatively, you can click and drag with the Text tool to draw a text block. By drawing a text block, you can define the width of multiline text. If you click and drag a text block, you'll notice that the width changes while the height remains the same. The height is determined by the point size of the text, which is set in the Property Inspector.

> *For more information about setting text attributes, see "Character Attributes," later in this chapter, page 73.*

As you type, your text wraps and the text block becomes larger to accommodate its contents. In Flash, a handle that appears on text boxes identifies the type of text block and allows you to resize the text block. A square box that appears in the upper-right corner of text blocks, as shown in Figure 5.3, is a fixed-block text handle indicating that the height has been defined. A round handle on the upper right indicates a text block of undefined dimensions that expands as you type, produced when you create an insertion point on the Stage. A round handle on the lower right indicates a vertical text block. To resize a text block, be sure that the Text tool is selected and that there is an insertion point in the text block. Move your mouse pointer over the resize block so that horizontal arrows appear. Drag to the left or right to resize the text block.

> **Caution**
>
> Don't use the Width and Height fields in the Property Inspector to resize text blocks. This distorts text by stretching or condensing it to make it match your designated dimensions.

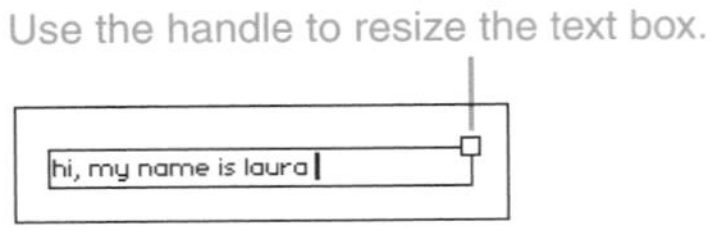

Use the handle to resize the text box.

Figure 5.3
Drag a text box's handle to resize a text box.

hi, my name is laura

THE PROPERTY INSPECTOR

Working with text requires using the Text tool, Arrow tool, and Property Inspector in tandem. The Text tool defines placement of text, dimensions for text blocks, and is used for selecting text within text blocks, whereas the Arrow tool is used to change the position of text blocks and to edit text blocks as a whole. The Property Inspector assigns text attributes, as shown in Figure 5.4. The Flash 5 Character and Paragraph panels have been replaced by the Property Inspector, making it much more convenient to edit text.

Figure 5.4
Use the Property Inspector to define and edit text attributes.

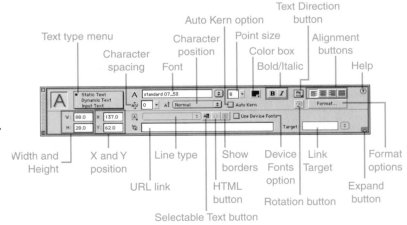

Text can be edited globally—affecting entire text blocks—or specifically—affecting letters or words within text blocks. The most efficient way to make global changes to text blocks—such as changing font, font color, point size or direction—is to use the Arrow tool to select a text block. After a text block is selected, changes made in the Property Inspector affect the entire text block. You cannot, however, make character-level changes or edits that affect letters individually—such as kerning, which determines the spacing between two characters—globally. To edit individual character attributes, you must select individual letters by clicking and dragging with the Text tool. Any subsequent changes made in the Property Inspector affect just the selected characters.

To quickly switch from the Arrow tool to the Text tool when editing text, double-click a text block with the Arrow tool. The arrow pointer changes to an insertion point, and the Text tool is active.

CHARACTER ATTRIBUTES

Text attributes can be divided into those that affect individual letters or characters and those that affect paragraphs. Character attributes affect individual letters and include font selection, point size, text direction, kerning, letter spacing, and character position. Attributes can be set prior to placing text on the Stage—by choosing the Text tool to access text properties in the Property Inspector—or can be changed after text is created.

To edit individual characters, click and drag with the Text tool to select letters on the Stage, as shown in Figure 5.5. Then change text settings within the Property Inspector.

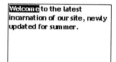

Figure 5.5

Click and drag with the Text tool to edit individual letters within text blocks.

Font Selection and Point Size

You can select a font directly by typing its name into the Font field, or you can use the pop-up arrows next to the Font field to select from the active fonts on your system. If you type in the font name, you'll need to click at the insertion point on the Stage to be able to type your text. Otherwise, Flash MX will enter your text into the Font selection field.

As with the Font name, you may either type directly into the Point size field or use the pop-up slider to select a size. Typing in a size is much easier than trying to manipulate the slider. The only time I use the slider is to preview text at different sizes. Then I select the text and move the slider, keeping my eyes on the text until I find a size I want.

Use the color box to select a font color. Click the color box to access the Web-safe pop-up palette. Click on a color to choose it. To create a custom, non–Web-safe color, you need to use the Color Mixer.

⇨ *For more information about the Color Mixer and working with color in Flash, see Chapter 3, "Drawing and Painting in Flash," page 37. Also see "Best Practices for Using Text," later in this chapter, page 83.*

Flash assigns the fill color to your text. You can also force font styles by using the Bold and Italic buttons. However, you will lose much of the subtlety of typefaces if you force styles upon them. Because typefaces are specifically designed in different weights and styles, choose a bold or italic version of a font for the best results, as shown in Figure 5.6.

Figure 5.6
For best results, use italic or bold versions of fonts, not the Bold or Italic button settings.

Text Direction

A new feature in Flash MX is the capability to control text direction, which provides support for Asian languages. Use the Text Direction button to create vertical text from left to right or from right to left, as shown in Figure 5.7.

Figure 5.7
The Text Direction button allows you to specify horizontal or vertical text.

Kerning and Character Spacing

Kerning refers to the amount of space between two letters or characters, and character spacing inserts a specified amount of space between selected characters or entire blocks of text. Both kerning and character spacing can be defined by positive or negative settings. Positive settings increase the amount of space between letters, and negative settings decrease space until letters eventually overlap, as shown in Figure 5.8. Zero is neutral. For general legibility in blocks of copy, it's best to work within a range of 0 to +5 or even less, depending on text size. The smaller the point size, the greater the effect of character spacing. Many fonts have desirable kerning built in; you can use this kerning by selecting the Auto Kern option.

Figure 5.8
Character spacing: +20 on the top, 0 in the middle, −5 at the bottom.

Use the Text tool to select letters, words, or entire text blocks to specify character spacing; then enter a positive or negative number in the character spacing field, or drag the slider to select the amount of spacing. When used with vertical text, character spacing determines the vertical amount of space between characters. You can also set a preference to turn off kerning of vertical text. When this preference is enabled, character spacing affects only horizontal text.

➪ *For more information about setting preferences, see "Setting Flash Preferences," page 32 (Chapter 2, "The Flash Interface").*

Character Position

Character position determines where text is positioned in relation to its baseline. The baseline is an invisible horizontal line that characters of a typeface sit upon, as shown in Figure 5.9. The character position options are normal, superscript, or subscript. Most of the time you will use the default of Normal, which places text squarely on the baseline. The superscript and subscript options are typically used with special characters or footnotes within text blocks. Superscript places text above the baseline and is used with special symbols such as trademark (™) or the registered trademark symbol (®). Subscript places text slightly below the baseline.

Figure 5.9
The baseline is an implied line that characters sit on. Superscript and subscript appear above or below the baseline.

PARAGRAPH ATTRIBUTES

Paragraph attributes allow you to format chunks of text, from individual paragraphs—blocks of text between hard, or manual, returns—to entire text blocks. These attributes are global in nature and affect blocks of text as opposed to individual letters or words. Paragraph formatting options include alignment, justification, margins, and indentation.

To format a paragraph, use the Text tool to click and drag within a text block to select an entire paragraph. Or, to format an entire text block, click with the Arrow tool to select the text block.

Alignment and Justification

Use the Alignment buttons to specify left-aligned, centered, right-aligned, or full justification of paragraphs. Full justification creates newspaper-style paragraphs that are aligned on both the left and right sides. When using full justification, be sure to check the amount of space that is created by the justification so that large, distracting gaps do not appear between words. These settings also apply to vertical text.

If you are using bitmap fonts, use the default left alignment. Right-alignment, centering, or full justification in particular can force bitmap fonts into sub-pixel alignment so that they appear blurry. The greatest culprit is full justification, which will stretch fonts onto sub-pixel coordinates even when Snap to Pixels is enabled, as shown in Figure 5.10.

5

Ut wisi enim ad minim veniam, quis nostrud exerci tation ullamcorper suscipit lobortis nisl ut aliquip ex ea commodo consequat. Duis autem vel eum iriure dolor in hendrerit in vulputate velit esse molestie consequat, vel illum dolore eu feugiat nulla facilisis at vero eros et accumsan et iusto odio dignissim qui blandit praesent luptatum zzril delenit augue duis dolore te feugait nulla facilisi.

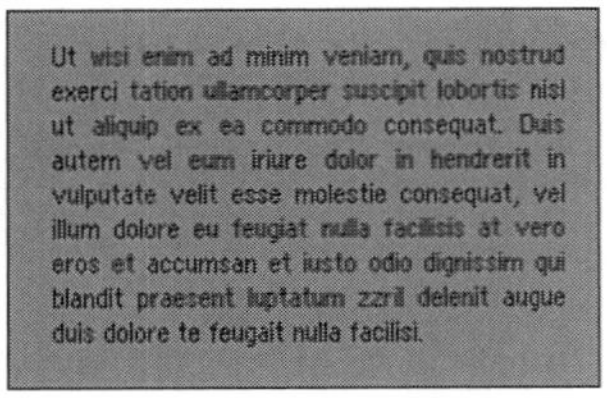

Figure 5.10
Do not use full justification with bitmap fonts, or they will stretch and become blurry.

Indents, Line Spacing, and Margins

Click the Format button to access the Format Options to specify indents, line spacing, and margins, as shown in Figure 5.11. You can enter pixel values directly in the fields, or click the sliders to select values. Changes are immediately previewed in the selected text on the Stage. Click Done when you're finished. Unfortunately, there is no Reset button for this dialog box, so be sure to double-check your settings before you click the Done button. You can revert to the original formatting by pressing Cmd-Z (Macintosh) or Ctrl+Z (Windows) to undo.

Format Options
Indent:
0 px
Done
Line Spacing:
2 pt
Left Margin:
0 px
Right Margin:
0 px
Help

Figure 5.11
The Format dialog box allows you to specify paragraph attributes.

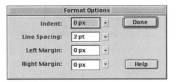

The Indent option of the Format Options dialog box specifies the amount of indentation, in pixels, at the beginning of each paragraph. The default is zero, or no indentation. Indents are used to enhance the visual separation between paragraphs. Entering a positive number in the Indent field moves the beginning of the first line of a paragraph to the right. You also can enter a negative number to create a hanging indent in which the first line "hangs" to the left compared to the rest of the paragraph, as shown in Figure 5.12. Specifying a negative indentation amount has an effect only if a left margin has been created; otherwise, there is no space to the left of the text block to create the hanging indent.

Welcome to the latest, greatest incarnation of our site, newly updated for summer 2002.

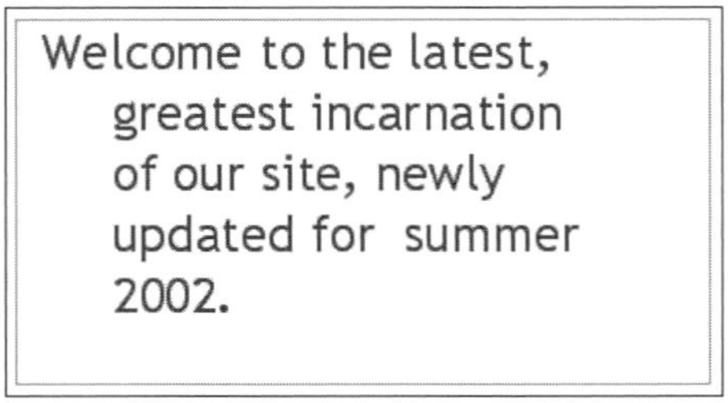

Figure 5.12
Specifying a negative number in the Indent field creates a hanging indent.

The Line Spacing option specifies the amount of space in points between lines of text, traditionally known as *leading*. It's important to pay attention to the amount of line spacing to ensure legibility. Too little space between lines results in crowded text that is difficult to read. Too much space can make lines of text appear to float and can also negatively affect readability. The default line spacing is approximately 120% of the point size of text and is generally acceptable for body copy. Large point sizes typically require less leading, so experiment with the line spacing settings to find the best amount.

Left Margin and Right Margin options specify the amount of indentation from either side for blocks of text. The defaults are zero, or you can specify an amount in pixels to add space on either side within a text block, as shown in Figure 5.13.

Figure 5.13
The Right and Left Margin options increase the amount of space on either side within a text block.

TEXT OPTIONS

With Flash, you are not limited to static text—text that displays in published movies exactly as it is entered in an FLA. Users can insert text into input fields or it can be added dynamically to a movie during runtime. So far, you have worked with static text, which is the default. Static text does not allow for any user input and, to update content, changes must be made in the FLA. Input and dynamic text fields are populated during runtime, and can be accessed and manipulated with ActionScript. When you're utilizing input and dynamic text, you create placeholder text fields within an FLA to designate where text will be placed and how it will appear during playback of the movie. Input and dynamic text attributes, like static text attributes, are assigned within the Property Inspector.

Input Text

Input text enables users to insert text, as in a form, while a movie is playing. Input text fields are assigned variable names so that the information entered into them can be saved and accessed using ActionScript.

For more information about using ActionScript with input text, see Chapter 16, "Interaction, Events, and Sequencing," page 303.

To use input text, make sure that the Text tool is active and select Input from the pop-up Text type menu in the Property Inspector. You must draw a text field on the Stage where the user can enter text, or you can convert an existing text block by selecting it and changing the text type to Input. The borders of input text fields appear as dotted lines. The text block handle is a filled square on the lower right, indicating an input or dynamic text box. Assign text attributes such as font, point size, and font color in the Property Inspector as you would with static text. To preview how text will appear as the user enters it, type something in your input text field, as shown in Figure 5.14.

Figure 5.14
Enter some text in your input text field to preview how the text will appear when a user types.

It is important to indicate to your users where they should click to enter input text. Unless your layout graphically indicates where the user should enter text, you'll need to turn on borders around your input text field. To do so, click the Show Borders button. One caveat, though, is to be aware that if you do turn on the borders, your input text field will appear with a black border and a white background. If this is undesirable, you can position an input field without borders over a shape that can indicate your input boundaries, as shown in Figure 5.15. Alternatively, you can use ActionScript to set the background and border colors.

Figure 5.15
Position your input text field over graphic elements to indicate the borders without having a white background appear.

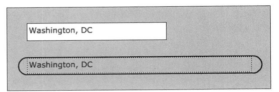

Dynamic Text

Dynamic text is loaded into your movie at runtime from an external source. "Dynamic" refers to content that is culled during playback rather than being assembled in advance in the FLA. This is a terrific option for content that changes frequently, such as news stories, because content can be updated without editing the FLA. A variable name must be assigned to the text field, as seen in Figure 5.16, to designate the source for the dynamic content.

To add dynamic text, follow these steps:

1. Select dynamic text from the Text type menu.

2. Click on the Stage to create a dynamic text field.

   Similar to input text fields, the borders of dynamic text fields appear as dotted lines on the Stage. The text block handle is a filled square on the lower right, indicating an input or dynamic text box.

You can also preview the appearance of dynamic content by typing in a dynamic text field.

Text Formatting Options

Several text formatting options are specific to input and dynamic text. You must give these text fields instance names to be able to access their properties using ActionScript. To do so, enter a unique instance name in the Instance name field, which is beneath the Text type pop-up in the Property Inspector, as shown in Figure 5.16.

For more information about using ActionScript to access text fields, see Chapter 16, "Interaction, Events, and Sequencing," page 303, and Chapter 20, "Using the Built-in Movie Objects," page 443.

Figure 5.16
Variable names allow you to access the contents of text fields using ActionScript.

Variable names allow you to access text field content programmatically to perform calculations. Variable names also allow you to access user-entered content in input text fields or assign content to dynamic text fields. To assign a variable name to a text field, enter a unique name in the Variable field (see Figure 5.16).

Using the Line type drop-down option, you can specify whether more than a single line of text can be entered into a text field. The options are Single Line; Multiline, which displays multiple lines of text; and Multiline No Wrap, which displays multiple lines only if the user enters hard breaks using Return (Mac) or Enter (Windows).

The Maximum Characters field, as shown in the lower-right corner of Figure 5.16, allows you to limit the number of characters that can be entered into an input text field.

The Render as HTML button preserves some of the HTML formatting of text when text fields are assigned variables or instance values that contain HTML formatting. When this option is selected, Flash applies the appropriate HTML tags to text when exporting SWF files. The supported tags are links, bold, italic, underline, paragraph, font color, font face, and font size. Supported HTML attributes are leftmargin, rightmargin, align indent, and leading. Render as HTML can also be set programmatically using the `html` property of the `TextField` object.

Finally, this panel contains an option to allow users to select dynamic text. It is turned on by default; if you don't want users to be able to select your text, such as to copy and paste it, be sure to deselect the Selectable Text button, as shown in Figure 5.17.

Figure 5.17
Deselecting the Selectable Text button prevents users from copying and pasting dynamic text.

Embedded and Device Fonts

When you create text in Flash, all the fonts installed on your system are at your disposal. However, different users may not have your installed fonts, and different fonts are available on different platforms. Does this mean that your careful formatting of text will go to waste? No, but you will need to take steps to ensure that users see the typefaces you intend them to see.

You have two options. One is to embed font outlines. Embedding allows you to save the outlines of your fonts so that text is displayed in the specified font even if it is not installed on a user's system. Flash will antialias embedded fonts. Embedding fonts does add to the overall file size of movies, but in some cases you may not need to embed all the characters in a given font.

With static text, you don't need to embed the fonts because the outlines are automatically saved. Fonts used in dynamic and input text fields are not embedded by default and, therefore, are not antialiased. To embed fonts, follow these steps:

1. Select a dynamic or input text field on the Stage.

2. In the Property Inspector, click the Character Options button. The Character Options dialog box launches and allows you to specify whether you want to embed fonts, as shown in Figure 5.18.

Figure 5.18
Using the Character Options dialog box, you can specify whether font outlines are embedded for dynamic and input text fields.

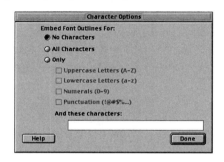

You have the option to embed font outlines for no characters, all characters, or only specified characters. This is how Flash helps you to keep file size down, so you should plan for which characters may be needed in a given text field. For instance, you don't need to embed characters other than numerals for a text field that will contain the year in four-digit format. So, for a date text field, select Only and then Numerals in the Character Options dialog box.

Not all fonts can be embedded and exported with your movie. Sometimes Flash doesn't recognize font outline information. To test whether a font can be embedded, select the text and choose View, Antialias Text. This action creates a preview, and if the text appears jagged, Flash does not recognize the font's outlines and will not export it.

The other font display option is device fonts. Computer operating systems include a limited number of fonts that are automatically installed. These fonts are different on Macintosh and Windows platforms, but each platform includes a sans serif, a serif, and a typewriter typeface. A serif typeface includes decorative lines along the main strokes of characters, as shown in Figure 5.18. Sans serif is Latin for "without serif." Typewriter typefaces are monospaced, meaning that each letter occupies an identical amount of space. Note that both the capital *A* and the lowercase *i* in the typewriter typeface in Figure 5.19 occupy equal amounts of space. Compare this to the serif and sans serif examples.

Figure 5.19
Device fonts utilize system fonts that include serif, sans serif, and typewriter typefaces.

When device fonts are specified, outlines are not embedded, and the Flash Player displays the most similar font that is installed on the user's system. Three device fonts are available: _sans, which typically uses Helvetica or Arial; _serif, which typically uses Times or Times New Roman; and _typewriter, which uses fonts similar to Courier. To specify device fonts, select them from the Font pop-up list, as shown in Figure 5.20.

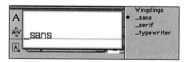

Figure 5.20

You can select device fonts from the Font pop-up list in the Property Inspector.

Device fonts produce smaller file sizes than embedded fonts, but there is an element of uncertainty; if a user doesn't have installed fonts that correspond to specified device fonts, strange and unexpected substitutions may occur. Device fonts are not antialiased, so they work best at small sizes where antialiasing can make characters appear fuzzy. They appear noticeably jagged at large sizes because they are not antialiased.

EDITING AND TRANSFORMING TEXT

You can use basic word processing techniques within Flash to edit your text. You can copy, cut, and paste within Flash and to other applications. Unfortunately, there is no spell checking. You have to copy Flash text into a word processing program to spell check it, and then copy it back if you make changes. The formatting of your text will be retained. Be sure to select and replace the original text when you copy corrected text back into Flash, or else a new text block will be created for the copied text and it will be at a different position and of different dimensions than the original.

Use the Text tool to select characters within text blocks. Click and drag to select multiple characters, or double-click to select an entire word. To make a long selection without dragging, click at the beginning and Shift+click at the end. To select all the words in a text block, press Cmd-A (Mac) or Ctrl+A (Windows).

To select a text box to be able to move or copy it, use the Arrow tool. Shift+clicking selects multiple text boxes. You can copy a text block by Option-clicking (Macintosh) or Alt+clicking (Windows) and dragging a text block with the Arrow tool.

Breaking Text Apart

With Flash MX, you can easily break apart text and place each character into a separate text block. Individual characters in words can then be animated separately, or text can be converted into shapes. In Flash 5, breaking apart a text box converted the text to shapes. In Flash MX, you can break text apart once to place each character into a separate text block. To break apart text, follow these steps:

1. Select a text block using the Arrow tool.

2. Choose Modify, Break Apart; then choose Modify, Break Apart again to convert the character text blocks into shapes, as shown in Figure 5.21.

Figure 5.21
Break apart text once to place each character into its own text box or a second time to convert text blocks to shapes.

After text is converted to shapes, it is no longer recognized as text and cannot be edited as text.

With text broken apart, MX allows you to quickly distribute the character blocks to separate layers. Select the text blocks with the Arrow tool and then choose Modify, Distribute to Layers. Flash places each letter on a separate layer, named for each character, as shown in Figure 5.22.

Figure 5.22
The Distribute to Layers option places each character block on a separate layer.

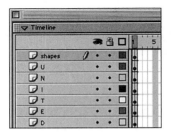

Naming Distributed Layers

Flash assigns each distributed layer the name of the letter it contains. If a word uses a letter more than once, you end up with several layers with the same name. This quickly becomes confusing, so be sure to add numbers or otherwise create distinctions between layers containing the same letters.

Transforming Text

After your text is broken apart into shapes, it can be dramatically transformed. You can use the Subselection tool to select points and move them, changing the shapes of letters, as shown in Figure 5.23. Such transformations can be used to create unique letter shapes and can be animated over time using shape tweens.

For more information about creating animation and shape tweens, see Chapter 7, "Animating in Flash," page 109.

Figure 5.23
After your text is broken apart into shapes, you can use the Subselection tool to drag anchor points and reshape letters.

You can also use the new Distort and Envelope transform modifiers to really push the boundaries of text distortion. You cannot use these modifiers on groups or symbols, so you must create text and break it apart twice to convert it to shapes. Then you use either the Arrow tool or the Transform tool and drag over shapes that create a word to transform the word as a whole. If you use the Arrow tool, select the Transform tool; then select the Distort or Envelope modifiers of the Transform tool at the bottom of the Toolbox, and select and drag the transform handles that appear around your word, as shown in Figure 5.24.

Figure 5.24
Use the Distort modifier of the Transform tool to create perspective text effects.

The Envelope modifier creates the most dramatic transformation and can completely change the shapes of letters, as shown in Figure 5.25. Use this powerful capability carefully because letters can become so misshapen that they are no longer recognizable or legible.

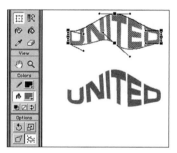

Figure 5.25
Use the Envelope modifier of the Transform tool for more psychedelic text effects.

BEST PRACTICES FOR USING TEXT

The essential criteria of using text is that it is legible. After all, the purpose of text is to be read in order to convey information. If it cannot be read, the information will not be conveyed. It is crucial to ensure that your text can be read.

Attributes that contribute to or impede legibility include the following:

- Contrast between text color and background color
- Serif typefaces
- Point size
- Letter spacing and line spacing

These attributes are especially important when bitmap fonts are used. The point size is predetermined for bitmap fonts and is often small. It is therefore even more important to ensure that there is sufficient contrast between font color and background color. Dark text on light backgrounds is most easily read, although light text can be used on dark backgrounds if the colors are carefully chosen to ensure sufficient contrast. Avoid combining text and background colors that are similar in brightness, especially with text at small sizes such as body copy set in bitmap fonts.

Another rule of thumb is to avoid the use of serif typefaces at small sizes. Serifs are delicate lines, much finer than the main strokes of letters, and at small sizes it is difficult to distinguish such fine detail. Antialiasing exacerbates the problem. Miniml offers a bitmap serif font, Cerif, which is more legible at small sizes.

⇨ *For more information about Miniml fonts and other bitmap fonts, see "Bitmap Font Resources," earlier in this chapter, page 71.*

If you are not using bitmap fonts, you can control the point size of your text. Preview your text at different sizes and formatting to find the optimum size, letter spacing, and line spacing. Also, have someone else read your text to ensure that a viewer who is unfamiliar with the content can comfortably read it.

TROUBLESHOOTING

Why do bitmap fonts placed on whole pixel coordinates in a movie clip appear blurry when placed on the Main Timeline?

Check to be sure that your movie clip is placed on whole pixel coordinates in the Main Timeline. Placement on the Main Timeline determines the coordinates of the text embedded within a movie clip. Even though your text may reside on whole coordinates (x.0) in a nested clip, if the clip is placed on sub-pixel coordinates on the Main Timeline (for example, x.5), the text is in fact displayed at the sub-pixel coordinate: x.0 + x.5 = x.5.

Also, when you publish a movie containing bitmap fonts, be sure to select No Scale from the Scale options within the HTML Publish Settings. If the movie is allowed to scale, its dimensions are determined by the size of the browser window, causing the SWF to stretch or shrink. Any text will also stretch or shrink and display at sizes different from those specified in your FLA. Bitmap fonts are mapped to specific pixels and must be displayed at precise sizes in order to render correctly.

Bitmap fonts are especially problematic when used in components. The reason is that the movie clips within components that contain text are not positioned on whole pixels. Branden Hall has scripted a workaround that rounds the pixel placement. You can find it at `http://www.waxpraxis.org/entry_blog-15.html`.

⇨ *For more information about publish settings, see Chapter 30, "Optimizing, Publishing, and Exporting Movies," page 643. For more information about using components, see Chapter 9, "Buttons, Menus, and User Input," page 143, and Chapter 22, "Components," page 511.*

Why am I unable to use bold or italic text in a dynamic text field?

You can run into problems if you use HTML formatting with a font that is embedded. Embedding fonts includes the font outlines in the published movie. However, bold and italic fonts are distinct, separate outlines that must also be embedded to display. Embedding bold and italic font outlines will significantly increase the size of your movie—you are tripling the font information that is contained in a movie. Also, you may have to trick Flash into including these outlines. To embed the outlines, you must create a text field to specify each outline. You can do so by creating pseudo text fields that specify alternative outlines—one for bold, one for italic, and so on—that are positioned outside the viewable Stage area. You don't want these text fields to be visible in the final movie. In some cases, you can limit the embedded characters if you know the types of characters that will be used in your dynamic text fields. Still, embedding additional outlines will noticeably increase the file size of your movie.

A simpler solution is to specify device fonts for your dynamic text field. This ensures the display of HTML text and does not add to the final file size. You do relinquish some control over the way your text is displayed, but the file savings and insurance that HTML text will display is generally worth the compromise.

FLASH AT WORK: COPYING TEXT BOXES

If you need to create several input or dynamic text fields that are the same size and have the same attributes, it's fastest to copy and paste a single text field. However, copied text fields have identical attributes, *including* instance and variable names. This will really mess up your scripting, so you must—I repeat *must*—then assign unique instance and variable names for each text field. Be compulsive about naming.

Similarly, if you're debugging scripts for multiple text fields and can't find any errors, check your instance and variable names for repetition. Because you can display the attributes of only one text field at a time in the Property Inspector, it's best to use the Movie Explorer, as shown in Figure 5.26, or the List Variables option in the Debugger to view the entire list of variables at once.

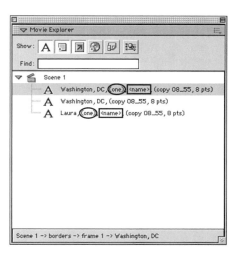

Figure 5.26
The Movie Explorer reveals that two text fields have the same instance names.

ANIMATION AND SOUND

IN THIS PART

SYMBOLS, INSTANCES, AND LIBRARY ASSETS

UNDERSTANDING SYMBOLS

Symbols are the cornerstones of Macromedia Flash, the building blocks of your movies. Any time you draw a shape, place an imported bitmap, or animate an object, Flash must store the information required to render these elements in your published movie. As with any Web-delivered content, minimizing file size while maximizing content is crucial, and is a tightrope that must continually be negotiated. Symbols are archetypes—objects that are stored and can be used repeatedly.

Symbols are stored in the Library, and instances are dragged from the Library to the Stage. Each individual symbol instance on the Stage is a copy that is independent of its original and any other instances, and can be manipulated freely without changing the original. Because the original is stored and reused with each instance, you can create as many instances as you want with minimal impact on file size. Symbols also enhance playback because the Flash Player needs to download a symbol only once.

Think of symbols as Flash Legos. Not only do they decrease file size, but when used properly, they also increase your efficiency as you work. The trick is to learn to separate the elements of your movies into component parts—Legos—that can be snapped together to form complex animations and interface systems. Then, when you need to make changes, you can make them in a single place and affect many parts of your movie.

Any object on the Stage can be converted to a symbol. Given the tremendous file savings if an element is to be reused, it saves time to make any element that could potentially be reused into a symbol. There are three types of symbols: graphic, button, and movie clip. Each has its own timeline, Stage, and layers.

Graphic Symbols

Graphic symbols are the most basic and least powerful symbols. Graphic symbols are tied to the Main Timeline, and are best used with static images, such as backgrounds. Graphics can be animated but cannot contain sounds or interactive elements. Further, because they are controlled by the Main Timeline, a graphic symbol will play only for the duration of frames that exist on the Main Timeline. With all the power of movie clips at your disposal for animation, you should reserve your graphic symbols for static elements that are reused.

Button Symbols

Buttons are interactive symbols that respond to user interaction, such as mouse clicks and rollovers. Buttons have unique timelines containing Up, Over, Down, and Hit frames, as shown in Figure 6.1. These frames represent various button states. Button timelines don't unfold over time like other timelines, but instead respond and move among the four frames according to user interaction.

The Up state defines how the button appears on the Stage, with no user interaction. Over provides a rollover state when the user's mouse pointer hovers over the button. Down is the state or appearance of the button when it is clicked. Hit allows you to establish the physical boundaries of your button, defining the area that will respond to the user's mouse. Anything placed in the Hit frame will not be visible on the Stage. You don't need to create all four states for your buttons. Button states can contain graphics, sounds, and even movie clips.

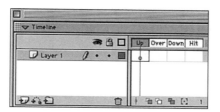

Figure 6.1
Buttons have unique timelines containing Up, Over, Down, and Hit states.

To learn more about buttons, see Chapter 9, "Buttons, Menus, and User Input," page 143.

Movie Clips

Movie clips are self-contained movies—mini-movies, if you will—with their own, independent time-lines that are not tied to the Main Timeline. This capability to place timelines within timelines is a hallmark of Flash, and the key to its capacity for complex interactivity and multilinear narrative flow. Think of the Main Timeline as a master movie clip. Movie clips can contain graphics, buttons and scripted interactive controls, sounds, videos, and even other movie clips.

To learn about the Movie Clip object within ActionScript, see Chapter 17, "Unlocking the Power of Movie Clips," page 331.

CREATING SYMBOLS

So, how do you begin to build movies with your Flash Legos? First, you need to build Legos for a particular movie.

You can create symbols directly or convert objects on the Stage to symbols. The more you use Flash, the more adept you will become at planning symbols in advance. If you know before you create art-work that it will be reused, create a new symbol and then create the artwork as a symbol. Alternatively, you may develop a movie element and then realize that it will be reused. In this case, you can easily convert artwork to symbols.

To create a new, empty symbol, make sure that nothing is selected on the Stage and then choose Insert, Symbol or press Cmd-F8 (Mac) or Ctrl+F8 (Windows). The Create New Symbol dialog box appears, as shown in Figure 6.2.

Type in a name for your symbol, and choose the type of symbol: movie clip (the default), button, or graphic. Then click OK. Your symbol is added to the Library and is opened in the work area in symbol-editing mode. The name of your symbol appears in the Information bar above the upper-left corner of the Stage, and a cross-hair icon appears in the middle of the Stage indicating the symbol's registration point, as shown in Figure 6.3. You can now add content to your symbol.

Always be on the lookout for opportunities to convert artwork into component parts that can be reused. Symbols increase your efficiency, so take the fullest possible advantage of them.

6

Figure 6.2
In the Create New Symbol dialog box, you can name your symbol and choose its type.

Figure 6.3
When you create a new symbol, it is placed in the Library and opened in symbol-editing mode.

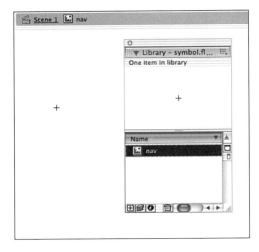

Registration

The registration point is the point of reference used when positioning a symbol numerically. There are nine standard points of registration: each of the four corners, the center point, and the midpoint on each edge of an object. The registration point determines the 0,0 point—0x and 0y—for that symbol.

To learn how to change a symbol's registration point, see "Editing Registration Points," later in this chapter, page 100.

Coordinate systems map a two-dimensional plane, allowing you to plot objects to specific coordinates. Flash uses an inverted Cartesian coordinate system, with 0,0 (x,y) marking the upper-left corner of the Stage or, in a published movie, the screen. The x-axis is the horizontal axis, and the y-axis is the vertical axis. Before you have nightmarish flashbacks to high school algebra, all you need to grasp is that as an object moves to the right, its x-value increases, and as it moves down, its y-value increases. Moving to the left decreases the x-value, until its values become negative when it crosses to the left of the y-axis and moves off the Stage (or screen). Moving up decreases the y-value until it becomes negative when it crosses above the x-axis and moves off the Stage (or screen), as shown in Figure 6.4.

Flash needs to know the internal reference point for each object to be able to position it precisely on the Stage. If you have a square that is 10 pixels × 10 pixels that you want to place at the upper-left corner of the Stage (0,0), Flash needs to know which part of the square should be positioned at 0,0.

The nine standard points of registration are the available options when you convert artwork to a symbol. However, a symbol can be edited to change its registration to any point within the symbol.

If the registration point is at the center, the center will be placed at 0,0 and most of the square will be off the Stage (or screen), as shown in Figure 6.5.

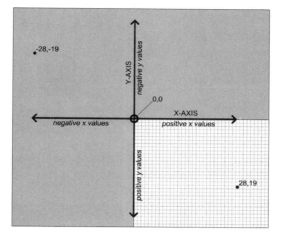

Figure 6.4
In the Flash coordinate system, the upper-left corner of the Stage is 0,0.

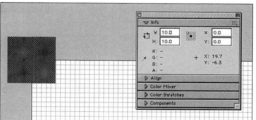

Figure 6.5
If an object's registration point is its center, it will be positioned according to its center point.

If the registration point is the upper left, the upper-left corner is placed at 0,0, keeping the square positioned within the Stage or screen, as shown in Figure 6.6.

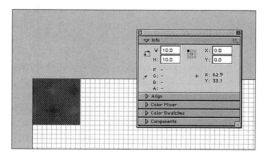

Figure 6.6
If an object's registration point is one of its corners, it will be positioned according to that corner point.

Convert to Symbol

To convert an existing object on the Stage to a symbol, select it and choose Insert, Convert to Symbol, as shown in Figure 6.7, or press F8.

Figure 6.7
Choose Insert, Convert to Symbol
to convert an object on the Stage
to a symbol.

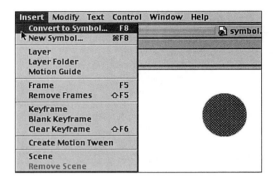

Choosing this option launches the Convert to Symbol dialog box, which is nearly identical to the
Create New Symbol dialog box with an important exception—it contains a Registration setting, as
shown in Figure 6.8.

Figure 6.8
The Convert to Symbol dialog box
allows you to convert an object
on the Stage to a symbol and set
its registration point.

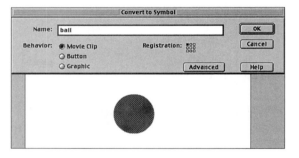

Click one of the squares in the Registration grid to set the registration point. In general, positioning
objects according to their upper-left corner is much easier. I almost always change the registration to
the upper left as that is typically the best reference point for positioning objects. When you convert
an object to a symbol, the default registration is the center point. However, if you change it in the
Convert to Symbol dialog box, that setting becomes the default for the duration of your work
session.

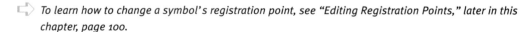 *To learn how to change a symbol's registration point, see "Editing Registration Points," later in this
chapter, page 100.*

Give your symbol a name, select the type of symbol, and then click OK. The symbol is added to the
Library, and the selection on the Stage becomes an instance of the symbol, as indicated by the
square bounding box that appears, as shown in Figure 6.9. The cross-hair within a circle indicates
the registration point of the symbol.

Figure 6.9
When you use Convert to Symbol,
the selection on the Stage
becomes an instance with a rectangular bounding box.

You can also duplicate an existing symbol to use it as a template for a new symbol. Select an instance on the Stage and choose Modify, Duplicate Symbol. You can name the new symbol in the Symbol Name dialog box that appears, as shown in Figure 6.10. You can then edit the new symbol.

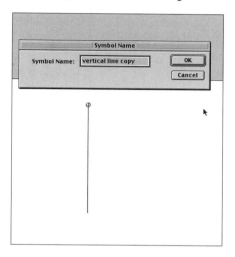

Figure 6.10
To duplicate a symbol, select an existing instance and choose Modify, Duplicate Symbol.

Say you want to create a tic-tac-toe game in Flash. You can create the game grid using symbols. Your first symbol is a vertical line. You can then duplicate the vertical line symbol, as shown in Figure 6.11, to create the horizontal lines.

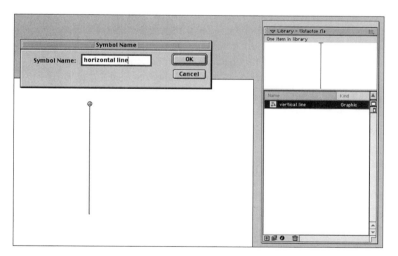

Figure 6.11
In the Symbol Name dialog box, you can name the new duplicate symbol.

After you've duplicated the vertical line, you can rotate it to create a horizontal line symbol, as shown in Figure 6.12.

6

Figure 6.12
You can then edit the duplicate to create a unique symbol.

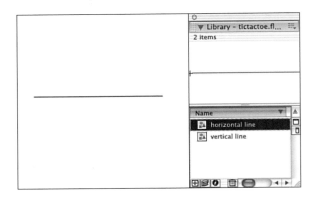

EDITING SYMBOLS

Over the course of a project, changes will be made and symbols will need to be edited. Color schemes, graphics, and even the navigation structure of a movie may change. Because symbols are archetypes, editing a symbol changes every instance of that symbol. This is the beauty of symbols. If a client dislikes a particular color, using symbols allows you to quickly change the color in a few symbols and update the color throughout an entire movie. You can edit symbols in three ways: in place, in a new window, or in symbol-editing mode.

Edit in Place

As its name implies, the Edit in Place command allows you to edit a symbol within the context of the Stage. This capability is useful for tweaking size, color, and shape. To edit in place, double-click a symbol on the Stage, or select a symbol and choose Edit, Edit in Place, or Ctrl-click (Mac), or right-click (Windows) and select Edit in Place from the pop-up menu, as shown in Figure 6.13.

Using the tic-tac-toe example, the circle symbol is too big for the tic-tac-toe grid. The Edit in Place command enables you to scale the circle within the context of the grid, ensuring it is in proportion with other elements, as shown in Figure 6.14.

After you finish editing, click the back button or the current scene name in the Information bar above the upper-left corner of the Stage, click the current scene in the scene pop-up menu, or choose Edit, Edit Document.

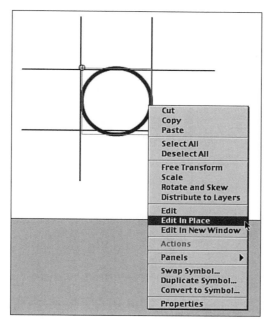

Figure 6.13
To edit in place, select a symbol and choose Edit in Place from the pop-up menu.

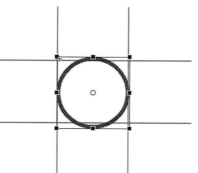

Figure 6.14
Edit in Place allows you to edit symbols within the context of other objects on the Stage.

Edit in New Window

You can also edit symbols in a new window. Editing in a new window launches the symbol's time-line in a new window while the main movie remains open in the original window. This allows you to refer to other elements within a movie—even those in frames other than the frame where a symbol resides—as you edit a symbol.

To edit a symbol in a new window, select the symbol on the Stage and Ctrl-click (Mac) or right-click (Windows) and select Edit in New Window from the pop-up menu, as shown in Figure 6.15.

6

Figure 6.15
Select Edit in New Window from
the pop-up menu to edit a symbol
in a new window.

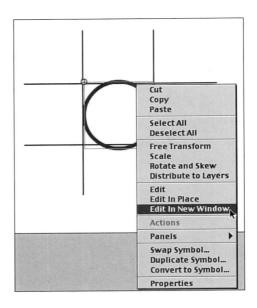

Figure 6.15
Select Edit in New Window from
the pop-up menu to edit a symbol
in a new window.

The symbol opens in a separate window, as shown in Figure 6.16. Edit as needed and then click the
Close button in the upper-left corner (Mac) or the upper-right corner (Windows) to return to the Main
Timeline.

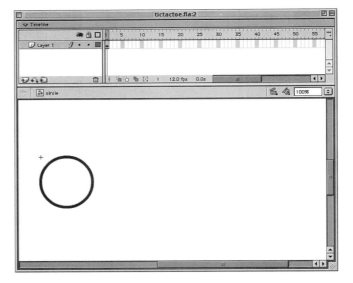

Figure 6.16
The Edit in New Window command opens the symbol in a
separate window.

Symbol-Editing Mode

Editing in symbol-editing mode takes you from the main work area—whichever timeline you may be working in—into the symbol's timeline. If you need to make extensive changes to a symbol, it can be easiest to edit it in isolation. You can access symbol-editing mode as follows:

- Select the symbol on the Stage. Then Ctrl-click (Mac) or right-click (Windows) and select Edit from the pop-up menu.

- Select the symbol on the Stage and choose Edit, Edit Symbols.

- Double-click the symbol's icon (located to the left of the symbol's name, as shown in Figure 6.17) in the Library.

Figure 6.17
To access symbol-editing mode, double-click a symbol's icon in the Library.

- Select the symbol in the Library and choose Edit from the Library options pop-up menu, as shown in Figure 6.18. Alternatively, Ctrl-click (Mac) or right-click (Windows) and select Edit from the pop-up menu.

Edit as needed and then click the back button in the Information bar, or choose Edit, Edit Document to return to the Main Timeline.

6

Figure 6.18
Alternatively, you can select Edit
from the pop-up menu.

Editing Registration Points

Because Flash uses a symbol's registration point as the axis for transformations and positioning, you may need to change the registration point of certain symbols. A common example is in scripted status bars, which are most often used in preloaders to indicate the progress of a download to users. In this example, a status bar consists of a symbol—a graphical shape, usually a rectangle—that is scripted to extend, or grow wider, to represent the progress of a download. If the registration point is the center of the status bar symbol, changes in the width of the progress bar occur from the center in either direction, as shown in Figure 6.19, which is probably not the effect you intend.

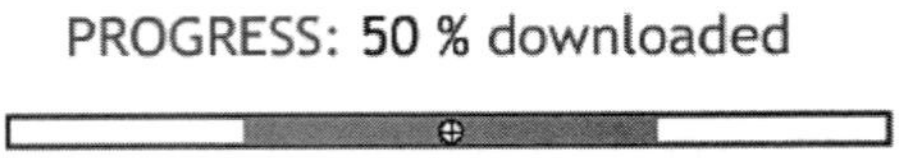

Figure 6.19
If a symbol's registration point is
its center, any transformations
occur from that point.

PROGRESS: **50** % downloaded

For a progress bar to grow wider to the right only—the standard representation of a progression—the registration point of the status bar symbol must be the center point of the left side of the graphic, as shown in Figure 6.20.

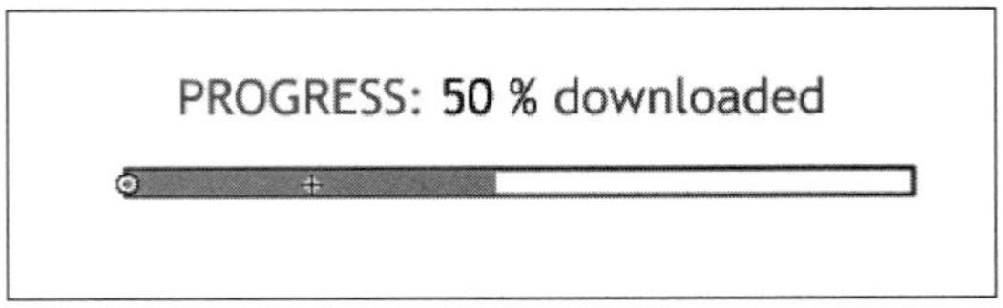

Figure 6.20
The status bar symbol's registration point is the center of the left
side, so changes in its width
occur from the left.

PROGRESS: **50** % downloaded

A quick way to change to a symbol's registration point that allows you to position the registration point visually is to select a symbol on the Stage and then select the Transform tool in the Toolbox. A circle appears within the selected symbol to indicate the registration point, as shown in Figure 6.21. You can click and drag the circle to relocate the registration point.

Figure 6.21
Select the Transform tool and click and drag the white circle to change a symbol's registration point.

⇨ *For more information about registration points, see "Registration," earlier in this chapter, page 92.*

INSTANCES

Symbols reside in the Library. Any time you place a symbol on the Stage, you are actually placing an *instance* of the symbol, not the symbol itself. This is an important distinction. Changing the original symbol within the Library changes the archetype and every instance of that symbol. However, instances are independent of their original symbols. You can edit an instance without changing the symbol itself or affecting any other instances of the same symbol.

To edit an instance, simply select it and make changes. If you select an instance and use the Transform tool to scale it, you change the dimensions of that instance only. To change the dimensions of the symbol itself, you would need to edit the symbol using one of the methods outlined previously in this chapter.

You can also change an instance's type of behavior. Say you have an instance of a graphic symbol that you want to animate independently of the Main Timeline. You can easily change that instance from a graphic to a movie clip. Select the instance and, in the Property Inspector, use the drop-down menu to change the instance type, as shown in Figure 6.22.

Figure 6.22
Use the Instance type drop-down menu in the Property Inspector to change instance behavior.

Changing Instance Properties

An instance has several properties that are independent of its original symbol. They are brightness, tint, alpha, and advanced color settings. You access these properties by using the Color drop-down menu on the Properties Inspector, as shown in Figure 6.23.

Figure 6.23
The Color drop-down allows you to manipulate an instance's color properties.

Use the Brightness option to make an instance lighter or darker. Enter a value directly in the Brightness field or drag the slider to change the relative brightness of an instance from 100% (white) to –100% (black), as shown in Figure 6.24.

Figure 6.24
Changing the brightness of an instance makes it lighter or darker.

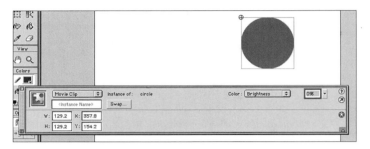

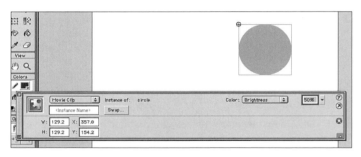

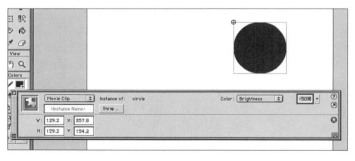

The Tint option allows you to change the hue of an instance by manipulating its red, green, blue, and alpha values. First, select the color you want to tint with, and either enter its values in the red, green, and blue fields or use the Color box to select a Web-safe color. Then adjust the alpha setting to change the saturation of the tint, as shown in Figure 6.25.

Figure 6.25
Change the red, green, blue, and alpha settings within the Tint option to change an instance's hue.

The Alpha option changes the transparency of an instance, from 100% (opaque) to 0% (completely transparent). Enter a value in the Alpha field or use the slider to select a setting.

The Advanced option allows you to separately manipulate the red, green, blue, and transparency values of instances, producing more subtle effects than tint. Select Advanced from the Color pop-up menu. A Settings button appears next to the Color pop-up menu, as shown in Figure 6.26. Click the Settings button to launch the Advanced Settings dialog box.

Figure 6.26
To launch the Advanced Settings dialog box, select Advanced from the Color pop-up menu, and a Settings button appears.

You can adjust these values either by percentages (using fields in the left column) or by absolute values (using fields in the right column), as shown in Figure 6.27.

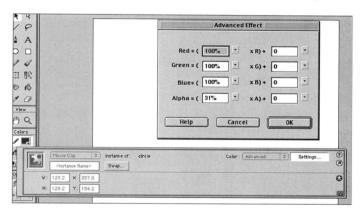

Figure 6.27
In the Advanced Effects dialog box, you can manipulate settings by percentages or by numeric values.

Advanced Effects work by taking the current red, green, and blue values and multiplying them by the percentages entered in the left column. These amounts are then added to the values in the right column, producing new color values. Don't be intimidated by the Advanced Color settings; just take the time to experiment with them. You'll find these subtle effects work best with the range of color values found in bitmaps.

For more information about using bitmaps, see Chapter 4, "Using Bitmaps in Flash," page 55.

Swapping Symbols

As you develop a movie, you may want to swap an instance of one symbol for an instance of a different symbol—for example, to swap graphics. Like Legos, symbols are easily interchanged. To swap a symbol instance, select the instance and click Swap in the Property Inspector to launch the Swap Symbol dialog box. The Swap Symbol dialog box displays all the symbols in the Library, as shown in Figure 6.28. Select one to swap to and click OK.

Figure 6.28
In the Swap Symbol dialog box, you can swap the symbol that is represented in a particular instance.

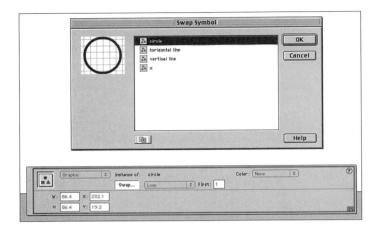

Instance Names

Movie clip and button instances can be given unique instance names, which allow you to access symbol instances using ActionScript. Symbol instances can then be manipulated programmatically. Scripting provides much greater control over symbol instances and allows you to create content that can change in response to user actions.

▷ *For more information about using ActionScript to access instances, see Chapter 17, "Unlocking the Power of Movie Clips," page 331.*

To assign an instance name, select a button or movie clip instance on the Stage and type a unique name in the Instance Name field, as shown in Figure 6.29.

Figure 6.29
Instance names allow you to access individual movie clip and button instances with ActionScript.

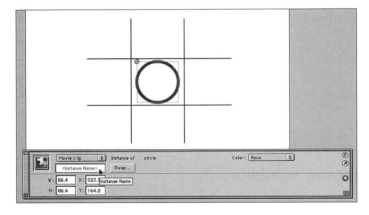

THE LIBRARY

Symbols are housed and organized in the Library. Think of the Library as your Lego toy chest. And your mother was right: It's best to keep your toy chest neat and tidy. The more organized your Library is, the more efficiently you can work.

To open the Library, choose Window, Library or press F11. You'll need to have the Library open to drag symbol instances to the Stage, so you may even want to dock the Library with the other panels you keep open as you work. The Library panel consists of a preview window and a scrolling list of symbols and imported assets. You can expand the Library by clicking the Wide Library View button, as shown in Figure 6.30, to see how symbols are organized.

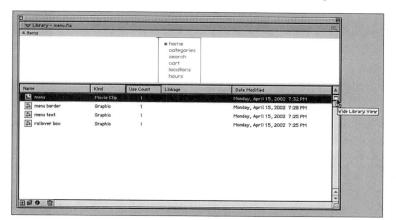

Figure 6.30
Click the Wide Library View button to expand the Library panel.

The first column lists symbols by name in alphabetical order by default, including symbol type icons, and is visible when the Library is in narrow view mode. To change the sort order in the Library, click on the column headers to sort by name, type, use count, linkage, or date modified.

The Use Count column reflects the number of times a symbol is used in a movie. Sorting by use count is helpful in identifying symbols that may no longer be used in your movies, and can also help you to optimize a movie. If your movie's file size is too large, you may find that a particular symbol is bulky and may be used repeatedly. Click the Use Count column header to sort your assets by the number of times they're used. By default, the Use Count is not updated, but you can choose Keep Use Counts Updated from the Library options pop-up to get the current use count, as shown in Figure 6.31.

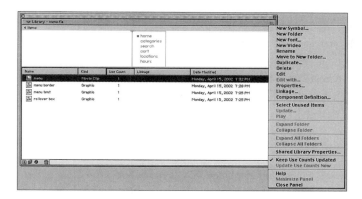

Figure 6.31
The Library options pop-up menu.

The contents of the Library can be organized into folders. Simply click the New Folder icon at the bottom of the Library panel to create a new folder. As with layer folders, using Library folders helps to conserve scarce screen real estate. You can also use folders to organize the contents of the Library. You might have a folder for imported assets, one for navigation symbols, and so on. The number of items in the Library can quickly mushroom when you're working on big projects, and you can waste a lot of time scrolling through the contents of the Library to locate a particular symbol if you do not utilize folders to organize your symbols and assets.

TROUBLESHOOTING

How can I copy a symbol from one movie into another movie?

In Flash MX, you can easily copy symbols from one movie into another. If you have more than one FLA open, simply open the Library panel, and the Libraries for any open documents appear within the Library panel. The title bars within the Library panel display the name of each FLA, as shown in Figure 6.32, and each Library can be expanded or minimized by clicking the arrow to the left of the title.

Figure 6.32
Libraries for any open FLAs are displayed within the Library panel.

To copy a symbol from one Library to another, simply click to select the symbol and drag it to the desired Library. Alternatively, you can drag a symbol onto the Stage in another FLA, which also places an instance on the Stage and also adds the symbol to the Library.

If you want to use multiple symbols from another movie, you can also open an FLA as a Library, which opens just the Library of a selected FLA and not the timeline or Stage. Choose File, Open as Library and select an FLA to open.

Why do I receive the prompt `Resolve Library Conflict`*?*

Flash MX makes it easy to replace an existing symbol with a new symbol of the same name. If you attempt to drag a symbol with the same name as an existing symbol from a different FLA into a Library, you will be prompted to resolve the conflict. Flash makes sure you don't inadvertently overwrite symbols. The Resolve Library Conflict dialog box allows you to replace an existing symbol, as shown in Figure 6.33.

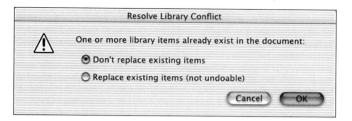

Figure 6.33
The Resolve Library Conflict dialog box allows you to replace an existing symbol.

FLASH AT WORK: NESTING SYMBOLS

I've referred to symbols as Legos, but how do you snap these Flash Legos together? Symbols can be nested within other symbols. Say you want to build a drop-down navigation menu in a Web site for a retailer. One way to build this menu is to start with a graphic symbol that makes up the borders for the drop-down menu. You can then convert the border symbol into a movie clip that contains the border on one layer, text symbols for the menu items on another layer, and rollover graphic symbols on another layer, as shown in Figure 6.34.

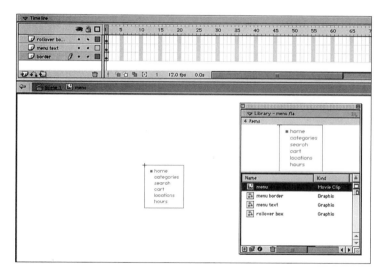

Figure 6.34
Symbols can be nested, creating complex graphics that can be easily modified.

Snapping symbols together in this manner allows for quick revision. If the text items in the menu change or are reordered, you need to change the text only in the menu text symbol even if the menu movie clip is used in several different places in your movie. The change is reflected wherever that symbol is used—in the menu text symbol, in the menu movie clip, and wherever the menu movie clip is used.

ANIMATING IN FLASH

IN THIS CHAPTER

UNDERSTANDING ANIMATION

Animation is the illusion of movement created by a progressive sequence of still images. The emphasis is on the *sequence*. In producing the illusion of movement, the quality of the sequence is the crucial ingredient, and is more important than the quality of the images. This is true because animation is not the art of moving objects and drawings, but instead is the art of drawing and capturing motion. The art is in the action.

Macromedia Flash is uniquely equipped to produce animation. The vector format is perfectly suited for cartoon-like animation. Vector graphics produce shapes that can be easily and precisely transformed while maintaining small file sizes. Vector graphics offer the capability to zoom in and out on shapes, which helps to create convincing animation. Bitmaps can also be animated within Flash. Flash's symbol system is also ideal for animation. Symbols allow animations to be broken into component parts that can be reused, which streamlines both production time and file size.

➪ *For more information about vector graphics, see Chapter 3, "Drawing and Painting in Flash," page 37. For more information about bitmaps, see Chapter 4, "Using Bitmaps in Flash," page 55. To learn more about symbols, see Chapter 6, "Symbols, Instances, and Library Assets," page 89.*

FRAMES AND KEYFRAMES

Flash utilizes a Timeline to help you organize and control your movie and your animation. The Timeline is divided horizontally into frames—discrete units of time—and vertically into layers—discrete units of space that are stacked. Animation unfolds over time and through space. The timeframe of an animation is determined by the total number of frames, and the space it occupies is determined by the dimensions of the Stage, although a nearly unlimited number of layers can be stacked within the Stage dimensions.

The Magic Number: 16,000

Have you ever wondered how big a Flash movie can be? Well, 16,000 is something of a magic number within Flash. Movies can have up to 16,000 frames—any more and playback will stop. The maximum number of symbol instances per movie is also 16,000, as is the maximum number of layers that can be exported and the maximum number of loaded movies that can be supported.

A frame is a static slice of time—the contents of the Stage at a particular moment. Keyframes are critical junctures when the contents of the Stage change. This is a crucial distinction. Animation portrays action, and the essence of action is change. Flash creates animation by tracking change: where the contents of the Stage change—keyframes—and how long the contents remain the same—frames. Frames indicate content, whereas keyframes signal action, or change.

The playhead displays a single frame at a time, although an unlimited number of layers can be displayed within a single frame. It's important to separate content into different layers to be able to animate objects individually. You might have a static background that remains stationary, and several layers with content that animate at different points in your movie. Although you may have content on numerous layers, it is unlikely that you will want to display all your content on every frame of your movie. Frames exist within a layer only when that layer's content is visible on the Stage.

Adding, Editing, Deleting, and Copying Frames

When you create a new document, Flash provides a single layer with one frame, as shown in Figure 7.1. Adding frames defines when the contents of a layer are visible. The overall length of a movie is determined by the highest frame number that occurs in any layer. Adding frames to a layer keeps content on the Stage longer. Deleting frames shortens the amount of time that content is visible. As you add content and layers to a movie, you'll likely need to manipulate the length of time that different objects appear on the Stage.

Figure 7.1
A new document contains a single layer and a single frame.

To add frames to a layer, click to select a frame in the Timeline and then press F5 to insert frames, as shown in Figure 7.2.

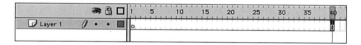

Figure 7.2
To add frames, select a frame and press F5.

When content is added to the Stage, Flash converts the current frame to a keyframe. Frames display the content of the keyframe that precedes them. Content remains static between keyframes unless a tween has been added.

Tweening

"Tween" comes from the classic animation term "inbetweening." Senior artists would sketch frames where crucial action occurs, and junior artists would fill in the intermediate frames, or inbetweens. Flash can do the tweening for you. The crucial frames are keyframes, and you can specify a motion or shape tween and have Flash interpolate the changes between keyframes.

To add a keyframe, click to select a frame in the Timeline; then press F6 to insert a keyframe, which is displayed as a hollow circle in a frame on the Timeline, as shown in Figure 7.3.

Figure 7.3
Blank keyframes are displayed as hollow circles, and keyframes with content are shown as filled circles.

7

You can easily edit or make changes to frames and keyframes as you work. To delete frames or keyframes, select a frame or frames, Ctrl-click (Mac) or right+click (Windows), and select Remove

Frames from the context menu. To change a keyframe to a frame, removing the changes that occur on the Stage in that keyframe without deleting the frame, select a keyframe and choose Clear Keyframe from the context menu.

To select multiple frames, click and drag across frames. You also can copy and paste frames. Select frames and/or keyframes, Ctrl-click (Mac) or right+click (Windows), and select Copy Frames from the context menu. Select another frame in the Timeline, and Ctrl-click (Mac) or right+click (Windows) and select Paste Frames from the context menu. You can copy and paste frames across layers, for example, frames 4 through 12 in layers four and five, and paste into other layers. Copying frames in multiple layers pastes those frames into multiple layers.

Manipulating Keyframes

Keyframes can be added anywhere within a layer. Flash inserts frames, if necessary, to fill the distance between an existing keyframe and a new keyframe. Keyframes display the content of preceding keyframes, and allow that content to be changed. To clear the contents of the Stage, you can add blank keyframes. Simply select a frame and press F7 to insert a blank keyframe.

You can also convert existing frames to keyframes or blank keyframes. Select a frame and Ctrl-click (Mac) or right+click (Windows) to access the context menu, as shown in Figure 7.4. Release to select Convert to Keyframes or Convert to Blank Keyframes.

Figure 7.4
Ctrl-click (Mac) or right+click (Windows) a frame in the Timeline to access the context menu.

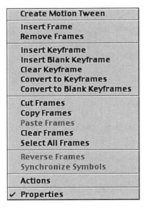

To move keyframes in the Timeline, click to select a keyframe. Release and the keyframe is highlighted. Click and drag it to a new position, even to a new layer.

Frame Rate

The speed of an animation is a factor of both the frame rate of your movie and the number of frames over which an animation takes place in the Timeline. Variable frame rate is a digital concept. Animation in traditional media, such as film, occurs over fixed frame rates. Flash allows you to set the frame rate, in number of frames per second, for your movie. It's best to set the frame rate for a document as soon as you open it, or you may have to tweak the length of your animations later if you change the rate. To set the frame rate of a movie, follow these steps:

1. Click an unoccupied portion of the Stage. The document properties appear in the Property Inspector, as shown in Figure 7.5.

Figure 7.5
The frame rate of a movie is accessed in the document settings displayed in the Property Inspector.

2. Click in the Frame Rate field and enter a number. The default fps (frames per second) is 12, and anything between 8 and 18 is acceptable for the Web.

The higher the frame rate, the more information is conveyed, the smoother the animation, and the higher the file size. If you know your audience has higher bandwidth and faster computers, you have the luxury of using higher frame rates. In most cases, however, it's best to err on the side of caution and use slower frame rates. If a download takes too long, your audience may leave in frustration and never see your animation.

With the frame rate set, you can focus on the timing of your animations. Animations that unfold over a greater number of frames appear slower, whereas those that take place over few frames appear rapid. You must experiment with the length of your animations to perfect their speed.

TWEENING

There are two types of animation in Flash: frame-by-frame and tweened. Frame-by-frame animation changes the contents of the stage in every frame and consists of a series of keyframes. Frame-by-frame animation is both labor and file-size intensive and is best reserved for animation that evolves and is more organic, requiring individual manipulation of shapes.

Tweened animation is punctuated by intermittent keyframes, when critical change occurs on the Stage, with in-between frames that are created by Flash. Flash takes the content of two keyframes in the same layer and creates the intermediate steps to change the Stage contents from one state to the next. This process of interpolating differences in keyframes is known as in-betweening, or more commonly, tweening.

To create a simple animation of a ball bouncing, follow these steps:

1. Open a new document by choosing File, New or by pressing Cmd-N (Mac) or Ctrl+N (Windows).

2. Select the Oval tool and choose a red fill with no stroke.

Strokes and Animation

When animating solid shapes, use strokes only when necessary, that is, when the stroke is a different color than the fill. A stroke that is the same color as the fill is indistinguishable from the fill and requires Flash to perform unnecessary calculations that increase rendering time and file size.

7

3. Shift+drag with the Oval tool near the top of the Stage to draw a red circle, as shown in Figure 7.6.

Figure 7.6
When content is first added to the Stage in a new document, Flash converts the single, existing frame to a keyframe.

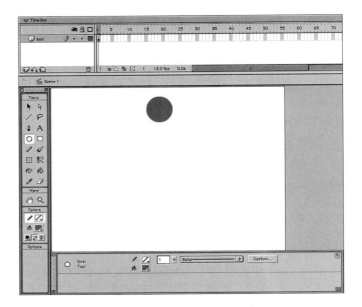

4. Select the circle and convert it to a symbol by pressing F8. Name the symbol **ball**, choose Graphic for the behavior, and click the center square in the registration grid. Click OK to close the Convert to Symbol dialog box.

5. Now that you have your ball, you need to make it move. To make it appear to bounce, you need to change its position on the Stage. In the Timeline, go to frame 12 and press F6 to insert a keyframe. Notice that nothing on the Stage has changed yet.

6. Select the Arrow tool and, with the ball on the Stage selected, move the ball to the bottom of the Stage, as shown in Figure 7.7.

7. Play your movie within the work area by pressing Return (Mac) or Enter (Windows). Notice that the ball is positioned at the top of the Stage for 11 frames and jumps to the bottom of the Stage only in frame 12. Remember, frames display the content of the keyframe that precedes them.

8. To make your ball appear to gradually fall to the bottom of the Stage, select any frame between frames 1 and 12. Ctrl-click (Mac) or right+click (Windows) to access the context menu. Select Create Motion Tween.

9. Play your movie again by pressing Return (Mac) or Enter (Windows). The ball now gradually falls over the course of all 12 frames.

10. Save your animation as **ball.fla**. You will be using it again later in the chapter.

➪ *For more information about drawing simple shapes, see Chapter 3, "Drawing and Painting in Flash," page 37. For more information about symbols, see Chapter 6, "Symbols, Instances, and Library Assets," page 89.*

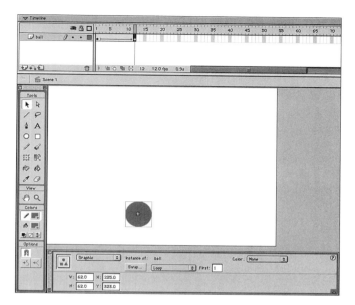

Figure 7.7
Insert a keyframe in frame 12 and use the Arrow tool to move the ball to the bottom of the Stage.

You could have created the ball animation using frame-by-frame animation, but given the simple path of the animation, it's best to save the effort and file size and let Flash do the work for you. The ball animation takes advantage of tweening.

Motion Tweens

There are two types of tweens: motion and shape. Motion tweens interpolate changes in position, scale, rotation, color, and transparency of a single shape located in different positions in multiple keyframes. Shape tweens interpolate differences between two shapes, allowing you to morph or change one into the other. Tweens occur across a single layer only. The ball animation used motion tweening. If you want to create a motion tween, objects within keyframes must be symbols or groups and exist on the same layer. If you attempt to tween simple shapes without converting them to symbols, a dotted line appears between keyframes and a caution symbol appears in the Property Inspector, as shown in Figure 7.8.

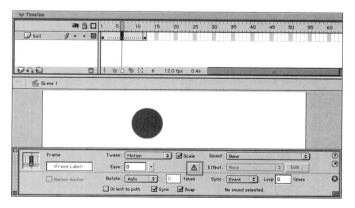

Figure 7.8
A dashed line in the Timeline and a caution symbol in the Property Inspector indicate incomplete tweens.

7

These symbols indicate that the tween is incomplete, and if you preview your animation, you'll see that your intended tween does not occur.

Motion Guides

When you create a motion tween, Flash follows the shortest path between positions in keyframes. This saves file size but isn't always desirable. To use the ball animation example, change it so that the ball bounces instead of merely falling. You need to create a motion guide, so follow these steps:

1. Open ball.fla.

2. To create the illusion of the ball bouncing, you need to offset the place where the ball hits the ground. Click in the Timeline and select frame 12.

3. Use the Arrow tool to drag the ball instance to the right on the Stage.

4. Play your animation by pressing Return (Mac) or Enter (Windows). The ball travels at an unnatural angle from the top of the Stage to the lower right, as shown in Figure 7.9. You need to create a motion guide to overcome this problem.

Figure 7.9
With motion tweens, Flash follows the shortest path between positions in keyframes, as revealed in Onion Skin mode.

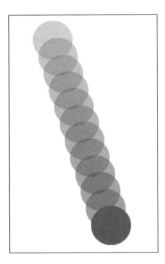

5. Select the ball layer and choose Insert, Motion Guide. A motion guide layer is added above the selected layer, as shown in Figure 7.10.

Figure 7.10
To create a motion guide, select a layer and choose Insert, Motion Guide.

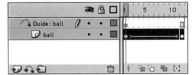

6. Select the Pen tool and then click and drag on the Stage to draw two points to create an arc from the top of the Stage to the bottom, in a realistic bounce shape, as shown in Figure 7.11.

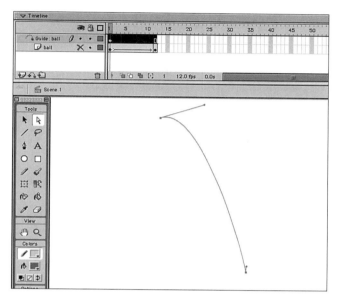

Figure 7.11
Use the Pen tool to draw an arc to move the ball along to create a bounce effect.

7. Select frame 1 in the ball layer and check the Property Inspector to ensure that Snap is checked, as shown in Figure 7.12. When Snap is selected, the registration point of a tweened object is snapped to the path of the motion guide. Your ball should appear snapped to the end of the motion guide.

Figure 7.12
Select Snap in the Property Inspector to snap the registration point of a tweened object to a motion guide.

8. Select frame 12 in the ball layer and use the Arrow tool to move the ball on the Stage over the motion guide path until it snaps to the end, as shown in Figure 7.13.

9. Save your file as **ball2.fla**. Play your animation by pressing Return (Mac) or Enter (Windows). Your ball should follow the arc of your motion guide, as shown in Figure 7.14.

A motion guide works only if objects are snapped to the beginning and end of the motion guide path. The path is not visible in your published movie, so feel free to draw it in a color that contrasts with your tweened object to facilitate the snapping process.

7

For more information about motion guides, see the "Troubleshooting" section at the end of this chapter, page 126.

Figure 7.13
In frame 12, use the Arrow tool to move the ball over the end of the motion guide path.

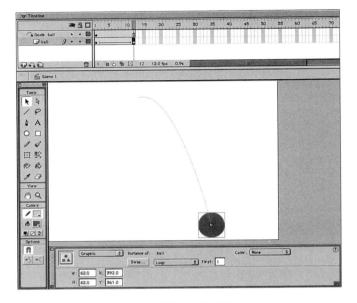

Figure 7.14
When the ball is snapped to either end of the motion guide path, it follows the arc of the guide.

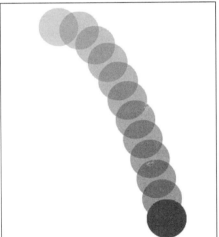

Easing

The frame rate of a Flash movie is constant. When Flash creates a motion tween, it spaces the movements evenly over the number of frames between keyframes. However, few natural motions occur at consistent rates. Most motion begins gradually and ends gradually unless another force, such as gravity in the case of the bouncing ball, intercedes. To mimic the natural variations in speed, you can adjust easing in your tweens. Easing adjusts the rate of change between tweened frames. Negative easing values (between –1 and –100) cause motion tweens to start quickly and decelerate near the end. This is known as easing in. Positive easing values (between 1 and 100) create tweens that speed up as they progress, known as easing out.

To change the Ease settings in the bouncing ball animation, follow these steps:

1. Open ball2.fla.

2. Click in the ball layer to select a frame in the motion tween.

3. Click the Onion Skin button in the Timeline so you can preview your animation, and click the Onion Marker button and select Onion All from the pop-up menu, as shown in Figure 7.15.

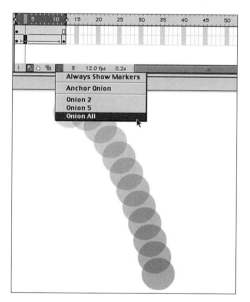

Figure 7.15
Onion skinning options allow you to preview your animations by showing the contents of multiple frames simultaneously.

4. In the Property Inspector, click on the Ease slider and drag it upward until the animation on the Stage appears faster near the end, as shown in Figure 7.16. With onion skinning turned on, you'll notice changes in speed represented by varying distances between objects in different frames. For the ball, an ease amount of approximately 30 seems best.

5. Save your file as **ball3.fla** and test your movie by choosing Control, Test Movie.

Figure 7.16
Onion skinning reveals changes in easing as varying distances between objects in different frames.

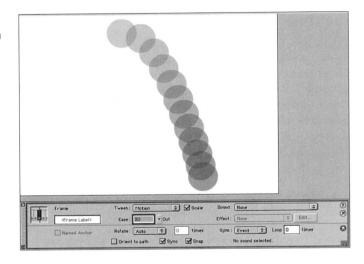

Onion Skinning

Normally only one frame at a time is visible on the Stage. Onion skinning, however, allows you to see many frames simultaneously as you saw in the preceding exercise. This capability to see frames in context is invaluable when you're creating animations. Turn on onion skins frequently as you create tweens to check alignment and easing.

Onion skins are also helpful in perfecting the timing of animations. Figure 7.17 shows a ball falling over varying numbers of frames at varying speeds.

Figure 7.17
Onion skins provide clues to the speed of animations.

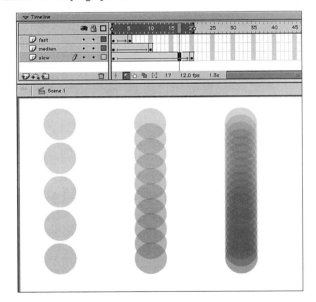

The ball on the left falls quickly. When onion skins show no overlap in objects across frames, the animation is so rapid that it appears to jump, and detecting the continuity of movement is difficult. The ball on the right falls slowly, with substantial overlap across frames, whereas the ball in the middle falls at a medium pace. Any of these speeds may be desirable depending on the type of motion you are attempting to portray.

Shape Tweens

Flash can also interpolate dramatic changes in the shapes of objects. Shape tweens create the illusion of morphing from one shape into another. Unlike with motions tweens, shape tweens work only with simple shapes. Symbol instances, groups, or bitmaps must be broken apart for you to be able to apply a shape tween.

To create a simple shape tween, follow these steps:

1. Open a new document by pressing Cmd-N (Mac) or Ctrl+N (Windows).

2. Click on the Stage and change the movie dimensions to 400×200 in the Property Inspector.

3. Select the Rectangle tool, and choose a fill color and no stroke. Click and drag on the Stage to draw a large rectangle.

4. Press Cmd-K (Mac) or Ctrl+K (Windows) to open the Align panel. Select the rectangle on the Stage, and in the Align panel, select To Stage and center the rectangle horizontally and vertically, as shown in Figure 7.18, by clicking the second and fifth buttons in the Align row.

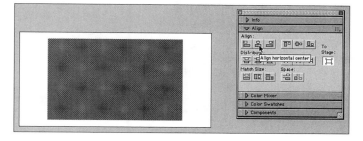

Figure 7.18
Select To Stage in the Align panel and center the rectangle vertically and horizontally.

5. Select frame 15 in the Timeline and press F7 to insert a blank keyframe.

6. Select the Text tool and a bold typeface in the Property Inspector. Click with the Text tool on the Stage and type your name.

7. Click the text with the Arrow tool to select it. Use the align panel to center it horizontally and vertically as you did in step 4.

8. With the text selected, choose Modify, Break Apart to break the text block into letters, as shown in Figure 7.19.

9. Choose Modify, Break Apart a second time to break letters apart into shapes, as shown in Figure 7.20.

Figure 7.19
Select the text block and choose Modify, Break Apart to break the text into letters.

Figure 7.20
Break a text block apart a second time to convert letters to shapes.

10. Select a frame between keyframes, and in the Property Inspector, choose Shape from the Tween pop-up menu, as shown in Figure 7.21.

Figure 7.21
Select a frame between keyframes and choose Shape from the Tween pop-up menu in the Property Inspector.

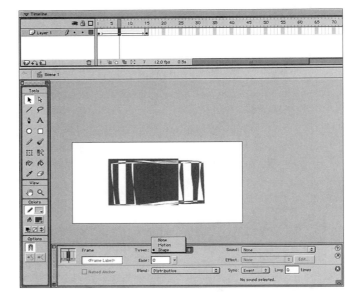

11. Save your movie and test it by choosing Control, Test Movie. The rectangle morphs into your name, as shown in Figure 7.22.

Figure 7.22
The rectangle morphs into your name.

Easing can be applied to shape tweens as it is to motion tweens. There is an additional option for blending, as shown in Figure 7.23. Blending is either distributive, which smoothes shapes during interpolation, or angular, which preserves the hard edges of shapes. Angular is appropriate only for shapes with pronounced edges and angles.

7

Figure 7.23
Shape tweens have a blending option, which preserves angles during tweening.

Shape tweens are very powerful, and consequently can inflate file sizes. Use them sparingly for best effect and experiment with simple shape tweens. Sometimes the best effects are subtle.

Shape Hints

In shape tweens as in motion tweens, Flash creates the simplest interpolation between shapes. This can produce some strange and sometimes undesirable effects, as you might have noticed in the shape tween of your name. Portions of some shapes can turn inside out during interpolation. Fortunately, you can identify points that should correspond in beginning and ending shapes. Flash allows you to designate shape hints in your shape tweens.

To use shape hints, follow these steps:

1. Select the first shape in a shape tween sequence.

2. Choose Modify, Shape, Add Shape Hint. The beginning shape hint appears as a red circle containing the letter *a*.

3. Click on the shape hint with the Arrow tool and drag it to the point you want to mark, as shown in Figure 7.24.

Figure 7.24
Shape hints appear as red circles containing letters. Move them to points of shapes you want to mark during tweens.

4. Click in the final frame of the shape tween. The corresponding shape hint appears in a similar position on the final shape, as shown in Figure 7.25.

Figure 7.25
A corresponding shape hint appears on the final frame of the tween in a similar position.

5. Test your movie again, choosing Control, Test Movie, and see how the shape hint affects the tween. You can add additional shape hints, up to a maximum of 26.

SCRUBBING THROUGH THE TIMELINE

Movement is the essence of animation, so previewing your animations in motion as you work is essential. Scrubbing refers to manually moving the playhead back and forth within the Timeline, allowing you to preview the progression of a movie. Simply click on the playhead above the Timeline, as shown in Figure 7.26, and move it across frames to preview them. A red line extends from the playhead down through frames in the Timeline to indicate the current frame. Scrubbing is especially useful for perfecting animation because it allows you to move through a movie as quickly or slowly as you choose, depending on how quickly you drag the playhead.

Figure 7.26
Click and drag the playhead, the red rectangle above the Timeline, to scrub through the Timeline.

The Control menu, as shown in Figure 7.27, also allows you to preview your movie as you work. Choose Play, or press Return (Mac) or Enter (Windows), to preview a movie at the specified frame rate. An especially useful option is the capability to step through a movie a frame at a time using the period key—to go forward—and comma key—to go backward.

Figure 7.27
By choosing options from the Control menu, you can preview your movie as you work.

CARTOON ANIMATION IN FLASH

Flash's vector format is ideally suited to cartoon animation. Vector graphics resemble cartoon-style drawings and can be easily and accurately transformed within Flash. Many traditional cartooning techniques can be translated into Flash.

Panning

A classic animation strategy that can be translated to the Web is panning. Panning creates the illusion of depth of field and a continuous background. In film this would be achieved by panning the camera, or moving the camera across a scene at a fixed height to capture the full sweep of a distant background. In animation, this effect is simulated by moving the background across the fixed Stage.

The secret to creating a convincing pan is to create background elements that are animated at different rates. The most distant element should move at the slowest rate. Objects in the foreground appear to move relative to the scene behind them, creating the illusion of depth.

7

To produce a pan effect, follow these steps:

1. Create a background element that is wider than the Stage. Ideally, the left and right edges of the background should match up so that the background appears seamless when it loops while in motion.

2. Tween the background element across the Stage so that in the first keyframe the right edge of the background is flush with the right edge of the Stage. In the final keyframe, the left edge of the background should be flush with the left edge of the Stage. This effect creates the illusion of continuous motion and a sprawling, vast backdrop.

Symbol Cycles

The easiest way to create complex character animation is to use nested symbols. Symbol hierarchy is ideal for breaking complex animations into mechanical parts that can be cycled or reused. Plan for how an object or character should move, and isolate each moving part into a separate symbol that can be reassembled in the master symbol.

The human walk cycle is one of the most difficult animations to achieve realistically. With care, you can construct it in nested symbols for maximum efficiency and realism. To make it easiest, dissect a person walking in profile. The highest level is a movie clip symbol for the walking cycle. It contains layers for the head, torso, and legs. The head could be a single graphic. The torso movie clip contains two animated instances of an arm symbol, and the legs movie clip consists of two animated instances of a leg symbol. Collectively, the symbols that comprise the walking cycle make up a complete stride that can be repeated without having to redraw.

ANIMATION GUIDELINES

Any style of animation—from classic cartoon-style characters to scripted physics-based movement—can benefit from some classic animation principles:

- **Timing and Motion**—Timing gives meaning to movement. The speed at which a movement happens can imbue the same motion with different meaning. Think of a punch. If it is delivered rapidly, with the person on the receiving end snapping back, it is a painful event. The same motion, delivered more slowly with a minimal reaction from the receiver, could be seen as playful.

  Timing and pacing are critical for creating realistic and interesting motion. You can manipulate timing to give objects life and convey their attributes: Heavy objects are difficult to move and take longer to accelerate and decelerate. Few objects move at identical paces, so you should vary the speeds at which action occurs.

  Pacing is also crucial. There is a delicate balance between anticipation, action, and reaction. If the pace is too slow, the viewer will lose interest, but if it is too fast, the action may be confusing and open to misinterpretation. Also, experiment with the length of each stage—they should not be of equal lengths or carry the same emphasis. Action typically is the focus, but you can confound that expectation to great effect. Lengthy anticipation followed by quick action and reaction can produce comic or dramatic effect.

7

- **Anticipation**—Movement is most dynamic and realistic if it is anticipated. Runners lean backward slightly before hurtling themselves forward. Try adding slight movement in the opposite direction at the beginning of a motion.

- **Follow-through**—Movement does not stop instantaneously. Runners do not stop as soon as they cross the finish line, but continue on as they decelerate. Think of the follow-through of a pitcher's arm after a ball is released. Whenever you initiate a movement, try to follow it through slightly beyond the point where you want it to ultimately finish.

- **Squash and Stretch**—Few objects are completely rigid while in motion. Most objects are slightly deformed by motion and collision. To make our ball bounce even more realistic, we could add a shape tween so that the ball stretches as it falls—accomplished by scaling the ball to make it taller and thinner—and squashes on impact—scale again to make it shorter and fatter.

- **Overlapping Action**—Action is most interesting if it is varied, so you should avoid actions that begin and end simultaneously. Stagger movement—have a second object begin to move before the first object has stopped—when possible.

- **Secondary Action**—No man is an island, and animation shouldn't be either. Animation is most effective if it produces a ripple effect; movement should rarely happen in isolation. Secondary action results directly from primary action, echoing and reinforcing the main action. Allow objects to interact to produce more complex animation.

TROUBLESHOOTING

I've created a motion guide layer and motion path to animate along. Why isn't it working?

Animation moves along motion guides only if shapes are snapped to the beginning and end of the guide path. Check your beginning and ending keyframes and ensure that your shapes are squarely snapped to the path.

I'm unable to add a shape tween. Why isn't it working?

Check whether the objects you're attempting to tween are symbols. Although objects need to be symbols or grouped for motion tweens, you cannot perform a shape tween on groups or symbols. You can work around this problem by breaking apart a symbol instance. Simply select the instance on the Stage and press Cmd-B (Mac) or Ctrl+B (Windows) to convert a symbol to an object. If a symbol contains nested symbols, you may need to break it apart more than once. This affects just the symbol instance; the symbol itself remains intact in the Library.

Any tips for managing the pacing of complex animations?

If a movie contains significant amounts of complex animation—particularly character animation—your best bet is to storyboard the action. Grab a pencil and sketch out your animation. For extremely complex animation, you may need to sketch it frame by frame. Otherwise, sketch the highpoints of the action. That way, you can plan interactions between objects and finesse the timing.

FLASH AT WORK: "UN-PERFECTING" ANIMATION

The mathematical precision of Flash's vector graphics places animation within the grasp of anyone who can master a graphics program. Think of the caliber and quantity of artists who were required to create early Disney cartoons. Flash truly makes animation accessible.

The downside to the awesome power of Flash's vectors is that they can be so exact as to become impersonal and therefore less interesting. In the natural world, shapes have imperfections and movement is often irregular. To create the most compelling animations with Flash, use its capabilities as a starting point. Tweak shapes to make them slightly irregular. Take full advantage of easing to create variety in pacing of movement. Introduce intermediate keyframes in tweens and combine frame-by-frame and tweened animations for more realistic effects. Above all, take inspiration from the imperfect world around you.

7

USING SOUND

8

UNDERSTANDING SOUND

Sound adds depth and resonance to your Macromedia Flash movies. Even before it was possible to incorporate sound tracks with movies, live music was used as accompaniment to accent action and stir emotion during silent movies. Imagine *Jaws* without the menacing sound track to appreciate all that sound adds to visual experiences.

There are some critical differences in the way you perceive visual information and the way you perceive sound. Because you blink somewhere in the neighborhood of 20 times per minute, with each blink lasting approximately a quarter of a second, your brain is accustomed to interruptions in the flow of visual data and is extremely adept at filling in gaps in visual information. This ability to connect the visual dots is what allows you to perceive film, which is composed of a collection of static images that are shown in quick succession, as continuous motion.

Your brain is not nearly so forgiving of or able to compensate for gaps in audio information. On the contrary, you are especially sensitive to variations in sound. Whereas film visuals are delivered in static frames, film sound is delivered in a continuous stream or sound track. Content delivery over the Web, however, makes it difficult to emulate a continuous sound track.

Sound is produced when objects vibrate. These vibrations displace air particles and travel across space as sound waves. When these waves hit your eardrums, the brain perceives the vibrations as sound. You differentiate between sounds according to variations in frequency—how quickly the air pressure fluctuates; higher fluctuations are more frequent and are perceived as being higher in pitch—and amplitude—the level of air pressure; higher levels are perceived as louder, as shown in Figure 8.1. This is important because Flash must reproduce these sound waves to be able to deliver sound.

Figure 8.1
The anatomy of a sound wave:
Frequency determines pitch and
amplitude determines loudness.

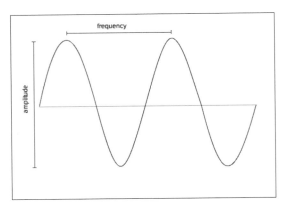

PREPARING SOUNDS FOR FLASH

To be able to reproduce sound, sound waves are sampled. Sampling is a process of splicing sound waves into increments—sound bites—and reproducing those increments, or samples, as closely as possible, as shown in Figure 8.2. The number of samples captured per second is known as the sampling rate and is measured in hertz (Hz).

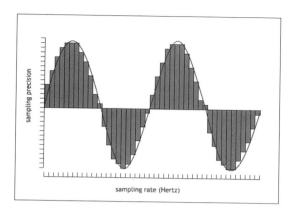

Figure 8.2
Sound sampling: The gray bars represent samples of a sound wave.

The sampling process should sound familiar as it echoes the process of creating animation using frames. The sampling rate is similar to the frame rate of a movie, in frames per second. It is also similar to pixel resolution. The denser the sampling rate—the greater the number of samples that are taken—the better the sampling as the original sound wave is more closely reproduced. Table 8.1 shows standard sampling rates and the associated fidelity, or sound quality.

Table 8.1 Sound Sampling Rates

Sampling Rate	Sound Quality
44.1kHz	CD quality
22.05kHz	FM radio quality; popular Web playback choice
11.025kHz	Lowest recommended quality for short music clips; high quality for speech
5kHz	Minimum quality for speech

Sampling precision, or bit depth, determines how many different gradations or discrete amplitude levels are possible when sampling a sound. This is analogous to the bit depth of bitmap images. The higher the bit depth, the more information is stored about each waveform. Table 8.2 shows standard sound bit depths and the comparable sound quality.

Table 8.2 Sound Bit Depth and Associated Quality

Bit Depth	Sampling Rate (Pulses Per Second)	Sound Quality
16	65,536	CD
12	4,096	Moderate, near CD
8	256	FM radio
4	16	Lowest acceptable for music

As you might expect, higher sampling rates and bit depth result in larger sound file sizes. However, these two components of reproduced sound can be independently manipulated to create smaller files. Speech has far fewer variations in pitch compared to music, but has greater fluctuation in amplitude or volume because of pauses between words and sentences. Unwanted hissing or noise can occur during these pauses. Therefore, speech requires a lower sampling rate with a higher bit depth to reduce the occurrence of noise or hissing during pauses.

Conversely, music has a much greater range in pitch, or frequency, requiring a higher sampling rate to reproduce the pitch variation. Music typically has a narrower range of volume than speech does, so the bit depth can be lower.

Similarly, the choice between stereo and mono sound has a large impact on file size. Mono sound is recorded in a single audio track or channel. If you have two speakers, the single mono channel is played over both speakers. Stereo sound is recorded on two audio channels to better reproduce the effect of human hearing, which detects sound through two sources: ears. Clearly, two audio channels make for twice the file size.

IMPORTING SOUNDS

Flash allows you to import assets that cannot be created within Flash, such as sounds or bitmaps, and use them within your movies. Sounds that are imported into Flash are placed in the Library. The following sound file formats can be imported into Flash MX:

- WAV (Windows only)—The Waveform Audio File Format was developed for the Windows platform and is the standard sound file format for Windows.

- AIFF (Macintosh only)—The Audio Interchange File Format developed by Apple is the standard sound file format used on the Macintosh.

- MP3 (Macintosh and Windows)—(MPEG-1 Audio Layer-3) offers tremendous compression of sound data without sacrificing sound quality. Original CD data can be compressed by a factor of 12 using MP3 compression.

If you have QuickTime 4 or higher installed, you can also import the following formats:

- AIFF (Windows or Macintosh)

- Sound Designer II (Macintosh only)

- Sound Only QuickTime Movies (Windows or Macintosh)

- Sun AU (Windows or Macintosh)

- System 7 Sounds (Macintosh only)

- WAV (Windows or Macintosh)

MP3 is the only sound format you can import that is precompressed. Therefore, MP3 file sizes are smaller than WAV or AIFF files. To import a sound, choose File, Import to Library and use the Import to Library dialog box to locate the sound file, as shown in Figure 8.3.

Select a sound and click Open. The sound is added to the Library, as shown in Figure 8.4. To preview a sound, select it in the Library and click the black arrow that appears over the sound waveform in the window.

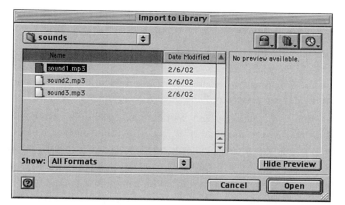

Figure 8.3
To import sounds into the Library, choose File, Import to Library.

Figure 8.4
Imported sounds are added to the Library.

The best approach is to place a sound on its own layer. Add a new layer to your movie (by choosing Insert, New Layer or using the New Layer icon below the layers on the timeline). With that layer selected, drag a sound from the Library onto the Stage. (Flash MX comes with sample sounds that you can access by choosing Window, Common Libraries, Sounds.fla. A library of sounds will open.) The sound is placed on the selected layer, as shown in Figure 8.5.

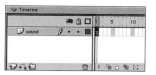

Figure 8.5
Dragging a sound to the Stage places it on a selected layer.

Sound properties are shown in the Property Inspector, as shown in Figure 8.6. Notice that the sound sampling rate, number of sound channels, and bit depth are displayed (22kHz Mono 16 Bit in this case) in the bottom right of the Property Inspector.

Figure 8.6
Sound attributes are accessed and edited in the Property Inspector.

8

SYNCHRONIZING SOUNDS

It is important to realize that sound is time-based, not frame-based like animation. Sound is delivered at a steady rate; it must be delivered this way to be able to preserve the integrity of the sound. Change the delivery speed, and you change the frequency, which produces a different sound. This is in sharp contrast to animation, which can start, stop, and jump among frames.

So, how can you synchronize sound to animation, when the two operate so differently? There is no way to precisely and seamlessly sync sound and visuals as you can with a sound track embedded in a filmstrip. The most you can do is place sounds where they need to occur, and work to optimize your sound delivery.

Compromises have to be made with Web-delivered content. With sampling rates in the thousands per minute, sound is second only to video in adding to the file size of your Flash movies. To create animations with sound at file sizes that can be delivered over the Internet, either the animation (frame) or sound delivery must take precedence.

Who Leads? Sound Versus Animation

Flash has two methods for incorporating sound that allow you to establish which drives your movie, the animation or the sound. Event sounds are subordinate to animation. They are triggered by events such as the mouse rolling over a button or when a particular frame in the timeline is reached during playback. Once triggered, event sounds play in their entirety independently of the timeline, even if the movie stops. If the triggering event is repeated while the event sound is playing, the first sound continues and a second instance of the sound will play simultaneously.

Event sounds must download completely before they play, so you should take this fact into account when using them. If you place an event sound on the first frame of your movie, the user will likely have to wait for the sound to download.

The other synchronization method is streaming. Streamed sounds approximate sound tracks. Sounds take precedence, and Flash will force the animation to keep up with the sounds, dropping animation frames if necessary. Streamed sounds are tied to the timeline. They play and stop as the movie plays and stops, and if the timeline has fewer frames than a sound occupies, the sound will end when the last frame has played. Streamed sounds begin to play as soon as they begin to download, so they are often used for continuous background sounds.

When you place a sound on the Stage, you must select a synchronization option in the Property Inspector, as shown in Figure 8.7.

Figure 8.7
Sound synchronization options are accessed in the Property Inspector.

Synchronization Options

The synchronization options are Event, Start, Stop, and Stream. Event synchronizes the sound to the keyframe in which it is placed, which can include a button state frame. Start designates an event sound and prevents the sound from overlapping if the triggering event is repeated; Start sounds play only one at a time. Stop silences any event sounds. Stream synchronizes the sound to the animation.

When you placed your sound on the Stage, you may have noticed that the sound instance occupied just a single frame in the timeline (refer to Figure 8.5). That happens because event sounds require just a single frame on the timeline to play in their entirety. Streaming sounds, however, play for the duration of the number of frames that contain the sound. Flash has no way of knowing how you plan to synchronize your sound when you place it on the Stage. If you are using streamed sound, you'll need to add frames to your sound layer to display and play the sound fully, as shown in Figure 8.8. Select a frame in the sound layer, try somewhere around 30, and press F5 to insert frames. The waveform of your sound will appear across the frames it occupies. You may need to add more frames or remove some to encompass the length of your sound.

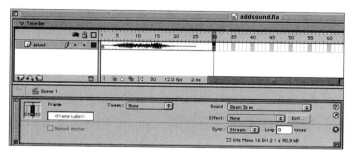

Figure 8.8
With streamed sounds, you must add frames to the timeline to encompass the length of your sound.

EDITING SOUNDS

After you place your sound, you have several editing options. Although Flash does not allow for true sound editing—where the sound wave itself can be changed—you can change how Flash plays a sound. The Effect pop-up menu in the Property Inspector, as shown in Figure 8.9, allows you to manipulate volume effects such as fading in and out.

Figure 8.9
The Effect pop-up menu in the Property Inspector allows you to apply basic effects to sound instances.

None, the default option, applies no effects or removes previously set effects. Left Channel/Right Channel allows you to play only one of the sound channels. Fade Left to Right/Fade Right to Left shifts the sound from one sound channel to the other, creating a pan effect. Fade In gradually increases the volume (amplitude) of a sound over its duration. Fade Out gradually decreases the volume of a sound.

Selecting Custom or clicking the Edit button allows you to access the Edit Envelope dialog box for more sophisticated volume controls, as shown in Figure 8.10.

To change when in a soundwave a sound begins to play, drag the Time In control in the middle of the Edit Envelope dialog box. You'll find a corresponding Time End control at the end of the sound. These settings allow you to shorten or use only parts of sounds.

Envelope handles, draggable square icons that appear on a sound channel, allow you to control the volume in a given channel. Each channel has a single Envelope handle when the Edit Envelope dialog box is launched. Click and drag the Envelope handle up or down to change the overall volume of

8

the sound. To create a fade in or fade out, click on the envelope lines to create additional Envelope handles, up to a maximum of eight total handles. These additional handles allow you to independently drag and control the volume for portions of your sound.

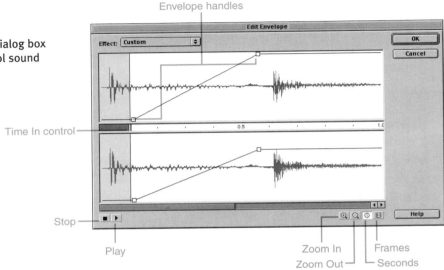

Figure 8.10
The Edit Envelope dialog box allows you to control sound effects.

Use the Zoom buttons to zoom in on portions of your sound or zoom out to view a sound in its entirety. Click the Seconds or Frames buttons to view your sound in seconds or according to the number of frames. Use the Play and Stop buttons to preview your edits. When you're satisfied with your edits, click OK.

Sounds can also loop or play repeatedly. With a sound selected, enter a number in the Loop field in the Property Inspector, as shown in Figure 8.11. If you want a sound to play continuously, be sure to enter a number large enough to make your sound play for an extended duration.

> **Caution**
>
> If you loop streamed sounds, frames will be added to the end of your movie to accommodate the looping. This will increase the file size of your movie.

Figure 8.11
Enter a number in the Loop field of the Property Inspector to play a sound repeatedly.

CONTROLLING SOUND

You can control when a sound plays and ends by using keyframes in the timeline or by accessing the Sound object using ActionScript. Although sound is time-based, you can force it to begin and end in relation to content in other frames by utilizing keyframes. In this way, you can synchronize sound to animation. The Sound object allows you to extend some control of sound playback to the user.

Keyframes

You use keyframes to start and stop sounds in synchronization with animation. To add a sound to an animation, follow these steps:

1. Create a new layer for the sound and then insert a keyframe in the sound layer to correspond with the place where you want your sound to begin, as shown in Figure 8.12.

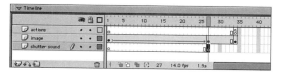

Figure 8.12
Add a keyframe to your sound layer where you want your sound to begin.

2. With the keyframe on the sound layer selected, drag your sound from the Library to the Stage to add the sound to the timeline, as shown in Figure 8.13.

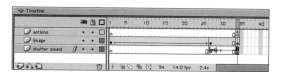

Figure 8.13
With the keyframe in the Sound layer selected, drag an instance of your sound from the Library to the Stage.

3. Insert a keyframe in your sound layer where you want the sound to end, as shown in Figure 8.14.

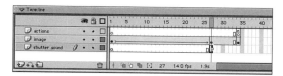

Figure 8.14
Insert a keyframe in the sound layer to stop the sound.

4. Select a synchronization setting for your sound in the Property Inspector, and press Return (Mac) or Enter (Windows) to preview your sound in the timeline.

It is especially important to preview your sound if you're truncating it—stopping it before the sound is over—to be sure it sounds acceptable. You don't want it to seem like a mistake, which will draw the user's attention away from your content. Experiment with the placement of a keyframe that stops a sound so that it does not seem to end prematurely or abruptly—unless, of course, that is the desired effect.

Linkage and the Sound Object

You can also add and control sounds by using the Sound object in ActionScript. Using the Sound object, you can allow your users to control the delivery of sound in your movies. The Sound object allows you to turn sounds on and off, change the volume or the panning of sounds, or start a sound after another sound ends.

➪ *To learn how to use ActionScript to control sound, see "Sound Events," page 324 (Chapter 16, "Interaction, Events, and Sequencing") and "The Sound Class," page 453 (Chapter 20, "Using the Built-in Movie Objects").*

To access a sound using the Sound object, you must assign an identifier to your sound in the Library. Open the Library panel and select your sound. To access the Linkage Properties dialog box, Ctrl-click (Mac) or right-click (Windows) the symbol name and choose Linkage from the pop-up menu, as shown in Figure 8.15, or choose Linkage from the Library options pop-up menu at the upper-right corner of the Library panel.

> **Caution**
>
> All exported sounds are loaded in the first frame of a movie—*not* when they are attached or played. This can result in long downloads and delays before a movie begins playing.

Figure 8.15
Ctrl-click (Mac) or right-click (Windows) a symbol name in the Library to access the Linkage Properties dialog box.

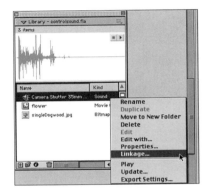

Click in the Export for ActionScript check box. Selecting this option places the symbol name for your sound in the Identifier field and also automatically selects the Export in First Frame check box, as shown in Figure 8.16.

Figure 8.16
Select Export for ActionScript to enter a Linkage Identifier in the Linkage Properties dialog box.

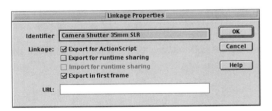

You may need to edit the Identifier string that is automatically filled in with your symbol name, as shown in Figure 8.17. Keep your Identifier name simple and descriptive, and don't use spaces if there is more than one word.

Figure 8.17
You may need to edit the Identifier name that is automatically entered when you select Export for ActionScript.

When you're finished, click OK to close the Linkage Properties dialog box.

An alternative to attaching sounds is to place sounds in separate movies—external SWF files—that can be imported and loaded as necessary using loadMovie. This approach allows your main movie to play while sounds are being loaded.

OPTIMIZING SOUNDS

8

Because sounds can add significantly to the file size of your Flash movies, it is very important to optimize them. Optimization truly begins before you import your sounds. Flash provides modest sound-editing capabilities, so take advantage of sound-editing programs if you have access to them.

Sounds can be compressed individually and should be able to create the smallest possible files. To create individual compression settings, double-click a sound symbol's icon in the Library, or Ctrl-click (Mac) or right-click (Windows) and select Properties from the context menu to launch the Sound Properties dialog box, as shown in Figure 8.18.

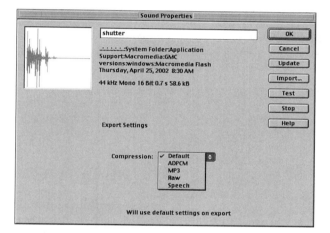

Figure 8.18
By selecting settings in the Sound Properties dialog box, you can compress sounds individually.

You can choose from several compression options. The first, Default, uses the global compression settings selected in the Publish Settings dialog box when you export your movie. The default sound compression for Flash is MP3 16-bit mono, although you can change that default within the Publish Settings dialog box. If you select Default in the Sound Properties dialog box, no further compression options are available.

ADPCM

ADPCM, or Adaptive Differential Pulse Code Modulation, compresses 8-bit or 16-bit sound data. Use this setting, as shown in Figure 8.19, to export short event sounds, such as those used for button clicks.

Figure 8.19
ADPCM compression options.

Selecting Convert Stereo to Mono compresses two mixed sound channels into one. Mono sounds are unaffected by this setting.

8

A sample rate of 22kHz is standard for the Web and is half the standard CD rate of 44kHz. You cannot increase a sound's original kHz rate.

You can also decrease the bit depth, reducing the range of variation within sound samples. Lower bit depths and sample rates reduce file size and also decrease sound quality. Be sure to click the Test button to preview your sound at different settings.

MP3 Compression

You can refine MP3 compression for individual sounds within the Sound Properties dialog box. MP3 offers the best quality at the smallest file sizes, so it is the setting you will choose most often. It is the best option for longer and streamed sounds.

Choose MP3 from the Compression menu. You can choose either to use the original MP3 compression settings of your imported sound (check Use Imported MP3 Quality) or refine those settings, as shown in Figure 8.20.

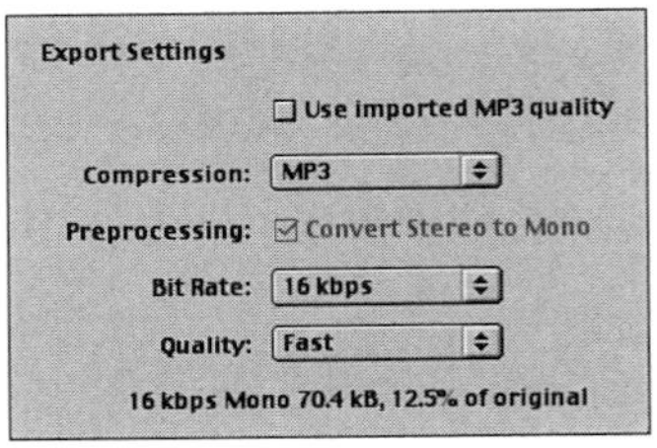

Figure 8.20
MP3 compression options.

To edit the settings, be sure that Use Imported MP3 Quality is not checked; then select a bit rate to determine the bits per second for your exported sound. Choose 16Kbps or higher to maintain sound quality.

You can also compress stereo tracks into mono using MP3. Finally, you can choose from three quality settings: Fast, Normal, and Best. Test your sound at various quality settings to find the best compression.

Carefully compressing streamed sounds is particularly important. Even though you can set individual compression for streamed sounds, all streamed sounds within a movie are exported together in a single stream file using the highest setting of all those applied to individual stream sounds. You must compress your streamed sounds well; otherwise, your file size can become huge.

TROUBLESHOOTING

Why do event sounds seem to have higher quality than streamed sounds?

You may notice that sounds synched to events sound better than streaming sounds. This is true because event sounds are fully downloaded before they begin to play, ensuring that all sound data is preserved. Streaming sounds begin as soon as they begin to download, and they must share bandwidth with images, animations, and video that are concurrently downloaded. Streaming sound takes priority, but some sound data can still be lost to ensure that the sound arrives on time.

Is there any way to prevent frames from being dropped when using streamed sound?

With streamed sound, the sound takes precedence, and frames may be dropped to ensure that animation keeps pace with sounds. However, you may be able to preserve animation frames by using a slower frame rate. Playback will attempt to meet the specified frame rate but will not exceed it. Slower playback allows more time for movie elements to download.

What's the best way to synchronize sound to animation?

It's easiest to control sounds by triggering them from the timeline. Whenever possible, break sounds into short segments that can be placed in frames and coordinated with animated sections of a movie. Due to their brevity, shorter sounds are more easily controlled and tied to specific frames. Imagine synchronizing the song *Happy Birthday* to an animated, singing character. Now imagine synching the unabridged version of *American Pie*. In these examples, the best strategy is to break the songs into individual words and verses that can be individually synchronized to the animation.

You can even mix short sounds manually within Flash by placing sounds on individual layers and overlapping portions of the sound layers. This approach takes advantage of the control offered by short sounds and creates a more intricate and sophisticated audio experience, where sounds are not only synchronized with animation but can also be synchronized with each other.

FLASH AT WORK: TURNING OFF SOUND

Because sound is such a powerful addition to your movies, you need to empower the user to turn off your sounds. The last thing you want is to drive visitors away from your Flash sites because they dislike your music.

Whenever you use streamed sound, be sure to include a button to turn off your sound. You can easily provide this option, even if you're not much of a coder. To turn off your sound, follow these steps:

1. Create a button and select it on the Stage.

2. Launch the Actions panel by clicking F9. You can use Normal mode—press Cmd-N (Mac) or Ctrl+N (Windows)—if you're not accustomed to writing ActionScript.

3. In the left pane of the Actions window, double-click the Actions folder to open it; then double-click the Movie Control folder within the Actions folder. Double-click stopAllSounds.

   This step adds the stopAllSounds action to the right pane, adding it to your selected button, as shown in Figure 8.21.

4. Test your movie by pressing Cmd-Return (Mac) or Ctrl+Enter (Windows). Press your button, and all sounds should stop.

Figure 8.21
Adding a stopAllSounds action to a button enables users to turn off sound in your movie.

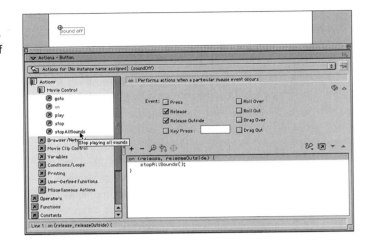

BUTTONS, MENUS, AND USER INPUT

FLASH INTERACTIVITY

Macromedia Flash offers a unique fusion between graphics, animation, and interactivity. You can not only use Flash to create intricate graphics and animated content, but you can also use ActionScript, Flash's scripting language, to enable the users to control the delivery of that content.

⇨ *For more information about ActionScript, see Chapter 11, "Getting Started with ActionScript," page 169.*

You can script Flash movies to respond to a variety of user behaviors, from mouse clicks to typed input in text fields. Interactivity can be as simple as a button click shifting the playback to a different frame or as complex as dynamically loaded menus.

Creating interactivity is easier than ever in Flash MX. You can easily use symbols to create interactive buttons and movie clips. In addition, Flash MX comes with prebuilt components: movie clips with predefined parameters for standard elements such as buttons and form elements. Simply drag and drop them into your movies; then define the parameters for the associated scripts to quickly create forms and gather user input.

BUTTONS

Buttons are interactive, four-frame movie clips. They provide feedback to users by changing in reaction to the users' actions, alerting the users that they can perform some new action. When you create a button symbol, Flash automatically opens a four-frame button timeline. The four frames represent the Up, Over, Down, and Hit states of a button. These frames can contain simple graphics, animated movie clips, or sounds. Although you can use different graphics for the different button states, it is important to maintain some sort of consistent button appearance. If a button changes dramatically in response to users' mouse movements, it can confuse the users so that they are unable to discern the purpose of the button.

⇨ *For more information about using the drawing tools to create graphics, see Chapter 3, "Drawing and Painting in Flash," page 37.*

Simple Buttons

Simple buttons employ graphic variation, such as changes in color, to create the different button states—Up, Over, and Down—and provide visual cues to the users that they can perform an action and exercise some control over the playback of the movie. To create a simple button containing static graphics, follow these steps:

1. Choose Insert, New Symbol or press Cmd-F8 (Mac) or Ctrl+F8 (Windows). The Create New Symbol dialog box launches.

2. Type a name for your button in the Name field and select Button for the behavior, as shown in Figure 9.1.

Figure 9.1
Choose Insert, New Symbol to create a new button symbol.

3. Click OK. A four-layer button timeline is created with a keyframe in the first frame, the Up state. The Up state defines the appearance of your button on the Stage.

4. Use the drawing tools to create a visual form for your button in the Up frame. Button symbols can have multiple layers, so you can separate button graphics onto separate layers, as shown in Figure 9.2.

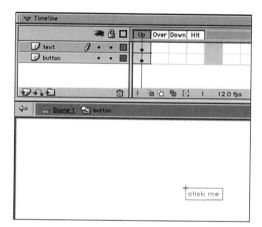

Figure 9.2
Use any of the drawing tools to create a graphic form for your button in the Up frame.

5. The Over state enables you to create rollovers. Click to select the frame beneath the Over label. If you want to change graphics in multiple layers to create your rollover effect, Shift+click to select frames in more than one layer. Choose Insert, Keyframe or press Cmd-F6 (Mac) or Ctrl+F6 (Windows) to add keyframes to those layers. Your button graphics from the first frame appear on the Stage.

6. Select the button graphics on the Stage and make changes to create a rollover state, as shown in Figure 9.3.

Figure 9.3
Insert a keyframe in the Over frame and make changes to your graphic to create a rollover for your button.

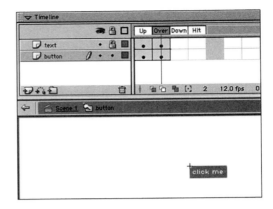

7. To create a click state for your button, select the frame(s) beneath the Down label; then repeat steps 5 and 6. Try offsetting your graphics by moving them down and to the right by a few pixels in the Down frame. This movement creates the illusion that a button is being depressed.

8. The Hit state defines the clickable area of your button. Add a keyframe beneath the Hit label in the layer that contains your button shape, as shown in Figure 9.4. Be sure that your shape covers the entire area that will register a button click. You might need to draw a separate shape in the Hit frame to cover the entire button area.

Figure 9.4
Insert a keyframe in the Hit frame to define the clickable area of your button.

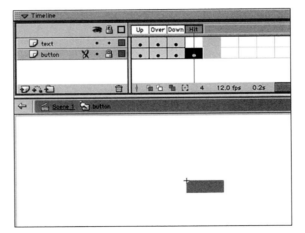

9. Click the Back arrow beneath the folder icons or choose Edit, Edit Document to exit symbol-editing mode and return to the Main Timeline.

10. Choose Window, Library or press Cmd-L (Mac) or Ctrl+L (Windows) to open the Library panel.

11. Locate your button in the Library and drag an instance onto the Stage.

Hit Me

Hit states must be well defined for your site to be usable. Often a button graphic defines the area you want to be clickable, such as a rectangular box behind your button text. Then it's easy to use the same graphic in the Hit frame.

However, if a button consists solely of text, it's vital to draw a generous shape in the Hit frame that encompasses the text. Otherwise, users must click exactly within the letterforms for a click to register.

12. Choose Control, Enable Simple Buttons to preview your button on the Stage. Move your mouse cursor over the button and click to see the Over and Down states. The Hit state is not visible during playback, but it defines the area of your button graphic that responds to the mouse and triggers the Over and Down states.

Your simple button graphics are complete, but your button doesn't actually do anything at this point. You need to add ActionScript so that your button does more than change appearance in response to the user's mouse.

To assign a simple action to a button, follow these steps:

1. Select the button instance on the Stage. If you've enabled simple buttons, you'll need to use the Arrow tool to drag a selection marquee around your button to select it.

2. Choose Window, Actions or press F9 to launch the Actions panel.

3. Double-click the Actions folder in the left column of the Actions panel.

4. Double-click the Movie Control folder and double-click on to add an on action to your button and send the on script to the right side of the Actions panel.

5. Working in Normal mode, choose the appropriate on event(s) to add to your button, as shown in Figure 9.5. Release is the default for buttons.

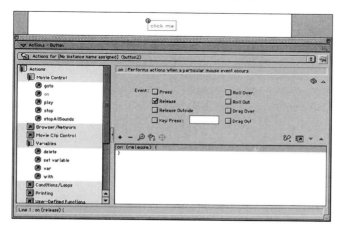

Figure 9.5
Add an on action to your button instance.

6. With the on line of code selected, double-click goto under Movie Control in the left Actions column.

7. Click to select either Go to and Play or Go to and Stop.

8. Select Frame Number, Frame Label, Expression, Next Frame, or Previous Frame in the Type pop-up menu. Enter a Frame number or label if you have selected either of those options from the Type pop-up, as shown in Figure 9.6.

Figure 9.6
Insert a keyframe in the Hit frame to define the clickable area of your button.

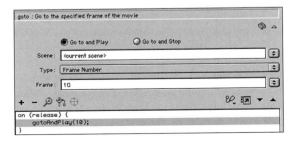

9. Select Control, Test Movie to test your button.

⇨ *For more information about writing scripts, see Chapter 11, "Getting Started with ActionScript," page 169. To learn more details about button events, see Chapter 16, "Interaction, Events, and Sequencing," page 303.*

Advanced Buttons

Buttons can react to user interaction in myriad ways. Advanced buttons go beyond simple graphics and use sound or animated movie clips to denote button states. You can add sound to any of the button frames in place of or in addition to simple graphics. Sound is typically added to the Over or Down frames. Follow these steps to add sound to a button:

1. Insert a new layer in your button symbol. Name it **sound**. It's best to place a sound on its own layer.

2. Within the sound layer, insert a keyframe under the button state you want to add your sound to.

3. With the keyframe selected, drag an instance of a sound from the Library to the Stage. The sound is added to the button frame, as shown in Figure 9.7.

4. In the Property Inspector, set the sound synchronization to Event.

⇨ *For more information about sound, see Chapter 8, "Using Sound," page 129.*

You can also create animated buttons by placing movie clips in button frames. It's best to use short animations and to limit your animations to a single button state; otherwise, the animations can become distracting and make it difficult to differentiate the different button states. To add an animation to a button state, follow these steps:

1. Create a movie clip for a button state.

⇨ *For more information about creating animated movie clips, see Chapter 7, "Animating in Flash," page 109.*

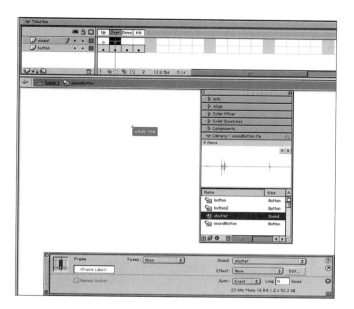

Figure 9.7
To add a sound to a button, insert a keyframe in a button frame and drag a sound from the Library to the Stage.

2. Create a button and add a keyframe to the frame where you want to create an animated state.

3. Drag an instance of your movie clip from the Library to the Stage. Be sure to align your movie clip with graphics in other button frames so that the button appears in a consistent form. Use guides to mark the placement of your button across frames. You don't want a button to move several hundred pixels when clicked or rolled over.

→ *For more information about using guides and alignment, see Chapter 2, "The Flash Interface," page 17.*

4. After your other button frames are completed, return to the Main Timeline and drag an instance of your button onto the Stage.

5. Test your movie by choosing Control, Test Movie.

You can also create invisible buttons—buttons that consist of a Hit state only. Why would you use an invisible button? There are fewer reasons to use invisible buttons in Flash MX than there were in previous versions of Flash. Invisible buttons have been used to create hotspots, or clickable areas of graphics or movie clips. As you can do with imagemaps in HTML, you can place a series of invisible buttons over graphics that you want to use as buttons rather than creating individual buttons. However, the improved MX object model allows you to assign button interactivity directly to movie clips. Also, using invisible buttons to create imagemaps is a disaster in terms of accessibility: Screen readers and other assistive technologies do not recognize invisible buttons as buttons, so any text beneath an invisible button is ignored.

Alignment of elements, particularly text, across button frames is crucial. If elements are not aligned, they appear to jump between button states.

Caution

You cannot preview embedded movie clips in the Flash editor, which displays a single timeline at a time. Only the first frame of an embedded movie clip is visible within the Main Timeline.

To learn more details about the Movie Clip object, see Chapter 17, "Unlocking the Power of Movie Clips," page 331. For more information about Flash accessibility, see Appendix A, "Making Flash Accessible," page 663.

MENUS

Menus allow users to navigate through your movies and to choose when and in what order content is delivered. A menu provides the key to accessing the content of your movie.

Navigation is vital to any Web-delivered content. There is no single standard for navigating Web content, such as turning pages in a book, or for neatly chunking Web content into easily indexed sections, such as individual pages within a book. However, with Flash there is an even greater responsibility to ensure that your movies can be readily navigated. The flexibility that Flash offers for creating new interfaces with complex nesting of timelines muddies these waters even further, and can potentially strand users.

If users can't find your content, they will never hear your message and will likely not return to your site. Flash's capacity for nested timelines means that there can be multiple paths through movies, and Web conventions such as breadcrumbs, which detail a user's path to a particular Web page, are not standard within Flash. Flash content can also be separated into individual SWFs, which can be loaded on demand to conserve bandwidth. For example, an online clothing retailer would be wise to separate different clothing lines into separate movies so that users need only wait for the desired Women's line to download, not the entire line from Men's to Children's. It's important to plan your movies well, with navigation that allows users to maneuver both within SWFs as well as between them.

Structuring Documents Using the Timeline

A simple way to structure interactions within your movie, requiring minimal scripting, is to place movie clips containing sections of your Flash content at keyframes on the timeline. These keyframes can be given corresponding frame labels, which can then be accessed using ActionScript.

Content sections of your movie can be placed into separate movie clips. For example, you could have Home, Services, Portfolio, About, and Profiles movie clips to correspond with menu items for a Flash site. You can then assemble the sections of your site on separate layers on the Main Timeline, as shown in Figure 9.8.

Figure 9.8
Sections of your movie can be assembled on separate layers on the Main Timeline.

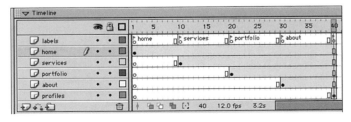

Each section needs its own layer, keyframe, and frame label. So, create a layer for each section. It's important to isolate each section on a different frame number so that you can write a script instructing the playhead to stop on a particular frame to access that section's content. Doing so requires staggering keyframes for the sections so that each occurs on a different frame number. Create a new layer for your labels, and add keyframes with labels corresponding to each of your section keyframes. You could simply assign your scripts according to frame number, but should you need to add new sections to your site, you'll have to change your scripts. Using labels allows you to easily add new content without having to update your existing scripts.

You can stagger the content keyframes so that the sections are placed on consecutive keyframes, but if you do, you won't be able to read the corresponding frame labels on the timeline. However, you can space out the keyframes so that your labels are legible within the timeline for quick reference.

Then, when you create your navigation system, you can assign button actions to access the different sections of your site by moving the playhead to the different section frame labels.

Track as Button and Track as Menu Item

Two important criteria for creating a Flash menu are available space and type of menu data. How much physical space does your layout allow for menu items? Will menu items change? If so, how often? Will menu data need to be dynamically loaded from external sources?

A simple series of menu buttons—the classic Web menu—can be used if your site is small, with few menu items that should not require frequent updates, as shown in Figure 9.9.

Figure 9.9
Simple, static menus can consist of a series of buttons.

When you create a button instance, you can set its properties to Track as Button or Track as Menu Item, as shown in Figure 9.10. Track as Button, the default, defines a button's events independently of any other buttons. If a user clicks and drags from one button to another, the rollover is triggered only on the original button; the second button is independent of the first and does not track mouse events that occur on other buttons. Track as Menu Item, however, allows button events to be triggered by mouse events that may have started on other buttons. If a user clicks and drags from one button to another, releasing the mouse over the second button, the second button's rollover and click states are triggered. Buttons that are menu items should be set to Track as Menu Item.

Figure 9.10
Button instances can be tracked as buttons or as menu items.

Menus can also be extremely complex, triggering advanced scripts, and even involving the loading of external data and XML. Dynamic menus can be completely generated on demand.

To learn more details about integrating XML data into Flash movies, see Chapter 28, "XML Data," page 611.

USING COMPONENTS

Components are a fantastic new feature in Flash MX. An outgrowth of Flash 5 Smart Clips, components provide a variety of prebuilt interface elements. Seven components, which are common form elements, ship with MX. Many more components are available for download from Macromedia, and the greatest potential is in the ability to create custom components.

➡ *To learn more information about creating custom components, see Chapter 22, "Components," page 511.*

Components are housed in the Components panel, as shown in Figure 9.11. To open the Components panel, choose Window, Components, or press Cmd-F7 (Mac) or Ctrl+F7 (Windows).

Figure 9.11
Flash MX provides prebuilt interface components, which are located in the Components panel.

Seven components ship with Flash MX:

- **PushButton** is a simple button with pre-assigned button states.

- **CheckBox** is a traditional form element that allows for the selection of multiple items within a form question.

- **RadioButton** is another traditional form element that allows for the selection of single or multiple items within a form question.

- **ComboBox** is a scrollable drop-down list that allows for the selection of a single item.

- **ListBox** is a scrollable drop-down list that allows for both single- and multiple-item selection.

- **ScrollBar** is a vertical or horizontal scrollbar element that can be added to dynamic and input text fields, allowing them to accept large amounts of text within small text fields.

- **ScrollPane** is a scrolling window pane that adds vertical and horizontal scrollbars to display movie clips. ScrollPane works only with movie clips.

Adding Components

To add components, you simply drag and drop components onto the Stage. Or you can double-click a component in the Components panel, and an instance of the component is placed on the Stage, where you can reposition it as needed.

Follow these steps to add a ComboBox component:

1. Click to select the ComboBox component in the Components panel. Drag an instance to the Stage. The Property Inspector displays the ComboBox component parameters, as shown in Figure 9.12.

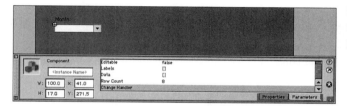

Figure 9.12
Component attributes are displayed in the Property Inspector.

2. Assign an instance name of `month` to the ComboBox.

3. The Editable parameter is set to `false` by default, meaning that the contents of the ComboBox list are static. When this parameter is set to `true`, users can select items in the list and enter a term to search for within the list. Leave Editable set to `false`.

4. Double-click in the column next to Labels to launch the Values dialog box. Click the plus sign 12 times to create 12 values for the 12 months, as shown in Figure 9.13. Click each `defaultValue` and type in a list item, the months `January` through `December`.

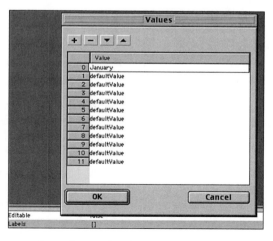

Figure 9.13
Enter list items for the ComboBox component in the Values dialog box.

5. Save your movie, and test it by choosing Control, Test Movie. The values you added to the ComboBox component are displayed in a drop-down list, as shown in Figure 9.14.

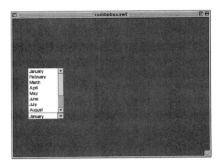

Figure 9.14
The ComboBox component produces a scrollable drop-down list in your exported movie.

Editing Components

When you add a component to a movie, a Flash UI Components folder is added to the Library, as shown in Figure 9.15. This folder contains the symbols that comprise each component.

Figure 9.15
When a component is added to a movie, a Flash UI Components folder is added to the Library.

The Flash UI Components folder contains the selected component; a Component Skins folder, which contains the graphic symbols that make up the chosen component; a Global Skins folder, which contains graphic elements that are common to all components; and a Core Assets folder, which contains advanced scripting elements.

You can edit the appearance of components by accessing the Component Skins folder. Double-click to open the Component Skins folder and then double-click the Skins folder of the component you want to edit. You can double-click the desired movie clip skin to edit the movie clip, or you can delete the movie clip and replace it with a new clip. When you're satisfied with your edits, return to the Main Timeline and drag an instance of your edited component onto the Stage. Finally, test your movie to see the new skin.

TROUBLESHOOTING

Can I edit component text styles?

Yes, you can access component color and text styles using ActionScript. See Chapter 22, "Components," to learn more details about using the `setPropertyStyle` method with components.

If a component instance is resized, it looks stretched. How can I scale components?

Resizing a component instance scales it. It will appear misshapen when viewed on the Stage, but components aren't actually created until a movie is exported. Then the parameters, including size, are applied. Test your movie, and you'll see that the component is scaled as you have specified.

FLASH AT WORK: OPEN AS LIBRARY

The easiest way to share assets among team members is to create a project .fla that contains the major assets for a given project. Be sure to include any customized components, design elements, and menus. Updated asset files can be distributed to team members, who can open the file as a library by choosing File, Open as Library. This opens the contents of an .fla as a library. Team members can then drag assets from the opened library into any working files. This approach helps to ensure that everyone is using the same assets, prevents duplication of work, and can dramatically increase efficiency while decreasing development time.

INTEGRATING VIDEO

VIDEO IN FLASH

For the first time in Macromedia Flash, MX offers true video support—the capability to embed and play video through the Flash Player without requiring any external plug-ins. Now video can be imported into Flash and transformed much like any other object. You can incorporate live action content such as corporate announcements, movie trailers, instructional videos, and news and sports coverage into your Flash movies.

As with other imported artwork, the quality of video in a published Flash movie depends on the quality of the imported video. Plan for how you will use video within Flash and edit it accordingly in a video-editing program prior to import into Flash. For best results, do not attempt to edit video within Flash. The file size of imported video remains the same in a published movie regardless of any editing that removes frames or content, just as with bitmaps that are scaled within Flash. As always, the goal is the highest quality with the lowest file size.

IMPORTING VIDEO

Flash can import video in a variety of formats if either QuickTime 4 (QT) or DirectX 7 or higher (Windows) is installed, as shown in Table 10.1. Macromedia Flash Video format, .flv, the format created by Sorenson Spark, can be imported without QT or DirectX installed.

Table 10.1 Video Import File Formats

File Type	Required Drivers	Platform
Audio Video Interleaved (.avi)	QuickTime 4, DirectX 7 or higher	Macintosh, Windows
Digital Video (.dv)	QuickTime 4	Macintosh, Windows
Motion Picture Experts Group (.mpg, .mpeg)	QuickTime 4, DirectX 7 or higher	Macintosh, Windows
QuickTime Movie (.mov)	QuickTime 4	Macintosh, Windows
Windows Media File (.wmv, .asf)	DirectX 7 or higher	Windows

Flash imports and exports video using the Sorenson Spark codec. *Codec* is an abbreviation for *coder-decoder*, the process of compressing and decompressing video. Video compression is accomplished by reducing the number of bits needed to represent video data and then decompressing, or recovering the original data, during playback. Video files are notoriously data intensive, so compression is vital.

Video data can be compressed in two ways: spatially and temporally. Spatial compression, or intraframe, compresses data in each frame independently of other frames. Temporal, or interframe, compression compares data in successive frames and stores only the differences between frames. Sorenson Spark takes advantage of both types of compression. Whenever possible, Sorenson Spark utilizes temporal compression to create the smallest file sizes. However, when significant changes occur in a video frame, a video keyframe is made using spatial compression. Video keyframes mark points of change and are similar to Flash keyframes. A video keyframe becomes the reference point for subsequent interframe or temporal compression. Video keyframes are created during import into Flash.

Sorenson Spark

Sorenson Spark is a powerful compression application. Video files are huge—far too large for Internet delivery without intensive compression being applied. Codecs compress data for faster downloads and then decompress video data during playback. The Spark codec is integrated into the Flash 6 Player, so no external players or plug-ins are required to display video content.

The standard edition of Sorenson Spark is integrated into Flash MX and is used to import and compress video files. A professional edition is also available; it provides more robust compression options, including two-pass Variable Bit Rate compression. You can purchase Sorenson Spark Pro at http://www.sorenson.com.

Embedded Versus Linked Video

With Flash MX, video can either be embedded directly into Flash movies or linked to a Flash movie. If you import a QuickTime video, it can be linked to instead of embedded within the Flash movie. Embedded videos become part of the Flash document. If you link to a QuickTime video, you must publish your Flash movie as a QuickTime movie. Video content is then displayed in QuickTime, outside the Flash Player. Embedding video integrates it seamlessly into your Flash movies, and no external players are required to view video content.

For more information about publishing options, see Chapter 30, "Optimizing, Publishing, and Exporting Movies," page 643.

Sorenson Spark Compression Options

To import and embed a video clip into Flash, follow these steps:

1. Choose File, Import or press Cmd-R (Macintosh) or Ctrl+R (Windows). The Import dialog box launches.

2. Navigate to the location of the file you want to import.

3. Select your file and click Open. If the imported file is a QuickTime movie (.mov), an Import Video dialog box opens, as shown in Figure 10.1. Select Embed Video in Macromedia Flash Document.

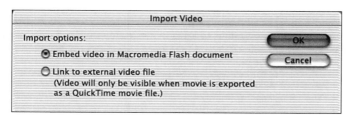

Figure 10.1

If you import a QuickTime movie, you are prompted to choose to embed or link to the video.

4. The Import Video Settings dialog box appears, as shown in Figure 10.2.

Figure 10.2
You can specify video compression settings during import using the Sorenson Spark codec.

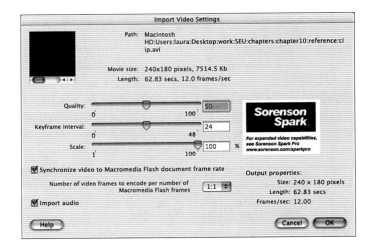

The top of the Import Video Settings dialog box displays the properties of the source video, including dimensions, file size, duration, and frame rate. The following are the options available in the dialog box:

- The Quality slider specifies the quality at which the video will be exported, and is similar to the JPEG export settings. The quality range is from 0 to 100, although 60 is the minimum setting for acceptable output. The default is 50, so be sure to increase it to at least 60.

- The Keyframe interval slider determines how often Sorenson Spark creates keyframes. Remember, complete frame data is stored only where keyframes occur. More keyframes result in larger file sizes. A setting of 0 inserts no keyframes. Lower values insert more keyframes, with the exception of zero. Experiment with this setting to find the best balance between image quality and file size.

- The Scale slider allows you to reduce the pixel dimensions of the imported video. The Output properties displayed in the lower right of the dialog box update to reflect changes in the Scale setting. The default is 100%.

- The Synchronize Video to Macromedia Flash Document Frame Rate check box, which is selected by default, adjusts the source video's frame rate to match the specified frame rate of the Flash movie. If this option is deselected, each frame in the imported video occupies one frame within the Flash Timeline.

- Select a value in the Number of Video Frames to Encode Per Number of Macromedia Flash Frames check box. This setting specifies the ratio of video frames to Flash Timeline frames, with a default of 1:1 that preserves the original frame rate of the imported video. Try not to go below a frame rate of 12fps, or the video may appear choppy.

- The Import Audio check box allows you to import or discard audio tracks in imported video. It is checked by default.

The maximum dimensions for an imported video are 360×240. Anything larger will be displayed as 360×240.

5. Click OK. An Importing dialog box with a status bar then appears.

6. If the Timeline does not contain a sufficient number of frames to display the imported video, you will be prompted to extend the Timeline, as shown in Figure 10.3. Click Yes to extend the Timeline or No to maintain the current number of frames. Any frames in the imported video that exceed the number of frames in the Timeline will not be displayed during playback.

> **Caution**
>
> Video is highly memory intensive, especially on the Macintosh. In operating systems prior to OS X, allocate as much RAM to Flash as possible. Otherwise, you may be unable to import video.

Figure 10.3
You will be prompted to extend the Timeline if it does not contain enough frames to display the imported video.

10

The video is imported to the Library and an instance is placed on the Stage. To import directly into the Library, choose File, Import to Library and follow steps 2 through 5 in the preceding series of steps. If you import to the Library, you will not be prompted if the current Timeline contains fewer frames than the imported video.

> The number of frames required to display a video is equal to the duration of the video in seconds multiplied by the frame rate of the Flash movie.

To check the size of your imported video, save your movie and test it by choosing Control, Test Movie. Choose View, Show Bandwidth Profiler to preview your movie. Also, choose View, Show Streaming to preview how long users will have to wait for content to download.

⇨ *For more information about testing and optimizing a movie, see Chapter 30, "Optimizing, Publishing, and Exporting Movies," page 643.*

WORKING WITH IMPORTED VIDEO

Embedded video instances can be transformed much like other objects. You can rotate, skew, apply color effects, mask, and even tween a video instance. Simply select the video instance and use the Free Transform tool to apply transformations. To mask a video, move the layer containing the video beneath a mask layer. To animate or apply color effects to a video instance, embed the video in a movie clip symbol and apply color effects or a tween to the symbol. Combine animation and video sparingly, though, as both can increase file size dramatically.

For more information about transforming objects, see Chapter 2, "The Flash Interface," page 17, and to learn more about masks, see Chapter 3, "Drawing and Painting in Flash," page 37. To learn more about creating tweens and color effects, see Chapter 7, "Animating in Flash," page 109.

After a video is imported, you can replace or update it like other symbols. To replace an embedded video clip, follow these steps:

1. Within the Library, click to select the embedded video clip.

2. Click the upper-right corner of the Library panel to launch the Library Options pop-up menu, and choose Properties. The Embedded Video Properties dialog box appears, as shown in Figure 10.4.

Figure 10.4

In the Embedded Video Properties dialog box, you can replace or update a video clip.

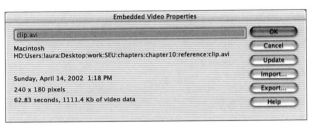

3. Click Import to open the Import dialog box and navigate to a video file to replace the embedded clip. Then follow the steps in the "Sorenson Spark Compression Options" section earlier in this chapter.

To update a clip that has been edited externally since import into Flash, select the clip in the Library and access the Embedded Video Properties as outlined in the preceding steps. Instead of clicking Import, click Update.

You can place video clips on the Stage and move them about like other objects. The Property Inspector allows you to assign an instance name for a clip and to access its coordinates and dimensions, as shown in Figure 10.5.

Figure 10.5

The Property Inspector displays video clip properties and allows you to swap a symbol instance.

CONTROLLING VIDEO PLAYBACK

After video is embedded, it can be controlled much like any other content that is on the Stage. Video frames are converted to Flash frames, and you can drag the playhead to scrub through the Timeline and preview video content. If your video content is lengthy, such as a presentation, it's a good idea to add buttons to allow users to control the playback of the video. You control video playback by using ActionScript to control the playback of the Timeline in which the video is placed. To rewind a video, you can simply send its Timeline back to frame 1. To fast-forward or rewind, increment or decrement the frame number.

To create simple playback buttons to control a video clip, follow these steps:

1. Open a new Flash document and name the existing layer **Video**.

2. Import a video clip by selecting File, Import. A sample video, video.avi, is included on the book CD. Select a video clip and import to the Stage. Be sure that the instance of your movie is placed on the Main Timeline.

3. Add a new layer to your document and name it **Controls**.

4. Choose Window, Common Libraries, Buttons.fla, as shown in Figure 10.6. Buttons.fla, which contains sample buttons in various graphic styles, opens as a library. Browse through the buttons and find a style that complements your movie.

Common Libraries	▶	Buttons.fla
Sitespring		Learning Interactions.fla
		Sounds.fla

Figure 10.6

Choose Window, Common Libraries, Buttons.fla to access the sample buttons.

5. With the Controls layer selected in the Main Timeline, drag instances of Play, Stop, Fast Forward, and Rewind buttons from the Buttons.fla library to the Stage, as shown in Figure 10.7.

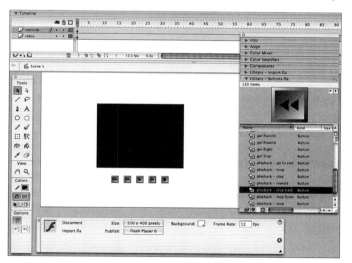

Figure 10.7

Place playback control buttons on the Controls layer.

6. Select the Play button—the single arrow pointing to the right—and choose Window, Actions or press F9 to open the ActionScript Editor.

7. Click the arrow in the upper right of the Actions panel; be sure Expert Mode is selected.

8. In the Script pane, type the following, as shown in Figure 10.8:

```
on (release) {
    play();
}
```

Figure 10.8

A simple play action added to a button can control the playback of a video clip.

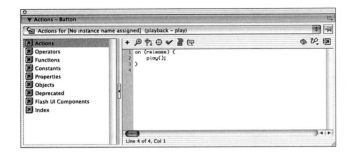

9. Select the Stop button—the square—and click in the Actions panel or press F9 to relaunch it.

10. Type the following code, as shown in Figure 10.9:

```
on (release) {
     stop();
}
```

Figure 10.9

Add a stop action to the Stop button.

11. Save and test your movie by pressing Cmd-Return (Macintosh) or Ctrl+Enter (Windows).

Flash movies loop automatically, so the video should begin to play as soon as it loads even without the Play button being clicked. (You can prevent the movie from automatically playing by inserting a `stop();` action in frame 1.) To test your buttons, click the Stop button to make the video stop. Click Play, and the video plays from the point it stopped.

To complete the playback controls, follow these steps:

12. Return to your saved movie in Editing mode. Click the Rewind-to-the-Beginning button—the double arrow pointing to the left against a vertical line—and type the following code into the ActionScript Editor:

```
on (release) {
     gotoAndStop(1);
}
```

13. Return to the Stage and click on the Rewind button—the double arrow pointing to the left—and type the following code into the ActionScript Editor:

```
on (release) {
     prevFrame();
}
```

14. Return to the Stage and click on the Fast Forward button—the double arrow pointing to the right—and type the following code into the ActionScript Editor:

```
on (release) {
    nextFrame();
}
```

15. Save and test your movie. Click each button to change the playback of the movie.

For more information about buttons, see Chapter 9, "Buttons, Menus, and User Input," page 143. For more information about writing scripts, see Chapter 11, "Getting Started with ActionScript," page 169.

TROUBLESHOOTING

Can video have its own sound properties?

Unfortunately, no. Video does not support event sounds, and only one streamed audio track is available per SWF.

If I try to export to QuickTime, I get the following error: "The installed version of QuickTime does not have a handler for this type of Macromedia Flash movie."

Translation: The installed version of QuickTime does not support Flash Player 6. Until QuickTime 6 comes out, QuickTime does not support Flash Player 6 content. You'll have to go to the Publish Settings. Just choose File, Publish Settings; click the Flash tab, and then select Flash Player 5 from the version pop-up menu.

FLASH AT WORK: VIDEO INTERACTIVITY

The capability to embed video in Flash MX means that users can control the delivery of video content—and not simply by using playback controls. As an example, with careful editing and compression to keep file size down, multiple video clips can offer user-controlled non-linear narratives. Further, it is possible to employ Flash text to offer optional video subtitles in multiple languages. Combining the capabilities of video and Flash can provide a highly individualized user experience.

10

ADDING ADVANCED INTERACTIVITY WITH ACTIONSCRIPT

IN THIS PART

GETTING STARTED WITH ACTIONSCRIPT

ADDING INTERACTIVITY WITH ACTIONSCRIPT

ActionScript is a programming language, a way of sending both commands and questions to Flash about timelines, movie clips, and other objects such as buttons.

> ActionScript is based on the ECMA-262 standard, which was in turn derived from JavaScript. ActionScript is essentially JavaScript adapted and optimized for the Flash environment.

Often, you can accomplish tasks easily with ActionScript that would be difficult or impossible without it. Without ActionScript, you can access only a small portion of Flash's capabilities. For example, you need some ActionScript to get any kind of interactivity, such as responding when the user clicks on a button or presses a key on the keyboard. ActionScript is also the only way to get Flash to go to a particular frame of a timeline and either start or stop playing. These simple examples, however, don't communicate the richness, flexibility, and endless possibilities that ActionScript opens up to the Flash developer. ActionScript is Flash's native language; if you don't speak at least a little of the language, it's like being in a foreign country and having to gesture and point to get what you want. Very often, you have to settle for less than what you want.

In addition, ActionScript usually gives you smaller SWF files and better performance than tweening. Another advantage is that you can perform tasks with more precision, such as moving a movie clip to a precise position on the Stage.

ActionScript offers endless possibilities, and you can easily get started using it. The place to start is the Actions panel.

Accessing the Actions Panel

To display or maximize the Actions panel, do one of the following:

- From the Window menu, choose Actions.

- Press F9.

The Actions panel, as shown in Figure 11.1, maximizes or becomes visible. Or, if it was behind another window, it comes to the front. In the default layout, the Actions panel is docked with the Properties panel. (If you want to restore the default layout, choose Window, Panel Sets, Default Layout.)

Pin current script button

Figure 11.1

The Actions panel is Flash's built-in ActionScript Editor.

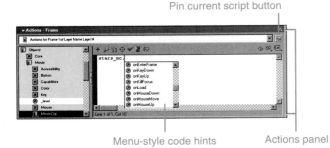

Menu-style code hints   Actions panel

The Actions panel is Flash's built-in ActionScript Editor. It displays menu-style code hints if you use appropriate suffixes for object instances, such as _mc for movie clips. You can "pin" the current script (keep it in the Actions panel) by using the pin current script button.

USING THE ACTIONS PANEL

You enter all your ActionScript in the Actions panel. Click on the frame, button, or movie clip in which the ActionScript will reside; then go to the Actions panel and enter actions into the Actions pane on the right side of the panel.

Selecting Frame Actions or Object Actions

A given block of actions can be attached either to an object (button or movie clip) or to a frame. The type of action you're currently entering is indicated in the gray title bar at the top of the Actions panel, which says either "Actions — Frame," "Actions — Movie Clip" or "Actions — Button." The appropriate mode is selected when you click on an object or a frame.

In general, frame actions execute when the playhead reaches the frame to which the actions are attached. Object actions, on the other hand, are executed when a designated event occurs involving that object. For instance:

- **Frame action**—Suppose you put a trace action in a frame, such as

  ```
  trace("hello");
  ```

  The word hello will be displayed in the Output window each time the playhead reaches that frame.

- **Object action**—Movie clips have an "enter frame" event that occurs every time the clip enters a frame. For example, this event occurs 12 times per second if your movie is running at 12 frames per second (fps). You tell Flash which event you want to trigger your code by putting your code inside an "event handler." The traditional "enter frame" event handler looks like this:

  ```
  onClipEvent(enterFrame) {
       // your code goes here!
  }
  ```

That's how things work, generally. There are two notable exceptions:

- A *function* is a named block of code that implements a particular procedure. For instance, gotoAndPlay() is a built-in movie clip function that causes a movie to go to a particular frame in its Timeline and start playing.

- You can define your own custom functions anywhere that you can write code—within a frame or within an event handler. When the playhead reaches a frame or executes an event handler containing a custom function definition, the function becomes defined and available, but it does not actually execute. You have to *call* the function to cause it to execute.

⇨ *For more information on functions, see Chapter 15, "Combining Statements into Functions," page 267.*

11

■ In addition, Flash MX has a new format for event handlers that allows you to enter the event-handler code in a frame. For example, the new-style "enter frame" event handler looks like this:

```
myClip.onEnterFrame = function () {
        // your code goes here!
};
```

When the playhead reaches the frame with the event handler code, Flash starts "listening" for the event. However, the event handler "fires" (executes the code it contains) only when the event occurs.

➩ *In the preceding example, myClip is the instance name of a movie clip. Movie clip instance names are covered in Chapter 6, "Symbols, Instances, and Library Assets" page 89.*

➩ *You'll find more details on frame actions and object actions in Chapter 16, "Interaction, Events, and Sequencing," page 303.*

Selecting Normal or Expert Mode

You can create and edit code in two modes: Expert and Normal.

With the exception of multiline comments (which are possible only in Expert mode), you can write the same statements in either mode. Normal mode is most appropriate for short, simple blocks of code. Expert mode is faster for more complex code structures.

Flash Helps You Code

Giving instructions for creating code in Normal mode can take up a lot of space. Thus, to keep explanations concise, I assume Expert mode in this book. However, when you're trying to remember the format of an action, don't forget that you can always switch into Normal mode and let Flash coach you.

In addition, Flash MX has a new feature, *code hints*, that makes Expert mode a lot easier to use. Code hints come in two forms: *tooltips* and menu-driven *code completion*. Tooltips show you formats after you have typed a portion of the action. Code completion saves you typing by displaying a menu of possible choices, as shown in Figure 11.1.

To get the menu-style code hints for instances of various classes of objects (such as movie clips, buttons, or text fields), you must add a class-specific suffix to each instance name. For instance, in Figure 11.1, the suffix _mc has been added to the instance name stars, forming the name stars_mc. (All the suffixes are listed in Table 11.1.)

Both types of code hints are enabled by default but can be disabled by selecting Edit, Preferences, ActionScript Editor and clicking in the Code Hints check box. If code hints are enabled, you can enable and disable just Tooltips by selecting Edit, Preferences, General and clicking in the Show Tooltips check box.

Table 11.1   Actions Panel Code Hint Suffixes

Suffix	Object Class
Array	_array
Button	_btn
Camera	_camera(*)
Color	_color
Date	_date
Microphone	_mic(*)
MovieClip	_mc
NetConnection	_connection(*)
NetStream	_stream(*)
SharedObject	_so(*)
Sound	_sound
String	_str
TextField	_txt
TextFormat	_fmt
Video	_video(*)
XML	_xml
XMLSocket	_xmlsocket

(*)Although listed in Macromedia documentation, these suffixes do not currently bring up any code hints.

Normal mode takes a "fill-in-the-blanks" approach to ActionScripting. When you click once on an item in the Actions toolbox (the list on the left side of the Actions panel), a description of the item appears at the upper right of the panel. When you double-click an item, the parts of the action that are always the same appear in the Script pane on the right side of the panel. This saves you typing and gives you a head start on getting the syntax of the action right.

You use text boxes at the top of the Script pane to fill in the parts of an action that are not always the same. For example, the gotoAndPlay() action causes the playhead to go to a specific frame of a movie clip and start playing the clip from there. When you double-click on gotoAndPlay in the Actions toolbox, here's what pops up:

```
<not set yet>.gotoAndPlay();
```

The <not set yet> is a placeholder for a movie clip name, which you must provide in the text box at the top of the Actions panel. In another text box, you provide the frame number. Ultimately, something like this ends up in the Action pane:

```
myClip.gotoAndPlay(4);
```

You don't type anything directly into the Actions pane; it's just used as a viewer. You can also add, delete, or change the order of statements in Normal mode. Use Normal mode when you're not sure of the syntax of the statements you're using and want something to jog your memory or help you avoid mistakes.

In Expert mode, you can still select items in the Actions toolbox (by double-clicking), but there are no text boxes at the top of the Actions pane. You also have the options of just typing text in the Actions pane or else cutting and pasting from another document—options you don't have in Normal mode. In Expert mode, you can usually get the same code out with fewer keystrokes and mouse clicks.

To select Normal or Expert mode, do one of the following:

- Click on the options menu in the upper-right corner of the Actions panel and select Normal Mode or Expert Mode.

- Press Cmd-Shift-E (Mac) or Ctrl+Shift+E (Windows) for Expert mode, or Cmd-Shift-N (Mac) or Ctrl+Shift+N (Windows) for Normal mode.

Whichever mode you set—Normal or Expert—is used for all code editing in all movies from that point on, until you change it again. This holds true even if you exit and restart Flash.

Hiding and "Un-hiding" the Actions Toolbox

You can hide the Actions toolbox, thus gaining more space for the Actions pane, by clicking the triangle between the Actions toolbox and the Actions pane.

To "un-hide" the Actions toolbox, click the triangle to the left of the Actions pane.

UNDERSTANDING OBJECT-ORIENTED LANGUAGES

ActionScript is an object-oriented programming (OOP) language. For approximately the last 40 years, OOP has been gaining ground as the programming paradigm of choice. In this chapter, I'll explain why and give some simple examples. Later chapters, starting with Chapter 15, go into more detail.

➡ *Chapter 15, "Combining Statements into Functions," introduces the basic object-oriented programming (OOP) concept of classes in "Functions as Classes: Constructor Functions," page 279. Most subsequent chapters show you how to use built-in objects and/or discuss issues around creating custom objects.*

"Object-oriented" means "based on objects." An *object* is a data structure that allows you to do in programs what you do in everyday life: group complex phenomena under simple headings.

For instance, suppose I want my friend Joe to come to my party and bring his guitar. Both Joe and his guitar have many capabilities and characteristics, but I just call Joe and say, "Hey, are you free Saturday night? Great! Come to my party and bring your guitar!" I don't have to tell him how to come to my party or what his guitar is; Joe already knows those things.

Joe, in this case, is analogous to a programming object. I'm dealing with two of his properties: One property is a function, namely, coming to a party. The other property is an object: Joe's guitar. (Joe, in this analogy, is also an object. So you have an object as a property of an object.)

You can use objects in ActionScript to organize the complex behaviors and characteristics of your programs and give yourself simple interfaces to them. Like Joe, an object is something that you can refer to by a single name, even though it may have many properties and behaviors. By summarizing related functions and data properties under object names, you make your programs easier to work with and understand.

Every movie clip in Flash is an object. Thus, if you have even a little experience with Flash, the terminology of objects may be new, but objects themselves are not.

Let's look at the three basic building blocks of objects: primitive data, functions, and data structures. This discussion will constitute a whirlwind tour of the elements that make up an ActionScript program. Most of the remainder of this book will be devoted to filling in the details.

The simplest form of data—data primitives—includes numbers and character strings. For instance, the number 6 is a primitive datum (piece of data), as is the string "Hello world!". A third primitive data type is Boolean. A Boolean datum can have only one of two values, namely, true or false.

> *If you want more information about primitives, see Chapter 12, "Managing Variables, Data, and Datatypes," page 187.*

A *function* is a named block of code embodying a procedure.

Primitive data and functions can be grouped into data structures. One type of data structure is an *array*, which is basically a numbered list, starting at zero. Thus, myArray[0] is the first element in the array named myArray. In an array containing the names of months, you would have myArray[0] = "January".

> *If you want more information about arrays, see Chapter 19, "Using the Built-in Core Objects," page 393.*

Objects are another way of grouping data and functions into structures. Instead of accessing things via numbers, as you do in an array, you access the items (called *properties*) in an object using names.

The following are examples of some movie clip properties. They are all "read-write" properties: You can read them to determine the current state of the movie clip, or you can change them and thus control the movie clip.

- _currentFrame—A number; the movie clip's current frame on the Timeline.

- _rotation—A number; the number of degrees the movie clip has been rotated from its original position.

- _visible—A Boolean; controls the visibility of the movie clip.

- _name—A string; the name of the movie clip instance.

You access the elements of an array via the square bracket notation: myArray[0]. You typically access the properties of an object via "dot syntax," in which the name of the object and the name of the property are separated by a dot, as in these examples:

```
myClip._currentFrame
myClip._visible
myClip._name
myClip._rotation
myClip.gotoAndPlay()
```

In summary, objects are collections of properties. Each object has a name, and each property within an object has its own separate name. The property name refers either to a function or to data. The data may be a data primitive or a data structure such as an array or another object.

11

Data can also be stored in a *variable*, which is a container that is outside any data structure. For instance, the following statement stores the number 10 in a variable named x:

```
x = 10;
```

Functions in Objects Are Methods

Both arrays and objects can contain functions. However, object properties that refer to or contain functions are called *methods*. A function that is an element of an array is still just called a *function*.

Methods come under the grab-bag term *actions*, which also include global functions such as eval that are not associated with any object, statements such as break that control program flow, and directives such as include that give instructions to the ActionScript compiler. *Methods* is a more precise term.

THE THREE R'S: READABILITY, REUSABILITY, AND REACHABILITY

Each Flash programmer tends to develop his or her own style of writing, organizing, and commenting programs. Companies that employ Flash programmers also have different standards. However, whatever your individual style, you probably want to write code that is readable, reachable, and perhaps reusable. The longer and more complex your programs are, the more important it is to think about these goals before and as you write.

Readability: Writing Readable Code

When you go back to change, enhance, or debug a program, it's nice to have code that you can decipher without too much strain on your eyes or brain. Readability is partly just a matter of spacing, indentation, and capitalization. Comments can also add a lot to readability, as can the use of meaningful names for functions, variables, arrays, and objects. Finally, the best (and hardest) way of making code more readable is by solving coding problems in more elegant, simpler ways.

Spacing, Indentation, and Capitalization

With a few exceptions, ActionScript is fairly flexible about spacing, indentation, and capitalization.

> For some unusual but important examples of Flash's inflexibility in capitalization, see Chapter 16, "Interaction, Events, and Sequencing," page 303.

For example, these two functions look the same to the ActionScript interpreter (the software that interprets SWF files):

```
function addonetobasescore(basescore){return basescore+1;}

function addOneToBaseScore (baseScore) {
    return baseScore + 1;
}
```

Whitespace, capitalization, and indentation make the second significantly more readable, and thus make it easier for you to understand and edit your program.

Adding Comments to Your Script

Just formatting the code is seldom enough to allow you to easily understand what's going on in a complex program. Comments are usually necessary to make the elements clear. Single-line comments are marked by double slashes:

```
// input: base score, returns: one more than the base score
```

A comment can also follow code:

```
baseScore += 1; // baseScore declared frame 1, main timeline
```

Enclose multiline comments like this:

```
/*
ADD ONE TO BASE SCORE
Michael Hurwicz  - January, 2002 - www.maximpulse.com
baseScore is an integer
*/
```

Some people prefer double slashes on every line because they make it clear that each line is still part of the comment:

```
///////////////////////////////////////////////////////////
// ADD ONE TO BASE SCORE
// Michael Hurwicz  - January, 2002 - www.maximpulse.com
// baseScore is an integer
///////////////////////////////////////////////////////////
```

In the Actions pane, comments are color-coded, so you know where they start and stop. You can customize the color coding by selecting Edit, Preferences, ActionScript Editor and clicking in a color swatch in the Syntax Coloring section. A selection of color swatches pops up, and you can select one. In this way, you can use colors for displaying foreground, background, keywords, comments, identifiers, and strings.

Flash permits you to store code in external files, as well.

> *For more information on storing code in external files, see Chapter 24, "Sharing ActionScript," page 551.*

Not all external editors are "ActionScript-smart," so they may not give you any help in distinguishing comments from code. In that case, double slashes on every line may be more readable, especially if comments are long. Double slashes on every line may also be clearer when you paste your code into an e-mail message, for instance.

> *Problems with comments? See the "Troubleshooting" section later in this chapter, page 183.*

11

Creating Readable Names

You've seen that ActionScript programs have several types of elements, such as functions, arrays, objects, and variables, that require names. What makes such names readable?

You've already encountered one aspect of readability for names: capitalization. Reading addOneToBaseScore is easier than reading addonetobasescore. Traditionally, by the way, most names in Flash begin with lowercase letters. An initial capital indicates a class.

Another good technique is to give things names that you (and others, if necessary) will understand intuitively. For instance, you probably won't have to examine the details of the addOneToBaseScore function to remember what it does.

Simplifying, Standardizing, and Optimizing Code

The best way to make your code more readable is to come up with straightforward ways of accomplishing your programming goals. Simple code will make your life as a programmer much easier. Of course, creating masterfully elegant code is easier said than done, but it's a worthy objective.

Trying to standardize your code is also helpful so that you can use the same techniques or syntax over and over. You'll understand blocks of code at a glance because you'll be so familiar with the techniques and syntax involved.

Simpler code also usually performs better than more complicated code. Because you will, of course, standardize on your best code examples, standardization is likely to make your program run better all around. A more concise approach to code will also permit faster debugging and easier editing.

In some cases, however, a conflict occurs between fast code and easy-to-read code. In those cases, one approach is to actually use the fast code in the program but retain the easy-to-read code as a comment.

Reusability: Modularizing Code

Most programmers reuse code to some extent. After all, programming is essentially problem-solving. If you've solved a problem before, why reinvent the wheel? The techniques used to achieve reusability also make code more readable, and tend to make you a better programmer, as well.

The two main vehicles of reusability are functions and objects. Both allow you to package functionality in modules that you can reuse both within a program and among multiple programs. Arrays can also play the same role, if you want access via numeric indices.

In addition, packaging functionality in functions and objects makes your code more readable. For instance, suppose you find this code inside an "enter frame" event handler attached to the left leg of a figure:

```
degrees++;
if (degrees < 30) {
    _rotation++;
}
```

You know that every time the movie clip enters a frame, the ActionScript interpreter is going to do whatever this code says. But what is that exactly?

Compare that example to the following line, which invokes a lift() function, passing it an argument of 30.

```
lift (30);
```

An *argument* is data that you pass to a function, enclosed in parentheses after the function name.

You don't need to be a genius to guess that the figure is probably lifting its left leg, and that the argument, 30, has something to do with how much it's lifting the leg. You get that increase in readability just by putting the less intuitive code in a function with an intuitive name.

Now, let's make that leg part of an object named guy, with a leftLeg property. The leftLeg property is also an object, with a lift() method:

```
guy.leftLeg.lift(30);
```

It's practically a full sentence, with subject, object, verb, and adverb: A guy is lifting his left leg.

How do you make the leg part of an object named guy? You take advantage of the fact that movie clips are objects. Here, guy is a movie clip, and leftLeg is a clip within it. The lift() function becomes a method of leftLeg when it is defined in an event handler associated with that clip.

Both lift() and guy.leftLeg.lift() assume that somewhere else in your program you have defined a function called "lift" that does something similar to the less intuitive code shown on page 178. If you look at that function definition, you can get a more precise idea about what lifting means in this context—namely, that it has to do with rotating the clip:

```
function lift (degrees) {
    if (_rotation > degrees) {
        _rotation--;
    }
}
```

Add a comment to the function definition—"used to lift leftLeg"—and you have some very readable code.

The sample program leglift.fla shows a slight elaboration of this approach. It adds a second part to the lift() function so that the function lowers the leg if _rotation is less than degrees and raises the leg if _rotation is greater than degrees. If degrees equals _rotation, the function does nothing; that's the basis for stopping the leg.

```
// used to raise, lower and stop left leg
    function lift(degrees) {
        if (_rotation < degrees) {
            _rotation++; // lower the leg
        }

        if (_rotation > degrees) {
            _rotation--; // raise the leg
        }
    }
```

The sample also defines three functions that change the `degrees` variable, thus raising, lowering, or stopping the leg:

```
function raise() { degrees = 20; }
function lower() { degrees = 68; }
function halt() { degrees = _rotation; } // lift() will do nothing
```

These three functions are invoked from three buttons on the Stage. The "enter frame" event handler of the leg clip is constantly executing the `lift()` function, so the appropriate action is triggered as soon as `degrees` changes.

Using functions and objects also tends to make you a better programmer. This goes back to the fact that programming is problem-solving, and the first steps in problem-solving are defining the problem domain and defining the problem itself.

In the process of defining objects, you also define problem domains precisely. In the leg lift example, for instance, the domain of your problem is `guy.leftLeg`. Similarly, in the process of defining a function, you also define the problem. For instance, the previous function defines the problem as lifting the leg a certain number of degrees.

Functions and objects also help you break down large problems into smaller problems. Suppose you want a cartoon figure to walk across a room. A `walkAcrossTheRoom()` function might be relatively complicated. Perhaps you could write a `takeOneStep()` function and repeat it until the figure gets across the room. So, what is involved in taking one step? The figure has to swing an arm, move a leg, and move a certain distance forward.

If you keep going like this, eventually you'll come to problems that are small and precise enough to get your mind around and solve. You may start by implementing your solutions as functions. You could then combine these functions into more complex functions, objects, or sections of code. Objects and functions are great problem-solving tools because they help you solve dauntingly complex problems one simple step at a time.

Ready to start programming, but don't know where to start? See the "Troubleshooting" section later in this chapter, page 183.

Avoiding the supposed complexities of functions and objects is like avoiding the complexities of folders when you're managing e-mail or files on a hard disk. As the number of messages or files grows, the lack of organization begins to hamper your ability to work efficiently. Similarly, objects and functions are basic to organizing ActionScript. They should make your life easier, not harder.

Reachability: Organizing and Centralizing Code

There are two aspects to reachability: the interpreter's ability to find functions and variables at runtime (when your program is running) and your ability to find physical lines of code when you need to edit them.

By bundling functions and variables into objects and classifying objects in different classes, OOP provides the infrastructure that allows the ActionScript interpreter to find what it needs while your program is running. For instance, there is a `concat()` method (function) for arrays and a `concat()` method for text strings. In each case, the definition of the method is stored in the class definition, so the interpreter knows just where to look for it and doesn't get the two confused.

See "Functions as Classes: Constructor Functions," page 279 (Chapter 15, "Combining Statements into Functions").

There are also *scoping* rules that determine whether a variable, function, or object in one part of the program is directly "visible" from another part of the program. By centralizing code—putting as much of it in one place as possible—you avoid possible scoping problems.

For instance, if all your code is within a single frame, you don't have to worry about scoping. Putting all your code in one frame was sometimes difficult or undesirable in Flash 5. In Flash MX, due to in-line event handlers, it is much easier and generally has few drawbacks. (In-line or *dynamic* event handlers are defined in frames rather than having to be attached to movie clips.)

In-line event handlers are introduced in "Selecting Frame Actions or Object Actions," earlier in this chapter, page 171. They are discussed at more length in Chapter 16, "Interaction, Events, and Sequencing," page 303.

Having problems converting an old Flash file to use the new-style event handlers? See the "Troubleshooting" section later in this chapter, page 183.

Another important issue is your ability to find and conveniently edit code. In any somewhat complex program, Flash provides many nooks and crannies where you can "hide" code. If code is scattered around in too many places, maintaining your program can become hard.

Suppose you need to add a second argument to a function. The function itself is defined in just one place, so you can change it easily enough. However, you must also find every reference to that function in your program and add a second argument there, as well. If all your code is centralized in one place, you can search on the function name and probably find all the references in minutes. If your code is scattered around in 20 different places, you have a longer, more tedious job in front of you. Of course, if you had to do it only once or twice, such a change would be no big deal. If you spend a lot of time doing these kinds of things, you want a better system.

Centralizing code is perhaps the most important factor in easy program maintenance. Through in-line event handlers, Flash MX makes it easier to avoid the "scatter-gun" effect that makes programs difficult to maintain.

Have you centralized all your ActionScript and now want to keep it in the Actions panel while working on graphics in other frames? See the "Troubleshooting" section later in this chapter, page 183.

Organizing Data and Functions Using Movie Clips

Prior to Flash MX, nearly every scripted Flash program used movie clips for organizing code. The clips containing code were often "dummy" clips with no graphical content. Although you may still find it convenient to attach code to movie clips from time to time, this strategy is much less necessary in Flash MX than it was in Flash 5. Anything that you would formerly have put in an onClipEvent(enterFrame) event handler (attached to a movie clip) can now go in an in-line onEnterFrame event handler (in a frame). Similarly, there are in-line formats for other event handlers.

When considering whether to attach code to movie clips, think about this: If you have 20 movie clips on the Stage in frame 1 of your movie, you can put an action in the "enter frame" event handler of every movie clip, and the Flash interpreter will execute every one of those actions, round-robin style, before going on to frame 2. Or, you can put one in-line onEnterFrame event on the first frame of the Main Timeline and put all the actions in that one clip. Flash will execute all the actions in the in-line event handler before going on to frame 2. In other words, exactly the same thing gets accomplished, but your program may be 20 times easier to maintain.

Using Timelines to Organize Code

You can also use a timeline to organize code. Each frame can serve the purpose of a function, holding a block of code that accomplishes a particular task. You "invoke the function" with a play(), gotoAndPlay(), or gotoAndStop() action that sends the playhead to the appropriate frame.

At the same time, you can animate, add, or remove movie clips in that frame.

Better yet, put each block of code into a function and just call the function on the frame. This makes each frame more readable. It also allows you to centralize the bulk of the code. For instance, you can put all the functions in the first frame of a single layer.

Organizing code on a timeline is a more visual approach than implementing the same behaviors in functions. However, because you must edit code separately in each frame, organizing code on a timeline doesn't really centralize the code. It's almost as tedious to "peek" into multiple frames on a timeline as multiple movie clips.

Though still used, this technique is largely a holdover from earlier versions of Flash, which did not support functions. It is a viable technique, especially for simple movies, but it can become a hindrance in more complex ones.

Using the Movie Explorer to Find ActionScript

The Movie Explorer can help you find the ActionScript in Flash source (.FLA) files. Start by deselecting all the buttons except the ActionScript button in the Show section near the upper left of the Movie Explorer panel (see Figure 11.2). The Movie Explorer then displays only movie clips and buttons that contain ActionScript.

For more details about the Movie Explorer, see Chapter 2, "The Flash Interface," page 17.

The buttons in the Show section in the upper left of the Movie Explorer panel determine which types of movie elements the Movie Explorer displays. From left to right, they control text; buttons, movie clips, and graphics; ActionScript; video, sounds, and bitmaps; frames and layers. The hourglass on the right provides a single panel for customizing all aspects of the Movie Explorer display.

To display the ActionScript in a particular button or movie clip, highlight the button or movie clip, click on the options menu (in the upper-right corner of the Movie Explorer panel), and select Expand Branch. Alternatively, you can click on the plus sign to the left of the movie clip or button icon in the display list. However, you might have to click on several plus signs before you get down to the ActionScript.

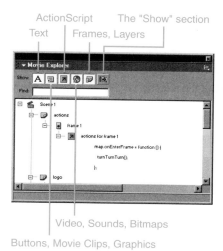

ActionScript

Text

Frames, Layers

The "Show" section

Video, Sounds, Bitmaps

Buttons, Movie Clips, Graphics

Figure 11.2
The buttons in the Show section near the upper left of the Movie Explorer panel determine what kinds of program elements appear in the panel.

TROUBLESHOOTING

I know what I want my program to do, but where do I start?

If you find yourself completely stymied about how to approach a problem in ActionScript (or any programming language), you may not have broken down the problem into small enough component problems yet. Define subproblems and sub-subproblems. When you hit tasks that you can accomplish with a few lines of code, you're on your way.

A related approach is to attempt to solve a greatly simplified version of the problem you're really interested in. Then approach your goal by successive approximations.

Okay, I've centralized all my ActionScript. Now, how do I keep it in the Actions panel while I'm working on graphics in other frames?

Normally, when you click on a frame, the Actions panel displays whatever ActionScript is in that frame—even if that's no ActionScript at all. Then you have to go back and click in the frame that does have ActionScript in it. Annoying.

There is a solution: the pin current script button. It's the button with the push pin symbol on it in the upper-right corner of the Actions panel, just under the Options menu (refer to Figure 11.1). While your ActionScript is in the Actions panel, click on the pin current script button. Your ActionScript is "pinned" in the Actions panel and will stay there, no matter what frame you are in, until you click the button again to "unpin" the ActionScript.

11

I'm converting an old Flash project to use the new in-line event handlers. But they're just not working! What's wrong?

Most probably, Flash MX recognized a Flash 5 FLA and automatically configured the `Publish Settings` to output a Flash 5 file (SWF). The new-style event handlers don't work in Flash 5, naturally—thus, your problem. The solution: Choose File, Publish Settings and, on the Flash tab, select Flash Player 6 in the Version combo box.

Can comments cause errors?

Yes! One place where comments cause errors with great consistency is just before the `else` in an `if-else` statement:

```
if (myVar) trace("if");
 // any comment on this line causes an ERROR !!!
else {
    trace("else");
}
```

If you're having a problem you think may be related to a comment, try moving the comment to a new location or eliminating it temporarily.

Also consider the possibility that you might have commented something out inadvertently, or forgotten to uncomment something that you commented out for debugging purposes.

FLASH AT WORK: READABLE, REUSABLE, REACHABLE CODE: A "BEFORE AND AFTER" AD

Here's an example of making your code more readable, reusable, and reachable.

The movies created using unimportant1.fla and unimportant2.fla on the CD look exactly the same (see Figure 11.3). However, unimportant1.fla was just thrown together, while unimportant2.fla was designed for readability, reusability, and reachability.

Figure 11.3

An animated cartoon created for irthlingz.com based on a saying from the Tao Te Ching.

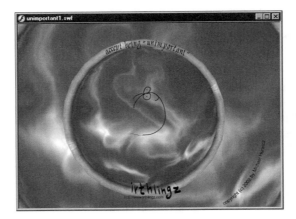

The code for unimportant1.fla, arrived at by the time-honored technique of "messing around," is fairly mysterious:

```
onClipEvent(load) {
    var frame=1;
    var rotate=5;
    var radian;
}


onClipEvent(enterFrame) {
    rotate2=Math.round((rotate/10)+(5*rotate*(Math.abs(Math.cos(radian)))));
    this._rotation+=rotate2;
    radian=(Math.PI/180)*(this._rotation);
    if (Math.abs(Math.cos(radian))<.01) {
        frame=(frame+5);
        if (frame>20) {frame=1;}
        this.gotoAndPlay(frame);
        rotate=-rotate;
    }
}
```

In unimportant2.fla, I did four things: created a function, pendulumSwing(), that does everything that needs to be in the "enter frame" event handler; converted to the new in-line event handler format; gave the movie clip instance a name, happyPerson, so that I can control the movie clip using ActionScript; and added comments.

```
_root.happyPerson.frame = 1;
// seed value for rotation
_root.happyPerson.rotate = 5;
// rotation in radians
_root.happyPerson.radian;
////////////////////////////////////////
// pendulumSwing() function
////////////////////////////////////////
// back and forth pendulum-like motion
// starting rotation should be in approx. range -65 to +65
// (otherwise swing is inverted)
_root.happyPerson.pendulumSwing = function () {
    with (_root.happyPerson) {
        // 10 and 5 are "magic numbers", found by experimentation
        rotate2 = Math.round((rotate/10)+(5*rotate*(Math.abs(Math.cos(radian)))));
        this._rotation += rotate2;
        // convert to radians for use with Math.cos
        radian=(Math.PI/180)*(this._rotation);
        // true at each extreme of the swing
        // wag the tail and reverse direction
        if (Math.abs(Math.cos(radian))<.01) {
            frame += 5;
            if (frame>20) {frame = 1;}
```

11

```
                this.gotoAndPlay(frame);
                rotate=-rotate; // reverse rotation direction
            }
        }
    }
_root.onEnterFrame = function () {
    _root.happyPerson.pendulumSwing();
};
```

It's now fairly clear, just from looking at the code, what the program does. In addition, I have a function that I can easily reuse as a "black box," without having to understand it or remember how I arrived at it.

For this tiny program, how readable or reusable it is might not matter much. In a complex program, with dozens or hundreds of such bits of code, readability and reusability can matter a great deal.

MANAGING VARIABLES, DATA, AND DATATYPES

WORKING WITH VARIABLES

A variable is a name that you assign to a datum. It's called a *variable* because what it names can vary. For instance, a variable named myScore may equal 10 now. A moment later, after you've scored a point in a game, myScore may equal 11. However, in ActionScript, the variability of variables goes far beyond that: You could assign the same variable first to the number 11, then to the string "foo", and then to an array of strings and numbers.

You can *declare* variables using the var keyword, as follows:

```
var x; // declares the variable x with no initial value
var y; // declares the variable x with no initial value
```

You declare a variable, at most, once. Then you can use it as many times as you want throughout your program. For example:

```
var x = 10; // declares the variable x and sets it equal to 10
trace  (x); // displays "10" in the Output window
y = x + 10;
trace (y); // displays "20" in the Output window
```

In many programming languages, you must declare a variable before you can use it. In ActionScript, if you use a variable that has not been declared, the ActionScript interpreter creates the variable on the fly (*implicitly*).

It's good to get into the habit of declaring variables explicitly, however, and including a comment about how and where you use each variable. This coding practice makes your code more readable, and more importantly, it allows you to explicitly control the scope of variables—that is, where within a program a variable is defined or accessible.

> *This chapter touches on the issue of scope. Chapter 15, "Combining Statements into Functions," deals with scope in more depth. See "Explicit Scoping," page 292, and "Automatic Scoping," page 296.*

In addition, explicit declarations can be more centralized and thus easier to find. Declaring variables implicitly is like leaving tools scattered around a workshop. You can never find the one you need when you're looking for it, and you are liable to trip over one you don't want when you least expect it.

> *For more details on declaring variables, see "Where to Declare Variables," later in this chapter, page 189.*

Assigning Values to Variables

You can assign values to variables by using the assignment operator (=) or the set statement. For example, both of the following statements set the variable firstName equal to "John":

```
firstName = "John";
set (firstName , "John");
```

The value on the right can also be a complex expression:

```
x = y + 10;
set (x, y + 10);
```

In the preceding examples, `set` offers nothing but unnecessary complexity. However, if you want to use an expression to form the variable name, `set` allows you to do that, whereas the assignment operator alone does not. For example, this `set` statement works fine:

```
i = 4;
set("day"+i+"night", "a French movie");
trace (day4night); // "a French movie"
```

But this statement will generate an error:

```
"day"+i+"night" = "a French movie"; // ERROR!!!
```

With the help of the `eval` function, you can use the assignment operator and still use an expression to form the variable name. But using `eval` is at least as complex as using `set`:

```
eval("day"+i+"night") = "a movie";
trace (day4night); // "a movie"
```

For more details on the assignment operator, see Chapter 13, "Using Operators," page 215.

Where to Declare Variables

No simple set of rules about where to declare variables is optimal for all programs and all programmers. However, two issues generally predominate when you're deciding where to declare variables:

- Your ability to find, understand, and edit your variables as you work on the program. This is an issue of program design.

- What you must do to make sure the ActionScript interpreter can find variables when you want it to—and *can't* find them when you don't want it to. This is an issue of variable *scope*.

The first consideration—your ability to find your code—would lead you to put all or most of your code in one frame, such as the first frame of the top layer of the Main Timeline. This type of code centralization is, in fact, a Macromedia-recommended "best practice."

You can access Main Timeline variables from subclips by using `_root` as the path. For instance, suppose this line is on the Main Timeline:

```
myVar =  20;
```

Then you can access `myVar` from a subclip like this:

```
trace(_root.myVar); // displays "20"
```

In a couple of situations, total centralization doesn't work. To the extent that it does work, there remains the question of how to organize your code within that single container to maximize readability and minimize errors.

When *Not* to Centralize Code

Program design works against code centralization in at least two situations:

- **When you use a preloader**—When you use a preloader, the idea is to get the preloader up as quickly as possible and then, in the background, do other things necessary to initialize your program. In this case, the preloader will typically take up one or more frames at the beginning of the movie. Any variables associated with the preloader will be defined in those beginning frames. The main movie will start, and variables associated with the main movie will be defined, on frame 2 or later.

- **When you use components**—A component combines graphics and code. When you use components, you cannot centralize the code that is in the components. In addition, a set of components is likely to be based on a class hierarchy, in which all components in the set belong to a single superclass and various subsets of components belong to appropriate subclasses. In this case, each class and subclass has its own code in its own location. The idea is that the typical programmer will never need to delve into this code.

How to Organize Variables on the Main Timeline

To the extent that you are able to centralize your variables on the Main Timeline, some issues arise. First, keeping a huge list of individual variables in a timeline can be like keeping kitchen utensils, piano-tuning accessories, and car repair tools all in the same drawer.

The confusion can be somewhat reduced by dividing variables into categories using comments. Code for each category can also be stored and edited in an external file and loaded using the `#include` directive.

⇨ *For more details on storing ActionScript in external files, see "Including External ActionScript," page 558 (Chapter 24, "Sharing ActionScript").*

Commenting and external files alone don't address all issues, however. For instance, each movie clip, including both its timeline and its event handlers, defines a single *scope*. The same applies to the Main Timeline.

In some ways, a timeline is like a file folder on a computer, except that a timeline contains program elements such as variables, objects, arrays, and functions. As with a file folder, no two program elements in the same timeline can have the same name. If they do, the more recently defined element will usually overwrite the one that existed previously. (In some cases, the existing name incapacitates the newer name.)

If you just declare variables on the Main Timeline without explicitly assigning a *scope* to each variable, they will all be scoped to the Main Timeline. In that case, each variable must have a unique name, so you may end up with complex variable names to distinguish floor wax (`kitchenWax`) from piano wax (`musicWax`) and car wax (`autoWax`). In addition, you may inadvertently reuse a variable name, thus overwriting the previous value of the variable.

In addition, if you use `loadMovie()` to load a SWF into the Timeline containing your variables, the variables will be lost as the new movie clip's Timeline replaces the existing Timeline. On the other hand, if you use `attachMovie()`to load a clip from the Library, and the instance name you assign the new clip matches the name of an existing variable, object, array, or function on the same Timeline, the existing name will continue to work properly, but you will not be able to control the attached movie clip because its instance name will be "hijacked" by the existing name.

Code in any timeline is vulnerable to such namespace conflicts. If your strategy for finding things in your movie is to dump everything in the Main Timeline, you need to be careful to avoid collisions.

Using Movie Clips to Organize Variables

One strategy for namespace conflict avoidance uses movie clip timelines and event handlers as containers for code. For instance, you can create a clip named `kitchen`, with the following event handler:

```
onClipEvent (load) {
    var wax =  true;  // we have floor wax
}
```

Variables declared in a traditional-style event handler such as this are scoped to the movie clip. You can reference them directly from that clip's Timeline and its other traditional-style event handlers:

```
onClipEvent (enterFrame) {
    wax = false; // out of floor wax
}
```

Declaring variables in a traditional-style `load` clip event allows you to use the same variable name, such as wax, in multiple movie clips. However, if you have code in any other clip that references a variable in the `kitchen` clip, you must include the full path:

```
_root.kitchen.wax = false; // reaching into the kitchen from another clip
```

There is a downside to storing code in movie clips: If you have many clips, and you end up with variables scattered in all those clips, editing will be difficult.

One solution is to use a *container* movie clip (also called a *code* clip) as a central code container for several other movie clips, or even for all the movie clips in your program. Having all your variables in a single `load` event handler isn't so different from having them all in a single frame on the Main Timeline. However, if you remember never to load or attach movies in your code clip, you'll avoid one major cause of namespace conflicts. In addition, parceling variables out among a small number of container clips can be effective.

Another good idea is to create one or more movie clips solely as targets for loading and attaching movies. These clips are empty, so nothing will be displaced by the newly attached or loaded movie.

To make editing easier, you can put all the code that creates variables in one place but specify paths to movie clips that will have the variables as properties. From the point of view of the ActionScript interpreter, the variables are part of the movie clips that they are assigned to. For instance, assume you have movie clips named `kitchen`, `shop`, and `musicRoom` on the Main Timeline:

```
_root.kitchen.wax = true;
_root.shop.wax = false;
_root.musicRoom.wax = true;
```

12

The ActionScript interpreter will look for these wax variables in the kitchen, shop, and musicRoom clips, respectively. This approach helps avoid namespace conflicts, while still allowing you to centralize your code.

However, if you load an external SWF into the root, all the movie clips in the root, and all the variables associated with them, will be wiped out.

Using Objects to Organize Variables

Wherever you put your code, you can also store variables in objects as properties. In this case, only your top-level object names are vulnerable to namespace conflicts. For example, you might have three top-level objects in the Main Timeline: kitchen, shop, and musicRoom. You need to be careful not to load or attach a movie clip with one of those three names into the Main Timeline.

Other property names, such as wax, are "protected" inside their respective objects, just as they were inside movie clips. And your references to them could look identical:

```
_root.kitchen.wax = true;
_root.shop.wax = false;
_root.musicRoom.wax = true;
```

However, whereas an empty movie clip takes up 800 bytes in memory, a new object takes up only 340 bytes.

You can protect even your top-level objects from namespace conflicts that involve movie clip instances. In Flash 5, programmers sometimes did this by making top-level objects properties of the global Object object like this:

```
Object.kitchen = new Object();
```

Object.kitchen is safe from accidental interference from movie clips because you can't load or attach movie clips into Object (or any object other than a movie clip). One disadvantage of this approach is that you can never refer to any of your variables simply by the variable name. You always have to use names like Object.kitchen.wax.

Flash MX provides a better means of accomplishing the same goal: the _global identifier, which is a reference to the global object that holds the built-in ActionScript objects and classes, including Object itself, as well as others such as Array, Math, and String.

You can store variables as global properties, like this:

```
_global.myGlobalVar = 10;
```

Or you can create a few high-level global objects, such as _global.kitchen, _global.shop, _global.musicRoom, and put all your other variables, functions, arrays, and objects within those objects. For instance:

```
_global.kitchen = new Object();
_global.kitchen.wax = true;
```

This provides a safe and comprehensible storage system for all the elements of your program.

Global variables and objects are available throughout your program. The code creating these elements can be centralized on the Main Timeline or anywhere you want. Global variables and objects cannot be destroyed by loading an external SWF, no matter which timeline you load it into.

In addition, you can read global variables and objects just by using their names; you don't have to include the _global identifier. For instance:

```
trace(myGlobalVar); // displays "10"
```

When you want to change a variable or property, you have to use the _global identifier. For instance:

```
_global.myGlobalVar = 11;
_global.kitchen.wax = true;
```

Using objects entails a small performance penalty. One workaround, if you'll be referring to a particular property repeatedly at some point in your program, is to create a temporary variable pointing to the property. For instance:

```
kWax = Object.kitchen.wax;
```

Using kWax instead of making the interpreter find the object property over and over again can improve performance substantially. In addition, the shorter variable name will save you some typing.

Movie clips, objects, and the _global object address design and scope issues simultaneously in a way that comments and external files alone cannot. For instance, when you categorize variables with comments, the interpreter doesn't understand those categories. Similarly, if you load multiple files into a single timeline using the #include directive, the interpreter sees the variables in one big list. Movie clips, objects, and _global provide a structure that both you and the interpreter understand.

Many programmers tend to use either movie clips or objects or both to organize variables in any program with a lot of code. However, to encourage code centralization, it is a Macromedia-recommended "best practice" to minimize the amount of code attached to movie clips and buttons. Using custom objects opens up a new world of possibilities, with issues and complications of its own.

For more details on custom objects, see Chapter 21, "Packaging Data and Functions Using Custom Objects," page 489.

Another type of object that you can use to store variables is the array. Storing variables in arrays as elements also opens up new possibilities for manipulating and retrieving the variables.

For more information on the Object object and arrays, see Chapter 19, "Using the Built-in Core Objects," page 393.

Rules for Naming Variables (and Other Things)

A variable name is an *identifier*, a series of alphanumeric characters used to represent a datum or a function.

All variable names are identifiers. However, not all identifiers are variable names. For example, function names are identifiers, but they are not variables because they hold a specific, unchanging datum (the function), not an arbitrary datum.

You must follow three absolute rules for forming identifiers. Violating these rules may generate errors or cause serious problems:

- Use only letters, numbers, underscores, and dollar signs. Do not use spaces; punctuation marks such as periods, commas, hyphens, parentheses, brackets, exclamation points, or question marks; or symbols such as the following:

  ~ @ # % ^ & * = + / \ < >

- Use a letter, underscore, or dollar sign for the initial character. Do not use a number.

- Do not use reserved words.

ActionScript's reserved words are as follows:

add (*)	else	instanceof	super	with
and (*)	eq (*)	le (*)	switch	
break	for	lt (*)	tellTarget (*)	
case	function	ne (*)	this	
continue	ge (*)	new	typeof	
default	gt (*)	not (*)	var	
delete	if	or (*)	void	
do	in	return	while	

(*) Flash 4 reserved words deprecated since Flash 5

The following list shows words that may become reserved words in the future; you can use a word from this list now, but your program may "break" if a future version of ActionScript claims the word as its own.

abstract	enum	int	static
boolean	export	interface	synchronized
byte	extends	long	throw
catch	final	native	throws
char	finally	package	transient
class	float	private	try
const	goto	protected	volatile
debugger	implements	public	
double	import	short	

Other things being equal, you should follow these rules for movie clip instance names, too. Even though they are *not* officially identifiers, movie clip instance names often play the role of identifiers when you use them in ActionScript, and you may get errors if you don't follow the rules.

⇨ *Having trouble with code that involves a movie clip name? See the "Troubleshooting" section later in this chapter, page 212.*

Many programmers also follow identifier-naming rules for other names such as frame labels and layer names.

In general, ActionScript identifiers are not case sensitive. Thus, the following three statements do *not* define different variables:

```
myVar = 6;
myvar = 10;
Myvar = "Hello";
```

Lack of case sensitivity, required for compatibility with earlier versions of Flash, is a departure from the ECMA-262 standard and a potential stumbling point for JavaScript programmers, who are used to full case sensitivity. In JavaScript, the preceding three statements *do* create three separate variables.

In ActionScript, only the reserved words shown previously in this section are case sensitive.

That being said, there is at least one case-related guideline that most programmers follow: Identifiers traditionally begin with lowercase letters. The one exception is constructor function names.

➪ *See Chapters 15 (page 267), 19 (page 393), 20 (page 443), and 21 (page 489) for more information on constructor functions.*

Following some consistent capitalization rules is also a good idea, to make your programs more readable.

CATEGORIZING DATA USING DATATYPES

The most basic piece of information to know about a variable is its datatype. For instance, many problems result from using a text string where ActionScript requires a number, or vice versa.

➪ *Mysterious errors often result from using the wrong datatype. See the "Troubleshooting" section later in this chapter, page 212.*

Keeping track of datatypes can be tricky because the ActionScript interpreter sometimes does automatic datatype conversions to try to make things work. You need to understand the logic of those conversions to predict which datatypes you will end up with.

The Nine ActionScript Datatypes

ActionScript has nine basic types of data. The five *primitive* datatypes, of which the most common are number and string, contain just a single primitive datum. For instance, the _currentFrame property of a movie clip contains just a single number indicating the current position of the playhead on the Timeline. Similarly, the _name property of a movie clip contains a single text string.

The four *composite* datatypes (object, array, movieclip, and function) contain multiple pieces of data. For instance, a movie clip contains a _currentFrame property, a _name property, a _visible property, and many others.

You can determine the datatype of any variable by using the typeof operator, as follows:

```
typeof expression
```

Consider this example:

```
var x = 2;
trace (typeof x); // displays "number" in the Output window
```

Manipulating Data with Operators

The most common and basic way of manipulating data is by using *operators*. Operators are symbols and keywords that accept one or more existing values as *operands* and return a new value. Many operators, including plus (+), minus (-), and divide (/), are familiar from basic arithmetic. Operators are covered in detail in Chapter 13, "Using Operators."

Table 12.1 shows the ActionScript datatypes, with their `typeof` return values, examples of variable assignments, and legal values for the datatypes.

Table 12.1   ActionScript Datatypes

Datatype	typeof Value	Assignment Example	Legal Values
number	"number"	var x = 6;	Any number
string	"string"	var x = "foo";	Any character string
Boolean	"boolean"	var x = true;	true, false
object	"object"	var x = myObj;	Any object
array	"object"	var x = myArray;	Any array
null	"null"	var x = null;	null
movieclip	"movieclip"	var x = myClip;	Any movie clip instance
function	"function"	var x = myFunc;	Any function
undefined	"undefined"	var x;	undefined

Note that the variable assignment examples in Table 12.1 assume that the object, array, movie clip, and function already exist.

⇨ *Chapter 15 describes creating objects (including arrays, movie clips, and functions). See "Functions as Classes: Constructor Functions," page 279.*

You create movie clips either by dragging and dropping symbols from the Library onto the Stage or by using the `attachMovie()`, `duplicateMovieClip()`, or `loadMovie()` functions.

The Power of Numbers

Most aspects of a scripted movie are controlled through numbers. Animation with ActionScript depends primarily on effective manipulation of numbers. For example, out of 19 properties of the MovieClip object, 13 are numerical. Numbers control movie clip transparency, position, rotation, scale, size, and position on the Timeline.

The first step in using numbers effectively is to understand the kinds of values that the number datatype can represent. The two most important kinds of numbers are *integers*, which have no fractional component (such as –10, 0, 2, 856), and *floating-point numbers* (*floats*) which do have a fractional component (such as –10.2, .01, 635.8916).

Special values for the number datatype include

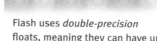

Flash uses *double-precision* floats, meaning they can have up to 15 *significant digits*. Thus, in scientific notation, Flash will never use more than 15 digits in the base.

- NaN ("not a number") identifies non-numeric data in a datum of the number datatype.

- Number.MAX_VALUE is the largest number that ActionScript can represent (1.79769313486231e+308).

Scientific Notation

To represent very large or very small floats (whether positive or negative), ActionScript uses scientific notation, consisting of a base and an exponent, separated by the letter e (*exponent*). To get the base, put the decimal point after the first digit and drop any trailing or leading zeros. For instance, both 123,000,000,000,000 and .000000000000123 give a base of 1.23. The exponent indicates how many places the decimal point was moved. Thus, you arrive at 1.23e+15 and 1.23e-15 in the preceding examples. You can use scientific notation in your programs, too, using any float as a base. For instance, you can write 126e+3 instead of 126,000.

- Number.MIN_VALUE is the smallest positive number that ActionScript can represent (5e-324).

- Infinity (positive infinity) is an indeterminate number larger than Number.MAX_VALUE.

- -Infinity (negative infinity) is an indeterminate number more negative than -Number.MAX.VALUE.

- Constants, such as pi and the square root of 2, may be stored as properties of the Math object.

⇨ *For more information on the Math object as well as more details on manipulating numbers with built-in functions, see "The Math Object," page 426 (Chapter 19, "Using the Built-in Core Objects").*

You can manipulate numbers with operators or built-in functions.

⇨ *For more details on manipulating numbers with operators, see "Understanding Arithmetic Operators," page 219 (Chapter 13, "Using Operators").*

Using Strings

If a user inputs data into your program, you end up with a string variable. If you retrieve the name of a movie clip, it is a string. In fact, of the six non-numeric properties of a movie clip, four are strings. Your ability to manipulate strings is key to successful ActionScript programming.

12

The `string` datatype is simple to define: A string is any sequence of alphanumeric characters enclosed in quotation marks.

Flash MX supports the double-byte character set (DBCS), or Unicode character set, for text and user interface strings. Unicode is required for a variety of languages such as Chinese and Hindi. Unicode includes, as a subset, character sets that can be coded in one byte, such as Latin-1 (ISO-8859). Latin-1 will probably accommodate your needs if you're working on a standard computer in a widely used Western European language (such as English, French, German, Italian, Portuguese, Spanish, and so on). Flash MX also continues to support (as did Flash 5) Shift-JIS for Japanese characters. Shift-JIS is a workaround that offers the equivalent of the double-byte (16-bit) characters required for Japanese.

> Alphanumeric: "consisting of alphabetic and numerical symbols and of punctuation marks, mathematical symbols, and other conventional symbols used in computer work." *American Heritage Dictionary*.

> (See http://www.unicode.org for more details on Unicode, Latin-1, and Shift-JIS.)

Let me add a couple of points relating to Unicode characters:

- To display a font, such as the character sets for Chinese, Hebrew, Hindi, Japanese, or Korean, either you must have the font installed on your computer, or the font must be embedded in the Flash movie.

- To load Unicode characters from a file, including an XML file, the file must be saved in Unicode format. Most full-featured word processors have a "save as Unicode text" option. For instance, in the following example, if you want to load Unicode characters from the test.xml file, be sure to save it as Unicode text:

```
var myXML = new XML();
myXML.load("test.xml");
```

- You can use the undocumented `System.useCodepage` property to enable the display of Unicode characters not loaded from a file. The following example displays a string of double-byte characters:

```
System.useCodepage = true;
aeioun="%E1+%E9+%ED+%F3+%FA+%F1";
trace(unescape(aeioun)) ;
```

You may be able to use a multi-character-set Flash generator, such as the swfx.org generator, to build Flash movies dynamically containing any of the million possible Unicode characters, assuming you have a font with those characters that you can embed in a SWF.

To encode Unicode characters in ActionScript, you can use long or short Unicode escape sequences. The long form is a backslash and a small u followed by four hexadecimal digits. The short form is a backslash and a small x followed by two hexadecimal digits. The following are some examples:

```
trace ("\u00A3"); // the English pound sign: £
trace ("\xA3"); // the English pound sign: £
trace ("\u00A9"); // the copyright sign: ©
trace ("\xA9"); // the copyright sign: ©
```

Strings can be joined together, or *concatenated*, using the plus operator (+), as follows:

```
trace ("This "+"works!"); // displays "This works!"
```

The assignment operator (=), the equality operator (==), the inequality operator (!=), the strict equality operator (===), and the strict inequality operator (!==) also work with strings. For example:

```
x = "foo";
y = "foo";
trace (x == y); // "true"
trace (x === y); // "true"
trace (x != y); // "false"
trace (x !== y); // "false"
```

You manipulate strings with both operators and built-in functions.

> For more details on manipulating strings with operators, see Chapter 13, "Using Operators," page 215.

> For more information on manipulating strings with built-in functions, see "The String Class," page 410 (Chapter 19, "Using the Built-in Core Objects").

Control and Decision-Making Using Booleans

The Boolean datatype is extremely simple, permitting only two values: true and false. It is commonly used for decision-making, to test whether a particular condition is true or false to decide what needs to happen next. For instance, this statement tests whether the movie clip myClip is visible:

```
if (myClip._visible == true)
```

If the clip is visible, the ActionScript interpreter resolves the expression (myClip._visible == true) to the Boolean value true. If not, the expression resolves to false.

Similarly, the following statement resolves to true if myClip is *not* visible:

```
if (myClip._visible == false)
```

Notice that Booleans are used in two different ways in these statements: as the value of the _visible property of a movie clip and as the interpreter's answer to your questions.

In the following statement, you use a Boolean as a value of a property, but not as an answer to a question:

```
myClip._visible = true; // make the clip visible
```

A Boolean does not appear in the following two-line program, but the ActionScript interpreter will respond to the second line by displaying a Boolean true:

```
x = "Barbara";
trace ( x == "Barbara" ); // "true"
```

You usually manipulate Booleans with operators, though built-in functions may be applied to Booleans, as well.

12

⇨ *For more details on manipulating Booleans with logical operators, see "Using Logical (Boolean) Operators," page 236 (Chapter 13, "Using Operators").*

⇨ *For more details on manipulating Booleans with built-in functions, see "The Boolean Class," page 409 (Chapter 19, "Using the Built-in Core Objects").*

Modeling Problem Domains Using Objects

`object` is the most flexible ActionScript datatype, and the most fundamental composite datatype. The simplicity and flexibility of the `object` datatype make it suitable for modeling almost anything you might want to include in your program, no matter what the real-world problem domain may be.

The structure of the `object` datatype is extremely simple: an unordered collection of properties, each of which is a *name:value* pair. An object property can contain any type of data that ActionScript supports.

Many of the operators commonly used with primitive datatypes don't apply to objects or other composite datatypes. For instance, you can't add, subtract, or multiply objects.

On the other hand, one operator applies only to objects (including movie clips): You use the dot (`.`) operator—officially known as the "object property access" operator—to...how did you guess...access object properties. You can also use square brackets—officially the "array-element/object-property" operator—to access object properties. The general format is as follows:

`object[property name string]`

Note that the property name must be a string, meaning it must be enclosed in quotation marks. So, `root.myObj["name"]` is the same as `_root.myObj.name`. Remember that objects are properties of the timelines they are on, so a third way of writing the same thing is `_root["myObj"]["name"]`.

You create a datum of the `object` type by using the `new` operator. Other operators that you can use in connection with objects include `delete`, `typeof`, equality (`==`), strict equality (`===`), inequality (`!=`), strict inequality (`!==`), and assignment (`=`).

⇨ *For more information on operators that can be used with objects, see Chapter 13, "Using Operators," page 215.*

Comparing Objects

Two objects will *not* compare as equal just because they have the same properties with the same values. Two object names compare as equal only if they refer to *the same object*.

⇨ *For more details on comparing objects, see "Automatic Datatype Conversions for Comparisons," page 234 (Chapter 13, "Using Operators").*

⇨ *For a discussion of some of the advantages of using objects in your programs, see Chapter 11, "Getting Started with ActionScript," page 169.*

⇨ *Chapter 19, "Using the Built-in Core Objects," page 393, goes into more detail on the built-in Object object, which is the foundation for all other objects in ActionScript.*

⇨ *To learn how to create custom objects, see "Functions as Classes: Constructor Functions," page 279, (Chapter 15, "Combining Statements into Functions").*

Array

An *array* is an ordered list. For instance, you could use an array to store the names of days of the week or months of the year. Items in the list (*elements*) are accessed via numerical indices. The initial index is always 0. Here, you assign a value, `"Monday"`, to the first element of an array, `myArray`, and display that value in the Output window:

```
myArray[0] = "Monday";
trace (myArray[0]); // "Monday"
```

The array is actually a special case of the `object` datatype. As with objects, you create arrays using the new operator. You can use all the same operators with arrays as with objects, with the exception of the dot (`.`) operator, which is reserved for objects (including movie clips).

As with the `object` datatype, having the same contents does not make two arrays equal in the eyes of the ActionScript interpreter. If `arr1` and `arr2` refer to arrays, the following expression is true only if `arr1` and `arr2` are two names for *the same array*:

```
(arr1 == arr2)
```

⇨ *For more information on comparing arrays, see "Automatic Datatype Conversions for Comparisons," page 234 (Chapter 13, "Using Operators").*

Like objects, arrays can hold any kind of ActionScript data.

⇨ *The numerical indices used to access arrays offer some possibilities that do not exist with objects. These possibilities are discussed in "The Array Class," page 395 (Chapter 19, "Using the Built-in Core Objects").*

12

null

The `null` datatype permits just one value: the primitive value `null`. You assign this value to a data container (such as a variable, object property, or array element) to indicate that the container is empty. You can also assign the `null` value to an identifier used as a function name, thus disabling the function.

The `null` datatype is closely related to the `undefined` datatype, as shown by the fact that the ActionScript interpreter sees them as equal:

```
trace (null == undefined); // "true"
```

There is nothing else (except null itself) that the interpreter considers equal to null. For example:

trace (null == ""); // "false" – the empty string is not equal to null

⇨ *For more information on the distinction between null and undefined, see "Using null and undefined," later in this chapter, page 211.*

movieclip

The movieclip datatype is familiar to every Flash programmer. Its distinguishing feature is graphical content, which can be manipulated via the movie clip's properties. Thus, for instance, a movieclip is the only built-in object in Flash that has color, position, rotation, scale, size, or transparency. Adding this datatype is one of the ways in which the ECMA-262 standard was adapted to Flash. The movieclip datatype doesn't exist in ECMA-262 or JavaScript.

You can use six operators with movie clips: the dot (.) and square bracket operators for accessing properties, and the equality (==), inequality (!=), strict equality (===), and strict inequality (!==) operators for comparisons. As with objects and arrays, if (myClip1 == myClip2), then myClip1 and myClip2 are two names for the same movie clip.

⇨ *For more details on comparing movie clips, see "Automatic Datatype Conversions for Comparisons," page 234 (Chapter 13, "Using Operators").*

You cannot create movie clips using the new operator, nor can you destroy them using the delete operator.

⇨ *You create movie clips through Flash's graphical user interface, using the techniques described in Chapter 6, "Symbols, Instances, and Library Assets," page 89, or using the techniques described in Chapter 17, "Unlocking the Power of Movie Clips," page 331.*

⇨ *You can create new instances of existing movie clips and remove those new instances, as well as load and unload external SWFs, using the techniques described in Chapter 17, "Unlocking the Power of Movie Clips," page 331.*

Function

A *function* is a named block of ActionScript code that performs a particular task. A number of *global* functions, such as trace(), are not properties of any object. Functions that are properties of objects are called *methods*. For instance, gotoAndStop() is a MovieClip method that causes a movie clip to go to a particular frame in its Timeline and stop.

Often, a function takes one or more *arguments* as input and returns a datum. For example, isNaN() is a global function that takes any expression as an argument and returns a Boolean true if the expression, when treated as a number, resolves to the special value NaN (not a number), or false if the expression does not resolve to NaN.

Although it's not usually as evident as it is with arrays, the `function` datatype is actually a special case of the `object` datatype, too. For example, although programmers often don't take advantage of this capability, functions can have properties, accessible via the same dot and square bracket operators used for the `object` datatype.

The fact that a function is a special type of object turns out to play a very important role in object-oriented programming (OOP). Is it a problem that functions are objects and can also be properties of objects? Not at all. Objects can have other objects, including functions, as properties.

Despite these object-like characteristics, you can't create or remove functions programmatically: The `new` and `delete` operators do not work with functions. However, you can disable a function by assigning its name to `null`:

```
function foo() { // now you see it
}
foo = null; // now you don't
```

> For more information on functions, including constructor functions used to create objects, see Chapter 15, "Combining Statements into Functions," page 267.

undefined

Like the `null` datatype, the `undefined` datatype indicates an absence of data. However, whereas you assign the `null` value yourself, the intention is that only the ActionScript interpreter will assign the `undefined` value as a default when you don't assign a value to a variable or other data container. For example:

```
var middleName;
trace (typeof middleName);  // "undefined"
```

The ActionScript interpreter also returns `undefined` if you reference a variable or other data container that does not exist. (JavaScript generates an error under these conditions.)

ActionScript departs from the ECMA-262 standard, and differs from JavaScript, in its treatment of `undefined` in string contexts. When the ActionScript interpreter encounters `undefined` where it expects a string, it usually converts `undefined` to the empty string (`""`). When you attempt to display a datum that is equal to the empty string, nothing is displayed.

In Flash MX, there is an exception to this rule, when the undefined element occurs alone. For instance, in the following example, continued from the previous example, Flash MX displays `"undefined"`, while Flash 5 displays nothing (the empty string) :

```
trace (middleName); // Flash MX displays "undefined"
```

The JavaScript interpreter, in accordance with the ECMA-262 standard, also displays `"undefined"` in a similar case.

However, in the following example, both Flash MX and Flash 5 display the empty string, not `"undefined"`, when `middleName` is encountered:

```
trace ("my "+middleName);  // Flash displays just "my"
```

12

ActionScript departs from the standard in this instance to maintain backward compatibility with Flash 4 ActionScript programs. Flash 4 did not have an `undefined` datatype. Therefore, programmers often used the empty string to test for an absence of data:

```
if (middleName eq "")
```

This test would cease to work if `undefined` translated to anything but the empty string.

Because of this peculiarity, it's usually best to use the `typeof` operator to determine whether a datum is of the `undefined` datatype:

```
if (typeof middleName == "undefined"); //  true
```

⇨ See "Using null and undefined" later in this chapter for more details on the distinction between null and undefined, page 211.

Implicit and Explicit Data Conversion

In *strongly typed* languages, such as Java, when you create or *declare* a variable, you must declare its datatype, such as `integer` or `string`, as well. Unless you explicitly change the datatype (*typecasting*), Java enforces your original declaration, generating an error, for example, if you try to assign a string to an integer variable.

In contrast, ActionScript (like JavaScript) is *weakly typed*. The ActionScript interpreter can assign a new datatype to a datum at any point in the program based on its own assessment of what the situation requires, without the programmer doing any explicit typecasting. This is called *implicit* datatype conversion.

Not *all* datatype conversion in ActionScript is implicit: You can perform the equivalent of typecasting by explicitly assigning a datatype to a datum. For instance, you can convert a string to a number by using the `Number()` function. Similarly, you can convert a number to a string by using the `String()` function or the `toString()` function.

⇨ For more details on converting a number to a string, see "Converting to a String," later in this chapter, page 208.

Such *explicit* datatype conversion isn't likely to cause too much trouble because you are conscious of what you're doing. Implicit datatype conversion, on the other hand, can happen without your being aware of it and therefore may produce results you aren't expecting.

By knowing the rules of implicit datatype conversion, however, you can eliminate surprises and even use the rules to your advantage. You've already encountered one of these rules—namely, that `undefined` is converted to the empty string when it is used as a string.

In general, whenever the ActionScript interpreter expects one datatype, and you use a different datatype, the interpreter creates a new value of the expected type. For instance, suppose your program contains the following statements:

```
x = 63 - "my dentist";
trace(x); // ??
```

What will the interpreter display? What is x to the interpreter?

If you ask the ActionScript interpreter to subtract a string from a number, it attempts to comply by implicitly converting the string to a number and then subtracting. In this case, the string `"my dentist"` cannot be successfully converted to a number. It was for cases such as this that the NaN value was created. The ActionScript interpreter converts `"my dentist"` to NaN, which is officially of the number datatype. Any mathematical operation involving NaN also results in NaN. Therefore, x is equal to NaN.

In this case, implicit datatype conversion didn't do much good, except that it allowed the program to continue functioning (the alternative to implicit conversion being an error, as in Java). Then again, you gave the ActionScript interpreter an impossible job. On the other hand, if you give it a string like `"3"` that *can* be converted to a number, the ActionScript interpreter does something quite helpful:

```
x = 63 - "3";
trace(x); // 60
```

The result of an implicit datatype conversion is always a primitive datatype: string, number, or Boolean. Table 12.2 shows the rules for converting to a number.

Table 12.2   Implicit Conversion to a Number

Supplied Value	Value After Conversion
undefined	0
null	0
Boolean false	0
Boolean true	1
A numeric string that can be converted to a base-10 number. (Can contain numerals, a decimal point, a plus sign, a minus sign, and whitespace.)	The equivalent numeric value. (Exception: The + operator concatenates all strings, including numeric strings. See Chapter 13.)
A non-numeric string. (Includes the empty string and any string containing an alphabetic character, including strings starting with "x", "0x", and "FF".)	NaN
"Infinity"	Infinity
"-Infinity"	-Infinity
"NaN"	NaN
Any array	NaN
Any object	NaN
Any movie clip	NaN

Table 12.3 shows the rules for converting to a string.

12

Table 12.3 Implicit Conversion to a String

Supplied Value	Value After Conversion
`undefined`	`""` (the empty string)
`null`	`"null"`
Boolean `false`	`"false"`
Boolean `true`	`"true"`
`NaN`	`"NaN"`
`0`	`"0"`
`Infinity`	`"Infinity"`
`-Infinity`	`"-Infinity"`
Any other numeric value	The string equivalent of the numeric value.
Any array	A comma-separated list of element values.
Any object	The return value of the object's `toString()` method. The default is `"[object Object]"`. The built-in `Date` object returns a date.
Any movie clip	The absolute path to the movie clip instance; for example, `"_level0.myClip"`.

Table 12.4 shows the rules for converting to a Boolean.

Table 12.4 Implicit Conversion to a Boolean

Supplied Value	Value After Conversion
`undefined`	`false`
`null`	`false`
`NaN`	`false`
`0`	`false`
`Infinity`	`true`
`-Infinity`	`true`
Any other numeric value	`true`
Empty string	`false`
Any string that can be converted to a valid nonzero number	`true`
Any string that *cannot* be converted to a valid nonzero number. (Departs from ECMA-262 standard to maintain compatibility with Flash 4.)	`false`
Any array	`true`
Any object	`true`
Any movie clip	`true`

Using Explicit Datatype Conversion

Most of the time, implicit datatype conversion is all you need. Flash automatically converts your data to whatever datatype you need at the moment. Occasionally, however, the easiest way to make sure that you get what you want is to explicitly tell Flash what kind of datum it's dealing with.

For instance, any information that a user types into an input text box is initially a string. If you want to arithmetically add the numbers represented by two such strings, you have to convert the strings to numbers first. Otherwise, if you use the + operator, Flash will assume that you want to concatenate the two strings.

You can explicitly convert any datum to a number, string, or Boolean. The conversion will follow the rules shown in Tables 12.2, 12.3, and 12.4.

Converting to a Number

You convert to a number by using the global `Number()` function. For instance, if a user types his or her age into an input text box, it is initially a string. You convert it to a number like this:

```
user1Age = Number(user1Age);
```

If the user types in "23", the interpreter sees the preceding line as follows:

```
user1Age = Number("23");
```

The interpreter sets the `user1Age` variable to the number 23.

The `Number()` function assumes decimal numbers with optional trailing exponents:

```
Number("2.637e-4"); // 0.0002637
```

You can use hexadecimal numbers if you prefix the string with 0x, as in this instance:

```
greenColor = "0x00FF00"; // hex representation of green color, a string
hexGreen = Number(greenColor); // 65280, the decimal form of 0x00FF00
```

The `parseInt()` and `parsefloat()` functions also convert strings to numbers, but the string must have the following format: The first nonblank character must be the first character of the number you want, and the first character after the number you want must be non-numeric. The following examples use `parseInt()`:

```
1: parseInt("12years") ; // extracts 12
2: parseInt("   12years") ; // extracts 12
3: parseInt("12 years") ; // extracts 12
4: parseInt("12 1 year olds") ; // extracts 12
5: parseInt("twelve 1 year olds") ; // NaN
```

Looking at line 1, the first character after the number is y, which is non-numeric. Line 2 shows that leading blank characters don't matter. Lines 3 and 4 demonstrate that a following blank character counts as non-numeric. In line 5, the first non-blank character is not the first character of a number; therefore, NaN is extracted from this string.

12

The parseInt() function can also take a second argument that specifies the *radix* (base) of the result. For instance:

```
parseInt("10",16); // extracts 16 - hex 10 (base 16)
parseInt("10",8); // extracts 8 - octal 10 (base 8)
parseInt("10",10); // extracts 10 - decimal 10 (base 10)
```

---

parseInt() **and Hexadecimal Numbers**

parseInt() *always* assumes that numbers starting with 0x are hexadecimal:

```
parseInt("0x10"); // 16
```

Trying to override such an implied hexadecimal yields results that aren't usually useful:

```
parseInt("0x10", 10); // 0
parseInt("0x10", 8); // 0
```

Numbers starting with 0 (but not with 0x) are octal by default:

```
parseInt("010"); // 8
```

Unlike with the hexadecimal 0x, you *can* override the implied octal radix and get useful results:

```
parseInt("010", 10); // parsed as decimal, equals 10
```

Don't forget the quotation marks around the string. Sometimes, you can get by with leaving them off, but not always:

```
trace(parseInt(010)); // 0 - not what you want !!!
```

The following examples show how to use parseFloat():

```
trace(parseFloat("12.5years")) ; // extracts 12.5
trace(parseFloat("   12.5years")) ; // extracts 12.5
trace(parseFloat("12.5 years")) ; // extracts 12.5
trace(parseFloat("12.5 1 year olds")) ; // extracts 12.5
trace(parseInt("twelve and a half 1 year olds")) ; // NaN
```

The last example is NaN because the first nonblank character is not numeric.

Converting to a String

You can convert to a string by using either the toString() method or the String() global function. By default, the two accomplish the same thing, though they use different syntax:

```
var x = 6;
x.toString(); // "6"
String(x); // "6"
```

Although methods belong only to objects, implicit datatype conversion allows the toString() method to work with any datatype, according to the rules in Table 12.3:

```
var x = 6;
trace(x.toString()); // "6"
```

```
y = true;
trace(y.toString()); // "true"
z = null;
trace(z.toString()); // "undefined"
trace(Math.toString()); // "[object Object]" - Math is a built-in object
```

The `toString()` method has an optional argument that sets the radix (base) of the result, if the supplied datum is a number. For instance, if the number and the radix are the same (such as the number 6 in base 6, the number 7 in base 7), the result is `"10"`:

```
trace(x.toString(x)); // "10" - true if x is any number
```

The following is another example. Note the parentheses required around the number 65280:

```
(65280).toString(16); // "ff00"
```

Using Implicit Datatype Conversion

You can use a couple of tricks to take advantage of implicit datatype conversion. Their advantage is their very concise syntax. On the downside, when you're reading the code, what they do may not be intuitively obvious.

For instance, the "add and reassign" operator (+=) can accomplish the same thing as the `toString()` method or the `String()` global function. It's more obvious with `toString()` or `String()` that you are converting to a string, but the "add and reassign" operator is more concise.

Any datum will be converted to a string, following the rules of Table 12.3, if you add the empty string to it. For example, the second line here accomplishes the same thing as `String()` or `toString()`:

```
x = 77; // x is a number
x += ""; // x is now a string: "77"
```

"Add and Reassign" and "Subtract and Reassign"

The "add and reassign" operator (+=) adds a second operand to a first operand and assigns the result to the first operand. For example, `x += ""` is the equivalent of `x = x + ""`.

The "subtract and reassign" operator (-=) subtracts a second operand from a first operand and assigns the result to the first operand. For example, `x -= 0` is the equivalent of `x = x - 0`.

Similarly, subtracting 0 from any datum converts it into a number, according to the rules of Table 12.2. For instance:

```
x = new Object(); // x is an object
x -= 0; // x is a number: NaN
```

Numbers and Strings Versus Numeric and String Literals

A *variable* is an abstract representation of a datum. It in no way resembles the datum itself. Thus, the variable x can represent any datum under the sun. In contrast, a *literal* represents a datum literally, not abstractly. A literal depicts a datum with complete accuracy, and the ActionScript interpreter actually creates the datum using only the literal as a blueprint.

In the following example, the variable x is first set to a numeric literal and then to a string literal. The variable x is the same, but the value it contains changes, and therefore its datatype changes, too.

```
var x;
trace (typeof x);        // "undefined"
// 6 is a numeric literal
x = 6;                   // x now refers to a numeric literal
trace (typeof x);        // "number"
// "Howdy Pete!" is a string literal
x = "Howdy Pete!"        // x now refers to a string literal
trace (typeof x);        // "string"
```

A variable is a number if its assigned value is a numeric literal. It is also a number if its assigned value is a complex expression that can be reduced to a numeric literal. For instance:

```
x = 3 + 3; // can be reduced to a numeric literal: 6
```

As you have seen, strings can also be formed using complex expressions:

```
x = "Howdy" + "Pete!"; // resolves to a string literal: "Howdy Pete!"
```

Literals cannot span multiple lines of code. For instance, the following will not work:

```
test = "Howdy
Pete!";
```

You can use the plus (+) operator to get around this limitation:

```
test = "Howdy" +
    "Pete!";
```

A string or numeric literal may be used for a temporary purpose, without being stored. If you want to reuse the datum represented by a string or numeric literal, you must store it in a variable, array element, or object property. Unless it is stored, a literal does not persist and is of no further use.

Object and Array Literals

An *array* is a named, ordered list whose elements are accessed via numeric indices. An *array literal* is a comma-separated list of the elements, enclosed in square brackets, without the array name or the indices. For instance, here are the first three values of an array of strings representing the months:

```
months[0] = "January";
months[1] = "February";
months[2] = "March";
```

The corresponding array literal looks like this:

```
["January" , "February" , "March"]
```

You can create an array by assigning the anonymous, nameless array literal to a variable, which thereby becomes an array name:

```
months = ["January" , "February" , "March"];
```

> The object literal format provides a good visual representation of an object, and the *property:value* syntax is a concise way of referring to objects and properties.

Similarly, an *object* is a named, unordered list whose properties are accessed by name. For instance, here are the properties of a `computer` object:

```
computer.monitor = "SVGA";
computer.processor = "Pentium 4";
computer.price = 1700;
```

The corresponding object literal is a comma-separated list of properties enclosed in curly braces, without the object name. Each property consists of a name and a value, separated by a colon. For instance:

```
{ monitor : "SVGA" , processor : "Pentium 4" , price : 1700 }
```

You can assign the object literal to a variable, which thereby becomes an object name:

```
computer = { monitor : "SVGA" , processor : "Pentium 4" , price : 1700 };
```

As with string and numeric literals, array and object literals are lost if they are not assigned to a variable or stored in an array element or an object property.

Using `null` and `undefined`

Both `null` and `undefined` are extremely useful to the programmer, but their uses are different, even though both indicate an absence of data. The `null` value is used in messages from the programmer to the interpreter. The `undefined` value should be reserved for messages from the interpreter to the programmer.

The ActionScript interpreter assigns the `undefined` datatype as a default when you don't assign any content to a declared variable. A declaration of this sort is shown in line 1 in the following example. The interpreter also returns `undefined` if you ask for the type of a variable that does not exist. This is illustrated in line 7.

Assigning the value `undefined` to a variable is legal but not recommended. (This poor practice is shown in line 5.) If you refrain from assigning the `undefined` datatype, you will always know when you see it that the interpreter has assigned it automatically. When you want to assign a value to a variable to indicate that it contains no data, use `null`. Then `undefined` will always indicate exactly what the word implies: something that has never been defined.

```
1: var x;                  // good
2: trace (typeof x);       // "undefined"
3: x = null;               // good
4: trace (typeof x);       // "null"
```

12

```
5: x = undefined;            // legal but poor practice !!!
6: trace (typeof x);         // "undefined" : no value assigned
7: trace (typeof y);         // "undefined" : doesn't exist
```

TROUBLESHOOTING

Why can't I reference a variable on the Main Timeline from a subclip?

If you store variables in the Main Timeline and access them from subclips, don't forget to use _root when referencing the variables. Here's a common error: You look at the variable where it is declared in the Main Timeline and don't see _root there, so you forget to include _root when you reference the variable.

Tired of having to put _root before all those variable names? Define global variables using the _global identifier. You can access a global variable for read operations by using just the variable name.

Can using a particular variable or movie clip instance name cause problems?

Yes! Using a reserved word for a variable name, function name, or object name is a common source of error. Though you may never use all the ActionScript keywords, it's worthwhile familiarizing yourself with them so that you can avoid using them.

Using a reserved word as a movie clip instance name can produce hard-to-track errors. For instance, le is a reserved word. However, Flash will allow you to assign le as a movie clip instance name. When you try to use that name in ActionScript, however, you're likely to run into trouble. For instance, in the following example, the movie clip is named le, a reserved word. This code would normally change the color of a shape in the movie clip to green. Because of the reserved name, the code doesn't do anything.

```
var green = 65280 // numerical code for green
myColor = new Color("le"); // "le" is a movie instance name
myColor.setRGB(green); // THIS DOES NOT WORK!
```

➯ *This technique for setting colors is covered in "The Color Class," page 447 (Chapter 20, "Using the Built-in Movie Objects").*

The preceding example fails silently. The following statement will generate an error (Expected a field name after '.') and will not work:

```
_root.le.gotoAndStop(1); // ERROR!!!
```

Will I always get an error message when things go wrong?

Unfortunately, no. For instance, using an inappropriate datatype can generate mysterious "silent" errors, in which the ActionScript interpreter generates no error messages. Instead, things just don't work the way you expect them to. For instance, this statement duplicates the `myClip` movie clip, creating a copy named `myClip1`:

```
duplicateMovieClip ("myClip", "myClip1", 1);
```

This statement fails silently:

```
duplicateMovieClip ("myClip", myClip1, 1);
```

The reason for the failure? Without quotation marks, `myClip1` isn't a text string, nor is it a variable that refers to a string. One of the two is required.

FLASH AT WORK: VERSION DETECTION

The variable `$version`, introduced in version 4.0r11 of Flash, can be accessed programmatically, in addition to being displayed using Cmd-Option-V (Mac) or Ctrl+Alt+V (Windows) (in the authoring environment, while the program is running). The `$version` variable cannot be used to determine whether a Flash Player is present because it can be used only from within an already-executing Flash program. JavaScript in the HTML page is the standard way to check whether the Flash Player is present. However, the `$version` variable has its own advantages: For instance, it works in browsers that don't support scripting or that have scripting disabled.

Flash 5 introduced a new function, `getVersion()`, that evaluates `$version` and returns the result. But, of course, if you want to be able to detect the Flash 4 Player, you must use something that works in Flash 4.

The following script obtains the version of the Flash Player from `$version` and puts its three main components—platform, major version, and minor version—into other variables.

You can copy this script from the sample movie, detect.fla, and paste it into the first frame of a new movie. To make the script most useful, you can branch off to alternate content or an upgrade page, for instance, based on the version that you find.

```
// Sample $version strings:
// "WIN 6,0,21,0"
// "MAC 4,0,11,0"
// "UNIX 5,0,30,0"

// divide $version into 2 parts, at the " " (space) character
// and put those parts in an array named platformVersionArray
platformVersionArray = $version.split(" ");

// You get:
// platformVersionArray[0] ==  e.g WIN or MAC
// platformVersionArray[1]) == e.g. 6,0,10,0
```

12

```
// assign the first element to the "platform" variable
platform = platformVersionArray[0]; // WIN or MAC

// divide the second element into 4 parts, at the "," (comma) characters
// and put those parts in an array named versionArray
versionArray = platformVersionArray[1].split(",");

// assign first and third elements to appropriate variables
majorVersion = versionArray[0]; // 6
minorVersion = versionArray[2]; //10

// Here is where you would branch off
// based on major/minor versions:
if (majorVersion >= 4) {
    if (majorVersion >= 6) {
        // Latest and greatest!
    }
    if ((majorVersion >= 5) && (minorVersion>=41)) {
        // Player versions 5.0r41 and 42 handle XML files better.
    }
    // Player version is 4.0r11 or later.
    if ((majorVersion >= 4) && (minorVersion >= 20)) {
        // Player version 4.0r20 supports printing.
    }
} else {
    // A version preceding 4.0r11
}
```

USING OPERATORS

WORKING WITH OPERANDS, EXPRESSIONS, AND STATEMENTS

Operators are symbols and keywords that change, access, create, remove, analyze, and organize data. Most operators come from the fields of mathematics and logic. A number of them are old friends from grade-school arithmetic. For instance, the multiplication operator (*) multiplies two values; the addition operator (+) adds two values; the division operator (/) divides one value by another.

In some instances, an operator's form in ActionScript is different from that of grade-school arithmetic. For instance, the ActionScript multiplication operator is an asterisk (*), not ×. Similarly, the division operator is a forward slash (/), not the ÷ symbol.

Although operators are very basic, they're also powerful and can be tricky. There are a lot of them—52 in all, 51 of which are listed in Table 13.1.

 ⇨ *The super operator, new in Flash MX, is covered in "Accessing the Superclass Using super,"*
page 497 (Chapter 21, "Packaging Data and Functions Using Custom Objects").

Forty operators fall into five major categories:

- *Arithmetic* operators operate on numeric operands to produce a numeric result.

- *Assignment* operators assign a result to a variable, object property, or array element; *reassignment* operators also include an arithmetic or bitwise operation with the assignment.

- *Bitwise* operators operate on individual bits within a byte.

- *Comparison* operators compare two values.

- *Logical* (Boolean) operators reduce expressions to Boolean values (`true` or `false`) and return results based on those values.

In addition, 12 "one-of-a-kind" operators don't fall into any category: array-element/object-property, comma, conditional, `delete`, dot, function call, grouping, `new`, `typeof`, `instanceof`, `void`, and `super`.

Table 13.1 ActionScript Operators

Operator	Category	Usage	Precedence	Associativity
x++	arithmetic	postfix increment	16	L-R
x--	arithmetic	postfix decrement	16	L-R
.	N/A	object property access	15	L-R
[]	N/A	array-element/object-property	15	L-R
()	N/A	parentheses, grouping	15	L-R
function()	N/A	parentheses, function call	15	L-R

Operator	Category	Usage	Precedence	Associativity
++x	arithmetic	prefix increment	14	R-L
--x	arithmetic	prefix decrement	14	R-L
-	arithmetic	unary negation	14	R-L
~	bitwise	bitwise NOT	14	R-L
!	logical	logical NOT	14	R-L
new	N/A	create object/array	14	R-L
delete	N/A	remove object/property/array element	14	R-L
typeof	N/A	determine datatype	14	R-L
void	N/A	return undefined value	14	R-L
*	arithmetic	multiply	13	L-R
/	arithmetic	divide	13	L-R
%	arithmetic	modulo divide	13	L-R
+	arithmetic string	add (number) concatenate (string)	12	L-R
-	arithmetic	subtract	12	L-R
<<	bitwise	bitwise left shift	11	L-R
>>	bitwise	bitwise signed right shift	11	L-R
>>>	bitwise	bitwise unsigned right shift	11	L-R
<	comparison	less than	10	L-R
<=	comparison	less than or equal to	10	L-R
>	comparison	greater than	10	L-R
>=	comparison	greater than or equal to	10	L-R
instanceof	N/A	determine class	10	L-R
==	comparison	equality	9	L-R
!=	comparison	inequality	9	L-R
===	comparison	strict equality	9	L-R
!==	comparison	strict inequality	9	L-R
&	bitwise	bitwise AND	8	L-R
^	bitwise	bitwise XOR	7	L-R
|	bitwise	bitwise OR	6	L-R
&&	logical	logical AND	5	L-R
||	logical	logical OR	4	L-R
?:	N/A	conditional	3	R-L
=	assignment	assignment	2	R-L
+=	assignment	add and reassign	2	R-L

13

Table 13.1 Continued

Operator	Category	Usage	Precedence	Associativity
-=	assignment	subtract and reassign	2	R-L
*=	assignment	multiply and reassign	2	R-L
/=	assignment	divide and reassign	2	R-L
%=	assignment	modulo divide and reassign	2	R-L
<<=	bitwise	bit-shift left and reassign	2	R-L
>>=	bitwise	bit-shift right and reassign	2	R-L
>>>=	bitwise	bit-shift right (unsigned) and reassign	2	R-L
&=	bitwise	bitwise AND and reassign	2	R-L
^=	bitwise	bitwise XOR and reassign	2	R-L
|=	bitwise	bitwise OR and reassign	2	R-L
,	N/A	comma	1	L-R

Defining Simple Data Relationships Using Expressions

Operands are what operators operate on. Operators combined with operands form *expressions*. An expression is a section of code that resolves to a single value. For example, the following are all expressions:

```
3 + 7 // operands are 3 and 7, operator is +, result is 10
"Bed #"+6 // operands are "Bed #" and 6, operator is +, result is "Bed #6"
a - b // operands are a and b, operator is -, result is a less b
x++ // operand is x, operator is ++, result is x + 1
```

The *statement* is the smallest unit of ActionScript code that can actually cause something to happen in the program. Often, all that's required to turn an expression into a statement is a semicolon, as in these examples:

```
x++; // a complete statement, increments x by 1
x--; // a complete statement, decrements x by 1
```

Many expressions, when terminated with a semicolon, become *legal* statements, but not *useful* ones. For instance, these statements produce a result but don't do anything with it:

```
3 + 7;
a - b;
```

The following, on the other hand, are useful statements:

```
x = 3 + 7; // stores result in variable x
trace(a - b); // displays result in Output window
```

> **Caution**
>
> If you leave out the semicolon in a statement, the ActionScript interpreter will try to guess where it should be. However, leaving out this punctuation can cause errors and is not a good practice.

Understanding Precedence, Associativity, and Operator Grouping

When one statement includes multiple operators, the ActionScript interpreter has two simple rules by which it determines which operators to evaluate first:

■ Each operator has a precedence value, as shown in Table 13.1. The interpreter evaluates operators in order of precedence, higher precedence operators first.

■ Operators with the same precedence are evaluated according to their *associativity*, either left to right (L-R) or right to left (R-L). Table 13.1 also shows the associativity of each operator.

Examples of precedence include the following:

```
1 + 2 * 10 // 21 - multiplication happens before addition
--6 * 100 // 500 - decrement happens before multiplication
```

Parentheses can be used as *grouping operators*, to override the default order of operation, as in the following examples:

```
(1 + 2) * 10 // 30 - addition happens before multiplication
--(6 * 100) // 599 - multiplication happens before decrement
```

You can also use parentheses to make the order of evaluation more obvious, even if they don't actually change anything. For instance:

```
1 + (2 * 10) // 21 – doesn't really change anything
```

Here's an example of associativity: The "add and reassign" (+=) and "subtract and reassign" (-=) operators have the same precedence and right-to-left associativity. Therefore, in the expression a += b -= c, the interpreter starts by evaluating the operator on the right, so a += b -= c is the same as a += (b -= c). For instance, in the following example, the interpreter evaluates b -= c first, making b equal to –1. Then it evaluates a += b, making a equal to 0, as shown here:

```
a = 1;
b = 2;
c = 3;
a += b -= c; // result: a == 0, b == -1, c == 3
```

⇨ *The "add and reassign" and "subtract and reassign" operators are covered later in this chapter in the "Assignment and Compound Assignment" section, page 231.*

UNDERSTANDING ARITHMETIC OPERATORS

Arithmetic operators perform mathematical operations on numeric operands to produce numeric results. The ActionScript interpreter automatically converts non-numeric operands to numbers for use with arithmetic operators.

⇨ *For the rules governing such conversions, see Table 12.2, "Implicit Conversion to a Number," page 205 (Chapter 12, "Managing Variables, Data, and Datatypes").*

13

The Special Value NaN ("Not a Number")

If an operand used with an arithmetic operator cannot be converted into a number, the ActionScript interpreter will change it to the special value NaN ("not a number").

It is possible, though rare, to get NaN as a result of manipulating numbers. For instance, if you divide zero by zero, you get NaN:

```
trace(0/0); // NaN
```

More commonly, NaN results from an unsuccessful attempt to convert a string to a number.

⇨ *You can find an example of NaN resulting from an unsuccessful attempt to convert a string to a number in "Implicit and Explicit Data Conversion," page 204 (Chapter 12, "Managing Variables, Data, and Datatypes"). You'll find more discussion of this phenomenon in "Automatic Datatype Conversions for Comparisons," later in this chapter, page 234.*

Any mathematical operation involving an operand whose value is NaN yields a final result of NaN.

Incrementing and Decrementing

The increment operator, which is two plus signs (++), adds 1 to the operand. The decrement operator, which is two minus signs (- -), subtracts 1 from the operand, as in these examples:

```
x = 1;
x++; // x is now equal to 2

y = 2;
y--; // y is now equal to 1
```

Both the increment and the decrement operator can be used as a *prefix* or a *postfix*—that is, before or after the operand. It doesn't matter whether you use the prefix or the postfix form, if you're only incrementing or decrementing the statement (as shown in the previous example), although postfix is favored by tradition.

If, in the same statement, however, you're doing something with the result (storing it in a variable, for instance, or displaying it in the Output window), prefix and postfix act differently. The prefix form changes the operand first and then does something with it. The postfix does something with the operand first and then changes it.

For instance, in the following two statements, the operand x always changes in the same way: It starts with a value of 2 and ends up with a value of 3. With the postfix increment, the variable y ends up with the initial value of x because the assignment is made before x changes. With the prefix increment, y ends up with the final value of x because the assignment is made after x changes. (Visually, when the operator is near y, it affects y. When the operator is away from y, it doesn't affect y.)

```
x = 2;
y = x++; // postfix, result is  x : 3, y : 2
y = ++x; // prefix, result is x : 3, y : 3
```

The same rule applies to the decrement operator. In the following statements, the final and initial values of x are 2 and 1, respectively. The variable y ends up with the initial value of x with the post-fix decrement, and the final value of x with the prefix decrement.

```
x = 2;
y = x--; // x : 1, y : 2
y = --x; // x : 1, y : 1
```

Again, for a simple assignment, a decrement operator that faces a variable affects it. In contrast, when x faces y, y just gets the value of x.

Similarly, in the following examples, when the operator faces the trace keyword, it affects what is displayed:

```
x = 2;
trace(x++); // displays 2 , x changes, but it doesn't affect the trace
```

```
x = 2;
trace(++x); // displays 3 , x changes, and it does affect the trace
```

Increment and decrement operators are commonly used with variables for counting loops in looping sequences.

> To learn more details about loops, see "Repeating Actions Using Loops," page 259 (Chapter 14, "Working with Data: Using Statements").

Addition and Subtraction

Addition and subtraction differ from incrementing and decrementing in two ways:

- They require two operands.

- They do not change the operands. They just produce a result.

Consider this example:

```
a = 6;
b = 2;
c = 1
d = a - b + c; // Now d is 5. No change in a, b or c, still 6, 2 and 1.
```

> For a discussion of statements containing multiple operators, see "Understanding Precedence, Associativity, and Operator Grouping," earlier in this chapter, page 219.

Operands can be any expressions that resolve to real numbers. Operands that don't resolve to real numbers are converted to NaN.

If you want the absolute (positive) difference between two numbers, subtract and then apply the Math.abs function to the result:

```
c = Math.abs(a - b); // if b is greater than a, c is still positive
```

⇨ *For more information on the Math object, see Chapter 19, "Using the Built-in Core Objects," page 393.*

Working with the Polymorphic + Operator

With numeric operands, the + operator performs simple addition. For instance:

```
2 + 2 // yields 4
```

However, the + operator is *polymorphic*. That is, it performs different operations with different datatypes or classes. Specifically, it concatenates strings and adds numbers. Whenever one of the operands is a string, the result is a string, as in these examples:

```
x = "1" + 6; // "16"
trace(typeof x); // string

x = 6 + "1"; // "61"
trace(typeof x);   // string
```

You can change this behavior by explicitly converting strings to numbers as follows:

```
x = 6 + Number("1"); // 7
trace(typeof x);   // number
```

Other arithmetic operators are not polymorphic and will always yield numbers, even if all the operands are strings, as shown here:

```
x = "3" * "7"; // 21, a number; multiplication is not polymorphic
x = "7" - "3"; // 4, a number; subtraction is not polymorphic
x = "6" / "3"; // 2, a number; division is not polymorphic
```

Working with the Overloaded - Operator

Although the – (minus and unary negation) operator is not polymorphic—it does not perform different operations with different datatypes or classes—it is *overloaded*. That is, it performs different operations within a single datatype or class, depending on the number of operands. In fact, it is considered a different operator depending on the number of operands.

With a single operand, it is the *unary negation* operator, which reverses the sign of a numeric value. A positive value becomes negative, and a negative value becomes positive, as shown in this example:

```
x = 8;
trace(-x); // displays -8 (negative 8)
```

With two operands, it is the familiar *subtraction* operator, as shown here:

```
2 - 2 // yields 0 (zero)
```

Multiplication and Division

Multiplication and division present few problems or peculiarities. They work just as they do in ordinary arithmetic. As usual, ActionScript relies on automatic datatype conversions (rather than errors or exceptions, as in some other languages, such as Java) to deal with illegal operations. For instance, division by zero yields an undefined result in ordinary arithmetic. In Flash, it yields Infinity:

```
x = 0;
y = 8;
z = y / x; // z is Infinity
```

Integer division can produce a fractional result. This point might not even be worth mentioning, except that Macromedia's Lingo (the programming language for Director) always produces an integer result if both operands are integers. The following example illustrates the fact that, in ActionScript, you can get a fractional result by dividing integers:

```
x = 17;
y = 8;
z = x / y; // z is 2.125
```

Modulo (%) Division

The modulo operator gives you the remainder of a division operation. That is, it performs *modulo division*, in which the result is the remainder, or *modulus*, of the division operation. For instance, 11 % 3 equals 2, because 11 divided by 3 is 3, with a remainder of 2. More examples include the following:

```
4 % 3 // 1
16 % 8 // 0
200 % 100 // 0
18 % 10 // 8
10 % 9.5 // .5
```

Note from the final example that, unlike some other languages (C and C++, for instance), ActionScript can use floats as operands in modulo division.

You also can use modulo division to perform a task at a regular interval, such as the following:

```
onClipEvent (load) {
    var interval = 5;
    var frameCounter = 0;
}
onClipEvent (enterFrame){
    if( ++frameCounter % interval == 0){
        // Do something here. It will happen every five frames.
    }
}
```

13

For instance, sample movie leglift2.fla is a slightly modified version of leglift.fla from Chapter 11. Here, you make the leg move half as fast by using modulo division:

```
onClipEvent(load) {
    var slowdown = 2; // ADDED
    var frameCounter = 0; // ADDED
    var degrees = _rotation;
    function raise() { degrees = 20; }
    function lower() { degrees = 68; }
    function halt() { degrees = _rotation; }
    function lift(degrees) {
        if (_rotation < degrees) _rotation++;
        if (_rotation > degrees) _rotation--;
    }
}
onClipEvent(enterFrame) {
    if( ++frameCounter % slowdown == 0){ // ADDED
        lift(degrees);
    }
}
```

UNDERSTANDING BITWISE OPERATORS

Bitwise operations provide an efficient and concise alternative to tracking large numbers of binary variables—variables that can have only two values. Using bitwise operators will give you a smaller SWF. In addition, if you often want to set or get multiple values simultaneously, using bitwise operators will probably speed up your program significantly.

Unfortunately, code that incorporates bitwise operators can be hard to read. In addition, to use bitwise operators effectively, you need to understand binary (base 2) arithmetic. Bitwise operators are never an absolute necessity: You can always achieve the same result by using logical (Boolean) operators. Therefore, many programmers avoid bitwise operators. However, bitwise operators are much more concise and efficient for some jobs. You'll almost certainly benefit from having them in your ActionScript toolkit.

Binary arithmetic is based on the *bit*, which is a unit of information that can have just two states. You can think of these states as 0 and 1, on and off, true and false, set and cleared, or whatever other dichotomy you might want to represent.

ActionScript binary arithmetic is based on 32-bit binary numbers, as shown in Figure 13.1. The power of these numbers comes from the fact that you can look at them in two completely different ways:

- You can get and set them as integers, changing all 32 bits in one operation.

- You can use each number to represent 31 binary variables, which you can get or set in any grouping or combination you want.

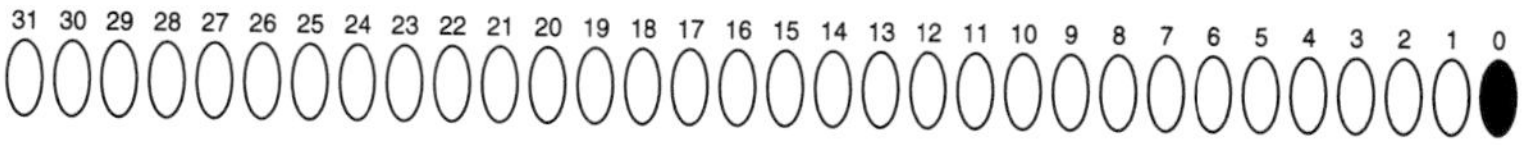

31 30 29 28 27 26 25 24 23 22 21 20 19 18 17 16 15 14 13 12 11 10 9 8 7 6 5 4 3 2 1 0

Figure 13.1
A 32-bit binary number. The number shown here is 1 because the only digit that is "on" is the ones place.

Why limit yourself to 31 binary variables if you have 32 bits to work with? See the "Troubleshooting" section at the end of this chapter, page 245.

You can switch back and forth between these modes at will, using ordinary arithmetic operators for the first type of operation and the bitwise operators for the second type. It's the second way of looking at binary numbers, in which each digit represents a separate variable, that makes them so powerful in ActionScript.

A Very Short Course in Binary Arithmetic

In base 10, the value of the digits from right to left goes up by powers of 10: 1, 10, 100, 1,000, 10,000, and so on. Each place is 10 times greater than the one to its right. In the binary system, the value of the digits goes up by powers of 2: 1, 2, 4, 8, 16, 32, 64, and so on. Each place is 2 times greater than the one to its right.

This is 1 represented as a 32-bit binary number:

```
00000000000000000000000000000001
```

This is 2:

```
00000000000000000000000000000010
```

This is 4:

```
00000000000000000000000000000100
```

In base 10, each digit can contain a number from 0 to 9. In base 2, each bit can contain either a 0 or a 1. Each place is either on or off. If it's on, you add the value of the place to the number. If it's off, you add nothing.

Consider these examples:

11 in binary is 3: $1 \times 2 + 1 \times 1$.

100 in binary is 4: $1 \times 4 + 0 \times 2 + 0 \times 1$.

1001 in binary is 9: $1 \times 8 + 0 \times 4 + 0 \times 2 + 1 \times 1$.

Figure 13.2 shows binary counting from 0 to 8, using four bits. A black oval indicates a 1; a white oval, a 0. At the same time, these bits can be viewed as four on-off switches.

13

Figure 13.2

Binary counting from 0 to 8. The four digits can also be viewed as four on-off switches.

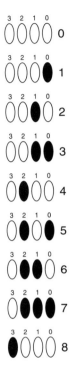

With that background, let's look at the bitwise operators. They fall into two basic categories: I'll refer to the first as "bitwise logical." (They're usually just called "bitwise," to avoid confusion with the Boolean logical operators.) The other category is "bit-shift."

In addition, each bitwise logical and bit-shift operator can be combined with an assignment in the same way that arithmetic operators can.

Bitwise Logical Operators

The four bitwise logical operators are AND (&), NOT (~) OR (|), and XOR (^).

The bitwise NOT operator simply reverses every bit of a 32-bit binary number. So, if all the bits of a number are set to 1, they will all be set to 0, and vice versa.

The other three bitwise logical operators compare two 32-bit binary numbers and yield a third 32-bit binary number as a result. They do a bit-by-bit comparison of the two input numbers and use the result of each bitwise comparison to determine the value of the corresponding bit in the third number. You can most easily visualize this comparison by arranging the two input numbers vertically, with the result underneath.

The Bitwise AND Operator

With the bitwise AND operator, the result bit is a 1 only if both input bits are 1. Figure 13.3 illustrates this using four bits. In the figure, only the least significant bit (LSB), bit 0, is a 1 in both input numbers. Therefore, only the LSB is 1 in the result.

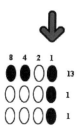

You can use the bitwise AND operator to check whether a particular bit or group of bits is on. For instance, consider this code, which embodies the comparison in Figure 13.3:

```
x = 13;
y = 1;
result = x & y; // result is 1
```

> The symbol for the bitwise AND operator is a single character (&),whereas the logical AND operator uses two characters (&&).

The result answers the question, "Is the LSB (bit 0) on in x?" If the result is 1, the LSB is on. If the result is 0, the LSB is off. In this case, it's on.

You could also look at the result the other way around, as answering the question, "Are bits 0, 2, or 3 on in y?" Whichever bits are on in the result are on in y. In this case, that is just bit 0.

If you set y = 3, then result = x & y answers the question, "Is either bit 0 or bit 1 on in x?" Table 13.2 shows the possible results and their meanings.

Table 13.2   Using the Bitwise AND Operator to Determine the On/Off States of Bits

Result	Bit 1 in x	Bit 0 in x
3	on	on
2	on	off
1	off	on
0	off	off

For example, in a database of houses for sale, bits 0 and 1 could represent a garage and a carport, respectively. With one query, you could find out whether the house in question has just one or the other (and, if so, which one), or if it has both or neither.

Using two bits, you can check four possible combinations. With three bits, you can check eight combinations. Each additional bit doubles the number of combinations you can check. How many combinations can you check with 31 bits? The answer is 2 to the 31st power, or 2,147,483,648! (Check this result in Flash with `trace(Math.pow(2,31))`.) Not bad for four bytes of information.

The Bitwise OR Operator

With the bitwise OR operator, the result bit is a 1 if either input bit is 1, as illustrated in Figure 13.4.

Figure 13.4
The result bit of the bitwise OR
operator is a 1 if either input
bit is 1.

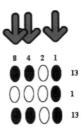

You can use the bitwise OR operator to turn on a particular bit or group of bits. For instance, consider this code, which embodies Figure 13.4:

```
x = 13;
y = 1;
result = x | y; // result is 13
```

The symbol for the bitwise OR operator is a single character (|), whereas the logical OR operator uses two characters (||).

Bit 0 will be on in result, no matter what x is. As it happens, bit 0 is already on in x, so there is nothing to turn on, and result and x are the same.

If the bits in operands x and y represent newspaper articles in online databases, the preceding example would represent the question, "Does either database contain the article represented by bit 0?" If bit 0 is on in result, one of the databases has the article. If bit 0 is off in result, neither database has the article.

Another way of thinking about the bitwise OR operator is that it combines two sets of information. For instance, in the example of the two databases, result combines the information in x and y.

The Bitwise XOR Operator

With the bitwise XOR operator, the result bit is a 1 only when the input bits differ, as illustrated in Figure 13.5. The symbol for the bitwise XOR operator is the caret (^), Shift+6 on most keyboards.

Figure 13.5
The result bit of the bitwise XOR
operator is a 1 only when the
input bits differ.

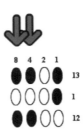

You can use the bitwise XOR operator to reverse a particular bit or group of bits. For instance, consider this code, which embodies Figure 13.5:

```
x = 13;
y = 1;
result = x ^ y; // result = 12, because LSB toggled from 1 to 0
```

Bit 0 in result will be reversed from whatever it was in x. In this case, it was on in x, and it is off in result.

If you have on-off buttons in a program, you could track the states of up to 31 buttons in one 32-bit binary number and set the states of multiple buttons simultaneously by using the bitwise XOR operator.

The Bitwise NOT Operator

The bitwise NOT operator reverses each bit of a 32-bit binary number. If you have on-off buttons in a program, for instance, with their on-off states represented in a 32-bit binary number, you could toggle the state of all your buttons in one operation by using the bitwise NOT operator.

Using Multiple Bitwise Logical Operators

You can use multiple bitwise logical operators in a single statement as follows:

```
x = 13;
y = 1;
z = 2;
result = x & (y | z); // result = 1
```

The final line answers the question, "Is either bit 0 or bit 1 on in x?" Whichever of these two bits is on in result is also on in x.

Using the same values for x, y, and z as in the preceding example, the following line of code answers the question, "Are both bit 0 and bit 1 on in x?"

```
result = (x & (y | z)) == (y | z); // result is false
```

In this case, bit 0 is on in x, but bit 1 is not, so result is false.

To understand the logic of this expression, consider that (y|z) is some group of bits; call it g. Then (x & (y | z)) is the overlap between x and g—the bits that are on in both. This means that result answers the question, "Is the overlap between x and g equal to g?" If so, that is the same as saying that all the on bits in g are also on in x. In this case, y is 1, so bit 0 is on in y; z is 2, so bit 1 is on in z. So g in this example includes both bits 0 and 1. But x is 13, in which bits 3, 2, and 0 are on, but not bit 1. So the overlap between x and g is only bit 0, which is not equal to g.

Bit-Shift Operators

The three bit-shift operators move the value in each bit a certain number of steps to the right or left. Bits at the end of the line fall off and are lost.

Shifting bits one step to the right is the equivalent of dividing by 2. Shifting bits one step to the left is the equivalent of multiplying by 2.

Shifting bits is analogous to the base-10 phenomenon, in which shifting digits to the right or left divides or multiplies by 10. For instance, if you start with 100 and shift digits one step to the right, you get 10. In other words, you have just divided by 10. The final 0 in 100 falls off and is lost.

Similarly, if you start with binary 100 (which is 4) and shift digits one step to the right, you get binary 10 (which is 2). In this case, you have just divided by 2. The final 0 in the binary 100 falls off and is lost.

Using bit-shift operators to divide or multiply an integer is significantly faster than using the division (/) or multiplication (*) operators. In some tests that I have run, the difference has been about 30%. Of course, using bit-shift operators to divide or multiply works only if your divisor or multiplier is a power of 2. Also, if you bit-shift right (divide) with an odd operand, the result is rounded down because the LSB falls off. Positive results become smaller, and negative results become more negative.

Signed Right Shift

The signed right shift divides by 2, dropping any remainder. It preserves the sign of a negative number.

Preserving the Sign When Shifting Right

Computers set the most significant bit (MSB) to 1 when making a number negative in "twos complement" notation. In positive numbers, the MSB is 0.

As a binary number is shifted to the right, bits fall off on the right, and new bits appear on the left. For negative numbers, the bitwise signed right shift operator sets the new bits to 1. For positive numbers, it sets the new bits to 0. In this way, the signs of numbers are preserved even if you reverse the process and shift left the same number of steps that you shifted right.

The general form of the signed right shift is

```
result = value >> steps
```

Consider these examples of the signed right shift:

```
x = 10;
y = 1;
result = x >> y ; // result = 5, which is 10 / 2, no remainder

x = 13;
y = 2;
result = x >> y ; // result = 3, which is 13 / 4, rounded down

x = -13;
y = 2;
result = x >> y ; // result = -4, which is 13 / 4, rounded down
```

The symbol for the signed right shift is formed by two greater than signs together: >>.

Unsigned Right Shift

The unsigned right shift shifts digits to the right. However, unlike the signed right shift, the unsigned right shift always adds zeros on the left. Therefore, the result is always positive.

The symbol for the unsigned right shift is formed by three greater than signs together: >>>.

The general form of the unsigned right shift is

```
result = value >>> steps
```

The symbol for the signed left shift is formed by two less than signs together: <<.

The unsigned right shift sometimes comes in handy when you're "twiddling bits." However, it doesn't have any obvious arithmetic applications. For positive numbers, it yields the same results as the signed right shift. For negative numbers, the 1s in the high bits yield results that are not related to the original number in any obvious way. For instance:

```
x = -13;
y = 1;
result = x >>> y ; // result = 2,147,483,641
```

Signed Left Shift

The signed left shift multiplies by 2, preserving the sign of a negative number.

The general form of the signed left shift is

```
result = value << steps
```

Consider these examples of the signed left shift:

```
x = 13;
y = 2;
result = x << y ; // result = 52, which is 13 * 4

x = 10;
y = 1;
result = x << y ; // result = 20, which is 10 * 2

x = -13;
y = 2;
result = x << y ; // result = -52, which is -13 * 4
```

ASSIGNMENT AND COMPOUND ASSIGNMENT

The assignment operator (=) stores the result of an expression in a variable, array element, or object property, as in these examples:

```
x = 2; // stores the number 2 in the variable x
month[11] = "December";// 12th element of the month array is "December"
car.color = 0xFF0000; // color property of car object is 0xFF0000 (red)
```

Ten *compound assignment operators* provide a concise notation for combining the assignment operator with various arithmetic or bitwise operators. For instance, the "add and reassign" operator (+=) combines assignment and addition. Each compound assignment operator performs an operation using two operands and stores the result in the left operand. For instance, x += 2 adds 2 to x and stores the result in x. This is equivalent to x = x + 2.

Table 13.3 lists the compound assignment operators with examples and equivalent expressions.

Table 13.3   Compound Assignment Operators

Name	Operator	Example	Equivalent Expression
add and reassign	+=	i += 2	i = i + 2
subtract and reassign	-=	balance -= debit	balance = balance - debit
multiply and reassign	*=	rate *= increase	rate = rate * increase
divide and reassign	/=	price /= discount	price = price / discount
modulo divide and reassign	%=	frameCounter % slowdown	frameCounter = frameCounter % slowdown
bit-shift left and reassign	<<=	answer <<= num	answer = answer << num
bit-shift right and reassign	>>=	result >>= 1	/result = result >> 1
bitwise AND and reassign	&=	test &= 4	test = test & 4
bitwise XOR and reassign	^=	finalMask ^= initialMask	finalMask = finalMask ^ initialMask
bitwise OR and reassign	|=	onOff |= on	onOff = onOff	on

The compound assignment operators are not more efficient computationally than their longer equivalents, nor do they result in smaller SWFs. They are strictly a notational convenience.

Note that

x *= y + z

is equivalent to

x = x * (y + z)

not

x = x * y + z

which is the same as

x = (x * y) + z

COMPARISON OPERATORS

The comparison operators are used to determine whether two operands are equal, or whether one operand is greater than or less than another. The eight comparison operators are as follows:

- Equality (==)
- Inequality (!=)
- Strict equality (===)
- Strict inequality (!==)
- Less than (<)
- Less than or equal to (<=)
- Greater than (>)
- Greater than or equal to (>=)

The first four are also known as *equality* operators, and the last four as *relational* operators. All eight compare two strings or numbers and return `true` or `false`, depending on whether the relationship indicated in the comparison is accurate.

In addition, the relational operators return `undefined` if at least one of the operands is NaN. The equality and strict equality operators return `false` in this case, whereas the inequality and strict inequality operators return `true`.

Understanding Equality Operators

Both the equality (==) and strict equality (===) operators test for "sameness," but the equality operator performs datatype conversions when necessary before comparing. The strict equality operator insists that the operands already be of the same datatype, or else it returns `false`.

For instance, `null == undefined` is true, but `null === undefined` is false. Because `null` and `undefined` are of different datatypes, they are not strictly equal. However, the equality operator converts them both to 0, so they are equal.

The inequality (!=) and strict inequality (!==) operators return the opposite of the equality and strict equality operators. Whenever the former returns `true`, the latter returns `false`, and vice versa.

The equality operator is perhaps the most commonly used operator, and also the source of one of the most common mistakes: using a single equal sign (the assignment operator) when you mean to use two equal signs (the equality operator).

⇨ *For more details about the common error of confusing the equality operator with the assignment operator, see the "Troubleshooting" section at the end of this chapter, page 245.*

Numbers are compared mathematically. For instance, these expressions all yield `true`:

```
1 + 2 == 3
-20 < -1
80.5 != 80
```

13

In contrast, these expressions all yield `false`:

```
6 <= 5
5 >= 6
-200 > 0
```

Strings are compared using the "code points" of the ISO-8859 (Latin-1) or Unicode character set. The code point is the number or "character code" associated with each character. For instance, these expressions all yield `true`:

```
"A" < "a" // capital letters come before lowercase
"A" > "1" // numbers come before capital letters
"<" <= ">" // the "less than" sign comes before the "greater than" sign
```

If you want to use the character code of a letter to compare it with a number, use the `charCodeAt()` function. For instance, the character code for a blank space is 32. Therefore, the following expression yields `true`:

```
" ".charCodeAt(0) == 32 // true, the first (0) character is a blank
```

This expression yields `false`:

```
" " == 32
```

Automatic Datatype Conversions for Comparisons

The expression `" " == 32` is false because of the way the ActionScript interpreter performs automatic datatype conversion. For primitive datatypes, the interpreter converts operands to ensure that it ultimately compares either two strings or two numbers. Note that the interpreter makes temporary copies of the operands and converts the copies; it does not change the original data that is being compared.

A character string converts to a number only if it literally spells out a number. For example, the following yields `true`:

```
"32" == 32
```

> ⇨ *Rules for converting other data types to numbers are shown in Table 12.2 in Chapter 12, "Managing Variables, Data, and Datatypes," page 187.*

In all other cases, strings are converted to NaN. If either operand (or both) is converted to NaN, the comparison yields `false` for all the comparison operators except `!=` and `!==`. As counterintuitive as it seems, even `NaN == NaN` is a false expression, as far as the ActionScript interpreter is concerned! By the same token, `NaN != NaN` is true. This makes comparison operators an extremely nonintuitive means of determining whether a datum is NaN. The `typeof` operator doesn't help either; it just yields `number`. To test whether a value is NaN, use the `isNaN()` function:

```
x = NaN;
trace(x); // NaN(
trace(x == NaN); // false
trace(typeof x); // number
trace(isNaN(x)); // true
```

The preceding discussion assumes two primitive datatypes. If just one of the operands in a comparison is a composite datatype (`object`, `array`, or `function`), the ActionScript interpreter invokes the `valueOf()` method of the operand. If `valueOf()` returns a primitive value, that value is used in the comparison. If not, the comparison yields `false`.

In Flash 5, the `valueOf()` method was used in comparing *two* composite types, as well. This is no longer true for equality/inequality comparisons in Flash MX.

In Flash MX, if *both* operands are composite types, equality/inequality comparisons are made *by reference*. This means they are equal only if they reference *the same object*.

Thus, if `f1` and `f2` refer to function literals, (`f1 == f2`) is true only if both refer to the same function literal, as is the case in the following example:

```
myfunc = function (){};
f1 = myFunc;
f2 = myFunc;
trace(f1==f2); // true
```

On the other hand, `func1` and `func2` in the following example are identical in form but do not refer to the same function literal:

```
function func1(){}
function func2(){}
trace(func1 == func2); // false
```

Movie clips have always been compared by their instance names, and this is still true in Flash MX. Only the equality/inequality comparisons yield meaningful results with movie clips. The >=, <=, >, and < operators yield `undefined`.

Automatic datatype conversion for comparisons favors numbers over other datatypes: If one operator is a number and the other is a string, Boolean, `null`, or `undefined`, the non-numeric operand is converted to a number. This includes non-numeric operands returned by `valueOf()` functions.

Deprecated Flash 4 Comparison Operators

The Flash 4 comparison operators eq, ne, lt, gt, le, and ge are equivalent to ==, !=, <, >, <=, and >= except that lt, gt, le, and ge are string-specific. As of Flash 5, the Flash 4 operators are "deprecated," meaning supported but not recommended, unless you're exporting to Flash 4 format.

You may find situations in which the deprecated objects work better than the newer ones. Rather than use the old ones, you might be wise to create new functions of your own, based on the new operators but compensating for whatever behavior is creating a problem.

Macromedia will drop support for deprecated operators and functions as soon as it is practical to do so. Programs using deprecated syntax live on borrowed time.

13

Using Comparison Operators with Objects and Arrays

By default, >=, <=, >, and < do not yield meaningful results with objects and arrays as operands.

Newly created objects test unequal:

```
trace(o == o2); // false
trace(o != o2); // true
```

However, the results of the following statements, taken together, would lead to the conclusion that the objects are equal:

```
trace(o); // [object Object]
trace(o2); // [object Object]
trace(o <= o2); // true
trace(o >= o2); // true
trace(o > o2); // false
trace(o < o2); // false
```

For instance, if o >= o2 is true (o is either greater than or equal to o2) and o > o2 is false (it's not greater than), o must be equal to o2, right? (Wrong. You'll see why in a moment.)

Results for two newly created arrays are similar, except that they display nothing where objects display [object Object].

These results, however, are simply artifacts of the way Flash tests for >= and <=. In both cases, under the covers, Flash actually uses < in the final comparison and then reverses the answer. For example, for o <= o2, Flash asks, "Is o2 < o?" If not, it concludes that o <= o2 must be true! For o >= o2, Flash asks, "Is o < o2?" If not, it concludes that o >= o2 must be true!

These conclusions are valid, assuming numeric operands, or strings that can be reduced to numeric code points. In the case of objects, however, the interpreter converts both objects to NaN. The result of (NaN < NaN) is undefined:

```
trace(typeof (NaN < NaN));  // undefined
```

The ActionScript interpreter converts undefined to false in comparison results. So the interpreter reverses that result and deduces true for the original comparisons, in both cases!

Clearly, by default, >=, <=, >, and < do not produce generally useful results with objects or arrays as operands. However, you can create valueOf() methods for objects or arrays that return numeric or string primitives that can be usefully compared using the >=, <=, >, and < operators.

Note that objects and arrays differ from functions in this respect. The valueOf() method does not come into play when comparing two functions. It plays a role only when comparing a function with a primitive datatype.

USING LOGICAL (BOOLEAN) OPERATORS

Logical operators allow you to make decisions based on evaluating two or more expressions. Typically, you use expressions that naturally and intuitively yield Boolean values.

The three logical operators are AND (&&), OR (||), and NOT (!).

The logical NOT operator returns the Boolean opposite of the single operand that it precedes. Thus, if an expression returns `true`, with the logical NOT operator, you get `false`. For instance, say you have a movie clip, myClip, on the Stage, and it is visible:

```
trace(myClip._visible); // true
trace(!myClip._visible); // false
```

Similarly, if an expression returns `false` and you prefix it with the logical NOT operator, you get `true`. For instance, say you have a function, `checkKillList()`, that returns `false`:

```
trace(checkKillList()); // false
trace(!checkKillList()); // true
```

The AND operator answers the question, "Are both of these expressions true?"

The OR operator answers the question, "Is either of these expressions true?"

The following four pseudocode examples involve two expressions that are either true or false:

Example #1:

```
IF
starting point is San Francisco
AND
destination is Berkeley
THEN
take Bay Area Rapid Transit
```

Example #2:

```
IF
user hits Cancel
OR
an error occurs
THEN
cancel operation
```

Example #3:

```
IF
user provides correct password
AND
user is NOT on "kill" list
THEN
grant user access
```

Example #4:

```
IF
movie clip does NOT exist
OR
movie clip is NOT visible
THEN
tell user "Sorry, that movie clip is unavailable! "
```

13

The preceding four examples might look like this in ActionScript:

Example #1:

```
if ((start == "San Francisco") && (end == "Berkeley") )
{
    wayToGo = "BART";
}
```

Example #2:

```
if ( (input == cancel) || (input == error) ) {
    cancelOperation();
}
```

Example #3:

```
if ( (checkPassword() ) && (!checkKillList() ) {
    grantAccess();
}
```

Example #4:

```
if ( (!myClip) || (!myClip._visible) ) {
    returnError(unavailable)
}
```

> The symbol for OR is two vertical lines. On most keyboards, you produce the vertical line by using the Shift key plus the backslash (\) key, at the far right of the QWERTY row.

You can always duplicate the logic of logical operators by using multiple if statements. For instance, the AND operator is the equivalent of two nested if statements. Examples #1 and #3 look like this converted into nested if statements:

```
if (start == "San Francisco") {
    if (end == "Berkeley") {
        wayToGo = "BART";
    }
}

if (checkPassword()) {
    if (!checkKillList()) {
        grantAccess();
    }
}
```

Mostly, programmers think of the choice between AND and nested if statements as just one of taste. Some programmers find nested if statements more readable. The AND operator is more concise.

You can replace the OR operator with an if-else-if statement. For example, Example #2 looks like this converted into an if-else-if statement:

```
if (input == cancel) {
    cancelOperation();
}
```

```
else if (input == error) {
    cancelOperation();
}
```

In this case, the if-else-if statement has nothing to recommend it. The OR operator is both more concise and more readable.

For more information on if-else-if statements, see "Making Decisions Using Conditionals and switch," page 256 (Chapter 14, "Working with Data: Using Statements").

Actually, if statements do not exactly replicate the functionality of the AND or OR operator. The if statements return Boolean values, true or false. The AND and OR operators, on the other hand, actually return one of their operands. The AND operator returns its second operand if both operands resolve to true; otherwise, it returns whichever operand resolves to false. The OR operator returns its first operand, if it resolves to true: otherwise, it returns its second operand. The AND and OR operators are usually used in an if statement, and the if statement converts the returned operand to a Boolean.

Table 12.4, "Implicit Conversion to a Boolean," page 206, shows the rules the ActionScript interpreter follows when deriving Booleans from the operands in AND and OR statements or returned by OR statements.

Table 13.4 gives some examples of OR statements, their return values as displayed by a trace() statement, and which Boolean the return value resolves to.

Note that what is actually returned by the OR statement in each example is identical to one side of the OR statement. For instance, in the statement ["one", "two"] || "hi", the array ["one", "two"] becomes true when converted to a Boolean; therefore, the OR statement returns the array, which a trace() statement displays as one, two.

In practice, the values returned by AND and OR statements are seldom utilized directly. They're just converted into Booleans by if statements.

Table 13.4   OR Statements, Their Returns, and Boolean Equivalents

OR Statement	Trace (Return)	Boolean Equivalent of Return
"ho" || "hi"	hi	false
"32" || "hi"	32	true
32 || "hi"	32	true
Infinity || "hi"	Infinity	true
["one", "two"] || "hi"	one, two	true
myClip || "hi"	_level0.myClip	true
{eyes : "green", age : 32} || "hi"	[object Object]	true

THE CONDITIONAL OPERATOR

The conditional operator is a slightly optimized way of implementing if-else logic. It's like an if that *requires* an else, in contrast to the normal if statement, for which the else is optional.

The conditional operator always specifies both a true and a false condition, making it a *ternary* operator, meaning it has three arguments. Because it is the only operator that always has three arguments, it is sometimes also called *the* ternary operator. Its format is

```
condition ? result_if_true : result_if_false;
```

The first part of the conditional expression (`condition`) is a test that returns true or false. The next two parts are possible return values. If the condition is true, the operator returns part two. If the condition is false, the operator returns part three. In pseudocode, here's a condition that says, "If the journey is greater than 1,000 miles, then fly; if it is not greater than 1,000 miles, then drive."

```
journey is greater than 1000 miles ? fly : drive
```

Here's how that example might look in ActionScript:

```
distance = 2000;
howtoGo = distance > 1000 ? "fly" : "drive";
trace(howToGo); // fly
```

The third line is the equivalent of

```
if (distance > 1000) {
    howtoGo = "fly"
} else {
    howtoGo = "drive"
}
```

You can use functions in the second and third parts, too, thus using the conditional operator to control program flow. For instance:

```
function fly() {
    trace("fly");
}
function drive() {
    trace("drive");
}
miles = 2000;
miles > 1000 ? fly() : drive(); // displays "fly"
```

You can check multiple conditions with nested conditional operators. For instance, suppose you want to fly if the distance is more than 1,000 miles, walk if it's 3 miles or less, and drive otherwise. In that case, you would add a walk() function to the previous program:

```
function walk() {
    trace("walk");
}
```

Then you can do all this in a single line of code:

```
Ask "Is the distance greater than 1000 miles?"
If yes, fly.
If no, ask, "Is the distance greater than 3 miles?"
If yes, drive.
In no, walk.
```

In the following example, the distance is not greater than 3 miles, so the `walk()` function is executed:

```
miles = 3;
miles > 1000 ? fly() : miles > 3 ? drive() : walk(); // displays "walk"
```

In this case, the conditional operator is faster and produces a smaller SWF than `if`/`else`, but not by much.

In the following instance, `if-else` would be slightly lighter and faster, but the conditional operator is more readable:

```
(day == "Monday")    ? trace("is fair of face")  :
(day == "Tuesday")   ? trace("is full of grace") :
(day == "Wednesday") ? trace("is full of woe")   :
(day == "Thursday")  ?  trace("has far to go")   :
(day == "Friday")    ? trace("is loving and giving")  :
(day == "Saturday")  ? trace("works hard for a living"):
(day == "Sunday")    ? trace("is bonny and blithe and good and gay.") : null;
```

Notice the use of `null` as the final option. The conditional operator must always return something, so the choice is between using something like `null` or choosing one of the `trace` actions as a default. For instance, to make the final `trace` the default, change the last line to look like this:

```
trace("is bonny and blithe and good and gay.");
```

Using the final `trace` as a default implies that the variable `day` will always have a valid day of the week as a value. Thus, if it isn't `"Monday"` through `"Saturday"`, it must be `"Sunday"`.

⇨ *Compare the conditional operator's functionality with the identical functionality implemented using if-else, in the section "Making Decisions Using Conditionals and switch," page 256 (Chapter 14, "Working with Data: Using Statements").*

13

THE COMMA OPERATOR

The comma operator is used primarily to declare two or more variables in a single statement, as in this example:

```
var x=1, y=2, z=3;
```

The preceding is equivalent to

```
var x=1;
var y=2;
var z=3;
```

This operator can come in handy when you want to initialize two or more index variables in a `for` loop, as in this example:

```
for (i = 0, j = 0,  k = 0; i < 50;   i++, j -= i, k--) {
    trace(i+" "+j+" "+k);
}
```

The output is as follows:

```
0 0 -10
1 -1 -11
2 -3 -12
3 -6 -13
. . .
```

> *For more details about the for loop, see "The for Statement," page 261 (Chapter 14, "Working with Data: Using Statements").*

The return value of the comma operator, which is the resolved value of the final operand, isn't used in either of the preceding cases. In general, the return value of the comma operator is not useful. For instance, it is useless (though not illegal) to have several comma-separated terms in the middle (test) portion when you're setting up a `for` loop because only the final term would be evaluated. For instance, the following does exactly the same thing as the previous `for` loop because `j >= k, k < i` is ignored and only `i < 50` is tested on each loop:

```
for (i = 0, j = 0,  k = -10; j >= k, k < i, i < 50;   i++, j -= i, k--) {
    trace(i+" "+j+" "+k);
}
```

NAMED OPERATORS

A number of operators are referred to by names instead of symbols. They include `new`, `typeof`, `instanceof`, `delete`, and `void`.

The `new` Operator

You use the `new` operator with a constructor function to create a datum of the `object` or `array` datatype. For instance, in the following examples, the constructor functions are `Object()`, `Array()`, and `Date()`:

```
myObj = new Object();
myArray = new Array();
myDate = new Date();
```

> *The new operator is introduced in "Modeling Problem Domains Using Objects," page 200 (Chapter 12, "Managing Variables, Data, and Datatypes"). The new operator is discussed further under "Functions as Classes: Constructor Functions," page 279 (Chapter 15, "Combining Statements into Functions").*

The `typeof` Operator

The `typeof` operator returns a string indicating the datatype of an operand. Its format is

`typeof` *expression*

where *expression* is any legal expression.

➡ *The typeof operator is introduced and used extensively in Chapter 12, "Managing Variables, Data, and Datatypes," page 187.*

The `instanceof` Operator

The `instanceof` operator determines whether an object belongs to a class. Its format is as follows:

object `instanceof` *class*

In ActionScript, a class is embodied in a constructor function. Therefore, the `class` operand on the right should be the name of a constructor function. The `instanceof` operator follows the inheritance chain, to determine whether the object inherits from the class. In the following example, for instance, a is an instance of `Object` because a is an array, which is an object, and all objects inherit from `Object`. On the other hand, a is not an instance of _global because _global is not a constructor function.

```
a = new Array();
trace(a instanceof Array); // true
trace(a instanceof Object); // true - this is true for all objects
trace(a instanceof _global); // false - _global is not a constructor function
```

In the following example, 6 is not an instance of Number because 6 is a primitive datum, not an object. On the other hand, n is an object whose value is 6, and n is an instance of Number.

```
trace(6 instanceof Number); // false -  6 is not an object
n = new Number(6);
trace(n instanceof Number); // true
```

The `delete` Operator

The `delete` operator attempts to delete a variable, object (including a function), object property, array, or array element. The format is simply

`delete` *identifier*

Here's an example of its use:

```
myVar = "three"; // create a variable
delete myVar; // remove it
```

The `delete` operator returns `true` or `false`, depending on whether the deletion was successful. In the following example, `delete` returns `false` when you try to delete a property a second time:

```
myObj = {a : "one", b : "two"} // create an object
trace(delete myObj.a); // true
trace(delete myObj.a); // false - it's already gone
```

13

The void **Operator**

I have not been able to find any instances of anyone actually using the ActionScript void operator. It's just there for ECMA compatibility, apparently. Its format is

```
void(expression)
```

It causes the interpreter to throw away the results of the expression and return undefined.

The Flash ActionScript Dictionary says that the void operator "is often used in comparisons using the == operator to test for undefined values." I can't find any real-life examples; however, the following does work:

```
a = undefined;
b = 1;
trace(void(b) == a); // true
```

Still, using the following approach is easier:

```
a = undefined;
trace(undefined == a); // true
```

OTHER OPERATORS

The rest of the operators were introduced in Chapters 11 and 12, and will be demonstrated extensively in coming chapters. I mention them here for completeness and as a quick reference.

Object Property Access: The Dot Operator

The dot (.) operator indicates a property of an object or a nested movie clip. For instance, you set a property of an object to a value as follows:

```
myObject.myProperty = "myValue"; // set a property to a string value
```

Here, you set a variable, clipVar, equal to a movie clip instance name:

```
clipVar = myClipParent.myClipChild; // set a variable to a movie clip name
```

The dot operator is introduced in "Modeling Problem Domains Using Objects," page 200 (Chapter 12, "Managing Variables, Data, and Datatypes"). The dot operator is used extensively in Chapter 19, "Using the Built-in Core Objects," page 393, and Chapter 21, "Packaging Data and Functions Using Custom Objects," page 489.

The Array-Element/Object Property Operator

Square brackets can indicate an element of an array or a property of an object. For instance, the following is an array element:

```
months[0] = "January";
```

⇨ *For more details on arrays, see Chapter 19, "Using the Built-in Core Objects," page 393.*

The following is an object property:

```
computer["display"] = "SVGA";
```

⇨ *For more information on objects, see Chapter 19, "Using the Built-in Core Objects," page 393, and Chapter 21, "Packaging Data and Functions Using Custom Objects," page 489.*

The Parentheses/Function Call Operator

In addition to using parentheses for grouping other operators, you can use them as the function call operator, to invoke a function.

⇨ *For more information on the use of parentheses for grouping operators, see "Understanding Precedence, Associativity, and Operator Grouping," earlier in this chapter, page 219.*

The format for *calling*, or invoking, a function is

```
identifier(list)
```

where `identifier` is the name of the function and `list` is an optional comma-separated list of *arguments*, or parameters, passed to the function. The operator here is the parentheses that enclose the arguments.

⇨ *For rules for forming identifiers, see "Rules for Naming Variables (and Other Things)," page 193 (Chapter 12, "Managing Variables, Data, and Datatypes").*

⇨ *Declaring or creating functions and retrieving values from functions using the return statement are discussed in Chapter 15, "Combining Statements into Functions," page 267.*

⇨ *For more information on the return statement, see "Forming Standalone Statements," page 252 (Chapter 14, "Working with Data: Using Statements").*

⇨ *For more details on functions, see Chapter 15, "Combining Statements into Functions," page 267.*

TROUBLESHOOTING

13

The operands are not equal, so why do they test equal?

One of the most common mistakes in ActionScript is using the assignment operator (=) when you should use the equality operator (==). The assignment operator sets a variable, array element, or object property equal to a value. The equality operator tests whether two expressions are equal. Your familiarity with standard arithmetic notation works against you here. Too often, you write `if (x = 10)`, a statement that the ActionScript interpreter sees as always true, when you mean `if (x == 10)`, a statement that is true only when x equals 10.

Can using all 32 bits for bitwise operations cause problems?

Yes! It is better not to use the most significant bit (MSB)—the largest bit, on the far left—in 32-bit binary numbers for bitwise operations. Computers use this bit to represent negative numbers internally (in "twos complement" notation), and using this bit may give incorrect results, particularly on Macintoshes.

FLASH AT WORK: APPLYING BITWISE OPERATORS TO TIC-TAC-TOE

Bitwise operators can make a difference in speed in a tic-tac-toe game because they can be used for repeated operations.

At the very least, you need to check once for each of the winning patterns each time a player makes a move, to determine whether the player has just created a winning pattern. If you want the computer to play an intelligent game, you also need to determine whether the player will be able to create one of these patterns in the next move. Bitwise operators allow you to make these calculations very quickly.

Using nine bits to represent the nine squares of a tic-tac-toe board, you can use a single integer to record where all the xs have been placed. Similarly, a single integer records the positions of all the os. When you want to compare these positions to winning patterns (to check whether one of the players has won), a single integer can represent each winning pattern, as well.

Note that you would use standard ActionScript 32-bit binary integers, but you would actually use only the first nine bits because you don't need the others.

For instance, here are the winning patterns in tic-tac-toe, shown by the letter *X*:

XXX	OOO	OOO	XOO	OXO	OOX	XOO	OOX
OOO	XXX	OOO	XOO	OXO	OOX	OXO	OXO
OOO	OOO	XXX	XOO	OXO	OOX	OOX	XOO

You treat each position as a bit, starting in the upper-left corner with 0. So bits 0 through 8 correspond to the tic-tac-toe board like this:

```
012
345
678
```

Table 13.5 shows the winning positions as decimal (base 10), binary (base 2), and octal (base 8) numbers. Note how each octal digit represents three binary digits. Each group of three binary digits, in turn, is like a row of the tic-tac-toe board.

Table 13.5   Winning Tic-Tac-Toe Positions

Decimal	Binary	Octal
7	000 000 111	7
56	000 111 000	70
448	111 000 000	700
73	001 001 001	111
146	010 010 010	222
292	100 100 100	444
84	001 010 100	124
273	100 010 001	421

Listing 13.1, sample movie tictactoe.fla (a simplification of Ralf Bokelberg's oxo.fla on the CD), shows how you can use an array of numbers representing these eight winning patterns with bitwise opera-tors. In sample movie tictactoe.fla, the computer plays both sides (x and o), randomly choosing free squares. In oxo.fla, the computer plays one side and the user plays the other, and the computer looks ahead and blocks the player if the player can win in the next turn.

Listing 13.1   Sample movie tictactoe.fla

```
// abridged and adapted from oxo by Ralf Bokelberg, www.QLOD.com (c) 2002

onClipEvent(load) {
    // an array of squares
    squares = new Array(_root.s0, _root.s1, _root.s2,
        _root.s3, _root.s4, _root.s5,
        _root.s6, _root.s7, _root.s8);
    // find a free square, random
    function getFreeSquare() {
        // random start from 0 to 8 inclusive
        do {
            i = Math.random();
        } while (i == 1); // if the random value is 1, don't use it
        i = Math.floor(i * 9);
        // if the space is free, take it
        // if not, take the next free one
        if (squares[i] != null) return i; // it's available
        else {
          for(var j = 0 ; j < 9; j++){
                i++;
                if (i==9) i = 0; // at top square? start from bottom
                if (squares[i] != null) return i; // it's available
            }
        }
    }
```

13

Listing 13.1 Continued

```
// the o player makes a move
function omove(num) {
    squares[num].attachMovie("o","o",(num*2)+20);
    o |= Math.pow ( 2, num );
    squares[num] = null;
}
// the x player makes a move
function xmove(num) {
    squares[num].attachMovie("x","x",num+1);
    x |= Math.pow ( 2, num );
    squares[num] = null;
}
// determine whose move it is
var whoseMove = true;
function move(num) {
    if (whoseMove) xmove(num);
    else omove(num);
    whoseMove = !whoseMove;
}
// array of winning patterns in octal notation
 wins = new Array( parseInt("0111"),
     parseInt("0222"),
     parseInt("0444"),
     parseInt("07"),
     parseInt("070"),
     parseInt("0700"),
     parseInt("0124"),
     parseInt("0421"));
// o holds positions of o
    var o = 0;
// x holds positions of x
    var x = 0;
// check to see if anybody has won
 function checkResult(){
    for(var i = 0;i < 8; i++){
        if((o & wins[i]) == wins[i]){
            trace(" o wins :"+o);
            j = 8; // stop the game
            return;
        }
         if((x & wins[i]) == wins[i]){
            trace("x wins :"+x);
            j = 8; // stop the game
            return;
        }
    }
}
```

```
    var j = -1;
}

onClipEvent(enterFrame) {
    j++; // count the moves
     if (j < 9) { // nine moves max
        num = getFreeSquare(); // find a free square
        move(num); // make a move
        checkResult(); // check for a winner
    }
}
```

WORKING WITH DATA: USING STATEMENTS

FORMING STANDALONE STATEMENTS AND CONTROL BLOCKS

A *statement* is the "sentence" of coding; that is, it is the smallest unit of code that communicates a complete command to the ActionScript interpreter (the software that reads and executes ActionScript). Therefore, to accomplish anything in a movie, you must use a statement.

Syntactically, there are two basic kinds of statements: standalone statements and control blocks. A control block is a statement that can contain other statements.

There are two kinds of control blocks: looping (or *iterative*) and non-looping. The looping control blocks (`while`, `do-while`, `for`, and `for-in`) repeat the statements they contain until a condition is met. The non-looping control blocks (`if-else`, `ifFrameLoaded`, and `with`) execute the statements they contain just once.

Forming Standalone Statements

A standalone statement consists of

- An optional keyword, one of a number of reserved words that ActionScript has earmarked for its own use
- Zero or more expressions and operators
- A semicolon

The simplest standalone statement is the *empty* statement, which consists of just a semicolon:

```
;
```

By itself, the empty statement doesn't do anything. However, the *evaluate* action, available when you're in Normal mode in the Actions panel, creates an empty statement as a placeholder, into which you can enter an expression to be evaluated, including a custom function to be called.

Theoretically, a standalone statement can consist of just an expression and a semicolon, although such a statement doesn't accomplish anything:

```
"hi"; // doesn't do anything
```

To be useful, a statement must change something (or invoke a function that changes something). Often, an operator causes the change, as when you set a variable using the assignment operator:

```
heSays = "hi";
```

Just as frequently, a keyword defines the action to take. A standalone keyword-based statement starts with a single keyword and ends with a semicolon. In two cases, `break` and `continue`, that's all there is to the statement:

```
break;
continue;
```

The `break` statement breaks out of (cancels) the currently looping control block, whereas the `continue` statement restarts the currently looping control block.

In the case of the `call` statement, which executes the script on a frame, the keyword is followed by a parenthesized expression that resolves to the frame number. For instance, in this example the expression just represents the number literally:

```
call(4);
```

The `return` statement, which exits a function, may optionally be followed by an expression. The interpreter resolves the expression to a value, which the function returns. Thus, the first of the following statements simply exits a function. The second exits the function and returns the value myValue.

```
return;
return myValue;
```

The `set` statement, which assigns a value to a variable, is followed by a parenthesized pair of comma-separated parameters: the variable name and an expression. The interpreter resolves the expression to a value and assigns that value to the variable. For instance, this statement assigns the value 6 to the variable myNumber:

```
set(myNumber, 6);
```

➩ *For more information on the set statement, see "Assigning Values to Variables," page 188 (Chapter 12, "Managing Variables, Data, and Datatypes").*

In the case of the `var` statement, which declares and optionally initializes a variable, the keyword is followed by the variable name, and optionally by the assignment operator and an initial value for the variable. Thus, the first statement here declares a variable without initializing it. The second declares it and initializes it.

```
var myVar;
var myVar = myValue;
```

➩ *For more details on the var statement, see Chapter 15, "Combining Statements into Functions," page 267.*

Combining Statements into Control Blocks

A typical control block consists of

- A keyword

- A parenthesized control construct

- A body consisting of zero or more statements

A typical control block is shown in the following example:

```
if (allDone) quit;
```

In the preceding statement, `if` is the keyword, `(allDone)` is the control construct, and `quit;` is the body. The *keyword* defines the type of statement, the *control construct* determines under what conditions the body is executed, and the *body* determines what actions the control block performs.

14

If two or more statements appear in the body, they must be enclosed in curly braces. Here are the four basic formats for a control block:

Format 1:

```
keyword ( expression ) statement;
```

Format 2:

```
keyword ( expression ) {
    statement;
}
```

Format 3:

```
keyword ( expression ) {statement1; statement2;}
```

Format 4:

```
keyword ( expression ) {
    statement1;
    statement2;
}
```

Statement1 and *Statement2* represent a list of any length.

The third and fourth formats accomplish exactly the same thing, but the fourth is easier to read and is the standard multi-statement format. The choice between the first and second formats is one of taste. This book uses the fourth format when defining formats for control blocks.

The do-while, for-in, and if-else statements contain two keywords. In a do-while or if-else statement, the second keyword follows the body. In the case of for-in, the second keyword is in the control construct.

Table 14.1, which lists keywords used in statements, shows each of these formats.

The keyword and the control construct together make up the *header* of the control block.

The following example displays numbers from 0 to 49:

```
for (i = 0; i < 50; i++) {
    trace(i);
}
```

Here, for is the keyword, (i = 0; i < 50; i++) is the control construct, and trace(i); is the single statement in the body. Therefore, for (i = 0; i < 50; i++) is the header.

Table 14.1 The ActionScript Statement Keywords

Keyword(s)	Format	Description	Flow Control	Chapter
break	break;	Cancel the current loop	loop	14
call	call(frame)	Execute the script on another frame	call	14
continue	continue;	Restart the current loop	loop	14

Keyword(s)	Format	Description	Flow Control	Chapter
do-while	do { *statements* } while (*expression*)	Repeat statements while *expression* is true	loop	14
none (empty statement)	;	Hold a place for a statement in Normal mode	default	14
for	for (*init*; *test*; *next*) { *statements* }	Repeat statements while *test* is false	loop	14
for-in	for (*property in object*) { *statements* }	Enumerate properties of *object*	loop	19, 20, 21
function	function *name* (*parameters*) { *statements*}	Declare a function	call	15
if/else – if/else	if (*condition1*) { *statements* } else if (*condition2*) { *statements* } else { *statements* }	Execute statements based on one or more conditions	conditional	14
ifFrameLoaded	ifFrameLoaded (*frame*) { *statements*}	Execute statements if *frame* has been loaded	conditional	14
return	return;return *expression*;	Exit a function Return a value from a function	call	15
set	set (*variable, value*)	Assign a *value* to a dynamically named *variable*	default	12, 14
switch/case/ default	switch(*expression*) {case *value* : *block* default : *block*}	Execute statement(s) starting with *block* where *value* matches *expression* (if no match, execute default)	conditional	14
var	var *variableName*; var *variableName* = *expression*;	Declare a variable, optionally assigning a value	default	15
while	while (*expression*) { *statements* }	Repeat statements while *expression* is true	loop	14
with	with (*objectName*) { *statements* }	Execute statements in the context of a given object	loop	19, 20, 21

UNDERSTANDING PROGRAM FLOW CONTROL

By default, the ActionScript interpreter executes statements sequentially, from top to bottom. However, most statements can change the default program flow. The exceptions are the empty statement, set, and var, which don't affect program flow.

The three basic types of flow control in ActionScript are *conditional*, *loop*, and *call*. *Conditional* and *loop* flow control are the focus of the following pages.

The *call* paradigm of flow control is represented by the `call` and `function` statements. In this paradigm, the statement initiates a call that interrupts the interpreter's sequential processing. The interpreter executes a block of code elsewhere in the program and then returns and continues processing at the point where it left off.

⇨ *The call statement is covered under "Forming Standalone Statements," earlier in this chapter, page 252.*

⇨ *Functions are introduced in Chapter 11, "Getting Started with ActionScript," page 169. They are dealt with in depth in Chapter 15, "Combining Statements into Functions," page 267.*

MAKING DECISIONS USING CONDITIONALS AND SWITCH

When the ActionScript interpreter encounters a conditional statement, it evaluates a condition in the control structure and, if the condition is true, executes the statements in the body.

There are two types of conditional statements: `if-else` and `ifFrameLoaded`. `if-else` can be broken down into simple `if` statements and `if-else` statements.

The `if` Statement

The simplest conditional is an `if` statement. The syntax is straightforward:

```
if (expression) {
    statement1;
    statement2;
}
```

The interpreter converts *expression* to a Boolean. If *expression* resolves to `true`, the statements in the body are executed. Otherwise, they are not executed.

⇨ *The rules for converting expressions to Booleans are given in Table 12.4, page 206.*

Note that any array, object, or movie clip evaluates to `true`. Therefore, you can use an `if` statement to test for the existence (or nonexistence) of an array, object, or movie clip. For instance:

```
// if movie clip does not exist, handle error condition
if (!myClip) {
    // code to handle error condition goes here
}
// if array exists, set variable len to length of array
if (myArray) {
    len = myArray.length;
}
```

The `if-else` **Statement**

An `if-else` statement is actually two separate but related statements: An `if` statement tells the interpreter what to do if the expression is true, and an `else` statement tells the interpreter what to do if the expression is false. For instance, in the following example, if the array `myArray` already exists, the program sets variable `len` to the length of the array. If the array does not exist, the program creates it first and then sets the variable.

```
if (myArray) {
    len = myArray.length;
} else {
    myArray = new Array();
    len = myArray.length;
}
```

> *To see a number of if-else statements, refer to "Using Logical (Boolean) Operators," page 236 (Chapter 13, "Using Operators"). You'll also find an important note about comments and if-else statements in the "Troubleshooting" section at the end of Chapter 11, "Getting Started with ActionScript," page 183.*

Nesting Conditionals

Conditionals can be nested to any desired depth, allowing you to test for a number of different conditions sequentially. For instance:

```
if (day == "Monday") {
    trace("is fair of face");
} else if (day == "Tuesday") {
    trace("is full of grace");
} else if (day == "Wednesday") {
    trace("is full of woe");
}
```

To make the last `trace` action a default, substitute the following for the last three lines:

```
} else trace("is full of woe");
```

> *The same type of nesting can be achieved using the conditional operator. See "The Conditional Operator," page 240 (Chapter 13, "Using Operators").*

The `switch/case` **Statement**

In the previous example, each conditional statement uses the variable `day` in an equality test. This type of nested conditional logic can also be expressed using a `switch` statement, like this:

```
switch (day) {
    case "Monday":
        trace("is fair of face");
```

14

```
        break
case  "Tuesday":
        trace("is full of grace");
        break
case  "Wednesday":
        trace("is full of woe");
}
```

The interpreter tests the same expression (in this case, the variable day) against each of a series of expressions (in this case, the string literals "Monday", "Tuesday", and "Wednesday"). When it finds a match, it starts executing statements, beginning with the statement following the matched value.

If the interpreter does not find a match, it looks for a default statement. For instance, to make the last trace action the default, substitute the following for the last three lines:

```
default:
        trace("is full of woe");
}
```

The default statement does not have to be the last statement in the switch body, though it almost always is.

Unlike the nested conditionals in the previous section, the switch statement uses strict equality (===) in comparing values.

The switch statement is a notational convenience and does *not* execute faster than nested conditionals. In the byte code of the SWF, they both look exactly the same. This allows movies using the switch statement to be backward compatible to Macromedia Flash 4. However, a Flash 4 SWF uses equality (==), whereas Flash 5 and Flash MX use strict equality (===). This is inevitable because Flash 4 can't determine the datatype. Checking the datatype is the chief defining feature of strict equality.

➪ *For more details on strict equality, see Chapter 13, "Using Operators," page 215.*

Both the test value (day) and the case values ("Monday", "Tuesday", and "Wednesday") can be any valid expressions. This means they could be objects, arrays, functions, or complex mathematical formulas, as long as each one resolves to a single value. However, the values are usually just string or numeric literals.

Note the break statement in each case. Each case statement specifies a beginning point for code execution. It does *not* specify any ending point. The break statements cause the interpreter to exit the switch statement after executing the statements associated with a single case. If multiple cases are executing one after another, you may have omitted break statements.

➪ *If a case statement isn't executing as expected, see the "Troubleshooting" section at the end of this chapter, page 262.*

The `ifFrameLoaded` Statement

The `ifFrameLoaded` statement is deprecated (supported for now but not forever), but it is still popular. The `ifFrameLoaded` statement offers compatibility with Flash 3. The recommended substitute, `_framesLoaded`, requires at least Flash 4.

The `ifFrameLoaded` statement is a special case of the `if` statement, which checks whether a specific frame (optionally in a specific scene) has loaded yet. It is used to make preloaders for movie clips.

For instance, if you put the following code on the first two frames of a movie clip, it will loop through the first two frames until frame 60 has loaded. Then it will start playing from frame 5.

```
//frame1:
ifFrameLoaded (60) {
    gotoAndPlay (5);
}
//frame2:
gotoAndPlay (1);
```

The recommended substitute for `ifFrameLoaded (60)` is simply

```
if (_framesLoaded == 60)
```

With `ifFrameLoaded`, you can also include a scene name:

```
ifFrameLoaded ("intro", 60) {
```

One limitation of `ifFrameLoaded` is that it does not support an `else` statement (whereas `_framesLoaded` does). The two-frame structure essentially implements an `else` using a two-frame loop.

REPEATING ACTIONS USING LOOPS

The loop statements, `while`, `do-while`, `for`, and `for-in`, are used to perform repetitive actions. Each repeatedly evaluates a condition and uses the result of the evaluation to decide whether to continue looping through the body. For example, a loop could be used to repetitively check whether a certain amount of time has elapsed, or to repetitively duplicate a movie clip until a certain number of clips have been created.

The four loop statements are closely related. The `while` and `for` statements are basically two ways of doing the same thing: Which you use is often a matter of taste. The Flash compiler translates both into `while` loops in the SWF. And `do-while` is just a minor variation of `while`.

The `while` Statement

The `while` statement is the basic statement for performing repetitive actions. The format for the `while` statement is

```
while ( expression ) {
    statement1;
```

14

```
    statement2;
    statement3;
}
```

The interpreter loops through the statements as long as the expression is true, unless it encounters a break statement, in which case it exits the loop. For instance, the following while loop puts a half-second (500 millisecond) delay into the program. It is based on the fact that elapsed time is the current time minus the initial time:

```
initialTime = getTimer();
while (elapsedTime < 500) {
    (elapsedTime = getTimer() - initialTime);
}
```

The following is a common application of while, making multiple duplicates of a movie clip, giving each one a name and putting it on its own level. This example creates nine duplicates of myClip: myClip1 on level 1, myClip2 on level 2, and so on up to myClip9:

```
var i = 1;
while (i < 10) {
    duplicateMovieClip("myClip", "myClip"+i, i);
    i++;
}
```

This example also illustrates a very common structure for while loops: A counter (i) is initialized before the while loop and incremented within the loop. The condition becomes false when the counter reaches a certain number.

while loops are often used to access arrays. The following program takes elements from the menu array and puts them into the myOrder array, until it comes to the "pie" element, at which point it stops.

```
menu = ["potatoes", "steak", "peas", "salad", "pie", "ice cream"];
myOrder = []; // an empty array to start
i = 0; // initialize counter
while (menu[i] != "pie") {
    myOrder[i] = menu[i];
    i++; // increment counter
}
trace(menu); // potatoes,steak,peas,salad,pie,ice cream
trace(myOrder); // potatoes,steak,peas,salad
```

The do-while Statement

The body of a while loop will not execute even once if the condition is false from the beginning. To make the while loop execute at least once, use the do-while statement.

For example, the following code accomplishes the same task as the previous while loop, except that it will start running through the loop even if "pie" is the first item in the menu array, menu[0] .

```
// BAD !!! danger of infinite loop
do {
```

```
    myOrder[i] = menu[i];
    i++;
} while (menu[i] != "pie");
```

However, note the danger here! If "pie" is the first element in the menu array, menu[0], the do-while loop will put "pie" into myOrder[0]. Then it will increment i to 1 and check whether menu[1] equals "pie". It doesn't, so the condition (menu[i] != "pie") is true. As i increments, the condition will continue to be true forever, and the interpreter will go into an *infinite loop*.

⇨ *For more details on infinite loops, see "Some Simple Examples of Recursion," page 278 (Chapter 15, "Combining Statements into Functions").*

⇨ *Think you might have run into an infinite loop in an enterFrame clip handler? See "Troubleshooting" later in this chapter, page 262.*

The for Statement

Most while loops have a counter that is initialized and updated. The for statement makes initialization and updating part of the parenthesized control structure. The format of the for statement is as follows:

```
for (initialization; condition; update) {
    statement1;
    statement2;
    statement3;
}
```

For instance, the following is the while loop for duplicating movies, shown previously, put into the form of a for loop:

```
for (var i = 1; i < 10; i++) {
    duplicateMovieClip("myClip", "myClip"+i, i);
}
```

The two loops are not just functionally the same: The resulting code in the SWF is identical for each of them. Therefore, whether you use the while loop or the for loop is a matter of taste. The for loop is more concise. Its structure also reminds you to include the increment. Leaving the increment out of a while loop is a common error that leads to an infinite loop. On the other hand, the while loop allows you to comment the initialization, condition, and increment expressions separately.

Here's the previous array access example converted into a for loop:

```
for (i = 0; menu[i] != "pie"; i++) {
    myOrder[i] = menu[i];
}
```

⇨ *A for statement can have multiple counters. See "The Comma Operator," page 241 (Chapter 13, "Using Operators").*

14

The `for-in` Statement

The `for-in` statement enumerates or lists the properties of an object. It can be extremely useful for investigating existing objects that you did not define, such as built-in objects or objects associated with components. Its format is as follows:

```
for (variable in objectName) {
    statement1;
    statement2;
}
```

Here is a simple example of a `for-in` loop:

```
myObj = {prop1 : "a", prop2 : "b", prop3 : "c"}
for (prop in myObj) {
    trace(prop+" : "+myObj[prop]);
}

/*
output:
prop1 : a
prop2 : b
prop3 : c
*/
```

The `for-in` statement does not state a condition explicitly. However, the implied condition is, "Is there another property in the given object?" If there is, the interpreter executes the body of the `for-in` statement in the context of that property.

Note that the variable in the control structure contains the *name* of the property (such as `prop1`), not the value of the property (such as `"a"`). You can easily access the value when you have the name. For instance:

```
trace(myObj.prop1); // a
```

`myObj["prop1"]` is another way of expressing `myObj.prop1`. In the example, `myObj[prop]` is equivalent first to `myObj["prop1"]`, then to `myObj["prop2"]`, and finally to `myObj["prop3"]`.

⇨ *See Chapter 19, "Using the Built-in Core Objects," page 393, for more examples using the for-in statement.*

TROUBLESHOOTING

Why is my switch statement failing to execute any case statement?

Remember, `switch` comparisons use strict equality. Are you sure your test value and `case` value are of the same datatype? If you're using a variable as a test value, an error may have caused your test value to be `undefined`. As a debugging measure, use the `typeof` operator to confirm the datatype of your test value just prior to the `switch` statement.

Help! I'm going into an infinite loop in an `enterFrame` *event handler!*

Here's a common mistake that leads to an infinite loop in a movie clip "enter frame" event handler. The enter frame event handler happens once each frame, so you can put a counter in it, and it will automatically get updated each frame. For instance:

```
onClipEvent(enterFrame) {
    frameCounter++;
    // do things
}
```

So far, so good.

Now, you decide to use that counter in a `while` loop, like this:

```
onClipEvent(enterFrame) {
    frameCounter++;
    while (frameCounter < 10) {
        // INFINITE LOOP !!!
    }
}
```

The result is an infinite loop. The interpreter dives into the `while` loop and never comes out because the counter is never updated inside the loop. The moral: The `while` loop needs its own counter, updated *inside* the loop.

FLASH AT WORK: USING A FOR LOOP TO GENERATE A LIST

Sample movie dropdownmenu.fla on the CD generates a drop-down menu using a SQL database to provide the menu items. The menu items in this case happen to be the names of the 50 states plus the District of Columbia.

The drop-down menu is used during the registration process on `http://www.asexpressedbyyou.com`.

The drop-down menu is just one small part of the site, and I'm going to look at only one small part of the drop-down menu here: the `generateList()` function, the heart of which is a `for` loop. Dropdownmenu.fla on the CD is fully functional, however, generating a Flash 5–compatible drop-down menu. The CD also contains sqllookup.php, which is required for accessing the SQL database. It is written in PHP 4.0.6, a server-side scripting language. (See `http://www.php.com` for more details on PHP.)

The drop-down menu displays state names, 10 names at a time. The `generateList()` function goes through the elements in an array (the `items` array), 10 elements at a time.

For a description of this site, see "one part gin, two parts branding: Bacardi USA's Flash application generates buzz," by Michael Hurwicz, *New Architect* magazine, March 2002 (`http://www.newarchitectmag.com/documents/s=2286/na0202cs1/index.html`).

14

Each element contains a reference to an object. Each object has two properties: id is an integer that uniquely identifies the object; name is the name of the state in a string.

Each selection on the drop-down menu is a movie clip. There are 10 such clips, named entity0, entity1, and so on, up to entity9. The clips are manually laid out on the Timeline of the menu component, starting at frame 12. To see this, double-click the menu component in the Movie Explorer to get to the menu component's Timeline.

On each iteration of the for loop, the generateList() function takes one object in the items array and transfers the values in the object properties into the text and id properties of one of the 10 entity movie clips. This happens in lines 13 and 14 of the following code listing. In addition, on line 12, the function makes the menu selection visible.

The second half of the program, starting with line 18, makes the up and down arrows (used to go up and down in the list) visible and invisible appropriately, depending on whether there are more names to display before or after the currently displayed batch of 10 names.

```
// used by permission of Mass Transmit (http://www.masstransmit.com)
 1: var maxdisplay = 10;
 2: function generateList(pagenum) {
 3:   var startnum = maxdisplay * pagenum;
 4:   for(i = startnum; i < startnum + maxdisplay; i++) {
 5:     var entity = eval("entity" + (i % maxdisplay));
 6:     var entityObj = items[i];
 7:
 8:     if (i >= items.length) {
 9:       entity._visible = false;
10:     }
11:     else {
12:       entity._visible = true;
13:       entity.text = entityObj.name;
14:       entity.id = entityObj.id;
15:     }
16:   } // end for loop
17:
18:   if (pagenum == 0) {  // set up arrow
19:     uparrow._visible = false;
20:   }
21:   else {
22:     uparrow._visible = true;
23:   }
24:
25:   if ((startnum + maxdisplay) >= items.length) {  // set down arrow
26:     dnarrow._visible = false;
27:   }
28:   else {
29:     dnarrow._visible = true;
30:   }
31:
32: }
```

For those wanting to delve deeper, there are some points that need to be made.

The PHP script residing at `http://www.masstransmit.com/demo/sqllookup.php` is hard-coded to return the list of states. It is not the same as the PHP file included on the CD. The PHP script on the CD can be used for any SQL `select` lookup initiated from a Flash file.

In your own application, you can change the SQL `select` statement in the clip parameters for the menu component. If you change the SQL `select` statement, you need to program the Flash application to accommodate the data it returns.

As is, the dropdownmenu.fla movie can be used with any SQL table that has an `id` field that is an integer and a `name` field that is a string. For instance, the `state` table in the mySQL database accessed via `http://www.masstransmit.com/demo` has the following fields:

```
state_id: integer
name: varchar(64)
```

If the fields are not named `id` and `name`, respectively, in the SQL table, you can use `as` in the `select` clause to rename the field to `id` or `name`. In the following example, `indexnumber` is renamed to `id`, and `stringvalue` is renamed to `name`:

```
select indexnumber as id, stringvalue as name from mytable;
```

In dropdownmenu.fla, the SQL statement is

```
select state_id as id, name from state where state_id > 0;
```

Click on the component on the Main Timeline and open the Properties panel to see the SQL statement.

There is not necessarily a database file residing on the Web server itself. When PHP performs a database lookup, it connects to the MySQL daemon running on the same server. PHP logs in, passes the SQL statement, and waits for the response from the MySQL daemon. The daemon connects to a mySQL database, which may be on the same server or a different one. The response is a database table laid out as a series of rows with a number of fields in each row. The PHP script takes this table, formats it appropriately for Flash, and sends the formatted data to the calling Flash application.

If you attempt to view the source of the PHP file (or any other PHP or CGI script) online, you won't see the actual code. Instead, you'll see only the text generated by the execution of the PHP or CGI script. In this case, the text begins

```
result=1&numitems=51&id0=1&name0=Alabama.....
```

You can actually take this text, save it on a Web server as a text file (for instance, `http://your.domain.com/states.txt`), and have the dropdownmenu.fla load the text file. You'll get the same list of states without a database lookup.

"One thing that is driving me up the wall with Flash: A Flash movie accessed via browser can only contact a CGI or PHP application that is in the same subdomain from which the Flash movie was served," notes Mark Lewis, the technical lead at Mass Transmit for developing the application. This same-subdomain limitation does not apply if you're running the Flash movie from your local hard disk without using a browser. In a browser, however, the Flash movie and the CGI or PHP script must be on the same server. This limitation, implemented by Macromedia for security reasons, is documented in the ActionScript Reference under `LoadVariables`.

14

"I wish Macromedia would have left the security up to the server-side programmer instead of enforcing it by default," Lewis said. "It actually is preventing us from developing some Flash applications."

To use dropdownmenu.fla on your own site in such a way that others can use it via a browser, you'll have to set up a MySQL database and edit the PHP script, inserting information similar to the following to permit access to your database:

```
$dbname = "genericdb";  // name of database to use
$dbuser = "username";  // username for database
$dbpass = "passwd";  // password for username
```

COMBINING STATEMENTS INTO FUNCTIONS

15

WRITING BETTER CODE WITH FUNCTIONS

A *function* is an entire block of code that you can call, or invoke, from anywhere in a program. Calling the function causes the code in the function to execute. You can call a function using its name, if it has one. You can also call functions via variables, array elements, or object properties. All these ways of referring to a function are much more concise than the function itself. Thus, functions effectively give you short, convenient "handles" for potentially complex behaviors.

Functions make it much easier to maintain programs. For instance, suppose you create a `displayError()` function to display error messages. If you ever want to change your error display function, you can make the change in only one place, in the `displayError()` function declaration. If you had instead repeated a block of code multiple times, you would have to edit each duplicate block individually.

Functions greatly improve both readability and reusability. They also make SWF files smaller by substituting a short function call for a longer repeated block of code. In addition, object-oriented programming (OOP) is founded on functions.

➡ *Functions, readability, reusability, and OOP are introduced in Chapter 11, "Getting Started with ActionScript," page 169.*

➡ *OOP is used extensively in Chapter 19, "Using the Built-in Core Objects," page 393, Chapter 20, "Using the Built-in Movie Objects," page 443, and Chapter 21, "Packaging Data and Functions Using Custom Objects," page 489.*

FUNCTION BASICS: CREATING FUNCTIONS

There are two basics in using a function: creating it and calling it.

You can create a function in one of two ways, depending on whether or not you want it to have a permanent name of its own:

- To create a function with its own permanent name, you *declare* the function.

- To create a function with no permanent name of its own, you create a *function literal*. A function literal must be stored in a variable, an array element, or an object property to be referenceable.

Declaring Functions

When you declare a function, you permanently associate a function name with a block of code. The basic format for declaring a function is

```
function identifier(list) {
    statement1;
    statement2;
}
```

where function is a keyword, *identifier* is the name of the function, *list* is an optional comma-separated list of *arguments* passed to the function, and *statement1* and *statement2* represent a series of ActionScript statements. The series can contain any number of statements.

⇨ *The name of the function must be a valid identifier, formed according to the rules set forth in "Rules for Naming Variables (and Other Things)," page 193 (Chapter 12, "Managing Variables, Data, and Datatypes").*

For instance, here is a declaration of a function with no arguments:

```
function displayError() {
    errorText = "Error!";
}
```

The idea is that this function updates a timeline variable that is displayed in a text field, notifying the user of an error.

Using Functions Without Names: Function Literals

A literal is an expression that represents a datum *literally*, as opposed to *abstractly*. It embodies the datum rather than naming it.

⇨ *You learned about numeric, string, array, and object literals in "Numbers and Strings Versus Numeric and String Literals," page 210 (Chapter 12, "Managing Variables, Data, and Datatypes").*

A function literal is a function that you write out without giving it a name. Here's an example of a function literal:

```
function () {
    errorText = "Error!";
}
```

It looks just a like a function declaration with no name.

As with other literals, you need to store the function literal somewhere as soon as it's created, or it will be lost. You can store function literals in variables, for instance. When you do so, it's correct syntax to include a semicolon after the curly brace to terminate the statement, although omitting the semicolon won't actually cause any problems. For instance:

```
displayError = function () {
    trace("Error!");
}; // this semicolon terminates the assignment statement
```

In addition, you can store function literals as properties of objects, providing the most common and convenient syntax for creating methods. In the following example, the functions are not assigned using assignment statements; therefore, no semicolons are used after the final curly braces of the two function bodies. However, there is still a semicolon at the very end to terminate the assignment statement:

```
myObj = {prop1 : function(){trace("prop1");} ,
         prop2 : function(){trace("prop2");} };
```

The following is another way of accomplishing the same thing. The first line creates an empty object. The second and third lines add properties to it. Each property refers to a function. In this example, the functions *are* assigned using assignment statements; therefore, semicolons are used after the final curly braces of the two function bodies:

```
myObj = {}; // create empty object
myObj.prop1 = function(){trace("prop1");};
myObj.prop2 = function(){trace("prop2");};
```

The following example assigns the same functions as properties of an array:

```
myArray = []; // create empty array
myArray[0] = function(){trace("prop1");};
myArray[1] = function(){trace("prop2");};
```

CALLING FUNCTIONS

Declaring a function doesn't actually make anything happen in the program. To do that, you need to *call* or run the function.

You call a function by using the function call operator, which is a pair of parentheses: ().

⇨ *The function call operator is covered in Chapter 13, "Using Operators," page 215.*

The syntax for calling a function is straightforward:

```
identifier(list);
```

Here, *identifier* is the name of the function, and *list* is an optional comma-separated list of arguments.

Many ActionScript "actions" are built-in functions that you can call without declaring them. For example, `nextFrame()` is a built-in function that sends the playhead to the next frame and stops it. If a function has no arguments, the parentheses are left empty. Adding a semicolon completes the statement, as shown here:

```
nextFrame();
```

You call custom functions (ones that you have created) in exactly the same way:

```
displayError(); // invokes displayError() function
```

The `displayError()` function is trivial and lacks the advantage of summarizing complex functionality under a simple descriptive name. In this case, `errorText = "Error!"` is nearly as concise and easy to read as `displayError()`. The main argument here for using `displayError()` is easier maintenance. If you use `errorText = "Error!"` directly throughout your program and later decide you want to implement a more complex error display method, you must change it everywhere it appears in the program.

You can also use the `call()` and `apply()` methods of the `Function` object to call any function.

⇨ *For more information on the call() and apply() methods, see "Using Function.apply() and Function.call()" later in this chapter, page 290.*

USING VAR TO CREATE LOCAL FUNCTION VARIABLES

Most functions contain one or more variables used only within the function. For instance, suppose you're writing a function, greet(), that returns one of three greetings ("good morning," "good afternoon," or "good evening") depending on the time of day. To determine the time in ActionScript, you create both a Date object (such as myDate) and a variable to hold the time (such as hours). You want to use myDate and hours only within the greet() function, but you may want to use those *names* again elsewhere in the program to refer to different objects or variables. Looking to the future, you also want to be able to drop this function into other programs and know that it will not cause a "name conflict" by using a name that is already in use in that program and therefore affect the items (such as variables or objects) in the other program with which it is now inadvertently sharing the name.

In a situation like this, you can use the var keyword to declare a *local* variable within a function. A local variable is available only within the function. A local variable does not change or refer to a variable of the same name outside the function. For instance:

```
function greet() {
    var hours;
    var myDate;
    // code to get the time and return greeting
    // all uses of hours and myDate remain local to the function
}
```

In the following example, the trace (myVar) statement displays the local variable, not the timeline variable of the same name:

```
myVar = "timeline";
function myFunc() {
    var myVar = "local";
    trace (myVar); // "local"
}
```

If you leave out the var keyword in the preceding example, the myVar = "local" statement will *refer to and change* the timeline variable of the same name! If you have a variable that you want to use just within a function, always declare it with var. Declaring it this way will prevent you from inadvertently changing a timeline variable of the same name.

⇨ *Arguments are also treated as local variables. Arguments are discussed later in this chapter, in the "Passing Information to Functions in Arguments" section, page 272.*

The `var` Keyword Doesn't Work Outside Functions

The `var` keyword has no effect outside a function. This includes event handlers! You can use `var` in an event handler, but it doesn't change anything. For instance, if you create a variable in a `load` event handler, as shown in the following example, it *can* be changed by statements on the movie clip timeline, in other event handlers, or on associated buttons:

```
onClipEvent(load) {
    var c = 10; // the "var" doesn't change anything
}
```

Accessing Timeline Variables Within a Function

If you have a function on a timeline, and you create a local variable within a function using `var`, you can refer to a timeline variable of the same name by using the `this` keyword. For example:

```
myVar = "timeline";
function myFunc() {
    var myVar = "local";
    trace  (myVar); // "local"
    trace (this.myVar); // "timeline"
}
```

PASSING INFORMATION TO FUNCTIONS IN ARGUMENTS

The `displayError()` function in the "Calling Functions" section earlier in this chapter can display only one message: `"Error!"`. Suppose you want to give the user more specific information about the error. You can do that, without creating a separate function for each error, by passing an *argument* to the `displayError()` function. In the following example, the argument is named `arg`. The `arg` parameter exists in memory only for the duration of the function. When the function terminates, `arg` disappears. It completed its task in changing the `errorText` variable.

```
function displayError(arg) {
    errorText = arg;
}
```

Then you can call the function for different errors like this:

```
displayError("Error: required field, cannot be left blank");
displayError("Error: password must be 8 or more characters");
displayError("Error: invalid zip code");
```

The `displayError()` function will display the argument that is passed to it. Adding arguments like this makes `displayError()` much more flexible and useful. In addition, it makes the function more reusable. For instance, you could easily plug in different error messages for a different program.

Note that declaring arguments does not limit the number of arguments that you can pass to a function. However, only arguments that are declared can be referred to within the function by name. You can access other arguments via the `arguments` object, as described in the section after next.

Passing Arguments by Value and by Reference

When a primitive datum is passed to a function as an argument, it is passed *by value*. That is, the interpreter allocates a new space in memory and copies the value of the datum into it. The function never sees the original datum, only the copy. If you change the copy within the function, the original is not affected.

The following example shows how you can pass a string primitive to a function and alter the passed value without affecting the original. In this case, the function adds two exclamation points to the passed value, but the original string doesn't change:

```
str = "string";
function myFunc(arg) {
        arg += " !!";
        return(arg);
}
result = myFunc(str);
trace (result); // displays "string !!"
trace(str); // displays "string" -- the original doesn't change
```

On the other hand, composite data types (objects, arrays, functions) are passed *by reference*. That is, the interpreter creates a pointer to the original item and passes it to the function. Any changes made within the function *do* affect the original. The following example shows how, when you pass an object to a function and change a property of the object, the original does change. In this example, the function changes a string property named `str` belonging to an object named `obj`. When the function changes the property's value to `"changed"`, it changes the value of the property in the original object:

```
function myFunc(arg) {
    arg.str = "changed"; // change the original value
}
obj = new Object();
obj.str = "property";
myFunc(obj);
trace(obj.str); // displays "changed"- object has new value
```

The `arguments` Object

When a function is invoked, it automatically gets a property named `arguments`, which is an array (or, in Macromedia Flash 5, an array-like object), with elements that can be accessed via numeric indices (starting with 0), and a `length` property specifying the number of array elements.

Each time a function is called, `arguments` is created and populated with all the arguments passed to the function. In addition, `arguments.length` is set to the number of arguments.

The `arguments` object is supported in both the Flash 6 and the Flash 5 Player. The two players don't handle the `arguments` object identically. For instance, in the Flash 5 Player, array methods such as `push()` and `pop()` do not work with the `arguments` property. In the Flash 6 Player, `arguments` is a real array with all the associated methods. In addition, the `arguments.callee` property shows up in a `for-in` loop in the Flash 5 Player, but not in the Flash 6 Player.

`arguments.caller` is available only in the Flash 6 Player, not the Flash 5 Player.

The `arguments` property is available only inside the function, while the function is executing. It can be referred to simply as `arguments`. Alternatively, it can be preceded by the function name—for instance, `myFunc.arguments`.

In the following function, `myFunc()`, the `trace(arg1)` statement and the `trace(arguments[0])` statement do exactly the same thing, namely, display the value of the first (and only) argument:

```
function myFunc(arg1) {
    trace(arg1); // displays "this is the argument"
    trace(arguments[0]); // displays "this is the argument"
}
myFunc("this is the argument");
```

The `arguments` object has three properties:

- `length`—The length of the `arguments` array

- `callee`—The function that is currently executing

- `caller`—The function that called the currently executing function

The preceding are *properties* of the object, not *elements* of the array. These three properties are present even if the `arguments` array has no elements—that is, even if no arguments are passed.

Using the `arguments.length` Property

One use of the `arguments.length` property is to make sure that the correct number of arguments was passed to a function. The following example shows how you can assign a `length` property to a function. This property contains the expected number of arguments, namely, one. When the function is invoked, it checks whether the actual number of arguments matches the expected number. If not, it returns an error message. In the example, `myFunc()` displays "Wrong number of arguments! expected 1, got 0."

```
function myFunc(arg) {
    if (myFunc.length != arguments.length) {
        err = "Wrong number of arguments! expected ";
        return (err + myFunc.length + ", got " + arguments.length);
    }
}
myFunc.length = 1; // expected number of arguments
trace ( myFunc(arg1, arg2) ); // this will result in an error message
```

The `arguments` array, with its `length` property, can also be helpful when a variable number of arguments may be passed to a function. For instance, the following `avg()` function returns the average of any number of arguments. The `arguments` array and the `arguments.length` property allow the `avg()` function to cope with a variable number of arguments:

```
function avg() {
    var sum = 0;
    // add up all the arguments
    for(var i = 0; i < arguments.length; i++) {
        sum = sum + arguments[i];
    }
    // divide the sum by the number of arguments -- that's the average
    var average = sum/arguments.length;
    return average;
}
trace("Average = " + avg(2,4,6)); // display "Average = 4"
trace("Average = " + avg(10,20,30,40,50)); // display "Average = 30"
```

Using the `callee` Property

The `arguments.callee` property gives you a way of calling a function from within the function, without using the function name.

One use of `arguments.callee` is to make code more generic so that you can cut and paste more easily within and between programs. For example, the argument-checking code in the preceding section, as it is written, works only for `myFunc()`. However, you could substitute `arguments.callee` for `myFunc`. You could cut and paste the resulting code into any function with a `length` property, and it would work.

With ordinary, named functions, using `arguments.callee` to create generic code is just a convenience. Each function has a fixed name, and you can always use it.

In contrast, an anonymous function created by a function literal has no fixed name. At any given moment, it may be assigned to a particular variable, array element, or object property. But that assignment could change. In this case, using `arguments.callee` to create generic code is a safety measure.

Here's an example of the type of problem that `arguments.callee` can prevent: You create a function literal, initially assigning it to a variable, `firstVar`. You want the function literal to call itself, so you include a reference to `firstVar()` in the function literal:

```
var firstVar = function (i) {
    if (i < 3) {
        trace(i);
        return firstVar(i+1);
    }
};
firstVar(0);
/*Output
0
```

```
1
2
*/
```

You then reassign the function literal to a different variable, `secondVar`, and get rid of `firstVar`:

```
secondVar = firstVar;
delete firstVar;
secondVar(0);
/*Output
0
*/
```

Now, when you invoke `secondVar()`, it invokes `firstVar()` within the function literal, but that no longer calls the function literal as you intended.

If, on the other hand, you include a reference to `arguments.callee()`, the function literal will call itself no matter what variable the function literal is assigned to. Here's what the function literal looks like. Assign and reassign it to any variable, and it will work:

```
function (i) {
        if (i < 3) {
            trace(i);
            return arguments.callee(i+1);
        }
};
```

Functions that call themselves are *recursive*. Therefore, `arguments.callee` allows you to make "unbreakable" anonymous recursive functions.

For more details on recursion, see "Some Simple Examples of Recursion" later in this chapter, page 278.

Reassignment to a different variable name is not the only thing that can "break" a recursive anonymous function with a hard-coded reference in it. Even if you keep the same variable name, the variable may be out of scope within the anonymous function.

Whether a function literal can "see" the variable that is serving as its name and thus execute itself is a question of scope. In the following two situations, a variable assigned to a function literal is out of scope within the function literal:

- When the function literal is assigned to a local variable within a function

- When the function literal is used in a constructor function

The following example illustrates the first case.

In `myFunc()`, `localFunc` is a local variable to which a function literal is assigned. First, you call `myFunc()` (line 12). Then `myFunc()`, as it returns (line 9), calls `localFunc()`. At the point where `localFunc()` calls itself (line 5), the `localFunc()` variable is undefined. On the other hand, `arguments.callee` successfully executes `localFunc()`.

The myFunc() function doesn't do anything useful, but it does illustrate a type of situation in which arguments.callee can come in very handy.

```
// thanks to Tatsuo Kato (http://tatsuokato.com) for this idea!
 1: myFunc = function (i) {
 2:    var localFunc = function (i) {
 3:        if (i < 3) {
 4:            trace(i);
 5:            return arguments.callee(i+1); // localFunc() undefined here!
 6:        }
 7:        else return i;
 8:    };
 9:    return localFunc(i);
10: };
11:
12: r = myFunc(0);
13: trace ("r = "+r);
/*
Output
0
1
2
r = 3
*/
```

Though localFunc() alone won't work on line 5, this.localFunc() would work in this case. Nevertheless, arguments.callee is the one thing that will always allow an anonymous function to call itself and so is the easiest and safest thing to use.

Using the caller **Property**

The caller property gives you a way to call the function that called the currently executing function. For instance:

```
function calleeFunc() {
    arguments.caller(); // call the caller back
}
```

⇨ *For a useful application of the arguments.caller property, see the mySuper() function in "Using the constructor Property to Run Constructor Functions," page 504 (Chapter 21, "Packaging Data and Functions Using Custom Objects").*

In using arguments.caller, be sure that the caller will not call you right back, creating an infinite loop.

15

Some Simple Examples of Recursion

Recursion occurs when a function calls itself. In most cases, you can create recursion just by using the name of the function within the function, like this:

```
function infiniteLoop() {    // DON'T EXECUTE THIS!
    infiniteLoop();
}
```

You can accomplish the same thing by using `arguments.callee()`, like this:

```
function infiniteLoop() {  // DON'T EXECUTE THIS!
    arguments.callee();
}
```

The loop will be infinite even if you insert a `return` statement, like this:

```
function infiniteLoop() {  // DON'T EXECUTE THIS!
    return arguments.callee();
}
```

In the last example, when the interpreter attempts to calculate the return value, it executes the `infiniteLoop()` function. That cycle goes on forever.

The `infiniteLoop()` function is a clear example of recursion because all the function does is *recurse*—call itself over and over. This is not only useless but also harmful because it eats up infinite amounts of memory and can crash applications and computers.

 The Flash MX authoring tool automatically aborts such a script with an error message in the Output window, after 256 cycles. The Flash 6 Player aborts with no error message. The Flash 5 authoring tool and player both display error messages and allow you to abort. With browsers, results vary depending on factors such as the operating system, but it's safe to say that none of the results are useful, and you may well end up rebooting.

Recursion itself can be useful, however. You just have to make sure you provide a way to break out of it!

For an example of useful recursion, see "Flash at Work: Calculating Factorials—An Example of Recursion," at the end of this chapter, page 300.

RETRIEVING RESULTS USING RETURN VALUES

Sometimes, you want a function not only to perform a task but also to return a value to you. For instance, if you write a function to double numbers, you don't just want it to double the numbers; you want it to pass the doubled numbers back to you so that you can do something with them. Functions supply return values using a `return` statement. A `return` statement with a return *value* returns that value to the caller, as in the following example, in which a function returns twice the value passed to it:

```
function doubleIt(numberToBeDoubled) {
    return numberToBeDoubled * 2;
}
```

A function does not need to have a `return` statement. If it doesn't have one, the function will just execute its statements sequentially, top to bottom, and terminate when it comes to the final curly brace. A `return` statement terminates the function before the final curly brace.

A `return` statement with no return value returns `undefined`. For example, the following function, `myFunc()`, returns `undefined` if no argument is passed to it. Otherwise, it returns the argument.

```
function myFunc(arg) {
    if (!arg) return;
    return (arg);
}

result = myFunc();
trace (result); // undefined
```

    ➭ *Does part of your function seem "disabled"? Perhaps you're suffering from a premature return statement. See the "Troubleshooting" section at the end of this chapter, page 298.*

There are two ways to use a return value:

- Assign the return value to a variable and use the variable in some way.

- Use the function call itself as an expression and use the var that is equivalent to the return value.

For example, using the `doubleIt()` function, this is an example of the first approach:

```
twicefour = doubleIt(4);
trace(twicefour); // displays 8
```

And this is an example of the second approach:

```
trace(doubleIt(4)); // displays 8
```

Both examples accomplish the same task. The second approach is half the size of the first, both in the source code and in the SWF. However, the second approach does not create a variable that you can continue to use. The first approach does.

    ➭ *Not getting the return you expect? See the "Troubleshooting" section at the end of this chapter, page 298.*

FUNCTIONS AS CLASSES: CONSTRUCTOR FUNCTIONS

One of the most important types of functions in Flash is the constructor function. The constructor function, in combination with the `new` operator, is the way that Flash creates new objects.

The constructor function looks like a normal function, and, in fact, it is a normal function. However, you use the constructor function in a very specialized way, and therefore you take advantage of function characteristics that normally go unused.

In particular, all functions have a `prototype` property. Normally, you don't make any use of it. With a constructor function, on the other hand, the `prototype` property is of key importance because it allows all objects in a class to share properties and also allows one class to inherit properties from other classes.

This section covers three basic topics:

- Creating new objects using the `new` operator

- Using the `prototype` property to share properties

- Setting up inheritance chains using the `new` operator

These three topics constitute some of the basics of object-oriented programming (OOP).

More advanced topics pertaining to OOP are covered in Chapter 21, *"Packaging Data and Functions Using Custom Objects,"* page 489.

Creating Objects Using the `new` Operator

To create an object, you first define a constructor function and then use the `new` keyword to create the object. The following constructor function for a `Ball` class assigns just one property, `col` (short for "color") to objects it creates:

```
function Ball (col) {
    this.col = col;
}
```

To create an object in the `Ball` class, you invoke the `Ball()` function using the `new` operator:

```
myBall = new Ball("blue");
```

Except for the keyword `new`, this statement looks like a normal function call. You can guess, therefore, that this statement calls the `Ball()` function, takes the return value, and assigns it to the `myBall` variable. That would be the behavior of a normal function, and it is indeed what happens here, too.

That being said, there is something strange here: You're invoking the function as if it returns something, yet there is no `return` statement! What is being returned? The `new` keyword tells the function to create a new object. That object is what gets returned and assigned to the `myBall` variable.

Considering how simple this line of code looks, `myBall = new Ball("blue")` triggers a surprisingly complex chain of events:

- First, the ActionScript interpreter creates a new "generic" object and passes it to the `Ball()` function. For the moment, consider the generic object to be empty, without properties.

- Inside the `Ball()` function, the object (which is still "anonymous" or nameless) is referred to as `this`. So what does the statement `this.col = col` do? The `col` on the right side of the statement refers to the argument that was passed to the function, in other words, the string `"blue"`. The part on the left, `this.col`, creates a new property named `col` for the anonymous object. Therefore, the result of the whole statement is an object `{col: "blue"}`.

- The `Ball()` function returns the still-nameless object, sporting its brand-new `col` property. This part of the process is somewhat "hidden" because the constructor function doesn't have a `return` statement. Instead, the `new` operator causes the object to be returned. At that point, the anonymous object finally gets a name, `myBall`.

- The ActionScript interpreter sets a hidden property of `myBall`, the `__proto__` property, to point to the `prototype` object of the `Ball()` constructor function. This property allows `myBall` to find its shared properties in the `prototype` object.

⇨ *The __proto__ property is discussed in Chapter 21, "Packaging Data and Functions Using Custom Objects," page 489.*

Now you can check whether what you just did worked:

```
trace (typeof myBall); // "object"
for (a in myBall) trace(a); // enumerate properties: displays "col"
trace(myBall.col); // "blue"
```

Everything looks good!

The `col` property is contained locally in the `myBall` object. Similarly, every object created by the `Ball()` constructor function will be given a `col` property, and each one of those properties will be local to each object created. This means that if you change the value of the `col` property in one of the objects, it will not affect the `col` values in any of the other objects. It's not a shared property.

The `prototype` **Property**

The ActionScript interpreter automatically assigns a `prototype` property to every function when the function is created. The `prototype` property is an object, so it can have properties of its own. When you create a new object using the `new` operator (as described in the previous section), any properties in the constructor function's `prototype` object are shared by the newly created object.

Say you create a `Dog` class, embodied in a function named `Dog()`:

```
function Dog () {}
```

This example doesn't look like much of a function, but, nevertheless, it has a `prototype` object. Now assign some properties to the `prototype` object of the `Dog` class:

```
Dog.prototype = {legs: 4, says: "bow wow", food: ["bones", "steak"]};
```

The idea is that the prototypical dog has four legs, says "bow wow," and eats bones and steak.

Alternatively, you can assign the same properties to the `prototype` object like this:

```
Dog.prototype.legs =  4;
Dog.prototype.says = "bow wow";
Dog.prototype.food = ["bones", "steak"];
```

The `prototype` object can also have functions as properties. A function that is a property of an object is a *method*.

Class names are capitalized by tradition.

None of the properties in this particular example are methods. I'm going to save methods for later, because there are some special considerations when assigning methods to the prototype object.

⇨ *The syntax for assigning a method to a prototype object is shown in the next section in this chapter, "Assigning Methods to a Class," page 282.*

After you create these three properties in the Dog.prototype object, any object in the Dog class will automatically have all three of these properties. You could create 100 objects in the Dog class, and each of them would "know" that it has four legs, says "bow wow," and may eat bones or steak. But you need to store that information in only one place.

Flash developer Robin Debreuil, whose Web site (www.debreuil.com) contains an excellent tutorial on object-oriented programming in ActionScript, came up with a good analogy for this situation: Imagine that you're looking through a double pane of glass. The first pane has some decals on it. So does the second pane. But when you look through the glass, you can't distinguish the first pane from the second pane. You just see a bunch of decals. The first pane is the object itself, and the decals on that pane are its properties. The second pane is the prototype object of the constructor function, and the decals on that pane are its properties. When you, as an ActionScript programmer, access a property, you don't know or care whether it is a local property (first pane) or a prototype property (second pane). This analogy breaks down when you have multiple objects in the same class—which would all somehow have the same second pane behind them—but it works quite nicely for one object.

What's really going on is this: When the ActionScript interpreter needs to find a property for an object (because your program has referenced something like myDog.col), it looks in the object first (myDog). If the object doesn't contain the property, the interpreter looks in the prototype of the object's constructor function (Dog.prototype). This process is normally transparent to you as a programmer. When you refer to myDog.col, you don't have to specify whether that property is local to the object or stored in the constructor's prototype.

⇨ *The ActionScript interpreter may pursue its search even beyond the constructor's prototype, as you'll see later in this chapter, in "Using Inheritance to Create Reusable Code," page 285, and "Using the new Operator to Create Inheritance Chains," page 287.*

You haven't put anything in the Ball.prototype object yet, so there are no shared properties for this class yet. Now create a shared property:

```
Ball.prototype.className = "Ball"; // add className property
for (a in myBall) trace(a); // displays "className" and "col"
trace(myBall.className); // "Ball"
```

Notice that the syntax for referring to myBall.className is exactly the same as the syntax for referring to myBall.col, even though className is in the prototype object of the constructor function, and col is local to myBall.

Assigning Methods to a Class

Theoretically, you can assign a method to a class in one of four ways, as shown in Table 15.1.

Table 15.1   Four Ways to Assign a Method to a Class

Local (in Each Instance)	Shared (in Prototype)
Function declaration	Function declaration
Function literal	Function literal

As you can see from Table 15.1, you assign a method in one of two basic ways: using a function declaration or using a function literal. Each approach can be used to create either a local method stored in each instance of the class or a shared method stored just once in the prototype object.

In reality, there is almost never a good reason for each object to have its own local copy of a method. An object needs to have its own copy of a property only when it may have an individual value for that property. For instance, if you have many objects of different colors belonging to the Dog class, you don't want all these members of the Dog class to share just one copy of the col property because that would mean having just one value for the property and, therefore, just one color. But a method is almost always identical for all objects in a class. When that's the case, the method can be shared, and it belongs in the prototype object of the constructor function. In this chapter, you'll just assign methods to the prototype object.

⇨ *"Overriding Properties in Individual Instances," page 496, (Chapter 21, "Packaging Data and Functions Using Custom Objects") illustrates assigning properties to individual instances.*

As Table 15.1 shows, you can assign a method using a normal function declaration or a function literal. Let's look at the syntax for each one first. Then I'll discuss when it's appropriate to use each of them.

Assigning a Method Using a Function Declaration

Assigning a method to the prototype object starting with a normal function declaration is a two-step process: First, you declare the function (whatColorAmI() in this case). Then you assign the function to a property of the prototype object of the constructor (getColor in this case):

```
// first declare the function
function whatColorAmI() {
    return this.col;
}
// then assign the function identifier to a property in the prototype
Ball.prototype.getColor = whatColorAmI;
// it works!
trace(myBall.getColor()); // displays "blue"
```

Notice that when you're assigning a function, you don't use any parentheses:

```
Ball.prototype.getColor = whatColorAmI;
```

You use parentheses only when you're *executing* a function:

```
myBall.getColor();
```

Also notice that you can use the `this` keyword in the function, and it will automatically refer to the object on which the method is invoked. That means you can conveniently assign the same function to multiple objects. For instance, the following listing creates a `Cat` constructor function, creates a `getColor` property in the `Cat` prototype, and assigns the `whatColorAmI()` function to the `getColor` property. Notice that this is the same `whatColorAmI()` function that was used for the `Ball` class:

```
function Cat (col) {
    this.col = col;
}
Cat.prototype.getColor = whatColorAmI;
// create a gray Cat
myCat = new Cat("gray");
// check the color of myCat
trace(myCat.getColor()); // displays "gray"
```

Assigning a Method Using a Function Literal

You can assign a method to the `prototype` object in a single step by using a function literal. Take this function literal, for example:

```
function () {
    return this.col;
};
```

You can write the same thing in a single line:

```
function () {return this.col;};
```

You must store the function literal somewhere as soon as it's created, or it will be lost. In this case, that "somewhere" is a property of the `prototype` object:

```
// assign function literal to getColor property
Ball.prototype.getColor = function () {return this.col;};
// it works!
trace(myBall.getColor()); // displays "blue"
```

Here are a couple of other examples of property assignments using function literals, the second of which includes a `col` argument to allow you to set a new color for the ball:

```
Ball.prototype.getClassName = function () {return this.className;};
Ball.prototype.setColor = function (col) {this.col = col;};
trace(myBall.getClassName()); // displays "Ball"
myBall.setColor("red");
trace(myBall.getColor()); // displays "red"
```

Using a Function Literal Versus a Function Declaration

If you're going to assign a function to only one class, and you're not using the function in any other context, using a function literal is more efficient. In this case, a function declaration just adds extra lines of code to your program.

On the other hand, if you're assigning the same function to several classes, or using the function in some other context, declare it in one place and reference it each time you want to use or assign it. If you use function literals in this case, you'll be using extra memory unnecessarily because each class will store its own copy of the function.

Using Inheritance to Create Reusable Code

The capability of one object (such as myBall) to effectively borrow properties from another object (its constructor's prototype object) provides the basis for a key OOP capability: inheritance.

The basic idea of inheritance is pretty simple: Just as an object like myBall can effectively borrow properties from the prototype object of its constructor function, so one class can borrow properties from another class. In ActionScript, the constructor function is the embodiment of the class, so inheritance involves one constructor function borrowing from another constructor function. More specifically, it involves the prototype object of one constructor function borrowing properties from the prototype object of another constructor function.

Though I am pointing out the similarity between the way objects borrow properties and the way classes borrow properties, you'll notice that I haven't said that an object "inherits" properties from a class. In languages that have statically defined classes such as Java, you can be detained by the OOP police and possibly executed for saying that an object "inherits" properties from a class. Inheritance is something that happens only between classes. When an object is *instantiated* (created as an instance of a class), the constructor function assigns various properties to the object. Some of the properties may have been inherited by the class before being assigned to the object. But objects themselves don't "inherit."

This clear-cut distinction does not reflect the realities of ActionScript very well. In ActionScript, the mechanism by which an object, such as myBall, gets some perfectly good properties without working for them, just by virtue of the circumstances of its birth, is exactly the same mechanism used to pass "unearned" properties from class to class. That mechanism is the prototype object. Instances and classes receive "loaner" properties in the same way, and so it is sometimes natural to use the term *inheritance* in both cases.

The relationship between a class that loans properties and a class that borrows them is a "parent-child" relationship. The prototype object of a constructor function loans properties to instances of the class in a similar fashion. In ActionScript, it may be convenient to refer to the prototype-instance relationship as a parent-child relationship.

Any given parent-child relationship is just a two-level hierarchy. On the top level is the parent object. On the lower level are one or more child objects. In ActionScript, a parent can have any number of children, though each child can have only one parent.

You can build multi-generation inheritance chains: Parents can have parents, and children can have children. You'll see in a minute how to do this.

First, though, consider why you would want to create such a chain. Going back to the Ball() function for a moment, why would you want to use a constructor function to create balls? It's a lot of trouble to go to, just to create a ball with a couple of properties. In fact, if all you want to do is create a couple of balls with a few properties, OOP is probably overkill. On the other hand, the more balls you want to create, the handier it is to be able to create them with a single line of code each. In other words, the value of the constructor function increases as you reuse it within the program.

And if you need balls in another program, your time and effort in creating the Ball() constructor function are even more richly rewarded. Thus, the value of the constructor function increases as you reuse it across programs.

You also can let other programmers use your constructor functions in their programs. They don't have to analyze all the inner workings of your constructor functions. All they have to do is understand simple interfaces embodied in methods. Thus, more reuse, and still more value, can be realized from your original effort.

This last kind of reuse is what Macromedia has done with ActionScript: It has created a number of different classes that are likely to be useful to a broad spectrum of Flash programmers. You, as a programmer, can now take those classes and use them in your own programs. You can use them as is. You may also be able to change or extend them to suit your own needs. This kind of reuse is probably the most frequently mentioned benefit of OOP.

Not every class, however, has equal potential for reuse. Therefore, programmers have an incentive to create broadly applicable "generic" classes. That's the major motivation for creating multi-generation inheritance chains: It allows you to create some highly generic, highly reusable classes.

Good examples of this strategy can be seen in the user interface components, such as the scroll bar, combo box, and list box, that Macromedia provides with Flash MX. For instance, if you drag and drop a ListBox object onto the Stage and use the Movie Explorer to browse the ActionScript, you'll find comments such as the following:

```
FSelectableListClass
        EXTENDS FUIComponentClass
CLASS FSelectableItemClass
        EXTENDS FUIComponentClass
FListBoxClass
        EXTENDS FSelectableListClass
        IMPLEMENTS FListItemClass
FScrollSelectListClass
        EXTENDS FSelectableListClass
FListItemClass
        EXTENDS FSelectableItemClass
```

These comments reflect a three-tier inheritance hierarchy:

- Tier 1—FUIComponentClass is at the top.

- Tier 2—FSelectableListClass and FSelectableItemClass inherit from FUIComponentClass.

- Tier 3—FScrollSelectListClass inherits from FSelectableListClass, and FListItemClass inherits from FSelectableItemClass.

Properties needed by all components can be put in the FUIComponentClass and shared by all the classes in the hierarchy. Properties needed by all selectable lists can be put in the FSelectableListClass and shared by FScrollSelectListClass. Finally, properties needed by all selectable items can be put in the FSelectableItemClass and shared by FListItemClass.

An object created using a class constructor function will share all the properties in its particular line of inheritance, all the way back to FUIComponentClass. For instance, an object in the FListItemClass class shares properties from FSelectableItemClass and FUIComponentClass.

Using the new **Operator to Create Inheritance Chains**

You can set up inheritance hierarchies of your own, using classes that you create or reusing existing classes. For instance, if you want to create your own components, you might want to reuse some of Macromedia's existing classes.

You can set up multi-generation hierarchies in two basic ways. If you think of prototype objects as chains that link parents and children, the approach covered in this chapter involves forging new chains. This is the standard and recommended way of going about this process.

> *The other approach, which involves relinking existing chains (think of it as "adoption"), is covered in "Creating Class Hierarchies Using the __proto__ Property," page 502 (Chapter 21, "Packaging Data and Functions Using Custom Objects").*

Suppose you have four constructor functions: Bird, Raptor, Eagle, and BaldEagle. Obviously, these four classes belong in a hierarchical relationship. How can you link them in parent-child relationships?

You have seen how objects get linked to the prototype object of their constructor functions. This happens automatically, when you instantiate an object using the new operator. But you're not trying to create any instances yet. You just want to link existing classes hierarchically.

Start by thinking about just the top two classes in the hierarchy: Bird and Raptor. Pretend for a moment that you're going to create some instances in the Raptor class, and you want each of them to have all the properties of the Bird class. You can accomplish that if you can get all the properties of the Bird class into the prototype object of the Raptor class. Basically, that means you want Raptor.prototype to be a member of Bird. In other words, you want to say:

```
Raptor.prototype = new Bird();
```

Would that work? Yes! This approach may seem a little strange because, so far, you've seen the prototype only as something that is created automatically when a function is created. In this case, you're creating a new prototype object as a member of an existing class.

Now look at the details. The following shows the constructor function for Bird and a statement that assigns a movement property to the Bird prototype object:

```
function Bird ( )  {
    // local "covering" property
    this.covering = "feathers";
}
// shared "movement" property
Bird.prototype.movement="fly";
```

Any object constructed with the Bird function will have two properties:

- A local property, covering:"feathers"

- A shared property, movement:"fly"

Here's the `Raptor` constructor function:

```
function Raptor ( ) {
    // statements would go here
}
```

The `Raptor` constructor function is just an empty shell at this point. Nevertheless, like all functions, `Raptor` already has a `prototype` object. It was given one as soon as it was created. Macromedia did not make this fact very easy to confirm. For example, the `prototype` object doesn't normally show up in a `for-in` loop:

```
for a ( in Raptor) trace(a); // displays nothing
```

Nevertheless, it is there, as you can confirm by using the undocumented `ASSetPropFlags()`—"ActionScript set property flags"—function:

```
ASSetPropFlags(Raptor, null, 8, 1); // "unhide" hidden properties
for (a in Raptor) trace(a); // displays "prototype"
```

Nothing appears in the `Raptor prototype` yet. You can confirm this by using a `for-in` loop as follows:

```
for (a in Raptor.prototype) trace(a); // displays nothing
```

> For more details on hidden prototype properties, see *"Creating Class Hierarchies Using the __proto__ Property,"* page 502 (Chapter 21, *"Packaging Data and Functions Using Custom Objects"*).

You need to create a new `prototype` object for `Raptor`, one that has all the properties of the `Bird` class. To do this, you use this statement: `Raptor.prototype = new Bird()`. Now if you check the contents of the `Raptor.prototype`, even with no `ASSetPropFlags()`, you find two properties, both inherited from the `Bird` class:

```
for (a in Raptor.prototype) trace(a); // "movement" "covering"
```

You have accomplished your initial goal! Any objects created with the `Raptor` constructor function will have all the properties of the `Bird` class.

Remember that you were only pretending that you wanted to create instances of the `Raptor` class. In reality, `Raptor` is still too generic a class to have instances. First, you want to link the `Eagle` class to `Raptor` in the same way that you just linked `Raptor` to `Bird`. Then you want to link `BaldEagle` to `Eagle`. Finally, you'll create instances of the `BaldEagle` class. The following skeleton program does all that and then tests to make sure it worked:

```
// Bird constructor function
    function Bird ( ) {
        // local "covering" property
        this.covering = "feathers";
    }
```

What if you used `ASSetPropFlags()`? Might that not reveal hidden properties in `Raptor.prototype`, just as it did in `Raptor`? Actually, yes. But for now, the half-truth of the standard `for-in` loop is sufficient.

```
      Bird.prototype.movement="fly"; // shared "movement" property

// Raptor constructor function
    function Raptor ( ) {
        // statements would go here
    }

    Raptor.prototype = new Bird(); // make Raptor inherit from Bird

// Eagle constructor function
    function Eagle ( ) {
        // statements would go here
    }

    Eagle.prototype = new Raptor(); // make Eagle inherit from Raptor

// BaldEagle constructor function
    function BaldEagle ( ) {
        // statements would go here

    }

    BaldEagle.prototype = new Eagle(); // make BaldEagle inherit from Eagle

baldEagle1 = new BaldEagle(); // create a BaldEagle instance
for (a in baldEagle1) trace(a); // displays "movement" and "covering"
trace(baldEagle1.movement); // displays "fly"
trace(baldEagle1.covering); // displays "feathers"
```

The last three lines of this program show that you have accomplished your ultimate goal: All the properties of the `Bird` class are passed down through `Raptor`, `Eagle`, and `BaldEagle` and appear in instances of `BaldEagle`.

This inheritance chain is just a skeleton because the bottom three classes don't add or delete any properties. In a real program, each class would have to do something useful to justify its existence. In this example, it would probably add properties specific to its subclass. For instance, raptors have qualities that are not shared by all birds, eagles have qualities that are not shared by all raptors, and bald eagles have qualities that are not shared by all eagles.

For more information on inheritance chains, see "Creating Class Hierarchies Using the __proto__ Property", page 502 (Chapter 21, "Packaging Data and Functions Using Custom Objects").

Functions as Data

Every function is an object and thus can have properties. For instance, the following example shows how you can declare a function, `myFunc()`, and give it a property named `counter`, which you set to `0`:

```
function myFunc () {}
myFunc.counter = 0;
```

Normally, you don't assign properties to functions, but you may want to when you're working with classes. One natural place to store information about the class is in the constructor function. In the following example, `MyClass()` is a constructor function. The `MyClass.counter` property might, for example, count the number of instances of the class that have been created:

```
function MyClass () {}
MyClass.counter = 0;
```

The technique of storing data in a constructor function is discussed in "Using a Constructor Function for 'Safe' Storage," page 501 (Chapter 21, "Packaging Data and Functions Using Custom Objects").

USING FUNCTION.APPLY() AND FUNCTION.CALL()

The `apply()` and `call()` methods, which are defined for all functions, allow you to call a function or method as if it were a method of any designated object. You specify the object as the first argument of the `apply()` or `call()` method. Inside the called function, the `this` keyword will refer to the designated object.

Without the `apply()` and `call()` methods, when you call a function or method, you're stuck with a default value for `this`. For example, if you call a method, `this` refers to the object that the method belongs to. If you call a function on a timeline, `this` refers to the timeline.

For more details on this, see "Explicit Scoping with the this Keyword" later in this chapter, page 293.

With `apply()` and `call()`, you can make `this` refer to any object you want.

You can also pass any number of parameters to the called function. The only difference between `apply()` and `call()` is that `apply()` passes parameters in an array, whereas `call()` passes a comma-delimited list.

The format looks like this:

```
myFunction.apply(myObject, myArray);
myFunction.call(myObject, myArg1, myArg2, myArg3);
```

The `apply()` or `call()` method will receive whatever return value the function normally returns.

If the first argument is `null`, the default value of `this` will be used. In this case, `apply()` and `call()` behave like normal function calls, except that `apply()` passes its parameters in an array.

You can also set the second argument to `null`, to show that you're deliberately not passing any parameters. This technique has the same effect as omitting the second argument completely.

The following example uses the `apply()` method to reset counters in three classes.

See the previous section, "Functions as Data" on page 289, for more information on using the class to store a counter.

First, declare the `resetCounter()` function, designed to set the `counter` property in some object (represented by `this`) to `0`.

Then create three classes—Class1, Class2, and Class3—and give each one a counter property. Set the counter properties to nonzero values so that resetCounter() will have something to do.

Finally, use a for loop and the apply() method to pass the classes one-by-one to resetCounter(). The second argument of the apply() method is set to null because resetCounter() does not take any arguments.

```
// declare the resetCounter function
function resetCounter () {
    this.counter = 0;
}
// create three classes, each with a "counter" property
function Class1() {}
Class1.counter = 1;
function Class2() {}
Class2.counter = 2;
function Class3() {}
Class3.counter = 3;
// use apply() to pass the classes one-by-one to resetCounter()
for (i = 1; i < 4; i++) {
    className = eval("Class"+i); // form the class name
    resetCounter.apply(className, null);
}
```

The following example creates three counter properties in each class and sets the value of counter1 to 1, counter2 to 2, and counter3 to 3. The values for the counters are passed to setCounters() in an array as the second argument of the apply() method. The setCounters() function retrieves these values using its arguments property, which stores the arguments passed to a function.

> The arguments object is discussed earlier in this chapter, in the section "Passing Information to Functions in Arguments," page 272.

```
// define function
function setCounters () {
    this.counter1 = arguments[0];
    this.counter2 = arguments[1];
    this.counter3 = arguments[2];
}
// define classes
function Class1() {}
function Class2() {}
function Class3() {}
// create and initialize three counters in each class
for (i = 1; i < 4; i++) {
    className = eval("Class"+i);
    setCounters.apply(className, [1,2,3]);
}
```

The apply() method does not support associative arrays as its second argument. The named properties of the associative array will be lost, and only numerically indexed elements will be received by the called function.

For more information on associative arrays, see "Named Array Elements: Associative Arrays," page 399 (Chapter 19, "Using the Built-in Core Objects").

You can use the arguments property of a function as the second argument of apply(). For instance, the following example first calls the myHandler() function with two arguments: 1 and 2. The myHandler() function, in turn, calls the myDelegate() function. The myHandler() function "forwards" its arguments by using its arguments property as the second argument of the apply() method.

Notice how the return value returns from myDelegate() to myHandler() and then back to the original call.

The this keyword in myDelegate() refers to the timeline because the first argument of the apply() method was null. Thus, in the final trace action, p0 and p1 show up as ordinary timeline variables.

```
function myDelegate () {
    this.p0 = arguments[0];
    this.p1 = arguments[1];
    return true;
}

function myHandler() {
    ret = myDelegate.apply (null, arguments); // "forwarding" arguments
    return ret;
}

result = myHandler(1,2);
trace (result); // true
trace (p0 + " " + p1); // 1 2
```

EXPLICIT SCOPING

Scoping is telling the ActionScript interpreter where to look for a variable, movie clip, object, or array. The interpreter can look in a *function*, in an *object*, in a *timeline*, in the Object object, or in _global. You can tell it specifically where to look, and then it looks just in that one place. That is *explicit* scoping, the subject of this section. Or you may deliberately *not* tell the interpreter where to look, and then it follows its own automatic scoping rules. That type of scoping is covered next in the "Automatic Scoping" section.

Scope is like a sophisticated filing system. You can use it both to find things and to keep things private. Unfortunately, misfiling is also possible: Subtle bugs can result when the ActionScript interpreter is unable to find something or finds the wrong thing.

15

⇨ *For more details on _global, see "Where to Declare Variables," page 189 (Chapter 12, "Managing Variables, Data, and Datatypes").*

One way to avoid this type of problem is to use explicit scoping to tell the ActionScript interpreter exactly where to look. With explicit scoping, you use dot syntax (or deprecated *slash* syntax) to tell the ActionScript interpreter where to look for the data item that you're referencing. For instance:

> In this section, *timeline* or *movie clip* means a movie clip timeline and any attached event handlers and buttons.

```
_root.myClip.myFunc(); // tells interpreter to look in a movie clip "myClip"
_global.myVar = 10; // look in _global
```

The Limitations of Hard-Coding

Using the name of a movie clip, function, object, or the _global identifier to specify the *path* (location) of a datum, as in the previous examples, is an example of *hard-coding*. Though clear and often easy to use, hard-coded paths make code less reusable. In the root.myClip.myFunc(); example, for instance, if you want to use the myFunc() function in another project but need to use it somewhere other than a movie clip named myClip in _root, you need to do some recoding. The same holds true in the second example, if you want to reuse myVar but don't want it to be a global variable.

You may be able to avoid hard-coding by using *relative references* or by using the this keyword. Another possibility is to use automatic rather than explicit scoping.

Explicit Scoping Using Relative References

When you're scoping to a movie clip, a common way of making code more reusable is to use r*elative references*. That is, use the _parent property of the current movie clip to indicate the movie clip to look in. For instance:

```
_parent.myFunc(); // look in the parent of the clip this appears in
_parent._parent.myFunc(); // look in the "grandparent" of this clip
```

Suppose, for example, myFunc() is in a movie clip named mc1 on the main timeline, making the *absolute* path of the clip _root.mc1. (Any path that begins with _root is called an "absolute path," because it gives you the location of the movie clip starting from the Main Timeline, not relative to any other movie clip.) Now, if you want to reference myFunc() from a child clip—say, _root.mc1.mc2—you can use _parent.myFunc(). In a grandchild clip—say, _root.mc1.mc2.mc3—you can use _parent._parent.myFunc(). Later, if you use this code with movie clips myClip1, myClip2, and myClip3, nothing about the code needs to change to accommodate the different instance names of the movie clips.

Explicit Scoping with the this Keyword

The third type of explicit scoping uses the this keyword. With one major exception, this refers to the movie clip where the statement is located. The next section gives some examples of the general rule. The section after that covers the exception.

Using the `this` Keyword: Basics

In a timeline (including attached event handlers and buttons), `this` usually refers to the timeline. You can use the `this` keyword in movie clips to get the ActionScript interpreter to recognize that you're invoking a `MovieClip` method, as opposed to the global function of the same name. For instance, if you put this code on a timeline, the ActionScript interpreter thinks you're invoking the global `duplicateMovieClip()` function and generates an error:

```
duplicateMovieClip("myClip",1); // ERROR!!!
```

By inserting the `this` keyword, you invoke the `MovieClip` method, and all is well:

```
this.duplicateMovieClip("myClip",1); // no problem
```

⇨ *For more information on duplicateMovieClip(), see Chapter 17, "Unlocking the Power of Movie Clips," page 331.*

The following example shows three uses of `this` on a timeline, each of which causes a variable to scope to the timeline:

- The variable is in a property of an object on the timeline.

- The variable is referenced inside a function.

- The variable is referenced in the movie clip directly.

The three `trace` statements at the end prove that the interpreter sees `this` as the timeline in each case. If c equals 300, you can conclude that the statement is "seeing" a and b on the timeline. If it were seeing the a and b properties in the myObj object, for example, c would equal 3, not 300.

```
a = 100; // variable declared on movie clip timeline
b = 200; // variable declared on movie clip timeline
c = a + b; // variable declared on movie clip timeline
myObj = {a : 1, b : 2, c : this.a + this.b} // #1 "this" in a property
function myFunc() {
    trace(this.c); // #2 this in a function
}
trace(this.c); // # 3 this on the timeline - displays 300
trace(myObj.c); // displays 300 - in an object
myFunc(); // displays 300 - in a function
```

The variable scopes to the timeline that it is on, even if it is used inside an object or function. Perhaps surprisingly, the interpreter does *not* check within the object first for properties that match the referenced name.

Exception: Scoping to the Object

In the previous section, you saw that, in most situations, if you see `this` as the path of a variable on a timeline, `this` means the timeline. There is one notable exception—namely that *within a method of an object*, `this` scopes to the object.

Other than that, the scoping rules for functions are the same as for variables. That is, on a timeline (or associated event handlers and buttons), or within a function on the timeline, `this.myFunc()` scopes to the timeline.

The following example does basically the same thing as the previous example, using functions instead of variables. The four function calls at the end (lines 10–13) tell the story. The first one shows that when you reference `this.a()` on the timeline, the interpreter looks for `a()` on the timeline. Similarly, when you reference `a()` within `b()`, as in the function invoked on line 11, the interpreter looks for `a()` on the timeline. The third function call (line 12) shows that invoking `this.a()` from within a function, `myFunc()`, on the timeline, doesn't change anything: The interpreter still looks for `a()` on the timeline. The final function call, however, shows that when you say `this.a()` within a method, the interpreter looks for `a()` in the object the method belongs to.

```
1: function a () {trace ("function a");}
2: function b () {this.a();} // "this" scopes to timeline here
3: myObj = {
4:     a : function () {trace ("object function a");},
5:     b : function () {this.a();} // this scopes to the object!
6: };
7: function myFunc() {
8:     this.a(); // "this" scopes to timeline here
9: }

10: this.a(); // displays "function a" - "this" scopes to timeline here
11: b();// displays "function a"
12: myFunc(); // displays "function a"
13: myObj.b(); // displays "object function a"
```

Function Aliases Retain Their Own Scope

If you set a variable equal to a function or method, the variable maintains its own scope as a variable. It does *not* adopt the scope of the function or method. For instance, in the following example, `myAliasFunc` is set equal to `myObj.myFunc`. Executing `myObj.myFunc()` displays `prop1` correctly because it uses the method, which scopes to the object. However, executing `myAliasFunc()` displays `undefined` (or, in Flash 5, a blank line) because `myAliasFunc` scopes to the timeline, where there is no such variable as `prop1`.

```
myObj = new Object();
myObj.myFunc = function () {
  trace(this.prop1);
}
myObj.prop1 = 1;
myAliasFunc = myObj.myFunc;
myObj.myFunc(); // displays "1"
myAliasFunc (); // undefined, this.prop1 is undefined in the timeline
```

AUTOMATIC SCOPING

With automatic scoping, you simply make a direct reference to the variable, function, object, or array, with no dot syntax. You let the ActionScript interpreter scope your datum automatically.

For example, this is a direct reference:

```
myFunc(); // does not tell the interpreter where to look for myFunc()
```

In this case, the interpreter starts its search wherever you make the data reference. From there, it may search in movie clip timelines (including associated event handlers and buttons), functions, or objects, including inheritance chains. As a last resort, it looks in _global.

By default, ActionScript *scope chains* are very simple. The scope chain is the list of objects to be searched. Unless you create a more complicated structure using the object-oriented programming (OOP) techniques discussed earlier in this chapter, the scope chain is usually _global-Object-timeline or _global-Object-timeline-function. The interpreter searches these chains from right to left—for instance, the function first, then the timeline, then Object, and finally the _global object.

Longer chains do occur, such as _global-Object-timeline-outer function-inner function, in which the inner function is declared within the outer function.

You temporarily lengthen the scope chain when you use the with statement, which tacks on another object at the lowest level of the scope chain. That tacked-on object (the object in the with statement) is always checked first within the with statement. It is removed from the scope chain when the with statement terminates.

The following three examples show a starting point (where the variable or function is declared) and the typical resulting scope chain:

- Start on a *timeline* (or attached event handler or button).

  Example:

  ```
  myFunc(); // on a timeline
  ```

  Scope chain: _global-Object-timeline.

  Note: The scope chain does not include other timelines.

- Start in an *object property* or *array element* on a timeline.

  In this example, the myVar variable is declared on the timeline and referenced as the myObj.myProp1 property. That property is then displayed in two ways: using a method of the object, myMethod(), defined on line 4 and called on line 5; and using a trace statement on the timeline, on line 6.

  ```
  1: myVar = "main";
  2: myObj = { myVar : "myVarObj",
  3:           myProp1 : myVar,
  4:           myMethod : function () {trace(this.myProp1);}};
  5: myObj.myMethod(); // displays "main"
  6: trace(myObj.myProp1); // displays "main"
  ```

Scope chain: _global-Object-timeline.

Note 1: If the value of myProp1 on line 3 is this.myVar (note the added this), the scope chain is still _global-Object-timeline.

Note 2: The scope chain does not include "sibling" properties or elements. For instance, line 2 contains a myObj.myVar property, but it is ignored.

■ Start in a *function* or *method* declaration.

In the following example, the myVar variable, after being declared on the timeline (line 1), is referenced first in a function declaration that is on the timeline (line 3) and then in a method myObj.myFunc() (line 5).

```
1: myVar = 10;
2: function myFunc() {
3:        trace(myVar);
4: }
5: myObj = {myVar : 99 , myFunc : function() { trace(myVar);} }
6: myFunc(); // 10
7: myObj.myFunc(); // 10
```

Scope chain: _global-Object-timeline-function.

Note: The scope chain does not include "sibling" properties. For instance, the interpreter ignores the myVar : 99 property (line 5) .

The last statement (line 7), myObj.myFunc(), works identically in Flash 5 and Flash MX, assuming it is on the same timeline as the declaration of myObj above it (line 5). However, if you tried to execute the myObj.myFunc() method from another timeline, it would fail in Flash 5 (or display a myVar variable on the other timeline, if one existed). In Flash MX, you can execute the myObj.myFunc() method from another timeline, and it will display the myVar variable on the timeline where myObj is defined.

For instance, suppose the preceding code is on the Main Timeline, and you have a "circle" clip on the Main Timeline with the following statements on its timeline:

```
myVar = "circle";
_parent.myObj.myFunc(); // displays "circle" in Flash 5, 10 in Flash MX
```

The second statement will display "circle" if you use the Flash 5 authoring tool. It will display "10" if you're using the Flash MX authoring tool. In Flash MX, a method consistently takes the scope of the timeline where it is defined, never the timeline it is called from. (Flash MX conforms to ECMA-262 in this respect, whereas Flash 5 deviated from it.)

Also new in Flash MX, a function literal defined within a function now takes the scope of the outer function. In Flash 5, it took the scope of the timeline.

In the following example, innerFunction() refers to a function literal within outerFunction(). In Flash MX, the function literal is scoped to outerFunction() and thus has access to the parameter arg. Therefore, when the function literal is returned in line 4, it includes the argument, which is displayed when the function executes in line 5. In Flash 5, innerFunction() is scoped to the timeline, on which arg is undefined, so line 5 displays "Argument was: ".

```
1: function outerFunction (arg) {
2:     return innerFunction = function () {trace ("Argument was: "+arg);}
3: }
4: myFunc = outerFunction("myArg");
5: myFunc(); // in Flash MX, displays "Argument was: myArg"
```

This is an example of a five-link scope chain: _global-Object-timeline-outer function-inner function.

The following makeHandler() function shows how you can use this new functionality to attach event handler functions to a movie clip programmatically. The makeHandler() function returns the name argument in Flash MX. In Flash 5, it would return undefined (assuming there is no name variable on the timeline) because the inner function would not scope to the outer function.

```
// thanks to Gary Grossman, principal engineer, Macromedia Flash team!
function makeHandler(name) {
  return function () {
    trace("Handler  "+ name +"  invoked.");
  };
}
function makeHandlers(mc, names) {
  for (var i=0; i<names.length; i++) {
    mc[names[i]] = makeHandler(names[i]);
    mc[names[i]](); // displays "Handler  onPress  invoked." etc.
  }
}
makeHandlers(mc, ["onPress", "onRelease", "onReleaseOutside",
            "onRollOver", "onRollOut", "onDragOver", "onDragOut"]);
```

> *See the next section, "Troubleshooting," for a discussion of the possibility of timing (position on the timeline) making a variable or function inaccessible even within a single timeline.*

TROUBLESHOOTING

Why can't I access a variable or function on the same timeline?

If the playhead has never once entered the frame containing a particular variable or function, the ActionScript interpreter won't know about that variable or function.

Say you put this event handler on frame 1:

```
_root.onEnterFrame = function() {
    trace(x);
};
```

You also put the statement x = 10; on frame 2 of the same timeline. In that case, the trace(x) statement in the event handler will display undefined the first time it executes (in the first frame) because x hasn't been defined yet. After the interpreter "sees" x (that is, after the playhead enters the second frame), it will always "remember" it, and the trace(x) statement in the event handler will display "10" upon entering all frames, even frame 1, from then on.

Note that all functions in a frame become known to the ActionScript interpreter as soon as it enters the frame. Thus, you can execute a function before you declare it, within a single frame:

```
test(); // displays "hi"
function test() {
    trace("hi");
}
```

Why am I getting an undefined return?

Functions return undefined when there is no return statement or when there is a return statement without a return value. Check for one of these situations. In both of the following cases, what you want is return result;.

No return statement:

```
function doubleIt(numberToBeDoubled) {
    result = numberToBeDoubled * 2;
}
```

No return value:

```
function doubleIt(numberToBeDoubled) {
    result = numberToBeDoubled * 2;
    return;
}
```

Part of my function never runs! Why?

If part of your function never seems to run, perhaps a return statement is getting in the way. Here's a simple example of the problem:

```
1: function showRoomNumber(floor, num) {
2:     if (num < 0)
3:         err = "negative numbers not supported";
4:         return(err);
5:     return ("Your room number is "+floor+num); // this line never executes
6: }
```

The problem is that there are no curly braces around the two statements that are intended to be the error return (lines 3 and 4). Thus, line 4 always executes, causing the function to return. Line 3 is skipped if num is greater than or equal to 0. If line 3 doesn't execute, err isn't defined, and line 4 returns undefined. Meanwhile, line 5, which would return the room number, never executes at all.

The function should look like this:

```
function showRoomNumber(floor, num) {
    if (num < 0) {
        err = "negative numbers not supported";
        return(err)
    }
    return ("Your room number is "+floor+num);
}
```

FLASH AT WORK: CALCULATING FACTORIALS—AN EXAMPLE OF RECURSION

Recursion is frequently illustrated through a function that calculates factorials. Factorials are often used to determine how many different ways you can order or arrange a set of things.

The factorial of a number is

(number) × (number − 1) × (number − 2)...

and so on until you reach the last multiplier, which is 1. Thus, the factorial of 4 is

$4 \times 3 \times 2 \times 1$

or 24.

The factorials of 0 and 1 are both defined to be 1.

In pseudocode, a `factorial()` function works as follows:

if (number < zero) reject it
if (number is not an integer) round it down to an integer
if (number is 0 or 1) factorial = 1
if (number > 1) factorial = number × factorial (number − 1)

The last line makes the function recursive: To get the factorial of a number, you multiply the number by the factorial of the next lowest integer. That starts the loop again.

Here's what the factorial function looks like in ActionScript:

```
 1: function factorial(myNumber){
 2:     myNumber = Math.floor(myNumber); // Round down to nearest integer.
 3:     if (myNumber < 0){ // If number < 0, reject it.
 4:         return ("factorials not defined for negative numbers");
 5:     }
 6:     if (myNumber < 2 ) { // If number is 0 or 1
 7:         return 1; // factorial = 1  Also breaks the recursion loop!
 8:     }
 9:     else return (myNumber * factorial(myNumber - 1)); // recursion
10: }
11: trace(factorial(4)); // displays "24"
```

When the `factorial()` function is called with the argument 4, the first line that really does anything is line 9. It starts to return `4*factorial(3)`, but, of course, the interpreter must calculate `factorial(3)` before it can return that value.

Again, when the `factorial()` function is called with the argument 3, the `else` statement on line 9 executes. The function starts to return `3*factorial(2)`, but the interpreter needs to calculate `factorial(2)` before it can return that value.

The `factorial()` function is called with the argument 2. In the `else` statement on line 9, the interpreter starts to return `2*factorial(1)` but needs to calculate `factorial(1)` first.

Finally, when the interpreter executes `factorial(1)`, the `if (myNumber < 2 )` statement on line 3 is true. It returns 1.

The interpreter now completes all the `return` statements that have been "left hanging." The most recent round resolves to 2. That makes the previous round resolve to 6, and the round before that to 24, which is the value returned by the `factorial()` function.

INTERACTION, EVENTS, AND SEQUENCING

IN THIS CHAPTER

TRIGGERING ACTION: THE TIMELINE AND EVENT HANDLERS

The ActionScript interpreter is linear by nature. Unless you tell it differently, it simply executes statements sequentially. In the preceding chapter, you saw that function calls allow you to break out of that sequential lockstep. They allow you to interrupt the sequential program flow, execute a series of statements defined elsewhere in the program, and then return to the place you left off.

⇨ *For more details on function calls, see Chapter 15, "Combining Statements into Functions," page 267.*

This chapter discusses two other ways to alter program flow, one using timelines and the other using *events*. Each object has particular events it watches for. For instance, a button generates an `onPress` event every time the user clicks on the button. You can *trap* such events by using special-purpose functions called event *handlers*. The timeline-based approach, also called "frame-based," takes advantage of the fact that, when a frame plays, the interpreter executes the code on that frame.

⇨ *Another way to alter program flow is to use the setInterval() global function, covered in Chapter 17, "Unlocking the Power of Movie Clips," page 331.*

A possible source of confusion is the fact that the most commonly used event also happens to relate to frames: A movie clip generates an `onEnterFrame` event each time it enters a frame. The `onEnterFrame` event allows you to execute the same code every time a particular movie clip enters a frame, *without* having to put that code in every frame. In contrast, frame-based programming executes code that *is* in a frame when the playhead enters that frame.

⇨ *The distinction between frame-based and event-based program flow control is introduced in "Selecting Frame Actions or Object Actions," page 171 (Chapter 11, "Getting Started with ActionScript").*

Most of this chapter is devoted to event-based programming. First, however, let's take a brief look at timeline-based programming.

TIMELINE-BASED SCRIPTING

Sometimes, the timeline is the most natural means of organizing your programs. A good example is a drop-down menu, in which the collapsed state of the menu is on one frame (such as frame 1), and the expanded state is on another frame (such as frame 2). Sample movie timeline.fla on the CD provides an example of such a menu. Figures 16.1 and 16.2 show the expanded state as it appears in the SWF and in the FLA, respectively.

⇨ *The timeline is introduced in Chapter 2, "The Flash Interface," page 17.*

If an action is associated with one of the menu states (collapsed or expanded), it makes sense to put the action on the frame the action is associated with.

For example, Figure 16.1 shows an "Art Gallery" application in which each menu option allows the user to select a different graphic for display. When the menu expands, the graphic currently being displayed is "grayed out" (by setting its _alpha to 50) so that it is less distracting.

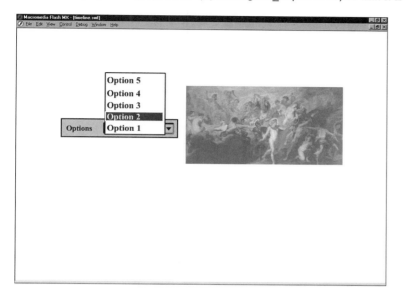

Figure 16.1
The expanded state of a drop-down menu, achieved with frame-based programming by sending the playhead to frame 2.

Figure 16.2 shows the FLA for this "Art Gallery" application. The timeline contains a two-frame pop-up menu with the playhead on frame 2 in layer 1. The collapsed state of the menu is on frame 1; the expanded state, on frame 2. When the menu expands (by going to frame 2), it triggers the code in that frame, currentPicture._alpha = 50;, and dims the graphic.

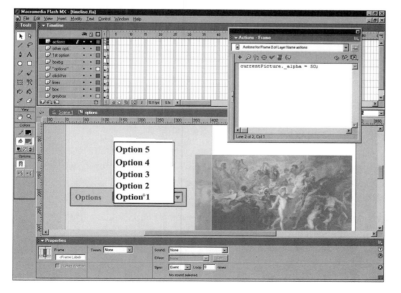

Figure 16.2
The FLA that created the drop-down menu shown in Figure 16.1. The playhead is on frame 2.

In addition, if you have code that executes sequentially but logically consists of two or more discrete sections, you can use the timeline to lay out that code. If you put each section in a different frame in the top layer and label each code-bearing frame, the location of your code and its basic structure can be immediately apparent as soon as someone opens the file. Figure 16.3 shows the timeline of Macromedia Flash developer Robin Debreuil's MovieClass.fla, which is laid out this way. (Don't worry about what MovieClass.fla does. It's just used here to show the layout. The file is on the CD if you want to delve into it.)

16

Figure 16.3
Using the timeline to lay out code that logically consists of two or more discrete sections.

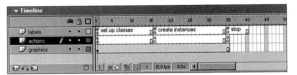

You can construct quite complex applications by putting code on various frames (ideally, with descriptive labels) and sending the playhead to the appropriate frame at the appropriate time. Until Flash 5, this was the only way of simulating function calls in Flash. With the arrival of real functions in Flash 5, timeline-based program flow control is used much less. However, the two are not incompatible; they can easily be combined.

EVENT-BASED SCRIPTING

The Flash Player generates an event to signal you that something potentially significant has happened to an object in your program. For instance, the user may have clicked on a button or resized the Stage; a movie clip, XML file, or sound may have completed loading; or the user may have changed the contents of a text field.

Nothing happens in your movie when the player generates an event. To make something happen, you must *trap* the event by creating an event handler or *callback* function for it. The Flash Player will then call your function when the event occurs.

For instance, the callback function might display a new graphic when a button is pressed; rearrange items on the Stage when the Stage is resized; check the value of a variable after a movie clip containing the variable has loaded; or check the contents of a changed text field and take action based on the text.

All callback functions are methods of objects. If the object is a movie clip, button, or text field, the callback function will execute only if the object is currently on the Stage.

The names of callback functions are predetermined: They always begin with on, as in onEnterFrame. The circumstances under which they are called are also predetermined. However, it is totally up to you to decide whether to create a particular handler for a particular object and what statements to put in the callback function.

For instance, you can define an onEnterFrame event handler for a movie clip, myClip, by putting this line of code in a frame on the timeline containing myClip:

```
myClip.onEnterFrame = function () {trace("just testing");};
```

The Flash Player will call your callback function every time the movie clip enters a new frame. In this case, it will display "just testing" in the Output window once per frame.

Flash MX Event Handling Enhancements

In Flash 5, the only documented events were those attached to buttons, movie clips, and instances of the XML and XMLSocket classes. Button and movie clip event handlers had to be object actions, not frame actions.

> *"Selecting Frame Actions or Object Actions," page 171, (Chapter 11, "Getting Started with ActionScript") explains the difference between object actions and frame actions. Chapter 11 also shows how to create movie clip event handlers using object actions.*

In Flash 5, you needed to attach button and movie clip events while you were authoring the movie. This method of defining events still works. You click on the button or movie clip on the Stage; then you use the Actions pane to create an on (for buttons) or onClipEvent (for movie clips) event handler. In Flash 5, you could not attach button or movie clip event handlers programmatically while the movie was running, nor could you change or delete them at runtime. They were *static* or immutable.

In contrast, events associated with XML and XMLSocket, in both Flash 5 and Flash MX, are attached programmatically while the movie is running. For instance, to use the XML onLoad event handler, you first create an XML object programmatically and then attach the event handler, also programmatically, like this:

```
myXML = new XML(); // create XML object
myXML.onLoad = function(success) {trace("loaded !")}; // attach handler
```

> *For more information on XML, see Chapter 28, "XML Data," page 611.*

Event handlers that are created programmatically can also be changed or deleted programmatically at runtime. They are *dynamic*.

The on, onClipEvent, and XML-related event handlers work the same in Flash MX as in Flash 5. In addition, Flash MX introduces a number of significant enhancements to event-based programming:

- Custom objects that you create can now have event handlers and receive event notifications. An object that is explicitly registered to receive a particular class of events is called a *listener*. You can also register a built-in object as a listener if you want it to receive events that it would not normally receive.

- You can create an event handler dynamically for any event that you want to trap, whether it's associated with the Button, LoadVars, MovieClip, Sound, Stage, TextField, XML, or XMLSocket class. Every static on and onClipEvent event has a dynamic equivalent. For instance, onEnterFrame is the dynamic equivalent of onClipEvent(enterFrame).

> *LoadVars is covered in Chapter 27, "Communicating with the Server," page 600.*

- Movie clips can now take all the same events and have all the same behaviors as buttons, with the fortunate exception of scope. A *button movie clip* is a movie clip that acts like a button but offers more flexibility and retains its own scope rather than scoping to the timeline it's on. Some Flash MX users have declared that they will never use "old-style" buttons again.

■ You can define event handlers for four classes of objects that never received events before: LoadVars, Sound, TextField, and Stage. LoadVars, TextField, and Stage are new object types in Flash MX.

■ With the new object types come new events: onLoad for LoadVars; resize for Stage; and onChanged, onScroller, onSetFocus, and onKillFocus for TextField.

■ Text fields and buttons now have instance names, a requirement for assigning dynamic event handlers to them.

➡ *For more details on the TextField object, see Chapter 20, "Using the Built-in Movie Objects," page 443.*

■ The existing Sound object, which defined no event handlers in Flash 5, now defines two: onLoad and onSoundComplete.

■ A new Button class makes buttons "real" objects and allows you to apply all the techniques of object-oriented programming (OOP) to them. The Button class has dynamic equivalents for all the static on events that buttons have always had. For instance, the Button class has an onPress method equivalent to on(press). In addition, the Button class has two new events: onSetFocus and onKillFocus. Buttons also have instance names now, a requirement for attaching dynamic events.

■ The MovieClip class also supports onSetFocus and onKillFocus, as well as dynamic equivalents for all the static onClipEvent events. For instance, the onEnterFrame method is equivalent to onClipEvent(enterFrame).

Table 16.1 shows all the events that the Flash 6 Player considers potentially significant.

Table 16.1 Flash MX Events

	Button	Key	LoadVars	MovieClip	Mouse	Selection	TextField	Sound	Stage	XML	XML Socket
on	E										
onResize									L(n)		
onChanged							E(n),L(n)				
onScroller	E			E			E(n),L(n)				
onSetFocus	E			E		L(n)	E(n)				
onKillFocus	E			E			E(n)				
onRollOver	E			E							
onRollOut	E			E							
onPress	E			E							
onRelease	E			E							
onReleaseOutside	E			E							

	Button	Key	LoadVars	MovieClip	Mouse	Selection	TextField	Sound	Stage	XML	XML Socket
onDragOut	E			E							
onDragOver	E			E							
onMouseUp				E	L(n)						
onMouseDown				E	L(n)						
onMouseMove				E	L(n)						
onKeyUp		L(n)		E							
onKeyDown		L(n)		E							
onClipEvent				E							
onUnload				E							
onEnterFrame				E							
onLoad			E(n)	E				E(n)		E	
onData				E						E	E
onConnect										E	E
onClose										E	E
onSoundComplete								E(n)			

Legend: E = event, L = Listener, (n) = new in Flash MX

System Events and User Input Events

The two basic kinds of events in Flash are *system* events and *user input* events. System events are generated by the movie. They include a movie clip entering a frame, for example, or an external data load operation completing.

User input events, on the other hand, begin with a mouse click or a keypress. Or, more precisely, they arrive through the mouse or keyboard interfaces, which can also accommodate other input methods such as voice. User input events include all events associated with the Button, Key, Mouse, Stage, and TextField classes. Many movie clip events are also user input events because they duplicate the functionality of Button, Key, Mouse, and TextField events.

Registering Listeners

Every dynamic event handler function is a property of an object. The object may belong to one of these built-in classes: Button, LoadVars, MovieClip, Sound, TextField, Stage, XML, or XMLSocket. In that case, the object receives one or more events by default. You just create the callback function for the particular object instance, and you're done.

If you want an object that belongs to a built-in class to receive events it doesn't receive by default, or if you want a custom object that you have created to receive events, another step is involved: You must register the object as a listener. Five classes generate events that an object can register to receive: Key, Mouse, Selection, Stage, and TextField.

You register an object as a listener using the `addListener` method of the class you're registering with. For example, a movie clip normally receives `onKeyUp` and `onKeyDown` events only when it has keyboard focus. To make it receive these events under all circumstances, you create callback functions and register the movie clip as a listener with the `Key` class, like this:

```
myClip.onKeyUp = function () {trace("onKeyUp fired");};
myClip.onKeyDown = function () {trace("onKeyDown fired");};
Key.addListener(myClip);
```

The following code creates an object named `myObj`, provides it with an event handler for the `onMouseUp` event (releasing the mouse button), and then registers as a listener with the `Mouse` class:

```
myObj = new Object();
myObj.onMouseUp = function () {trace("mouseUp");};
Mouse.addListener(myObj);
```

From that point on, `myObj.onMouseUp` will fire whenever the mouse button is released.

You can accomplish the same result using an empty movie clip with a static `onClipEvent(mouseUp)` event handler. However, the dynamic approach has a number of advantages:

First, the dynamic approach is more flexible because you can decide programmatically at runtime which listeners to register and which events to create event handlers for. With the static approach, you need to decide which objects get which event handlers when you're authoring the movie.

Second, the dynamic approach allows you to put your code wherever you want. It doesn't force you to attach it to the movie clip. You might be able to centralize all your code on the Main Timeline, for instance, making it easier to find and edit.

Third, dynamic event handlers are real functions, whereas static event handlers are not. That means that, unlike static event handlers, dynamic event handlers allow you to define local variables within them, call them explicitly, and pass them parameters.

Fourth, there are just 9 static movie clip events, implemented as parameters to `onClipEvent`. There are 18 dynamic movie clip events.

Fifth, for both movie clips and buttons, there are no static equivalents for `onSetFocus` and `onKillFocus`. Thus, you can't programmatically control the way the static event handlers relate to keyboard focus.

Sixth, the dynamic `onPress` and `onRelease` event handlers can make a movie clip act like a button, firing its events only when it has focus, and displaying a hand icon. Achieving the same effect with the static `mouseUp` and `mouseDown` events takes more work.

Finally, using a movie clip just to trap events is like using a Swiss Army knife for the corkscrew. A custom object uses less memory than an empty movie clip because it doesn't contain movie clip properties that are irrelevant to trapping events.

The only compelling reason to use static clip events is for `onClipEvent(load)` for movie clips that are manually placed on the Stage at authoring time. The dynamic `onLoad` event does not work in this case.

⇨ *For more details on onLoad and onClipEvent(load), see "Movie Clip Events," later in this chapter, page 320.*

Scoping and the `this` Keyword with Event Handlers

Inside the static event handlers, on and onClipEvent, both the `this` keyword and direct references refer to the timeline of the clip to which the event handler is attached. For instance, the following are equivalent:

```
onClipEvent(enterFrame) {
    _x++;
}
onClipEvent(enterFrame) {
    this._x++;
}
```

With dynamic event handlers, however, the situation is more complex. Every dynamic event handler is a method of an object, and inside the event handler, `this` refers to the object. Direct references, on the other hand, scope to the timeline on which the event handler function is defined. Thus, if the following code is placed on the Main Timeline, `this.myVar` refers to `myClip.myVar`, whereas `myVar` refers to `_root.myVar`:

```
_root.createEmptyMovieClip("myClip",1);
myVar = "main timeline";
myClip.myVar = "myClip";
myClip.onMouseUp = function() {
    trace(this.myVar); // "myClip"
    trace(myVar); // "main timeline"
}
```

As with other methods, you can define local variables in dynamic event handlers. For example, you could add the following as the first line of the `myClip.onMouseUp` function in the preceding example:

```
var myVar = "local";
```

The `trace(myVar)` statement in the last line will then display `"local"` rather than `"main timeline"`.

You can point another object's event handler at `myClip.onMouseUp`, and the value of the `this` variable inside `myClip.onMouseUp` will change to the other object. The direct reference to `myVar`, on the other hand, still scopes to the timeline on which the function literal is defined.

For instance, suppose you create another clip named `myClip2`, give it its own `myVar` property, and give it an `onMouseDown` property referencing the `myClip.onMouseUp` event handler defined in the previous example. Here's the code:

> When the scope of a variable or other data item is the scope in which it is defined, the item is said to be *lexically* scoped.

```
myClip2.myVar = "myClip2";
myClip2.onMouseDown = _root.myClip.onMouseUp;
```

16

Although `myClip.onMouseUp` and `myClip2.onMouseDown` refer to the same function literal, `myClip2.onMouseDown` fires when the user *depresses* the mouse button, and `this` means `myClip2` inside the function. It displays `"myClip2"` and `"main timeline"`. On the other hand, `myClip.onMouseUp` fires when the user *releases* the mouse button, and `this` means `myClip`, so it displays `"myClip"` and `"main timeline"`. In both cases, direct references still refer to the Main Timeline. To summarize: The value of the `this` variable is the object associated with the calling method, while the direct reference to `myVar` scopes lexically.

Calling Event Handlers Explicitly

Even though event handlers have the special property of being called automatically by the Flash Player under predetermined circumstances, invoking event handlers explicitly is also legal. You might want to invoke them, for instance, if you have created an event handler in one object and want to execute it on another object. Using the `Function.apply()` or `Function.call()` method allows you to specify the meaning of `this` within the call.

For example, extending the examples from the preceding section, the following code creates an object named `myObj` (line 1), gives it a `myVar` property (line 2), gives it an `onMouseDown` event handler that first executes `myClip.onMouseUp` and then executes one additional line of code (lines 3–6), and finally (line 7) makes `myObj` a listener of the Mouse object so that `myObj.onMouseDown` will fire when the mouse is clicked:

```
1: myObj = new Object();
2: myObj.myVar = "myObj";
3: myObj.onMouseDown = function () {
4:     myClip.onMouseUp.apply(myObj); // displays "myObj", "main timeline"
5:     trace("this "this.myVar); // displays "myObj"
6: };
7: Mouse.addListener(myObj);
```

`this.myVar` always displays `"myObj"` within `myObj.onMouseDown`. You need to use the `Function.apply()` or `Function.call()` method when you explicitly invoke `myClip.onMouseUp` if you want `this` to refer to `myObj` inside `myClip.onMouseUp`. If you invoke `myClip.onMouseUp` using a regular function call, `this` will always refer to `myClip`.

Extending the examples in the preceding section, suppose you now place the following code on a third movie clip:

```
// on myOtherClip
onClipEvent(load) {
    _root.myClip.onMouseUp();
}
```

This code displays `"myClip"` and `"main timeline"` because it is called as a method of `myClip`; therefore, it executes in the context of `myClip`.

Calling event handlers explicitly opens up a third possibility, other than using a regular function call, and using `apply()` or `call()`. The third option is pointing a variable at the method and then using the variable to execute the method. In this case, `this` will be the timeline where the variable is defined. The direct reference to `myVar` in `myClip.onMouseUp` still scopes lexically; that's consistent among all three ways of calling the method. This third option is illustrated in the following code, which is on the timeline of `myClip2`:

```
myVar = "myVar in myClip2";
f = _root.myClip.onMouseUp;
f(); // displays "myVar in myClip2", "main timeline"
```

⇨ *For more information on function scoping, see Chapter 15, "Combining Statements into Functions,"*
page 267.

Event Handlers and Focus

Text fields, buttons, and button movie clips all support the `onSetFocus` and `onKillFocus` events. By default, `onKeyUp` and `onKeyDown` event handlers associated with these objects will not fire unless the object has keyboard focus—that is, unless the keyboard cursor is on the object. (The static equivalents, `onClipEvent(keyUp)` and `onClipEvent(keyDown)`, fire regardless of keyboard focus.)

Alternatively, you can use an `addListener` statement to register an object to receive a particular class of events. In that case, the object's dynamic event handlers for that class will always fire, whether or not the object has focus.

Thus, say you have a movie clip, `myClip`, and you want it to trap `onKeyUp` and `onKeyDown` events. First, create the callback functions:

```
myClip.onKeyUp = function () {trace("onKeyUp");};
myClip.onKeyDown = function () {trace("onKeyDown");};
```

Then you have two options. One possibility is to make `myClip` into a button movie clip. The callback functions are enabled when `myClip` has keyboard focus.

⇨ *The process for creating a button movie clip is described in "Movie Clip Events," later in this chapter,*
page 320.

The other possibility is to make `myClip` a listener of the `Key` class, like this:

```
Key.addListener(myClip);
```

The callback functions are continuously enabled.

Disabling and Deleting Event Handlers

Deleting an event handler is easy because it's just an ordinary variable. Here's an example:

```
delete myClip.onKeyDown;
```

If you've registered a listener for a class from which you're no longer going to trap any events, you should remove the listener, as well, like this:

```
Key.removeListener(myClip);
```

You might want to temporarily disable an event handler so that it doesn't use up processor cycles when it isn't performing any useful function. For instance, a number of `enterFrame` event handlers just checking an `if` condition and returning can slow down your program noticeably.

One possibility is setting the event handler itself to `null`. Suppose you define an `onEnterFrame` event handler like this:

> To enable line numbers in the Actions panel, click in the upper-right corner of the panel and select View Line Numbers. Enabling line numbers makes it easy to find a particular line.

```
myClip.myFunc = function () {
    // function statements
};
myClip.onEnterFrame = myFunc;
```

When you want to disable the event handler, you can use a statement like this:

```
myClip.onEnterFrame = null;
```

Sample movie ondata.fla on the CD uses this technique. See line 25 in the program:

```
else { _root.attachTarget.onEnterFrame =  null;}
```

To start the event handler again, use the following statement:

```
myClip.onEnterFrame = myFunc;
```

If setting `onEnterFrame` to `null` has unwanted side effects, you can achieve a close equivalent by setting a variable equal to `myFunc` and using the variable to run `myFunc()` in the `onEnterFrame` event handler. You can then switch the variable back and forth between `null` and `myFunc` to stop and start. Here's how you set things up:

```
myClip.myFunc = function () {
    // function statements
};
doNow = myClip.myFunc;
myClip.onEnterFrame = function () {
    doNow();
};
```

Now, when you want to stop, you use a statement like this:

```
doNow = null;
```

And when you want to start up again, you use the following:

```
doNow = myClip.myFunc;
```

Button Events

Flash has eight static button events: `press`, `release`, `releaseOutside`, `rollOver`, `rollOut`, `dragOut`, `dragOver`, and `keyPress`.

It has nine dynamic button events: onPress, onRelease, onReleaseOutside, onRollOver, onRollOut, onDragOut, onDragOver, onKillFocus, and onSetFocus.

Notice that buttons do not receive dynamic Key events by default. However, you can make a button a listener of the Key class so that it can receive onKeyUp and onKeyDown events, the dynamic equivalents of keyPress.

All button events fire only in response to the primary mouse button. There is no reaction to a secondary mouse button.

All mouse-related button events (which include all button events except keyPress) fire just once, at a transition point. For instance, even though the user holds down the mouse button, the press event occurs just once, when the button is first pressed.

Except for the first paragraph on focus events, each of the following paragraphs covers just a single event, which may be trapped by either a static or a dynamic event handler. Thus, referring to "the press and onPress events," for example, is a bit like saying "the radio and TV news." There is just one event, but you're finding out about it through two different channels. You can also say "the press events," meaning "the press event, whether captured statically or dynamically."

onKillFocus **and** onSetFocus

The onSetFocus event occurs when a button gets keyboard focus. Keyboard focus changes when the user presses the Tab or Shift+Tab keys to navigate among text fields and buttons on a page. The onKillFocus event occurs when the button loses keyboard focus. Focus events were implemented primarily for input text fields. They provide a convenient hook for any necessary pre- and post-processing as the user fills in the fields. These events can also be useful for buttons and button movie clips. For instance, if you're using a "Submit" button, when the button gains focus, you could check to make sure the user has filled in all the fields properly. When the button loses focus, you could generate a "Thank You" message.

press **and** onPress

The press and onPress events occur when the user presses the primary mouse button while the mouse pointer is within the hit area of the button. This event provides the fastest possible reaction because it fires when the mouse button is pushed down, as opposed to when it is released. On the other hand, this does not allow the user to change his or her mind after pushing the mouse button. This event is most appropriate for games (where reaction time is critical), and it also works for radio buttons, where the user can undo the choice just by pushing the button again.

release **and** onRelease

The release and onRelease events occur when the primary mouse button is both pressed and released while the mouse pointer is within the hit area of the button. These events allow the user to change his or her mind by moving the pointer outside the hit area before releasing the mouse button.

releaseOutside **and** onReleaseOutside

The releaseOutside and onReleaseOutside events occur when the user presses the mouse button while the pointer is within the hit area, and then moves the pointer outside the hit area and releases the button. If the user needs to drag something from one place to another, for instance, you could put actions within these event handlers to determine whether the mouse pointer is in the correct place when the user releases it.

rollOver **and** onRollOver

The rollOver and onRollOver events fire when the mouse pointer moves into the hit area while the mouse button is up (not depressed). Although the *Up* state of the button and the corresponding _up frame of a button movie clip handle the visual aspects of rollover, the event handler allows you to do something programmatically at this point, as well. For instance, if you want to do something just before the user presses a button, you can use these events.

rollOut **and** onRollOut

The rollOut and onRollOut events fire when the mouse pointer moves out of the hit area while the mouse button is up (*not* depressed). Again, *Up* and _up handle the visual aspects of rollout, but the event handler allows you to do something programmatically. This event can be used, for instance, to do something after the user finishes interacting with a particular button.

dragOut **and** onDragOut

The dragOut and onDragOut events fire when the mouse pointer moves out of the hit area while the mouse button *is* pressed.

dragOver **and** onDragOver

The dragOver and onDragOver events fire when the user performs a dragOut-type action, does *not* release outside, and then moves the pointer back inside the hit area and releases.

keyPress

The keyPress event occurs when the user presses a key on the keyboard. The format is as follows:

```
on (keyPress key) {
    statement1;
    statement2;
}
```

key is a string in quotation marks representing the key pressed. For alphanumeric keys, *key* represents the key literally, like this:

```
on (keyPress "a") {
    trace("a pressed");
}
```

Alternatively, *key* can be one of 14 special keywords representing nonalphanumeric keys, such as arrow keys, the spacebar, and the Enter key:

<Backspace>	<Delete>	<Down>	<End>	<Enter>
<Home>	<Insert>	<Left>	<PgDn>	<PgUp>
<Right>	<Space><Tab>	<Up>		

You use the keywords like this:

```
on (keyPress "<Space>") {
    trace("space bar pressed");
}
```

Unlike mouse-related button events, `keyPress` typically occurs repeatedly if the user holds down the key, though this could vary with the keyboard and the operating system configuration.

The `keyPress` event handler must be attached to a button instance. In addition, the Flash Player must have mouse focus for key-related event handlers to fire. Movies get mouse focus automatically in the Flash Player or in a projector, but not in the browser. Therefore, for browser compatibility, you might want to make users click a button before beginning keyboard input.

In almost every way, the `keyPress` event is more limited and less flexible than the `onKeyUp` and `onKeyDown` events associated with the Key object. For instance, `keyPress` doesn't support function keys, Caps Lock, or Cmd (Mac) or Ctrl (Windows). Nor does it support listeners. Probably most importantly, `keyPress` requires that you check for a specific key; it does not allow you to get an event when any key is pressed and then determine which one it was. The Key object overcomes all these limitations.

The `keyPress` event does have one unique capability that the Key object events don't: It can disable the Tab key for focus shifting. To prevent users from using the Tab key to shift focus in the standalone player, projector, and browser, you attach the following to a button:

```
on(keyPress "<Tab>") {
    // must have some statement here
    dummy = null;
}
```

In the Flash authoring environment, you may need to click in an input text field to give the movie keyboard focus.

Then, if you want, you can use Key object events to detect the Tab key and `Selection.setFocus` to explicitly change focus.

The Key object events, on the other hand, allow you to capture the Tab key without disabling it for focus shifting.

Because keyboard focus behaves differently in the authoring environment, Flash Player and browser, you should test any movie that involves keyboard focus in all the environments where it may be used.

Key Events

The Key object was introduced in Flash 5, with `onClipEvent(keyDown)` and `onClipEvent(keyUp)` movie clip events. `keyDown` fires when the user presses any key on the keyboard; `keyUp`, when the user releases any key.

Four methods associated with the `Key` object allow you to determine which key was pressed:

- `Key.getCode()` returns the keycode of the last key pressed.
- `key.getAscii()` returns the ASCII code of the last key pressed.
- `Key.isDown(keycode)` returns `true` if the specified key is being pressed now.
- `Key.isToggled(keycode)` returns `true` if the specified key (Caps Lock or Num Lock) is toggled on now.

You can use the `Key.isDown()` method by itself in an `enterFrame` event handler, to check for a key on every frame. For instance, this code checks for the Tab key on every frame:

```
myClip.onEnterFrame = function () {
    if (Key.isDown(Key.TAB)
        trace("Tab key pressed");
}
```

This code could be appropriate in a game, for example, where catching keypresses as fast as possible is a primary design goal.

Notice the use of the `TAB` constant in caps.

Unless you're checking on every frame, using `Key.isDown()` alone is an unreliable method of detecting keypresses because the user could press the key in a frame where you're not checking for it. To get around this problem, use a `Key` event handler to detect the keypress and one of the `Key` methods to find out which key it was. The following example uses the `onKeyDown` event handler with the `Key.getAscii()` method—and the `String.fromCharCode()` method—to translate the ASCII code into an alphanumeric character:

```
myClip.onKeyDown = function () {
    trace( String.fromCharCode(Key.getAscii()) );
};
```

Flash MX adds no new events or methods, but adds dynamic handlers (`onKeyUp` and `onKeyDown`) and listener functionality, which permits objects other than movie clips to receive Key events.

When the Flash Player has focus, `on(keyPress)` will always fire when the appropriate key is pressed. Events associated with the `Key` object, however, may or may not fire, depending on two factors: keyboard focus and listener registration.

➡️ *Focus, listeners, and events are discussed in "Event Handlers and Focus," earlier in this chapter, page 313.*

> A number of constants representing commonly used keys are listed in the Toolbox list of the Actions panel, under Objects, Movie, Key, Constants.

> The Flash Player must have mouse focus for key-related event handlers—including `on(keyPress)`—to fire.

You can get Key-related event handlers to fire in two ways:

- Any object's Key-related event handlers will fire, regardless of keyboard focus, if the object is registered as a listener with the Key object, as in the following example:

```
myClip.onKeyDown = function () {trace("onKeyDown fired");};
Key.addListener (myClip); // works for any object, ignores keyboard focus
```

- If a button or button movie clip has keyboard focus, its Key-related event handlers will fire. It does *not* have to be registered as a listener with the Key object.

Table 16.2 summarizes these two rules.

Table 16.2   When Key-Related Event Handlers Fire

	Object Registered as Key Listener	Object Not Registered as Key Listener
Object has keyboard focus	Any object's Key events will fire.	Button and button movie clip's Key events will fire.
Object doesn't have keyboard focus	Any object's Key events will fire.	Key events will not fire.

Mouse Events

The Mouse object was introduced in Flash 5, with onClipEvent(mouseDown), onClipEvent(mouseUp), and onClipEvent(mouseMove) movie clip events. mouseDown fires when the user presses the primary mouse button, mouseUp fires when the user releases the button, and mouseMove fires whenever the mouse moves. mouseMove may also fire when a movie loads.

Flash MX adds dynamic versions of these events: onMouseUp, onMouseDown, and onMouseMove. It also adds listeners so that objects other than movie clips can receive these events. Although Mouse events can now be associated with buttons, they fire no matter where the mouse pointer is on the Stage, ignoring both keyboard focus and button hit areas. In addition, unlike Button events, Mouse events do not change the mouse pointer to a hand cursor.

One use of mouseMove or onMouseMove is to "wake up" a program after an idle period. If you're using mouseMove or onMouseMove in a limited context like this, consider setting them equal to null while they're not being used. Otherwise, they can generate large numbers of events in a short time, taking up a lot of processor cycles.

For more details on setting event handlers to null, see "Disabling and Deleting Event Handlers," earlier in this chapter, page 313.

One common use of Mouse events—in conjunction with the two Mouse methods, show() and hide(), which make the mouse pointer visible or invisible—is to create a custom mouse pointer. You hide the standard pointer, use _root._xmouse and _root._ymouse to check for mouse position whenever a Mouse event occurs, and then consistently display the custom mouse pointer at that position.

Movie Clip Events

Movie clips receive all the `Button`, `Key`, and `Mouse` events. In addition, movie clips receive *enter frame*, *load*, *unload*, and *data* events.

One new capability in Flash MX is that the dynamic forms of these events—`onEnterFrame`, `onLoad`, `onUnload`, and `onData`—can be associated with the Main Timeline. The static forms can be attached to movie clips, but not to the Main Timeline. Movie clip events on the Main Timeline don't offer any revolutionary new capabilities, but sometimes they make things more straightforward. For instance, they eliminate the need to put code on a movie clip just because you want to execute some action on every frame.

enterFrame

The `enterFrame` event has already appeared many times in this book. It occurs each time the playhead enters a frame, and it is the most commonly used event in Flash.

data and onData

The `data` and `onData` events fire when external data loads into a movie as a result of a `loadVariables()` or `loadMovie()` function.

> *The XML class also has an onData event, which is covered in Chapter 28, "XML Data," page 611.*

The `loadVariables()` function fires a single `data` event when an entire batch of variables finishes loading. In contrast, `loadMovie()` fires a series of `data` events up to a maximum of one per frame, as the movie loads. Thus, with `loadVariables()`, the `data` event tells you that you have all the data and can start to work with it. With `loadMovie()`, a `data` event tells you that some portion of the loaded movie has arrived, but you may need to check whether enough of it has arrived for your purposes. To check, you can use the `getBytesLoaded()` and `getBytesTotal()` functions, the `_framesloaded` and `_totalframes` movie clip properties, or—for Flash 4 compatibility—the deprecated `ifFrameLoaded()` function.

> *For more information on _ framesloaded and ifFrameLoaded(), see Chapter 14, "Working with Data: Using Statements," page 251.*

Sample movie ondata.fla provides a simple example of using the `onData` event with `loadVariables()`.

> *The data event is covered in "loadVariables and loadVariablesNum," page 600 (Chapter 27, "Communicating with the Server."*

load and onLoad

The `load` or `onLoad` event fires when a movie clip is initially loaded into your movie.

> *The LoadVars object also has an onLoad event. See Chapter 27, "Communicating with the Server," page 600.*

The Sound object has an onLoad event, too, covered in "Sound Events," later in this chapter, page 324.

The clip may have been manually created using the authoring tool, created by duplicating another clip using `duplicateMovieClip()`, loaded from the Library using `attachMovie()`, or loaded as an external SWF using `loadMovie()`.

Flash MX: No Load Event When a Clip Unloads

In Flash 5, the `unloadMovie()` function, paradoxically, also caused a `load` event to fire because an empty movie clip loaded into the space created by the unloaded movie. Thus, suppose you had a clip in the Library with the linkage ID `myMC`, and you put this code on the Main Timeline:

```
attachMovie("myMC", "myMC",1);
```

Suppose you also had this code on a button:

```
on(press) {
    _root.myMC.unloadMovie();
}
```

Pressing the button caused the `Error opening URL ...` error message to be displayed because Flash apparently attempted to load a nameless movie clip.

This is no longer true. In Flash MX, the button will work with no error message. Apparently, Flash MX doesn't generate a `load` event when a clip unloads.

In most cases, dynamic and static event handlers provide almost identical functionality. Dynamic event handlers provide advantages such as greater flexibility, easier code centralization, and local scoping.

For more details on the advantages of dynamic over static event handlers, see "Registering Listeners," earlier in this chapter, page 309.

Still, anything that can be done with dynamic event handlers can usually also be done with static event handlers, and vice versa. Not so with the `load` and `onLoad` events. In fact, when you first start trying to apply the `onLoad` event, it appears nearly useless. Why?

The problem is that the `onLoad` event handler must be created before the clip loads. However, if the clip hasn't loaded, there is nothing to assign the `onLoad` event handler to. Thus, if a clip named `myClip` is manually created on the Stage, and you place the following code on the first frame of the Main Timeline, the clip will already have loaded by the time the interpreter gets to your code:

```
myClip.onLoad = function () {trace("myClip loads");}; // will never fire
```

On the other hand, if you're going to load the clip programmatically, using `attachMovieClip()`, should you declare the `onLoad` event handler before or after the attach? If before, the clip does not exist yet, so you can't define an event handler for it. If after, the clip has already loaded, and it's too late.

It turns out there is one, and only one, way to use the dynamic onLoad event successfully: The event must be inherited from the `prototype` object of the constructor function—that is, from the class. When the interpreter creates a new object, there is a time when the object is still unnamed and "unborn" but already endowed with all the shared methods and properties from the `prototype` object.

⇨ *The process of creating a new object is described more fully in "Creating Objects Using the new Operator," page 280 (Chapter 15, "Combining Statements into Functions").*

When the object is "born," if one of those shared methods is an onLoad event handler, it will fire.

Sample movie onload.fla, for which part of the code follows, demonstrates this. The basic strategy of this program is to put an onLoad event handler in the `prototype` object of MyMCclass and then use an `Object.registerClass` statement to register a movie clip in the Library with MyMCclass.

⇨ *For more details on the Object.registerClass statement, see "Using Object.registerClass() to Subclass a New Movie Clip," page 351 (Chapter 17, "Unlocking the Power of Movie Clips").*

When the attachMovie statement loads the movie clip from the Library, the movie clip is assigned to MyMCclass and the onLoad event handler fires:

```
MyMCclass = function () {} // define the class
MyMCclass.prototype = new MovieClip(); // make it inherit from MovieClip
MyMCclass.prototype.onLoad = function () { // put onLoad in prototype
    trace(this+" loaded");
}
Object.registerClass("mc", MyMCclass); // register movie clip
_root.attachMovie("mc","mc",2);
```

Sample movie onload2.fla, also on the CD, created by Erica Norton, senior quality assurance engineer on the Macromedia Flash team, uses the same strategy, putting all the code between the #initclip and #endinitclip compiler instructions. These instructions make the statements into *clip initialization* actions that execute before any code on frame 1.

⇨ *Clip initialization is common with components, covered in Chapter 22, "Components," page 511.*

unload **and** onUnload

The unload and onUnload events occur when you use unloadMovie() or unloadMovieNum() to unload a clip that has been loaded.

The unload event is a good place to free up resources, such as listeners, that have been associated with a movie clip. For instance:

```
onClipEvent(load) {
    Mouse.addListener(this);
}
onClipEvent(unload) {
    Mouse.removeListener(this);
}
```

⇨ *Can't get a dynamic movie clip event to work? See the "Troubleshooting" section at the end of this chapter, page 328.*

Creating a Button Movie Clip

In Flash 5, movie clips could not receive button events. In Flash MX, movie clips receive button events by default. This provides the foundation for creating a button movie clip. There are three other pieces of functionality that you want in a button:

- A *hand cursor*, so that the user gets a visual indication when the button is clickable. By default, if you assign a button event handler to a movie clip, the clip immediately starts displaying the hand cursor when the mouse pointer is over it.

- A *hit area* defining the area of the Stage in which the button is clickable. Movie clips now have a hitArea property that allows you to designate any movie clip as the hit area of the button movie clip.

⇨ *For more details on the movie clip hand cursor, as well as the hitArea property, see "Flash MX's New Properties for Movie Clips," page 336 (Chapter 17, "Unlocking the Power of Movie Clips").*

- *Up, over, and down states*, so that the button changes appearance when the user enters the hit area and when he or she presses the button. You can give _up, _over, and _down labels to frames in the button movie clip's timeline, and they will automatically provide the desired behaviors. Alternatively, you can use onRollOver, onRollOut, and onRelease or onPress event handlers to implement these behaviors.

Sample movie buttonMovie.fla demonstrates the use of a hitArea clip and the _up, _over, and _down labels.

Web designer and i-Technica (http://i-Technica.com) owner/operator Helen Triolo's dynamicButtonMovie.fla on the CD demonstrates an alternative approach, using the default hit area and onRollOver, onRollOut, and onRelease. This program creates a button movie clip 100% programmatically.

After using the drawing API and createEmptyMovieClip() to create a movie clip named triangle, dynamicButtonMovie.fla gives triangle button functionality with the following lines:

```
triangle.c = new Color(triangle);
triangle.onRollOver = function() {
    this.c.setRGB(0xff0000);  // red on rollover
}
triangle.onRollOut = function() {
    this.c.setRGB(0x0000ff);  // original blue on rollout
}
triangle.onRelease = function() {
    trace("button clicked");
}
```

16

The first line gives the `triangle` clip a property, `triangle.c`, that belongs to the `Color` class and is used in the subsequent `onRollOver`, `onRollOut`, and `onRelease` event handlers to change the color of the movie clip to achieve the *up*, *down*, and *over* behaviors. The `onRelease` event handler makes the button clickable.

Selection Events

The primary purpose of the `Selection` object is to help you manage keyboard focus.

Any object can receive notification of all focus changes if you register the object with the `Selection` object using `addListener` and define an `onSetFocus` event handler.

The `Selection.onSetFocus` event handler has the following format:

```
onSetFocus (oldFocus, newFocus) {
    statements
}
```

The following sample code creates an object and makes it listen for all `onSetFocus` events:

```
myObj = new Object();
myObj.onSetFocus = function() {trace("focus set event occurred");};
Selection.addListener(myObj);
```

This is different from the `onSetFocus` event handlers available by default (without using `addListener`) for instances of the `Button`, `MovieClip`, and `TextField` classes. A default `onSetFocus` event handler fires only when *the instance it belongs to* gets focus. Therefore, a default `onSetFocus` event handler needs only one argument, which is the old focus. The new focus is always the instance that the handler belongs to. So the format for a default `onSetFocus` event handler is as follows:

```
onSetFocus (oldFocus) {
    statements
}
```

If an instance of `Button`, `MovieClip`, or `TextField` registers with the `Selection` object using `addListener`, its `onSetFocus` event handler will receive both kinds of notifications. This "double-barreled" `onSetFocus` event handler will fire *twice* when the instance gets focus but only once when any other object gets focus.

Sample movie selection.fla illustrates these points.

 Selection and focus are discussed earlier in this chapter in "Event Handlers and Focus," page 313, "Button Events," page 314, and "Key Events," page 317.

Sound Events

 The Sound object has two events: `onLoad` fires when the sound loads, and `onSoundComplete` fires when the sound completes playing.

As shown in the following code, summarized from sample movie sound.fla, you simply create the Sound object, define the event handlers, and load the sound.

```
music = new Sound(this); // create the sound object
music.onLoad = function () {
    this.start(); // start playing the sound
                //when the sound loads
};
music.onSoundComplete = function() {
    trace("music finished playing");
};
music.loadSound ("electro.mp3", true); // "true" means streaming mode
```

> For more details on the Sound object, see Chapter 20, "Using the Built-in Movie Objects," page 443.

The Stage onResize Event

The ability to manipulate the Stage as an object is a new feature in Flash MX.

The Stage object has just one event: onResize, occurring when the user resizes the Stage. The user can resize the Stage by clicking on boxes in the upper left (Mac) or upper right (Windows) of the Flash Player or the browser. The user can maximize the Stage or restore down or up. All these actions trigger an onResize event. Another way to resize is to drag the edges of the Player or browser window. This triggers multiple onResize events as the window continuously changes size. In the Flash Player or authoring environment, selecting View, Magnification, 100% also triggers an onResize event, but minimizing or zooming in or out does not. In addition, one or more Stage.resize events may fire when a movie is initially loaded, whether in a browser or in the Flash Player or authoring environment.

The scaleMode property of the Stage object determines how graphics are scaled and cropped as the Stage resizes. In the browser, parameters in the HTML file also affect scaling and cropping.

> For details on the scaleMode property, see "The Stage Object," page 457 (Chapter 20, "Using the Built-in Movie Objects").

Although there are many combinations of scaleMode and HTML settings, here's a setup that will generally yield good results:

Choose File, Publish Settings. On the HTML tab, select Percent in the Dimensions combo box, leaving Width and Height at the default values of 100%. Also on the HTML tab, select Default (Show All) in the Scale combo box.

Set Stage.scaleMode to "noScale" and Stage.align to "TL". You set these programmatically as shown in the code following the next paragraph.

Any object can be a listener for the Stage.resize event. In this simple example, the Stage registers with itself as a listener, eliminating the need to create a separate object to listen to this event.

```
Stage.scaleMode = "noScale";
Stage.align = "TL";
Stage.onResize = function() {
    // your code goes here!
};
Stage.addListener(Stage);
```

Defining the event handlers *before* loading the sound is essential.

16

The Stage.resize event is typically used to adjust the dimensions, layout, or contents of the movie to fit the new size of the Stage.

TextField **Events**

The four TextField events in Flash are as follows:

- onSetFocus occurs when the keyboard focus is not on the text field and the user gives focus to it by clicking on it or entering it using the Tab or Shift+Tab keys. It has one argument, the previous focus.

- onKillFocus occurs when the keyboard focus is on the text field and the user takes focus away from it by clicking outside it or leaving it using the Tab or Shift+Tab keys. It has one argument, the new focus.

For more information on onKillFocus and onSetFocus, see "Selection Events," earlier in this chapter, page 324.

Pressing Tab to change focus, but nothing is happening? See the "Troubleshooting" section at the end of this chapter, page 328.

- onChanged fires each time text in the field changes. Thus, it occurs every time the user types a letter in the text field and every time the user deletes a letter. Cutting a block of text or pasting in a block of text triggers just one onChanged event. This event has one argument, the text field instance name.

- onScroller fires when the scrollbar in a text field is moved, either by clicking the mouse on the scrollbar itself or automatically as the user enters text into the text field. This event has one argument, the text field instance name.

Sample movie textfieldEvents.fla demonstrates each of these events. It contains a single text field, myText, with a ScrollBar component added from the Components window. (Choose Window, Components to get to the Components window.) onChanged and onScroller increment variables (myScrollBarChanged and myScrollBarScroller) that are displayed in dynamic text fields. Here's the code:

```
myScrollBarChanged = 0;
myScrollBarScroller = 0;
myText.onSetFocus = function(oldFocus) {
    trace(oldFocus);
    trace("set focus");
};
myText.onKillFocus = function(newFocus) {
    trace(newFocus);
    trace("kill focus");
};
```

```
myText.onChanged = function(textfieldName) {
    trace(textfieldName);
    myScrollBarChanged++;
};
myText.onScroller = function(textfieldName) {
    trace(textfieldName);
    myScrollBarScroller++;
};
```

SEQUENCING ACTIONS USING EXECUTION ORDER

System events execute in a definite order in relation to the Main Timeline and the timelines of any child movie clips. Three main factors must be taken into account: first, the relative positions of the layers the events occur in; second, the position in the clip hierarchy (such as main movie, child clip) of the clip containing the event; and, finally, the type of event, such as *data load* using `attachMovie()`, `loadMovie()`, or `duplicateMovieClip()`, *clip initialization* using `#initclip` and `#endinitclip`, *clip loading and unloading* using `onClipEvent(load)` and `onClipEvent(unload)`, `onLoad` and `onUnload`, or *enter frame* using `onClipEvent(enterFrame)` and `onEnterFrame`.

Here are some basic rules governing the sequence of system events:

- When you load a movie, any clip initialization code in the loaded movie executes before anything else in that frame.

- Static load events (`onClipEvent(load)`) execute in the frame in which the clip loads and before any timeline code in that clip executes.

- Dynamic load events (`onLoad`) execute in the frame *after* the frame in which the clip loads and *after* any timeline code in that clip executes.

- Loading or unloading a movie pre-empts the enter frame event for that movie. Thus, `enterFrame` and `onEnterFrame` events don't start until the frame *after* the frame in which the clip appears onstage.

- Within a single timeline, code executes from the top layer to the bottom layer.

- Nonevent code on the parent timeline executes before nonevent code on child timelines.

- If more than one clip loads in the same frame, their code initially executes according to the load order defined in File, Publish Settings on the Flash tab (Bottom Up, which is the default, or Top Down). In subsequent frames, this execution order is reversed.

With all these rules interacting, execution order can get quite complex. This is another reason why it's worthwhile to try to centralize code as much as possible and to limit the number of child clips containing code.

TROUBLESHOOTING

Why isn't my event handler firing?

Here's one possibility: Perhaps you've used a static parameter name instead of a dynamic event handler name. For instance, `mouseDown` is a static parameter, properly used with a static event handler, like this:

```
onClipEvent(mouseDown) {
    // statements
}
```

If you used static event handlers often in Flash 5, you may have a tendency to write something like this in Flash MX:

```
myClip.mouseDown = function () { // NOT AN EVENT HANDLER!
    // statements
};
```

What you need is `onMouseDown`, not `mouseDown`:

```
myClip.onMouseDown = function () {
    // statements
};
```

I'm pressing Tab to change focus, but nothing is happening.

This is standard behavior in the authoring environment. Try testing your SWF in the browser and in the Flash Player.

FLASH AT WORK: GENERAL-PURPOSE FLASH EVENT ENGINES

The documented event model in Flash MX allows you to listen for a limited set of events: key presses, mouse clicks, text field changes, and Stage resizing. However, situations may arise in which you want to listen for other events, associated either with built-in objects or with objects that you have created. A general-purpose event engine allows you to do this.

For instance, suppose you have a movie with a puppet and a puppet-master. The user manipulates the puppet-master. The actions of the puppet-master in turn trigger responses in the puppet. You want to define events associated with the puppet-master, and you want the puppet to listen for those events. You can accomplish this in four basic steps:

- Represent puppet and puppet-master by custom objects (or by movie clips or other built-in objects).

- Give the user a way to control the puppet-master.

- Give the puppet-master object the necessary properties and methods to track listeners, add listeners, remove listeners, and send notifications for one or more events.

- Give the puppet appropriate callback functions (matching those defined for the puppet-master) and add the puppet as a listener of the puppet-master.

The third step requires a general-purpose event engine. There are several available as free downloads on the Web, including Tatsuo Kato's Event Engine or Branden Hall's FLEM (Flash Event Model). You can find links to the download sites on http://www.flashoop.com.

There is also an undocumented general-purpose event engine, ASBroadcaster, built into Flash MX. It's quite similar to FLEM. The following program, puppets.fla on the CD, uses ASBroadcaster to make two puppets respond to a puppet-master. The basic structure is that the puppet-master listens for the onKeyDown event and fires its assumeDefaultPosition event when the user presses the spacebar. The two puppets listen for the assumeDefaultPosition event by registering as listeners with the puppet-master and defining assumeDefaultPosition() callback functions. When the callback functions run, the following lines are displayed in the Output window:

```
puppet1 assumes default position
```

```
puppet2 assumes default position
```

Here's how each line of the program corresponds to the four basic steps:

- The puppet-master object is created on line 1, the puppet objects on lines 12 and 13.

- Lines 2–7 create an onKeyDown() callback function for the puppet-master, such that the puppet-master fires its assumeDefaultPosition event (line 5) when the user presses the spacebar.

- The initialize statement on line 8 endows the puppetMaster object with four properties: a _listeners array, an addListener() method, a removeListener() method, and a broadcastMessage() method. The addListener() and removeListener() methods add objects to and remove objects from the _listeners array. The broadcastMessage() method executes a callback function in all objects in the _listeners array.

- The defaultPosition() function defined on lines 9–11 is used by the puppet objects as a callback function. Lines 14 and 15 make the two puppets listen to the puppet-master. Lines 16 and 17 give each of the puppets an assumeDefaultPosition() method.

```
 1: puppetMaster = {};
 2: Key.addListener(puppetMaster);
 3: puppetMaster.onKeyDown = function(){
 4:  if(Key.isDown(Key.SPACE)){
 5:   this.broadcastMessage("assumeDefaultPosition");
 6:  }
 7: }
 8: ASBroadcaster.initialize(puppetMaster);
 9: function defaultPosition (name){
10:  trace(this.name+" assumes default position");
```

```
11: }
12: puppet1 = {name: "puppet1"};
13: puppet2 = {name: "puppet2"};
14: puppetMaster.addListener(puppet1);
15: puppetMaster.addListener(puppet2);
16: puppet1.assumeDefaultPosition = defaultPosition;
17: puppet2.assumeDefaultPosition = defaultPosition;
```

The first argument of the ASBroadcaster.broadcastMessage() method is the name of the event. In addition, you can add any number of other arguments. In the following program, puppets2.fla on the CD, the puppet-master responds to any one of three keys: the spacebar, K, and P. Depending on which key the user presses, the puppet-master executes ASBroadcaster.broadcastMessage() with a different second parameter (or, in the case of the spacebar, with no second parameter). The second parameter (or lack thereof) tells the puppets which position to assume.

```
 1: puppetMaster = {};
 2: Key.addListener(puppetMaster);
 3: puppetMaster.onKeyDown = function(){
 4:  if(Key.isDown(Key.SPACE)){
 5:   this.broadcastMessage("assumePosition");
 6:  }
 7:  if(Key.isDown(75)){  //  75 is keycode for the letter K
 8:   this.broadcastMessage("assumePosition", "kneeling");
 9:  }
10:  if(Key.isDown(80)){  //  80 is keycode for the letter P
11:   this.broadcastMessage("assumePosition", "prone");
12:  }
13: }
14: ASBroadcaster.initialize(puppetMaster);
15: function assumePosition (arg){
16:   if (arg == undefined) arg = "default";
17:   trace(this.name+" assumes "+arg+" position");
18: }
19: puppet1 = {name: "puppet1"};
20: puppet2 = {name: "puppet2"};
21: puppetMaster.addListener(puppet1);
22: puppetMaster.addListener(puppet2);
23: puppet1.assumePosition = assumePosition;
24: puppet2.assumePosition = assumePosition;
```

I learned about ASBroadcaster on the "flashcoders" mailing list. My code is based on a contribution by Peter Hall. Check out the archives or subscribe at http://chattyfig.figleaf.com.

Warning! As an undocumented feature, ASBroadcaster could change or disappear in future versions of Flash. It is relatively easy to code a substitute for it in ActionScript. For more information on ASBroadcaster, go to http://chattyfig.figleaf.com/flashcoders-wiki and click on Undocumented Features and then Flash MX Features.

UNLOCKING THE POWER OF MOVIE CLIPS

INTRODUCING THE MOVIE CLIP

The movie clip is by far the most important and commonly used type of object in Macromedia Flash. It is also unique. Although the `MovieClip` class was created to bring movie clips under the umbrella of the object-oriented programming (OOP) framework introduced in Flash 5, movie clips are not like other objects and require special treatment in many ways.

> Buttons also have a specialized type of Timeline, although this Timeline does not support ActionScript. Nor are any methods, properties, or events associated with it.

For example, you can't create new `MovieClip` instances using the new operator, as you can for most other classes. This statement, for instance, does *not* create a new movie clip:

```
myClip = new MovieClip(); // does NOT create a new movie clip!!
```

A new `MovieClip()` statement can still be useful. For instance, you can use such a statement to make a subclass that inherits from the `MovieClip` class. But, unlike other constructor functions, the `MovieClip` class alone doesn't come close to being a complete factory for making movie clips.

⇨ *For more details on making a subclass that inherits from the MovieClip class, see "Using Object.registerClass() to Subclass a New Movie Clip," later in this chapter, page 351.*

In fact, in Flash 5, you could not create a brand new empty movie clip programmatically. In Flash MX, the `createEmptyMovieClip()` method of the `MovieClip` class fulfills this function. The `createEmptyMovieClip()` method is necessary because, although the movie clip participates via the `MovieClip` class in the new object-oriented programming (OOP) framework introduced with Flash 5, it has its roots in the pre-OOP era, and many of the most basic properties of a movie clip (such as _x, _y, _xscale, _yscale) have no connection to the `MovieClip` class but are built into the interpreter.

Movie clips are also unique in having a *timeline* with one or more *keyframes*—that is, frames in which you either add ActionScript or add or change a graphic, a button, a text field, or another movie clip. Many movie clip methods (such as `gotoAndPlay()`, `stop()` and `prevFrame()`), three properties (_currentframe, _framesloaded, and _totalframes), and the ubiquitous `onEnterFrame` event relate to the Timeline.

Other than the Stage, the only objects that can contain graphical content in Flash are buttons and movie clips. Graphic symbols contain graphics, but graphic symbols are not objects.

Table 17.1 lists all the `MovieClip` methods, except the drawing methods.

⇨ *Drawing methods are covered in Chapter 18, "Drawing with ActionScript," page 367.*

Table 17.1   MovieClip Methods

Method	Format	Description
attachAudio	myClip.attachAudio(*stream*);	Attaches an audio stream to a movie clip.
attachMovie	myClip.attachMovie(*idName*, *newName*, *depth* [, *initObject*])	Attaches a movie in the Library to myClip, with the specified depth. The attached movie has all the local properties of the init object. Returns a reference to the attached movie.
attachVideo	(n/a)	(n/a)
createEmptyMovieClip	myClip.createEmptyMovieClip (*instanceName*, *depth*)	Creates an empty movie clip as a child of myClip, with the specified depth.
createTextField	myClip.createTextField (*instanceName*,*depth*,*x*,*y*,*width*,*height*)	Creates an empty text field, with the specified instance name, depth, x and y coordinates, width, and height.
duplicateMovieClip	myClip.duplicateMovieClip (*newName*, *depth* [,*initObject*])	Duplicates myClip, creating a sibling at the specified depth. The new movie has all the local properties of the init object.
getBounds	myClip.getBounds (*targetCoordinateSpace*)	Returns the minimum and maximum x and y coordinates of myClip in relation to a specified coordinate space.
getBytesLoaded	myClip.getBytesLoaded()	Returns the number of bytes loaded for myClip.
getBytesTotal	myClip.getBytesTotal()	Returns the size of myClip in bytes.
getDepth	myClip.getDepth()	Returns the depth number of myClip.
getURL	myClip.getURL(*URL* [,*window*, *variables*])	Loads a document into a browser window from the specified URL, sending all the variables from the root of myClip using GET or POST, as specified in the *variables* string.
globalToLocal	myClip.globalToLocal(*point*)	Converts the *point* object from main movie Stage coordinates to the local coordinates of myClip.
gotoAndPlay	myClip.gotoAndPlay(*frame*)	Sends the playhead to a specific frame in myClip and then starts playing the movie.
gotoAndStop	myClip.gotoAndStop(*frame*)	Sends the playhead to a specific frame in myClip and then stops the movie.

17

Table 17.1   Continued

Method	Format	Description
hitTest	myClip.hitTest(*x*, *y*, *shapeFlag*)	Returns true if myClip's bounding box overlaps the point specified by the x and y coordinates. *shapeFlag* is a Boolean value that determines whether the entire shape of myClip is evaluated (true), or just myClip's bounding box (false).
	myClip.hitTest(*target*)	Returns true if myClip's bounding box intersects the bounding box of the target movie clip.
loadMovie	myClip.loadMovie("*url*" [,*variables*])	Loads the movie or JPEG specified in "url" into myClip, using GET or POST, as specified in the *variables* string.
loadVariables	myClip.loadVariables("*url*", *variables*)	Loads variables from a URL or other location into myClip.
localToGlobal	myClip.localToGlobal(*point*)	Converts a point object from the local coordinates of myClip to the global Stage coordinates.
nextFrame	myClip.nextFrame()	Sends the playhead to the next frame of myClip.
play	myClip.play()	Plays myClip.
prevFrame	myClip.prevFrame()	Sends the playhead to the previous frame of myClip.
removeMovieClip	myClip.removeMovieClip()	Removes myClip from the Timeline if it was created using attachMovie(), duplicateMovieClip(), or createEmptyMovieClip().
setMask	myClip.setMask (*maskMovieClip*)	Specifies a movie clip as a mask for myClip.
startDrag	myClip.startDrag([*lock*, [*left*, *top*, *right*, *bottom*]])	Makes myClip draggable and begins dragging myClip. If the value of *lock* is true, the mouse pointer remains centered on myClip's registration point. The *left*, *top*, *right*, and *bottom* values specify coordinates beyond which myClip cannot be dragged.
stop	myClip.stop()	Pauses myClip.
stopDrag	myClip.stopDrag()	Stops the dragging of any clip that is being dragged (not just myClip). Exact equivalent of global function stopDrag().

17

Method	Format	Description
swapDepths	myClip.swapDepths(*depth*)	Puts myClip at the specified depth. If there is a movie clip at that depth, it is moved to myClip's former depth level.
	myClip.swapDepths(*target*)	Swaps the depth levels of myClip and the target movie clip.
unloadMovie	myClip.unloadMovie()	Removes myClip if it was loaded with loadMovie(). Also works for JPEGs loaded with loadMovie().

Legend: (na) not available (undocumented method)

Table 17.2 lists all the MovieClip properties.

Table 17.2 MovieClip Properties

Property	Description
_alpha	Transparency/opacity, an integer from 0–100.
_currentframe	Current frame number, an integer, read-only.
_droptarget	A read-only string containing the absolute path in slash syntax notation of the movie clip instance on which a draggable movie clip was dropped.
enabled	A Boolean that determines whether a button movie clip is enabled.
focusEnabled	A Boolean that determines whether a movie clip can receive focus.
_focusrect	A Boolean that determines whether a focused movie clip has a yellow rectangle around it.
_framesloaded	An integer, the number of frames that have been loaded into memory, read-only.
_height	The height of a movie clip instance, in pixels, a floating-point number.
hitArea	The movie clip that defines the hit area for a button movie clip.
_quality	A string that determines rendering quality: LOW, MEDIUM, HIGH, BEST.
_name	The instance name, a string.
_parent	A reference to the movie clip's parent clip.
_rotation	A floating-point number, the number of degrees of rotation from the clip's original orientation.
_soundbuftime	An integer, the number of seconds of sound to prebuffer before starting to play the sound.
tabChildren	A Boolean, determines whether the children of a movie clip are included in automatic tab ordering.
tabEnabled	A Boolean, determines whether a movie clip is included in tab ordering.
tabIndex	Determines the tab order of the clip.
_target	The target path of the clip.
_totalframes	The total number of frames in the clip.

Table 17.2 Continued

Property	Description
trackAsMenu	A Boolean that determines whether, if the user presses the mouse button over this button movie clip (or button) and releases it over a different one, the second one receives a release event.
_url	A read-only string, the location of the SWF file from which the clip was downloaded.
useHandCursor	A Boolean that enables and disables the display of the hand cursor for a button movie clip.
_visible	A Boolean value that determines whether a clip instance is hidden or visible.
_width	The width of a movie clip instance, in pixels, a floating-point number.
_x	The x coordinate of a clip instance, a floating-point number.
_xmouse	The x coordinate of the mouse cursor within a clip instance, a floating-point number.
_xscale	A floating-point number specifying a percentage for horizontally scaling a clip instance.
_y	The y coordinate of a clip instance, a floating-point number.
_ymouse	The y coordinate of the cursor within a clip instance, a floating-point number.
_yscale	A floating-point number specifying a percentage for vertically scaling a clip instance.

FLASH MX'S NEW PROPERTIES FOR MOVIE CLIPS

Flash MX adds nine new movie clip properties. Six of them—_focusrect, enabled, focusEnabled, hitArea, trackAsMenu, and useHandCursor—enable and disable button-like functionality for movie clips and button movie clips. Flash 5 had a _focusrect global variable, which still exists in Flash MX. In addition, buttons and movie clips now have a _focusrect property.

⇨ *For more information on _focusrect, see this chapter's sidebar "Enabling and Disabling the Yellow Focus Rectangle," page 337.*

⇨ *For more information on button movie clips, see "Creating a Button Movie Clip," page 323 (Chapter 16, "Interaction, Events, and Sequencing").*

Three of the new movie clip properties—tabChildren, tabEnabled, and tabIndex—control *tab ordering*, the sequence of text fields, buttons, and/or movie clips that receive keyboard focus as the user presses Tab or Shift+Tab. The typical application is filling out a form and using the Tab key to move from one field to the next.

If you do nothing about tab ordering, Flash will implement *automatic* tab ordering. That is, it will set up a default order in which items will take focus. For example, if you create a form with a number of input text fields in a single column, the default tab ordering, which is simply top-to-bottom, may be perfectly acceptable. Alternatively, you can explicitly set up a *custom* tab order, which disables automatic tab ordering for the entire document, including any SWFs loaded with loadMovie() or loadMovieNum(). This might be required in a more complex form.

Enabling and Disabling the Yellow Focus Rectangle

Flash displays a yellow rectangle over a button or button movie clip that has keyboard focus, unless you've done something to suppress this feature. You can enable and disable the yellow focus rectangle on a global basis using the global _focusrect property. If _focusrect is set to true (the default), the yellow rectangle appears. If _focusrect is set to false, as in the following example, the yellow rectangle does not appear. In that case, buttons and button movie clips display their *Over* state when they have keyboard focus.

```
_focusrect = false; // focus rectangle is disabled globally
```

 In Flash MX, you can enable and disable the yellow focus rectangle for an individual movie clip or button instance using the _focusrect property of the instance. If _focusrect is set to true (the default), the yellow rectangle appears when the instance gets focus. If _focusrect is set to false, as in the following example, the yellow rectangle does not appear when the instance gets focus. In that case, a button or button movie clip displays its *Over* state when it has keyboard focus.

```
myButton._focusrect = false; // focus rectangle is disabled for myButton
```

---

enabled

The enabled property enables and disables button-type functionality in a movie clip. The default is true. Set enabled to false, as shown in the following example, and the hand cursor does not appear; button event handlers are no longer called; and _over, _down, and _up frames are disabled:

```
myButtonClip.enabled = false; // no more button functionality
```

Even when enabled is false, the movie clip continues to be included in tab ordering, and MovieClip, Mouse, and Key event handlers continue to function.

focusEnabled

The focusEnabled property allows you to enable and disable focus-related event handlers for movie clips.

Text fields, buttons, button movie clips, and ordinary movie clips can all have onSetFocus and onKillFocus event handlers that fire in response to Selection.setFocus(). For text fields, buttons, and button movie clips, these two focus-related event handlers are *enabled* by default. For ordinary movie clips, these event handlers are *disabled* by default. If you set the focusEnabled property of an ordinary movie clip to true, its onSetFocus and onKillFocus event handlers will fire in response to Selection.setFocus().

The following example is based on sample movie focusenabled.fla:

```
myClip.onSetFocus = function(oldFocus) {
    trace("focus was "+oldFocus+ ", new focus is myClip");
};
myClip.focusEnabled = true; // allows myClip.onSetFocus above to fire
Selection.setFocus(myClip); // myClip.onSetFocus fires
```

Here are four facts about the `focusEnabled` property:

- By default, it is `undefined`, which is equivalent to `false`.

- It is unnecessary if `tabEnabled` is `true`. (`tabEnabled` enables focus.)

- It has no effect on a text field, button, or button movie clip.

- It enables event handlers associated with a *single* movie clip—`myClip` in the preceding example. It will fire `myClip.onSetFocus` only when `myClip` gets focus. If you want `myClip.onSetFocus` to fire on *every* change of focus (for other objects, as well as `myClip`), define a listener instead of or in addition to setting `focusEnabled` to `true`:

```
Selection.addListener(myClip);
```

⇨ *For more information on listeners, see Chapter 16, "Interaction, Events, and Sequencing," page 303.*

If you both define a listener and set `focusEnabled` to `true`, `myClip.onSetFocus` will fire twice when `myClip` gets focus.

You can also use `focusEnabled` to enable a movie clip to take focus, even though that clip has no `onSetFocus` event handler. In the following example, focusenabled2.fla on the CD, the movie clip (myMc) takes focus but another object (myObj) listens for the event.

```
function MyClass () {}
MyClass.prototype.onSetFocus = function(){
 trace("MyClass.prototype.onSetFocus");
}
myObj = new MyClass();
myMc.focusEnabled=true;
Selection.addListener(myObj);
Selection.setFocus(myMc) ;
```

hitArea

The `hitArea` property allows you to designate any movie clip as a hit area. For button movie clips, as in this example, when the mouse is over the hit area clip, the mouse pointer changes to a hand cursor, and the button movie clip is clickable:

```
myButtonClip.hitArea = myButtonClip.myHitClip;
```

You can reassign `hitArea` to a different clip at any time. You can change the size or shape of the `hitArea` clip. And you can make the `hitArea` clip invisible, without affecting the button movie clip's clickability. If you don't assign a `hitArea` clip, or you assign one that doesn't actually exist, the button movie clip itself will become the hit area by default.

> **Enabling the Hit Area Feature**
>
> Just assigning a hit area to an ordinary movie clip has no effect. Even if you add useHandCursor = true (as described in the "useHandCursor" section later in this chapter), you will see no effect. You can achieve clickability and get a hand cursor by assigning a button event handler to the movie clip, making it a button movie clip. Then the hit area feature is functional, as well.

tabChildren

The tabChildren property allows you to exclude a movie clip's children from tab ordering and later to re-include them. This capability could be useful, for instance, if certain fields in a form need to be filled in only under certain conditions. When those conditions were met, you would set the tabChildren property to true.

By default, the children of a tab-*enabled* movie clip are tab-*disabled* (not included in tab ordering). So if you have a user interface component made up of multiple movie clips, for instance, and you always want to treat it as a single tab stop, you don't have to do anything special.

If you sometimes want the children tab-enabled and sometimes tab-disabled, you first tab-enable them (for instance, using the tabEnabled property). Then, if you later want to disable them again, set tabChildren to false. When you want to re-enable them, set tabChildren to true.

If tabChildren is undefined (the default), the children *are* tab-enabled as soon as you set the tabEnabled property to true or make the movie clip into a button movie clip.

tabEnabled

The tabEnabled property causes the movie clip to be included in either automatic or custom tab ordering, whichever is currently in force in the document. The movie clip will also be able to take focus.

tabIndex

Changing the tabIndex property to a positive integer (from its default, which is undefined) causes the movie clip to be included in custom tab ordering and enables the movie clip to take focus. The movie clip's place in the tab sequence is determined by the integer: A movie clip with a lower tab index receives focus before a movie clip with a higher tab index.

Setting even one tabIndex property in a document disables automatic tab ordering for the entire document.

trackAsMenu

Normally, an onRelease event occurs when the user *presses and releases* the mouse button over a single button or button movie clip. With a drop-down menu, you may want the user to press the mouse button over one button, causing the drop-down menu to appear, and then move the mouse to the button representing the desired selection and release it there. The "track as menu" option enables this behavior.

17

You assign an `onPress` event handler to the button or button movie clip that reveals the drop-down menu. To the other buttons or button movie clips, you assign an `onRelease` event and the "track as menu" tracking behavior.

You can assign the "track as menu" behavior to a button in two ways: through the Properties panel or by using ActionScript and the `trackAsMenu` property. With a button movie clip, you must use ActionScript.

In sample movie options.fla, the "track as menu" tracking behavior is assigned to buttons using ActionScript for one option, as shown in the following example, and the Properties panel for the others. Sample movie options2.fla uses button movie clips and ActionScript. Sample movie wapsec.fla demonstrates the default "track as button" behavior.

```
option1.trackAsMenu =  true;
```

useHandCursor

Button movie clips display the hand cursor by default. You can suppress this behavior by setting the `useHandCursor` property to `false`, as shown in the following example, and re-enable it by setting the `useHandCursor` property to `true`:

```
myButtonClip.useHandCursor = false;
```

⇨ *For an example of useHandCursor in action, see spacelisten.fla, later in this chapter, in "startDrag() Options," page 360.*

The hand cursor is also suppressed if you set the movie clip's `enabled` or `tabEnabled` property to `false`.

Just setting `useHandCursor = true` on an ordinary movie clip has no effect. You can achieve click-ability and get a hand cursor by assigning a button event handler to the movie clip, making it a button movie clip. Then you can use `useHandCursor = false` to suppress the hand cursor, if you want.

CREATING AND REMOVING MOVIE CLIPS

You can create movie clips in four ways. Each has implications for how the new clip fits into the hierarchy of clips and where it is positioned on the Stage.

You can also remove a movie clip, displace it with another clip, or remove just the graphical contents of a clip, while the movie clip object remains.

⇨ *The registration point is introduced in Chapter 6, "Symbols, Instances, and Library Assets" page 89.*

⇨ *For more details on the visual stacking order, see "Controlling the Visual Stacking Order of Movie Clips," later in this chapter, page 345.*

Clip positioning is managed via the *registration point*, indicated by a cross-hatch when editing a clip in the Library. By default it's in the center of a clip, but in the upper left of the Main Timeline.

The Parent-Child Hierarchy

The hierarchy of clips in Flash, which determines their *visual stacking order*, is based on *parent-child* relationships.

A parent-child relationship between two movie clips is a "container-contained" relationship: The parent contains the child. A parent can have any number of children, but a child can have only one parent. Two children of the same parent are *siblings*.

Creating Movie Clips

As mentioned earlier, you create a clip in one of four ways. Each of the following examples creates clip2 as a child of clip1. The last three examples also give clip2 a *depth number* of 1.

⇨ *For more information on depth numbers, see "Visual Stacking for Siblings: Depth Numbers," later in this chapter, page 346.*

The four ways of creating a clip are as follows:

- **Manually**—For instance, while you're authoring, if clip1 and clip2 already exist in the Library, you open clip1 in the Library panel by double-clicking on the symbol icon, and then you drag and drop clip2 into clip1. You can also create and select a graphic inside clip1; select Insert, Convert to Symbol; type **clip2** in the Name field; click the Movie Clip radio button; and click OK to convert the graphic into a movie clip named clip2.

- **Using the `attachMovie()` method of the MovieClip class**—At runtime, if clip1 is on the Stage and a clip in the Library has the linkage ID clip, for example, the following statement will create a clip named clip2, position clip2 on the Stage with its registration point aligned with the registration point of clip1, and make clip2 a child of clip1:

  ```
  clip1.attachMovie("clip", "clip2", 1);
  ```

- **Using the `duplicateMovieClip()` method of the MovieClip class or the `duplicateMovieClip()` global function**—At runtime, if myClip is on the Stage and is a child of clip1, either of the following statements will create a clip named clip2, position clip2 on the Stage with its registration point aligned with the registration point of myClip, and make clip2 a child of clip1:

  ```
  myClip.duplicateMovieClip("clip2", 1);
  duplicateMovieClip("myClip", "clip2", 1);
  ```

- **Using the `createEmptyMovieClip()` method of the MovieClip class**—At runtime, if clip1 is on the Stage, the following statement will create a clip named clip2, position clip2 on the Stage with its registration point aligned with the registration point of clip1, and make clip2 a child of clip1:

  ```
  clip1.createEmptyMovieClip("clip2",1);
  ```

  If you use `createEmptyMovieClip()` to create a movie clip in the root, the new clip's registration point will be aligned with the upper-left corner of the Stage.

`attachMovie()`, `duplicateMovieClip()`, and `createNewMovieClip()` return references to the clips they create. This is an undocumented new feature of Flash MX.

In Flash 5, developers often created references to frequently used movie clips because evaluating a reference is less processor-intensive than evaluating a string. For example, the second of the following two statements creates such a reference:

> Buttons can be attached using `attachMovie()`. They can't be duplicated programmatically. In addition, they cannot be removed. Neither `removeMovieClip()` nor `unloadMovie()` works with buttons.

```
clip1.attachMovie("clip", "myClip"+i, i); // attach movie
ref = clip1["myClip"+i]; // create reference
```

In Flash MX, you can accomplish the same thing by using a single statement, as follows:

```
ref = clip1.attachMovie("clip", "clip"+i, i);
```

Removing Movie Clips

You can use the `removeMovieClip()` method of the `MovieClip` class to remove a clip created using `attachMovie()`, `duplicateMovieClip()`, or `createEmptyMovieClip()`. If you no longer need the graphics or code contained in a movie clip, removing it will give Flash a chance to reclaim the memory that the clip is using, and (especially if there are a lot of such clips to be removed) make your program run more efficiently. Here's an example:

```
myClip.removeMovieClip(); // myClip is gone
```

In addition, you can displace any existing clip by creating a new sibling with the same depth number as the existing clip.

You can remove the graphical content from a movie clip, leaving an "empty" movie clip object behind, using `unloadMovie()`. The empty clip could be used as a "container" to attach clips from the Library, for instance, or to load external content.

In contrast, `removeMovieClip()` completely removes the clip, leaving nothing behind. If you remove a clip using `removeMovieClip()`, you can't attach anything to it or load anything into it; it is simply not there.

LOADING AND UNLOADING EXTERNAL CONTENT

With the advent of `attachMovie()` in Flash 5, loading external SWFs became much less of a necessity. However, in some situations, you still might want to load external SWFs.

Suppose a Flash application provides access to several SWFs and/or JPEGs, and each user is likely to access only a small portion of the content. It doesn't make sense to force every user to download all the content, as happens when you store the content in the Library and use `attachMovie()`.

Or you might want to provide alternative "skins" for an application, each of which will be used only by a minority of users.

Or you might be asked to "frame" an existing SWF, perhaps adding an introduction, new music, or credits at the end. The easiest way to accomplish this task may be to write an application that contains the additional material and loads the existing SWF.

Another reason to load external SWFs might be to give the user a choice between different versions of your content—for instance, a large, high-resolution image and a small, low-resolution one.

Loading an External SWF or JPEG

You can load an external SWF or JPEG in three ways: using the `loadMovieNum()` and `loadMovie()` global functions or the `loadMovie()` method of the `MovieClip` class. Here's an example of each:

```
loadMovieNum("test.swf", 1); // global function
loadMovie("test.swf"," myClip"); // global function
myClip.loadMovie("test.swf"); // MovieClip method
```

With `loadMovieNum()`, either you assign the SWF or JPEG to an existing level, or you can create a new level for it. With the `loadMovie()` method of the `MovieClip` class, the external file loads into an existing clip, so its level is that of the existing clip.

➡ For more details on levels, see "Controlling the Visual Stacking Order of Movie Clips," later in this chapter, page 345.

You can use the `loadMovie()` global function to load content into a *movie clip*, as shown in the preceding example. You can also use the `loadMovie()` global function to load into a *level*, using a string or a numeral to indicate the level:

```
loadMovie("test.swf","_level1"); // string "_level1"
loadMovie("test.swf", 1); // numeral 1
```

You can't use a variable to indicate the level. For instance, the following code doesn't work:

```
x = 15;
loadMovie("test.swf", x); // DOESN'T LOAD !!
```

Some reasonable-looking nonstring values cause the `loadMovie()` global function to load the content into level 0, replacing everything in your movie. For instance, the following is an innocent-looking implement of mass destruction:

```
loadMovie("test.swf",_level1); // LOADS INTO LEVEL 0 !!
```

You Can't Duplicate Clips Containing External Content

After you load content into a movie using `loadMovie()`, you cannot duplicate that movie.

There is one minor exception to this rule: If you execute `duplicateMovieClip()` in the same code block as `loadMovie()`, you can use `duplicateMovieClip()` to duplicate the clip *with its original content* (not the newly loaded content). For instance, the following example does work but does *not* duplicate the loaded content as you might expect:

```
loadMovie("test.swf", _root.clip1);
_root.clip1.duplicateMovieClip("dupetest", 1);
```

Neither the rule nor the exception applies to `loadMovieNum()`, which does not load into a movie clip.

Loaded Movies Attach *Only* from Their Own Libraries

If you load content into `myClip` using `loadMovie()`, you can no longer attach clips from `myClip`'s Library to `myClip`. You *can* attach content from the Library associated with the loaded content.

Suppose you load test.swf into `_root.myClip` with a statement like this:

```
loadMovie("test.swf", _root.myClip);
```

Then you put this line in an `onRelease` button event:

```
_root.myClip.attachMovie("linkageID", "newClip", 1);
```

If `linkageID` is the linkage ID of a clip in the same Library where `myClip`'s symbol is defined, the preceding statement does not work. On the other hand, if `linkageID` is the linkage ID of a clip in test.swf's Library, pressing the button will attach that clip to `myClip`, creating `_root.myClip.newClip`.

> ⇨ *If you're having trouble attaching a movie from the Library of a loaded SWF or accessing a variable, movie clip, or function in a loaded SWF, see the "Troubleshooting" section at the end of this chapter, page 364.*

Unloading SWFs and JPEGs

External SWFs or JPEGs loaded with `loadMovie()` can be unloaded using `unloadMovie()`. You can use the global function for both loading and unloading, the `MovieClip` method for both, or the global function for one and the `MovieClip` method for the other. Here are some examples

```
loadMovie("test.swf", _root.clip1); // load "test.swf" into _root.clip1
_root.clip2.loadMovie("test.swf"); // load "test.swf" into _root.clip2
unloadMovie("_root.clip2"); // unload whatever is in _root.clip2
clip1.unloadMovie(); // unload whatever is in clip1
```

Similarly, you can load with `loadMovieNum()` and unload with `unloadMovieNum()`:

```
loadMovieNum("test.swf", 1);
unloadMovieNum(1);
```

`unloadMovie()` leaves an empty movie clip. For instance, even after you have executed the `clip1.unloadMovie()` statement, `clip1` remains and you can attach content to it again:

```
clip1.loadMovie("new.swf");
```

You can also just load the new content without ever having executed `clip1.unloadMovie()`. Loading new content into a clip automatically unloads the old content.

You can use `unloadMovie()` to unload the graphical content from a manually created clip, leaving an empty movie clip.

The `unloadMovie()` **Global Function**

It is generally best to use a string to specify a movie to `unloadMovie()`.

The `unloadMovie()` global function can also take as a parameter a reference to a movie clip, rather than a string. For instance, this statement is legal:

```
unloadMovie(_root.clip2); // unload whatever is in _root.clip2
```

However, if you provide a reference to a clip that does not exist, the `unloadMovie()` global function will unload the content from whatever Timeline the statement is on. It's safer to use only strings as parameters for the `unloadMovie()` global function.

CONTROLLING THE VISUAL STACKING ORDER OF MOVIE CLIPS

Movie clips in a Flash document appear as if on clear pieces of acetate, so that where there is no graphical content at a higher stratum, elements on lower strata are visible. To control which movies appear in front of or behind other movies on the Stage, referred to as the *visual stacking order*, you need to understand how clips in a Flash document are arranged hierarchically.

The movie clip hierarchy combines two paradigms: the "sandwich" and the "tree." Specifically, a Flash document is organized into one or more sandwich-like *levels*. Within each level, clips are organized into a tree-like hierarchy, with clips vertically organized in a *parent-child hierarchy*, and the visual stacking order of siblings (child clips of the same parent) managed using depth numbers. Thus, the overall Flash document is a "sandwich of trees." If a movie has only one level, you deal only with a tree-like structure.

The `_root` identifier refers to the base of each tree. Each level has its own `_root`, or Main Timeline. Thus, two references to `_root.myClip1` refer to two entirely different clips if the references occur on two different levels. For instance, one of the clips might be `_level0.myClip1`, and the other might be `_level1.myClip1`. References that begin with a level are unambiguous.

The initial hierarchical arrangement of movie clips is determined by five factors:

- The chronological order in which you manually place multiple clips into any single Timeline layer

- The relative positions of Timeline layers containing clips

- Parent-child relationships among clips

- Whether the clip was created using `duplicateMovieClip()`, `attachMovie()`, or `createEmptyMovieClip()`

- Which levels clips reside on

17

Visual Stacking Using Levels

The overall Flash document hierarchy consists of one or more numbered *levels*, starting with
_level0. The level hierarchy is a simple "sandwich" structure, with a higher level number indicating a higher position in the hierarchy. For instance, _level2 is in the foreground compared to
_level1, and _level1 is in the foreground compared to _level0.

Every document must have a _level0, and beyond that it can have any number of levels up to a
total of 16,534. There is no harm to having gaps in level numbers. For instance, you can have content on levels 0, 100, and 1,000, with nothing on other levels.

You assign—and perhaps create—levels beyond _level0 when you load an external SWF or JPEG
using the loadMovieNum() or loadMovie() global function.

⇨ *The three ways to load external files are covered in "Loading an External SWF or JPEG," earlier in this chapter, page 343.*

Unless you deliberately create a new level using the loadMovieNum() or loadMovie() global function, your document will have only one level, _level0.

Visual Stacking for Nonsiblings: The Parent-Child Hierarchy

Within each level, the visual stacking order is determined by two factors: the parent-child hierarchy
and depth numbers.

In the parent-child hierarchy, every sibling is the founder of a "family line." When you look vertically
within a family line, the visual stacking order of parents and children is simple: A child always
appears in the foreground in comparison with its parent.

Each family line forms a unit for purposes of visual stacking order, just as it does for setting rotation,
scale, or position. When you're working with two sibling movie clips, you don't have to think about
the fact that each one may be composed of child clips and grandchild clips and so on. The way that
visual stacking order works is consistent with other operations in Flash: If you rotate a clip, any family line within it is rotated, too. If you move a clip, the whole family line is moved. Similarly, if one
clip is placed "behind" another clip in the visual stacking order, that placement applies to any family
line within each of those clips, too. In short, when you're working with a clip, you can treat it as a
unit.

That's it for the parent-child hierarchy, which determines the visual stacking order for nonsiblings.

Visual Stacking for Siblings: Depth Numbers

The other factor determining the visual stacking order within each level is *depth numbering*. Flash
uses depth numbers to track several factors that together determine the visual stacking order of siblings. A sibling with a higher depth number appears in the foreground, in comparison with a sibling
with a lower depth number.

The maximum number of depths that can be assigned in a single Timeline is 16,384.

Legal depth numbers range from −16,384 to 0x7EFFFFFD (or 2,130,706,429). Testing is warranted to
make sure you can remove clips with depth numbers higher than 1,048,575.

When developers use very high depth numbers, it is typically in an attempt to make sure that they don't accidentally use an existing depth number for a new clip, which would cause the new clip to displace an existing clip.

Automatic and Explicit Depth Numbering   Depth numbers may be assigned automatically or explicitly:

- Flash automatically assigns depth numbers to movie clips that you manually place on the Stage at authoring time. The numbering depends on three factors: the chronological order in which you place multiple clips into any single Timeline layer, the relative positions of Timeline layers containing clips, and parent-child relationships among clips. Automatically assigned depth numbers are always negative, starting at –16,384 for _root and going up, possibly with gaps (for example, –16,383, –16,382, –16,380).

- You must explicitly assign a depth number to each movie clip that you create using duplicateMovieClip(), attachMovie(), or createEmptyMovieClip(). Flash reserves numbers in the range from 1 to 16,384 for this purpose and does not automatically assign numbers in this range.

- You can explicitly "swap" the depth numbers of two existing clips, or assign a currently unused depth number to a clip, using the swapDepths() method of the MovieClip class.

  For instance, the following line assigns myClip a depth number of 1. If a sibling already has a depth number of 1, the sibling will be assigned myClip's current depth number.

  ```
  myClip.swapDepths(1);
  ```

  The following line gives otherClip's depth number to myClip and vice versa:

  ```
  myClip.swapDepths(otherClip);
  ```

If you explicitly assign only depth numbers greater than 0, automatically assigned numbers and explicitly assigned numbers will never conflict because automatically assigned numbers are never greater than 0.

Using getDepth()   You can determine the depth of any movie clip using the getDepth() method of the MovieClip class. Using that information, you could, for example, deliberately assign any existing depth number (negative or positive) to a new sibling to displace a manually or programmatically created movie clip. The following code, which assumes the existence of a Library symbol with the linkage ID clip, destroys myClip1 in the process of creating myClip2:

```
dep = _root.myClip1.getDepth(); // get myClip1's depth number
_root.attachMovie("clip", "myClip2", dep); // myClip2 displaces myClip1
```

> Flash 5 apparently put no lower limit on depth numbers, but a Flash 6 SWF can't go below –16,384. The Flash 6 Player will make exceptions for older SWFs.

> The swapDepths() method was unreliable in Flash 5. It is much more reliable in Flash MX.

17

Assigning _root's Depth to Create New Backgrounds Dynamically   You can dynamically place a background behind all content, including author-time content, by giving a new clip the depth of the _root (–16,384), like this:

```
_root.attachMovie ("newBackground", "myBG", -16384);
```

For automatically assigned depth numbers, "higher" means "less negative." For instance, –16,380 is higher than –16,382.

Automatic Depth Numbering   Flash follows just two key rules when automatically assigning depth numbers:

- A sibling in a higher Timeline layer gets a higher depth number than a sibling in a lower Timeline layer.

- A new sibling gets a higher depth number than any existing sibling. This means, for instance, if you manually place multiple clips into a single Timeline layer, Flash will automatically put the more recently placed clips higher in the visual stacking order.

Notice that I didn't say anything about the relative depth numbers of parents and children. They don't matter. Depth numbers determine only how clips "stack up" in relation to their siblings. In fact, if you create a family line with no siblings, all the clips in the line may have the same depth number. Nonsiblings can have the same depth number because the parent-child hierarchy determines their visual stacking order.

Explicit Depth Numbering   When you explicitly assign depth numbers, take these two steps if you want to make sure that you don't displace any existing content:

- First, make sure no existing clips will be siblings of the clip you're creating. With attachMovie() and createEmptyMovieClip(), make sure that the parent-to-be has no existing children. With duplicateMovieClip(), make sure the duplicated clip has no existing siblings.

- Give each new clip a new instance name and a higher depth number than the previous clip. For instance, the following block of code creates 10 duplicates of myClip: myClip0 at depth 1, myClip1 at depth 2, and so on.

```
for (i = 0; i < 10; i++) {
    myClip.duplicateMovieClip("myClip"+i,i+1);
}
```

If existing clips will be siblings of the clip you're creating, know their depth numbers. Assign new depth numbers to achieve the desired visual stacking order, and to either displace or not displace existing siblings, as required.

Remember these points:

- A clip created with attachMovie() becomes a *child* of the movie to which it is attached. For instance, this line creates the clip _root.myClip1.myClip2:

```
_root.myClip1.attachMovie("clip", "myClip2", 1);
```

Caution

Don't reuse a movie clip instance name; otherwise, the existing clip will become unaddressable.

- A clip created with `createEmptyMovieClip()` becomes a *child* of the movie in which it is created. For instance, this line creates the clip `_root.myClip1.myClip2`:

  ```
  _root.myClip1.createEmptyMovieClip("myClip2",1);
  ```

- A clip created with `duplicateMovieClip()` becomes a *sibling* of the movie that it duplicates. For instance, this line creates the clip `_root.myClip2`:

  ```
  _root.myClip1.duplicateMovieClip("myClip2", 1);
  ```

Applying Levels and Depths

You can load an external SWF or JPEG into a *level* using the `loadMovie()` or `loadMovieNum()` global function. Alternatively, you can load external SWFs into *movie clips* using the `loadMovie()` method of the `MovieClip` class or the `loadMovie()` global function.

With Timeline layers, depth numbering, the parent-child hierarchy, and the object-oriented framework to help you organize content, using levels as an organizing tool may seem unnecessary. Here are some reasons why you might prefer to use movie clips rather than levels as load targets:

- A movie clip can have a meaningful name, making your program more readable. Levels always have the generic names `_level0`, `_level1`, and so on.

- Movie clips offer more fine-grained control of the visual stacking order via layers, the parent-child hierarchy, and depth numbers. If you load into a movie clip, the `_root` of the loaded SWF becomes the clip into which it is loaded, displacing anything that was there previously but retaining the movie clip's depth number, layer position, and position in the parent-child hierarchy. (Similarly, a JPEG loaded into a movie clip effectively becomes the movie clip.)

- You can't specify a depth, and you can't use depth to control what you displace, when you load into a level. The `_root` of an SWF loaded into a level using the `loadMovieNum()` or `loadMovie()` global function becomes the `_root` of the level into which it is loaded, visually displacing anything that was there previously.

On the other hand, levels can have some advantages:

- Sometimes loading into a level provides the kind of "clean sweep" change that you want. For instance, if you load a movie into `_level0`, all levels are unloaded, and the new movie becomes `_level0`. If you then load movies into other levels, the movie in `_level0` sets document properties such as frame rate, background color, and frame size for all levels. Loading into `_level0` can thus provide some basic consistency for a team of developers, for instance.

- Movie clip properties such as `_visible` and `alpha` can be applied to a level without affecting other levels. This capability provides an easy way to change properties for multiple clips, while still excluding other clips.

- You can get a streaming sound to play across multiple scenes if you load the SWF containing the sound into a level.

17

- If you're loading an SWF that uses the _root identifier in ActionScript statements, the loaded SWF has the best chance of working unchanged if loaded into a level because the _root of the loaded SWF becomes the _root of the level. Loading into a movie clip can cause many problems in this case. For instance, the SWF's _root variables could overwrite existing _root variables of the same name.

USING INIT OBJECTS TO GIVE PROPERTIES TO NEW MOVIE CLIPS

Both the attachMovie() and duplicateMovieClip() methods of the MovieClip class allow you to specify an *init object* when creating a movie clip. Flash automatically gives the new clip all the local properties of the init object. This feature is an advantage of the duplicateMovieClip() method over the duplicateMovieClip() global function.

In the following example, myClip is the clip you're attaching to, linkageID is the linkage ID of a clip in the Library, newInstance is the name of the new clip, 1 is the depth of the new clip, and initObj is the name of an object:

```
myClip.attachMovie("linkageID", "newInstance", 1, initObj);
```

The result is that the newly created movie clip, newInstance, will have all the local properties of initObj. newInstance will *not* have properties that initObj inherits from its class prototype object.

You can use a function literal for an init object, like this:

```
myClip.attachMovie("linkageID", "newInstance", 1, {_x:300, _y:200 } );
```

Another option is to use a new statement with a constructor function to create a new init object. The following discussion assumes familiarity with the fundamentals of object-oriented programming (OOP) in Flash.

> For an introduction to OOP, see "Understanding Object-Oriented Languages," page 174 (Chapter 11, "Getting Started with ActionScript") and "Functions as Classes: Constructor Functions," page 279 (Chapter 15, "Combining Statements into Functions"). For more in-depth information, see Chapter 21, "Packaging Data and Functions Using Custom Objects," page 489.

Using a new statement with a constructor function to create a new init object allows you to give a new movie clip the local properties that a class normally gives to its instances, without assigning the new clip to the class. As usual when you're using the new statement, within the constructor function the this keyword refers to the object being created. In this case, that's the init object.

In the following example, a new, anonymous (unnamed) instance of the MyClass constructor function is used as the init object so that the new clip, instance, gets the local property of the class, instanceVar, but not the property in the class prototype, prototypeVar:

```
MyClass = function() {
    this.instanceVar = "instanceVar";
}
MyClass.prototype.prototypeVar = "prototypeVar";
```

```
depth = 1;
this.attachMovie("clip", "instance", depth, new MyClass());
for (a in instance) trace(a); // instanceVar
trace(typeof instance); // movieclip
```

`instance` gets the local properties normally given to instances of `MyClass`, but `instance` remains a movie clip instead of becoming a member of `MyClass`.

Thus, the init object provides a way of partially blending two classes within a particular instance. In a stricter object-oriented language, such as Java, you would have to create a new subclass for `instance`. You may find that creating a new subclass, rather than having members of the same class with different types of properties, keeps your class system more manageable.

The init object feature can come in handy even if you *do* want to subclass your new movie clip. I'll discuss this topic in the next section.

USING OBJECT.REGISTERCLASS() TO SUBCLASS A NEW MOVIE CLIP

Although `registerClass()` is officially a method of the `Object` class, it is used only with movie clips. It doesn't work with other types of objects, such as buttons.

The `registerClass()` method provides a convenient way of subclassing a new clip. This approach, which is used by Macromedia in its components, "preregisters" a movie clip for membership in a particular class.

Suppose you have a symbol named `clip` in the Library, and you want to use it to create a new movie clip named `myClip`, which you want to belong to the subclass `MyClass`. Give `clip` a linkage ID—for instance, `linkageID`—and then use `registerClass()` as follows:

```
Object.registerClass("linkageID", MyClass);
```

When `clip` is *instantiated*, Flash invokes `MyClass()` with no arguments, and with the `this` variable pointing to the new movie clip object that is being created—in this case, `myClip`. (Instantiation occurs when `clip` is placed on the Stage, either manually at author time or programmatically at runtime, using the `attachMovie()` method or the `duplicateMovieClip()` method or global function.) The result of invoking `MyClass()` is that `myClip` becomes a member of `MyClass`—without losing any of its movie clip methods or properties, including graphical content.

Understanding `registerClass()`

To understand the importance of `registerClass()`, recall that a movie clip is a very special kind of object in Flash. Its base properties—the ones that were there in versions of Flash before Flash MX—are "hard-wired" into the interpreter and can be acquired only through the normal processes of creating a clip, either manually or using `createEmptyMovieClip()`, `attachMovie()`, or `duplicateMovieClip()`. Even though there is a `MovieClip` class, these base properties have no connection to the `MovieClip` class. Properties included in this group include `_x`, `_y`, `_height`, `_width`, `_alpha`, `_rotation`, `_xscale`, `_yscale`, and `_name`, among others—properties a movie clip cannot do without.

On the other hand, all the movie clip methods (such as `play()`, `gotoAndPlay()`, and `prevFrame()`) *are* inherited from the `MovieClip` class and therefore are available only to members of the `MovieClip` class.

You are therefore faced with a dilemma if you want a movie clip to also belong to a custom class, such as `MyClass`. For instance, a seemingly hopeful approach that leads nowhere is making your custom class inherit from the `MovieClip` class (`MyClass.prototype = new MovieClip()`) and using the `new` operator to create a new object in your class (`myClip = new MyClass()`). This approach gives `myClip` the methods and properties that are provided by the `MovieClip` class and makes `myClip` a full-fledged member of `MyClass`, inheriting from the `MyClass` prototype object. However, `myClip` will *lack* the basic movie clip properties, without which a movie clip is nonfunctional.

On the other hand, if you use a constructor function as an init object to give a movie clip properties from a custom class, as described in the previous section, it will remain a full-fledged, functional movie clip but will *not* become a member of `MyClass`. In particular, it will *not* inherit from the `MyClass` prototype.

`registerClass()` can make `myClip` a full-fledged member of `MyClass`, inheriting from its prototype object, *and* preserve myClip's basic movie clip properties. You can then make `MyClass` inherit from the `MovieClip` class, and voila, you have a fully functional movie clip subclass, with everything that `MyClass` offers and everything you expect in a movie clip.

Using `registerClass()` with `attachMovie()`

The easiest way to use the `registerClass()` method is with `attachMovie()`. In the following example, `linkageID` is the linkage ID of a clip in the Library, and `MyClass` is the name of a constructor function:

```
Object.registerClass("linkageID", MyClass);
MyClass.prototype = new MovieClip();
_root.attachMovie("linkageID", "myClip", 1);
```

You now have a fully functional new movie clip, `myClip`, which is a member of `MyClass`, which in turn inherits from `MovieClip`.

Using `registerClass()` with a Manually Created Movie Clip

Using `registerClass()` with a manually created movie clip can be tricky. You *cannot* use the instance name of the clip in place of the linkage ID in the `registerClass()` statement.

Sample movie regclass.fla implements a solution that is consistent with the way Macromedia implements its own components. It gives the movie clip a linkage ID and puts initialization code similar to the following on the Timeline of the movie clip:

```
#initclip
function MyClass(){
    trace("constructor is executing");
}
MyClass.prototype = new MovieClip();
```

```
MyClass.prototype.myFunc = function(){
    trace("myFunc is executing");
};
object.registerclass("linkageID", MyClass);
#endinitclip
```

Giving a linkage ID to a movie clip that's already on the Stage is counterintuitive, but it works.

When the SWF runs, you'll see `constructor is executing` in the Output window.

If the manually created movie clip is `_root.myClip`, you can execute `myFunc()` like this:

```
_root.myClip.myFunc();
```

In this case, you'll see `myFunc is executing` in the Output window.

Using `__proto__` Instead of `registerClass`

In some situations, `registerClass()` does not work. For instance, there is no obvious way to apply `registerClass()` to clips created using `createEmptyMovieClip()`. One way around this problem is to use the `__proto__` property of the instance to make it a member of a subclass of `MovieClip`.

> ⇨ For more information on the `__proto__` property, see Chapter 21, "Packaging Data and Functions Using Custom Objects," page 489.

Using the same subclass as in the previous example (`MyClass`), sample movie proto.fla creates a new empty movie clip, `myHighlight`, and makes it a member of `MyClass` without affecting any of its movie clip properties. Here are the central lines of code. Line 1 creates the clip. Line 2 makes it a member of `MyClass`. Line 3 executes `MyClass` with `this` referring to `myHighlight`. (If `MyClass` conferred local properties, it would happen at this point.) Line 4 just proves that `myHighlight` really is a member of `MyClass`.

```
1: createEmptyMovieClip("myHighlight",1);
2: myHighlight.__proto__ = MyClass.prototype;
3: MyClass.apply(myHighlight); // displays "constructor is executing"
4: myHighlight.myFunc(); // displays "myFunc is executing"
```

> ⇨ For more details on the apply() method, see Chapter 15, "Combining Statements into Functions," page 267.

A Workaround for `registerClass`'s Lack of Parameter Passing

`registerClass()` does not allow you to pass any arguments to the constructor function. You can use an init object to compensate for this deficiency. The init object does not actually pass any arguments to the constructor. Instead, you modify the constructor so that it knows where to look in the init object for the values it would normally get in arguments.

In the listing that follows, based on sample movie regclassinit.fla, line 1 registers the linkage ID `clip` with the `MyClass` class. Notice that you can register the ID before the class exists.

The registerClass() function has a return value, which is supposed to be true if the operation is successful and false otherwise. However, registerClass() returns true even in extreme cases, such as both the movie clip and the class not existing. The example doesn't bother to check the return.

Lines 2–11 define the MyClass constructor function. If arg0 is undefined, the function looks in this.args.zero for a value. Similarly, if arg1 is undefined, the function looks in this.args.one for a value. Remember that the init object becomes this inside the constructor function. So, in this case, this.args.zero means initObj.args.zero.

Line 11 makes MyClass inherit from MovieClip.

Line 12 creates an init object with an args property that will be used to pass values to MyClass. (The name initObj is arbitrary.)

Line 13 attaches a movie from the Library, using initObj as an init object.

That's the end of the functional part of the program. Line 14 shows that myClip is a movie clip. Line 15 shows that myClip has access to the basic movie clip properties. Line 16 shows that myClip has access to inherited MovieClip properties. Lines 17 and 18 show that you can still create objects with the MyClass constructor.

```
 1: Object.registerClass("clip", MyClass);
 2: function MyClass (arg0, arg1) {
 3:     if (arg0 == undefined)
 4:         this.arg0 = this.args.zero;
 5:     else this.arg0 = arg0;
 6:     if (arg1 == undefined)
 7:         this.arg1 = this.args.one;
 8:     else this.arg1 = arg1;
 9:     this.localVar = "locVar";
10: }
11: MyClass.prototype = new MovieClip();
12: initObj = {args : { zero : "z" , one : "o" } };
13: _root.attachMovie("clip","myClip", 1, initObj);
14: trace(typeof _level0.myClip); // movieclip
15: trace(typeof _level0.myClip._x); // number
16: trace(typeof _level0.myClip.play); // function
17: myObj = new MyClass("argument 0", "argument 1");
18: trace(typeof _level0.myObj); // object
```

DETECTING MOVIE CLIP COLLISIONS

You can use the hitTest() method of the MovieClip class to determine whether any part of a movie clip overlaps either another movie clip or a particular point. The hitTest() method returns true if they coincide, otherwise false. Either or both of the clips, or any child clip, can have its _visible property set to false without affecting the hit test.

In the case of two movie clips, hitTest() checks whether their *bounding boxes* overlap. The bounding box is the smallest rectangle that contains all the graphics in the clip.

Determining a Movie Clip's Bounding Box

To find the bounding box of a movie clip, use the `getBounds()` method of the `MovieClip` class. Here's an example:

```
boundsObject = myClip.getBounds(coordinateSpace);
```

`boundsObject` is an object with four properties—`xMin`, `xMax`, `yMin`, and `yMax`—that contain the left, right, top, and bottom coordinates, respectively, of `myClip` relative to the registration point of the Timeline named by `coordinateSpace`. Thus, in the example, `boundsObject.yMin` is the top of `myClip`.

If you don't supply a value for the coordinate space, the clip itself (`myClip` in the example) is used. If you don't supply a value for the clip itself, the current Timeline is used. Thus, these two statements are equivalent:

```
getBounds();
this.getBounds(this);
```

If you need to find only one of the four properties, you can get it like this:

```
topOfMyClip = myClip.getBounds().yMin;
```

You can use `MovieClip.getBounds()` for collision detection. In comparison with `hitTest()`, `getBounds()` is more flexible, both because it allows you to test separately for each of the four bounds of the clip, and because you are free to adjust the test point. Instead of testing using `yMin`, for example, you could use `yMin-10` or `yMin+10`.

Sample movie getbounds.fla on the CD illustrates the use of `getBounds()`.

17

The format for checking for a collision between two movie clips is as follows:

```
myClip1.hitTest(myClip2)
```

When checking for a collision between a movie clip and a point, you can use either the bounding box of the movie clip or just the areas that actually contain graphics. Set the Boolean "shape flag" parameter to `false` to use the bounding box or to `true` to use just the graphics. The format is

```
target.hitTest(x, y, shapeFlag)
```

For instance, you can use the "point-check" approach to check whether the mouse pointer is over a movie clip:

```
myClip1.hitTest(_xmouse, _ymouse, true)
```

The "point-check" approach can also be used to check whether a movie clip overlaps the registration point of another movie clip.

⇨ *If you're having trouble using the "point-check" hitTest approach to check whether a movie clip overlaps the registration point of a movie created using createEmptyMovieClip(), see the "Troubleshooting" section at the end of this chapter, page 364.*

The hitTest() method is typically used with an if statement. In addition, you usually need to test for the collision repetitively. That means putting the test in an event handler. The following block of code will check in every frame whether any part of the graphics in myClip overlaps the point (100, 200) on the Timeline where the block of code resides.

```
_root.onEnterFrame = function () {
    if (myClip.hitTest(100, 200, true)) {
        // do something
    }
};
```

The x and y values used in a "point-check" hit test are interpreted as x and y points on the main Stage. If you want to check whether one movie clip has collided with a point in another movie clip, you need to use the localToGlobal() method of the MovieClip class to translate the coordinates of the point into main Stage coordinates.

The localToGlobal() and globalToLocal() Movie Clip Methods

Local movie clip coordinates are measured from the movie clip's registration point. Global coordinates are measured from the upper-left corner of the main Stage. To convert from local to global coordinates, or vice versa, you first create an object with two properties, x and y:

```
myObj = new Object();
myObj.x = 100;
myObj.y = 200;
```

Then you use this object as a parameter to the localToGlobal() or globalToLocal() method of the MovieClip class. The localToGlobal() method treats the x and y values as local coordinates and changes them to global ones. The globalToLocal() method treats the x and y values as global coordinates and changes them to local ones.

The methods do not return anything. Instead, they convert the actual x and y values in the object. For example, the following statement converts myObj.x and myObj.y from local coordinates within myClip to global coordinates:

```
myClip.localToGlobal(myObj);
```

Reducing Hit Test "Misses" with "Invisible Children"

If you check for a collision only once per frame, movie clips that are small in comparison with their relative speed can easily appear to "go through" each other without triggering a hit. For instance, suppose you have two movie clips, each 10 pixels square, moving toward one another at a rate of 20 pixels per frame. If the movie clips are 10 pixels apart in frame three, they will have "gone through" one another by frame four. No hit will be detected.

One way to reduce the number of "misses" is to create an invisible child clip (a clip with its _visible property set to false) inside one or both of the clips involved in the hit test. If the children are bigger than the parents, the bounding boxes of the parents will be those of their invisible children. If the parents are moving at a constant rate relative to one another, you should be able to find some size for the children that consistently triggers hits. If the relative speed of the parents is variable, you can scale the children up as the relative speed increases.

Creating the Illusion of a Perfect Hit

When an "invisible child" or a "hit distance" is larger than a visible graphic, your program may detect a collision before the visible graphics collide. If the movie clips are moving fast enough, the fact that the graphics do not actually "touch" may not be obvious to the eye. On the other hand, there is usually a limit to how large "invisible children" or "hit distances" can be before the illusion of the graphics "bumping into one another" is no longer convincing.

You can address this problem by moving the movie clips into the desired positions immediately after detecting the collision. The paddle() function, taken from the "reward actions" section of sample movie ecoball.fla, demonstrates this technique.

The paddle() function is a hitTest-like function that tests the x and y distances between the registration points of two movie clips. When the distances are small enough, it is considered a hit. As the movie clips speed up, the "hit distances" are increased. This approach may be less processor-intensive and less prone to "misses" than hitTest().

The paddle() function bounces a ball off a paddle. Line 4 of the function ensures that it detects hits only when the ecoball instance, ecoballi, is moving from right to left—that is, when its x velocity, vx, is negative (_root.ecoballi.vx < 0).

In line 6, the paddle() function adjusts the hit distance, hitDx, upward as paddle speed, paddleVx, and ball speed, ecoballi.vx, increase. This makes it less likely that they will pass through one another.

The Math.max() function in line 2 ensures that paddle speed is never less than the "hit constant," HC. Thus, paddleVx/HC is always greater than or equal to 1. Thus, in line 6, multiplying by paddleVx/HC can only increase—never reduce—the hit distance.

```
1: function paddle() {
2:  paddleVx = Math.max(_root.paddlei._x-oldPaddlex, HC);
3:  oldPaddlex = _root.paddlei._x;
4:    if (_root.ecoballi.vx < 0) {
5:    // hitDx adjusts upward but is never greater than 100
6:    hitDx=Math.min(Math.abs((root.ecoballi.vx/12)*(paddleVx/HC)),100);
7:    if ( (Math.abs(_root.paddlei._x - _root.ecoballi._x) < hitDx) &&
8:        (Math.abs(_root.paddlei._y - _root.ecoballi._y) < hitDy) ) {
9:        // bring ball to paddle - create illusion of perfect hit
10:        _root.ecoballi._x = _root.paddlei._x;
11:        // bouncing it back
12:        _root.ecoballi.vx = -_root.ecoballi.vx;
13:    }
14:  }
15: }
```

Executing Multiple Hit Tests per Frame

An option that may work in some applications is to put the hit test in a mouse event handler, such as onMouseMove. Mouse event handlers can fire multiple times per frame.

Another possibility is to use the setInterval() global function to both move the movie clips and execute a hit test multiple times per frame. Performing a new hit test is useless, of course, if you haven't moved the clip since the last test. You should also use the updateAfterEvent() function to refresh the screen.

> The setInterval() global function is covered in the next section, "Calling a Function Repetitively Using setInterval()."

Caution

Executing hit tests multiple times per frame is processor-intensive and runs the risk of slowing down your application to an unacceptable degree.

CALLING A FUNCTION REPETITIVELY USING SETINTERVAL()

The setInterval() global function calls a function or method repetitively at regular intervals while a movie plays. You provide a parameter that specifies an interval in milliseconds. The two formats are as follows:

```
setInterval(function,interval[,arg1, arg2, ...,argn] )
setInterval(object, methodName,interval[,arg1,arg2, ..., argn] )
```

For instance:

```
setInterval(myFunc,100);
setInterval(myObj, myMethod, 100);
```

This function looks straightforward enough. In reality, however, as the following two examples illustrate, the relationship between the interval you specify and the actual interval of execution is anything but obvious.

- If the specified interval is less than the frame length (the time required to play one frame), the function or method is called at some point after the interval expires. However, the actual interval is often *10 times* the specified interval.

  For instance, a frame rate of 1 frame per second (fps) is equivalent to a frame length of 1000 milliseconds (1 second). If you specify an interval of 10 milliseconds at 1 fps, the actual interval may be 100 milliseconds—10 times the interval you specified.

  In addition, the interval can vary depending on how processor-intensive the function or method is, what other processing is competing with it, and how powerful the computer is.

- If you specify an interval that is greater than the frame length, the function will execute on the next frame transition. For example, at 1 fps, if you specify 1500 ms (a frame and a half), the function will execute every other frame.

Determining the Actual Interval

You can use the following function to determine the actual interval resulting from any given specified interval. Just change the `interval` value in the first line.

```
interval = 100;
clearVal = setInterval(measureInterval, interval);
function measureInterval () {
    if (restart == undefined) restart = 0;
    else restart = start;
    start = getTimer();
    var elapsed = start - restart;
    trace("interval:  "+ elapsed);
    updateAfterEvent();
}
```

Note the `updateAfterEvent()` function in the last line, which refreshes the screen.

Caution

`setInterval()` can degrade the performance of your movie. The more intervals that you run simultaneously, the more the performance of your movie is likely to suffer.

Stopping or "Clearing" the Repeating Function Call

`setInterval()` returns an *interval identifier* that you can pass to the `clearInterval()` method to stop the function from executing. For instance, in the code in the previous section, the interval identifier is `clearVal` in the second line. Thus, the following line will cancel the execution of `measureInterval()`:

```
clearInterval(clearVal);
```

DRAGGING AND DROPPING MOVIE CLIPS

The capability to "pick up" a graphic on the screen, move it to another location, and "drop" it is useful in graphical user interfaces and also in games.

 Creating drag-and-drop behavior was straightforward in Flash 5 but is even easier in Flash MX, due to the introduction of button movie clips—movie clips with button event handlers, such as `onPress` and `onRelease`.

⇨ *For more information on button movie clips and event handlers, see Chapter 16, "Interaction, Events, and Sequencing," page 303.*

`startDrag()` **and** `stopDrag()`

In Flash 5, you could implement drag-and-drop behavior by putting an invisible button inside a movie clip and attaching two event handlers to the button: an `on(press)` event handler containing a `startDrag()` statement and an `on(release)` event handler containing a `stopDrag()` statement. The same basic strategy works in Flash MX, except that now you can attach `onPress` and `onRelease` event handlers directly to the movie clip.

In both cases, the result is the same from the user's point of view: When you press the mouse button, the movie clip named in the startDrag() statement (inside the onPress event handler) is "locked" to the mouse pointer and moves as the mouse pointer moves. When you release the mouse button, the stopDrag() statement in the onRelease event handler executes, and any currently draggable movie clip is no longer draggable. That is, the clip is no longer locked to the mouse pointer; the mouse can move, and the movie clip no longer moves.

Notice that the stopDrag() method does *not* apply just to the movie clip named in the stopDrag() statement. It disables dragging for any currently draggable clip. Thus, it is exactly equivalent to the stopDrag() global function. The movie clip name is like a comment, reminding you which clip you believe should currently be draggable.

The stopDrag() method takes no parameters. For instance, here's the stopDrag() portion of a typical drag-and drop implementation:

```
myClip.onRelease = function () {
    myClip.stopDrag();
};
```

Here's the startDrag() portion of a typical drag-and drop implementation:

```
myClip.onPress = function () {
    myClip.startDrag();
};
```

The optional parameters for startDrag() are discussed in the next section.

startDrag() **Options**

startDrag() has optional parameters to accomplish these two goals:

- Locking the movie clip's registration point to the mouse pointer. This locking occurs if the optional lock parameter is true. If lock is false, the movie clip and the mouse pointer retain the spatial relationship they had when the user first pressed the mouse button. For instance, in the following statement, myClip's registration point is locked to the mouse pointer:

  ```
  myClip.startDrag(true);
  ```

  If you don't supply a lock argument, it is treated as false.

- Constraining the area within which the movie clip can be dragged. The area is specified by four parameters: *left*, *top*, *right*, *bottom*. For instance, this statement constrains myClip to a rectangle starting at the upper-left corner of the stage and going 100 pixels to the right and 200 pixels down:

  ```
  myClip.startDrag(true, 0, 0, 100, 200]])
  ```

Flash developer Andy Hall's spacelisten.fla on the CD provides an interesting example of drag-and-drop functionality in Flash MX. Spacelisten.fla creates an empty movie clip (line 1) and uses drawing methods to associate a square graphic with it (lines 2–8). It makes the movie clip into a button movie clip by giving it an onRelease event handler and makes the movie clip "droppable" by putting a stopDrag() statement in the onRelease event handler (lines 9–11).

For a plain-vanilla drag and drop, you would now define an `onPress` event handler with a `startDrag()` statement in it, as shown in the previous section. Spacelisten.fla instead disables the hand cursor (line 12) and "hides" the `startDrag()` statement inside an `onKeyDown` event handler (lines 14–21), which is "watching" for the user to press the spacebar. Only when the user presses the spacebar is the hand cursor enabled (line 16) and an `onPress` event handler defined, containing the `startDrag()` statement (line 17–19).

This example also contains an `onKeyUp` event handler, such that when the user releases the key, the hand cursor is once again disabled (line 24) and the `onPress` event handler is set to `null`, disabling it (line 25) .

The result is a drag-and-drop feature that works only when the spacebar is down.

```
 1: _root.createEmptyMovieClip("a",1);
 2: a.moveTo(0,0);
 3: a.lineStyle(2,0x000000);
 4: a.beginFill(0x000000,30);
 5: a.lineTo(0,100);
 6: a.lineTo(100,100);
 7: a.lineTo(100,0);
 8: a.endFill();
 9: a.onRelease = a.onReleaseOutside = function() {
10:     this.stopDrag();
11: }
12: a.useHandCursor = false;
13: spaceListen = new Object();
14: spaceListen.onKeyDown = function () {
15:     if (Key.getCode() == Key.SPACE) {
16:         a.useHandCursor = true;
17:         a.onPress = function () {
18:             this.startDrag();
19:         }
20:     }
21: }
22: spaceListen.onKeyUp = function () {
23:     if (Key.getCode() == Key.SPACE) {
24:         a.useHandCursor = false;
25:         a.onPress = null;
26:     }
27: }
28: Key.addListener(spaceListen);
```

Using the _droptarget Movie Clip Property

When a user drags and drops something, *where* the user drops it is often critical. Dropping a file into the trash will trigger something quite different in a program than dropping it into a folder. The read-only _droptarget movie clip property gives you an easy way to test where a user has dropped, or may be about to drop, a movie clip.

If the registration point of a dragged clip is over any part of another clip (whether or not the mouse button has been released), the _droptarget property contains the path of that clip. If the dragged clip is not over any other clip, the _droptarget property is undefined.

The _droptarget property goes back to Flash 4, and it provides the path as a string in Flash 4 "slash notation," as shown in these examples:

```
/myClip
/myClip/child
```

WORKING WITH DYNAMIC MASKS

You can manually create a mask layer that reveals those portions of lower layers that are under graphics in the mask layer. Where the mask layer has no graphics, content in underlying layers is hidden.

 Masks are introduced in Chapter 3, "Drawing and Painting in Flash," page 37.

In Flash 5, you could set up masking only through the GUI, not through ActionScript. In addition, you could not control a movie clip in a mask layer using ActionScript; if you wanted to animate a mask, you had to use shape or motion tweening. You could use ActionScript with movie clips in *masked* layers, and you could use ActionScript with a movie clip that contained masking internally. All these features still work in Flash MX, as well.

In addition, in Flash MX, you can use ActionScript to animate masks. For instance, you can move, rotate, and scale masks. Check out ScriptableMask.fla, which comes as a sample with Flash MX, for some examples of what you can do with masks in Flash MX.

Also new in Flash MX is the setMask() method of the MovieClip class, which allows you to designate one clip as a mask for another clip programmatically. For instance, in the following statement, myMaskedClip is the instance name of a movie clip to be masked, and myMask is the instance name of the mask movie clip:

```
myMaskedClip.setMask (myMask);
```

Mask and maskee form an exclusive "monogamous" pair: You can have only one mask per maskee and only one maskee per mask. As soon as you set a new mask on a clip, any previous mask stops functioning as a mask. Usually, this limitation is not severe because both the mask and the masked movie clips can have multiple frames, multiple layers, and multiple scripted child clips internally.

If you want to turn off masking for a particular masked clip without designating a new mask, use null for the mask clip parameter, as shown here:

```
myMaskedClip.setMask (null); // myMaskedClip is no longer masked
```

Here are some points to remember about dynamic masking:

- Masks are always invisible, *while they are masks*. As soon as a mask clip is no longer being used as a mask, it becomes visible—not usually the behavior you want. Therefore, before taking a mask out of service, you should probably make it invisible, like this:

```
myMaskedClip.setMask (myMask);
myMask._visible = false;
myMaskedClip.setMask (null);
```

- You can use the drawing API to create masks. However, just as strokes (lines) have no effect in masks that you create manually, lines created with the drawing API are useless in masks. Only the filled portions of the clip have the ability to mask.

⇨ *The drawing API is covered in Chapter 18, "Drawing with ActionScript," page 367.*

- Device fonts in a masked movie clip are displayed but not masked. This means that they will show up, even though they are not under the mask! You can cure this problem by embedding fonts like this:

```
myTextField.embedFonts = true;
```

For Flash UI Components, you can set the `embedFonts` property globally:

```
globalStyleFormat.embedFonts = true;
```

- Setting a movie clip to mask itself accomplishes nothing, as in this example:

```
mc.setMask(mc); // does nothing
```

Movie Clips and Audio: The `attachAudio()` Method

The undocumented `attachAudio()` method of the `MovieClip` class allows you to attach an audio stream to a movie clip. It is analogous in function to the `attachVideo()` method of the `Video` class. (The `MovieClip` class also has an undocumented `attachVideo()` method, but I have not been able to obtain any information on it.)

Using only the initial release of Flash MX, the Flash Player can make local video and audio streams available for you to see and hear locally. You could use this to watch and listen to yourself rehearsing a speech, for instance. When attaching local video and/or audio streams, the Flash Player does not publish or record the video and audio; it just lets you view or listen to what's happening at the present moment.

The following example attaches an audio stream from a local microphone.

```
createEmptyMovieClip ("aud", 1);
inputMic = Microphone.get(); // capture audio stream
inputMic.setGain(2); // set loudness
aud.attachAudio(inputMic); // attach audio stream to movie clip
```

⇨ *For more details on Microphone.get() and the Video class, see Chapter 20, "Using the Built-in Movie Objects," page 443.*

The ability to attach audio and video streams becomes more interesting with the Flash Communication Server, which allows the Flash Player to publish video and audio to a remote audience over a network, enabling videoconferencing, for example. The Flash Player may also record the video and audio for later playback.

TROUBLESHOOTING

Why can't I access information in my loaded SWFs?

You should be able to attach a movie from the Library of a loaded SWF, and access variables, movie clips, and functions defined in the loaded SWF.

If you cannot, you might not be referring to the items correctly. To view the paths and identifiers associated with the items, do the following:

- Select Debug, List Variables or press Cmd-Option-V (Mac) or Ctrl+Alt+V (Windows) to list variables.

- Select Debug, List Objects or press Cmd-L (Mac) or Ctrl+L (Windows) to list objects.

If you're referring to the items correctly, you might be trying to access them before the SWF has loaded completely. Make sure the file has loaded completely by doing one of the following:

- Put in an adequate delay. For instance, you could put the code that accesses the items a number of frames after the code that loads the SWF. This assumes some level of predictability in load time, however.

- Use the `data` event of the `loadMovie()` function in combination with either the `getBytesLoaded()` and `getBytesTotal()` methods of the `MovieClip` class, the `_framesloaded` and `_totalframes` movie clip properties, or the deprecated `ifFrameLoaded()` function.

> *For more details on the data event of the loadMovie() function, see "Movie Clip Events," page 320 (Chapter 16, "Interaction, Events, and Sequencing").*

I'm using the "point-check" `hitTest()` approach to check whether a movie clip overlaps the registration point of a movie I created using `createEmptyMovieClip()`. Why isn't it working?

When you create movie clips manually, it is natural to create the graphics around the registration point and then position the movie clip on the Stage. Thus, you may become accustomed to the idea that the registration point is at the center of the graphics.

When using `createEmptyMovieClip()`, you use the drawing API to create the graphics, and you can create and position the graphics in one step without changing the registration point. For instance, using the `makeTriangle()` function in Helen Triolo's dynamicButtonMovie.fla sample movie from Chapter 16, you can create and position the triangle in one line without changing the registration point. If you change the registration point, three lines are required to achieve the same visual effect. For instance, in the following listing, the result looks the same whether you use lines 12 through 14 or just line 15:

```
 1: function makeTriangle(x1, y1, x2, y2, x3, y3, zdepth) {
 2:     this.createEmptyMovieClip ("triangle", zdepth);
 3:     with (triangle){
 4:             beginFill (0x0000FF, 50);
 5:             moveTo (x1, y1);
 6:             lineTo (x2, y2);
 7:             lineTo (x3, y3);
 8:             lineTo (x1, y1);
 9:             endFill();
10:     }
11: }
12: /* makeTriangle(0, 0, 60, 130, -50, 1);
13: triangle._x = 200;
14: triangle._y = 200; */
15: makeTriangle(200, 200, 260, 330, 250, 1);
```

You can easily forget, when using the more efficient syntax, that the registration point is nowhere near the graphic. Then, if you do something where the registration point is important, you may get surprising results. For instance, the following hit test will tell you when myClip overlaps triangle's registration point; however, myClip will be nowhere near the triangle graphic at that time:

```
makeTriangle(200, 200, 260, 330, 250, 1);
myClip.hitTest(triangle._x, triangle._y);
```

FLASH AT WORK: A SCRATCH-AND-WIN GAME

Peter Hall's scratch.fla on the CD uses the drawing API and dynamic masking to create a scratch-and-win game.

In scratch.fla, four covered windows hide a random selection of four symbols: an apple, a bell, a lemon, and a star. The player scratches the "wax" covering off the Windows, hoping to find a match. When scratching, the player actually creates a mask using the drawing API. As the player fills in the mask, the symbol under it appears because the parts of the mask that contain graphics are the parts that reveal whatever is under them.

The movie clip containing the symbols is named symbols. The mask movie clip's instance name is wax. Each scratch creates a child clip within wax, with names such as wax.1, wax.2, and so on.

The following line sets the wax movie clip to mask the symbols movie clip:

```
symbols.setMask(wax);
```

The following line creates the wax clip:

```
createEmptyMovieClip("wax",1);
```

The methods startScratch() and endScratch() are defined in the MovieClip prototype, so all movie clips can access them. Then they are called in the wax.onMouseDown and wax.onMouseUp event handlers. So wax.onMouseDown (pressing down the mouse button) starts the scratch, and wax.onMouseUp (releasing the mouse button) stops the scratch.

Thus, the core of scratch.fla consists of:

- Two methods in the `MovieClip` prototype: `startScratch()` and `endScratch()`. The `doScratch()` function is a helper for `startScratch()`.

- Two event handlers for the `wax` movie clip: `wax.onMouseDown` and `wax.onMouseUp`.

There is also a `startAgain()` function to begin the game again.

Here's a function-by function breakdown of the program:

- `MovieClip.prototype.startScratch = function(width)`

  Creates an empty movie clip (such as `wax.1`, `wax.2`, `wax.3`) and draws one "scratch" in it using `doScratch()`.

- `doScratch = function()`

  Uses the drawing API to draw in the current mask movie clip (such as `wax.1`). Draws with fills because lines do not work as a mask.

- `MovieClip.prototype.endScratch = function()`

  Deletes properties in the mask movie clip (such as `wax.1`). The properties were created in `startScratch()`. Properties deleted include the `onEnterFrame` event handler created in `startScratch()`.

- `wax.onMouseDown = function() { this.startScratch(6);};`

  Begins a new scratch every time the mouse button is pressed.

- `wax.onMouseUp = function(){this[this.i].endScratch();};`

  Ends the scratch when the button is released.

- `startAgain = function()`

  Clears all the drawing from the mask (`wax`).

> For reasons I haven't been able to determine, scratch.fla does not work on the Mac version of the Flash 6 Player.

DRAWING WITH ACTIONSCRIPT

INTRODUCING THE FLASH MX DRAWING METHODS

Programmatically controlled drawing is a new feature in Macromedia Flash MX, implemented via the drawing methods of the `MovieClip` class. These methods, which enable you to draw using ActionScript, are simple in format. They can be insanely fun. (On the CD, check out play.fla, Keith Peter's 3Dcube.fla, and test5.fla, as well as Millie Maruani's api_flower.fla and api_cube.fla.) The drawing methods simplify tasks that previously required kludgy workarounds.

For instance, although you could make a drawing program with Flash 5, it is much easier with Flash MX. Sample movie mouseDraw.fla, found on the CD, implements a very basic drawing function in five lines of code!

On the downside, getting the drawing methods to do exactly what you want is not always easy. In particular, controlling curve drawing with precision can require either trigonometry or some trial and error.

Basically, the drawing methods do the following:

- Draw lines
- Draw curves
- Fill in closed areas

Saving Drawings

Flash does not provide any means of programmatically creating a graphics file such as a GIF, PNG, or BMP file. However, you can easily save the data associated with a drawing in a *local shared object*. You can bring the data back into your Flash application and redraw the graphic, as illustrated in Peter Hall's saveDrawing.fla file on the CD. This file implements, in fewer than 75 lines of code, a simple drawing program that can save and retrieve drawing data.

For more details on shared objects, see Chapter 26, "Communicating Locally," page 577.

Table 18.1 lists the eight methods in the drawing API, their formats, and purposes.

The drawing methods can be referred to collectively as the *drawing API* (application programming interface).

Table 18.1 Drawing API Methods

Method	Examples	Description
beginFill	myClip.beginFill ();	If an open path exists, close it with a line and fill the enclosed space. Do not fill subsequent closed paths.
	myClip.beginFill (0x00FF00);	If an open path exists, close it with a line and fill the enclosed space. Fill subsequent closed paths with a solid green color.

Method	Examples	Description
	`myClip.beginFill (0xFF0000, 80);`	If an open path exists, close it with a line and fill the enclosed space. Fill subsequent closed paths with red at 80% transparency.
beginGradientFill	`myClip.beginGradientFill()`	If an open path exists, close it with a line and fill the enclosed space. Do not fill subsequent closed paths.
	`myClip.beginGradientFill (undefined, colorArray, alphaArray, ratioArray, transformationMatrix);)`	If an open path exists, close it with a line and fill the enclosed space. Do not fill subsequent closed paths.
	`myClip.beginGradientFill ("linear", colorArray, alphaArray, ratioArray, transformationMatrix);`	If an open path exists, close it with a line and fill the enclosed space. Begin filling subsequent closed paths with a linear gradient fill, blending the colors provided in the `colorArray`, at the transparency levels provided in the `alphaArray`, in the ratios provided in the `ratioArray`, and transformed according to the `transformationMatrix` transformation matrix.
clear	`myClip.clear();`	Remove all programmatically generated drawing from this clip, and cancel the current line style and the current fill.
curveTo	`myClip.curveTo (controlX, controlY, anchorX, anchorY);`	Draw a curve using the current pen position and (`anchorX`, `anchorY`) as anchor points and (`controlX`, `controlY`) as the control point.
endFill	`myClip.endFill();`	Complete and protect from future changes fills created since the previous `beginFill()` or `beginGradientFill()` statement. Do not fill enclosed areas until another `beginFill()` or `beginGradientFill()` statement is encountered.
lineStyle	`myClip.lineStyle ();`	Stop drawing lines.
	`myClip.lineStyle (6);`	Draw solid black lines six pixels thick.
	`myClip.lineStyle (6, 0xFF0000);`	Draw solid red lines six pixels thick.
	`myClip.lineStyle (6, 0xFF0000, 50);`	Draw red lines six pixels thick at 50% transparency.
lineTo	`myClip.lineTo (100, 50)`	Draw a line using the current line style. Start from the current pen position and go to a point 100 pixels to the right of and 50 pixels below the registration point of `myClip`.

18

Table 18.1 Continued

Method	Examples	Description
moveTo	myClip.moveTo (200,250)	Make the current pen position a point 200 pixels to the right of and 250 pixels below the registration point of myClip.

Basically, the line-drawing part of the drawing API imitates the Pen tool in the Toolbox. However, if you know how, you can actually duplicate anything that you can do with Flash's manual drawing tools: circles, rectangles, triangles, straight or squiggly lines, solid and gradient fills—you name it.

All the drawing functions are methods of the MovieClip class. That makes sense because movie clips are Flash's containers for graphics. You are always drawing in a particular movie clip or in the root. Everything you do in the drawing API is specific to one movie clip. For instance, if you specify a line style, it applies only to graphics programmatically created within one clip.

USING OBJECTS TO KEEP TRACK OF WHAT YOU'RE DRAWING

You can use objects to give meaningful names and groupings to the graphics that you're creating. These organized names are much more intelligible than raw numbers.

For instance, imagine you're drawing a circle. You'll need to specify a center point (an x and a y coordinate) and a radius.

You can use a Point class and a Circle class to group and name this information. As always in Flash, classes are embodied in functions, and new members of the class are created using the new operator.

➡ For an introduction to classes and the new operator, see "Functions as Classes: Constructor Functions," page 279 (Chapter 15, "Combining Statements into Functions").

To create the center point, use a Point class:

```
function Point (x , y) {
    this.x = x;
    this.y = y;
};
myCenter = new Point(100, 100);
```

Here's how you would provide the x and y coordinates of this point as parameters to the moveTo() method:

```
moveTo(myCenter.x, myCenter.y);
```

That line of code is much more meaningful than the following:

```
moveTo(100, 100);
```

The following `Circle` class creates a center point as a property of the circle. The only other property you need to define a circle is the radius:

```
function Circle (centerX, centerY, radius) {
    this.center = new Point(centerX,centerY);
    this.radius = radius;
};
```

DRAWING LINES AND CURVES

The workhorses of the drawing API are the `lineTo()` method, which draws straight lines, and the `curveTo()` method, which draws curved lines. The following points apply to both these methods:

- Graphics that you create with the drawing API are drawn underneath manually created graphics appearing in the same movie clip.

- Drawing methods assume a starting point ("current drawing position" or "current pen").

- If any parameters are missing, the method fails and the current drawing position doesn't change.

- Whenever you designate a point, you do so by providing an x and a y parameter. This point represents the x distance and the y distance from the registration point of the movie clip that you're drawing in. On the root, the registration point is the upper-left corner. Otherwise, it defaults to the middle of the clip.

Drawing Lines

To draw a line, you need to take these two steps:

- Specify a line style.

- Tell Flash the coordinates of the starting and ending point.

Flash draws a line from the current pen position to the ending point that you specify. The ending point then becomes the current pen position, used as a starting point if you draw another line without calling `moveTo()`.

Specifying a Line Style

You must specify a line style before you can start drawing a line. You specify a line style using the `lineStyle()` method. The style holds until you specify another one. You can change line styles within a path, after ending one line and before starting the next.

The `lineStyle()` method has three optional parameters, indicating the thickness, color, and transparency (alpha) of the line:

- Thickness is measured in pixels. A value of 0 means hairline thickness.

- Color is specified as a number, most readably expressed in hexadecimal (base 16) notation.

- Transparency or alpha is expressed as a number from 0 (invisible) to 100 (solid). If you omit this parameter or supply a value greater than 100, Flash uses 100. If you supply a negative value, Flash uses 0.

> Colors assigned to a movie clip using the `Color` object supercede colors assigned using the drawing API.

⇨ *For more information on using the Color object and expressing colors as hexadecimal numbers, see Chapter 20, "Using the Built-in Movie Objects," page 443.*

Although all three parameters are optional, each one is necessary to the next one: You can't specify color if you don't specify thickness, and you can't specify transparency if you don't specify color. The format is

> A continuous series of lines or curves formed without ever "taking the pen off the paper" is called a *path*.

```
myClip.lineStyle (thickness, color , transparency);
```

If you omit all the parameters, you are telling Flash to stop drawing lines in that movie clip.

See Table 18.1 earlier in this chapter for examples of the `lineStyle()` method.

Designating Starting and Ending Points

If you have just drawn a line, Flash assumes that the ending point of the last line will be the beginning of the next line. Unless you explicitly tell it to, Flash never "takes the pen off the paper."

If you haven't drawn a line yet, or if you don't want the ending point of the last line to be the beginning of the next, you need to tell Flash where to start the next line. To do that, you use the `moveTo()` method. `moveTo()` sets the current pen position. This is both your "start here" function and your "pick the pen up off the paper and put it down here" function.

⇨ *For an example of using a moveTo() statement when changing fills, see "Using Solid Fills," later in this chapter, page 378.*

See Table 18.1 earlier in this chapter for an example of the `moveTo()` method.

If you call a drawing method without having made any calls to the `moveTo()` method, the starting position defaults to the registration point (`0, 0`).

You give Flash the coordinates of the ending point using the `lineTo()` method. See Table 18.1 for a usage example.

Continuous Drawing with the Mouse

Basic drawing functions are easy to implement using the drawing API. Take sample movie mouseDraw.fla, for instance. In a few lines of code, this movie makes the mouse continuously draw a black, 6-pixel-wide line. Here is the code *in its entirety*:

```
lineStyle(6);
moveTo(_xmouse, _ymouse);
```

```
onMouseMove = function() {
    lineTo(_xmouse, _ymouse);
    updateAfterEvent();
}
```

The `updateAfterEvent()` statement is not an absolute necessity, but it makes the line a little smoother.

Drawing a Square

I'll demonstrate the line-drawing methods by drawing a square. Here's the code:

```
 1: function Point (x, y) {
 2:      this.x = x;
 3:      this.y = y;
 4: };
 5: function Square (centerX, centerY, side) {
 6:      this.center = new Point(centerX, centerY);
 7:      this.side = side;
 8:      top = this.center.y + (side/2);
 9:      this.bottom = this.center.y - (side/2);
10:      this.left = this.center.x - (side/2);
11:      this.right = this.center.x + (side/2);
12: };
13: createEmptyMovieClip("mySquareClip",1);
14: mySquareClip.mySquare = new Square(300,300,100);
15: with (mySquareClip) {
16:      with (mySquare) {
17:           lineStyle(6);
18:           moveTo(left, top);
19:           lineTo(left,bottom);
20:           lineTo(right,bottom);
21:           lineTo(right,top);
22:           lineTo(left,top);
23:      }
24: }
```

Line-by-line, here's what the program does:

- Creates a `Point` class (lines 1–4) and a `Square` class (lines 5–12). The `Square` class takes three parameters. The first two specify the x and y coordinates of the center of the square. The third specifies the length of a side of the square. From these values, the `Square` function calculates `top`, `bottom`, `left`, and `right` values, each half the length of a side from the center.

- Creates a movie clip to draw in (line 13).

- Creates a member of the `Square` class named `mySquare` (line 14).

■ Specifies a line style (line 17). The program just uses a raw number for line thickness. You could create a property in the `Square` class to hold values for the thickness, color, and transparency of the line, just like the `center` property that holds the x and y values of the center of the square. For instance, you could define an `LStyle` class as follows:

```
function LStyle (lineThickness, lineColor, lineTransparency) {
    this.lineThickness = lineThickness;
    this.lineColor = lineColor;
    this.lineTransparency = lineTransparency;
};
```

Then you would add `lineThickness`, `lineColor`, and `lineTransparency` as parameters to the `Square` class and create a member of the `LStyle` class within the `Square` class, following the example of `center`, which is a member of the `Point` class. For instance, this line inside the `Square` function would create a `line` property in each object constructed by the `Square` class:

```
this.line = new LStyle(lineThickness,lineColor,lineTransparency);
```

The new statement in line 14 would then look like this:

```
mySquareClip.mySquare = new Square(300,300,100,6,null,null);
```

And line 17 would be as follows:

```
lineStyle(line.lineThickness);
```

However, the existing statement, `lineStyle(6);`, is briefer and fairly readable.

■ Designates a starting point (line 18).

■ Draws the square (lines 17–22). The program uses nested `with` statements to avoid having to repeat the movie clip name (`mySquareClip`) and the name of the square object (`mySquare`). When it needs to evaluate a variable or execute a method, Flash will look first in `mySquare` and then in `mySquareClip` for a property or method of that name.

⇨ *For more details on the with statement, see Chapter 14, "Working with Data: Using Statements," page 251.*

Notice how readable the square drawing portion is. You can easily visualize starting at the left top, drawing a line to the left bottom, then a line to the right bottom, and so on until you complete the square. This is one of the rewards of implementing drawing functions within an object-oriented programming (OOP) framework.

Drawing Curves

You draw curves using the `curveTo()` method. Getting a handle on exactly how this function works can be a little difficult at first. Even after you understand it, creating complex shapes or creating shapes with mathematical precision can be tricky. Nevertheless, when you can visualize how `curveTo()` works, it's amazing what you can achieve with a little experimentation.

Luckily, a lot of basic groundwork has already been done by others. Look on the CD for Ric Ewing's drawMethods.fla, which contains functions that create basic shapes such as arcs (up to full circles), ovals, squares, rectangles, and regular polygons of any number of sides, as well as some more exotic shapes such as a gear, star, "burst," and circle with a wedge cut out of it. You can use and modify these functions to accomplish many strange, wonderful, and even useful tasks.

If you want to read more about Bezier curves in Flash, search on http://www.macromedia.com for a tech note about the Bezier Pen tool.

If you look at the code, you'll see that all the curved shapes require trigonometric functions. This chapter only goes as far as providing an example or two showing where and why trigonometry is required. If you want to delve more deeply into trigonometry, some examples in Chapter 19, "Using the Built-In Core Objects," can provide an introduction to the subject.

⇨ *For more details on trigonometric functions, see "Basic Trig Methods: Math.sin() and Math.cos()," page 431 (Chapter 19, "Using the Built-in Core Objects").*

Understanding the `curveTo()` Method

If you haven't already done so, spend some time playing around with the Pen tool in the Toolbox. The `curveTo()` method basically duplicates the functionality of the Pen tool.

⇨ *The Pen tool is covered in Chapter 2, "The Flash Interface," page 17, and in more detail in Chapter 3, "Drawing and Painting in Flash," page 37.*

Both the Pen tool and `curveTo()` method use Bezier curves, which define curves based on *anchor points* and *control points*. Two anchor points define the ends of each curve, and control points (on the ends of *handles*) act like magnets pulling the curve in the direction of the control point.

Figure 18.1 shows two kinds of Bezier curves: quadratic and cubic. Quadratic Bezier curves have one control point. Cubic Bezier curves have two. The Pen tool uses cubic Bezier curves while you're editing but converts them and stores them as quadratic Bezier curves in the SWF because they take up less space that way. The `curveTo()` method just uses quadratic Bezier curves from the start.

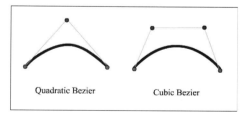

Figure 18.1
Quadratic and cubic Beziers.

Because the Pen tool uses cubic Beziers for editing, familiarity with the Pen tool, although definitely a good starting point, doesn't completely prepare you for using the quadratic Beziers of the `curveTo()` method. You may want to play with Andy Hall's curveTo.fla file on the CD. It will give you a good feel for how quadratic Bezier curves use two anchor points and a control point to define a curve.

Approximating Curves Through Triangulation

You can approximate any curve by setting the anchor points and then choosing a control point that forms a right triangle with them. Give the control point the x coordinate of one anchor point and the y coordinate of the other. Which anchor point contributes which coordinate determines the direction of the curve. If this approximated curve doesn't come close enough to what you want, move the control point a bit and see how it looks. Keep that up until you're satisfied.

You can use the triangulation technique, for instance, to draw a four-segment circle.

It is actually impossible to draw a perfect circle using Bezier curves. However, by dividing the circle into more and more segments, you can approximate a perfect circle more and more closely. For instance, Flash approximates circles using eight segments.

You can draw an approximation of a circle in four segments by using the `curveTo()` method and triangulation. The math is simple addition and subtraction. Figure 18.2 shows such a circle. (This figure is based on fourSegmentCircle.fla on the CD.)

Figure 18.2
A four-segment circle created using the `curveTo()` method and triangulation.

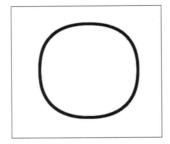

To see how the triangulation works, imagine a circle inscribed inside a square, as shown in Figure 18.3. The circle touches the square in four places. Take those places as the locations of the anchor points, the endpoints of the four arcs that make up the circle.

Figure 18.3
When you're drawing arcs using triangulation, start by imagining a circle inscribed in a square, as in this figure.

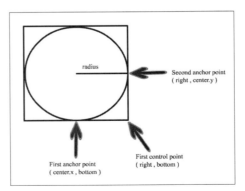

Now all you need to do is figure out where to put the control point for each arc. Each corner of the square forms a right triangle with two anchor points, so you'll use the corners of the square for triangulation.

Start by giving the `Circle` class that you defined earlier in this chapter four more properties—top, bottom, left, and right—which will make it easy to specify the top, bottom, left, and right-most points of the imaginary square around the circle. You can calculate these points easily because the top of the circle is one radius up from the center, the right-most point is one radius to the right from the center, and so on.

```
function Circle (centerX, centerY, radius) {
    this.center = new Point(centerX, centerY);
    this.radius = radius;
    this.top = centerY - radius;
    this.bottom = centerY + radius;
    this.left = centerX - radius;
    this.right = centerX + radius;
};
```

Using this `Circle` class, drawing an approximation of a circle is similar to drawing a square. The difference is that now you're drawing curves instead of straight lines. For each curve, you provide both the second anchor point (the first one is always the current pen position) and a control point.

The x and y coordinates of the control point are the first two parameters of the `curveTo()` method. As you can see, in the following code listing, they are the corners of the imaginary square around the circle.

```
 1: _root.createEmptyMovieClip( "circleClip", 1 );
 2: circleClip.fourSegmentCircle = new Circle(400,175,150);
 3: with ( _root.circleClip ) {
 4:     with (fourSegmentCircle) {
 5:         lineStyle( 6 );
 6:         moveTo( center.x, bottom );
 7:         curveTo( right, bottom, right, center.y );
 8:         curveTo( right, top, center.x, top );
 9:         curveTo( left, top, left, center.y );
10:         curveTo( left, bottom, center.x, bottom );
11:     }
12: }
```

The x and y coordinates of the second anchor point are the second two parameters of the `curveTo()` method.

Take a look at the first arc, which is the bottom right quadrant of the circle:

The first arc starts at the point where the bottom of the circle touches the square: (`center.x`, `bottom`). The `moveTo()` method on line 6 tells Flash to start there.

The first arc has its second anchor point at the point where the right side of the circle touches the square: (`right, center.y`). The `curveTo()` statement on line 7 specifies that.

The control point for the first arc is the bottom-right corner of the imaginary square: (`right, bottom`). The `curveTo()` statement on line 7 also specifies that.

The other four arcs follow this same triangulation strategy.

18

After you calculate points by triangulation, you can use trial and error to adjust them toward a more pleasing shape, if you want. For instance, Ric Ewings's 4SegCircle.fla on the CD uses a simple "fudge factor" to create a more circular-looking four-segment circle.

OPTIMIZING CURVE-DRAWING FUNCTIONS

If you're going to be drawing a lot of similar curves, consider optimizing your curve-drawing functions. Two common approaches are

- Paring down general-purpose methods to eliminate anything that's not needed for the particular curve that you're drawing

- Eliminating calculations by substituting constants

For example, in the `drawArc()` method in drawMethods.fla, if you're drawing only full circles, not partial arcs, you can substitute the constant 360 for `arc`. You can also substitute 0 for `startAngle` because it doesn't matter where you start drawing a circle. Finally, if you're drawing only circles, not ovals, you can eliminate `yRadius`, substituting `radius` wherever it appears.

You can gain more speed by precalculating the math functions. For instance, the following circle-drawing function has all the math precalculated. Because you're optimizing, substitute r for `radius`, as well. (Shorter names are more efficient.)

```
function fastCircle(r, x, y) {
    this.moveTo(x+r, y);
    this.curveTo(0.9991*r+x, 0.4151*r+y, 0.7071*r+x,0.7071*r+y);
    this.curveTo(0.4142*r+x, r+y, x, r+y);
    this.curveTo(-0.4151*r+x, 0.9991*r+y, -0.7071*r+x,0.7071*r+y);
    this.curveTo(-r+x, 0.4142*r+y, -r+x, y);
    this.curveTo(-0.9991*r+x, -0.4151*r+y, -0.7071*r+x, -0.7071*r+y);
    this.curveTo(-0.4142*r+x, -r+y, x, -r+y);
    this.curveTo(0.4151*r+x, -0.9991*r+y, 0.7071*r+x, -0.7071*r+y);
    this.curveTo(r+x, -0.4142*r+y, r+x, y);
}
lineStyle(6);
fastCircle(50,100,100);
```

When Flash compiles SWFs, it automatically substitutes constants for math functions whose parameters are constants. Thus, if you prefer `Math.cos(45*Math.PI/180)` to 0.7071, the result is exactly the same in the SWF.

⇨ *If you have a program that does a lot of drawing in a single movie clip, and you find that it is excessively slow, see the "Troubleshooting" section at the end of this chapter, page 386.*

USING SOLID FILLS

⇨ *Fills are introduced in Chapter 3, "Drawing and Painting in Flash," page 37.*

You can fill in closed paths with either solid or gradient fills, just as you can with the manual drawing tools. For solid fills, you use the `beginFill()` and `endFill()` methods of the `MovieClip` class. (See Table 18.1 earlier in this chapter for examples.)

A `beginFill()` statement stays in force, applying to everything you are drawing in that particular movie clip, until you execute `endFill()`, `clear()` or another `beginFill()` or `beginGradientFill()`.

Because `beginFill()` or `beginGradientFill()` closes any currently open path, often you don't need to use an `endFill()` statement. In many cases, results are the same with or without `endFill()`. For instance, if you draw a single curve while a fill is in force, Flash will automatically close the curve and fill the enclosed space, with or without an `endFill()` statement.

However, in some cases `endFill()` makes a dramatic difference. For instance, if you create two overlapping filled spaces with no `endFill()` between the `curveTo()` or `lineTo()` methods creating those spaces, fill will be canceled in the overlapping areas, and the background will show through, as illustrated by the two overlapping triangles on the left side of Figure 18.4. If you *do* put in an `endFill()` statement between the drawing methods (and a `beginFill()` statement so that the second graphic is also filled), both spaces will be completely filled, and the second shape will appear on top of the first, as illustrated on the right side of Figure 18.4. (This figure is based on fill-test.fla on the CD.) On the right, an `endFill()` statement was used after finishing one triangle and before beginning the next. Both spaces appear completely filled. On the left, no `endFill()` statement was used. Fill is canceled in the overlapping areas, and the background shows through.

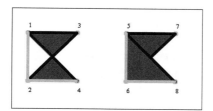

Figure 18.4
Two different ways of creating overlapping filled triangles.

In Figure 18.4, the graphic on the left was created by the following code, with no `endFill()` breaking up the `lineTo()` methods creating the two triangles:

```
this.beginFill(0xFF0000);
this.moveTo (one.x, one.y);
this.lineTo(three.x, three.y);
this.lineTo(two.x, two.y);
this.LineTo (one.x, one.y);
this.LineTo (four.x, four.y);
this.lineTo(two.x, two.y);
this.endFill();
```

The points used here are members of the `Point` class defined earlier in this chapter. The point numbered 1 in Figure 18.4 is named `one`, the point numbered 2 is named `two`, and so on.

The graphic on the right was created by the following code, with endFill(), beginFill(), and moveTo() breaking up the lineTo() methods creating the two triangles:

```
this.beginFill(0xFF0000);
this.moveTo (five.x, five.y);
this.lineTo(seven.x, seven.y);
this.lineTo(six.x, six.y);
this.endFill();
this.beginFill(0xFF0000);
this.moveTo(five.x, five.y);
this.lineTo (eight.x, eight.y);
this.lineTo (six.x, six.y);
this.endFill();
```

WORKING WITH GRADIENT FILLS

Gradient fills—bands of color that blend into each other—are by far the most complex feature in the drawing API. If you haven't already, start by familiarizing yourself with the manual procedures for creating gradients. Then you'll know what you're shooting for with their programmatic equivalents.

For gradient fills, you use the beginGradientFill() and endFill() methods of the MovieClip class. (See Table 18.1 earlier in this chapter for examples.)

A beginGradientFill() method stays in force, applying to everything you're drawing in that particular movie clip, until you execute endFill(), clear(), or another beginFill() or beginGradientFill().

Gradients can be either *linear* (parallel bars) or *radial* (concentric circles). A linear gradient fill is illustrated in Figure 18.5, and a radial gradient fill in Figure 18.6.

Figure 18.5
A linear gradient fill.

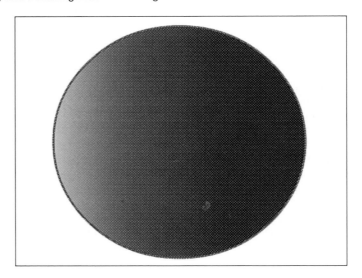

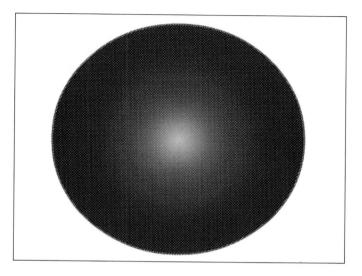

Figure 18.6
A radial gradient fill.

Working with the Three Gradient Arrays

Three properties of a gradient fill are stored in three different arrays. These properties are colors, alpha values, and ratios or widths.

The first array is an array of *colors* to be used in the fill. Each value in this array is a number from 0 to 0xFFFFFF.

The second is an array of *alpha values*. Each value in this array is a number from 0 to 100. Each value is applied to the corresponding color in the color array. Thus, `alphaArray[0]` specifies the transparency of the color in `colorArray[0]`.

The third is an array of *ratios* or *widths*. Each number in this array sets the point at which Flash starts filling in a particular color in its nonblended form. As you move to the left of that point, Flash blends in a greater and greater percentage of the neighboring color.

Setting these numbers is the programmatic equivalent of moving markers on the gradient definition bar in the Color Mixer panel to determine the width of each color band (for linear gradients) or ring (for radial gradients).

Each value in this array is a number from 0 to 255. To understand how these numbers work, imagine a ruler stretching the length of the gradient definition bar. The ruler has 255 marks on it. Each number in the ratio array refers to one of these marks, telling Flash to put the corresponding color's marker there. If you put in a number higher than 255, the entire function will fail.

Flash reads the numbers from left to right, with the result that colors that come earlier in the array have precedence over ones that come later. For instance, if multiple virtual "markers" are placed on the same virtual "mark," Flash displays only the color associated with the first marker. (Some blending from hidden colors may peek out.)

Flash always fills in the whole area to which the gradient fill has been assigned. It does this by giving any unclaimed area to the last color in the array. Thus, if you assign ratios of zero to all colors, the whole area will be filled in solidly with the last color in the array.

All three arrays must have exactly the same number of elements, or the entire function will fail. As a practical matter, the number of the elements will be at least two, and no more than eight. The arrays can actually have any number of elements, as long as it is the same number for all three. But at least two colors are required to make a gradient, so if each array has just one element, you get a solid fill, not a gradient fill. And colors after the eighth are not displayed. Thus, for instance, Flash displays the colors specified in `colorArray[0]` through `colorArray[7]`, but not the color specified in `colorArray[8]` .

The Transformation Matrix

The transformation matrix allows you to perform several standard transformations on gradient fills. These transformations include translation (which specifies the center point of the fill), scaling (which changes the size of the blended part of the fill), and rotation. Rotation changes the orientation of the whole fill; a 90-degree rotation, for example, makes the default vertical bars of a linear fill horizontal.

The matrix is an object and can be specified using an object literal or created using a custom class and the new operator.

> *For more information on object literals, see "Object and Array Literals," page 210 (Chapter 12, "Managing Variables, Data, and Datatypes").*

You define the matrix by creating an object whose properties become the elements in the matrix. You use this object as the last parameter supplied to the `beginGradientFill()` method.

The matrix object you create may contain either of the following:

- Nine properties specifying a 3-by-3 matrix as used in traditional matrix math. Macromedia provides an .AS file (an "include" file) that implements translate, rotate, and scale methods for a traditional matrix object. This makes the traditional matrix operations completely intuitive but requires a separate function call for each transformation (translate, rotate, scale).

- Six properties that provide parameters for translation, rotation, and scaling. You can perform one, two, or three operations with each call. This format is more concise and intuitive.

If all you want to do is translate, rotate, and scale, both formats can accomplish exactly the same thing. The 3-by-3 matrix is more efficient if you want to control the order of the scaling, translating, and rotating operations because you can transform the matrix multiple times and call `beginGradientFill()` just once.

The same operations performed in different orders give different results. Scaling-translating-rotating (in that order) is *not* the same as translating-rotating-scaling (in that order).

When you perform multiple transformations simultaneously with the more concise format, Flash always performs the operations in the following order: scale-rotate-translate. You can perform just one operation at a time, and thereby control the order, but you must call `beginGradientFill()` each time.

The traditional form is the way to go if you want to go beyond just translating, rotating, and scaling. For example, you could write your own matrix functions.

The Concise Transformation Matrix Format

The following statement creates a matrix object named m (the name is arbitrary) using the concise format:

```
m = { matrixType:"box", x:100, y:100, w:200, h:200, r:(45/180)*Math.PI };
```

The first property is always the string "box". Flash uses the x and y properties to perform translation, the w and h properties to perform scaling, and the r property to perform rotation.

Translation means moving the gradient. By default, Flash positions the center of the gradient in the upper-left corner of the clip where the fill is located. Then every point in the gradient is moved horizontally by the x value and vertically by the y value.

The following are some translation examples:

■ For a linear gradient that has not been rotated, and which is therefore a series of vertical color bands, shifting in the y direction does not affect the appearance of a gradient.

■ Shifting a nonrotated linear gradient in the x direction has the same effect as moving all the color markers on the gradient definition bar in the Color Mixer panel by the specified amount.

■ If you rotate a linear gradient by 90 degrees, you have a series of horizontal color bands, for which shifting in the x direction makes no difference. Shifting in the y direction is like moving color markers.

There's not a lot that needs to be said about scaling, except that what is being scaled is the *blended* part of the fill. As you increase the w and h values, more and more of the fill becomes blended. Less and less is pure 100% saturated color.

Note that rotation is specified in radians. The preceding example translates 45 degrees into radians by dividing by 180 and multiplying by pi.

⇨ *For more information on radians, see "The Math Object," page 426 (Chapter 19, "Using the Built-in Core Objects").*

Using the Traditional 3-by-3 Transformation Matrix

The traditional 3-by-3 transformation matrix is the underlying basis for every matrix operation in Flash, whether the interface is via the "box" format or the author-time GUI.

A 3-by-3 transformation matrix is commonly used in matrix mathematics for 2D and 3D transformations. It looks like this:

a	b	c
d	e	f
g	h	i

Table 18.2 lists the nine elements of a 3-by-3 transformation matrix and what each one does.

Table 18.2 Elements of a 3-by-3 Transformation Matrix

Element	Purpose
a	Sets xscale of gradient
b	Skews and scales x (used in rotation)
c	Always 0 for 2D transformations
d	Skews and scales y (used in rotation)
e	Sets yscale of gradient
f	Always 0 for 2D transformations
g	Sets x position of gradient center
h	Sets y position of gradient center
i	Always 1 for 2D transformations

For 2D transformations, c and f are always 0, and i is always 1. You would change these values only if you were doing 3D transformations, which are not possible for Flash gradients.

You can create a traditional 3-by-3 matrix object like this:

```
matrix = {a: 200, b:0, c:0, d:0, e:200, f:0, g:0, h:0, i:1};
```

Using Macromedia's include file, you start creating a transformation matrix like this:

```
#include "TransformMatrix.as"

_root.myMatrix = new TransformMatrix();
```

Continuing the preceding example using the include file, you perform scale, rotate, and translate transformations as follows:

```
_root.myMatrix.scale(300, 300);
_root.myMatrix.rotate(45);
_root.myMatrix.translate(300,300);
```

That's all you need to know to successfully use the traditional matrix object with `beginGradientFill()`.

The following listing puts together everything you've learned about gradient fills, using a traditional 3-by-3 matrix:

```
 1: #include "TransformMatrix.as"
 2:
 3: _root.myMatrix = new TransformMatrix();
 4: _root.myMatrix.rotate(45);
 5: _root.myMatrix.scale(350, 200);
 6: _root.myMatrix.translate(300,300);
 7: RED = 0xFF0000;
 8: YELLOW = 0xFFFF00;
 9: GREEN = 0x00FF00;
10: _root.createEmptyMovieClip("myGradientClip", 8);
11: with (_root.myGradientClip) {
```

The empty line between the include statement and the next line can be important. It's good practice always to separate include statements from other code by blank lines.

```
12:          colors = [RED, YELLOW, GREEN];
13:          alphas = [100, 100, 90];
14:          ratios = [0, 127, 255];
15:          beginGradientFill ( "linear", colors, alphas, ratios, _root.myMatrix);
16:          lineStyle(10,0x0000FF);
17:          moveTo(100,100);
18:          lineTo(400,100);
19:          lineTo(400,400);
20:          lineTo(100,400);
21:          lineTo(100,100);
22:          endFill();
23: }
```

Line 1 includes Macromedia's include file. Line 3 creates the matrix. Lines 4–6 transform the matrix. Lines 7–9 create some constants to make the color array more readable. Line 10 creates a new movie clip to draw in. Lines 12–14 create the arrays, and line 15 creates the gradient fill. The rest of the program draws a box and ends the fill.

⇨ *Getting weird results with fills? See the "Troubleshooting" section at the end of this chapter, page 386.*

Understanding the 3-by-3 Matrix

This section goes a little more deeply into the transformations using the traditional 3-by-3 transformation matrix. It gives you a more precise idea of what translation, rotation, and scaling mean in the context of a gradient. In addition, in combination with some study of Macromedia's include file, it gives you an idea of the steps involved in creating your own matrix functions. It involves some math, including trigonometry.

You use the 3-by-3 matrix to transform a point (x,y) into a point (x2,y2) by means of the following equations (written in ActionScript):

```
x2 = a*x + d*y + g;
y2 = b*x + e*y + h;
```

Flash transforms every single point in the gradient in this way.

The following sections describe briefly how Flash uses these equations to perform scaling, translation, and rotation. To see examples of these functions implemented in ActionScript, look in the transformation matrix .AS file provided by Macromedia.

Scaling

To scale using a 3-by-3 matrix, you set a to the x scale value and e to the y scale value. You set d, g, b, and h to zero. The result is that each x coordinate and each y coordinate is multiplied by the corresponding scale value, and nothing else happens.

Note that what is being scaled is the blended part of the fill. As you increase the a and e values, more and more of the fill becomes blended. Less and less is pure 100% saturated color.

18

Translation

To translate using a 3-by-3 matrix, you set both a and e to 1, so a*x equals x and e*y equals y. Then you set g and h to the x and y translation values, respectively. Every x coordinate becomes x+g, and every y coordinate becomes y+h. This moves every point in the gradient by the translation amounts.

Rotation

Rotation requires trigonometry:

Set a to the cosine of the rotation.
Set b to the sine of the rotation.
Set d to the opposite of the sine of the rotation.
Set e to the cosine of the rotation.
Set both g and h to zero.

Plugging these values into the two equations given at the beginning of this section, you get the following:

```
x2 = Math.cos(r)*x - Math.sin(r)*y;
y2 = Math.sin(r)*x + Math.cos(r)*y;
```

> *To get a visual idea of what the matrix rotation equations accomplish, and how it relates to the trigonometric functions, look at trigdemo.fla in Figure 19.2 in Chapter 19, "Using the Built-in Core Objects," page 432. This file shows a green line rotating like a clock hand counterclockwise around a circle.*

Each point in the gradient is rotated like the tip of a clock hand. Flash always treats positive rotation as clockwise rotation, although traditionally positive rotation is counterclockwise.

Combining Matrix Operations

If you want to combine matrix operations, for example, to create a single matrix that both scales and translates, you do so by using a process called *matrix multiplication*, or *concatenation*. The transformation matrix .AS file provided by Macromedia contains a concatenation function. In fact, the 3-by-3 matrix scaling, rotation, and translation functions are actually concatenation functions in disguise. If you look at these functions in the .AS file, you will see that each one creates a new matrix (initialized as described in the previous three sections for the appropriate operation) and then concatenates it with the matrix that you provide when you call the function.

TROUBLESHOOTING

Why is my drawing-intensive program getting choppy and slowing down to a crawl?

If you have a program that does a lot of drawing in a single movie clip, you may find that it becomes choppy and excessively slow. If you divide the same amount of drawing among multiple clips, you may find that you get a new lease on life each time you begin a new clip. Peter Hall's scratch.fla on the CD (discussed at the end of Chapter 17) uses this technique, for instance.

Help! I'm getting weird results with fills!

When you put in both `endFill()` and `beginFill()`, it's also a good idea to use a `moveTo()` method to start off the next shape, even if it is a `moveTo()` that doesn't change the current pen position and would therefore seem to be useless. It shouldn't be that way, but you may sometimes get undesired or unexpected results if you don't do this.

Another possibility is that you are using very small scaling numbers. A scale that is near 1-by-1 can cause anomalous results. The closer you get to that size, the worse the fill is likely to behave, especially when rotated.

Of course, there's no reason to specify a 1-by-1 gradient because it's really no gradient at all. For that reason, this behavior is officially labeled a Fact of Life (FOL), not a bug.

The following example, taken from matrixbug.fla on the CD, shows what to avoid. It yields red/green/red bars where you would expect red/yellow/green. (Matrix.fla on the CD provides an example of what you'd expect.)

```
// w:1, h:1 == unpredictable results !!
_root.m = { matrixType:"box", x:100, y:100, w:1, h:1, r:(0/180)*Math.PI};
RED = 0xFF0000;
YELLOW = 0xFFFF00;
GREEN = 0x00FF00;
_root.createEmptyMovieClip("myGradient", 8);
with (_root.myGradient) {
        colors = [RED, YELLOW, GREEN];
        alphas = [100, 100, 90];
        ratios = [0, 12, 255] ;
        beginGradientFill ( "linear", colors, alphas, ratios,_root.m);
        lineStyle(10,0x0000FF);
        moveTo(0,0);
        lineTo(300,0);
        lineTo(300,300);
        lineTo(0,300);
        lineTo(0,0);
        endFill();
}
```

FLASH AT WORK: DRAWING AN EIGHT-SEGMENT CIRCLE

Conceptually, drawing an eight-segment circle isn't very different from drawing a four-segment circle, except for one step: Now you have to inscribe your circle in an octagon, as shown in Figure 18.7, and figure out where the "corners" of the octagon are so that you can use them as control points. (This figure is based on eightSegmentCircle.fla on the CD.)

Figure 18.7
The process of creating an eight-segment circle can be understood by first imagining that you are inscribing the circle in an octagon.

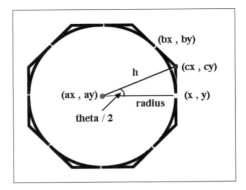

Figuring out the corners, though, requires trigonometry. In general, when you need to draw curves, creating regular, precise shapes is easiest using trigonometry. The alternative is to experiment with values until you find one that comes close enough, as in 4SegCircle.fla.

This is how you might go about determining the coordinates of one control point for an eight-segment circle. Look at the control point on the right side of the circle just above the middle. In Figure 18.7, it's labeled (cx, cy), and it's the top vertex of the triangle inside the circle. (The labels in the figure correspond to variables in the drawArc() method in drawMethods.fla on the CD.)

Determining the x Coordinate of the Control Point

The x coordinate of (cx, cy) is easy to see, so you don't need trigonometry to determine it. It is directly above the point (x, y), which is one radius to the right of the center of the circle. All you need to do is add the radius to the x value of the center, ax. For instance, if ax is 400 and the radius is 150, then cx is 550.

Determining the y Coordinate of the Control Point

To figure out how far up the control point is from the center (that is, the y coordinate, cy in Figure 18.7), you can use trigonometry. The calculation requires three basic steps. Referring to Figure 18.7, the steps are

- Determine the size of the angle labeled theta / 2.

- Determine the length of h, the hypotenuse.

- Use those two numbers to determine cy.

Determining the Size of the Angle Labeled theta / 2

When you divide a circle into eight parts, each part is 45 degrees (360 / 8). The variable name assigned to that angle in the drawArc() method is theta, the Greek letter traditionally used to indicate an angle. The angle labeled theta / 2 in Figure 18.7 is half of one of those parts. Therefore, theta / 2 is 22.5 degrees.

Determining the Length of h, the Hypotenuse

Okay, here comes the trigonometry. By definition, the cosine of `theta / 2` in Figure 18.7 is `radius` divided by the side labeled h (for "hypotenuse"). In ActionScript, `Math.cos(theta/2)` equals `radius / h`.

Multiply both sides of the equation by h and divide both sides by `Math.cos(theta/2)`, and you get h equals `radius / Math.cos(theta/2)`.

Determining cy

Also, by definition, the sine of `theta / 2` is cy divided by h. In ActionScript, `Math.sin(theta / 2)` equals `cy / h`.

Multiplying both sides by h, you get cy equals `Math.sin(theta / 2) * h`.

You know that h is equal to `radius / Math.cos(theta/2)`. So cy equals `Math.sin(theta / 2) * radius / Math.cos(theta/2)`.

Toward the end of the `drawArc()` method in drawingMethods.fla on the CD, you'll find an expression similar to that used in calculating cy. A similar formula also gives cx (which you obtained by "eyeballing" in this case).

The `drawArc()` method has a couple of other variables. For instance, `drawArc()` handles ovals as well as circles and therefore has both a `radius` and a `yRadius`, something you don't have to worry about for circles.

18

ADVANCED ACTIONSCRIPTING

IN THIS PART

USING THE BUILT-IN CORE OBJECTS

INTRODUCING BUILT-IN OBJECTS

Built-in objects are the most common means of exposing any sort of Macromedia Flash capability to the ActionScript programmer. Built-in objects are the workhorses of ActionScript, used to accomplish most basic day-to-day tasks, such as manipulating graphics, colors, sounds, keystrokes, and other elements of a Flash movie.

With Flash MX, built-in objects have become pervasive. There is now an object-oriented underpinning for text fields and text formatting, buttons, the Stage, custom additions to the Flash user interface (`CustomActions`), variables stored in local disk files as "shared objects," video, variables loaded from servers (`LoadVars`), local communications channels with other SWFs (`LocalConnection`), and connections to communications servers and application servers (`NetConnection/NetStream`).

Built-in objects fall into two main categories: *constructor functions* (or classes) and *global objects*. The main distinction between the two is this: With constructor functions, you can create new instances. With global objects, you can't.

A *global object* is also called a *singleton* because it is an instance of a class that allows just a single instance. For example, you can have only one Stage, one keyboard, one mouse, and one currently selected text box. Singletons are instances for which the constructor functions no longer work.

You cannot do three important things with global objects:

- Create new instances of them.
- Execute their constructor functions.
- Change the values of existing properties, including methods.

> *For more details on constructor functions and their role in creating objects, see "Functions as Classes: Constructor Functions," page 279 (Chapter 15, "Combining Statements into Functions").*

Typically, you execute a constructor function with the new keyword to create new instances. However, four "nonconstructive" constructor functions (my terminology)—`Button`, `Function`, `MovieClip`, and `Video`—can't create usable new instances, though they may have other uses. Instead, you can create instances of these classes in other ways.

You create a `Video` object in the Library panel by selecting New Video from the Library options menu (reached by clicking at the right side of the gray bar at the top of the panel).

> *You create movie clips, manually or programmatically, using the techniques described in Chapter 17, "Unlocking the Power of Movie Clips," page 331.*

You create buttons in one of two ways: manually (using the same technique you use to create movie clips) or using `attachMovie()`.

> *You create functions manually, using the techniques described in Chapter 15, "Combining Statements into Functions," page 267.*

THE CORE OBJECTS

Eight of Flash MX's built-in objects are defined in the ECMA-262 standard and also implemented in JavaScript. (However, Flash MX sometimes varies a bit from the standard and from JavaScript.) This chapter covers those eight objects, referred to in the Flash authoring tool's user interface as *core* objects.

The core objects provide basic data-manipulation capabilities useful for a wide variety of programming tasks, including creating Web animation. However, nothing about them is specific to Web animation. Table 19.1 lists the eight core objects.

Table 19.1 Core Objects

Object	Represents	Singleton or Constructor
Array	Ordered list	constructor
Boolean	True/false or other duality	constructor
Date	Calendar date/time	constructor
Function	A function	constructor(*)
Math	Math functions and constants	singleton
Number	Numbers	constructor
Object	Unordered collection	constructor
String	Alphanumeric data	constructor

(*) "Nonconstructive" constructor: You can't create usable new instances with the new keyword.

The Array Class

An *array* is an ordered, numbered collection of data items. You use an array like a filing cabinet for data. Each *element* (item in the array) is like a file drawer labeled with an *index* number. Indexes start at 0 and count up through the positive integers. The whole array also needs to be contained in a data item so that you can refer to it as a single object.

➡️ *For an example of what you can do with arrays, see "Flash at Work: Amazing Arrays," at the end of this chapter, page 439.*

Table 19.2 summarizes the three types of data required to work with an array: elements, indexes, and a data container for the whole array.

Table 19.2 Three Types of Data Needed for Working with Arrays

Type of Data	Filing Cabinet Analogy	Acceptable Values
The array *elements*	Each element is like the contents of one file drawer	Any valid expression
An *index* for each element	A numbered label on each file drawer	Any expression that resolves to an integer from 0 to Number.MAX_VALUE, inclusive

Table 19.2 Continued

Type of Data	Filing Cabinet Analogy	Acceptable Values
A data container for the whole array	A label for the entire filing cabinet	A variable, array element, or object property that refers to the array

An array element can contain any type of data that exists in ActionScript: a number, string, Boolean, function, object, array—any simple or composite data item. Any valid expression can be used to define an element of an array.

A single array can contain data items of various types.

An index can be any non-negative integer, or any expression that resolves to a non-negative integer. The highest valid index is Number.MAX_VALUE. If you go over Number.MAX_VALUE, Flash will use Number.MAX_VALUE as the index.

The data container that allows you to reference the entire array as a single object can be a variable, array element, or object property.

> An *expression* is an ActionScript phrase that resolves to a single datum.

> Number.MAX_VALUE is the largest number that ActionScript can represent (1.79769313486231e+308).

Creating Arrays

You can create arrays in two ways: using an array literal and using the Array() constructor function with the new keyword.

The format for creating an array using an array literal is

```
container = [expression1, expression2, expression3];
```

where *container* is the variable, array element, or object property that references the entire array, and the expressions inside the square brackets are the expressions defining the elements of the array. Here are some examples:

```
myArray = ["John", "Mary", "Peter", "Pat"]; // container is a variable

students = new Object();
students.scores = [98, 95, 87, 65]; // container is an object property

myMixedArray = ["John", 98, "Mary", 95]; // array with mixed data types
```

You can create an array in three ways using the Array() constructor function:

- You can call the constructor with no arguments:

  ```
  myArray = new Array();
  ```

  This approach creates an *empty* array—one with no elements.

- You can call the Array() constructor function with a single numeric argument:

  ```
  myArray = new Array(8);
  ```

All that actually happens here is that the array's `length` property is set to the number you specify. This approach has the effect of creating an array with the specified number of elements, each of which has the value `undefined`. However, an empty array will also return `undefined` for any element you reference, so the `length` property of the array is the only way to distinguish an empty array (no elements) from an array of empty elements (undefined elements).

■ You can call the `Array()` constructor function with arguments that provide values for array elements. The first argument becomes the value of the first element in the array. The second argument becomes the value of the second element in the array, and so on. For example:

```
myArray = new Array(8, 10, 12);
myArray = new Array("John", "Matt", "Mary", myVar, myArray, myObj);
```

If the `Array()` constructor function sees just one numeric argument, it assumes method 2 and sets the `length` property. If it sees one non-numeric argument or multiple arguments, it uses the arguments as values for array elements (method 3) .

Referencing Array Elements

You use the index to reference array elements. The format is as follows:

container[*index*]

Thus, the first element in `myArray` is `myArray[0]`, the second element is `myArray[1]`, and so on.

You can both read and write array elements using this format. Here are some examples of reading:

```
myVar = myArray[2]; // read the element into a variable
myObj.myProp = myArray[6]; // read the element into an object property
```

Here are some examples of writing:

```
myArray[2] = myVar; // write the variable into the element
myArray[6] = myObj.myProp; // write the object property into the element
```

Here's an example of reading from one array and writing into another:

```
myArray[3] = myOtherArray[0];
```

The fact that you can reference array elements using numbers gives arrays much of their power. A common technique is to use an index variable and the array's `length` property to set up a `for` loop that searches through all the elements in the array, tests each one in some way, and takes an action based on the result of that test. The following example searches through an array of names, testing each name to see if it equals a particular name, and then replaces that name after finding it:

```
nameArray = new Array("John Jones", "Mary Peterson", "Michael Smith");
for (i = 0; i < nameArray.length ; i++) { // the setup
    if (nameArray[i] == "Mary Peterson") {  // the test
        nameArray[i] = "Mary Laliberte"; // the action based on the test
 }
}
```

Notice that you need to say i < nameArray.length, not i <= nameArray.length, because the last index in an array is *one less* than the length property of the array.

If you have a particular array operation that you perform more than once, you can reduce it to a function. For instance, you could turn the "search and replace" operation shown in the previous example into a function like this:

```
function searchAndReplace(inThisArray, findThis, replaceWithThis) {
    for (var i = 0; i < inThisArray.length ; i++) { // the setup
        if (inThisArray [i] == findThis) {  // the test
        inThisArray[i] = replaceWithThis; // the action based on the test
    }
}
```

Notice the added var keyword in var i = 0;. This makes i a local variable to the searchAndReplace() function, preventing it from interfering with other uses of i as a variable elsewhere in the program.

⇨ *For more information on the var keyword, see "Using var to Create Local Function Variables," page 271 (Chapter 15, "Combining Statements into Functions").*

Adding Array Elements

You can add a new element to an array just by assigning a value to it. The following example creates an empty array and then adds an element at index position 4:

```
myArray = new Array();
myArray[4] = "testing";
```

This also sets myArray.length to 5.

The preceding example illustrates a *sparse* array, an array in which elements with values are interspersed among elements to which no value has been assigned. Flash allocates memory only for elements with assigned values. Thus, Flash imposes no penalty for using sparse arrays.

As illustrated in the previous section, the same syntax used for adding an element to an array will also replace an existing element at the specified index position.

Removing Array Elements

When removing an array element in the middle of an array, you want to accomplish these two goals:

- Change the value of the element to undefined.
- Deallocate the memory previously used to store the value in the element.

The delete operator takes care of both tasks. For instance:

```
delete myArray[6];
```

When removing the *last* element in an array, you want to perform both of these tasks and probably also reduce the `length` property of the array by one. You can accomplish all three objectives using the `pop()` method of the `Array` class:

```
myArray.pop(); // deletes last element, decrements length
```

The `pop()` method also returns the value of the element deleted.

> *For more details on the pop() method, see "pop() and push()" later in this section under "Array Methods," page 402.*

If you delete the last element manually, and you want to decrement the `length` property, you need to do that manually, too. For example:

```
myArray = new Array("John", "Matt", "Joe");
delete myArray[2]; // removes element containing "Joe", deallocates memory
trace(myArray[2]); // undefined
myArray.length = 2; // length was 3, reduce it by 1
```

Just setting the value of an element to `undefined` does *not* deallocate memory. For instance, the following code will cause memory usage on your computer to climb steadily. Uncomment line 4, and memory usage doesn't increase at all. (Both ways cause the Flash Player to display an error message saying that the script is causing the Player to run slowly and asking whether you want to abort the script. That's normal for an excessively long `for` loop like this.)

```
1: for (i=0 ; i < Number.MAX_VALUE ; i++) {
2:     myArray[i] = new Array(1000000000);
3:     myArray[i] = undefined;
4: //    delete myArray[i];
5: }
```

Named Array Elements: Associative Arrays

An array is actually an object in thin disguise. One result is that arrays can have named properties, just as objects can. An array with named properties is an *associative array* or *hash*.

You can assign or retrieve named properties in an array in these two ways: using a string in the square brackets, or using the dot operator and an identifier. The following example shows two ways to define a property named `"Mary"` in the `myPhones` array:

```
myPhones ["Mary"] = "555-555-1212";
myPhones.Mary = "555-555-1212";
```

Similarly, the property can be retrieved using either syntax:

```
trace( myPhones ["Mary"] ); // 555-555-1212
trace( myPhones.Mary ); // 555-555-1212
```

You can mix and match these two approaches. For instance, a property defined with a string can be retrieved using the dot operator. The property name must be a legal identifier, or an expression that yields a legal identifier, for both approaches. With the first approach, you supply the identifier as a string; in the second approach, as an identifier.

You can remove named properties using the `delete` operator. For instance, either of the following statements will remove the property named `"Mary"` and deallocate the memory associated with it:

```
delete myPhones["Mary"];
delete myPhones.Mary;
```

The `length` property of an array does not reflect any named properties. An array to which you have added 100 named properties but no numbered properties still has a `length` of 0. In addition, the array methods, such as `push()` and `pop()`, discussed in the next section, do not work with named array properties.

You can access the named properties of an array, like the properties of any object, using a `for-in` loop.

> The for-in loop is covered in "Repeating Actions Using Loops," page 259 (Chapter 14, "Working with Data: Using Statements").

You can also give an object numbered properties, as in this example:

```
myObj = new Object();
myObj[0] = "hello world";
```

However, assigning numbered properties does not make `myObj` an array. For instance, `myObj` still doesn't have a `length` property or work with the `Array` methods.

Array Methods

The Array class has 12 documented methods: `join()`, `pop()`, `push()`, `reverse()`, `sort()`, `sortOn()`, `concat()`, `slice()`, `splice()`, `shift()`, `unshift()`, and `toString()`. They are listed in Table 19.3. In addition, it inherits the documented and undocumented methods of the `Object` class.

Table 19.3　Array Methods and Property

Name	Method/ Property	Syntax	Description
concat	M	myArray.concat(*value0*,*value1*,...*valueN*)	Concatenates the arguments and returns them as a new array.
join	M	myArray.join([*separator*])	Joins all elements of an array into a string.
pop	M	myArray.pop()	Removes the last element of an array and returns its value.
push	M	myArray.push(*value0*,*value1*,...*valueN*)	Adds one or more elements to the end of an array and returns the array's new length.
reverse	M	myArray.reverse()	Reverses the direction of an array.
shift	M	myArray.shift()	Removes the first element from an array and returns its value.

Name	Method/ Property	Syntax	Description
slice	M	myArray.slice(*startIndex*, *endIndex*)	Extracts a section of an array and returns it as a new array.
sort	M	myArray.sort([*compareFunction*])	Sorts an array in place.
sortOn	M	myArray.sortOn(*fieldName*)	Sorts an array alphabetically based on a field in the array.
splice	M	myArray.splice(*start*, *deleteCount*, *value0,value1...valueN*)	Adds and/or removes elements from an array.
toString	M	myArray.toString()	Returns a string value representing the elements in the Array object.
unshift	M	myArray.unshift (*value1,value2,...valueN*)	Adds one or more elements to the beginning of an array and returns the array's new length.
length	P	myArray.length	Returns the number of elements in the array, including empty or undefined elements.

➪ *For more information on the methods of the Object class, see "The Object Class," later in this chapter, page 415.*

join() and toString()   The join() method converts all the elements of an array to strings and concatenates them. That much is exactly the same behavior as the Array.toString() method. However, with the join() method, you can specify a *delimiter* character or characters to separate the strings. The toString() method doesn't offer the delimiter option.

The format for join() is as follows:

myArray.join(*delimiter*);

If you don't specify a delimiter with join(), Flash uses a comma, exactly duplicating the toString() method. For example:

```
myArray = new Array("John", "Matt", "Joe");
names = myArray.join(); // names = "John,Matt,Joe"
```

I put quotation marks around the output in the comment to indicate that the output is a string. However, no quotation marks appear around the actual output. It is just John,Matt,Joe.

The delimiter option gives you some ability to format the output. For instance, if you want a space after the comma, you can specify a two-character delimiter that consists of a comma and a space:

```
myArray = new Array("John", "Matt", "Joe");
names = myArray.join(", "); // names = "John, Matt, Joe"
```

Any nested arrays (arrays within the array) are converted to strings using the toString() method. Therefore, these conversions use the simple comma delimiter, not any delimiter that you specify. For example:

```
myArray = new Array("John", "Matt", ["Peter","Mary","Sue"],"Joe");
names = myArray.join("--"); // names = "John--Matt--Peter,Mary,Sue--Joe"
```

The join() method does not change the array on which it operates.

pop() and push()   The pop() and push() methods treat an array as a *stack*, and more particularly, a *last-in-first-out* (LIFO) stack. Imagine a cook stacking pancakes on your plate as they come off the grill. Each time the cook puts one or more pancakes on the stack, that's a push(). When you eat the top pancake on the stack, that's a pop(). In this analogy, the *top* of the stack of pancakes is the *end* of the array.

Both of these methods operate on the array *in place*. That is, they modify the existing array.

The push() method appends one or more new elements to the end of an array. It returns the new length of the array, as in this example:

```
myArray = new Array ("John", "Matt", "Joe");
newLength = myArray.push ("Peter", "Mary", "Sue");
trace(myArray); // John,Matt,Joe,Peter,Mary,Sue
trace(newLength); // 6
```

When invoked with no arguments, the push() method appends an empty element to the array (one whose value is undefined). This is equivalent to incrementing the length property of the array (myArray.length++).

You can use any expression to determine the value to push onto the array. The expression is resolved before the value is assigned to the element. So if x is 3 and y is 4, these two statements have exactly the same effect:

```
myArray.push ( x + y );
myArray.push ( 7 );
```

The pop() method deletes the last element in an array and returns the value of the element that is deleted. In addition, it decrements the length property of the array.

reverse()   The reverse() method reverses the order of the elements in an array. It does the reversal in place, modifying the existing array. In addition, it returns the reversed array, as shown in this example:

```
myArray = new Array (3, 2, 1);
returnArray = myArray.reverse(); // myArray is now [1,2,3}
trace (returnArray); // 1,2,3
```

sort() and sortOn()   The sort()method sorts the elements of the array in place. It returns the sorted array. When called with no arguments, the sort() method sorts array elements in alphabetical order, *temporarily* converting them to strings first, if necessary. Any undefined elements are sorted to the end of the array.

To sort on some other basis, you need to provide a *comparison function* as an argument to the sort() method. The comparison function must take two arguments. They represent any two elements of the array. It's as if you have been asked, "Given any two elements of this array, which one should come first?" You must answer this question with your comparison function.

The function must return a negative number if the first element should come first in the sorted array. If the second element should appear first, the comparison function must return a positive number. If the comparison function returns 0, it says that it doesn't matter which element comes first.

In the following example, the `byVotes()` comparison function sorts an array of objects representing candidates according to which candidate object has the larger number in its `votes` property. The comparison function returns a positive number if the second object received more votes than the first. Thus, this function effectively says, "Put the object with the most votes first." The same thing could have been accomplished by returning a negative number if the first object received more votes than the second.

```
Abbey = {name: "Abbey", votes: 10};
Bob = {name: "Bob", votes: 2};
Charles = {name: "Charles", votes: 30};
Dave = {name: "Dave", votes: 100};
candidates = [Abbey, Charles, Bob, Dave];
function byVotes (a, b) {
    return b.votes - a.votes;
}
candidates.sort(byVotes);
for (i = 0; i < candidates.length; i++) {
    trace(candidates[i].name);
}
/* output
Dave
Charles
Abbey
Bob
*/
```

The `sortOn()` method provides a more concise notation for sorting objects in an array based on the value of a property of each object. However, `sortOn()` would not work in the previous example because `sortOn()` only sorts alphabetically. If you want to sort the array alphabetically by the candidate's name, `sortOn()` does the job:

```
candidates.sortOn("name"); // returns [Abbey, Bob, Charles, Dave]
```

⇨ *Having trouble sorting an array of numbers? See the "Troubleshooting" section at the end of this chapter, page 439.*

concat()   The `concat()` method appends one or more values to an array. It returns a new array rather than modifying an existing array. You provide the values to be appended as arguments to the `concat()` method, as in this example:

```
myArray = new Array (3, 2, 1);
myArray.concat(4,5,6); //  returns [3,2,1,4,5,6]
```

If one of the arguments is an array, it will be "flattened" and appended. Therefore, the following has the same result as the previous example:

```
myArray = new Array (3, 2, 1);
myArray.concat( 4, [5,6] ); //  returns [3,2,1,4,5,6]
```

Nested arrays, however, are not flattened:

```
myArray.concat( [ 4, [5,6] ] ); //  returns [3,2,1,4,[5,6] ]
```

slice()   The slice() method returns a new array that is a "slice" or subarray of the original array. It does not change the original array. The slice() method takes two arguments: The first specifies the index of the first element to be returned, and the second is one greater than the index of the last element to be returned. If you provide only one argument, the slice contains all the elements of the array starting at the index position indicated by the argument, and all subsequent arguments in the array. A negative argument indicates an index position relative to the end of the array, starting with -1 for the last element in the array. Here are some examples:

```
myArray = [1,2,3,4,5,6];
myArray.slice(1,2); // 2
myArray.slice(1,-1); // 2,3,4,5
myArray.slice(0,3); // 1,2,3
```

splice()   The splice() method can be used to add elements to or remove elements from an array. It can both add and remove elements in a single operation. It modifies an existing array rather than returning a new array. The format for the splice() method is as follows:

```
myArray.splice(startIndex, deleteCount, value0,value1...valueN)
```

All arguments except the first are optional. If you invoke splice() with only the *startIndex* argument, it deletes all elements beginning with the element whose index is *startIndex* and going to the end of the array. It returns the deleted elements. For instance:

```
myArray = [1,2,3,4,5,6];
trace(myArray.splice(1)); // returns : 2,3,4,5,6 -- these were deleted
trace(myArray); // 1 -- this is all that's left
```

The second parameter tells the splice() method how many elements to delete. Remaining elements are shifted downward (toward lower index numbers) in the array to fill the gap. For instance:

```
myArray = [1,2,3,4,5,6];
trace(myArray.splice(1,2)); // 2,3 -- it just deleted two elements
trace(myArray); // 1,4,5,6 -- leaving four elements in the array
```

The rest of the arguments provide values for elements to insert into the array, beginning at the index position following *startIndex*. Existing elements are shifted upward in the array to accommodate the new elements. For example:

```
myArray = [1,2,3,4,5,6];
trace(myArray.splice(1,2,"flowers","teakettles")); // 2,3
trace(myArray); // 1,flowers,teakettles,4,5,6
```

unshift() and shift()   The unshift() and shift() methods are similar to push() and pop(), except that they insert and remove elements at the *beginning* of the array rather than at the *end*.

The unshift() method inserts one or more elements at the beginning of the array and returns the new length of the array. Existing elements are shifted upward in the array. For example:

```
myArray = [1,2,3,4,5,6];
trace(myArray.unshift("flowers","teakettles")); // 8 -- the new length
trace(myArray); // flowers,teakettles,1,2,3,4,5,6 -- the new array
```

The `shift()` method removes the first element in the array. Existing elements are shifted downward in the array to fill the gap. It returns the deleted element, as in this example:

```
myArray = [1,2,3,4,5,6];
trace(myArray.shift()); // 1 -- returns the deleted element
trace(myArray); // 2,3,4,5,6 -- here's what's left
```

The `length` Property

The `length` property is the only property of the `Array` class. It is always one larger than the index number of the last element in the array. `length` may not reflect the number of data elements contained in an array because arrays can have undefined elements.

The most common use of the `length` property is as a test in loops, where you want to go through all the elements in an array.

Using the length property in a for loop is illustrated in "sort() and sortOn()," earlier in this section, page 402.

Boolean, Number, and String: **The Wrapper Classes**

The `Boolean`, `Number`, and `String` classes are "wrapper" classes for the corresponding primitive datatypes. An instance of a wrapper class contains a primitive datum in an inaccessible internal property. The difference between the primitive datum and an instance of a class is that the instance can have properties and methods, both local and inherited. In the three core wrapper classes, all the built-in methods and properties but one are inherited from the class prototype object. The one exception is the `length` property of the `String` class: Obviously, each string needs to have its own `length` property.

Table 19.4 shows the methods and properties of the wrapper classes.

Table 19.4   Methods and Properties of Wrapper Classes: `Boolean`, `Number`, `String`

Name	Method/ Property	Format	Description
Boolean.toString	M	myBoolean.toString()	Returns the string representation (`true`) or (`false`) of `myBoolean`.
Boolean.valueOf	M	myBoolean.valueOf()	Returns the primitive value type of `myBoolean`.
Number.toString	M	myNumber.toString()	Returns the string representation of `myNumber`.

Table 19.4 Continued

Name	Method/ Property	Format	Description
`Number.valueOf`	M	`myNumber.valueOf()`	Returns the primitive value of `myNumber`.
`Number.MAX_VALUE`	P	`myNumber.MAX_VALUE`	A constant, the largest number that ActionScript can represent: 1.79769313486231e+308.
`Number.MIN_VALUE`	P	`myNumber.MIN_VALUE`	A constant, the smallest positive number that ActionScript can represent: 5e-324.
`Number.NaN`	P	`myNumber.NaN`	"Not a Number," a constant representing a value that is not a number but is used in a context where a number is expected.
`Number.NEGATIVE_INFINITY`	P	`myNumber.NEGATIVE_INFINITY`	A constant representing a value more negative than `-Number.MAX_VALUE`.
`Number.POSITIVE_INFINITY`	P	`myNumber.POSITIVE_INFINITY`	A constant representing a value more positive than `Number.MAX_VALUE`. (Same as the global constant `Infinity`.)
`String.charAt`	M	`myString.charAt(index)`	Returns the character at a specific location in `myString`.
`String.charCodeAt`	M	`myString.charCodeAt(index)`	Returns the Unicode encoding of the character at `myString[index]` as a 16-bit integer between 0 and 65,535.
`String.concat`	M	`myString.concat(value1, ...valueN)`	Returns a new string resulting from concatenating (combining) `myString` and the strings specified in arguments (`value1–valueN`).
`String.fromCharCode`	M	`String.fromCharCode (charCode1,charCode2, ...charCodeN)`	Returns a new string made up of the characters specified as character codes in the parameters.

19

Name	Method/ Property	Format	Description
String.indexOf	M	myString.indexOf(substring, [*startIndex*])	Searches the string, starting at *startIndex*, and returns the index of the first occurrence of *substring*. Returns -1 if *substring* is not found.
String.lastIndexOf	M	myString.lastIndexOf (*substring*, [*startIndex*])	Searches the string, starting at *startIndex*, and returns the index of the last occurrence of *substring*. Returns -1 if *substring* is not found.
String.slice	M	myString.slice(*startIndex*, [*endIndex*])	Returns a substring of the original string, starting at the character whose position in myString is *startIndex*, up to but not including the character whose position in myString is *endIndex*. (The index of the first character in the string is 0.)
String.split	M	myString.split("*delimiter*", [*limit*])	Splits a string into substrings by breaking it wherever the *delimiter* string occurs, and returns the substrings in an array. If you use an empty string ("") as a delimiter, each character in the string is an element in the returned array. If *delimiter* is undefined, the first and only element in the returned array is the entire string. The optional *limit* argument specifies the maximum number of substrings that may be returned.

19

Table 19.4 Continued

Name	Method/Property	Format	Description
String.substr	M	myString.substr (*startIndex*, [*length*])	Returns a substring that starts at *startIndex* and includes the number of characters specified in the *length* argument, or the rest of the characters in the string (if there is no *length* argument). If *startIndex* is negative, the starting position is determined from the end of the string, with -1 indicating the last character, -2 the second to last, and so on.
String.substring	M	myString.substring (*startIndex*, *endIndex*)	Returns a substring starting at *startIndex* and ending one character before *endIndex*. If *endIndex* is omitted, the returned substring runs to the end of the string. If *startIndex* equals *endIndex*, the method returns the empty string. If *startIndex* is greater than *endIndex*, the Flash interpreter should swap them before running the function; in reality, it sometimes returns the empty string.
String.toLowerCase	M	myString.toLowerCase()	Returns a copy of myString, but with all characters in lowercase. The original value is unchanged.
String.toUpperCase	M	myString.toUpperCase()	Returns a copy of myString, but with all characters in uppercase. The original value is unchanged.
String.valueOf	M	myString.valueOf()	Returns the primitive value of the specified String object.
String.length	P	myString.length	The length of the string.

The Boolean Class

The Boolean class is the simplest class in ActionScript. Its only properties are `__proto__` and `constructor`, which are granted to every object when it is created. (In general, I won't bother to mention these two properties for other classes.)

 The __proto__ property is introduced in "Creating Objects Using the new Operator," page 280 (Chapter 15, "Combining Statements into Functions"). The constructor property is introduced in "The Object Class," later in this chapter, page 415. Both are discussed at more length in Chapter 21, "Packaging Data and Functions Using Custom Objects," page 489.

The Boolean class has just two methods, which are also common to every object:

- `toString()` returns the Boolean value (`true` or `false`) as a string.

- `valueOf()` returns the primitive Boolean datum, allowing you to compare the values contained in the objects.

 The `valueOf()` method was not needed for comparing the values of Boolean objects in Flash 5 because comparing the objects themselves effectively compared the values. This is no longer true in Flash MX.

 For more information on comparing objects, see the following sidebar, "Comparing Objects."

> ### Comparing Objects
>
> In Flash MX, two objects do *not* compare as equal just because they have the same properties with the same values. By default, two object references compare as equal only if they refer to *the same object*.
>
> Flash 5 was inconsistent in this regard, but Flash MX follows the ECMA-262 standard more strictly and is consistent in comparing objects by *reference*, not by *value*. In the following example, Flash MX compares by reference, whereas Flash 5 compares by value. Thus, they give opposite results:
>
> ```
> a = new Number(1);
> b = new Number(1);
> trace( a == b ); // false in MX, true in F5
> ```
>
> For Boolean, Date, Number, and String objects, you must use the `valueOf()` method in Flash MX to compare their contents:
>
> ```
> trace( a.valueOf() == b.valueOf() ); // true
> ```
>
> For other objects, a specific method may be required to get the values. To compare the colors stored in two instances of the Color class, for instance, you can use `getRGB()`.

 For more information on the valueOf() property and comparisons, see "Automatic Datatype Conversions for Comparisons," page 234 (Chapter 13, "Using Operators").

➪ *For more details on the distinction between "by reference" and "by value," see "Passing Arguments by Value and by Reference," page 273 (Chapter 15, "Combining Statements into Functions").*

The `toString()` method is seldom needed because ActionScript typically performs automatic conversion to the string datatype when appropriate. It can be used to force the use of a string or just to make absolutely sure that you are dealing with a string. However, the global `String()` conversion function performs the same task and allows you to use the same format with both objects and primitive data.

➪ *For more information on the toString() and valueOf() methods, see "The Object Class," later in this chapter, page 415.*

➪ *For more details on the global conversion functions String(), Number(), and Boolean(), see "Using Explicit Datatype Conversion," page 207 (Chapter 12, "Managing Variables, Data, and Datatypes").*

The Number Class

The Number class has `toString()` and `valueOf()` methods, which, respectively, return the string equivalent of the number and the primitive number datum.

In addition, the Number class has five constants: `NaN` ("not a number"), `Number.MAX_VALUE`, `Number.MIN_VALUE`, `Number.POSITIVE_INFINITY`, and `Number.NEGATIVE_INFINITY`.

➪ *The Number constants are discussed in "The Power of Numbers," page 196 (Chapter 12, "Managing Variables, Data, and Datatypes").*

The String Class

The `String` class has a `valueOf()` method, which returns the primitive string datum. Each member of the `String` class has a local read-only `length` property. In addition, the `String` class has a dozen string manipulation methods, which are among the most frequently used in ActionScript. They are also among the most processor-intensive, inspiring programmers to write alternative optimized methods. Overall, the string methods in Flash MX are faster than those in Flash 5.

String methods can be divided into four categories: searching for a character or character sequence, retrieving a portion or portions of a string, converting to lower- or uppercase, and generating characters from character codes or vice versa.

The `String.split()` method, which splits a string into substrings, has been brought into conformance with ECMA-262 in Flash MX by adding an optional second argument, *limit*, specifying the maximum number of substrings. In addition, when the first argument, *delimiter*, is the empty string, `String.split()` now returns an array in which each element is one character in the string. Flash 5, in the same situation, returned an array in which the only element was the whole string. The following code illustrates the difference:

```
myString = "Joe";
i = myString.split("");
```

```
trace (i); // J,o,e in MX, Joe in F5
trace (i.length); // 3 in MX, 1 in F5
```

The `String.substring()` method returns a substring starting at *startIndex* and ending one character before *endIndex*. The Flash 6 Player introduced a bug into this method. If *startIndex* is greater than *endIndex*, the Flash interpreter should swap them before running the function; in reality, it sometimes returns the empty string. It appears to do so consistently, for example, if *startIndex* equals the length of the string. For instance, in the following example, `subs` should equal `two12`. In fact, it equals the empty string.

```
str = "onetwo12"
subs = str.substring(8,3);
```

You can compensate for this bug by inserting the following code into your program at a point prior to using `String.substring()`:

```
String.prototype.substring = function(from, to) {
    var temp = from;
    if (to == undefined) to = this.length;
    if (from == to) return "";
    if (from > to){
        from = to;
        to = temp - from;
    }
    else to -= from;
    return this.substr(from, to);
};
```

This bug could be corrected in later versions of the Flash 6 Player.

The `Date` Class

The `Date` class allows you to determine the current time and date and store times and dates in objects. All times and dates in ActionScript are stored in the form of a single number: the number of milliseconds before or after midnight of January 1, 1970 UTC (Coordinated Universal Time, which is the same as Greenwich Mean Time). This number is returned by the `Date.valueOf()` method.

You can use `Date` class methods to get and set the date/time as a single object, or to get and set the year, month, date, day, hour, minute, second, and millisecond independently, in local or UTC time. You can also retrieve the number of minutes between UTC and local time by using `getTimezoneOffset()`.

There is also a `toString()` method, which returns full date information in a human-readable form like the following: `Sun Jun 16 18:04:58 GMT-0600 2002`. You can accomplish the same objective by using the `Date()` global function. Thus, `myDate.toString()` yields the same result as `Date(myDate)`. Neither is needed very often, due to automatic datatype conversion.

For a listing of Date methods, see Table 19.5.

Table 19.5   Methods of the Date Class

Name	Format	Description
Date.getDate	myDate.getDate()	Returns the day of the month from 1 to 31 according to local time.
Date.getDay	myDate.getDay()	Returns the day of the week from 0 (Sunday) to 6 (Saturday) according to local time.
Date.getFullYear	myDate.getFullYear()	Returns the four-digit year according to local time.
Date.getHours	myDate.getHours()	Returns the hour from 0 (midnight) to 23 (11 p.m.) according to local time.
Date.getMilliseconds	myDate.getMilliseconds()	Returns the milliseconds from 0 to 999 according to local time.
Date.getMinutes	myDate.getMinutes()	Returns the minutes from 0 to 59 according to local time.
Date.getMonth	myDate.getMonth()	Returns the month from 0 (January) to 11 (December) according to local time.
Date.getSeconds	myDate.getSeconds()	Returns the seconds from 0 to 59 according to local time.
Date.getTime	myDate.getTime()	Returns the number of milliseconds since midnight January 1, 1970, universal time.
Date.getTimezoneOffset	mydate.getTimezoneOffset()	Returns the difference, in minutes, between the computer's local time and the universal time.
Date.getUTCDate	myDate.getUTCDate()	Returns the day (date) of the month from 1 to 31 according to universal time.
Date.getUTCDay	myDate.getUTCDay()	Returns the day of the week from 0 (Sunday) to 6 (Saturday) according to universal time.
Date.getUTCFullYear	myDate.getUTCFullYear()	Returns the four-digit year according to universal time.
Date.getUTCHours	myDate.getUTCHours()	Returns the hour from 0 (midnight) to 23 (11 p.m.) according to universal time.
Date.getUTCMilliseconds	myDate.getUTCMilliseconds()	Returns the milliseconds from 0 to 999 according to universal time.
Date.getUTCMinutes	myDate.getUTCMinutes()	Returns the minutes from 0 to 59 according to universal time.
Date.getUTCMonth	myDate.getUTCMonth()	Returns the month from 0 (January) to 11 (December) according to universal time.
Date.getUTCSeconds	myDate.getSeconds()	Returns the seconds from 0 to 59 according to universal time.

Name	Format	Description
Date.getYear	myDate.getYear()	Returns an integer which, when added to 1900, gives the year according to local time. For instance, a return value of 0 means 1900.
Date.setDate	myDate.setDate(*date*)	Sets the day of the month to *date*, an integer from 1 to 31, according to local time. Returns the new time in milliseconds.
Date.setFullYear	myDate.setFullYear (*year* [, *month* [, *date*]])	Sets a four-digit *year*, and optionally also the *month* from 0 (January) to 11 (December), and the *date* from 1 to 31, all according to local time. Returns the new time in milliseconds.
Date.setHours	myDate.setHours(*hour* [, *minute* [, *second* [, *millisecond*]]])	Sets the *hour*, from 0 (midnight) to 23 (11 p.m.); and optionally *minute* from 0 to 59; *second* from 0 to 59; and *millisecond* from 0 to 999, all according to local time. Returns the new time in milliseconds.
Date.setMilliseconds	myDate.setMilliseconds (*millisecond*)	Sets the milliseconds according to local time from 0 to 999. Returns the new time in milliseconds.
Date.setMinutes	myDate.setMinutes(*minute* [, *second* [, *millisecond*]])	Sets *minute* from 0 to 59; and optionally *second* from 0 to 59; and *millisecond* from 0 to 999, all according to local time. Returns the new time in milliseconds.
Date.setMonth	myDate.setMonth (*month* [, *date*])	Sets the *month* from 0 (January) to 11 (December) and optionally the *date* from 1 to 31, both according to local time. Returns the new time in milliseconds.
Date.setSeconds	myDate.setSeconds(*second* [, *millisecond*]))	Sets the *second* from 0 to 59, and optionally the *millisecond* from 0 to 999, both according to local time. Returns the new time in milliseconds.
Date.setTime	myDate.setTime(*millisecond*)	Sets the date, expressed in milliseconds since midnight on January 1, 1970. Returns the same number you give it.
Date.setUTCDate	myDate.setUTCDate(*date*)	Sets the date according to universal time, from 1 to 31. Returns the new time in milliseconds.
Date.setUTCFullYear	myDate.setUTCFullYear (*year* [, *month* [, *date*]])	Sets a four-digit *year*, and optionally also the *month* from 0 (January) to 11 (December), and the *date* from 1 to 31, all according to universal time.

19

Table 19.5 Continued

Name	Format	Description
Date.setUTCHours	myDate.setUTCHours(*hour* [, *minute* [, *second* [, *millisecond*]]])	Sets the *hour*, from 0 (midnight) to 23 (11 p.m.); and optionally *minute* from 0 to 59; *second* from 0 to 59; and *millisecond* from 0 to 999, all according to universal time. Returns the new time in milliseconds.
Date.setUTCMilliseconds	myDate.setUTCMilliseconds (*millisecond*)	Sets *millisecond* from 0 to 999 according to universal time. Returns the new time in milliseconds.
Date.setUTCMinutes	myDate.setUTCMinutes(*minute* [, *second* [, *millisecond*]])	Sets *minute* from 0 to 59; and optionally *second* from 0 to 59; and *millisecond* from 0 to 999, all according to universal time. Returns the new time in milliseconds.
Date.setUTCMonth	myDate.setUTCMonth (*month* [, *date*])	Sets the *month* from 0 (January) to 11 (December) and optionally the *date* from 1 to 31, both according to universal time. Returns the new time in milliseconds.
Date.setUTCSeconds	myDate.setUTCSeconds(*second* [, *millisecond*]))	Sets the *second* from 0 to 59, and optionally the *millisecond* from 0 to 999, both according to universal time. Returns the new time in milliseconds.
Date.setYear	myDate.setYear(*year*)	Determines the value that will be retrieved by Date.getYear(). The *year* argument is an integer. If *year* is a one- or two-digit number, Date.getYear() will retrieve that number. If *year* is three or more digits, Date.getYear() will retrieve that number minus 1900.
Date.toString	myDate.toString()	Returns a string representing the date and time in this format: Sat May 4 12:42:19 GMT-0700 2002.
Date.UTC	Date.UTC(*year*, *month* [, *date* [, *hour*[, *minute* [, *second* [, *millisecond*]]]]])	Returns the number of milliseconds between midnight on January 1, 1970, universal time, and the date/time specified in the arguments *year*, *month*, *date*, *hour*, *minute*, *second*, and *millisecond*.

You can use the Date constructor in three ways:

- myDate = new Date(); sets myDate to the current date and time.

- myDate = new Date(1000000); sets myDate to the date and time one million milliseconds after midnight of January 1, 1970.

■ myDate = new Date(2002, 1, 2, 3, 4, 5, 6); sets myDate to January 2, 2002, at 3:04 a.m., plus 5 seconds and 6 milliseconds. Thus, the format is new Date (*year*, *month*, *date*, *hour*, *minute*, *second*, *millisecond*);.

In the last format, all parameters except *year* and *month* are optional and are set to zero if not supplied. Hours are set on a 24-hour clock, where midnight is 0 and noon is 12. For the year, a value of 0 to 99 indicates 1900 though 1999. For years beyond 1999, you need to specify all four digits of the year.

The Function **Class**

The Function class, which is new in Flash MX, brings functions into the class system, opening up the possibility of adding custom functions to Function.prototype, for example, or creating subclasses of functions. Because classes are embodied in functions in ActionScript, Function.prototype is also a logical place to put methods that may operate on any class. An example is an extends() method that sets up inheritance between a child class and a parent class.

⇨ *For an example of creating an extends() method in the Function.prototype, see "Creating Class Hierarchies Using the __proto__ Property," page 502 (Chapter 21, "Packaging Data and Functions Using Custom Objects").*

The Function class has just two built-in methods: apply() and call().

The Function class is a "nonconstructive" constructor: You can't create usable new instances with the new keyword.

⇨ *The apply() and call() methods, as well as the syntax for creating a function, are covered in Chapter 15, "Combining Statements into Functions," page 267.*

The Object **Class**

The Object class is the foundation for all other classes in ActionScript. All other classes inherit from it and thus share its properties and methods.

One of the hidden enhancements in Flash MX is an enrichment of the Object class, from 3 properties to 10. If you want to see these properties, use the undocumented ASSetPropFlags() function to "unhide" the properties of the Object class:

```
ASSetPropFlags(Object.prototype, null, 8, 1);
for (a in Object.prototype) trace (a);
```

This for-in loop reveals 10 properties: constructor, isPropertyEnumerable(), isPrototypeOf(), hasOwnProperty(), toLocaleString(), toString(), valueOf(), addProperty(), unwatch(), and watch(). Every object that you create with the new operator automatically inherits all these properties, the last 9 of which are methods. These properties are summarized in Table 19.6.

Table 19.6 Methods and Properties of the `Object` Class

Name	Method/Property	Format	Description
`addProperty`	M	`myObject.addProperty ("myProp", getMyProp, setMyProp )`	Creates a getter/setter property named `myProp`.
`constructor`	P	`myObject.constructor`	Points to the constructor function of the object.
`hasOwnProperty`	M	`myObject.hasOwnProperty ("myProp")`	Returns `true` if `myObject` has a local property named `myProp`; otherwise, returns `false`.
`isPropertyEnumerable`	M	`isPropertyEnumerable (property)`	Returns `true` if *property* is a local property that would be enumerated by a `for-in` loop
`isPrototypeOf`	M	`protoObject.isPrototypeOf (instanceObject)`	Returns `true` if *instanceObject* uses *protoObject* as the prototype object where it gets shared properties. Otherwise, it returns `false`.
`registerClass`	M	`Object.registerClass`	Preregisters a movie clip for member ship in a class. (See Chapter 17.)
`toLocaleString`	M	`myObject.toLocaleString()`	Returns a string appropriate to a particular country or area; by default, returns the string `[object Object]`.
`toString`	M	`myObject.toString()`	Returns the string `[object Object]`.
`unwatch`	M	See Table 19.8	Removes the registration that a `watch()` method created.
`valueOf`	M	`myObject.valueOf()`	In the `Object` class, returns the object itself by default. Child classes, such as `Boolean`, `Date`, `Number`, and `String`, may define more useful `valueOf()` methods.
`watch`	M	See Table 19.8	Registers a callback function to be invoked when a specified property of an object changes.

The first five properties in the list are undocumented. These undocumented properties are defined in ECMA-262—although `isPropertyEnumerable()` is `propertyIsEnumerable()` in ECMA-262. Nevertheless, you must assume that the behavior of any undocumented feature is subject to change in future versions of Flash. Theoretically, these functions might not even be supported in future versions of Flash.

In Flash 5, the `Object` class had only three properties: `toString()`, `valueOf()`, and `constructor`. If you want to enumerate these properties in Flash 5 using a `for-in` loop, the format for revealing hidden properties in Flash 5 is as follows:

```
ASSetPropFlags(Object.prototype, null, 2);
```

Of the 10 properties of the `Object` class, 7 are defined in the ECMA-262 standard and are also found in JavaScript. (Both have `propertyIsEnumerable()`, not `isPropertyEnumerable()`.) The 3 properties that are Flash-specific are `addProperty()`, `unwatch()`, and `watch()`.

constructor

The purpose of the `constructor` property is to point to the constructor function of the object. The `constructor` property can therefore be used to determine the class of an object:

```
mySound = new Sound();
if ((typeof mySound == "object") && (mySound.constructor == Sound))
    // then do something with the Sound object
```

Each instance of the class has its own local `constructor` property, and the `prototype` object of the class (like any other object) also has a `constructor` property.

> For more details on the constructor property, see Chapter 21, "Packaging Data and Functions Using Custom Objects," page 489. An undocumented __constructor__ property (with two underscores to the left and two to the right) is mentioned in "Creating Class Hierarchies Using the __proto__ Property," page 502 (Chapter 21).

toString()

The purpose of the `toString()` method is to return a string that represents the object in some manner. The ActionScript interpreter invokes this method when it needs to convert an object into a string. Some built-in objects come with class-specific `toString()` methods. They are listed in Table 19.7.

Table 19.7 Return Values of `toString()` Methods of Built-in Objects

Class	Return Value of `toString()` Method
Array	A comma-separated list of the array's elements converted to strings
Boolean	`true` or `false` as a string
Date	The full date and time in the form `Sun Jun 16 18:04:58 GMT-0600 2002(*)`
Button, MovieClip, TextField	The absolute path to the instance
Number	The number as a string
Object	The string `[object Object]`
XML node object or XML document	XML source code

(*) GMT is the Greenwich Mean Time (same as UTC) offset.

> For more specifics on converting a number to a string, see Table 12.3, page 206, in Chapter 12, "Managing Variables, Data, and Datatypes."

Classes that do not have class-specific toString() methods use the one they inherit from the Object class, which returns the string [object Object]. You can assign a class-specific toString() method to get a more meaningful return, as in this example:

```
Sound.prototype.toString = function () {return "Sound";};
```

When you create a custom class, you may want to create a toString() method that will return information that you can use either for debugging or in your program.

toLocaleString()

The toLocaleString()method is an alternate, implementation-specific version of the toString() method. Its purpose is to provide a *localized* version of the string representing the object. Localization refers to adapting to various countries and languages. The toLocaleString() method in the Object class prototype returns the same thing as the toString() method. However, you can define toLocaleString() methods for built-in classes. The toLocaleString() method is undocumented in ActionScript.

isPropertyEnumerable()

The isPropertyEnumerable()method takes one argument, which is a property of the object, and returns true if the property would be enumerated by a for-in loop. If the property does not exist, or if it would not be enumerated by a for-in loop, isPropertyEnumerable() returns false.

⇨ *The for-in loop is covered in "Repeating Actions Using Loops," page 259 (Chapter 14, "Working with Data: Using Statements").*

The isPropertyEnumerable() method does not consider properties in the prototype chain. This can give some counterintuitive results. For instance, the following code enumerates the properties of a new TextField instance and then invokes the isPropertyEnumerable() method for each property. You might think that, because you got the properties using a for-in loop, they must be enumerable using a for-in loop. You would be right, but the isPropertyEnumerable() method still returns false because it does not consider properties in the prototype chain, and all the properties of a new instance of the TextField class are shared properties from TextField.prototype. When you invoke the isPropertyEnumerable() method for each property directly in TextField.prototype, the isPropertyEnumerable() method returns true.

```
myTextField = new TextField();
for (a in myTextField) {
    trace (a);
    trace(myTextField.isPropertyEnumerable(a));
    trace(TextField.prototype.isPropertyEnumerable(a)) ;

}
/* Output
condenseWhite
false
true
```

```
restrict
false
true
textHeight
false
true
and so on …
*/
```

The `isPropertyEnumerable()` method is undocumented in ActionScript. Its equivalent in ECMA-262 and JavaScript is `propertyIsEnumerable()`.

isPrototypeOf()

The `isPrototypeOf()`method takes one argument, which is an object. The format is as follows:

protoObject.`isPrototypeOf(`*instanceObject*`);`

If *instanceObject* uses *protoObject* as the `prototype` object where it gets shared properties, `isPrototypeOf()` returns `true`. Otherwise, it returns `false`.

The `isPrototypeOf()` method depends on the `__proto__` property of the instance object to find the instance object's prototype. For example, the following uses the text field from the previous section. It shows that if you repoint the `__proto__` property of the instance object so that it no longer points to the class prototype, `isPrototypeOf()` no longer works properly:

```
trace(TextField.prototype.isPrototypeOf(myTextField)); // true
myTextField.__proto__ = null;
trace(TextField.prototype.isPrototypeOf(myTextField)); // false
```

valueOf()

Just as the `toString()` method represents the object as a string, the `valueOf()` method represents the object as another primitive datatype. The default `valueOf()` method in the `Object` class returns the object itself—which is something like buying a dollar bill for a dollar. For instance:

```
trace(myTextField.valueOf() == myTextField); // true
trace(typeof myTextField.valueOf() == typeof myTextField); // true
trace(typeof myTextField.valueOf()); // object
```

However, a class can define a useful `valueOf()` method. For instance, the `Date` class has a `valueOf()` method that returns the number of milliseconds between the time of the `Date` object and midnight, January 1, 1970. For dates prior to that time, the number is negative. (This method is equivalent to the `Date.getTime()` method.)

```
myDate = new Date();
trace (myDate.valueOf()); // 1024275924859
trace (myDate); // Sun Jun 16 18:05:24 GMT-0700 2002
```

The Boolean, Date, Number, and String classes define valueOf() methods that return the primitive datum, allowing you to compare these primitive values.

➡ *For more information on comparing objects, see the sidebar "Comparing Objects," earlier in this chapter, page 409.*

hasOwnProperty()

The undocumented hasOwnProperty()method takes one string argument specifying a name of a possible local property. The method returns true if the object has a local property with that name. Otherwise, it returns false. The format looks like this:

```
myTextField.hasOwnProperty("myProp")
```

The following example creates a global findValueOf() function, using the hasOwnProperty() method to determine whether an object or any of the prototype objects it inherits from has a valueOf() method. The findValueOf() method returns a number indicating how many levels up in the prototype chain it had to go to find a valueOf() method. A return of 0 means the object itself has a valueOf() method, a return of 1 means the parent of the object has a valueOf() method, and so on. Line 7 checks whether the valueOf() method was found in the Object class. If so, the findValueOf() method returns -1 (negative one).

If the prototype chain ends and no valueOf() method has been found, result will be undefined in line 5, the while loop will terminate (line 4), and the function will exit returning undefined (line 15). This could happen, for instance, if the prototype chain is broken before it reaches the Object class.

```
1: _global.findValueOf = function (obj) {
2:     var i = 0;
3:     var result = false;
4:     while (result != undefined) {
5:         result = obj.hasOwnProperty("valueOf");
6:         if (result == true) {
7:             if (obj == Object.prototype) return (-1);
8:             else return i;
9:         }
10:        else {
11:            obj = obj.__proto__; // one step up the prototype chain
12:            i++;
13:        }
14:     }
15:     return;
16: }
17:
18: createEmptyMovieClip("myClip",1);
19: trace (findValueOf(myClip)); // -1, valueOf in the Object.prototype
20: myDate = new Date();
21: trace (findValueOf(myDate)); // 1, valueOf in the parent class
```

addProperty()

The `addProperty()` method makes it easier to use get/set functions instead of changing properties of objects directly. First, I'll briefly discuss the advantages of get/set functions. Then I'll look at how the `addProperty()` method facilitates their use.

Say you create a class named `MyClass` that gives a property named `myProp` to instances that it creates:

```
function MyClass () {
    this.myProp = "myVal";
};
```

Now when you create an instance, it will have the `myProp` property:

```
myObj = new MyClass();
trace(myObj.myProp); // myVal
```

If you want to change the value of `myObj.myProp`, you can do so directly, like this:

```
myObj.myProp = "myNewVal";
trace(myObj.myProp); // myNewVal
```

However, it is considered a "best practice" to create a "set" function to change the value of `myObj.myProp`:

```
MyClass.prototype.setMyProp = function (newVal) {this.myProp = newVal;};
myObj.setMyProp("myNewVal");
trace(myObj.myProp); // myNewVal
```

The advantage is that, if you decide that you need to validate the data or take some other action based on the value provided, you can do it in the set function without having to change anything else in your program. In contrast, if you've used direct references everywhere, you'll have to change all of them (or substitute a set function for them).

Get functions provide similar advantages when retrieving data:

```
MyClass.prototype.getMyProp = function () {return this.myProp;};
trace(myObj.getMyProp()); // myNewVal
```

Get/set functions may be particularly important if you are working on a team because they give your team members a simple, consistent interface to your object, while still allowing you to make improvements and adjustments internally.

Most built-in properties, such as _x and _y for movie clips, are getter/setter properties.

However, there are two problems with get/set functions:

▪ The first problem concerns readability. The line

```
myObj.myProp = "myNewVal";
```

is more readable than

```
myObj.setMyProp("myNewVal");
```

19

■ The second problem is that just creating get/set functions doesn't enforce their use. When problems occur, you still have to wonder whether they might be due to a direct reference circumventing the get/set functions.

The `addProperty()` method addresses both of these problems. It allows you to add a property and associate get/set functions with it in one step. Thereafter, the direct reference syntax will actually call the get/set functions. Thus, you can use the more readable syntax with the assurance that the get/set functions are not being circumvented.

The format of the `addProperty()` method is as follows:

```
myObj.addProperty( "myProp", getMyProp, setMyProp )
```

Instead of the names of get and set functions, you can use function literals, as shown in sample movie addpropliteral.fla on the CD.

If you name both a get and a set function, both functions must exist. If you want to create a read-only property, put `null` in place of the set function. In the following example, you change x and y using other functions and use the `diff` property as a read-only property to keep track of the difference between x and y:

```
myObj = { x : 2 , y : 3 };
function getDiff() {
    return (this.x - this.y);
}
myObj.addProperty("diff", getDiff, null);
var difference = myObj.diff; // -1
```

Now if you try to set `myObj.diff`, you will find it doesn't work:

```
myObj.diff = 20;
trace(myObj.diff); // -1
```

The `addProperty()` method returns `true` if the property is successfully added, and `false` if it is not.

Note that the set function that you define *cannot actually change the value of the property*. It just receives the new value as an argument and gives you an opportunity to take related actions based on that value. The value is changed independently of your set function, and that is out of your control. In sample movie getset.fla (see Listing 19.1), the set function `setMyProp()` contains no statements, yet the value is still set—a dramatic demonstration that setting the value is done "under the covers."

Somewhat counterintuitively, your get function can change the property. The property will be set to whatever the get function returns. For instance, the following get function appends the string `"addon"` to the `myProp` property whenever the property is read:

```
MyClass.prototype.getMyProp = function () {
    this.myProp += "addon";
    return this.myProp;
};
```

The `addProperty()` method overwrites an existing property that has the same name as the property in the first argument. Therefore, the assignment on line 8 must take place *after* the `addProperty()` statement. Otherwise, `myProp` would be an existing property and would be destroyed, along with the value `myVal`.

Listing 19.1   getset.fla

```
1: function MyClass () {
2:       var getMyProp = function  () {
3:            return this.myProp;
4:       };
5:       var setMyProp = function (newVal) {
6:       };
7:       this.addProperty("myProp", getMyProp, setMyProp);
8:       this.myProp = "myVal"; // have to do this after addProperty
9: }
10: myObj = new MyClass();
11: trace(myObj.myProp); // myVal
12: myObj.myProp = "myVal2";
13: trace(myObj.myProp); // myVal2
```

The fact that your set function doesn't actually change the variable might seem like a significant loss at first because it means you cannot change the value being set. However, you can just treat the property being set as an instruction to perform other actions, not as a piece of data. Look at the value that has been set and then change other values as you want. The fact that you have "front end" objects and properties that provide the interface to the class and "back end" objects and properties that "do the work" is an implementation detail that can be hidden within the class.

In the following code listing, taken from sample movie addprop.fla, if the value passed to the set function is anything other than `"Bad Bart"`, the string `"okay"` is passed to a status display function (line 7), and the value is displayed in a text field (line 8).

On the other hand, if the value passed to the set function *is* `"Bad Bart"`, the strings `"error"` and `"Bad Bart"` are passed to the status display function (line 11), and the empty string (that is, nothing) is displayed in a text field (line 12). The getter/setter property `myObj.myProp` is successfully set to `"Bad Bart"`. Nevertheless, from the user's perspective (or the perspective of another programmer writing code that interfaces with your class), `"Bad Bart"` is rejected as input, and an error message is displayed.

```
1: function MyClass () {
2:       var getMyProp = function () {
3:            return this.myProp;
4:       };
5:       var setMyProp = function (newVal) {
6:            if (newVal != "Bad Bart") {
7:                 setStatus("okay");
8:                 setDisplayText(newVal);
```

```
 9:            }
10:            else {
11:                    setStatus("error", newVal);
12:                    setDisplayText("");
13:            }
14:        };
15:        this.addProperty("myProp", getMyProp, setMyProp);
16:        this.myProp = "Beautiful Betsy"; // have to do this after addProperty
17: }
```

Another option, if you want to change the value being set, is to use the `Object.watch()` method described in the next section. However, `Object.watch()` can take up a lot more processing cycles than `addProperty()`.

⇨ *If you are even thinking about trying to override a getter/setter property, see the "Troubleshooting" section at the end of Chapter 21, page 509.*

watch() **and** unwatch()

The `watch()` and `unwatch()`methods register and unregister a callback function that is called whenever an attempt is made to change a particular property. This is a powerful capability, but one that comes at a cost: If you watch a property that is constantly changing, the callback function will fire constantly, creating an excessive processing load.

The `watch()` method is useful for debugging. It can also be used as a kind of general-purpose event generator, like an `addListener()` for changes in properties. However, you can have only one watchpoint at a time on any given property. If you set a second watchpoint, it replaces the previous one. This contrasts with listeners: You can have as many listeners as you want for any given event. With `watch()`, you could implement your own event model so that any number of objects could "get the news" when the property changes.

⇨ *To learn more details about event generators, see the section "Flash at Work: General-Purpose Flash Event Engines," page 328, near the end of Chapter 16, "Interaction, Events, and Sequencing," and links to related sites on http://www.flashoop.com.*

The `watch()` method is not recommended for use with getter/setter properties. Although it may work to some extent, it could miss some changes, and there is a potential for creating excessive processing loads. Most built-in properties are getter/setter properties.

To start to watch a property, take these two steps: Define a callback function and execute the `watch()` statement. Table 19.8 shows formats for both steps, as well as the format for terminating the `watch()` with `unwatch()`.

19

Table 19.8   watch, callback, and unwatch

Method/ Function	Format	Parameters
watch	myObj.watch(*property*, *callback*,*userData*);	*property*—Specifies the property to watch (a string)
		callback—Specifies a callback function (a reference)
		userData(optional)—Specifies data to be sent to the callback function
callback function	function myFunc (*property*,*oldval*, *newval*,*userData*) { // *statements* }	*property*—Contains the property that changed *oldval*—Contains the previous value of *property* *newval*—Contains the new value of *property* *userData*—Contains data defined in the userData parameter of the watch() statement
unwatch	myObj.unwatch (*property*);	*property*—Specifies the property to stop watching

Both watch() and unwatch() return true if successful; otherwise, they return false.

The callback function is invoked as a method of the object containing the watched property (such as myObj in Table 19.8). Inside the callback function, this refers to myObj.

The object, such as myObj, that contains the property to be watched must exist when you set the watchpoint, and the watchpoint disappears if you delete the object. However, the watchpoint exists independently of the *property* it is watching. You can create a watchpoint on a property that does not yet exist, and the watchpoint will go into effect when you create the property. Similarly, you can delete a property for which a watchpoint has been set without destroying the watchpoint. If you later re-create the property, the watchpoint will still be in effect. To remove a watchpoint without deleting the object, use the unwatch() method.

The sample movie watch.fla contains a statusObj object with a property named isOkay:

```
statusObj = new Object();
statusObj.isOkay = "okay";
```

The following line sets a watchpoint on the isOkay property:

```
statusObj.watch("isOkay", setStatusText);
```

The callback function setStatusText() is as follows (I omitted the fourth parameter, *userData*, because it's not used):

```
function setStatusText (prop, oldval, newVal) {
    statusField.text = newVal;
    if (newVal == "okay") {
        statusField.setTextFormat(okayFormat);
    }
```

```
        else {
            statusField.setTextFormat(errorFormat);
            setDisplayText("");
        }
}
```

If the new value for the isOkay property is "okay", the status field text format is set to the okayFormat. If the new value for the isOkay property is anything other than "okay", the status field text format is set to the errorFormat, and the display field is blanked out by setting it to the empty string.

The callback function is triggered by an *attempted* change in a property value. However, any actual change in that property is under the control of the callback function. If the callback function does *not* return a value, the property value is set to undefined. This is always the case with the setStatusText() function just shown, for instance. It never returns anything, so the watched property is always undefined.

If the callback function *does* return a value, the property is set to the return value. Because the callback function gets the previous value as its second parameter, it can nullify the change simply by returning the previous value.

The watch() method's capability to control the value of the property or nullify the change distinguishes it from the addProperty() method. Sample movie watch2.fla illustrates this capability. When the callback function myPropHandler() gets an unacceptable new value, it returns the old value, nullifying the change (line 11).

```
 1: function myPropHandler (prop, oldval, newVal) {
 2:      if (newVal != "Bad Bart") {
 3:          myDisplayProp = newVal;
 4:          myStatusProp = "okay";
 5:          statusField.setTextFormat(okayFormat);
 6:          return newVal; // accept the change
 7:      }
 8:      else {
 9:          myStatusProp = "error";
10:          statusField.setTextFormat(errorFormat);
11:          return oldVal; // reject the change
12:      }
13: }
```

The Math **Object**

Often, mathematical functions are the best way to achieve a desired motion or effect, whether smooth and natural or wildly and wonderfully unnatural. Math functions are often the most "elegant" way to accomplish a particular goal; that is, they are simpler conceptually and in execution.

In addition, they are often more flexible than any other approach, including tweening; that is, you can accomplish a broader range of tasks with them.

The `Math` object has enough methods with varied uses to fill a book by itself. I'll give examples of some of the most common methods and some of the most powerful ones. For a full listing of math functions, see Table 19.9.

Combining the drawing methods and the math methods can yield marvelous results. On the CD, see examples from Keith Peters (3Dcube.fla and test5.fla) and Millie Maruani (api_flower.fla and api_cube.fla) from Chapter 18, "Drawing with ActionScript."

Table 19.9   Math Methods and Properties

Name	Method/ Property	Format	Description
abs	M	`Math.abs(x)`	Computes the absolute value of x.
acos	M	`Math.acos(x)`	Computes the arccosine of x.
asin	M	`Math.acos(x)`	Computes the arcsine of x.
atan	M	`Math.atan(x)`	Computes the arctangent of x.
atan2	M	`Math.atan2(y, x)`	Computes the arctangent of the ratio y/x, that is, the angle from the positive x-axis to the point (x, y).
ceil	M	`Math.ceil(x)`	Rounds x up to the nearest integer.
cos	M	`Math.cos(x)`	Computes the cosine of x.
exp	M	`Math.exp(x)`	Computes `Math.E` to the power x.
floor	M	`Math.floor(x)`	Rounds x down to the nearest integer.
log	M	`Math.log(x)`	Computes the natural logarithm of x.
max	M	`Math.max(x, y)`	Returns the larger of integers x and y.
min	M	`Math.min(x, y)`	Returns the smaller of integers x and y.
pow	M	`Math.pow(x, y)`	Computes x raised to the power y.
random	M	`Math.random()`	Returns a pseudo-random number between 0 and 1.
round	M	`Math.round(x)`	Rounds x to the nearest integer.
sin	M	`Math.sin(x)`	Computes the sine of x.
sqrt	M	`Math. sqrt(x)`	Computes the square root of x.
tan	M	`Math.tan(x)`	Computes the tangent of x.
E	P	`Math.E`	Euler's constant and the base of natural logarithms (approximately 2.718), traditionally notated as e.
LN2	P	`Math.LN2`	The natural logarithm of 2 (approximately 0.693).
LOG2E	P	`Math.LOG2E`	The base 2 logarithm of `Math.E` (approximately 1.442).

19

Table 19.9 Continued

Name	Method/ Property	Format	Description
LN10	P	Math.LN10	The natural logarithm of 10 (approximately 2.302).
LOG10E	P	Math.LOG10E	The base 10 logarithm of Math.E (approximately 0.434).
PI	P	Math.PI	The ratio of the circumference of a circle to its diameter (approximately 3.14159).
SQRT1_2	P	Math.SQRT1_2	The reciprocal of the square root of 2, that is, 1/Math.SQRT2 (approximately 0.707).
SQRT2	M	Math.SQRT2	The square root of 2 (approximately 1.414).

Common Math Functions

Among the most commonly used methods of the Math object are floor(), random(), and round().

floor()   The floor() method truncates a decimal number and returns just the integer portion. For example:

```
x = Math.floor (8.21) // result: 8
x = Math.floor (8.21) // result: 8
x = Math.floor (8.5) // result: 8
x = Math.floor (8.6) // result: 8
x = Math.floor (-8.21) // result: -9
x = Math.floor (-8.5) // result: -9
x = Math.floor (-8.6) // result: -9
```

random()   The random() method returns a decimal number greater than or equal to 0 and less than 1, usually with 14 to 17 digits. For example:

```
x = Math.random();
/*
Sample results:
0.236938397510414
0.102950482211518
0.274189059284604
0.585484127786702
0.00277895387391511
0.80261959452304
*/
```

round()   The round() method rounds a decimal number to the nearest integer. Here are some examples:

```
x = Math.round (8.21) // result: 8
x = Math.round (8.5) // result: 9
```

```
x = Math.round (8.6) // result: 9
x = Math.round (-8.21) // result: -8
x = Math.round (-8.5) // result: -8
x = Math.round (-8.6) // result: -9
```

In the following example, `mcPercent` is the integer percent of `myClip` that has been loaded:

```
mcPercent = Math.round((myClip.getBytesLoaded() / myClip.getBytesTotal()) * 100);
```

To round decimal fractions, first multiply by a power of 10, round, and then divide by the same power of 10. The power of 10 you use will determine the number of decimal places you round to. For instance, the following example rounds y to one decimal place:

```
y = .12;
yr = Math.round(10*y)/10; // yr is .1
```

In the preceding example, if y is any positive decimal fraction, yr will be `0.0`, `0.1`, `0.2`, `0.3`, `0.4`, `0.5`, `0.6`, `0.7`, `0.8`, `0.9`, or `1.0`.

⇨ *Rounding to a single decimal place is applied later in this chapter in "Using Trig to Get and Set Direction," page 435.*

Generating a Random Integer from 0 to 9, Inclusive

You can combine `random()` and `round()` to produce random integers. This code executes the steps one by one:

```
for (i = 0; i < 10; i++) {
    x = Math.random(); // generate random number less than 1
    x *= 10; // multiply by 10
    x = Math.round(x); // round off
    trace(x);
}
```

Here's a shorter, faster form replacing the whole body of the preceding `for` loop:

```
trace(Math.round(Math.random()*10));
```

Using `Math.sqrt()` to Get and Set Relative Positioning

The `Math.sqrt()` method can be used both to determine and to control the position of one movie clip relative to another, or relative to any known point on the Stage. For instance, `Math.sqrt()` can be used to keep a draggable movie clip a fixed distance from a point, thus constraining the clip's movement to an arc.

This use of the `Math.sqrt()` method to control position is founded on the fact that the position of a movie clip on the Stage is completely determined by two numbers: its x position and its y position. Therefore, you can constrain a draggable clip to any path if you can come up with a formula that will give you one of these numbers if you have the other.

In Figure 19.1, if I give you an x position within the range of the arc, you can tell at a glance what y position you would have to assign to the mouse to keep it on the arc.

Figure 19.1

The `Math.sqrt()` function keeps the mouse a constant distance from the center point of the arc, thus keeping it on the arc.

So perhaps it's not surprising that there is a mathematical equation that can do the same thing. By putting this equation into the mouse movie clip's *enter frame* event handler, you can force the mouse onto the arc in every frame where the x position permits it. This technique is demonstrated in sample movie constrain.fla.

The equation gets the mouse's _x property and then sets its _y property appropriately. The equation uses the fact that every point on the arc is the same distance from the center of the arc, namely, half the width of the `arc` movie clip. This distance is the `radius` of the arc, r in the formula. Here's the ActionScript:

```
onClipEvent(load){
    var r = _root.arc._width/2; // the radius of the arc
    var ctr_x = 400; // the x position of the arc's center
    var ctr_y = 300; // the y position of the arc's center
}
onClipEvent(enterFrame) {
    _y = Math.sqrt( (r * r) - ( (_x - ctr_x) * (_x - ctr_x) )) + ctr_y;
}
```

How was the formula derived?

Start from the fact that the distance between any two points on the Stage can be reduced to an x difference and a y difference. For example, in Figure 19.1, to get from the mouse to the center of the half circle, instead of going directly, you could go up (the y difference) and then left (the x difference)

Similarly, if you're given the x and y differences, the direct route is obvious. These three distances form a triangle, and given any two sides of a triangle, the third one is always obvious. Mathematically, if you know the direct distance from the mouse to the center of the arc and the x difference from the mouse to the center of the arc, you can calculate the y difference.

In this case, the distance from the mouse to the center of the arc is the radius of the arc, r; it is half the width of the arc movie clip (`arc._width / 2`). The x difference is `_x` minus `ctr_x`, `_x` being the x position of the mouse (you don't have to specify the movie clip instance name because the code is inside the mouse event handler), and `ctr_x` being the x position of the center point of the arc. Similarly, the y difference is `_y` minus `ctr_y`.

The equation that gives you the y difference is a form of the *Pythagorean theorem*, which says that $y^2 = r^2 - x^2$, where y is the y difference, r is the radius, and x is the x difference.

In ActionScript, the equation is as follows:

```
(y - ctr_y) * (y - ctr_y) = r * r - (x - ctr_x) * (x - ctr_x);
```

Taking the square root of both sides, you get the following:

```
y - ctr_y = Math.sqrt (r * r - (x - ctr_x) * (x - ctr_x));
```

Adding `ctr_y` to both sides gives the desired formula:

```
y = Math.sqrt( (r * r) - ( (_x - ctr_x) * (_x - ctr_x) )) + ctr_y;
```

Basic Trig Methods: `Math.sin()` and `Math.cos()`

The trigonometry methods, of which the most commonly used are sine (`Math.sin`) and cosine (`Math.cos`), are perhaps the most versatile methods of the `Math` object. This will be demonstrated in subsequent sections. For instance, sample movie treeshadow.fla will use the `_rotation` property of a movie clip to make a "tree" topple, and will animate its lengthening shadow as it falls using the cosine (`Math.cos`) method, while calculating how far the top of the tree is from the ground using the sine (`Math.sin`) method.

Sample movie enemy.fla uses trig to determine whether a gun is pointing at an enemy. You could use a similar approach to determine how many degrees (`_rotation`) to open a monster's jaws to accept an object of a given size.

The triangle in the circle on the left side of Figure 19.2 provides a visual representation of the sine and cosine functions. The sample movie, Helen Triolo's trigdemo.fla, brings it to life: On the left side of the figure, the sine and cosine functions are shown as legs of a triangle in a "unit circle," in which radius *r* is one unit in length. The radius is the hypotenuse (longest leg) of the triangle. The radius and the horizontal leg of the triangle form an angle, θ *(theta)*. As the radius rotates around the circle, the horizontal leg of the triangle is the cosine, and the vertical leg is the sine, of the angle θ (theta). On the right side of the figure, you see how the sine function, in going up and down, traces a sine wave over time.

Officially, the sine is the ratio of the vertical leg to the hypotenuse (y/r), but if the hypotenuse measures one unit ($r = 1$), then y/r is just y. Similarly, the cosine is the horizontal leg over the hypotenuse (x/r), which equals x if r equals 1.

theta

Figure 19.2
A screenshot from trigdemo.fla.
(Source: Helen Triolo)

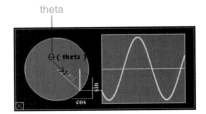

The lines representing the sine and cosine are in a single movie clip, mcSinCos. Their lengths are changed by scaling the y (sine) or x (cosine) dimension of the clip. These lines of code change their lengths:

```
mcSinCos._xscale = Math.cos(angle)*100;
mcSinCos._yscale = Math.sin(angle)*100;
```

The multiplier 100 is necessary because _xscale and _yscale are percentages from 0 to 100, while the sine and cosine functions yield results between 0 and 1.

Caution

Flash measures _rotation *clockwise*, while the unit circle assumes *counterclockwise* rotation. You can reverse Flash's natural rotation direction to get it to match trigonometry functions better.

Sizing Clips via Scale Instead of Height and Width

The usual formula for setting width using the cosine is width = cos(angle) * radius.

In trigdemo.fla, the dimensions of mcSinCos are changed via the _xscale and _yscale properties rather than via _width and _height. This requires multiplication by 100. The number 100 is derived from radius * 2, the mcRadius clip being 50 pixels wide.

If the mcSinCos clip were 100 pixels by 100 pixels, setting its _xscale would be the same as setting its _width. For instance, because 10% of 100 is 10, mcSinCos._xscale = 10 would be the same as mcSinCos._width = 10. In that case, the usual formula would work, and the correct multiplier would be the length of the radius—50 in this case.

However, mcSinCos is actually 50 pixels by 50 pixels. Therefore, its _width is always half its _xscale. For instance, mcSinCos._xscale = 10 is the same as mcSinCos._width = 5. Therefore, to set the correct width, amend the usual formula to scale = cos(angle) * radius * 2.

The horizontal dimension (cosine) is 100% when the angle is 0 radians because Math.cos(0) equals 1. It is 0% when the angle is Math.PI/2 radians (90 degrees) because Math.cos(Math.PI/2) equals 0.

▷ *Measuring angles in radians and degrees is discussed in the sidebar "Radians and Degrees," later in this chapter, page 434.*

▷ *Getting wildly erratic results with trigonometry functions? See the "Troubleshooting" section at the end of this chapter, page 439.*

Caution

The unit circle assumes that zero degrees rotation is at 3 o'clock on the circle. Zero degrees rotation for a movie clip is whatever position it starts in. If a movie clip representing a tree starts with the tree upright, the tree will point to 90 degrees (12 o'clock) on the unit circle when its _rotation is zero degrees.

The vertical dimension (sine) is 0% when the angle is 0 radians because `Math.sin(0)` equals 0. It is 100% when the angle is `Math.PI/2` radians (90 degrees) because `Math.sin(Math.PI/2)` equals 1.

The linear sine wave on the right in Figure 19.2 is created by duplicating a dot movie clip at the y positions of the changing sine. Code in the *enter frame* event handler of the "dot holder" movie clip moves each dot to the right and then removes it when it goes past the specified x position, `_root.nXStop`:

```
onClipEvent(enterFrame) {
    _parent._x += .5; // move dot to the right
    if (_parent._x > _root.nXStop) { //is dot beyond specified x position?
        _parent.removeMovieClip();    //if yes, then remove it
    }
}
```

By visualizing your movies within this unit circle, you can see how to produce the effects mentioned in the first paragraph of this section.

Using Trig to Get and Set Width and Height

Sample movie treeshadow.fla uses the `_rotation` property of a movie clip to make a "tree" topple, as shown in Figure 19.3, and animates the tree's lengthening shadow as it falls using the cosine (`Math.cos`) method, while calculating how far the top of the tree is from the ground using the sine (`Math.sin`) method.

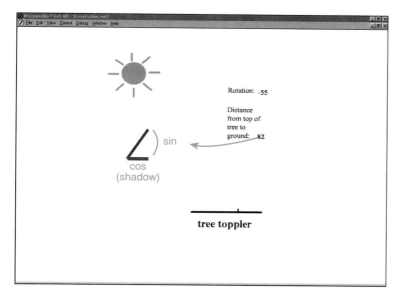

Figure 19.3

Using trig to lengthen a shadow and measure distance from the ground.

The toppling tree is the radius rotating (`treeHeight` in the program). This happens to be the *width* of the `tree` movie clip because the tree starts out lying down horizontally on the Stage. The shadow the tree casts is the cosine. The decreasing distance from the top of the tree to the ground as it falls is the sine.

Because this is not a unit circle (`treeHeight` is not equal to 1), you have to divide the horizontal leg of the triangle by the radius (`treeHeight`) to get the cosine. So, when the tree has fallen halfway to the ground (45 degrees), you get

```
shadow / treeHeight = cos(45)
```

Multiplying both sides by the length of the tree, you get

The number pi (π), represented in ActionScript by `Math.PI`, is the ratio of the circumference to the diameter of a circle, approximately 3.14.

```
shadow = cos(45) * treeHeight
```

The following line from sample movie treeshadow.fla uses `shadow._xscale` instead of an absolute value for setting the shadow width. However, because the `_root.shadow` clip is 100 pixels wide, setting its `_xscale` is the same as setting its `_width`. (See the sidebar "Sizing Clips via Scale Instead of Height and Width" earlier in this chapter.) The following code also converts the rotation measurement from degrees to radians for use by the cosine function:

```
_root.shadow._xscale = Math.cos(deg2rad(_root.tree._rotation))*treeHeight;
```

Radians and Degrees

In ActionScript, the trigonometry functions require angle measurements in *radians*. If you prefer to work in degrees, use a function that translates degrees into radians. The formula is

```
radians = degrees * pi / 180
```

Thus, in the sample movie, treeshadow.fla, to find the cosine of the rotation of a falling tree, you use

```
function deg2rad(degrees) {
    return degrees * Math.PI/180;
}
Math.cos(_root.deg2rad(_root.tree._rotation)
```

Table 19.10 gives some examples of rotation measurements in degrees and their radian equivalents.

Table 19.10   Degrees and Radians

Degrees	Radians
Full circle (360)	`2 * Math.PI`
Half circle (180)	`Math.PI`
Quarter circle (90)	`Math.PI/2`
Eighth circle (45)	`Math.PI / 4`

Similarly, the sine is the vertical distance divided by the radius, so you can start with

```
distance from ground / treeHeight = sin(45)
```

Multiplying both sides by the length of the tree, you get

```
distance from ground = treeHeight * sin(45)
```

The sample movie rounds off the distance to display it more easily. It also takes the absolute value using `Math.abs`, to compensate for Flash's reversed rotation direction. Finally, it subtracts 1, which causes it to round to 0 instead of rounding to 1 at each extreme of the tree's fall.

```
_root.distanceFromGround = Math.round(Math.abs
➥(Math.sin(deg2rad(_root.tree._rotation)) *_treeHeight)-1);
```

Using Trig to Get and Set Direction

To determine whether a gun is pointing at an enemy, use the gun's pivot point as the center of the unit circle, as shown in Figure 19.4.

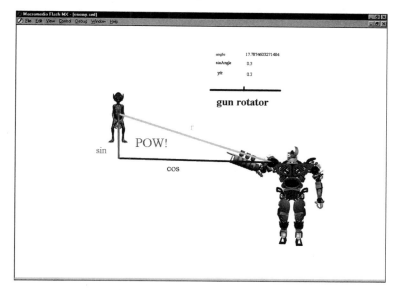

Figure 19.4
Sample movie enemy.fla uses the `Math.sin()` method to determine when a gun is pointing at any enemy. (Robot source: Poser 4, Curious Labs. Gremlin source: DAZ Productions.)

The unit is the direct distance from the gun to the enemy. Begin with the gun in a horizontal position and rotate the gun while checking in each frame whether the sine of the rotation equals the y difference between the enemy and the gun:

```
if (Math.sin(angle) == y)
```

In sample movie enemy.fla, it was necessary to add a couple of extra steps. For one, the movie starts with the gun at a nonzero rotation. The rotation is effectively "zeroed out" by subtracting the initial rotation before taking the sine:

```
angle = _root.gun._rotation - gunRotationStart;
```

Of course, there is the usual translation to radians:

```
sinAngle = Math.sin(deg2rad(angle));
```

The final test is completely straightforward:

```
if (sinAngle == yr)
```

The yr variable in this statement is the y difference between the gun and the enemy, expressed in terms of r:

```
var y = _root.gun._y - _root.enemy._y;
var yr = Math.round(((10*y) / r))/10;
```

Note the rounding of the y distance to one decimal place, using the round() method.

🔖 *Rounding to one decimal place is discussed in "round()," earlier in this chapter, page 428.*

The sine is similarly rounded:

```
sinAngle = Math.round(10*sinAngle)/10;
```

Both the sine and the y distance had to be rounded off, or they would never test equal due to minute differences.

Controlling Position with Math.sin()

Using the Math.sin() method, you can vary any property of a movie clip by substituting the property for y in this equation, which represents the general format of the Math.sin() method:

```
y = Math.sin(x);
```

Figure 19.5 shows the result of moving the butterfly to the right (incrementing the _x property of the movie clip) the same amount in each frame, while moving the butterfly vertically (incrementing or decrementing the _y property of the movie clip) using the Math.sin() function.

Figure 19.5

The Math.sin() method can control position, speed, and rotation to produce natural, gentle transitions and effects. Here, the Math.sin() method controls the vertical position of the butterfly. (Human figure produced with Poser 4, Curious Labs.)

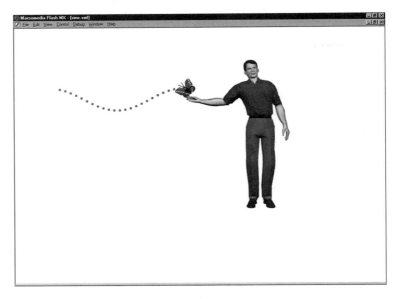

In the figure, the dots show the *sinuous* path followed by the butterfly. Here is the logic of the code controlling the butterfly's movement, expressed in pseudocode:

```
onClipEvent (enterFrame) {
    if (butterfly hasn't reached the target yet) {
        move butterfly one increment to the right;
        move b'fly vertically - amount depends on sine of x;
    }
}
```

The sine function goes through one full cycle (from peak to peak) as the x argument goes from 0 to 360 (traditionally visualized as the degrees of a circle). This example makes the butterfly go through one full sine wave by varying _x from 0 to 360.

Sample movie sine.fla expresses this logic in ActionScript. It has to make two adjustments: It adds a "y adjustment" variable (yadj), which increases the amplitude of the sine wave. Without this adjustment, the movement of the butterfly up and down would be very slight. It also uses the deg2rad() function to convert the degree measurement to radians. Here's the code:

```
// converts degrees to radians
function deg2rad (degrees) {
    return degrees * Math.PI/180;
}
bfly.startx = 0; // x starting point
bfly.endx = 360; // x ending point
bfly.starty = 112;
bfly._x = startx; // position the bfly at start
bfly._y = starty; // position the bfly at start
bfly.xinc = 16; // x increment for movement to the right in each frame
bfly.yadj = 8; // y adjustment - increases amplitude of sine wave
}
bfly.onEnterFrame = function() {
    if (bfly._x < bfly.endx) {
        bfly._x += bfly.xinc; // move bfly one increment to the right
        // move bfly vertically, amount depends on sine of x
        bfly._y += bfly.yadj * Math.sin(deg2rad(bfly._x));
    }
}
```

Controlling Speed with Math.sin()

You can apply the sine function to get the clip to speed up and slow down in a smooth, natural-looking way, too. Figure 19.6 shows what happens if, instead of moving the butterfly to the right the same amount in each frame, you vary the increment using the Math.sin() function. Instead of _x += xinc, you use _x += xinc + (xadj * Math.sin(deg2rad(_x))). This includes an x adjustment variable (xadj), set to 8 here, which exaggerates the amount of speed-up and slow-down. From 0 to 180 degrees, the sine is positive, so the butterfly speeds up while moving down. From 180 to 360 degrees, the sine is negative, so the butterfly slows down while moving up.

Remember that, in Flash, "moving down" means _y is getting larger. "Speeding up" means increasing the amount added to _x in each frame. Thus, a positive sine makes the butterfly move downward and speed up. Conversely, a negative sine makes the butterfly move upward and slow down. The changes in speed are indicated by the horizontal distances between the dots.

The slow-down means that the butterfly is in the 180 to 360 degree range for more frames than it is in the 0 to 180 degree range. (In Figure 19.6, each dot is one frame. Notice how many more dots there are in the second half of the butterfly's journey.) Thus, `_y += yadj * Math.sin(deg2rad(_x))` is executed more times with a negative sine than with a positive sine, making the butterfly move up farther than it moves down. Compensate for this by starting lower, substituting `var starty = 175` for `var starty = 112`. (See sample movie sine2.fla on the CD.)

Figure 19.6
Controlling speed using the `Math.sin()` method. The butterfly slows down as it moves right. (Human figure produced with Poser 4, Curious Labs.)

Other Trig Methods

Here are the other trig methods, specified in terms of the sine and cosine of a unit circle. Substitute `y/r` for `sin` and `x/r` for `cos` if `r` does not equal 1. The angle `theta` is specified in radians in all cases.

The arcsin (`asin`) method returns the angle given the sine:

```
theta = asin(sin)
theta = Math.asin(y/r);
```

The arccos (`acos`) method returns the angle given the cosine:

```
theta = acos(cos)
theta = Math.acos(x/r);
```

The tangent (`tan`) method returns the sine divided by the cosine:

```
sin/cos = tan(theta)
y / x = Math.tan(theta);
```

The arctangent (`atan`) method returns the angle given the tangent:

```
theta = atan(sin/cos)
theta = Math.atan(y/x);
```

TROUBLESHOOTING

Why isn't my array of numbers sorting correctly?

By default, the `Array.sort()` method sorts alphabetically. If you give it an array of numbers, it converts those numbers to strings and then sorts them alphabetically. According to this procedure, 2 is "higher" than 10,000.

To sort numerically, you need to give `Array.sort()` a *compassion function* as an argument. The following example sorts from lowest to highest:

```
numberArray = [3,2,6,3,8,3,9,5];
function byNumber (a, b) {
    return a - b;
}
numberArray.sort(byNumber);
trace(numberArray); // 2,3,3,3,5,6,8,9
```

➥ *For an explanation of how sort functions work, see "sort() and sortOn()," earlier in this chapter, page 402.*

Why are my trig functions going crazy?

One common reason, when trig functions give wildly unexpected results, is that you forgot to convert degree measurements into radians. Although Flash measures `_rotation` in degrees, all the Flash trigonometry functions require angles to be measured in radians.

➥ *Measuring angles in radians and degrees is discussed in the sidebar "Radians and Degrees," earlier in this chapter, page 434.*

FLASH AT WORK: AMAZING ARRAYS

It's amazing what you can do with arrays. For example, as demonstrated in amazingarrays.fla on the CD, you can chop yourself into 64 little pieces, shuffle them on the screen, and then bring them back together like a flock of birds landing in perfect formation.

"This is one of the oldest demos I did in Flash," says Fotios Bassayiannis (`http://fotios.cc`), a Greek Flasher living in Glasgow, Scotland.

"My picture is divided into 64 small pieces. Each piece gets an index number from 1 to 64, starting from top left and ending at bottom right of the picture. The pieces are given random initial placement each time the button is pressed. From then on, they try to reach their destination coordinates."

The program calculates the pieces' destination coordinates based on the index number of the piece and the position of the full picture.

I'm not going to try to explain the code line-by-line for this example, but just imagine trying to keep track of all these little bits of information without arrays!

There's a pic array to hold the 64 movie clip instance names.

There are maxX and maxY arrays for the initial x and y values for each picture "slice" (that is, each piece of the picture).

And there are two "limit" arrays, limitX and limitY, for keeping the x and y axis move limits for each slice. That is, the limit arrays hold the final x and y coordinates of each slice.

The array manipulation is accomplished through simple for loops and the assignment operator. This trio is one of the most powerful combinations in ActionScript.

To initialize the arrays, you use the following:

```
for (i = 1; i < 65; i++ )
{
  Pic[i] = "mc" + String(i);
  maxX[i] = random(450) + 100; //Randomize position for all slices
  maxY[i] = random(340) + 100;
  setProperty ( Pic[i], _x, maxX[i] );
  setProperty ( Pic[i], _y, maxY[i] );
}
```

Here's the code that determines limit values for the x and y coordinates for each picture slice:

```
for (i = 1; i< 65; i++)
{
  XmatrixPos = i % XSliceNum;
  YmatrixPos = Math.ceil(i / YSliceNum);
  if (XmatrixPos == 0) XmatrixPos = 8;
  if (YmatrixPos == 0) YmatrixPos = 8;
  limitX[i] = XmatrixPos * SliceWidth;  //x axis limit
  limitY[i] = YmatrixPos * SliceHeight; //y axis limit

}
```

Limit values are the coordinates where each slice needs to end up. The loop determines the matrix position of a slice by dividing its serial number—from left to right and for all rows—by the number of slices along the x and y axes.

The following description will help you dissect the program further, if you're so inclined. amazingarrays.fla is a three-frame movie, but the first frame is setup. After that, the movie loops on frames 2 and 3, which contain identical code.

On frame 1, all the arrays, as well as a number of variables, are created. Also, the program figures out where each slice belongs (the "slice matrix position," variables XmatrixPos and YmatrixPos) based on its index number (1–64). That's the second of the two preceding for loops. It's at the bottom of frame 1.

As the movie loops on frames 2 and 3, each piece must move toward its destination (in both the x and the y directions) or remain where it is, if it has already reached its destination.

Not all pieces reach their destination at the same time. The closer they get to it, the slower they move. (The x and y increment values change for each piece at different rates as it gets closer to its final x and y coordinates.) The increment value for the x and y axis for each slice at each frame is calculated separately and temporarily stored in the incX and incY variables.

Every time a piece moves in the x or the y direction, the program sets the value of the change variable to true. The change variable starts as false for each frame execution. If it remains false at the end of the frame execution, all pieces are in place. In that case, the movie stops with a stop() action and waits for the user to press the button. If change is set to true, at least one piece is still trying to get into place, and the movie should not stop playing.

19

USING THE BUILT-IN MOVIE OBJECTS

MOVIE-RELATED OBJECTS AND CLASSES

ActionScript defines a number of objects designed specifically for creating Web animation. Thirteen such objects are classified as Movie objects and listed under Objects, Movie in the Macromedia Flash MX Toolbox list (on the left side of the Actions panel). These 13 Movie objects are as follows: Accessibility, System.capabilities, Button, Color, Key, Mouse, MovieClip, Selection, Sound, Stage, System, TextField, and TextFormat.

These Flash-specific objects are not defined in the ECMA-262 standard or implemented in JavaScript. Nevertheless, they include some of the most widely used classes in ActionScript, such as MovieClip, TextField, and TextFormat.

⇨ *The TextField and TextFormat classes are covered later in this chapter, page 460.*

In addition, a number of objects that were undocumented in the initial release of Flash MX are covered later in this chapter. They include Camera, LocalConnection, Microphone, Video, and two objects (NetConnection and NetStream) associated with the Flash Communication Server.

All the classes and objects covered in this chapter are listed in Table 20.1.

Table 20.1 Movie-Related Objects

Object	Represent	Singleton or Constructor	Chapter
Accessibility(n)	Screen reader program	singleton	20
Button(n)	Onscreen buttons	constructor(*)	16, 17
Camera(n)	Video cameras (Webcams)	singleton	20
Capabilities(n)	Computer system capabilities, used with System object	singleton	20
Color	Colors	constructor	20
Key	Keystrokes	singleton	20, 16
LocalConnection(n)	Local inter-movie communication	constructor	20
Microphone(n)	Microphones	singleton	20
Mouse	Mouse cursor and clicks	singleton	20, 16
MovieClip	Movie clip	constructor(*)	17
NetConnection(n)	Connection to Flash Communication Server	constructor	20
NetStream(n)	Channel to Flash Communication Server	constructor	20
Selection	Edit text selection and focus	singleton	20
Sound	Sound/music	constructor	20
Stage(n)	The Stage	singleton	20
System(n)	Computer system	singleton	20

Object	Represent	Singleton or Constructor	Chapter
TextField(n)	Text fields	constructor	20
TextFormat(n)	Formatting for text in text field	constructor	20
Video(n)	Live video source	constructor(*)	20

(n) new in Flash MX

(*) "nonconstructive" constructor; can't create new instances with new keyword

The Accessibility **Object**

The Accessibility object represents the ability of the Flash Player to make Flash movies accessible to the visually impaired. Flash accessibility relies on screen reader software that supports Microsoft Active Accessibility (MSAA). Screen reader software interprets text and certain other screen elements and reads them out loud. Window-Eyes from GW Micro is currently the most popular screen reader that supports Active Accessibility.

The Accessibility object has only one documented property, the isActive() method, which checks whether an MSAA-compliant screen reader is active. Based on this information, you can load a more accessible interface into your movie or steer the user to a special accessible site.

You should wait a second or two after your movie has loaded to make the isActive() check. Otherwise, you may get a false return, even though a screen reader is active.

You can use the System.capabilities.hasAccessibility property to determine whether the system supports MSAA (even though the reader may not be currently active).

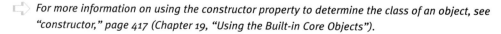 *For more details on accessibility, see Appendix A, "Making Flash Accessible," page 663.*

The Button **Class**

The Button class is new in Flash MX. There were buttons previously, but they were outside the class system. This class allows you, for instance, to programmatically determine whether an object is a button:

```
if ((typeof myObj == "object") && (myObj.constructor == Button))
    // then do something with the object
```

 For more information on using the constructor property to determine the class of an object, see "constructor," page 417 (Chapter 19, "Using the Built-in Core Objects").

Another new feature in Flash MX is instance names for buttons.

The Button constructor function is "nonconstructive." You create buttons manually or using attachMovie(). (However, the initObject argument of attachMovie() does not work with buttons.)

⇨ *The techniques for creating buttons are the same as the corresponding techniques for creating movie clips. See Chapter 17, "Unlocking the Power of Movie Clips," page 331.*

The Button class has only one method, getDepth(), which returns the depth of the button instance.

⇨ *For more details on depth numbers, see "Visual Stacking for Siblings: Depth Numbers," page 346 (Chapter 17, "Unlocking the Power of Movie Clips").*

The Button class has five properties (enabled, tabEnabled, tabIndex, trackAsMenu, and useHandCursor) and nine events (onPress, onRelease, onReleaseOutside, onRollOver, onRollOut, onDragOut, onDragOver, onKillFocus, and onSetFocus).

⇨ *Button events are covered in "Button Events," page 314 (Chapter 16, "Interaction, Events, and Sequencing"). The Button properties are the same as those described in "Flash MX's New Properties for Movie Clips," page 336 (Chapter 17, "Unlocking the Power of Movie Clips").*

The System.capabilities Object

The capabilities object is the only documented property of the System singleton. The capabilities object has 10 documented and 7 undocumented properties that reflect the capabilities of the system where the Flash Player is running. Table 20.2 lists these properties, starting with those that are documented. (Starting with language, they are undocumented.)

Table 20.2 System.capabilities Properties

Properties	Meaning	Example	Comment
hasAudio	Has audio capabilities	true	
hasMP3	Can play MP3 files	true	
hasAudioEncoder	Has an audio encoder	true	
hasVideoEncoder	Has a video encoder	true	
screenResolutionX	Gets horizontal screen resolution (pixels)	1024	
screenResolutionY	Gets vertical screen resolution (pixels)	768	
screenDPI	Gets screen dots per inch in pixels	72	
screenColor	Gets color, black & white (bw), or gray screen	color	
pixelAspectRatio	Gets the pixel aspect ratio	1	
hasAccessibility	Supports accessibility features	false	
language	Gets the language	en	English
os	Gets the operating system	Windows 2000	
input	Gets the input device	point	mouse

Properties	Meaning	Example	Comment
manufacturer	Gets the manufacturer's string	Macromedia Windows	
serverString	Gets the string to send to server	A=t&MP3=t&AE=t& VE=t&ACC=f&DEB=t& V=WIN%206%2C0%2C21%2C0& M=Macromedia Windows& R=1024x768&DP=72& COL=color&AR=1.0& I=point&OS=Windows 2000& L=en-US	
isDebugger	Is the debugger active	true	
version	Gets the version of Flash Player	WIN 6,0,21,0	

All the `System.capabilities` properties are effectively read-only. Although you may be able to set (change) them, it doesn't normally accomplish anything.

The `serverString` summarizes all the system capabilities in a single string that can be sent to a communications or application server. Note that `serverString` has been broken up into multiple lines to fit it into Table 20.2. In practice, you receive it as a single, unbroken string, and that is how it is sent to the server, as well.

The `Color` Class

Each instance of the `Color` class programmatically controls the color and transparency (alpha) of a particular movie clip or of the main movie. You can use color changes to simulate various conditions. For instance, continuously darken the color of an entire movie to simulate nightfall, or add yellow and white when a spotlight hits something. Alpha can be used for fade-ins and fade-outs, and to simulate something semi-transparent like a veil.

In Flash, color has four components: red, green, blue, and alpha (or transparency).

You can work with color in ActionScript in two basic ways:

▪ Set or get a new color, replacing any existing color and not affecting alpha. To do so, use the `setRGB()` and `getRGB()` methods.

▪ Use `setTransform()` to modify an existing color, or use `getTransform()` to determine how the color is currently transformed. Using the transform approach, you can set and get alpha in addition to color.

Either way, you first need to create a color object for a particular movie clip. Create a new color object by using the target movie clip's instance name as the single string parameter to the new statement:

```
myColor = new Color("myClip");
```

20

setRGB() **and** getRGB()

You can set the color of a movie clip using setRGB() and a six-digit hexadecimal number representing three pairs of digits. The pairs represent red, green, and blue values, respectively. Here are some examples:

```
myColor.setRGB(0xFF0000); // sets myColor to red
myColor.setRGB(0x00FF00); // sets myColor to green
myColor.setRGB(0x0000FF); // sets myColor to blue
```

⇨ *For more details on hexadecimal notation, see the following sidebar, "RGB Values and Hexadecimal (Base 16) Notation."*

RGB Values and Hexadecimal (Base 16) Notation

In hexadecimal (base 16) notation, there are 16 numerals: 0, 1, 2, 3, 4, 5, 6, 7, 8, 9, A, B, C, D, E, F. Thus, F is 15.

In base 10, the value of the digits from right to left goes up by powers of 10: 1, 10, 100, and so on. Each place is 10 times greater than the one to its right. In the hexadecimal system, the value of the digits goes up by powers of 16: 1, 16, 256, and so on. Each place is 16 times greater than the one to its right.

The RGB values associated with the Color object can be considered as three two-digit hexadecimal numbers, each one representing 256 values from 0 to 255. Thus, for instance, 0F as a two-digit hexadecimal number represents 15, and FF is 255. Precede the resulting six-digit hexadecimal number with 0x to indicate hexadecimal notation.

The result is the following format:

```
0xRRGGBB
```

Here, RR represents a two-digit hexadecimal number for red, GG represents a two-digit hexadecimal number for green, and BB represents a two-digit hexadecimal number for blue.

Web developers are familiar with hexadecimal numbers from HTML syntax like the following:

```
<BODY BGCOLOR="#00FF00">
```

In Flash, the fill-color box (indicated by a Paint Bucket icon in the Colors section of the Toolbox) gives you a handy way to determine the hexadecimal values of a variety of colors. Click on the fill-color box and then run the Eyedropper over the color swatches. As the Eyedropper passes over a color swatch, the hexadecimal value of the color appears in the input box at the top of the fill-color box.

The getRGB() method returns the currently assigned color. For instance, to compare the colors stored in two instances of the Color class, you can use getRGB().

The getRGB() method returns the color as a decimal number. To transform that into a hexadecimal number, use the toString() method of the Number class, like this:

```
hexColor = myColor.getRGB().toString(16);
```

setTransform() **and** getTransform()

The setTransform() method allows you to transform all the colors and the alpha of a given movie clip. For instance, if you have a movie clip that contains 100 other clips of various colors, you can remove a little red and add a little blue on all of them in one operation using setTransform(). In contrast, with setRGB(), you can only set them all to the same color. The setTransform() method is most useful for making changes to bitmaps, which contain many colors that you cannot address individually. The setTransform() method allows you to achieve subtle changes in tint exactly the same as those achievable via the Advanced Effect panel. (In the Property Inspector, select Advanced in the Color combo box, and then click the Settings button.)

Before you can use setTransform() and getTransform(), you need to create a *transform object*, which has eight properties corresponding to the eight input boxes on the Advanced Effect panel.

Both the Advanced Effect panel and the transform object contain four pairs of numbers, corresponding to red, green, blue, and alpha. The first number in each pair, the *transformation percentage*, is an integer from -100 to 100, which serves as a percentage multiplier for the existing color. The second number in each pair, the *offset*, is an integer from -255 to 255, which represents a color value. You take the result from the percentage multiplication and add the offset color value. Expressed in an equation, it looks like this:

```
newColor = ( oldColor × transformationPercentage ) + offset
```

This equation is, in fact, shown on each of the four lines in the Advanced Effect panel.

The transformation percentage multipliers are ra, ga, ba, and aa, for red, green, blue, and alpha, respectively.

The offset color values are rb, gb, bb, and ab, for red, green, blue, and alpha, respectively.

The following line of code creates a transform object, using an object literal:

```
myTransform = {ra:100,rb:255,ga:100,gb:255,ba:100,gb:255,aa:100,ab:255};
```

After you create a transform object, you can apply it to any instance of the Color class, as follows:

```
myColor.setTransform(myTransform);
```

The color of the movie clip associated with myColor changes.

Multiple setTransform() operations are *not* cumulative. Each transform operates on the original color values, assigned at author time or using the drawing API.

The getTransform() method returns a copy of the current transform object—the one set with the most recent setTransform().

The Key **Object**

The Key object represents user input via the keyboard. Flash MX brings a significant enhancement in this area: listeners. Listeners, available for onKeyDown and onKeyUp events, mean that you can trap all keypresses without having to check on every frame whether a key has been pressed. Instead, you can register an object to receive an event notification when a key is pressed. This is much less processor-intensive. Checking every frame via the on(keyPress) button event or the onClipEvent(keyDown) or onClipEvent(keyUp) movie clip events may give a shorter response time.

The Key object has just four methods: getAscii(), getCode(), isDown(), and isToggled().

⇨ *For an explanation of the four Key object methods, and for examples of using Key class methods with and without listeners, see "Key Events," page 317 (Chapter 16, "Interaction, Events, and Sequencing"). Just preceding the "Key Events" section in Chapter 16, the last item in the "Button Events" section is an explanation of the on(keyPress) button event, page 317.*

Eighteen constants such as Key.BACKSPACE and Key.TAB allow you to conveniently refer to commonly used keys without having to use their numeric codes. For instance:

```
if (Key.isDown(Key.UP)) {
    // then do things
}
```

For a listing of methods and constants associated with the Key object, see Table 20.3.

Table 20.3 Key Object Methods and Constants

Name	Method/ Property/ Event	Format	Description
Key.addListener	M	Key.addListener (myObject)	Registers myObject to receive notification when the onKeyDown and onKeyUp methods are invoked.
Key.getAscii	M	Key.getAscii()	Returns the ASCII value of the last key pressed.
Key.getCode	M	Key.getCode()	Returns the keycode of the last key pressed.
Key.isDown	M	Key.isDown(*charCode*)	Returns true if the user presses the key whose character code is *charCode*.
Key.isToggled	M	Key.isToggled(*charCode*)	Returns true if the key specified in *charCode* is activated. On the PC, *charCode* for Caps Lock is 20; for Num Lock, 144; and for Scroll Lock, 145. You can use Key.CAPSLOCK for Caps Lock.
Key.removeListener	M	Key.removeListener (myObject)	If myObject was previously registered with Key.addListener(), myObject is removed from the list of listeners.
Key.BACKSPACE	P	Key.BACKSPACE	Constant associated with the keycode value for the Backspace key (8).
Key.CAPSLOCK	P	Key.CAPSLOCK	Constant associated with the keycode value for the Caps Lock key (20).
Key.CONTROL	P	Key.CONTROL	Constant associated with the keycode value for the Control key (17).
Key.DELETEKEY	P	Key.DELETEKEY	Constant associated with the keycode value for the Delete key (46).

Name	Method/ Property/ Event	Format	Description
Key.DOWN	P	Key.DOWN	Constant associated with the keycode value for the Down Arrow key (40).
Key.END	P	Key.END	Constant associated with the keycode value for the End key (35).
Key.ENTER	P	Key.ENTER	Constant associated with the keycode value for the Enter key (13).
Key.ESCAPE	P	Key.ESCAPE	Constant associated with the keycode value for the Escape key (27).
Key.HOME	P	Key.HOME	Constant associated with the keycode value for the Home key (36).
Key.INSERT	P	Key.INSERT	Constant associated with the keycode value for the Insert key (45).
Key.LEFT	P	Key.LEFT	Constant associated with the keycode value for the left arrow key (37).
Key.PGDN	P	Key.PGDN	Constant associated with the keycode value for the Page Down key (34).
Key.PGUP	P	Key.PGUP	Constant associated with the keycode value for the Page Up key (33).
Key.RIGHT	P	Key.RIGHT	Constant associated with the keycode value for the right arrow key (39).
Key.SHIFT	P	Key.SHIFT	Constant associated with the keycode value for the Shift key (16).
Key.SPACE	P	Key.SPACE	Constant associated with the keycode value for the spacebar (32).
Key.TAB	P	Key.TAB	Constant associated with the keycode value for the Tab key (9).
Key.UP	P	Key.UP	Constant associated with the keycode value for the up arrow key (38).
Key.onKeyDown	E	myObject.onKeyDown = function() { };	Fires when a key is pressed.
Key.onKeyUp	E	myObject.onKeyUp = function() { };	Fires when a key is released.

If you need to determine the keycode of a particular key, you can create a keycode tester using the following code (also included on the CD as keytester.fla) :

```
_root.createTextField("myTextField", 1, 50, 50, 100, 50);
myTextField.variable = "kc";
myTextField.setNewTextFormat(new TextFormat(null,20,0x000000,true));
_root.onEnterFrame = function () {
    kc = String.fromCharCode(Key.getCode())+" : "+Key.getCode();
};
```

When you press a key, its numeric code will be displayed in the text field.

If you want to test keycodes within the authoring environment, select Control, Disable Keyboard Shortcuts while the movie is running. Disabling keyboard shortcuts allows the preceding code to pick up keys such as Backspace and Tab that are normally "trapped" by the keyboard shortcut feature.

The Mouse Object

The Mouse object represents user input via the mouse. Like the Key object, the Mouse object has been enhanced with listeners in Flash MX: onMouseMove, onMouseDown, and onMouseUp.

> For a discussion of Mouse events and listeners, see "Mouse Events," page 319 (Chapter 16, "Interaction, Events, and Sequencing"). Also see the "Button Events" section, page 314 (Chapter 16). Most button events are mouse-related.

Beyond its event-related capabilities, covered in Chapter 16, the Mouse object has two methods: show() and hide(). The hide() method allows you to hide the standard mouse cursor. Then you can substitute a custom mouse cursor.

For instance, say you want your cursor to look like a magic wand. Create a movie clip containing the magic wand graphic. Then, if the clip's instance name is magicWand, the code looks like this:

```
Mouse.hide();
_root.onEnterFrame = function () {
      magicWand._x = _root._xmouse
      magicWand._y = _root._ymouse
}
```

Then, to go back to the standard cursor, do this:

```
magicWand._visible = false;
Mouse.show();
```

The Selection Object

The Selection object controls the edit text selection and focus. Flash MX brings two enhancements that are relevant here: listeners and instance names for buttons and text fields.

> Listeners and events for the Selection object are covered in "Selection Events," page 324 (Chapter 16, "Interaction, Events, and Sequencing"). For more details on selection and focus, look in "Event Handlers and Focus," page 313; "Button Events," page 314; and "Key Events," page 317 (Chapter 16).

In addition to its event-based capabilities, the Selection object has three methods dealing with the currently selected text, or *selection span*. Each of these methods returns an index into the selected text. The index is zero-based. That is, the first position is 0, the second position is 1, and so on.

getBeginIndex() returns the index of the beginning of the selection span.

getEndIndex() returns the index of the end of the selection span.

In both cases, if the method fails to find a valid index (for example, because there is no currently focused selection span), the method returns -1.

getCaretIndex() returns the index of the blinking cursor position. If no blinking cursor is displayed, the method returns -1.

For instance, to find out if the cursor is at the end of a selected text field, you do the following:

```
if ( Selection.getCaretIndex() == Selection.getEndIndex() )
    // do something
```

The Sound Class

The Sound class represents sounds such as music, sound effects, or speech. Sound capabilities can be divided into five major categories: creating the sound object, loading sounds, getting information about sounds, controlling sounds, and using sound events.

 Sound events are introduced in Chapter 16, "Interaction, Events, and Sequencing," page 303. There are several examples of their use in this section.

Creating the Sound Object

You can create a new Sound object in two ways. One creates a sound object that will control all sounds in your movie. The other creates a sound object that controls sounds in a particular movie clip (or on the root). The following examples illustrate these two methods:

```
allSounds = new Sound(); // controls all sounds in your movie
mcSounds = new Sound("mc1"); // controls sounds in the "mc1" movie clip
```

Loading and Attaching Sounds

 You can attach sounds from the Library or load external MP3 files. A third option is to attach a sound stream using the MovieClip.attachAudio() method.

The external load capability is new in Flash MX. It works only for MP3 files. Attaching sounds from the Library results in a larger SWF and thus a longer initial delay. However, attached sounds will start to play almost immediately when you execute the Sound.start() method. Loading external sounds makes it difficult to control timing but gives you a smaller SWF.

Flash MX supports various types of compression: ADPCM, MP3, Raw, and Speech. They can also have an effect on timing. To change the compression of a sound or to see how large the sound file will be, use the Sound Properties dialog box.

 The Sound Properties dialog box is covered in "Optimizing Sounds," page 139 (Chapter 8, "Using Sound").

You load an external MP3 using the loadSound() method, as follows:

```
mySound.loadSound("techno1.mp3", false);
```

The first parameter, which is the name of the sound file to load, is in URL format. Here's an example of a full path to a local file, D:\sound\techno.mp3:

```
mySound.loadSound("file:///D||/sound/techno.mp3", 1);
```

Using a domain name:

```
mySound.loadSound("http:www.somedomain.com/somesound.mp3", 1);
```

And an IP address:

```
mySound.loadSound("http://205.188.234.33:8006", 1); // Shoutcast. Try it!
```

The second parameter to the loadSound() method determines whether the sound loads as a *streaming* sound (true or 1 in the second parameter) or an *event* sound (false or 0 in the second parameter).

A streaming sound starts playing as soon as the Flash Player has buffered enough of the sound file to play the number of seconds specified in the _soundbuftime global property—5 seconds, by default. You can change this time as follows:

```
_soundbuftime = 15; // buffer enough for 15 seconds of audio
```

An event sound doesn't start playing until it is completely loaded.

With a streaming sound, you don't have to tell it to start to play. It does so automatically. Thus, these two lines on a Timeline will start a sound playing:

```
mySound = new Sound();
mySound.loadSound ( "cantata.mp3", true ); // streaming
```

Event sounds, on the other hand, need an explicit call to the start() method to start playing. Because an event sound cannot start playing until it is fully loaded, the usual strategy is to put the start method inside an onLoad event handler. The event handler fires when the sound is fully loaded, triggering the start() method, as in this example:

```
mySound = new Sound(this);
mySound.onLoad = function () {
    this.start();
};
mySound.loadSound ( "cantata.mp3", 0 ); // event sound
```

You should define the onLoad handler *before* you load the sound.

The onLoad event will also fire if the sound fails to load. To check for failure, use the parameter that is passed to the onLoad callback function. The parameter is a Boolean, true for success and false for failure. For example:

```
mySound.onLoad = function (success) {
    if (success) {
        this.start();
    }
    else {
        // handle the error here
    }
};
```

You attach sounds from the Library using the `attachSound()` method, as follows:

```
mySound.attachSound("ByeBye.wav");
```

The single parameter for `attachSound()` is the linkage ID of the sound file in the Library. You must execute the `start()` method to start playing an attached sound.

There is a third potential source for audio material that can be associated with a sound object: a real-time audio stream, originating either from a local audio source such as a microphone or from the Flash Communication Server.

Here is a complete, working program that creates a movie clip (line 1), assigns the audio stream from the default local microphone to a variable (line 2), attaches the audio stream to the movie clip (line 3), creates a sound object that controls all sounds in the movie clip (line 4), and uses the sound object to set the volume of the sound to 0, thereby completely muting the sound (line 5) .

```
1: createEmptyMovieClip ("aud", 1);
2: inputMic = Microphone.get(); // capture audio stream
3: aud.attachAudio(inputMic); // attach audio stream to movie clip
4: mySound = new Sound("aud"); // controls all sounds in "aud " movie clip
5: mySound.setVolume (0); // set volume to zero
```

➡️ *Having trouble playing a sound in a movie loaded with MovieClip.loadMovie()? See the "Troubleshooting" section at the end of this chapter, page 484.*

Controlling Sounds

You can start and stop a sound, as well as control volume, speaker balance, and stereo separation.

When you start a sound, you can optionally specify a starting point in the sound file, in seconds. There is a second optional parameter, as well, which specifies the number of times to loop the file. The format for the `start()` method is as follows:

```
mySound.start(secondOffset, loop)
```

In the following example, the sound will start one second into the sound file and loop 10 times. The offset parameter does *not* cause a delay. The Flash Player simply skips over the designated amount of audio.

```
mySound.start(1,10); //
```

The `onSoundComplete` event will not fire until the sound has looped the specified number of times.

The `stop()` method has two formats. When executed without a parameter, the `stop()` method stops all sounds controlled by a particular sound object. For example:

```
mySound.stop(); // stops all sounds controlled by mySound
```

Which sounds are controlled by a particular sound object depends on how the sound object was created, as in these examples:

```
mySound = new Sound(); // controls all sounds in the movie
mySound.stop(); // stops all sounds in the movie
mySound = new Sound("mc1"); // controls all sounds in "mc1" movie clip
mySound.stop(); // stops all sounds in  "mc1" movie clip
```

> ⇨   *As described earlier in this chapter, in "Creating the Sound Object," page 453, a sound object may control either all sounds in your movie, or just sounds in a particular movie clip.*

You can also use a `stopAllSounds()` global function, which stops all sounds in a movie.

The `stop()` method has an optional parameter, used only with sounds attached using the `attachSound()` method. The parameter is the same linkage ID used to attach the sound originally:

```
mySound.attachSound("ByeBye");
mySound.stop("ByeBye");
```

When you use the `stop()` method with a linkage ID parameter, the sound object on which you execute the `stop()` method does not have to be the same sound object that the sound was attached to (mySound in the preceding example). However, it must be a sound object that controls the same sounds as mySound. For instance, in the following example, both `globalSound1` and `globalSound2` control all sounds in the movie. Therefore, `globalSound2` can be used to stop a sound that is attached to `globalSound1`.

```
globalSound1 = new Sound();
globalSound2 = new Sound();
globalSound1.attachSound("Techno.mp3");
globalSound2.attachSound("ByeBye");
globalSound1.start(0,2);
globalSound2.start();
globalSound2.onSoundComplete = function() {
    globalSound2.stop("Techno.mp3");
}
```

The same approach works if both sound objects control sounds in the same movie clip.

You set the volume using the `setVolume()` method, which takes as a parameter a number from 0 to 100, inclusive. The default is 100. For instance, the following sets the volume to half of full volume:

```
mySound.setVolume(50);
```

You control speaker balance, the relative loudness of each speaker, using the `setPan()` method. The `setPan()` method takes one argument, a number from `-100` to `100`, inclusive. If the parameter is negative, the amount is subtracted from the right speaker, while the left speaker remains at 100% of the maximum volume. Thus, `mySound.setPan(-50)` results in the left speaker being on at 100% of maximum, while the right speaker is on at 50% of maximum. Similarly, if the parameter is positive, the number is subtracted from the left speaker, and the right speaker remains at 100% of maximum. Thus, `mySound.setPan(25)` results in the right speaker being on at 100% of maximum, while the left speaker is on at 75% of maximum.

The maximum volume is either the default of 100 or whatever you have set via `setVolume()`. Thus, if you set the volume to 0 with a statement like `mySound.setVolume(0)`, it doesn't matter what you do with `setPan()` or `setTransform()`: No sound will be heard.

Here's an example:

```
mySound.setPan(100); // left speaker off, right speaker at 100% of max
```

With the `setPan()` method, if you are working with stereo sound, all the sound in the left speaker represents the left stereo channel, and all the sound in the right speaker represents the right stereo channel. You can control stereo separation using the `setTransform()` method.

To use this method, you first create a generic object with four properties: `ll`, `lr`, `rl`, and `rr`. Each property contains a number from 0 to 100, inclusive. The first letter in the property name indicates which speaker the property controls. The second letter indicates which stereo channel the property controls. Thus, `ll` is left speaker/left channel; `lr` is left speaker/right channel; and so on.

The following example creates a sound transform object using an object literal. This sound transform object, when applied to a sound object, will completely suppress the left speaker and put 100% of both the left and right channels in the right speaker. This is impossible to accomplish with `setPan()`, which will never put the left channel in the right speaker.

```
soundTransform = { ll : 0 , lr : 0 , rl : 100 , rr : 100 };
```

You apply the sound transform object to a sound object as follows:

```
mySound.setTransform(soundTransform);
```

Getting Information About Sounds

You can monitor the progress of loading sounds, determine when a sound has completed playing, and check speaker balance and stereo separation. You can also find out the duration of a sound and how much of the sound has already played.

 You monitor the progress of loading sounds by using the `getBytesLoaded()` method. You can combine it with the `getBytesTotal()` method to determine what percentage of the total sound has loaded:

```
percentLoaded = getBytesLoaded() / getBytesTotal() * 100;
```

You could, for instance, use the `percentLoaded` variable in the preceding example to determine the size of a progress bar in a sound preloader, providing a visual indication of progress in loading the sound.

 The read-only `duration` and `position` properties of the sound object tell you how long the sound is and how long it has been playing, respectively. Both provide a measure in milliseconds. Both are getter/setter properties, so you shouldn't use the `Object.watch()` method with either of them. In the following example, the `percentPlayed` variable could be used to provide a progress bar for playing a sound, as opposed to loading one:

```
percentPlayed = mySound.position / mySound.duration * 100;
```

The `Stage` Object

 The `Stage` object is new in Flash MX. One of its main purposes is to allow other objects to listen for the `Stage.onResize` event. The `Stage.onResize` event handler is typically used to adjust the dimensions or layout of the movie to fit the new size of the window.

> For more details on the Stage.onResize event, see "The Stage onResize Event," page 325 (Chapter 16, "Interaction, Events, and Sequencing").

The `Stage` object has five properties, two of which are read-only:

- `height`—Specifies the height in pixels (read-only).

- `width`—Specifies the width in pixels (read-only).

- `showMenu`—Determines whether the File-View-Control-Help menu bar is displayed at the top of the standalone Flash Player.

- `align`—A string property that determines how graphical content on the Stage is aligned. The eight possible values are Top Left (TL), Top (T), Top Right (TR), Left (L), Right (R), Bottom Left (BL), Bottom (B), and Bottom Right (BR).

Here's the arrangement:

```
TL  T   TR

L       R

BL  B   BR
```

For example:

```
Stage.align = "B"; // align at the bottom center
```

The ActionScript interpreter is extremely forgiving of extraneous elements in the string you provide: It simply looks for the first occurrence of one of the acceptable strings, as in this example:

```
Stage.align = "^&*&%$#@WBF"; // sets Stage.align to "B"
```

If none of the acceptable strings is present in the string you supply, Stage alignment is set to fully centered (the missing space in the middle of the others in the preceding text "diagram"), and the `Stage.align` property is set to the empty string. For example:

```
Stage.align = ""; // align fully centered
```

- `scaleMode`—Specifies the scaling mode of the Flash movie within the Stage. This string property has four legal values: `"exactFit"`, `"showAll"`, `"noBorder"`, and `"noScale"`. For instance:

```
Stage.scaleMode = "noScale";
```

In the standalone Flash Player (and in the authoring environment), the `scaleMode` property affects three characteristics of the graphics in a Flash movie: whether the graphics distort or remain proportional; whether the graphics scale when the user changes the size of the Player window; and if the graphics do scale, whether they scale to fit the larger or smaller dimension of the Player window, or both.

`"exactFit"` distorts to fill the Stage. That is, it scales to both the larger and the smaller dimension and does not crop the graphic.

`"showAll"` remains proportional and scales to prevent cropping. That is, it scales to fit the smaller dimension.

"noBorder" eliminates any "empty" border at the edges of the stage and scales to the larger dimension. Therefore, it may be cropped in the smaller dimension.

"noScale" does not scale and therefore may crop in both dimensions.

If you do not set a scaleMode value, it defaults to "showAll" in the standalone Flash Player and "noScale" in the authoring environment. In the browser, the default Stage.scaleMode is typically "showAll".

The behavior that the default scaleMode causes in the browser depends on the setting of the Scale option on the HTML tab in the Publish Settings dialog box.

Four options on the HTML tab in the Publish Settings dialog box parallel the scaleMode options. (Select File, Publish Settings, and the Scale combo box.) The option you select on the HTML tab affects only parameters in tags in the HTML file. They determine what happens if you edit the HTML file and change the original WIDTH and HEIGHT parameters in the OBJECT tag. The HTML Scale settings do *not* allow the Flash movie to adjust on-the-fly as the user changes the size of the browser window.

➭ *For more information on the Publish Settings dialog box, see Chapter 30, "Optimizing, Publishing, and Exporting Movies," page 643.*

The HTML tab setting and Stage.scaleMode do interact. There may be browser and platform (such as Windows versus Mac) dependencies. In general, if Stage.scaleMode is set to "noScale" and the HTML Scale setting is either No scale or Default (Show All), you can change the values of the WIDTH and HEIGHT parameters in the OBJECT tag of the HTML file, and the SWF will not distort to fit the new size.

Table 20.4 shows some sample settings and what happens in Internet Explorer 5.5 running under Windows if you change the values of the WIDTH and HEIGHT parameters in the OBJECT tag of the HTML file. For instance, the first row of the table tells you that, if Stage.scaleMode is exactFit and the Scale setting on the HTML tab in Publish Settings is No scale, Exact fit, or Default (Show All), the graphic will be scaled to fit both the WIDTH and HEIGHT parameters in the OBJECT tag of the HTML file, distorting the graphic if necessary. On the other hand, if the Scale setting on the HTML tab is No Border, the graphic will scale proportionally (no distortion allowed) so that it fully occupies the larger of the WIDTH and HEIGHT parameters in the OBJECT tag. For instance, if WIDTH is 50 and HEIGHT is 100, the graphic will be 100 pixels high. If the proportionately scaled width is more than 50 pixels, the graphic will be cropped in the horizontal direction.

Table 20.4   Stage.scaleMode and HTML Tab Scale Setting Interaction

Stage.scaleMode	HTML Tab "Scale" Setting	Result in IE 5.5
"exactFit"	No scale, Exact fit, or Default (Show All)	Nonproportional scaling (distort shape to fit height and width)
	No Border	Proportional scaling to larger dimension, cropping as necessary

20

Table 20.4   Continued

Stage.scaleMode	HTML Tab "Scale" Setting	Result in IE 5.5
"noScale"	Exact fit or No border	Proportional scaling to larger dimension, cropping as necessary
	No scale or Default (Show All)	No scaling
None (default)	No scale or Default (Show All)	No scaling
	Exact fit	Nonproportional scaling (distort shape to fit height and width)
	No border	Proportional scaling to larger dimension, cropping as necessary

The System Object

The System object represents the computer system. It has just one documented property: capabilities.

See "The System.capabilities Object" earlier in this chapter, page 446.

The TextField and TextFormat Classes

In Flash 5, ActionScript had a limited ability to control or monitor text fields. Text fields could only be created manually using the GUI, and almost all text field properties were set manually, as well, through the Text Options panel. Text fields were not objects and didn't have instance names.

In Flash MX, the text field has been fully integrated into the ActionScript environment. Anything that can be done with text fields manually through the GUI can now also be done using ActionScript.

To familiarize yourself with text fields and what you can do with them through the GUI, see Chapter 5, "Working with Text," page 69.

There are four possible steps to dynamically creating a text field. The first two will come into play for every text field that you create dynamically. You may or may not get to the third or fourth steps, depending on your requirements. The steps are as follows:

1. Create the text field.

2. Set one or more properties of the field.

3. Create a TextFormat object and apply it to the field.

4. Create and position a scrollbar component so that it "snaps" to the text field.

Dynamically Creating a Text Field

You create a text field dynamically using the `createTextField` method of the `MovieClip` class. The format is as follows:

```
myClip.createTextField ("myTextField",depth,x,y,width,height)
```

`myClip` is the movie clip in which you are creating the new text field. `myTextField` is the instance name of the new text field. *depth* is the depth of the text field. *x* and *y* are the x and y coordinates of the text field, measured in pixels from the registration point of `myClip`. *width* and *height* are the width and height of the text field, measured in pixels.

For instance:

```
myClip.createTextField ("myTextField",2,100,100,25,12);
```

This example creates a new, empty text field named `myTextField` that is a child of `myClip`, at a depth of 2, 100 pixels to the right of and 100 pixels down from `myClip`'s registration point. The text field is 25 pixels wide and 12 pixels high.

The newly created text field has a number of properties. For instance, Flash sets the `_x` and `_y` properties of the text field equal to the x and y parameters passed to `createTextField()`. Similarly, Flash sets the `_width` and `_height` properties of the text field equal to the `width` and `height` parameters passed to `createTextField()`. Flash also sets the `type` property to `dynamic`. All newly created text fields are dynamic unless and until you explicitly set the `type` property to `input`.

For a complete list of text field properties, methods, and events, see Table 20.5.

Table 20.5 TextField Properties, Methods, and Events

Name	Method/ Property/ Event	Format	Description
addListener	M	myTextField.addListener (myObject)	Registers myObject to receive notification of onChanged and onScroller events associated with myTextField.
getDepth	M	myTextField.getDepth()	Returns the depth of myTextField.
getFontList	M	TextField.getFontList()	Returns an array of font names. Note: TextField, *not* myTextField.
getNewTextFormat	M	myTextField.getNewTextFormat()	Returns a copy of the TextFormat object applied to new text inserted in myTextField manually or using replaceSel().
removeListener	M	myTextField.removeListener (myObject)	Removes myObject from the array of listeners associated with myTextField, that is, cancels myTextField.addListener(myObject).

20

Table 20.5 Continued

Name	Method/ Property/ Event	Format	Description
removeTextField	M	myTextField.removeTextField()	Removes myTextField, if it was created with MovieClip.createTextField().
setNewTextFormat	M	myTextField.setNewTextFormat (myTextFormat)	Sets myTextFormat as the text format object for new text inserted in myTextField manually or using replaceSel().
replaceSel	M	myTextField.replaceSel(newText)	Substitutes the newText string for currently selected text.
setTextFormat	M	myTextField.setTextFormat (myTextFormat)	Assigns myTextFormat to text that is already in myTextField.
_alpha	P	myTextField._alpha	The transparency value of myTextField, an integer from 0 to 100.
autoSize	P	myTextField.autoSize	A string specifying the anchor point for myTextField when automatically resizing it to fit text. See Table 20.6.
background	P	myTextField.background	A Boolean that shows (true) or hides (false) background fill.
backgroundColor	P	myTextField.backgroundColor	Specifies the color of the background fill. An integer, often in hexadecimal format, for example, 0xFF0000.
border	P	myTextField.border	A Boolean that specifies whether the text field has a border.
borderColor	P	myTextField.borderColor	Specifies the color of the border. An integer, often in hexadecimal format, for example, 0xFF0000.
bottomScroll	P	myTextField.bottomScroll	A read-only integer specifying the bottommost line in myTextField that is visible.
embedFonts	P	myTextField.embedFonts	A Boolean that specifies whether the text field uses embedded font outlines (true) or device fonts (false).
_focusrect	P	myTextField._focusrect	A Boolean that specifies whether a text field has a yellow rectangle around it when it has focus.
_highquality	P	TextField._highquality	References the global _highquality variable. Globally enables smoothing bitmaps and antialiasing. An integer. 0 : none. 1 : antialias, smooth bitmaps if no animation in movie (default). 2 : smooth bitmaps and antialias.

Name	Method/ Property/ Event	Format	Description
_height	P	myTextField._height	A read-write integer, the height of myTextField in pixels. Affects bounding box size only, not font size.
hscroll	P	myTextField.hscroll	An integer that specifies, in pixels, the current horizontal scroll position of myTextField.
html	P	myTextField.html	A Boolean that specifies whether myTextField contains HTML text. Must precede myTextField.htmlText.
htmlText	P	myTextField.htmlText	A string containing HTML-formatted text for myTextField.
length	P	myTextField.length	A read-only integer, the number of characters in myTextField.
maxChars	P	myTextField.maxChars	An integer. When myTextField contains this number of characters, Flash disables manual insertion of characters.
maxhscroll	P	myTextField.maxhscroll	A read-only integer value that specifies, in pixels, the maximum possible value of myTextField.hscroll, given the current text.
maxscroll	P	myTextField.maxscroll	A read-only integer value that specifies, in pixels, the maximum possible value of myTextField.scroll, given the current text.
multiline	P	myTextField.multiline	A Boolean that specifies whether myTextField can contain multiple lines.
_name	P	myTextField._name	A string, the instance name, for example, "myTextField".
_parent	P	myTextField._parent	A reference to the movie clip or button that is myTextField's parent.
password	P	myTextField.password	A Boolean that specifies whether myTextField is a password field. If it is true, Flash displays asterisks on the screen instead of input characters.

Table 20.5 Continued

Name	Method/Property/Event	Format	Description
_quality	P	TextField._quality	Global string property, specifies the rendering quality of a movie. LOW: Graphics not antialiased; bitmaps not smoothed. MEDIUM: Graphics antialiased using a 2×2 pixel grid, bitmaps not smoothed. Suitable for movies with no text. HIGH: Graphics anti-aliased using a 4×4 pixel grid, bitmaps smoothed if no animation in movie. (HIGH is the default.) BEST: Graphics antialiased using a 4×4 pixel grid, bitmaps always smoothed.
restrict	P	myTextField.restrict	A string specifying the set of characters that a user can enter into myTextField. A dash indicates a range. A caret (^) means the following characters are excluded, while preceding characters are allowed. The following example includes only lowercase letters, but excludes the lowercase letter w: myTextField.restrict = "a-z^w";
_rotation	P	myTextField._rotation	A read-write integer value that specifies the current degree of rotation of myTextField.
scroll	P	myTextField.scroll	A read-write integer value that specifies the current vertical scrolling position of myTextField, measured in lines of text.
selectable	P	myTextField.selectable	Boolean, specifies whether myTextField is selectable.
_soundbuftime	P	myTextField._soundbuftime	References the global _soundbuftime variable. Globally sets and gets the amount of time, in seconds, a sound must prebuffer before it streams. An integer, defaulting to 5.
tabEnabled	P	myTextField.tabEnabled	A Boolean that specifies myTextField is included in automatic tab ordering.
tabIndex	P	myTextField.tabIndex	Specifies the tab order of myTextField.
text	P	myTextField.text	A read-write string, the current text in the text field.

Name	Method/ Property/ Event	Format	Description
textColor	P	myTextField.textColor	A read-write integer, the color of the current text in the text field. Often in hex format, such as 0xFF0000.
textHeight	P	myTextField.textHeight	A read-only integer value that specifies the height of the actual text (not the bounding box).
textWidth	P	myTextField.textWidth	A read-only integer value that specifies the width of the actual text (not the bounding box) .
type	P	myTextField.type	A read-write string, dynamic or input, that specifies whether myTextField is an input text field or dynamic text field.
_url	P	myTextField._url	A read-only string, the URL of the SWF file that created the text field instance.
variable	P	myTextField.variable	A read-write string, the variable name associated with the text field.
_visible	P	myTextField._visible	A read-write Boolean value that determines whether myTextField is hidden (false) or visible (true).
_width	P	myTextField._width	A read-write integer, the width of myTextField in pixels. This affects only the bounding box of the text field; it does not affect the border thickness or text font size.
wordWrap	P	myTextField.wordWrap	A read-write Boolean that specifies whether the text field word-wraps.
_x	P	myTextField._x	A read-write integer, the x coordinate of myTextField.
_xmouse	P	myTextField._xmouse	A read-only integer, the x coordinate of the cursor relative to myTextField.
_xscale	P	myTextField._xscale	A read-write integer from -100 to 100, specifying the percentage for horizontally scaling myTextField.
_y	P	myTextField._y	A read-write integer, the y coordinate of myTextField.
_ymouse	P	myTextField._ymouse	A read-only integer, the y coordinate of the cursor relative to myTextField.

20

Table 20.5   Continued

Name	Method/ Property/ Event	Format	Description
_yscale	P	myTextField._yscale	A read-write integer from -100 to 100, specifying the percentage for vertically scaling myTextField.
onChanged	E	myTextField.onChanged = function (textfieldName) {}	Invoked when the text in the field is changed. See Chapter 16.
onKillFocus	E	myTextField.onKillFocus = function (newFocus) {}	Invoked when the text field loses focus. See Chapter 16.
onScroller	E	myTextField.onScroller = function (textfieldName) {}	Invoked when the scroll, maxscroll, hscroll, maxhscroll, or bottomscroll property of myTextField changes. See Chapter 16.
onSetFocus	E	myTextField.onSetFocus = function (oldFocus) {}	Invoked when the text field receives focus. See Chapter 16.

TextField.autoResize values are shown in Table 20.6.

Table 20.6   TextField.autoResize Values

Value	Single Line	Multiline
"none" or false	Do not automatically resize	Do not automatically resize
"left" or true	Expand right	Expand bottom
"center"	Expand right and left	Expand bottom
"right"	Expand left	Expand bottom

Setting Properties of the Text Field

A new text field needs to have at least one property set, and possibly several, before it becomes useful. At a minimum, you will do one or more of the following:

- Set the variable property for the text field.

   Because new text fields are automatically *dynamic* (as opposed to *input* or *static*) text fields, all you need to do is set the variable property, and the text field will immediately start displaying the value of the variable you specify.

- Set the text property for the text field.

   The text property determines what text will be displayed in the field. Both dynamic and input text fields display the text in their text properties.

- Make the field an input field by setting the type property equal to "input".

> You cannot create "static" type text fields dynamically. You can, however, use "dynamic" type text fields exactly like static text fields.

You can have both a `variable` and a `text` property associated with a single dynamic or input text field, and display the `variable` and `text` properties alternately.

Other text field properties you might want to set include the following:

- `border = true` to give the text field a border

- `multiline = true` to allow the text field to display multiple lines of text, as opposed to just a single line

- `wordWrap = true` so that lines of text that are too long for the text field will "wrap" (display on the next line down) automatically

Creating and Applying a `TextFormat` Object

The text field properties mentioned in the preceding section do not format the text. For example, they do not underline, bold, or italicize text. Nor do they set the font, size, or color of the text. To do these types of things, you can create a `TextFormat` object and apply it to the text field. `TextFormat` is a class or constructor function. Use it with the new keyword to create a `TextFormat` object, as follows:

```
myTextFormat = new TextFormat( font, size, color, bold, italic, underline, url,
➥ target, align, leftMargin, rightMargin, indent, leading);
```

All `TextFormat` parameters are optional and may be set to `null` to indicate that they are not defined. Trailing parameters (parameters that come after the last parameter you want to set) can be omitted entirely. Here's an example of creating a new `TextFormat` object, with red, bold text:

```
myTextFormat = new TextFormat(null,null,0xFF0000,true);
```

You can set `TextFormat` properties individually after creating the `TextFormat` object, as in this example:

```
myTextFormat.underline = true;
```

Though not as concise, setting properties individually is more readable.

See Table 20.7 for a listing of TextFormat properties and the only TextFormat method, getTextExtent().

Table 20.7 TextFormat Properties and Method

Name	Method/Property	Format	Description
getTextExtent	M	myTextFormat.getTextExtent(*text*)	Returns an object with two properties, `width` and `height`, that indicate the dimensions in points of the *text* string when formatted with `myTextFormat`. (Width may be inaccurate with embedded fonts.)
align	P	myTextFormat.align	A string indicating text alignment: `null`, `"left"`, `"right"`, or `"center"`.

Table 20.7 Continued

Name	Method/ Property	Format	Description
blockIndent	P	myTextFormat.blockIndent	An integer specifying, in points, an amount to indent all lines in a block of text.
bold	P	myTextFormat.bold	A Boolean indicating whether text is boldface.
bullet	P	myTextFormat.bullet	A Boolean indicating whether to format text in a bulleted list.
color	P	myTextFormat.color	An integer specifying the color of text. Often in hexadecimal format, for example, 0xFF0000.
font	P	myTextFormat.font	A string specifying the font name, for example, New Times Roman.
indent	P	myTextFormat.indent	An integer specifying, in points, the indentation from the left margin to the first character in each paragraph.
italic	P	myTextFormat.italic	A Boolean indicating whether text is italicized.
leading	P	myTextFormat.leading	An integer specifying, in points, the amount of leading (vertical space between lines).
leftMargin	P	myTextFormat.leftMargin	An integer specifying the left margin, in points.
rightMargin	P	myTextFormat.rightMargin	An integer specifying the right margin, in points.
tabStops	P	myTextFormat.tabStops	An array of positive integers specifying custom tab stops.
target	P	myTextFormat.target	Used with myTextFormat.url. A string specifying the browser window in which to display the hyperlinked page. Values match those of the HTML target attribute, for example, "_blank", "_self", "_top", "_parent".
size	P	myTextFormat.size	An integer specifying, in points, the size of the text.
underline	P	myTextFormat.underline	A Boolean indicating whether text is underlined.
url	P	myTextFormat.url	A string specifying the URL to which the text links.

You associate a new TextFormat object with a text field by using the setTextFormat method of the TextField class. For example:

```
myTextField.setTextFormat(myTextFormat);
```

To associate a new `TextFormat` object only with new text entered into a text field (for example, when a user is filling in an input field), use the `setNewTextFormat()` method of the `TextField` class, as shown in this example:

```
myTextField.setNewTextFormat(myTextFormat);
```

⇨ *Losing formatting when you load new text into a text field? See the "Troubleshooting" section at the end of this chapter, page 484.*

Text Format Tags Embedded in HTML Text

You can embed text format tags in HTML text. Embedded tags can be used in addition to, or as an alternative to, `TextFormat` objects. Embedded tags make it easy to apply an attribute to just part of the text. For instance, in sample movie htmltags.fla, which follows, the LEFTMARGIN and INDENT attributes apply to both paragraphs of HTML text, whereas the BLOCKINDENT attribute applies only to the second paragraph. Note that line 4 is one long line of code.

```
1: _root.createTextField("mytext", 1, 50, 50, 300, 100);
2: myText.html = true;
3: myText.wordwrap = true;
4: myText.htmlText = "<TEXTFORMAT LEFTMARGIN=\"12\" INDENT=\"6\">
➥<P ALIGN=\"LEFT\"><FONT FACE=\"_sans\" SIZE=\"20\" COLOR=\"#FF0000\">
➥This is the first paragraph, with no block indent.
➥</FONT></P><TEXTFORMAT BLOCKINDENT=\"30\">
➥<P ALIGN=\"LEFT\"><FONT FACE=\"_sans\" SIZE=\"20\"
➥COLOR=\"#000000\"> This is the second paragraph, with a block indent.
➥</FONT></P></TEXTFORMAT></TEXTFORMAT>";
```

Creating and Positioning a Scrollbar Component

You can dynamically create and position a scrollbar component so that it "snaps" into your text field. The following sample movie, textfield.fla, illustrates this, as well as other techniques discussed in this section.

```
 1: _root.createTextField("myTextField", 1, 50, 50, 100, 100);
 2: myTextField.border = true;
 3: myTextField.multiline = true;
 4: myTextField.wordWrap = true;
 5: myTextField.text = "When you drop a scroll bar onto a dynamic or"+
 6: "input text field on the Stage, the scroll bar automatically snaps"+
 7: "to the nearest side at the position where you place it.";
 8: _root.attachMovie("FScrollBarSymbol", "sc", 2);
 9: myTextFormat = new TextFormat(null,null,0xFF0000,true);
10: myTextField.setTextFormat(myTextFormat);
11: sc._x = 150;
12: sc._y = 50;
13: sc.setSize(101);
14: sc.setScrollTarget(myTextField);
```

⇨ *For more information on the scrollbar component, see Chapter 22, "Components," page 511.*

For the `attachMovie()` statement on line 8 to succeed, you need to have the scrollbar component in your library, with the linkage name `FScrollBarSymbol`. If you drag and drop the scrollbar component from the Components panel onto the Stage and then delete the instance from the Stage, the symbol will remain in the Library, properly linked.

Rich Media Objects: `Video`, `Microphone`, `Camera`

The `Video` class, which represents a real-time video/audio stream from a Webcam, was undocumented in the initial release of Flash MX. It will be most useful when used in combination with the Flash Communication Server MX, which is described briefly in the next section. Without a communication server, you can get only a local video stream, not one that originates at a remote location on the network.

To get the local video stream, create a new `Video` object using the top-right menu of the Library panel, and place an instance of it on the Stage. Give it an instance name in the Properties panel. If the instance name is `vid`, this code, placed on the Timeline, gets the video stream from the local default camera:

```
vid.attachVideo(Camera.get());
```

The `Camera.get()` method can be used either with a `Video` object, as in the preceding example, or with a `NetStream` object. The `NetStream` class is available only with the Flash Communication Server.

When a movie attempts to access the camera, the Flash Player displays a Privacy dialog box requiring the user to allow or deny access to the camera. The Stage must be at least 215 by 138 pixels to display the dialog box. When the user responds to the dialog box, the `Camera.onStatus()` event handler returns an information object indicating the user's response, as in the following example:

```
myCamera = Camera.get();
myVideoObject.attachVideo(myCamera);
myCamera.onStatus = function (infoMsg){
    if (infoMsg.code == "Camera.Muted")
        trace("User denied access to the camera");
    if (infoMsg.code == "Camera.Unmuted") {
        trace("User allowed access to the camera");
};
```

If the user checked the Remember check box the last time the Privacy dialog box was displayed, Flash will simply allow or deny access as appropriate, and the `onStatus()` event handler will *not* fire. To determine whether the user has denied or allowed access to the camera without using the `onStatus()` event handler, use the `muted` property of the camera object.

Tables 20.8 and 20.9 list the properties and methods, respectively, of the `Video` object.

Table 20.8 Video Properties

Property	Description
deblocking	A number that specifies the behavior for the deblocking filter applied by the video compressor when streaming video. 0 (the default) allows the video compressor to apply the deblocking filter as needed. 1 disables the deblocking filter. 2 forces the compressor to use the deblocking filter. Read-write.
smoothing	A Boolean; the default is `false`. Specifies whether video should be smoothed (interpolated) when it is scaled. The player must be in high-quality mode. Read-write.
height	Height in pixels. Read-only.
width	Width in pixels. Read-only.

The deblocking and smoothing properties of the video object configure video filters to mitigate the "blocky" appearance of highly compressed video. The deblocking filter degrades playback performance, especially on slower machines, and is usually not necessary for high-bandwidth video.

Table 20.9 Video Methods

Name	Format	Description
attachVideo	myVideoObject.attachVideo(*source* |null)	Specifies a video stream to be displayed within the boundaries of the Video object on the Stage. *source* is a NetStream object that is playing a video stream or a Camera object that is capturing a video stream. If *source* is null, the connection to the video object is dropped.
clear	myVideoObject.clear()	Clears the image currently displayed in the video object. Useful, for example, when the connection to the communication server breaks and you want to display standby information without having to hide the video object.

Tables 20.10, 20.11, and 20.12 list the methods, properties, and event handlers, respectively, of the Camera class.

Table 20.10 Camera Methods

Name	Format	Description
get	Camera.get([*index*])	Returns the video stream from the default camera or the camera specified by *index*. Returns null if no camera is available. (If more than one camera is installed, the user specifies the default camera in the Flash Player Camera Settings panel.)

20

Table 20.10 Continued

Name	Format	Description
setKeyFrameInterval	myCamera.setKeyFrameInterval (*keyframeInterval*)	An integer from 1 to 48, specifies which video frames are keyframes. All data is transmitted for keyframes, instead of only changes. *keyframeInterval* = 1 means every frame is a keyframe; 2 means every second frame is a keyframe, and so on. The default is 15. Used primarily with Flash Communication Server.
setLoopback	myCamera.setLoopback (*compressLocalStream*)	*compressLocalStream* is a Boolean that specifies whether to use a compressed video stream for a local view of what the camera is transmitting. Used primarily with Flash Communication Server.
setMode	myCamera.setMode(*width* , *height* ,*fps* [,*favorSize*])	Sets attributes of the camera capture mode, including height, width, and frames per second. *favorSize* is an optional Boolean value. To maximize frame rate at the expense of height and width, set *favorSize* to false. To favor maintaining height and width over frame rate, set *favorSize* to true.
setMotionLevel	myCamera.setMotionLevel (*sensitivity* [,*timeout*])	*sensitivity* is an integer from 0 to 100 that specifies how much motion is required to invoke Camera.onActivity(true). The default is 50. *timeout* specifies how many milliseconds must elapse without motion before Camera.onActivity(false) is invoked. The default is 2000 (2 seconds).
setQuality	myCamera.setQuality (*bandwidth*,*frameQuality*)	*bandwidth* specifies maximum bandwidth, in bytes per second, for the outgoing video stream. *frameQuality* is an integer from 0 to 100 that controls picture quality. If *bandwidth* is 0, the video stream gets bandwidth needed to maintain the *frameQuality* value. If *frameQuality* is 0, picture quality is adjusted to stay within the *bandwidth* setting.

Table 20.11 Camera Properties

Format	Description
myCamera.activityLevel	The amount of motion the camera is detecting, from 0 (none) to 100 (maximum). Read-only.
myCamera.bandwidth	The maximum amount of bandwidth the current outgoing video feed can use, in bytes. Read-only.

Format	Description
myCamera.currentFps	The rate at which the camera is capturing data, in frames per second. Read-only.
myCamera.fps	The rate at which you would like the camera to capture data, in frames per second. Read-only. Set using the setMode() method. (See Table 20.10.)
myCamera.height	The current capture height, in pixels. Read-only.
myCamera.index	The index of the camera, as reflected in the array returned by Camera.names. Read-only.
myCamera.keyFrameInterval	An integer from 1 to 48, specifies which video frames are keyframes. All data is transmitted for keyframes, instead of only changes. A value of 1 means every frame is a keyframe; 2 means every other frame is a keyframe, and so on. The default is 15. Used primarily with Flash Communication Server. Read-only.
myCamera.loopback	A read-only Boolean value that specifies whether a local view of the video stream is compressed or uncompressed.
myCamera.motionLevel	The amount of motion required to invoke Camera.onActivity(true). Read-only.
myCamera.motionTimeOut	The number of milliseconds between the time the camera stops detecting motion and the time Camera.onActivity(false) is invoked. Read-only.
myCamera.muted	A read-only Boolean value that specifies whether the user has allowed or denied access to the camera.
myCamera.name	The name of the camera as specified by the camera hardware. Read-only.
Camera.names	A class property, an array of strings containing the names of all available video capture devices, including video cards and cameras. Read-only.
myCamera.quality	A number from 1 to 100 that specifies the current level of picture quality. More compression means lower quality: 1 is lowest quality, maximum compression. 100 is highest quality, no compression. Read-only.
myCamera.width	The current capture width, in pixels. Read-only.

Table 20.12   Camera Event Handlers

Name	Format	Description
onActivity	myCamera.onActivity = function(*activity*) {}	Invoked when the camera starts or stops detecting motion. *activity* is a Boolean value set to true when the camera starts detecting motion, false when it stops.
onStatus	myCamera.onStatus = function(*infoObject*){}	Invoked when the user allows or denies access to the camera.

20

Tables 20.13, 20.14, and 20.15 list the methods, properties, and event handlers, respectively, of the Microphone class.

Table 20.13   Microphone Methods

Name	Format	Description
get	Microphone.get([*index*])	Returns a default or specified audio stream, or null if no microphone is available.
setGain	myMicrophone.setGain(*gain*)	Specifies the amount by which the microphone should boost the signal, from 0 to 100.
setRate	myMicrophone.setRate(*kHz*)	Specifies the rate at which the microphone should capture sound, in kHz.
setSilenceLevel	myMicrophone.setSilenceLevel (*level* [,*timeout*])	Specifies the sound level (from 0 to 100) required to activate the microphone. Optionally also sets *timeout*, specifying milliseconds of inactivity before Flash invokes Microphone.onActivity(false). The default value is 2000 (2 seconds).
setUseEchoSuppression	myMicrophone.setUseEchoSuppression (*suppress*)	*suppress* is a Boolean that specifies whether to use the echo suppression feature of the audio codec.

Table 20.14   Microphone Properties

Format	Description
myMicrophone.activityLevel	The amount of sound the microphone detects, from 0 to 100.
myMicrophone.gain	The amount by which the microphone boosts the signal before transmitting it, from 0 to 100. The default is 50.
myMicrophone.index	The index of the current microphone.
myMicrophone.muted	A Boolean value that specifies whether the user has allowed or denied access to the microphone.
myMicrophone.name	The name of the current sound capture device, as returned by the sound capture hardware.
Microphone.names	A class property, an array of strings containing the names of all available sound capture devices, including sound cards and microphones.
myMicrophone.rate	The sound capture rate, in kHz.

Table 20.15 Microphone Event Handlers

Name	Format	Description
onActivity	myMicrophone.onActivity = function(*activity*){ }	Invoked when the microphone starts or stops detecting sound. *activity* is a Boolean value set to true when the microphone starts detecting sound, and false when it stops.
onStatus	myMicrophone.onStatus = function(*infoObject*){}	Invoked when the user allows or denies access to the microphone. *infoObject* usage similar to that of Camera.onStatus.

Real-Time Network Connections: NetConnection and NetStream

The NetConnection and NetStream objects are associated with the Flash Communication Server MX, which enables two or more SWFs to exchange audio and/or video streams, as well as text, in real-time, over a corporate IP network or the Internet. For example, you can use Flash Communication Server MX to implement applications for videoconferencing, voice conferencing, and instant messaging.

The Flash Communication Server is intended only for real-time communication. For other types of data and content, Flash Communication Server can communicate with servers such as Macromedia ColdFusion MX Server, Macromedia JRun, or Microsoft .NET servers.

This book does not describe the Flash Communication Server in depth. This section provides an overview of how the Flash Communication Server relates to the Flash Player and the Flash MX authoring tool.

Flash Communication Server applications are implemented in two parts: the server module and the client module. The client module is an SWF running in the Flash 6 Player. Thus, you use the Flash MX authoring tool to create applications that use Flash Communication Server services. You can also use server-side scripting to add functionality to your application. In addition, Macromedia provides a NetConnection Debugger and a Communication App inspector for debugging.

To communicate with the Flash Communication Server, the Flash 6 Player first establishes a connection, represented by a NetConnection object, and then opens one or more communication channels on that connection. Each channel is called a *network stream* and is represented by a NetStream object. Each stream provides a one-way channel: It can either publish a stream to a server or play a stream coming from the server.

Table 20.16 lists client-side NetConnection methods, properties, and its single event handler.

Table 20.16   NetConnection Methods, Properties, and Event Handler

Name	Method/ Property/ Event	Format	Description
call	M	myConnection.call (*remoteMethod* , *resultObject* |null [,*param1* , ...*paramN*])	Invokes a command or method on the server.
close	M	myConnection.close()	Closes the connection with the server.
connect	M	myConnection.connect (*targetURI*,[,*param1* , ... *paramN*])	Connects to an application on the Flash Communication Server.
isConnected	P	myConnection.isConnected	A Boolean value indicating whether the Flash 6 Player is connected to the server.
uri	P	myConnection.uri	A string representing the target URI specified with NetConnection.connect().
onStatus	E	myConnection.onStatus = function(*infoObject*){ }	Invoked when a status change or error is posted for the NetConnection object. The *infoObject* has three properties: code, level, and description.

Table 20.17 lists NetStream methods, properties, and its single event handler.

Table 20.17   NetStream Methods, Properties, and Event Handler

Name	Method/ Property/ Event	Format	Description
attachAudio	M	myNetStream.attachAudio (*source*)	Publisher method; connects audio source to an outgoing stream.
attachVideo	M	myNetStream.attachVideo(*source* |null [,*snapShotMilliseconds*])	Publisher method; attaches video or a snapshot from the specified source to an outgoing stream. *source* specifies a Camera object to start capturing or null to stop capturing. *snapShotMilliseconds* specifies whether the video stream is continuous (if the *snapShotMilliseconds* parameter is omitted), a single frame (0 or any non-positive value), or a series of single frames used to create time-lapse photography (any positive value specifying the delay between captured frames).

Name	Method/ Property/ Event	Format	Description
close	M	myNetStream.close()	Stops publishing or playing on the stream, freeing the stream for another use.
pause	M	myNetStream.pause([*pauseResume*])	Subscriber method; pauses or resumes playback on a stream. *pauseResume* is an optional Boolean value specifying whether to pause (true) or resume (false). If you omit this parameter, the pause method toggles from pausing (the first time it is called on a stream) to resuming play.
play	M	myNetStream.play(*publishName* |false [,*start* [,*length* [, *flushPlaylists*]]])	Subscriber method; plays audio, video, and text from the Flash Communication Server. *publishName* is the name established using myNetStream.publish(*publishName*). *start* is an optional integer that specifies the start time in seconds and may also indicate whether the stream is live or recorded (see Table 20.18). *length* is an optional integer that specifies the duration of the playback in seconds (see Table 20.19). *flushPlaylists* is an optional Boolean value that specifies whether to flush (eliminate) any items on the current playlist and play this item immediately (true, the default) or to queue this item up and play it after existing playlist items (false) .

20

Table 20.17 Continued

Name	Method/ Property/ Event	Format	
publish	M	myNetStream.publish(*publishName* |false [,*howToPublish*])	Publisher method; sends streaming audio, video, and text from the client to the Flash Communication Server, optionally recording the stream. *howToPublish* is an optional string. If *howToPublish* is record, Flash both publishes the stream and records it to an .FLV file with the same name as the *publishName*. The file is stored in the application directory on the server, overwriting any existing file of that name. If *howToPublish* is append, Flash publishes and records but appends to any existing file instead of overwriting it. If *howToPublish* is omitted or live, Flash publishes without recording, and deletes any existing .FLV file with the same name as the *publishName* in the application directory on the server.
receiveAudio	M	myNetStream.receiveAudio(*receive*)	Subscriber method; *receive* is a Boolean that specifies whether incoming audio plays on the stream.
receiveVideo	M	myNetStream.receiveVideo (*receive* |*FPS*)	Subscriber method; *receive* is a Boolean that specifies whether incoming video will play on the stream. *FPS* specifies the frame rate of the video. Specify one or the other, not both.
seek	M	myRecordedStream.seek (*numberOfSeconds*)	Subscriber method; seeks to a position in a currently playing recorded stream.
send	M	myNetStream.send(*handlerName* [,*param1*,...,*paramN*])	Publisher method; allows the publisher to broadcast data to all subscribing clients. *handlerName* is the name of a method of the receiving NetStream object. The handler is invoked when the message is received. The parameters will be serialized and may be of any datatype.

Name	Method/ Property/ Event	Format	Description
NetStream. setBufferTime	M	myNetStream.setBufferTime (*numberOfSeconds*)	*numberOfSeconds* is an integer indicating how many seconds of data to buffer. For a published stream, Flash starts dropping frames when the buffer is full. For a subscribing stream, Flash buffers *numberOfSeconds* of data before starting to play the stream.
bufferLength	P	myNetStream.bufferLength	The number of seconds of data currently in the buffer.
bufferTime	P	myNeStream.bufferTime	The number of seconds assigned to the buffer using myNetStream.setBufferTime().
currentFps	P	myNetStream.currentFps	The current frame rate of the stream, in frames per second.
time	P	myNetStream.time	The number of seconds since a stream started playing or publishing.
onStatus	E	myNetStream.onStatus = function(*infoObject*){ }	Invoked when a status change or error is posted for the myNetStream object.

Table 20.18 The start Parameter of the NetStream.play() Method

Value	Description
-2 (the default) or any negative value other than -1	Flash looks first for a live stream and then for a recorded stream. If neither is found, it waits for a live stream.
-1	Flash looks only for a live stream. If no live stream is found, Flash waits for *length* seconds before going to the next item in the playlist. If *length* is -1, Flash waits indefinitely. (See Table 20.19 for more details on the *length* parameter.)
0 or a positive number	Flash looks for a recorded stream and starts playing it *start* seconds from the beginning of the stream. If no recorded stream is found, Flash immediately goes on to the next item in the playlist.

Table 20.19 The length Parameter of the NetStream.play() Method

Value	Description
-1 (the default) or any negative number	Flash plays a live stream continuously or an entire recorded stream.

20

Table 20.19 Continued

Value	Description
0	Flash plays the single frame that is *start* seconds from the beginning of a recorded stream (*start* must be 0 or positive).
Any positive number	Flash plays the first *length* seconds of a live or recorded stream. If the stream is less than *length* seconds, playback stops when the stream ends.

All communication between the Flash 6 Player and the Flash Communication Server uses the Real-Time Messaging Protocol (RTMP), not HTTP, which is used for communication with Web servers. RTMP provides a persistent socket connection for two-way communication.

There are five basic steps required to publish or play real-time audio and video using the Flash Communication Server. The first four steps are always similar. The fifth step differs depending on whether you are publishing or playing:

- Create a `NetConnection` object using `new NetConnection()`.

- Connect to the Flash Communication Server using `myNetConnection.connect("rtmp://serverName/appName/appInstanceName")`.

- Create a network stream over the connection using `new NetStream(connection)`.

- Attach a particular video and/or audio stream. If you are publishing, you can capture a local stream from a microphone or camera with statements such as `myNetStream.attachAudio(Microphone.get())` and `myNetStream.attachVideo(Camera.get())`. If you are playing a stream from the server, the commands are similar, but instead of `Microphone.get()` and `Camera.get()`, you use the *publish name* that was defined when the stream was published to the server.

- If you are publishing, use `myNetStream.publish(publishName)` to name this stream and send it to the Flash Communication Server. If you are playing, call `myNetStream.play(publishName)`.

The following example publishes audio and video on one stream and plays them back on another stream, using one connection (not a terribly useful feat but a quick way to demonstrate the capabilities):

```
1: myNetConnection = new NetConnection();
2: myNetConnection.connect("rtmp://mySvr.myDomain.com/App");
3: myNetStream_out = new NetStream(myNetConnection);
4: myNetStream_out.attachAudio(Microphone.get());
5: myNetStream_out.attachVideo(Camera.get());
6: myNetStream_out.publish("stock_quotes_082202");
7: myNetStream_in = new NetStream(myNetConnection);
8: myVideoObject.attachVideo(myNetStream_in);
9: myNetStream_in.play("stock_quotes_082202");
```

Note that the publisher connects the video and audio to the outgoing stream in two separate statements (lines 4 and 5). The subscriber, on the other hand, only attaches video (line 8). Audio is automatically played through the subscriber's standard audio output device. However, you can connect the audio stream to a movie clip using `MovieClip.attachAudio(myNetStream_in)`. You can then create a Sound object to control various properties of the audio stream.

 For examples using MovieClip.attachAudio(), see "Loading and Attaching Sounds," earlier in this chapter, page 453, and the sidebar "Movie Clips and Audio: The attachAudio() Method," page 363 (Chapter 17, "Unlocking the Power of Movie Clips").

The `LocalConnection` Class

The `LocalConnection` class, new and undocumented in the initial release of Flash MX, makes it possible for multiple SWFs running on the same computer to communicate. A movie can trigger an event handler in another movie, and movies can exchange arbitrary data. The local connection feature is browser-independent and thus works regardless of JavaScript support in the browser. It also works in the Flash 6 Player and in Flash projectors.

To enable a movie to communicate over a local connection, you must first create an instance of the `LocalConnection` class. You can use that one instance to communicate over any number of *connections* or virtual channels. Each connection has its own name and is a one-to-one communication channel with another movie. To send over a connection, you use the `send()` method of the local connection instance. To receive, you use the `connect()` method.

The format for the constructor function is straightforward:

```
myLocalConnection = new LocalConnection();
```

The `LocalConnection` class has four methods: `send()`, `connect()`, `close()`, and `domain()`. You use both `send()` and `connect()` whenever you use a local connection, using `send()` in SWFs that send and `connect()` in SWFs that receive. A SWF that both sends and receives uses both `send()` and `connect()`.

In addition, if the communicating movies are not in the same domain, you need to create an `allowDomain()` handler in the receiving movie to validate domains from which you are willing to receive. You can also define an `onStatus()` event handler in the sending movie, which will receive a notification of success or failure when you invoke the `send()` method. The `onStatus()` event handler is invoked when a `send()` command returns `true`. (The `send()` command returning `true` indicates that the format of the command was acceptable, but *not* that the data was actually dispatched.) The `onStatus()` event handler receives as a parameter an object with a string property named `level`. If the value of the level property is `status`, the data was dispatched successfully. If the value of the level property is `error`, the data was *not* dispatched successfully. This will occur, for instance, if there is no one "listening" on that connection.

The following code displays the connection status in a text field, along with a name identifying the SWF:

```
myName = "tictactotallyautomatic";
xLC.onStatus = function(infoObject) {
```

```
if (infoObject.level == "error") {
    _root.statusField.text = myName+" Connection xLC failed.";
}
else _root.statusField.text = myName+" Connection xLC succeeded.";
}
```

See Table 20.20 for a listing of LocalConnection methods and event handlers.

Table 20.20   LocalConnection Methods and Event Handlers

Name	Method/ Event Handler	Format	Description
send	M	myLocalConnection.send (connectionName, method[, p1... pN])	Sends data over connectionName. Returns true if the format of the command is acceptable.
connect	M	myLocalConnection.connect (connectionName)	Starts listening on connectionName.
close	M	myLocalConnection.close (connectionName)	Removes connection. Returns true if successful, false if no such connection exists.
domain	M	myLocalConnection.domain()	Returns a string containing the name of the domain of the SWF containing the LocalConnection instance. For example, macromedia.com.
allowDomain	E	myLocalConnection. allowDomain = function (senderDomain) { }	Created on the receiver, should return true if senderDomain is an acceptable sending domain.
onStatus	E	myLocalConnection.onStatus = function (infoObject) { }	Provides notification, via the infoObject.level property, of success or failure of a send() command.

The format for the send() method is as follows:

```
myLocalConnection.send(connectionName, method[, p1... pN])
```

Both *connectionName* and *method* are strings. The optional parameters supplied as *p1* through *pN* may be of any datatype. The movie that is "listening" on the connection named in *connectionName* will automatically execute the event handler named in *method*. Parameters *p1* through *pN* will be passed to the method.

Here's a send() example using a local connection instance named xLC, a connection named xmove, an event handler named move(), and a variable named num. (This example comes from the "Flash at Work" section at the end of this chapter.)

```
xLC.send("xmove", "move", num);
```

On the receiving end, the event handler method is associated with a particular connection using the connect() method. The format is simple:

```
myLocalConnection.connect(connectionName);
```

Here's an example using a local connection instance named oLC and a connection named xmove:

```
oLC.connect("xmove");
```

Receiving movies use the allowDomain() method to accept or reject connections, based on the sender's domain. The ActionScript interpreter passes the domain name to the allowDomain() event handler as a parameter. If the allowDomain() method returns true, the connection is allowed. In the following example, only connections from allowedDomain.com will be accepted:

```
xLC.allowDomain = function(senderDomain){
    return (senderDomain == "allowedDomain.com");
}
```

Senders and receivers can specify the sender's domain explicitly, as in the following examples:

```
xLC.send("flashoop.com:xmove", "move", num);
oLC.connect("flashoop.com:xmove");
```

If the connection name contains a colon, the ActionScript interpreter assumes that you have provided the domain name explicitly.

If the connection name does not contain a colon, by default it is prefixed with the domain of the movie containing the LocalConnection instance. Thus, two SWFs running in the same domain can use a connection name with no domain name, as in the following examples:

```
xLC.send("xmove", "move", num);
oLC.connect("xmove");
```

For SWFs loaded from the local hard disk, the domain is localhost. For example, the following two statements are equivalent if the sending movie was loaded from the local hard disk:

```
oLC.connect("xmove");
oLC.connect("localhost:xmove")
```

When you're loading SWFs from different domains, if you want to accept the connection without checking the domain name, take these two steps:

- Start the connection name with an underscore character. Messages will be sent with no domain name. Here are examples:

  ```
  oLC.connect("_myConnection");
  xLC.send("_myConnection ", "move", num);
  ```

- Create an allowDomain() handler for the receiver that always returns true, as in the following example:

  ```
  oLC.allowDomain = function(senderDomain){
      return true;
  };
  ```

Connections whose names begin with an underscore character will also be accepted if the actual domain is localhost, even with no allowDomain() method.

There is no built-in multicasting for local connections. Thus, for instance, if three movies must all communicate with one another, each movie will use three connections: one to "listen" on and one to talk to each of the other movies. For instance, one movie might be listening on a connection named incominga, one on incomingb, and one on incomingc. In that case, the relevant code in the first movie would look like this:

```
1: myLocalConnection = new LocalConnection();
2: myLocalConnection.connect("incominga");
3: myLocalConnection.onReceive = function(message) {
4:      // your event handler code goes here
5: }
6: function sendAll() {
7:      myLocalConnection.send("incomingb", "onReceive", _root.input.text);
8:      myLocalConnection.send("incomingc", "onReceive", _root.input.text);
9: }
```

The code in the second movie would look the same, except that it would have incomingb on line 2 and incominga on line 7. The third movie would have incomingc on line 2 and incominga on line 8.

TROUBLESHOOTING

Why can't I access the sound in my loaded movie up to a Web?

Here's a typical problem scenario: You have a movie—call it soundsInHere. The soundsInHere.fla movie has a sound file in its Library with the linkage name "ByeBye" and code on the Main Timeline that looks like this:

```
mySound = new Sound();
mySound.attachSound("ByeBye");
mySound.start();
```

When you test the soundsInHere movie on its own, the sound plays fine. But when you load the soundsInHere.swf file into another movie by using loadMovie(), the sound doesn't play.

The solution is to add the keyword this in the soundsInHere.fla file, as follows:

```
mySound = new Sound(this);
mySound.attachSound("ByeBye");
mySound.start();
```

If you publish the soundsInHere.swf file again, it should work.

This was an issue in Flash 5, and it's still an issue in Flash MX. You can find a tech note on it at www.macromedia.com/support/flash/ts/documents/attached_sound.htm

Why am I losing formatting when I load new text into a text field?

Say you've created a text field named myText, set the text property, and applied a format named myTextFormat. It works fine. When you change the text by assigning a new value to the text property, the text field reverts to its original configuration from the Property Inspector.

You need to use setNewTextFormat() in addition to setTextFormat(). This will set the format for new incoming text. You need to set it only once.

The following example shows the way to set the format. The problem, when the formatting reverts, is that you don't have a line like line 7.

```
1: _root.createTextField ("myText",2,100,100,200,20);
2: myTextFormat = new TextFormat()
3: myTextFormat.Color = 0xFF0000;
4: myTextFormat.font="verdana";
5: myText.text = "Original text";
6: myText.setTextFormat(myTextFormat);
7: myText.setNewTextFormat(myTextFormat);
8: myText.text="Here's some new text.";
```

FLASH AT WORK: TIC-TAC-TOTALLY AUTOMATIC WITH LOCALCONNECTION

The "local connection" feature, discussed in this chapter, allows two separate SWFs to communicate with one another. This opens up the possibility of writing separate programs that interact. For instance, two different programmers could create separate software "robots" to play a game. The robot whose ActionScript code implements the best strategy would tend to win.

Sample movies tictactoe_lc.fla and player_lc.fla in this chapter show how a tic-tac-toe game can be played between two SWFs over a local connection. Both movies are based on sample movie tictactoe.fla (discussed in the "Flash at Work" section of Chapter 13, "Using Operators"), which is a tic-tac-toe game played automatically within a single SWF, but still with two virtual "players," one making "x" moves and one making "o" moves. Sample movies tictactoe_lc.fla and player_lc.fla in this chapter basically split the functionality of the two players into two separate SWFs.

Tictactoe_lc.swf makes decisions about "x" moves. It also manages the display of the board and checks for a winning pattern after each move. Player_lc.swf makes decisions about "o" moves, though tictactoe_lc.swf actually carries out the moves on behalf of player_lc.swf. In both movies, a move() method associated with a local connection object is triggered when the movie receives a message over the local connection telling it what the other player's move was.

The basic flow of the action is as follows:

1. Tictactoe_lc.swf makes an "x" move and sends a message to player_lc.swf.

2. The message from tictactoe_lc.swf triggers a move() method associated with a local connection object (oLC) in player_lc.swf. This method records the "x" move locally in player_lc.swf, decides on an "o" move, and sends a message to tictactoe_lc.swf.

20

3. The message from player_lc.swf triggers a `move()` method associated with a local connection object (xLC) in tictactoe_lc.swf. This method carries out and records the "o" move, makes an "x" move, and sends a message to player_lc.swf.

Steps 2 and 3 repeat until tictactoe_lc.swf determines that someone has won or all nine squares have been filled.

Each move is based on getting a number from 0 to 8 (inclusive). The nine numbers correspond to the nine squares on the tic-tac-toe board. Both movies use identical `getFreeSquare()` functions to get this number. The choices are random, except for avoiding squares that are already filled. You could modify the `getFreeSquare()` functions so that the two players use different strategies to decide their moves.

Listing 20.1 shows the local-connection-related code from tictactoe_lc.fla.

Listing 20.1   From tictactoe_lc.fla

```
 1: xLC = new LocalConnection();
 2: xLC.move = function (num) {
 3:      j++;
 4:      if (j < 9) {
 5:          if (whoseMove) {
 6:              num = getFreeSquare();
 7:              xmoves(num);
 8:              xLC.send("xmove", "move", num);
 9:              whoseMove = !whoseMove;
10:              checkResult();
11:          }
12:          else {
13:              omoves(num);
14:              whoseMove = !whoseMove;
15:              checkResult();
16:              xLC.move();
17:          }
18:      }
19: }
20: xLC.connect("omove");
```

Line 1 creates the local connection object, xLC, that will be used for sending "x" moves from tictac-toe_lc.swf to player_lc.swf.

Lines 2–19 implement the `move()` method associated with the xLC local connection object. The `xLC.move()` method makes both "x" and "o" moves. (The message that determines which "o" move will be made comes from player_lc.swf.)

On line 2, the num parameter is supplied by player_lc.swf for "o" moves. The num parameter is not used for "x" moves because the number for each "x" move is determined on line 6.

The variable j, which is incremented on line 3 and tested on line 4, counts all moves and bypasses the statements in the `move()` method after nine moves have been made.

The whoseMove variable tested on line 5 is true when it is time for an "x" move and false when it is time for an "o" move.

Line 7 makes the "x" move.

Line 8 sends a message to player_lc.swf. Player_lc.swf will respond to this message. When the return message arrives from player_lc.swf, it will cause xLC.move() to fire, initiating an "o" move.

Line 9 changes the whoseMove variable from true to false so that when xLC.move() fires next time, the code for the "o" move (lines 13–16) will run.

Line 10 calls checkResult(), the function that checks whether the most recent move created a winning pattern. checkResult() ends the game if there is a winning pattern.

Line 13 makes an "o" move.

Line 14 changes the whoseMove variable from false to true so that when xLC.move() fires next time, the code for the "x" move (lines 6–10) will run.

Line 15, like line 10, calls checkResult().

Line 16 calls xLC.move(), triggering an "x" move. Note that no parameter is provided because none is required for an "x" move. (See the note for line 2.) Calling xLC.move() starts the entire process over again.

Line 20 uses the connect() method to prepare tictactoe_lc.swf to receive on the "omove" local connection. As a general practice, it is always best to execute a connect() method only after creating the method (xLC.move() in this case) that will handle the connection. Otherwise, you could miss a message on the connection because the handler doesn't exist yet. In this case, there is no chance of that actually happening because player_lc.swf sends messages only in response to messages initiated by tictactoe_lc.swf. Thus, there's no chance of player_lc.swf sending a message before tictactoe_lc.swf is fully prepared.

Listing 20.2 presents the local-connection-related code from player_lc.fla.

Listing 20.2   From player_lc.fla

```
 1: oLC.move = function(param) {
 2:      if (param == 10) { // game over
 3:          initArray();
 4:          _root.statusField.text = "game over";
 5:          return;
 6:      }
 7:      squares[param] = null; // record x move
 8:      num = getFreeSquare(); // get o move
 9:      squares[num] = null; // record o move
10:      oLC.send("omove", "move", num); // send o move
11: }
12: oLC.connect("xmove");   // prepare to receive on "xmove"
```

Lines 1–11 are the move handler specified in line 8 of Listing 20.1.

The two central lines in this listing are lines 10 and 12.

Line 10 sends on the omove local connection, on which tictactoe_lc.swf is prepared to receive (see line 20 in Listing 20.1).

Line 12 prepares player_lc.swf to receive on the xmove local connection, the connection on which tictactoe_lc.swf sends (on line 8 in Listing 20.1).

In addition, you see on line 2 that tictactoe_lc.swf passes the value 10 in the parameter when the game is over.

Also note on line 9 that, when a square is "taken," the value of the corresponding element in the squares array is set to null. When looking for a free square, getFreeSquare() looks for an array element that has not been set to null.

PACKAGING DATA AND FUNCTIONS USING CUSTOM OBJECTS

INTRODUCING CUSTOM OBJECTS

You create custom objects by creating a new constructor function defining a new class and then using the new keyword to create new objects belonging to that class.

> Basic techniques for creating custom objects are introduced in "Functions as Classes: Constructor Functions," page 279 (Chapter 15, "Combining Statements into Functions").

Custom objects allow you to extend the power and versatility of objects and classes to any problem domain. If built-in objects constitute OOP basic driver's ed, custom objects allow you to build on those skills to drive to work, to the store, or on vacation to the Grand Canyon. They allow you to use OOP to its full capability.

Using custom objects brings up a number of issues that usually don't arise when you're just using built-in objects. One such issue is having to make a decision about the level at which local properties should reside.

POSITIONING LOCAL PROPERTIES IN THE INHERITANCE HIERARCHY

A constructor function can endow the instances that it creates with both local and shared properties. For instance, the following Bird constructor function gives a local makingNoise property and a shared move() method to each of its instances. Each instance needs its own copy of the makingNoise property to indicate whether it is making noise or not at a given moment.

```
function Bird ( )  {
    this.makingNoise = false; // local "makingNoise" property
}
Bird.prototype.move = function () { }; // shared move() method
myBird = new Bird();
myBird.hasOwnProperty("makingNoise"); // true
```

The new operator, by the process described in Chapter 15, takes care of linking myBird to the shared move() method in the Bird.prototype, and of creating the local makingNoise property in the myBird instance. The makingNoise property is always set to false when a new instance is created.

If you don't always want to set the makingNoise property to false, you can pass the constructor function an argument to use as a value for the makingNoise property. The following example sets the myBird.makingNoise property to true:

```
function Bird (makingNoise)  {
    this.makingNoise = makingNoise; // local "makingNoise" property
}
Bird.prototype.move = function () { }; // shared move() method
myBird = new Bird(true);
myBird.hasOwnProperty("makingNoise"); // true
```

When you create multiclass inheritance hierarchies using the new operator, shared propertie still remain in the superclass `prototype` object. Local properties are created in the subclass `prototype` object. In other words, the subclass `prototype` object effectively becomes an instance of the superclass. Continuing the previous example:

```
function Raptor ( )  { }
Raptor.prototype = new Bird(false);
Raptor.prototype.hasOwnProperty("makingNoise"); // true
```

From this point on, `makingNoise` will be a shared property because it is in a `prototype` object. In this case, having `makingNoise` as a shared property doesn't work. You want to be able to determine whether each individual bird is making noise or is silent. You want every instance at the lowest level of the hierarchy to have its own copy of the `makingNoise` property.

You can accomplish this goal by inserting a `super` statement into the `Raptor` constructor function.

> The super operator is covered in more detail in *"Accessing the Superclass Using super," later in this chapter, page 497.*

You also need to add an argument to the `Raptor` constructor function, as in the following example, so that the lowest-level instances can set the value of the `makingNoise` property. Assuming that instances of `Raptor` represent the lowest level in the hierarchy, you will have accomplished your goal.

```
function Raptor (makingNoise)  {
    super(makingNoise);
}
Raptor.prototype = new Bird(false);
Raptor.prototype.hasOwnProperty("makingNoise"); // not useful, but true
myBird = new Raptor(true);
myBird.hasOwnProperty("makingNoise"); // true and useful
```

If `Raptor` has child classes, you can modify their constructor functions in the same way you modified the `Raptor` constructor function.

The following sample movie, newbird.fla on the CD, creates a `Bird`-`Raptor`-`Eagle`-`myBird` hierarchy, in which `myBird` has a `makingNoise` property equal to `true`, even though all the shared `makingNoise` properties up the line are `false`. The shared properties in `Raptor.prototype` and `Eagle.prototype` are probably useless to you, so you can delete them.

```
function Bird (makingNoise)  {
    this.makingNoise = makingNoise; // local "makingNoise" property
}
Bird.prototype.move = function () { }; // shared move() method
function Raptor (makingNoise)  {
    super(makingNoise);
}
Raptor.prototype = new Bird(false);
function Eagle (makingNoise)  {
    super(makingNoise);
}
```

```
Eagle.prototype = new Raptor(false);
myBird = new Eagle(true) ;
```

NEW "ORPHANS" THE EXISTING SUBCLASS PROTOTYPE

The new operator has a limitation that you should be aware of: If the subclass has an existing prototype object, it gets left behind when the subclass is linked to the new superclass.

What does "gets left behind" mean in this context?

The prototype object is a property. As such, it has two parts: a property name and a value. The property name represents a pointer to the value. The value itself is the object. Take away the pointer and the object is nameless, and therefore cannot be referenced or used—at least, not by that name. You can have two pointers to the same object. Then you can take away one pointer and still use the other. If all pointers to an object are destroyed, the object becomes totally useless. Then Macromedia Flash's "garbage collection" function should come along and reclaim the memory it was using, erasing the last vestiges of it.

In the process of linking it to the superclass, the subclass prototype property name is repointed at a new object. The property has the same name as before (*prototype*), but it no longer points to the same thing. Therefore, the class is cut off from its former prototype object.

For example, suppose you want to substitute a new top-level class in the Bird-Raptor-Eagle-BaldEagle hierarchy from Chapter 15. You want the new hierarchy to be Predator-Raptor-Eagle-BaldEagle. Could you accomplish this as follows?

```
function Predator () {
}
Raptor.prototype = new Predator();
```

No! But why not? This approach looks reasonable. You've linked Raptor to Predator, and you haven't changed anything below Raptor in the inheritance hierarchy. Will this give you Predator-Raptor-Eagle-BaldEagle? If so, a member of the BaldEagle class, baldy1, would no longer have access to properties, such as movement:"fly", in the Bird.prototype.

Almost the opposite happens. Instead of cutting Bird out of the inheritance chain, you cut out Raptor. Here's how it works. (This process is a bit involved. Figure 21.1 should help. In Figure 21.1, the arrows show the path the ActionScript interpreter uses to search for properties. The arrows serve the same function as the __proto__ property in ActionScript: They point to the prototype of the constructor function.)

The interpreter creates a new Raptor.prototype object and links it to Predator.prototype via the new Raptor.prototype.__proto__ property.

➡️ *See the sidebar "The __proto__ Property," page 493, in this chapter, for an explanation of the __proto__ property.*

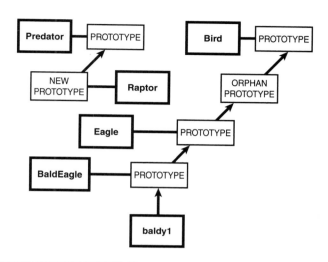

Figure 21.1
Arrows show the path the ActionScript interpreter uses to search for properties. Like __proto__, they point to class prototype.

The __proto__ Property

Every object that is created with the new keyword gets a __proto__ property (notice the double under-scores on each side). This property is normally hidden: For instance, it does not normally show up in a for-in loop. Nevertheless, the __proto__ property is the key to inheritance.

As part of the process of creating a new object, the ActionScript interpreter sets the __proto__ property to point to the prototype object of the constructor function. For instance, as part of the process of creating baldy1, the ActionScript interpreter sets the baldy1.__proto__ property to point to the prototype object of the BaldEagle constructor function. Thus, these two lines refer to the same object:

```
baldy1.__proto__
BaldEagle.prototype
```

The ActionScript interpreter looks in the prototype object of the constructor function when it can't find a property in the object itself. How does the interpreter make the jump from the object (baldy1) to the prototype object of the constructor (BaldEagle.prototype)? The baldy1.__proto__ property points the way.

You can subsequently "repoint" the __proto__ property to refer to a different object, if you want to. The interpreter will look wherever the __proto__ property points.

There is also a BaldEagle.prototype.__proto__. Just as the baldy1.__proto__ property tells the ActionScript interpreter where to look if it can't find a property in baldy1, the BaldEagle.prototype.__proto__ property points the way to the next prototype object to be checked, if the ActionScript interpreter doesn't find the property in BaldEagle.prototype.

So far, so good. However, `Eagle.prototype.__proto__` continues to point to the *former* `Raptor.prototype` object, which in turn continues to point to `Bird.prototype`. The inheritance chain remains unchanged, except for the following:

- Changes in `Raptor.prototype` do not affect `Eagle` (or `BaldEagle`) because `Eagle.prototype.__proto__` does not point to the new `Raptor.prototype`.

- Changes in `Bird.prototype` do not affect `Raptor` because the new `Raptor.prototype.__proto__` points to `Predator.prototype`.

In other words, `Raptor` and the new `Raptor.prototype` are completely disconnected from their former inheritance chain. The former `Raptor.prototype` object, now referenced only by `Eagle.prototype.__proto__`, remains in the chain. A member of the `BaldEagle` class, `baldy1`, sees no change whatsoever.

If the ActionScript interpreter looked for `prototype` objects as it went up the inheritance chain, linking `Raptor` to `Predator` would have accomplished the intended goal. The `Bird` constructor and "the object formerly known as `Raptor.prototype`" would be out of the inheritance chain.

But the interpreter doesn't look for `prototype` objects. It goes wherever `__proto__` points.

After you attach `Raptor` to `Predator`, if you want to push ahead and achieve the desired `Predator-Raptor-Eagle-BaldEagle` hierarchy using the new operator, you have to reattach `Eagle` to `Raptor` and `BaldEagle` to `Eagle`. Finally, you need to re-create `baldy1`, which otherwise continues to use the old inheritance chain, blithely unaware that anything has changed! It continues to reference the whole chain of former `prototype` objects formerly associated with `BaldEagle`, `Eagle`, `Raptor`, and `Bird`.

Sample movie new1.fla, which follows, shows the complete process. A cName property has been assigned to the initial `Predator` prototype for testing purposes.

```
function Predator () {
}
Predator.prototype.cName = "Predator";
Raptor.prototype = new Predator();
Eagle.prototype = new Raptor();
BaldEagle.prototype = new Eagle();
baldy1 = new BaldEagle();
trace (baldy1.cName); // "Predator"
```

You can also delete the `Bird` class, if you're not going to be using it anymore.

Following these steps gives you the hierarchy you want. You have paid a heavy price, however: destroying and re-creating all your prototypes and instances.

By "repointing" the __proto__ property, you can simply take `Bird` out of the inheritance chain and substitute `Predator`, without disturbing anything else.

➡ *Repointing the __proto__ property is discussed in "Creating Class Hierarchies Using the __proto__ Property," later in this chapter, page 502.*

Creating inheritance chains by directly manipulating the __proto__ property is not Macromedia's recommended practice. Nor is __proto__ defined in ECMA-262.

However, __proto__ is a documented property in ActionScript and is *not* deprecated. Some programmers prefer it, because in cases like the one just illustrated, it is more efficient and less destructive than the new operator.

OVERRIDING INHERITED PROPERTIES

The Bird-Raptor-Eagle-BaldEagle inheritance chain in Chapter 15 is just a skeleton because the bottom three classes don't do anything useful. One thing a subclass might do is add a new property. For instance, because raptors are birds of prey, the Raptor class might add a prey property, possibly an array of items on the Raptor menu, like this:

```
Raptor.prototype.prey = ["mice", "rabbits", "fish"];
```

If the subclass defines a property, and the parent class already has a property of the same name, the subclass property "overrides" the parent property. When you reference a property in an object within the inheritance chain, the ActionScript interpreter starts at the bottom of the inheritance chain and searches up to the top, looking for a property of that name. As soon as it finds a property with the name it's looking for, it stops. If a subclass has a property with the same name as a property in a superclass, the interpreter will never find the superclass property.

For instance, say you create a Bird class with a move() method, in which you put all the code necessary to make a bird fly:

```
function Bird () { }  // Bird constructor
Bird.prototype.move = function () {
    // statements to make the bird fly
    trace("fly"); // put this statement in for testing
};
```

Now you find that your program needs to include an auk. The auk, also called the "boreal penguin," is an almost featherless bird incapable of flying. Therefore, the standard move() method of the Bird class does not work for the auk. To accommodate this odd fellow in your system, you can create a new class with its own move() method, which will override the move() method of the Bird class:

```
1: function Auk ( ) { }   // Auk  constructor
2: Auk.prototype = new Bird(); // Auk inherits from Bird
3: auk1 = new Auk(); // instantiate an Auk
4: auk1.move(); // displays "fly" - but this isn't what we want
5: Auk.prototype.move = function () {
6:       // statements to make auk waddle
7:       trace ("waddle");  // for testing
8: }
9: auk1.move(); // displays "waddle" - that's better!
```

(Sample movie auk1.fla on the CD contains this test code.)

21

Note that you have to set up the inheritance from Bird (line 2) before you override (lines 5–8). If you created the Auk.prototype.move() method first and then set Auk.prototype = new Bird(), the new operator would repoint the existing Auk.prototype property to a new object in the Bird class, leaving the existing method stranded in an object that is no longer pointed to by Auk.prototype. Auk.prototype would end up with the move() method from the Bird class.

Frustrated trying to override get/set methods (methods set up via an addProperty() statement)? See the "Troubleshooting" section at the end of this chapter, page 509.

Overriding in a subclass (Auk) has no effect on the superclass (Bird) or any other classes that inherit from the superclass. The move() method remains intact in the Bird class. If you want to change the move() method in the Bird class, you need to *overwrite* it, not just *override* it.

Overwriting is discussed in "Overwriting Inherited Properties," later in this chapter, page 497.

Overriding Properties in Individual Instances

You can also override a property in just one instance, as opposed to a whole class. For instance, if auk1 happens to be swimming at the moment, you can define a local move() method for the auk1 instance, like this:

```
auk1.move = function () {
    // statements to make auk paddle
    trace ("paddle");  // for testing
};
auk1.move(); // displays "paddle"
```

When you do this, however, the auk1 instance will not be able to access the shared move() method as long as the instance property exists. If you delete the instance property, auk1 can access the shared property once again:

```
delete auk1.move;
auk1.move(); // displays "waddle" once again
```

A single-instance override may be convenient if almost all members of a class have a particular value for a property, while only one or two have a different value, or if you just want to temporarily change a behavior or value.

No Overriding for Global Objects

You can use global objects as is, and you can add properties to them. However, you cannot change the values of the built-in properties of global objects. For example, try to change the value of Math.PI, and you'll discover you can't do it:

```
Math.PI = 12;
trace(Math.PI);  // still 3.14159265358979
```

This is true when the property is a method, as well. For instance, this example tries to make the `Math.sqrt()` method multiply by 2 instead of taking the square root. If the change worked, `Math.sqrt(4)` would yield 8. As you can see, it doesn't work:

```
trace(Math.sqrt(4)); // "2" -- square root of 4 is 2
Math.sqrt = function (arg) {return arg * 2;} // multiply by 2 instead
trace(Math.sqrt(4)); // still "2", still took square root
```

It would seem that you are largely stuck with global objects. However, for a workaround, see the sidebar "Hijacking the `Math` Object," later in this chapter.

Overwriting Inherited Properties

The following two statements demonstrate the difference between overriding and overwriting. The first statement changes the `move()` method only for members of the Auk class. The second changes it for the `Bird` class and all its descendants—Raptor, Eagle, BaldEagle, and Auk. (Statements implementing the functions would go inside the curly braces.)

```
Auk.prototype.move = function () { }; // override in the subclass
Bird.prototype.move = function () { }; // overwrite in the superclass
```

ACCESSING THE SUPERCLASS USING SUPER

The following two situations commonly arise when you're working with inheritance hierarchies:

- You want to create a subclass with a method that overrides a superclass method. However, you occasionally want to access the superclass behavior, or you want your subclass method to combine the superclass behavior with its own added behavior.

- You have a parent class with instances and a subclass with instances. For example, you have a `Bird` class with instances and an Auk class with instances. The parent class gives its instances a local property. You want instances of the subclass to have a local copy of that property, too.

The `super` operator allows you to handle both of these situations. The `super` operator works only within a function. It has the special characteristic of referring to the superclass.

Accessing a Superclass Method with super

Say that, occasionally, you want your auk to make a supreme effort and fly. This means that you need to access the `move()` method of the parent `Bird` class. You can use the `super` operator to access the method in the parent, as shown here on line 3:

```
1: Auk.prototype.move = function (supremeEffort) {
2:      if (supremeEffort)
3:          super.move();
4:      else trace ("waddle"); // statements to make auk waddle go here
5: };
6: auk1.move(true); // executes Bird.prototype.move(), displays "fly"
7: auk1.move(); // displays "waddle"
```

21

Any value of the `supremeEffort` argument that resolves to `true` causes this version of `Auk.prototype.move` to execute the `move()` method of the superclass. This happens on line 6. If the `supremeEffort` argument does not resolve to `true`, `Auk.prototype.move` executes the `else` statement. This happens on line 7.

The `super` operator allows you to access a method in the superclass, even though you have overridden it in the subclass. You can use this ability to add something to the parent method, if you want. For instance, you can set things up as follows to cause the auk to waddle (the subclass-specific behavior) and then fly (the shared parent behavior):

```
Auk.prototype.move = function () {
    trace ("waddle"); // statements to make auk waddle
    super.move();
};
auk1.move(); // displays "waddle" and "fly"
```

This technique can come in very handy if you have complex functionality in the parent method and just want to add a little something in the subclass.

Getting Superclass Local Properties into Subclass Instances

The following `Bird` constructor function gives a local `singing` property and a shared `move()` method to each of its instances. Each instance needs its own copy of the `singing` property to indicate whether it is singing or not at a given moment. It is typical that a property indicating a state cannot be shared, whereas a method, which encapsulates a behavior, can easily be shared.

```
function Bird ( ) {
    this.singing = false; // local "singing" property
}
Bird.prototype.move = function () { }; // shared move() method
myBird = new Bird();
myBird.hasOwnProperty("singing"); // true
```

Now, you want to create an Auk constructor function, and you want each instance of the Auk class to have its own local `singing` property. You could, of course, replicate the code `this.singing = false;` from the `Bird` constructor in the `Auk` constructor. However, there is no need for this duplication of effort and code. Instead, you can use `super()` to access the superclass constructor from the subclass constructor, as follows:

```
function Auk () {
    super();
}
Auk.prototype = new Bird();
myAuk = new Auk();
myAuk.hasOwnProperty("singing"); // true
```

➡ *You can find more examples of super, including one use in a multilevel class hierarchy, in "Positioning Local Properties in the Inheritance Hierarchy," earlier in this chapter, page 490.*

⇨ *Getting unwanted properties from the superclass when using super()? See the "Troubleshooting" section at the end of this chapter, page 509.*

WORKING WITH THE CONSTRUCTOR PROPERTY

Every primitive datum and every object gets a `constructor` property when it is created, as part of its endowment from `Object`.

⇨ *The constructor property is introduced in "The Object Class," page 415 (Chapter 19, "Using the Built-in Core Objects").*

The `constructor` property is a reference to the class constructor function. Unlike `super`, however, the `constructor` property is available whenever the object is available, not just within methods and constructor functions.

The `constructor` property is undocumented in ActionScript, but it is defined in the ECMA-262 standard.

The following example shows how you can use the `constructor` property to execute the constructor function:

```
function MyFunc() {
    trace("running MyFunc");
}
myObj1 = new MyFunc();
myObj1.constructor(); // displays "running MyFunc"
```

The `prototype` object, being an object, also has a `constructor` property. When you first create a constructor function (or any other function), its `constructor` property points to the function itself, as you can see in this example:

```
MyFunc.prototype.constructor(); // displays "running MyFunc"
```

However, when you subclass a constructor function, you create a new `prototype` object for the subclass using the superclass constructor function. It is natural that the `constructor` property of the subclass `prototype` will now refer to the function that created it. For example:

```
function Bird () {}
function Raptor () {}
Raptor.prototype = new Bird();
myRaptor = new Raptor();
trace(Raptor.prototype.constructor == Bird); // true
trace(myRaptor.constructor == Raptor); //  true
```

Creating Object Siblings Using the constructor Property

The `constructor` property allows class members to create siblings for themselves, as in this example:

```
function Auk() {
    this.localProp = "local property";
```

21

```
}
Auk.prototype.sharedProp = "shared property";
sammy = new Auk();
susie = new sammy.constructor(); // sammy makes himself a sister, susie
```

The last line of the preceding example is the same as saying

```
susie = new Auk();
```

The form `sammy.constructor()` allows you to run a constructor given only the name of an object in the class. You don't have to know the name of the class itself. Thus, you can write a function in which an object creates other objects in its class, without having to hard-code the name of the class into the function. If you then pass the name of the object to the function in an argument, you have a generic "sibling creation" function:

```
function makeSib (objName) {
    sib = new objName.constructor();
    return sib;
}
susie = makeSib(sammy); // equivalent of susie = new sammy.constructor();
```

Using `constructor` to Convert Primitive Data Types into Objects

You can also use the `constructor` property to turn primitive data types into objects. Here's a function that does that:

```
function makeObj(primitive) {
    obj = new primitive.constructor(primitive);
    return obj;
}
```

It may seem strange that this approach works because primitives aren't objects, so you don't normally think of them as having properties such as `constructor`. However, the ActionScript interpreter thinks differently:

```
name1 = "Bob Smith";
trace(typeof name1); // "string" – a string primitive
trace(typeof name1.constructor); // "function"
```

The ActionScript interpreter knows that the `constructor` property is a function. If the string didn't have a constructor function, the `typeof` operator would yield `"undefined"`. So, under the covers, there is a little bit of "object-ness" even to primitives! In fact, primitives have a number of properties in addition to the constructor property:

```
trace(typeof name1.valueOf); // "function"
trace(typeof name1.toString); // "function"
trace(typeof name1.__proto__); // "object"
trace(typeof name1.length); // "number"
trace(name1.length); // 9
```

You may recognize `valueOf()` and `toString()` as properties inherited from `Object`. So it's not really surprising that you can turn primitives into objects.

But why would you want to?

Suppose you bring in a list of names from a text file and assign them to variables, as in the previous "Bob Smith" example. Now you want to add a property, such as a phone number:

```
name1.phone = "555-555-5555";
trace(name1.phone); // displays nothing
trace(typeof name1.phone); // "undefined"
```

It doesn't work. You can't add properties to primitives.

No problem. Use `makeObj()` to turn the string primitive into a string object:

```
name1 = makeObj(name1);
trace(typeof name1); // "object"
```

So far, so good. You've converted a string into an object. Now try adding that phone number:

```
name1.phone = "555-555-5555";
trace(typeof name1.phone); // "string"
trace(name1); // "Bob Smith"
trace(name1.phone); // "555-555-5555"
```

It worked!

Using a Constructor Function for "Safe" Storage

Functions are objects and can have properties. A constructor function can be a good place to store information about the class that does not need to be a property of class instances. For example, you might store the class name in a constructor function:

```
function Auk ( ) {
}
auk1 = new Auk();
Auk.cName = "Auk"; // store class name in property
```

Now you can use the `constructor` property to create a generic function to retrieve the value of the property:

```
function getObjectType (obj) {
    return obj.constructor.cName;
}
trace(getObjectType (auk1)); // "Auk"
```

Why would you want to store the function name in a property of the function? After all, you can store the function name in the `prototype` object, and you don't need to use the `constructor` property to retrieve it:

```
Auk.prototype.cName = "Auk";
trace(auk1.cName); // "Auk"
```

The prototype does offer more straightforward access and is probably the better choice in most cases. However, there is an advantage to using a function property for storage. Remember that the Auk prototype will be "orphaned" if you link Auk into an inheritance chain using the new operator. For example:

```
// Auk constructor function
function Auk() {}
// Bird constructor function
function Bird ( ) {}
Auk.prototype.cName = "Auk";
Auk.prototype = new Bird();
auk2 = new Auk();
trace(auk2.cName); // undefined
trace(typeof auk2.cName); // "undefined"
```

The old Auk.prototype.cName:Auk is part of the orphaned prototype object. The new Auk.prototype is empty; it doesn't have a cName property in it.

On the other hand, if you store the class name in a property of the constructor function, you don't have to worry if you use the new operator and thus orphan the class prototype: You can still access the class name in the class itself.

You can make getObjectType work with a global object, as follows:

```
Math.constructor.cName = "Math"; // store name in cName property
trace(getObjectType (Math)); // "Math"
```

Proving that the Math object is of type "Math" may not seem terribly useful. However, it could be useful to have a getObjectType function that "covers all the bases," giving a clear-cut return no matter what you throw at it. Supporting the global objects moves you closer to that goal.

CREATING CLASS HIERARCHIES USING THE __PROTO__ PROPERTY

You can create class hierarchies by pointing the prototype.__proto__ property of the subclass to the prototype property of the superclass. For example, the following line makes Raptor a subclass of Predator:

```
Raptor.prototype.__proto__ = Predator.prototype;
```

In fact, this single step accomplishes the essential task that proved so difficult earlier in this chapter: changing the Bird-Raptor-Eagle-BaldEagle hierarchy to Predator-Raptor-Eagle-BaldEagle.

⇨ *The problem of changing the Bird-Raptor-Eagle-BaldEagle hierarchy was introduced in "new 'Orphans' the Existing Subclass prototype," earlier in this chapter, page 492.*

Figure 21.2 illustrates the process of setting inheritance by repointing the __proto__ property.

21

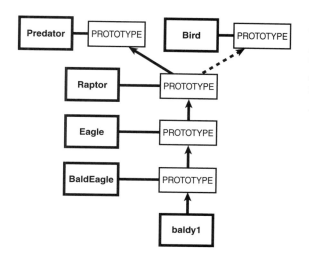

Figure 21.2
The arrows show the path the ActionScript interpreter searches for properties. At top, the dotted arrow is the former __proto__ link. The solid arrow is the new __proto__ link.

You can delete the Bird class if you're not going to be using it anymore.

The __proto__-based approach does not use the new operator. It does not create a new Raptor.prototype object. Nothing in the existing Raptor.prototype object changes, except that the __proto__ property is disconnected from Bird and attached to Predator.

You could also have created the entire original chain using __proto__. Assuming the constructor functions already exist, the code would look like this:

```
Raptor.prototype.__proto__ = Bird.prototype;
Eagle.prototype.__proto__ = Raptor.prototype;
BaldEagle.prototype.__proto__ = Eagle.prototype;
```

The result is the same Bird-Raptor-Eagle-BaldEagle hierarchy that was created in Chapter 15 using the new operator.

If you create inheritance using __proto__, the biggest issue to be aware of is getting desired local properties from superclasses into your bottom-level instances.

⇨ *The process of getting local properties from superclasses into instances is discussed in "Positioning Local Properties in the Inheritance Hierarchy," earlier in this chapter, page 490.*

Just repointing __proto__ doesn't get you any local properties at all because it doesn't run any constructor functions. Also, if all you do is repoint __proto__, the super operator will not work. You can use either of the following approaches to work around this problem:

- Use the constructor property to run constructor functions.

- Create a __constructor__ property (notice the double underscores on each side) in the prototype of the subclass and then use super as usual.

21

Whichever approach you use, you can make life a little easier for yourself by writing a function to contain the inheritance-setting code. In Java, the keyword extends is used in this context. You can use any function name in ActionScript, but extends will be widely understood. (extends is also reserved by ActionScript for possible use in the future. To avoid a future conflict, you could use myExtends.) Because both approaches are based on __proto__, the essence of your function will be as follows:

```
Function.prototype.extends = function (superclass)
{
     this.prototype.__proto__ = superclass.prototype;
}
```

Using the constructor Property to Run Constructor Functions

When you use the constructor property to run constructor functions, you can just use the standard, plain-vanilla extends() function. After you run it, you know that subclass.prototype.__proto__ = superclass.prototype—because that's what the extends() function does.

The goal then is to run the superclass constructor given only the subclass. Here's the reasoning that shows how you can do this:

- Because you haven't used the new operator to create inheritance for the superclass, the super-class prototype.constructor property should still point to the superclass constructor function itself.

- Because the subclass prototype.__proto__ points to the superclass prototype, an expression of the form subclass.prototype.__proto__.constructor points to the superclass prototype.constructor. As just noted, that means the superclass constructor function itself.

- Therefore, to execute the superclass constructor, you can use a statement of the form subclass.prototype.__proto__.constructor().

That's the basic approach. You can use it to build a mySuper() function that substitutes for the super() functionality. The essence of the function is as follows:

```
mySuper() {
     subclass.prototype.__proto__.constructor();
}
```

In this function, *subclass* is a pseudocode stand-in for the subclass. Because the mySuper() function will be called from the subclass constructor (Raptor in this case), you can use arguments.caller for the subclass. Now the function looks like this:

```
mySuper() {
     arguments.caller.prototype.__proto__.constructor();
}
```

You also want to be able to pass arguments to the superclass constructor so that your lowest-level instances can set the values of their local properties. The mySuper() function has not defined any arguments. Implicitly, however, all the arguments passed to any function are contained in the arguments object. Use that fact, plus the Function.apply() method, to produce a super() equivalent that looks like this:

```
mySuper() { // based on Robert Penner's superCon()
  arguments.caller.prototype.__proto__.constructor.apply (this,arguments);
}
```

> ➡️ *The arguments object and Function.apply() are both covered in Chapter 15, "Combining Statements into Functions," page 267.*

One last question is where to define this function. A number of different options could work. In sample movie newrap1.fla, which follows, the function has been placed in the Raptor.prototype.

```
 1: Function.prototype.extends = function (superclass)
 2: {
 3:  this.prototype.__proto__ = superclass.prototype;
 4: }
 5: function Bird (singing)  {
 6:  this.singing = singing; // local "singing" property
 7: }
 8: Bird.prototype.move = function () { }; // shared move() method
 9: Raptor.prototype.mySuper = function() {
10:   arguments.caller.prototype.__proto__.constructor.apply (this, arguments);
11: };
12: function Raptor () {
13:  this.mySuper(arguments);
14: }
15: Raptor.extends(Bird);
16: newRap = new Raptor(true);
17: trace(newRap.hasOwnProperty("singing")); // true
18: trace(typeof newRap.move); // function
19: trace(Raptor.prototype.hasOwnProperty("singing")); // false
20: trace(newRap.singing); // true
```

Everything before line 16 is the inheritance hierarchy setup. Everything after line 16 is testing.

Line 16 executes the Raptor constructor, starting the process of creating a new Raptor object.

Inside the Raptor constructor, this refers to the generic object, which is in the process of becoming a member of the Raptor class. This object has access to the Raptor.prototype and so is able to execute mySuper(). It does so on line 13, passing on the argument that was passed to the Raptor constructor by the statement in line 16.

Inside mySuper(), this still refers to the generic object, and the argument is also the same as before. On line 10, both this and arguments are used with the Function.apply() method to call the superclass constructor.

Creating a __constructor__ Property in the Subclass Prototype

Creating a __constructor__ property in the subclass prototype takes advantage of the undocumented fact that, after the extends() method based on __proto__ has been executed, if a subclass.prototype.__constructor__ object points to the superclass, the standard built-in super() functionality works correctly.

In newrap2.fla, the subclass.prototype.__constructor__ property is pointed at the superclass within the extends() method. The subclass.prototype.__constructor__ property is then hidden (so it won't show up in for-in loops) using the undocumented ASSetPropFlags() function, in an attempt to duplicate the way that Flash does things in response to a normal new statement. Outside the extends() method, the rest of the code is completely standard.

⇨ *Compare this code with the samples shown in "Positioning Local Properties in the Inheritance Hierarchy," earlier in this chapter, page 490.*

The newrap2.fla file is as follows:

```
1: Function.prototype.extends = function (superclass)
2: {
3:        this.prototype.__proto__ = superclass.prototype;
4:        this.prototype.__constructor__ = superclass;
5:        ASSetPropFlags(this.prototype, ["__constructor__"], 1);
6: }
7: function Bird ( )  {
8:      this.singing = false; // local "singing" property
9: }
10: Bird.prototype.move = function () { }; // shared move() method
11: function Raptor () {
12:      super();
13: }
14: Raptor.extends(Bird);
15: newRap = new Raptor();
16: trace(newRap.hasOwnProperty("singing")); // true
17: trace(typeof newRap.move); // function
18: trace(Raptor.prototype.hasOwnProperty("singing")); // false
```

DESIGNING GOOD SUPERCLASSES AND SUBCLASSES: "IS" VERSUS "HAS"

Much of the skill of OOP is in designing hierarchies of superclasses and subclasses that elegantly model a problem domain. Creating such hierarchies is far from a precise science, and no two programmers attacking the same problem will come up with exactly the same solution. Nevertheless, there is one general rule that will seldom, if ever, be broken: A subclass should have an "is" relationship to its superclass.

The "Is" Relationship

Each and every member of a subclass should belong to its superclass. For instance, a bald eagle "is" an eagle. An eagle "is" a raptor. A raptor "is" a bird. You will never find a bald eagle that is not an eagle, or a raptor that is not a bird.

If you find yourself having trouble creating a logical hierarchy, start by putting it to this simple test. If an "is" relationship doesn't exist between each subclass and superclass, you probably need to rethink your hierarchy.

The "Has a" Relationship

If you find that two objects in your program have a "has a" relationship, on the other hand, one may be a property of the other. For example, a bird "has a" covering, namely feathers. This relationship is called "composition," as in "A bird is composed of feathers (and a few other things)." Objects related by composition do not often make good superclasses and subclasses for each other.

Another "has a" relationship is the client relationship, in which one object uses another object. For instance, a bicycle rider uses a bicycle. Again, you would make "bicycle" a property of "bicycle rider," not a subclass. The client relationship is a very broad one that can also include relationships like student-teacher and employee-employer.

Clearing Up Difficult Cases

The distinction between "has" and "is" is not always as straightforward as you might think. For instance, you could say, "Every composer has a mathematician inside him or her." However, this is not much different from saying, "Every composer is also a mathematician."

One question that can help clear up difficult cases is "Could this relationship change?" If the relationship could change, it's probably a "has a" relationship. If not, it's probably an "is" relationship.

For instance, if you believe that, of necessity, every composer must also be a mathematician, you have an "is" relationship, even though you may choose to use the words "has a" in describing it.

Refining Class Hierarchies: Abstraction and Specialization

I mentioned in Chapter 15 that programmers have an incentive to create highly generic classes.

> *For a discussion of the advantages of creating generic classes, see "Using Inheritance to Create Reusable Code," page 285 (Chapter 15, "Combining Statements into Functions").*

However, it's not always immediately obvious what properties such classes should have. Often, it is easiest to create a number of specific classes first, note what properties they have in common, and then "abstract" a parent class with those properties from the existing classes. This particular type of abstraction, in which you "factor out" common properties, is called "factoring." Factoring eliminates duplication in subclasses and is generally a good thing.

Factoring results in subclasses with fewer properties. In some cases you create new subclasses, often with added properties, to accommodate unforeseen distinctions in the problem domain. For instance, you might create a highly generic move() method and assign it to the MovieClip class, giving you a standard way to move movie clips. However, in developing a ping-pong game, you might find that the ping-pong ball movie clip needs a highly specialized move() method, as well as other special properties, and you might create a pingPongBall subclass with its own move() method and properties. This type of hierarchy refinement is called "specialization." It complicates your hierarchy by creating new and more complex classes, so you should always have a pressing, practical reason for doing it.

Hijacking the Math Object

Generally, you cannot change the values of the built-in properties of global objects. This could be inconvenient. Suppose you have a program that uses a lot of Math functions involving integers, and you want to change its "precision" so that you round to the nearest tenth instead of the nearest integer. You could add several new methods to the Math object that round to the nearest tenth. Then you would have to change all the Math method references in the program. How much simpler life would be if you could just change the functions in the Math object!

A workaround accomplishes this goal. It takes advantage of the fact that the Math object is a property of the top-level Object. It involves "hijacking" the Math property name and pointing it at an object that you have created using the new operator.

Here's the code:

```
 1: x = 10.21
 2: trace("1 : "+Math.floor(x));  // "10" -- calls the original
 3: myMath = new Object();
 4: myMath.__proto__ = Math;
 5: myMath.oldFloor = Math.floor;
 6: myMath.floor = function (arg) {
 7:      arg *= 10;
 8:      var result = myMath.oldFloor (arg);
 9:      return result/10;
10: }
11: Object.prototype.Math = myMath;
12: trace("2 : "+Math.floor(x));  // "10.2" - calls the custom property
```

First, you create a new object (line 3). Then you use __proto__ to make your new object look in the Math object whenever it can't find a referenced property locally (line 4). This step is important because the "real" Math object is going to be "hidden" behind your object, and will not be accessible in any way other than via this __proto__ link. If you want to add a new property and still be able to access the old property as well, create a property in your new object that points at the old property (line 5). Now create your new math function (lines 6–10).

The "crime" takes place on line 11. Here, you "steal" the name "Math" in the Object.prototype and point it at your new object.

That's it. Line 12 just proves that this procedure worked: Math.floor() now rounds to one decimal place, unlike line 2, where it rounded to an integer.

TROUBLESHOOTING

Why can't I override my get/set methods?

It's not you! It's *them*! When you use `addProperty()` in the normal way, the getter/setter functions cannot be overridden. For instance, suppose you have a statement like this:

```
function MyClass () {
    this.addProperty("myProp",
        MyClass.prototype.getMyProp,
        MyClass.prototype.setMyProp);
}
```

`MyClass.prototype.getMyProp()` and `MyClass.prototype.setMyProp()` will be executed when `myProp` is read or written, respectively.

Now you create a subclass with methods with those same names in its prototype:

```
function MySubClass () {}
MySubClass.prototype = new MyClass();
MySubClass.prototype.getMyProp = function () {
// statements
};
MySubClass.prototype.setMyProp = function (arg) {
// statements
};
```

Finally, you create an instance of the subclass and get or set `myProp`:

```
myObj = new MySubClass();
trace(myObj.myProp); // get
myObj.myProp = "Gary Good"; // set
```

You would expect the *subclass* methods to execute. They don't. The methods of the *superclass* do. Apparently, it's not a bug, just a fact of life.

Why do I get unwanted properties from the superclass when I use super()?

Generally, you should run `super()` on the first line of your subclass constructor. That way, subsequent statements in your subclass constructor can override properties created by the superclass. If you run `super()` later in your subclass constructor, you run the risk that a statement in the superclass constructor might override a statement in the subclass constructor—not the way classes are usually intended to work.

For instance, suppose you have created a general-purpose `Window` class that provides all the basic functionality you need to create a windowing system in Flash. It gives its instances (among many other properties) two local properties: `minMax`, a Boolean property that indicates whether the

21

window is currently maximized or minimized, and bg, a six-digit hexadecimal number indicating a color for the background.

```
function Window () = {
    this.minMax = true; // maximized
    this.bg = 0xFFFFFF; // default white background
}
```

Now suppose that, for a particular site, you need to create windows that have bitmapped backgrounds. You create a new class, BitWindow; make it a subclass of Window; override the bg property from the parent; and run super() so that BitWindow instances will get all the other local properties (represented here by MinMax) from the parent.

But you make a mistake and run super() *after* you override bg. Instances of BitWindow will get the bg property from the parent rather than the bitmap bg property that you intended.

```
function BitWindow () {
    this.bg = "bg.jpg"; // default bitmapped background
    super(); // OOPs!
}
BitWindow.prototype = new Window();
win1 = new BitWindow();
trace(win1.bg); // 16777215 (same as 0xFFFFFF) - not what you want!
```

If you put the super() statement in the first line of the BitWindow constructor, instances of BitWindow will get the bitmap bg property.

COMPONENTS

IN THIS CHAPTER

USING BUILT-IN COMPONENTS

In Flash 5, Macromedia introduced Smart Clips, which were designed as a way to create animations with parameters. Smart Clips are movie clips with parameters assigned. By adding actions and scripts, you could create radio buttons, menus, and other elements that responded to mouse clicks. In Flash MX, this capability is taken to the next level with the introduction of components.

The problem with Smart Clips was that although they were beneficial in terms of your being able to create animations that helped with sharing information, reusability, and the all-important workflow, what they lacked—and was quickly picked up by Flash professionals—was the fact that they did not fit into the object-oriented framework of ActionScript. With ActionScript generally heralded as the best thing to ever happen to Flash, this was a major problem for many developers.

As well as being able to create a custom user interface for components, you also can use live preview. You therefore can see exactly how the component will look when it is used. You will create both a custom user interface and live preview later in the chapter when you create your own component.

The Components panel displays the built-in Flash components. You will immediately notice that these components are designed to be used in forms.

You can add Flash components into your files in two ways. The most obvious is to simply drag and drop an instance from the Stage into your files.

Alternatively, you can add your components programmatically using `attachMovie`. To do so, simply select the frame where you want the component to appear in the Timeline and, with the Action panel open in Expert mode, create a function to create an instance of the component. The following code shows how to add an instance of the CheckBox component, with an instance name of myCheckbox and the checked value set to unchecked:

```
_root.attachMovie("FCheckBoxSymbol", "checkBox1", Z);
_root.checkBox1.setValue(false);
_root.checkBox1.setLabel("myCheckbox");
```

You can create change handler functions for components; they are then called when the user chooses or clicks a menu item. It is best to create a single handler function that specifies the actions and then to use the handler function as the parameter for the component. A change handler always accepts at least one parameter, the changed instance of the component.

In the following example, `onChange` is the handler function for two check boxes. Each is a separate component. The function uses `if-else` statements to see which check box is selected and then enables the appropriate list box based on the selection:

```
function onChange(component)
{
if (component._name=="checkbox01") {
    Box1_mc.setEnabled(component.getValue());
} else if (component._name=="checkbox02") {
    Box2_mc.setEnabled(component.getValue());
}
}
```

Each component has a set of parameters that control the way the component looks and behaves. Figure 22.1 shows the CheckBox component with its available parameters.

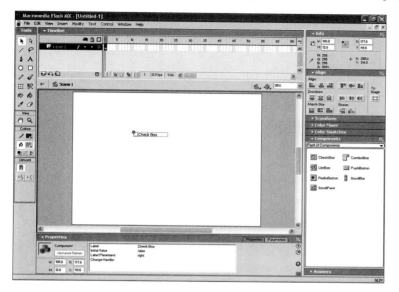

Figure 22.1
Every component has definable parameters to control the way it looks and works.

The ComboBox Component

The ComboBox component offers you a simple way to create a simple pop-up menu offering the user a list of choices.

The following steps configure the combo box to offer users a list of numbers to choose from. For example, when you're creating an order form, such a list would be appropriate for a quantity selection. Start by dragging an instance of the ComboBox component onto the Stage.

1. Select the combo box on the Stage to display the parameters in the Property Inspector and then name the instance.

2. Select the Labels parameter in the Property Inspector and click the magnifying glass to open the Values pop-up window.

    The Labels parameter contains the list of values a user can select from the pop-up menu.

3. In the Values pop-up window, click the plus (+) button to enter a new value.

4. Select the Default Value field and then type **1** for the first value. Click the plus (+) button to enter the next value.

5. Select the Default Value field and then type **2**. In the same manner, add **3**, **4**, and **5**.

6. Click OK to close the Values pop-up window.

7. Test the movie to check the .fla file. You should see the combo box with your selections available, as seen in Figure 22.2.

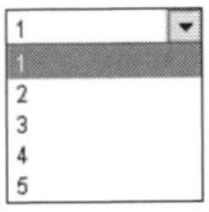

Figure 22.2

The combo box allows your visitors to make their selection from the menu based on the options you give them.

The ListBox Component

The ListBox component provides a list of items that can be selected. Users can choose their options from the list you present. With a list box, unlike a combo box, users can choose more than one option. The list box also displays the selections in a list format rather than as a menu. To set up your list box, start by dragging an instance of the ListBox component onto the Stage and then follow these steps:

1. With the Arrow tool, select the list box on the Stage.

   The parameters of the list box are displayed in the Property Inspector.

2. Name the instance **readoptions** in the Property Inspector.

3. Select the Labels parameter and then click the magnifying glass to open the Values pop-up window.

4. Click the plus (+) button to enter a new value.

5. Select the Default Value field and then type **Television** for the first value.

6. Click the plus (+) button to enter the next value.

7. Select the Default Value field and then type **Newspaper**. In the same manner, add **Magazine**, **Book**, **Internet**, or whatever options you need.

8. Click OK to close the Values pop-up window.

9. Select the Select Multiple parameter in the Property Inspector and then select True from the pop-up menu. Selecting this option allows users to select more than one option from the list.

10. Test the movie to see the list box in action. Note that users can choose more than one option. Figure 22.3 shows this component in action.

Figure 22.3

The ListBox component allows multiple selections. Note that the options are presented as a list, not as a menu.

The CheckBox Component

As well as allowing the user to simply choose yes or no—the most common use of the check box on the Internet—a check box can be used to allow the user to select or deselect all the options in a list box with a single click. In the case of a large number of options, selecting all the options may be easier for the user than having to work through a complete list box and choose each item individually.

As with all the components, you start by dragging an instance of the check box onto the Stage. Then you do the following:

1. Select the check box on the Stage and name the instance **chkbox_All**.

2. Select the Label parameter and then type **Select all options**. If all the label text isn't visible on the Stage, use the Free Transform tool to lengthen the check box.

3. Select the Change Handler parameter and then type **onSelectAll**.

The parameter you listed in step 3 is the name of a function that is called when the check box is selected or not.

The following sample script would perform this operation:

```
function onSelectAll(checkbox) {
    if(checkbox.getValue() == true) {
        readoptions.setSelectedIndices([0,1,2,3,4]);
        readoptions.setEnabled(false);
    } else {
        readoptions_lb.setSelectedIndices(null);
        readoptions_lb.setEnabled(true);
    }
}
```

In conjunction with the list box created in the previous section, this script works as follows: First, it checks to see if the list box has been selected by the user—that is, if checkbox.getValue == true—then the setSelectedIndices method for the ListBox component is called. This method is then passed an array of values that indicate the options in the list box. The number of indices needs to be equal to the number of options in the list box, with 0 being the first.

The setEnable method for the list box is then called and is passed the value false to disable the list box.

Testing the movie shows the list box from the previous component, as well as the check box. The Change Handler parameter is used to specify a change handler function that is called when a check box or radio button changes.

⇨ *Functions are discussed in Chapter 15, "Combining Statements into Functions," page 267.*

Radio Buttons

Radio buttons allow the user to select one of multiple options. Also known as option group buttons, they can be used to allow a user to select an age range or similar options where only one can be correct. Start by dragging three instances of the radio button component onto the Stage. Then follow these steps:

1. Select the first (top) radio button on the Stage and name the instance **Large_rb**.

2. Select the Label parameter and then type **Large**.

3. Select the Initial State parameter and then select True from the pop-up menu. The Large radio button is selected by default.

4. Select the Group Name parameter and then type **sizeGroup**.

5. Repeat steps 1 through 4 for the second (middle) radio button and configure its parameters as follows: type **medium_rb** for Instance Name, **Medium** for Label, **false** for Initial State, and **sizeGroup** for Group Name.

6. Repeat steps 1 through 4 for the third (bottom) radio button and configure its parameters as follows: type **small_rb** for Instance Name, **Small** for Label, **false** for Initial State, and **sizeGroup** for Group Name.

7. Test the .fla file. You should see the three radio buttons with the Large option selected. Click the others and make sure that only one can be chosen at a time. Figure 22.4 shows a completed option group.

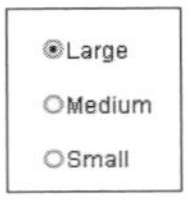

Figure 22.4
A radio button group allows only one selection. If you can choose multiple selections, check whether the Group Name parameter is the same for all buttons.

Pushbuttons

Pushbuttons are used to submit a form to the server or to reset form data. Regardless of whether a form is in Flash or any other type of Web page, the button is the last thing the user clicks before sending the form to you. Most forms have two buttons: one to submit the form and another to clear it in case of error. To create a pushbutton, follow these steps:

1. Drag an instance of a pushbutton onto the Stage and select it. Its parameters are displayed in the Property Inspector.

2. Type **btn_reset** in the Instance Name text box.

3. Type **Reset** for the Label parameter.

4. Type **onReset** for the Click Handler parameter. This is the name of a function that will be called when the user clicks the Reset button.

5. Repeat steps 1 through 4 for a second pushbutton and configure it as follows: type **btn_submit** for Instance Name, **Submit** for Label, and **onSubmit** for Click Handler. Figure 22.5 shows the two buttons with the properties for the Submit button visible.

6. Testing the movie will show you the two buttons, both of which are clickable. Try the Reset button to see it clear all the other components.

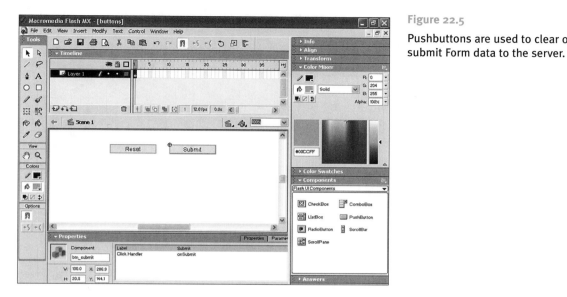

Figure 22.5

Pushbuttons are used to clear or submit Form data to the server.

The Scrolling Text Box

A scrolling text box at the bottom of a form displays a feedback message to the user or is used to accept free text from the user. The following steps set the component to display a message at the end of an ordering process. There is no specific component named Scrolling Text box, which may be a little confusing to start with; however, as you'll soon see, the process of inserting one is really straightforward.

1. Select the Text tool; then open the Property Inspector if it is not already visible. To do this, choose Properties from the Window menu.

2. Name the instance **txtmessage**.

3. From the Type pop-up menu, choose Dynamic and then click the Show Border Around Text button.

4. Select Multiline from the Line Type pop-up menu.

5. Use the Property Inspector to change the size of the message box to fit your form layout. The size can be whatever you think is appropriate.

6. Drag an instance of the ScrollBar component and release it near the right edge of the message box. The scrollbar automatically attaches itself to the text field, making it a scrolling text field.

7. Select the scrollbar that is attached to the Messages text box on the Stage. Its properties are displayed in the Property Inspector. Type **txtmessage** for the Target TextField parameter, as shown in Figure 22.6.

In Flash MX, dynamic and input text fields are instances of the ActionScript `TextField` object and can be assigned instance names, just like movie clips and other objects.

22

Figure 22.6
Properties for the scrollbar are added, and the target textfield matches the name of the text box into which you placed the scrollbar.

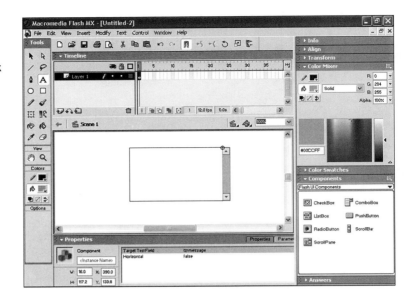

The ScrollBar

As the name implies, the ScrollBar component allows the user to scroll through a text field. As you saw with the creation of a scrolling text box in the preceding section, the ScrollBar component adds scrolling functionality.

Dragging a ScrollBar component from the Components panel and releasing it near the right edge of a scrolling text box causes the scrollbar to attach itself automatically to the scrolling text box.

The ScrollBar component's Target TextField parameter specifies the instance name of the TextField object the scrollbar applies to.

You don't need to assign an instance name to the scrollbar.

Using the Library Panel with Components

As soon as you add a component into your file, a Flash UI Components folder is added to the Library panel, as shown in Figure 22.7.

The elements in the Library are as follows:

- The component movie clip, represented by an icon for the component type

- A Component Skins folder, with a Global Skins folder containing graphic elements that apply to all components, and a Skins folder for the individual component type

- A Core Assets folder with assets for advanced developers, including a Data Provider API and the class hierarchy used by components

The Skins folders hold the graphic symbols that are used to display a component type in your file. The Global Skins folder holds information generic across all components as well as a Skins folder for each component type.

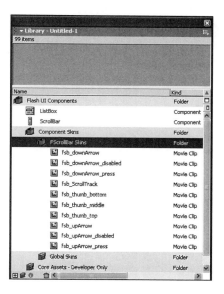

Figure 22.7
As soon as you use a component, the Library panel is populated with component information.

All the skins can be edited in the normal way. Obviously, editing the skins affects the appearance of the component in your documents.

Editing Skins

You can edit the skins to change the appearance of your components on the Stage as you would edit any other graphic, or you can create new graphics and break them into skin elements.

If you choose to create new graphics and break them apart, you need to register the elements to a component. You do so by editing the code in the first frame of the Read Me layer of each skin in the Library.

When you make these edits, you are changing all instances of the components that use the skins you edited. You cannot change skins for single instances of components.

CREATING A NEW COMPONENT

So far, you have looked at the built-in components that come with Flash MX. You might have noticed that they are all Form fields, which you can edit to suit the needs of your forms. However, components can be whatever you need them to be—programmable buttons, form fields, through to faders and shapes that you want control over, or as you will learn here, any type of element that you may want to use over again with different parameters. Check out the component buttons in the Flash Library to see one of these components at work.

In this section, you create a rectangle that has programmable options to change the height and width. There is no such thing as the right component to create, so for purposes of demonstrating the process, you will create a rectangle that has the following changeable properties: width, height, tint, and an additional option that allows control over whether the tint is applied.

Starting to Build Your Own Component

Every component starts the same way—with a movie clip. After the movie clip is created, you add the required ActionScript within the movie for the rectangle class, properties, and methods. You then link the movie clip with the class definition.

➡️ *For more information about movie clips, see Chapter 17, "Unlocking the Power of Movie Clips," page 331.*

Start by creating a movie clip. For the purposes of this exercise, name it **Rectangle Component**. Within the movie clip, draw a rectangle. You can fill the rectangle with any color you want. Use the Property Inspector to set the width and height of the rectangle to 30 pixels × 15 pixels.

Show the Align panel and align the rectangle to the center horizontally and the bottom vertically. Make sure that the Align To option is set to Stage. Because you are going to be able to scale the rectangle, you need to know that the base of the rectangle will remain static. Figure 22.8 shows the rectangle correctly sized and aligned.

Figure 22.8

Ensuring that the alignment is correct when you create your component means that the base will remain correctly positioned when you change the size of the rectangle.

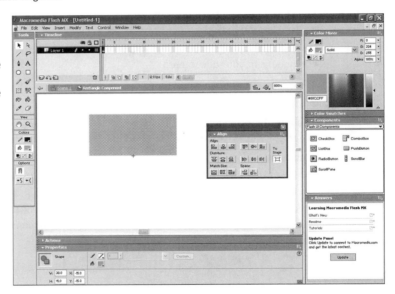

Defining a Rectangle Class

When you group information about an object, it is called a class. Creating a class involves defining the properties of the object. In this case, you will define the properties for your rectangle.

➡️ *For more information about classes, check out Chapter 15, "Combining Statements into Functions," page 267.*

The next step is to create a new layer in the movie clip and name it **Actions**. Open the Actions panel in Expert mode and then add the code as follows:

```
#initclip
function RectangleClass () {
```

```
    this.cobj = new Color(this);
    this.update();
}

// Allow RectangleClass to inherit MovieClip properties
RectangleClass.prototype = new MovieClip();

// Update draws the rectangle at the current base and height values.
RectangleClass.prototype.update = function () {
    if (this.applyTint) {
        this.cobj.setRGB(this.rcolor);
    }
    this._xscale = 30 * this.rbase;
    this._yscale = 15 * this.rheight;
}

// Connect the class with the linkage ID for this movie clip
Object.registerClass("FRectangle", RectangleClass);
#endinitclip
```

The code defines the component class. Before you move on, let me break down the code so that you can customize it for your components.

#initclip **and** #endinitclip

The #initclip and #endinitclip statements are new to Flash MX and are used exclusively when you're creating and defining components. When you create a component, you define a constructor for the class, define the methods, and then register the class with the movie clip.

These two statements mark the code for component definition. The code help within the statements is executed only once as the movie plays back. The code within the statements is always executed before anything else in the movie's Timeline. This is a huge progression from the limitations of Flash 5. Previously, you needed to wait for a full keyframe before your defined methods were available; now they are available immediately.

Defining the Constructor

The RectangleClass () function, shown here, defines the constructor for the component. When the component is created by Flash, the constructor is called and the actions are executed.

```
function RectangleClass ()
```

➡ *For more information about using constructors, see Chapter 15, "Combining Statements into Functions," page 267.*

Creating Inheritance

The following line of code must come immediately after the constructor; it must appear before you define any methods for your class:

```
RectangleClass.prototype = new MovieClip();
```

When you issue a command to connect a class definition to a movie clip, Flash automatically reassigns the type of the movie clip to the type (in this case, class) you defined. The problem with this functionality is that you actually want the movie clip to act like a movie clip.

The way around this problem is to use the code shown in this section, which tells the new class to inherit the methods and properties of movie clips.

Updating the Rectangle

The following method uses the current width and height of the rectangle. It looks to see whether you want to apply the tint and, if so, goes ahead and applies it. The multiplication values are set at 30 and 15 to correspond with the size of the rectangle you drew. This method will ensure that scaling works correctly:

```
RectangleClass.prototype.update = function () {
    if (this.applyTint) {
        this.cobj.setRGB(this.rcolor);
    }
    this._xscale = 30 * this.rbase;
    this._yscale = 15 * this.rheight;
}
```

Registering the Class

The final instruction is possibly the single most important one. It links the class with the clip in the Linkage ID:

```
Object.registerClass("FRectangle", RectangleClass);
```

Using Read and Write Methods

Now that you've looked at the code created so far, it's time to move on and add the other methods and properties you need for the Rectangle component. The routines come in two types—set and get. Get routines return a property value, whereas set routines redraw the rectangle when you change values.

You need to add the following code into the Actions panel. You should place it after the inheritance statement, but before the end of the #endinitclip code block. There is nothing in this code that has not been covered previously, so I won't break it down further. It should be self-explanatory at this point.

```
RectangleClass.prototype.setBase = function (b) {
    this.rbase = b;
    this.update();
}


RectangleClass.prototype.getBase = function () {
    return (this.rbase);
}


RectangleClass.prototype.setHeight = function (h) {
    this.rheight = h;
    this.update();
}


RectangleClass.prototype.getHeight = function () {
    return (this.rheight);
}


RectangleClass.prototype.setTintColor = function (c) {
    this.rcolor = c;
    this.update();
}


RectangleClass.prototype.turnOnTint = function () {
    this.applyTint = true;
    this.update();
}
```

Defining the Component Properties

You may be wondering why you have not yet done anything to turn your movie clip into a component. The simple reason is that there is a logical order to the creation of components, so adding the script and so on should come first. Now that you have your rectangle you can define the parameters.

Show the Library panel and select the Rectangle component movie. Open the Context menu and then choose Component Definition to open the Component Definition dialog box shown in Figure 22.9.

Figure 22.9

In the Component Definition dialog box, you can set the parameters for any component that you create.

You use the plus and minus symbols at the top of the dialog box to add parameters. By default, properties are added with the type `Default` and the value `default value`. The Type options available in Flash are as follows:

> Default
> Array
> Object
> List
> String
> Number Boolean
> Font Name
> Color

The window at the top of the dialog box is split into four columns. Name enables you to add the text to show in the component's Property Inspector. Variable allows you to set the name to be used in component scripts. The variable name must follow standard naming conventions for variables (no spaces and such). Value is the starting value for the property, and Type indicates the type of parameter from the preceding list.

For the Rectangle component you have created, you should add the properties shown in Table 22.1.

Table 22.1 Rectangle Component Properties

Name	Variable	Value	Type
Base Length	rbase	30	Number
Height	rheight	15	Number
Tint Color	rcolor	#000000	Color
Apply Tint	applyTint	false	Boolean

You also can add a text description for the component; this description will help others understand what the component does. To add your text description, click the Set button by the Description option and then add the description you want.

XML Descriptions

As an alternative to a text description, you can create an XML document to add a custom action to the Actions Panel toolbox. Placing the XML file in the Configuration/ActionsPanel/CustomActions folder makes it accessible.

Leave the component icon as the default for now and ignore the Live Preview and Custom UI options; those options will be described shortly.

The final options in the Component Definition dialog box allow you to control the locking of parameters; locking allows or disallows users from adding or removing parameters when the component is placed on the Stage. The final option allows you to display your component in the Components panel. For now, check the Display in Components Panel option; these options are described later in the chapter.

Adding Your Own Icon

One of the options you saw in the preceding section was to have your own icon for the component. If you choose to do this, the component will be displayed in the Library, Movie Explorer, or Components panel (if you choose to show the component there).

To add your custom icon, you should first create a graphic in either Fireworks or your chosen imaging application; you can even create the file in Flash and export it as a PNG file.

The icon should be no more than 20 × 20 pixels to ensure that it is displayed correctly.

After you create and save the file, you need to import it into the Library. To make sure that Flash recognizes this as a custom icon, you first need to create a new folder in the Library. Name this folder **FCustomIcons** and then import the image into the new folder.

Close and reopen the Library. The icon should now appear next to your component, as in Figure 22.10.

Figure 22.10
When you create your own icon, Flash displays it next to your component in the Library, Movie Explorer, and Components panel.

Setting the Linkage ID

The next step is to close the movie clip and return to the main scene in your movie. To create a Linkage ID, right-click on your new component in the Library and choose Properties from the context menu. The Symbol Properties dialog box opens. Click the Advanced button to ensure that you see the complete dialog box.

Enable the Export for ActionScript check box and leave all the others blank. Then in the Identifier text box, add the ID you created earlier for the rectangle. In this case, the ID is **FRectangle** as shown in Figure 22.11.

Figure 22.11

The Linkage Identifier is added in the Symbol Properties dialog box. This needs to match the ID created earlier—in this case, `Frectangle`.

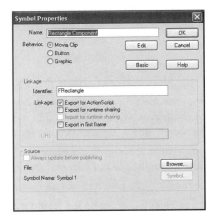

Testing

Okay, you have completed the design, albeit basic, and added the ActionScript. Now it's time to see what happens when you use your new component.

Drag an instance of the component onto the Stage from the Library. Testing the movie at this point will simply show the rectangle as it was originally drawn—amazing!

You can use the Property Inspector to edit the properties of the component. Edit the displayed values by clicking in the appropriate column and changing the numbers. Here, I have changed the width and height settings for the component. Note that the changes are displayed only when the movie is tested. They do not show up at design time. Figure 22.12 shows the changed rectangle. You can also play with the tint settings by changing the `false` value to `true` and choosing a tint color.

Figure 22.12

Changing the properties for the component controls the display when the movie is tested.

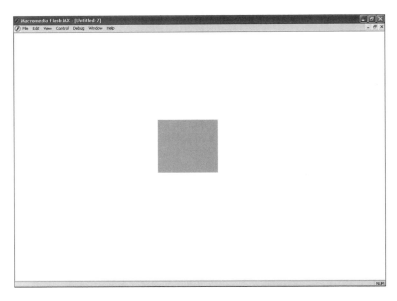

Installing the Component onto the Components Panel

To install the component onto the Components panel, start by adding the component, the icon, and any other symbols that are used with your component to a new folder in the Library. This step ensures that everything is correctly kept together.

Figure 22.13 shows the newly created folder complete with the movie clip, custom icons folder, and icon all neatly held together.

If you cannot see your Configuration\Components folder, make sure that you have hidden files and folders set to `visible`.

22

Figure 22.13

Putting all component elements into a single folder will make life easier for you as well as users of the component.

To install the component, you need to place your .fla file into the correct location. After the .fla file is in the correct place, Flash will load your component into the panel when it is launched.

Where you place your .fla file depends on the operating system and setup you're using. Data is stored in a per-user Configuration folder, wherever your operating system stores application data. Some examples are shown in Table 22.2.

Table 22.2   Where to Install Your Component

Operating System	Folder Name
Windows 2000 and XP	C:\Documents and Settings\User\Application Data\Macromedia\Flash MX\Configuration\Components\
Windows XP	C:\ Program Files\Macromedia\Flash MX\First Run\Components\
Windows 98 and Me	C:\Windows\Application Data\Macromedia\Flash MX\Configuration\Components\
Windows NT	C:\WinNT\Profiles\User\Application Data\Macromedia\Flash MX\Configuration\
Mac OS X	Hard Drive:Users:Library:Application Support:Macromedia:FlashMX:Configuration:Components
Mac OS 9.1	Hard Drive:Users:User:Documents:Macromedia:FlashMX:First Run:Components:
Mac OS 9.x (multiuser)	Hard Drive:Users:User:Documents:Macromedia:FlashMX:Configuration:Components:

Creating a Custom Interface

So far, you have created your component, looked at the properties, and introduced the code where needed. One of the best things about Flash MX is the way that you have so much control over usability issues. Creating a custom interface for components is one such example of this functionality at work.

A custom interface is a Flash movie file that allows users to enter values for properties such as height and width without recourse to the Property Inspector. When you create an interface, it can run from within the Property Inspector or from the Component Parameters panel.

The interface movie needs to have a way to get the values set by the user. In this case, they are rbase, rheight, rcolor, and ApplyTint.

The key element you need in your custom interface is a movie clip instance you create called xch. You pass values to your component by having the custom interface write values to properties of xch, such as xch.tbase = 75;.

The interface must allow users to enter the values they want so that when the component is either tested or published, the values on xch are copied to the component.

To create a custom interface, perform the following steps:

1. Create a new Flash movie and set the dimensions to 400 pixels × 70 pixels. This is the approximate dimensions of the Property Inspector.

2. Insert an empty movie clip into the movie and name it **Change**.

3. Place an instance of the clip onto the Stage and name it **xch**.

4. Create text in the movie for Width, Height, Red, Green, Blue, and 0–255.

5. Define the text fields you use to retrieve your rbase and rheight property values. Create base and height text fields as by Input Text fields; then place these fields above the corresponding Static Text field and set the instance names to **bs** and **ht**, respectively.

6. Define input text fields to retrieve the tint color. Create three more input text fields, naming them **rc**, **gc**, and **bc** (for red color, green color, and blue color), and place them above the corresponding Static Text field.

7. So that the user can preview the color, make a tile that shows the current tint setting. Use the drawing tool to create a square. Convert that square into a movie clip and name the instance **tintSq**.

8. You can use a predefined Flash component, FCheckBox, to set whether the user wants to apply the tint color. Open the Components panel and drag a check box into its place on the Stage. In the Properties window, set the text to Apply Tint? and its default value to false. Under the property named Change Handler, enter **tintApply**.

   The final step is to write the code for the custom user interface. In a new layer, enter the following into frame 1:

```
// Set the default property values
xch.rbase = 30;
```

```
xch.rheight = 15;
xch.rcolor = 0x000000;
xch.applyTint = false;
// Initialize the base and height text fields
bs.text = 30;
ht.text = 15;
// Initialize the tint tile and color text fields
tsc = new Color(tintSq);
rc.text = gc.text = bc.text = "0";
setTintSq(0, 0, 0);

// Given a red, green, and blue color value (0-255), create a composite
// color value, set the tint tile, and return the composite color value.
function setTintSq(r, g, b) {
    var col = r << 16 | g << 8 | b;
    tsc.setRGB(col);
    return col;
}

// Given an integer c, clamp it to values between 0 and 255
function boundColor (c) {
    if (isNaN(c))
        return 0;
    if (c < 0) {
        c = 0;
    } else if (c > 255) {
        c = 255;
    }
    return c;
}

// When the color text fields change, change the tint color
// and set the appropriate property in xch
rc.onChanged = function () {
    xch.tcolor = setTintSq(boundColor(this.text), ParseInt(gc.text),
➥ParseInt(bc.text));
}
gc.onChanged = function () {
    xch.tcolor = setTintSq(ParseInt(rc.text), boundColor(this.text),
➥ParseInt(bc.text));
}
bc.onChanged = function () {
    xch.tcolor = setTintSq(ParseInt(rc.text), ParseInt(bc.text),
➥boundColor(this.text));
}

// The check box (c) calls this function when the user checks or unchecks
// the box. Set the applyTint property of xch appropriately.
```

```
function tintApply (c) {
    xch.applyTint = c.getValue();

}

RectangleClass.prototype.getArea = function ()
{
    return (0.5 * this.tbase * this.theight);
}
```

> If you plan to save your compo-
> nent as a Flash 5 format movie,
> you will need to link to it as an
> external file rather than an
> embedded file.

9. Save the movie to your hard drive; then test it. This will create the .swf file in the same location you saved the file.

10. Integrate the custom user interface with the Rectangle movie. Go back to your Rectangle movie, open the Library, and select the Rectangle component. Next, open the Component Definition window, and to the right of Custom UI, click the Set button.

> If the custom user interface is not
> immediately visible, try closing
> and then relaunching Flash. Make
> sure that the custom user inter-
> face is visible before moving on to
> the live preview.

11. Next to Type, select Custom UI with .swf File Embedded in .fla File. The other option, Custom UI in External .swf File, allows you to keep the custom user interface outside the rectangle, which is good for testing rather than deployment. With this setting, you not only have to enter the absolute path to the file (which means that if you use the component on a different plat-form, this has to be adjusted), but you also must distribute both files.

12. Next to Display, select Display in Property Inspector.

13. Under Custom UI .swf File, click Browse to locate the .swf file, or Update if you have already located this file and want to reload your custom user interface.

14. Click OK. When you select the rectangle on the Stage and the Properties window is open, you will see your custom user interface.

That should take care of it! When you edit a component's properties, you should see the custom user interface displayed and working.

Creating a Live Preview Movie

A live preview movie allows the user to see how the component will look when published. As you have already seen, the changes made via the user interface are not displayed during design time. Using a live preview movie allows the user to make changes to the parameters and actually see them.

The live preview movie is designed for previewing only basic characteristics of the component, such as color and size—which suits you perfectly for this chapter's sample rectangle. It is not ideal for previewing animation, however, because the live preview movie runs at only 1 frame per second (fps).

Unlike the custom interface, which sets values within the xch object and transfers them to the component, live preview reads values from the object. The live preview works by invoking a function called onUpdate that you define.

Flash invokes the onUpdate function when changes are made, and the user is told when the preview needs updating.

Before you dive in and make a live preview, you need to stop awhile and think about any differences between the component and the preview. In most cases, there will be few if any differences, and using an instance of the actual component will work perfectly. However, when a tint color is applied to the rectangle, you are unable to remove it (only change the tint), so it would be handy if users could see the rectangle with or without the tint applied.

To achieve this goal, create two rectangles in the live preview—one that is displayed when the user applies the tint, and the original without. Then tell the preview which to display based on the user's choices. Follow these steps to create your live preview movie:

1. Create a new file in Flash with the same dimensions as the rectangle—30 × 15 pixels.

2. Add two layers to the file. Name one of them **Tinted** and the other **Plain**.

3. On the Plain layer, create a rectangle that is the same color, size, and so on as in the component.

4. Convert the rectangle to a movie clip named **plain rectangle** and name the instance **rp** (rectangle plain).

5. On the Tinted layer, place a copy of rp and then rename the instance to **rtint**.

6. Create an Actions layer to hold the onUpdate function mentioned earlier. This function will read the property values and adjust the size of the rectangle accordingly. The code tells the onUpdate function whether to display the tinted or plain rectangle.

7. Add the following code to keyframe 1 of the Actions layer:

```
// This routine is called when component properties have been changed.
// Redraw the rectangle with the new values. If the tint is applied,
// use the rtint rectangle. If it should not be applied, use rp.
function onUpdate(){
    var ac = _root.xch.applyTint, b = _root.xch.rbase,
➥h = _root.xch.rheight;

    tc._xscale = 30 * b;
    tc._yscale = 15 * h;
    tctint._xscale = rp._xscale;
    tctint._yscale = rp._yscale;

    if (ac) {
        rc_color.setRGB(_root.xch.tcolor);
    }

    rtint._visible = ac;
    rp._visible = !ac;
}
```

22

```
// There are two copies of the rectangle, rp, for previewing a plain
➥ untinted rectangle
// and rtint, for tinted previewing. The default shows only the plain
➥ rectangle.
rtint._visible = false;
// Make a Color for tint to apply.
rp_color = new Color(rtint);
```

8. Make sure that live preview is enabled. You should see a check next to the Enable Live Preview option at the bottom of the Control menu. If the check is not in place, add it now.

9. Save your file and then test it to generate the .swf file you need for linking to the component.

10. Open the Component Definition dialog box for the Rectangle component and click the Set button.

11. Choose Live Preview with .swf File Embedded as the option. Selecting this option connects your Preview file to the component. Click OK twice to close the Component Definition dialog box. When you return to the Stage, your preview movie will be running instead of the component.

TROUBLESHOOTING

I don't see my component in the Components panel. What should I do?

The Components panel shows the set of Flash UI Components by default. Next to the title is an arrow to trigger a drop-down menu. Click on that list, and see whether the file in which you saved the rectangle appears there. If so, choose it, and your component should be displayed in the box, with the icon you chose. If the file is there but your component is not, you probably forgot to check the Display in Components Panel check box on the Component Definition dialog box. If the filename is not in the drop-down list, you did not place the file in the correct folder.

I need to edit some of my code. Can I edit it directly from the directory?

If you find that you need to change the code, it is best to remove the existing file from the First Run directory and the special data storage area, make the correction to a separate copy, and then put it back into the First Run directory.

USING LEARNING INTERACTIONS

IN THIS CHAPTER

INTERACTIONS AND TEMPLATES

Building interactive courseware is currently a huge development area. Macromedia is aware of this fact, and the built-in learning interactions that come with Flash MX make it possible for anyone to create complex online learning applications in a standalone capacity or in applications that send information to a server-side Learning Management System (LMS). You can track a single learning interaction or one that uses the LMS to track cumulative results. Before you start planning and building your learning projects that need to be tracked, note that you must have a server-side LMS that meets Aviation Industry CBT Committee (AICC) or Shareable Content Object Reference Model (SCORM) standards.

In addition, your system must meet certain limitations in terms of browser compatibility for tracking learner interactions. Windows users must have Internet Explorer 4.0 or Netscape 4.0 or higher, whereas on a Macintosh, tracking does not work in Internet Explorer at all, and you must use Netscape version 4.5 or higher.

Using Learning Interactions

Flash MX learning interactions can be used in one of two ways. The quiz templates supplied with the application are fully editable in terms of design but have built-in ActionScript for tracking scores and passing them to either a SCORM- or AICC-compliant LMS.

Alternatively, you can use standalone style interactions that can be edited to fit into your style and layout. Again, you can edit these interactions from a graphical perspective.

Results from standalone interactions can be processed and passed to an AICC LMS only. To utilize SCORM tracking, you need to use a quiz template.

At this point, you may be panicking at the very idea of using a template. After all, in most cases when you think of a template used in an application, you are somehow stuck in a style and layout that everyone will know is a template. Don't worry about that; you have full control over the graphical aspects of the template as well as complete flexibility over the questions being asked. What a template does offer, however, is a fully functional quiz, complete with built-in navigation, that you can test immediately.

Flash MX ships with three learning templates; they are named quiz_style1, quiz_style2, and quiz_style3. You can locate them by selecting File, New from Template. Each template has the same content and is composed of the following elements:

- Introductory page
- Navigation structure
- Results page
- Learning interaction
- ActionScript for results tracking

Creating a quiz is a simple process in Flash. Just follow these steps:

1. Choose File, New from Template to open the New Document dialog box, as shown in Figure 23.1.

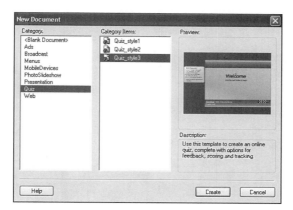

Figure 23.1
In the New Document dialog box, you can choose which of the three quiz_style templates you want to work with.

2. Select Quiz from the Category list. The three quiz_style options are displayed on the right of the dialog box.

3. In the Category Items list, look at the three template options. Moving the mouse cursor over each template gives you a preview of the style, as shown in Figure 23.2.

Figure 23.2
You can preview each quiz template before making your selection. Click on each one in turn to see the styles.

4. Choose the template that you want to work with and then click Create. Flash creates a complete working movie with all the quiz components in place.

5. Save your file.

After you create your file, you can see your quiz and interactions on the Stage. All the quiz layers are located on the Timeline, as shown in Figure 23.3.

The first time you save a file, Flash automatically prompts you to save a copy of the file because it has been created from a template.

Figure 23.3

As soon as your file is created, the quiz and interactions appear on the Stage. The layers are all visible immediately on the Timeline.

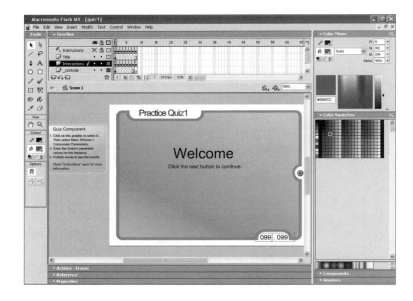

Adding Parameters

You cannot use a quiz without first adding parameters that control not only how the users see the quiz, but also how the questions appear and the order in which the questions are displayed. The questions can appear in numerical order or even randomly. The parameters also control the use of an LMS and whether the users see a results page.

The numerical option takes the users through questions in a normal, linear sequence. Choosing the Random option is handy if you want to present the same quiz to users on more than one occasion but change the order of the questions. Changing the order prevents people from being able to write down the answers for later use.

The movie contains an Instructions panel on the Stage. You use it to add and control your quiz parameters. Before you can set the parameters, though, you need to click on the Instructions panel to select the Quiz component.

To set the parameters for the quiz, you need to complete its Component Parameters panel. Start by opening the Component Parameters panel via the Window menu and resizing it if necessary.

Complete the panel as appropriate to your needs. The following information should help you get the best from your quiz:

- Add a check in the Randomize box to display questions in a nonsequential order.

- In the Questions to Ask text box, you can choose the number of questions that will be shown to the users.

  - Selecting 0 in this box will result in all questions always being shown to the users.

The Instructions panel is available only for your benefit or the benefit of your team. It is not displayed to the users at any time.

■ If you have 12 questions in the quiz but select a smaller number in this text box, the users will be shown your chosen number of questions.

■ If you put a higher number in the box than the number of questions, the users will see all your questions—the quiz will not show them twice.

■ If users need to log in to the quiz and you are not using an AICC-compliant LMS, Flash will redirect users to the login URL that you specify in this panel.

■ If you are using an LMS, enter the activity name and ID of the LMS. If you're not using an LMS, you can ignore these boxes.

■ To let the users see their results at the end of the quiz, add a check in the Show Results Page box.

The completed panel should look something like the one shown in Figure 23.4.

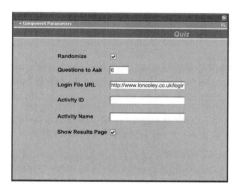

23

Figure 23.4
You complete the Component Parameters panel even before you create any questions for your quiz.

Adding Your Interactions

The Timeline created by the template has eight keyframes. They are made up of a welcome screen (keyframe 1), a results screen (keyframe 8), and six quiz keyframes. You can look at the template quiz at any time just by testing the movie.

Putting your questions into the quiz is a straightforward process. You add keyframes with interactions or remove existing ones at any time. The only rules to remember are that you must leave the first and last keyframes as the welcome and results screens, and that you must place your questions (interactions) into the Interactions layer on the Timeline in the correct sequential order.

You can edit the text on the welcome and results fields to match your site's style, colors, and so on. The only really important points to remember are that these pages cannot contain learning interactions and that even if you edit the text, you need to leave some kind of instructional text, making sure the users know to click Next to move to the next question. The dynamic text fields on the results page should be left intact. Changing these fields will prevent the quiz results from being displayed at all or cause them to be displayed incorrectly.

You can either delete or configure the interactions on the next screens to meet your needs and site layout. For this exercise, start with the easiest one.

Deleting an Interaction

Deleting an interaction is simple as long as you are careful to delete it as appropriate from all necessary layers. Select the keyframe with the unnecessary interaction on the Interactions layer. You can then perform one of two actions: delete the content by simply pressing the Delete or Backspace keys on the keyboard, and then reuse the keyframe and add a different interaction. Alternatively, you can delete the frame completely from the Timeline by selecting Insert, Remove Frame. Be sure to check that all the layers end at the same point on the Timeline.

Configuring an Interaction

The quiz template contains one of each of the six learning interaction types. They are stored in movie clips located in the Library. Each movie clip acts as a storage container for the elements that make up the interactions. Before you can edit the interaction to meet your needs, you must break it apart.

To configure your learning interaction, follow these steps:

1. Click in the keyframe on the Interactions layer containing the component you want to configure.

2. Select the learning interaction and then choose Modify, Break Apart. The Break Apart command is used to separate groups, instances, and bitmaps into single elements. In this case, the command allows you to work with the learning interaction to configure it.

3. Deselect everything on the Stage by selecting either Edit or Deselect All, or by pressing Ctrl+Shift+A.

4. Click on the Instructions panel for the learning interaction. The Instructions panel is clearly visible on the left of the Stage.

5. Open the Component Parameters panel by choosing Window, Component Parameters. Complete the fields on the Component Parameters panel as required with the name and ID for the interaction if you're using an LMS. Figure 23.5 shows the default panel for the True/False interaction.

6. Add a question or instructions for the users to complete; then click the Options button to open the Options screen where you can add Feedback, Knowledge Track, and Navigation parameters, as shown in Figure 23.6.

7. Use the Assets button to change the assets for the learning interaction.

> For documents created using a quiz template, you need to set Knowledge Track to On and Navigation to Off for each learning interaction.

After you customize the first interaction, it is a good idea to save and test the file.

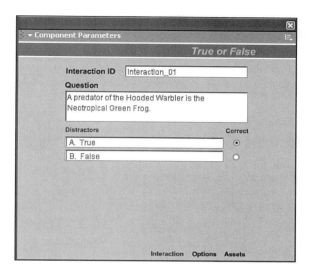

Figure 23.5
You use the Component Parameters panel to add your questions and set the possible answers.

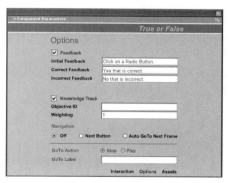

Figure 23.6
On the Options screen in the Component Parameters panel, you can add and change feedback to your users as well as set Knowledge Track and Navigation parameters.

Be Careful When Breaking Things!

Be careful when breaking apart learning interactions. You need to break apart the elements but not the actual component. Breaking apart the Learning Interaction component breaks the ActionScript and stops the correct functioning of your quiz. If you do this, the best solution is to delete the complete interaction, insert a new one from the Library, and start again.

The six types of learning interactions are described in more detail later in this chapter.

Adding an Interaction to the Timeline

If you're using a template, you must add your interactions sequentially into the Timeline. If you're adding the interactions into a Flash document that you have already created, you can add them into a single frame in the Timeline or sequential frames for sequential questions.

Adding an Interaction to the Timeline on a Template

If you want to add an interaction to the Timeline on a template, select the keyframe on the Interactions layer that has the question before the one you want to insert. Use the Insert menu to add a new blank keyframe. Select Insert Frame on the Interactions layer; then, with the new frame selected, choose Insert Blank Keyframe to convert the new frame to a keyframe. Then follow these steps:

1. Open the Document Library and then select the 2_learning Interactions folder, as shown in Figure 23.7.

Figure 23.7

The 2_learning Interactions folder contains the learning interactions you can add to your quiz.

2. Select the new keyframe you just inserted and drag one of the Learning Interaction components onto the Stage.

3. Position the component where you want it to appear and then configure the interaction.

⇨ *To learn how to configure an interaction, see "Configuring an Interaction," earlier in this chapter, page 538.*

Adding an Interaction to the Timeline in an Existing Document

The process for adding a learning interaction to an existing document is similar to the process outlined in the preceding section for adding a new interaction to a learning template.

Open the document into which you want to add a learning interaction and, on the appropriate layer, insert a blank keyframe. Open the Learning Interactions panel shown in Figure 23.8 by selecting Window, Common Libraries, Learning Interactions; then proceed in the same way as for adding and configuring a learning interaction within a template.

Figure 23.8
The Library panel contains interactions that can be added to any document, not just templates.

USING DRAG AND DROP

As the name implies, the Drag and Drop learning interaction enables the users to drag items across the screen and then drop them elsewhere. This functionality is commonly used to match shapes or to build jigsaw-type interactions where the result is vital.

A Drag and Drop learning interaction can support a maximum of eight objects and eight targets. For testing purposes, any of the objects can be dropped anywhere onscreen, and objects can have the same target; for example, both Object 1 and Object 3 can have a target of 7.

Targets need not have matching objects; this way, you can offer "distractors" for testing the users.

Configuring a Drag and Drop Learning Interaction

As with all the learning interactions, the first step after you place it on the Stage is to break it apart and then open the Component Parameters panel. Next, follow these steps to configure the interaction:

1. Complete the Drag Object Name column with instance names for the drag objects.

   Note that every drag object must have a unique name. Every time you add a new drag object into the learning interaction, you need to return to this panel to name it.

2. In the Matches Target Name column, list the matching target instance names, as shown in Figure 23.9. As with the drag objects, each target must have a unique name.

3. If you want the objects to return to their starting positions, in the case of being dropped away from the targets, add a check to the Snap to Start box.

> Each target and drag object is referred to as a *distractor*—one of a series of selectable choices.

Figure 23.9
All your instances must have unique names; this applies to both drag objects and targets.

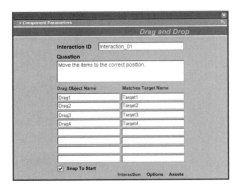

> **Matching Targets!**
>
> For every drag object named in the Drag Object Name column, you must have a target instance name in the Matches Target Name column.
>
> You can, however, have a target instance name without a matching drag object instance. This way, you can have targets that the users can snap objects into but that are not counted as correct matches.

Adding Drag and Drop Objects and Targets

The Drag and Drop learning interaction has a default of six objects and six matching targets. Flash MX allows you to add to or remove from this number to a maximum of eight objects and a minimum of one object.

For this exercise, create a movie clip symbol that contains the graphics for the drag object. If your quiz is about cars and you currently have five cars in the interaction, you must create a graphic for the sixth, seventh, and eighth cars that you require. Then do the following:

1. Place the new graphic or graphics in the Library. With the Drag and Drop learning interaction selected, drag the new symbol or symbols from the Library panel onto the Stage.

2. Use the Property Inspector to name the instance of each new symbol.

3. In the Component Parameters panel, add the instance name.

4. Repeat the naming process for each new instance that you add.

That's all you need to do. The component itself does the rest of the hard work when it is run. Just spend a minute or so saving and testing the file to make sure that there are no unexpected problems.

Removing Drag and Drop Objects

You can remove a Drag and Drop instance by selecting it on the Stage and deleting it. Remember that you need to remove the deleted object's instance name from the Component Parameters panel. If you forget this step and register any distractors that are not actually on the Stage, Flash will not warn you until you test the movie. At that point, you will see a trace output error message.

FILL IN THE BLANK

As you probably have concluded by now, the learning interactions in Flash MX are named pretty logically. The Fill in the Blank interaction enables the users to fill in a blank. How's that for a naming convention?

The Fill in the Blank learning interaction uses a question text field for your question to the users, a user entry text field where the users type their answers, a control button that allows the users to see whether they are correct, and a feedback text field that displays the information triggered by the control button.

Configuring a Fill in the Blank Interaction

You can easily configure a Fill in the Blank interaction. The first step is to open the Component Parameters panel for the interaction the same way as you did for other learning interactions. In the Component Parameters panel, you can have up to three correct answers for the question you are asking, as shown in Figure 23.10.

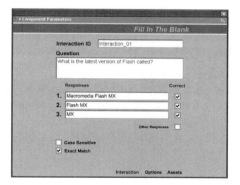

Figure 23.10

Complete the panel with a maximum of three acceptable answers. Alternatively, you can choose to specify only answers that are incorrect.

Alternatives for how you set the question are as follows:

- Type the correct answer or answers in the panel and then select the Correct check box on the panel.

- Tell the panel that all answers are correct other than those you specify. To do this, enter the wrong answers in the panel, deselect the Correct check box, and add a check in the Other Responses check box.

Choose whether the required answers are case sensitive by selecting the Case Sensitive box; then choose Exact Match if the users must type their response exactly as you entered it. With the Exact Match option turned off, the interaction works by recognizing a correct word from your settings. If the correct answer to a question is simply `Flash` and a user types `Flash MX`, `Flash` will be accepted. However, you cannot use Exact Match on multiword answers.

HOT OBJECTS

Hot Object may seem like a strange name for a learning interaction; the name is less obvious than some of the others. A Hot Object learning interaction allows you to ask a question and then allows the users to choose one or more correct answers from a series of graphics. For example, if you're using cars as the theme of your quiz, you can show the users between one and eight images of cars and ask a question that can have one or more correct answers. You may ask which cars are made by Ford or which cars are no longer in production.

Configuring a Hot Object Learning Interaction

If you want to configure a Hot Object learning interaction, starting with the broken-apart learning interaction, again open the Component Parameters panel. To complete the panel for a Hot Object, simply work through the Component Parameters panel for the interaction. Completing the component parameters should now be straightforward; the procedure for this task follows the same logic as the previous ones. Start by giving the interaction an ID; then type the question that users will be presented with. Finally, add a check to the Correct check box for each correct answer in the interaction.

Adding and Removing Hot Object Choices

You add and remove Hot Object choices in exactly the same way as you did with the Drag and Drop learning interaction earlier. You need to create additional graphics contained in movie clip symbols and then add them to the Library before they are placed on the Stage. You can then refer to the drag-and-drop instructions earlier in this chapter.

➪ *Drag-and-drop instructions are discussed in "Configuring a Drag and Drop Learning Interaction," earlier in this chapter, page 541.*

HOT SPOTS

Hot Spot learning interactions are set so that the users click on a region or regions onscreen to indicate the correct response to your question.

The only difference between a Hot Spot and a Hot Object is that a Hot Spot is a region, whereas a Hot Object is an actual object rather than a defined region.

As with all the interactions, you configure a Hot Spot by first breaking it apart and opening the Component Parameters panel. In the panel, mark each possible answer as correct or incorrect—you can have multiple correct answers.

The Up State Alpha allows you to set transparency before a user clicks an object. Complete transparency is a setting of 0.

You can have Down State Alpha as well; this setting controls the transparency of the Hot Spot after the user clicks it. You may want the selected answers to fade out, indicating they have been clicked.

You can add and remove Hot Spot distractors in the same way as with the other learning interaction types.

MULTIPLE CHOICE

Multiple Choice interactions allow the users to select a correct answer or answers from those offered onscreen. You can choose whether each question has a single correct answer, or whether more than one may be correct. Each multiple choice question starts with six possible correct answers (you don't have to offer this many selections). They are listed as A through F, rather than numerically, for the Multiple Choice interaction.

Again, you use the Component Parameters panel to configure the interaction. In the panel, add the possible answers and then type the question for your users. As appropriate, mark an answer or answers as correct.

Adding Multiple Choice Distractors

The default number of distractors (choices) for the multiple choice interaction is six, as mentioned in the preceding section; however, you can add additional distractors to a maximum of eight, or delete some existing ones to reduce the options.

To add Multiple Choice distractors, follow these steps:

1. In the Timeline, select the frame that contains the Multiple Choice interaction. Select Window, Library to open the Flash UI Components Folder located in the Library panel.

2. Drag a Check Box component onto the Stage and then use the Property Inspector to name the instance.

3. Open the Component Parameters panel and add the instance name you just created.

TRUE OR FALSE

A True or False learning interaction allows the users to choose either True or False as an answer to a question. The True or False interaction is made up of a question text field that holds the question presented to the users, two Radio Button components for the possible answers, a control button, and a feedback text field. The control button and feedback text field show the users whether they answered the question correctly and provide instructional text. You look at feedback options in the next part of this chapter.

Configuring a True or False Learning Interaction

To configure a True or False learning interaction, you use the Component Parameters panel to add the Interaction ID and the question you want to ask. Remember to select one of the radio buttons to identify the correct answer.

You can change the text from True and False to something more appropriate to your site and style by editing the text in the Distractors field. For example, you could have "A. Yes" and "B. No" as your chosen answers.

FEEDBACK, KNOWLEDGE TRACK, AND NAVIGATION

So far, you have looked at all the different types of learning interactions offered within Flash MX. As you can see, using them is simply a process of adapting the built-in functionality to address your needs. This chapter is devoted to the learning interactions and does not describe the specifics of customizing the graphical elements. By this stage of the book, I am sure that you are more than familiar with how to do that. The end of the chapter does, however, explain which parts can be customized and looks at the places where the scripts are held. This section describes what the users see, messages that are displayed, and the built-in navigation facilities.

For more general information about graphics in Flash, refer to Chapter 3, "Drawing and Painting in Flash," page 37.

Feedback, Knowledge Track, and Navigation are all controlled from that now-familiar Component Parameters panel. Clicking the Options button on the panel allows you to set these options for each interaction in your quiz.

Setting Feedback Options

The Feedback options control what the users see in response to the answers they give. You can show users a message after each question, indicating whether or not they are correct, as well as setting a number on the amount of tries allowed for each question. Feedback options can be set for each individual interaction in the quiz. Adding a check mark to the Feedback box enables you to show a message to the users after they have answered each question, while all interactions other than multiple choice have an option allowing the users to make multiple attempts to answer correctly.

Text in the initial feedback box is displayed to the users before they answer a question. This is a nice way to add instructional text, such as "select a radio button" or "click to select the correct answer."

The Correct and Incorrect Feedback options are used to show the users a message when they get the right or wrong answer. Use them both to send encouraging messages to the users. Even if the answer is wrong, encourage the users to try again and not get downhearted. When you're learning something new, there is nothing worse than simply being told something is not right! Additional incorrect feedback is displayed to the users each time they try to answer the question.

Setting Knowledge Track

Knowledge Track works with both AICC- and SCORM-compliant LMS. It is an automatic data-tracking feature that allows you to submit student performance data to an LMS or other back-end tracking systems.

To use Knowledge Track, you must embed your learning movie into an HTML page containing the required JavaScript. This page is generated based on the settings you choose in the publishing process.

⇨ *For more information on publishing and optimizing your movies, see Chapter 30, "Optimizing, Publishing, and Exporting Movies," page 643.*

> Weighting specifies the importance of a question. If all questions have equal difficulty, set all weighting to 1; otherwise, set weighting where 1 is easy and 3 is hard.

All data captured and tracked by Knowledge Track is based on the AICC standard.

In the Component Parameters panel for an interaction, you can set values for the data elements. To set Knowledge Track options, follow these steps:

1. Select the Instructions panel on the Stage and then open the Component Parameters panel.

2. Click the Options tab and a check to the Knowledge Track check box.

3. In the Objective ID field, specify an objective for the interaction. This ID is related to an objective set up within the LMS. Tracking still works if the optional field is left blank.

4. Specify a weighting value for the interaction. The options are now complete, as shown in Figure 23.11.

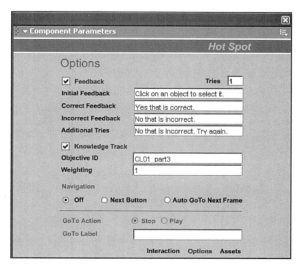

Figure 23.11
The complete Component Parameters panel has all the information required for successful tracking and weighting.

Basic Structure of the Learning Interaction Scripts and Components

The learning interactions are the core of the whole interactive process. The interactions themselves collect the user parameters and build the `SessionArray` and interaction event handling functions.

To dig deeper into the way these features work, it is best to look at the scripts within the Library panel.

The `LtoolBox` global class processes data storage and data formatting for interactions. Each interaction component also has its own script to initialize event-handling functions that are triggered by the interaction assets.

If you want to look at the scripts or to edit them, use the Library to open the script. All the scripts have been well commented by Macromedia to make them easy to follow and thus edit. Most of the script sections are built within functions.

With a script open in the Library panel, you can edit it in the normal way you work with ActionScript.

TROUBLESHOOTING

I added a new interaction, but everything is now wrong. What should I check for?

Make sure that the new frame you added for the interaction was a keyframe. Simply adding a normal frame will lead to problems.

Help! I broke apart the Learning Interaction component. What do I do now?

If you break apart the Learning Interaction component, the built-in interaction scripts will be lost or corrupt. You should delete the interaction completely and replace it with a fresh copy from the Library.

Why are some of the options different for the interactions?

Although most of the interactions perform in the same way, it is natural to have some differences. For example, you cannot possibly allow multiple attempts on a True and False interaction.

FLASH AT WORK: USING AN LMS

If you have little or no knowledge of what a Learning Management System (LMS) is or what it does, the following description should help provide an introduction to the student experience when an interactive learning experience is undertaken.

For an LMS-compliant quiz, the following events occur. Some are visible to the student, whereas others happen behind the scenes.

1. The LMS is launched and the student logs in.
2. The student chooses the learning activity to be undertaken.
3. The student launches the learning interaction.
4. The student works through the quiz questions.

5. The Flash file sends the data to the LMS via the HTML and JavaScript tracking files; the student does not see this action occur.

The user experience is basically the same regardless of the type of LMS.

Depending on whether you are sending your quiz data to an AICC or SCORM tracking system, the preparation is slightly different.

Preparing for AICC Compliance

Sending tracking data to an AICC-compliant LMS requires that you enable tracking for the quiz and then publish the movie using the Flash W/AICC tracking template. You need to place the HTML and SWF files that Flash creates in the same directory on the Web server. You also need to edit the Frameset file that is created to include the name of your quiz.

The steps required to prepare for AICC compliance are as follows:

1. Open the movie that contains your quiz in Flash. Choose File, Publish Settings to open the Publish Settings dialog box. Click the Formats tab and make sure that both Flash and HTML are checked.

2. Click the HTML tab and select Flash w/AICC Tracking from the drop-down menu, as shown in Figure 23.12.

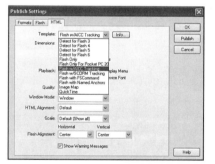

Figure 23.12

Choose the AICC template from the HTML Template drop-down menu to make sure the correct files are created.

3. Click the Publish button; then close the dialog box by clicking OK. Flash creates a SWF file and an HTML file. Place both of these files in the same directory on your Web server.

4. Use the File Management application to locate the Flash MX program folder and locate the First Run\HTML\Learning Extensions subfolder.

5. Open the folder from step 4 and copy the two HTML files as well as the Scripts subfolder to the same server directory that you used in step 3.

6. Use a text editor or Dreamweaver to open the frameset HTML file that you copied to your Web server.

7. Change the line that says `<frame src="Untitled-1.htm" name="content" frameborder="0">` so that Untitled-1.htm refers to the HTML file created when you published from Flash.

8. Launch the LMS system that references the frameset.htm page.

Preparing for SCORM Compliance

The main difference between preparing for AICC and SCORM compliance is the template you use during the publishing process. No editing of internal files is required. To prepare your movie for use with a SCORM-compliant LMS, follow these steps:

1. Open the movie that contains your quiz in Flash. Choose File, Publish Settings to open the Publish Settings dialog box.

2. Click the Formats tab and make sure that both Flash and HTML are checked.

3. Click the HTML tab and select Flash w/SCORM Tracking from the drop-down menu.

4. Click the Publish button; then close the dialog box by clicking OK. Flash creates a SWF file and an HTML file. Place both of these files in the same directory on your Web server.

5. Launch your LMS system and add the required reference for the HTML file created by Flash.

For the file to work correctly, you must make sure that you tell LMS to launch the SCORM tracking frameset.

SHARING ACTIONSCRIPT

SHARED LIBRARIES

A Shared Library allows media such as movie clips, graphics, sounds, and buttons to be used within multiple movies. A Shared Library can contain various buttons and sounds that are subsequently used in many movie files. You may have a sound or graphic set that you add to all client sites or a movie clip that you always include to signify your work.

In large Flash sites that are made up of multiple movies, the great thing about Shared Libraries is the savings that can be made in download time.

After a movie that contains the shared items is downloaded, the items don't need to be downloaded again. They are referenced in the subsequent files rather than the media actually being included multiple times.

The best part of using the Shared Library assets is the way they help you save time with your workflow and site or project management.

From simple acts such as sharing your logo to be shown on all sites to creating a large central library that allows you to update from a single location, Shared Libraries are beneficial to everyone using Flash.

Shared Library assets allow you to reuse assets from a source movie in as many destination movies as you like. There are (like most things in Flash MX) two ways in which you can achieve this result: You can either use runtime shared assets or author time-shared assets.

Runtime Shared Assets

When you work with runtime shared assets, you place the assets as symbols in the library of a single movie. This movie is known as the *source movie*. You then place a link to the shared assets in the source movie from the destination movie. The assets are then loaded when the movie plays back in the user's browser. For this to work, you must upload or publish the source movie to a specified directory. If the source movie is not uploaded, the shared assets will not be found and will thus not load at runtime.

To use runtime shared assets successfully, you need to make sure that the following workflow occurs: The authors of the movie that contains the shared assets must define the shared asset in their movie. The asset then needs a string and the URL where the file will be located.

You use the Symbol Properties dialog box to define the sharing properties of the asset in the source file.

The following steps take you through the process of setting up the source movie:

1. Open or create a movie that will contain the shared assets. In the case of a new movie, create or add the symbols to be shared.

2. Select a symbol to be shared and then show the Library Panel by selecting Window, Library.

3. Right-click to open the Library Option menu and then choose Properties. The Symbol Properties dialog box opens, as shown in Figure 24.1. If the dialog box does not look like the one shown here, click the Advanced button to expand it.

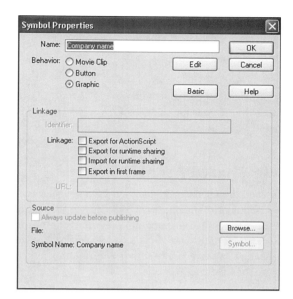

Figure 24.1
In the Symbol Properties dialog box, you can set Runtime Sharing options.

4. Select the Export for Runtime Sharing check box to make the asset available for linking to the destination movie.

5. In the Identifier field, type a name for the asset. Flash will use this name to identify the asset when linking to the destination movie.

6. Enter the URL where the SWF file containing the shared asset will be posted and click OK.

Now that the source movie has the sharing information in place, it is vital that the destination movie has exactly the same information included. If there are any differences in the information, the asset will not be shared or found correctly.

Again, you use the Symbol Properties dialog box to add the information. The following steps ensure successful linkage:

1. Open the Library panel in the destination movie.

2. Select a movie clip, button, or graphic symbol in the Library panel and then choose Properties from the Library options menu. Click the Advanced button to expand the Symbol Properties dialog box if the advanced properties aren't visible.

3. In the Linkage section, select Import for Runtime Sharing to link to the asset in the source movie.

4. Enter the same identifier as you did for the source movie—they must be exactly the same.

You must post the SWF file to the URL specified in step 6 so that the shared assets will be available to destination movies.

5. Enter the URL where the SWF source file containing the shared asset is posted. As stated previously, this information must be exactly the same as the information in the source movie.

6. Select Always Update Before Publishing to automatically update the asset if a new version is found at the specified source location and click OK.

> You can turn off linkage in the destination by selecting the linked symbol in the Library panel, opening the Symbol Properties dialog box, and deselecting the Import for Runtime Sharing check box.

Working with Author-Time Shared Assets

Author-time shared assets are used to replace (or update) symbols in your new movie with those from the shared resource. You can update symbols at any time during the authoring process. When you use author-time shared assets, you replace (or update) the contents of your symbol with those of the symbol from the shared resource. In this event, your symbol keeps the name and properties that you give it; only the contents change. When you use author-time sharing, any assets that the shared symbol uses are also imported to the destination movie.

This capability is handy if you want to use an updated logo image or to update links within a movie clip or component. Rather than have to search for each instance, you can merely update the contents of one symbol with that of the shared asset.

Updating or replacing symbols using author-time sharing is a simple process, as outlined in these steps:

1. With your destination movie open, select a movie clip, button, or graphic symbol and then choose Properties from the Library options menu. The Symbol Properties dialog box opens.

2. To select a new FLA file in the Symbol Properties dialog box, click Browse in the Source section.

3. In the resulting Open dialog box, navigate to an FLA file containing the symbol that you want to use to update or replace the selected symbol in the Library panel. Then click Open.

4. To select a new symbol in the FLA file, click Symbol in the Source section.

5. Navigate to a symbol in the resulting dialog box and then click Open.

6. Back in the Symbol Properties dialog box, select Always Update Before Publishing in the Source section to automatically update the asset if a new version is found at the specified source location.

7. The completed dialog box should look something like Figure 24.2.

8. Click OK to close the Symbol Properties dialog box.

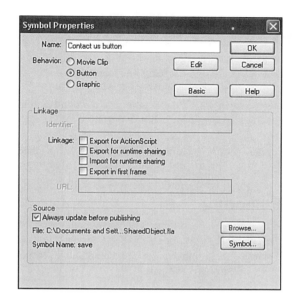

Figure 24.2
The completed Symbol Properties dialog box should contain the name of the source FLA and symbol.

FLASH REMOTING

Flash Remoting is yet another new function in Flash MX; it enables you to connect to remote services such as ColdFusion pages. Flash Remoting gives you, the developer, support for connecting to remote server objects.

In Part V, "External Communication with Flash," you will use dynamic data and connect to a server. This feature allows for the creation of shopping carts, message boards, and so on, in Flash by storing information in a database.

Flash Remoting supports object-based access such as Java objects, as well as document processing to exchange dates with remote services such as Java classes and JavaBeans.

To use Flash Remoting, you need to install the Flash Remoting Components and Jrun4 and make sure that you have Flash MX and the Flash 6 Player installed.

There are many benefits of Flash Remoting, as shown in Table 24.1. For a complete list of these benefits, check out the Macromedia Web site, `http://www.macromedia.com/FlashMX`.

Table 24.1 Benefits of the Flash Remoting Services

Feature	Benefit
Provides a single API for calling remote services and XML documents from within Macromedia Flash applications.	Simplifies the development process required to access remote services from Flash applications. Exposes remote service APIs to Flash applications as simple ActionScript APIs, enabling workflow between UI designers and application server developers.

Table 24.1 Continued

Feature	Benefit
Provides new ActionScript APIs for recordset handling and data binding.	Simplifies the use of recordsets in ActionScript, enabling Flash applications to serve as UIs for standard relational databases.
Supports a wide range of remote services, including EJBs, Java classes, JavaBeans, and MBeans.	Enables the use of a rich Flash interface as a UI for business logic.
Delivers high-performance transfer of data between Flash and remote objects.	Increases application performance by minimizing the amount of data needed to send over the wire.

Java Classes and Flash Remoting

To make Java application files available to Flash Remoting, you should either add new directories to the JVM Classpath on the server using the JMC, or else use the Server-Inf directory. The Server-Inf directory, when used for Java classes (including JavaBeans), should have classes placed under the `jrun_root/servers/jrun_server/SERVER-INF` path.

Using the correct structure means that classes are successfully available server-wide.

If you are creating a JavaBean, you must implement Serializable; however, this is not necessary when you're creating a Java object.

If you want to allow users to connect directly to your Java classes, you need to modify a policy file to set the required permissions to the package.

Assuming you have a package called com.myfiles and you want to allow the gateway to access the classes held within it, you need to edit the lib/jrun.policy file.

The following code will make the file accessible to everyone, so be careful what it contains before making such a change. As you can set permissions only at package level with Java, you will need to set permissions for any package that you want to make public.

```
// PERMISSIONS GRANTED TO EVERYONE

grant {
  // users should narrow or expand on this as they see fit
  // to grant wide-open security access to all code, uncomment this line
    //permission java.security.AllPermission;
  // to grant clients access to classes in the jrun packages, uncomment this line
    //permission java.lang.RuntimePermission "accessClassInPackage.jrun";
  // add this line
  permission java.lang.RuntimePermission "accessClassInPackage.com.myfiles";
  //snipped
}
```

ActionScript Classes and Flash Remoting

The ActionScript classes for Flash Remoting must be included in your movie at frame level. The NetServices.as fileincluded in the Flash Remoting Components download provides the main functionality.

Two other ActionScript classes are used with Flash Remoting. They are NetDebug.as, which is used purely in a development environment and, as the name suggests, is a debugging file; and DataGlue.as, which helps to format results that use the recordset object. The following three lines of code include the required ActionScript files:

```
#include "NetServices.as"
#include "NetDebug.as"
#include "DataGlue.as"
```

Making Service Calls to a Server from a Flash Movie

Before you can make a service call to an application server, you must first create the service object in the movie by using the NetServices functions creategatewayConnection and getService to create a connection object.

The following code will create a serviced object named FirstRemote:

```
#include "NetServices.as"

if (inited == null)
{
  // do this code only once
  inited = true;

  // set the default gateway URL (this is used only in authoring)
  NetServices.setDefaultGatewayUrl("http://localhost:8100/flashservices/gateway");

  // connect to the gateway
  gateway_conn = NetServices.createGatewayConnection();

  // get a reference to a service
  FirstRemote = gateway_conn.getService("FirstRemote ", this);
}
```

After you create the connection object, you can make service calls to the application server, as the following example shows:

```
FirstRemote.remoteServiceMethodName(param1, "param2");
```

Notice that the URL does not have the normal format for a link. In this case, the URL specifies the location and port of the Web server and the gateway servlet mapping for the Flash Remoting Server. It does not look or even translate to an actual directory structure.

To handle the results from the service function, you can either create a specific results handler or use generic ones.

For more details about event handlers, refer to Chapter 12, "Managing Variables, Data, and Datatypes," page 187.

INCLUDING EXTERNAL ACTIONSCRIPT

Although typing your scripts directly into the Actions panel of your movie is quite normal, you can save your script as an external file and reuse it whenever needed.

Simply use a normal text editor to create and edit the ActionScript; then paste it into the Actions panel, or use the Include action to add the external script at runtime.

Alternatively, you can create your ActionScript in the normal way (using the Actions panel) and then save it to a text file for later reuse or editing.

➪ *For more information about ActionScripting fundamentals, refer to Chapter 11, "Getting Started with ActionScript," page 169.*

You can export ActionScript to a text file in two steps. In the Actions panel, open the pop-up menu, as shown in Figure 24.3, and choose Export as File. Browse to the place where you want to keep the saved file, click Save, and you are all done.

Figure 24.3

The Actions panel pop-up menu has many useful features, including Export as File.

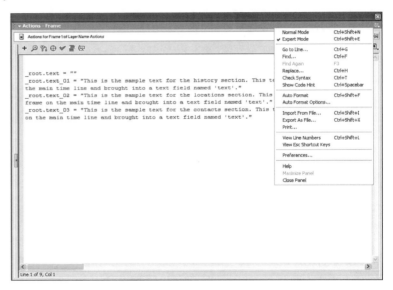

After the file is saved, you can use any text editor to make changes to the ActionScript.

After you save the text file, you can reimport it into the same FLA file or any other. This makes it a great way to share ActionScript that you want to use over and over. Make sure that you are working in Expert mode; and then from the same pop-up menu, choose Import from File, browse to your text file, and click Open.

Rather than pasting your ActionScript into the Actions panel, you can choose to include the text file when you export the movie by using the Include action.

Make sure that the insertion point is located in the correct place in the Script panel. This must be the place where you want the script included. Double-click Include from the Miscellaneous Actions category and type the path to the external file in the Path box.

Although this chapter is mainly about sharing, it is also a good place to talk about external files in general. Using Flash MX, you can load information from and send information to external sources. These sources include external scripts located on the server, text files, and, of course, XML files.

> The path you type must be relative to your FLA file. When your movie is exported, the Include action is replaced by the contents of the external file.

You can set your movies to load images and sound files during runtime. This capability allows you to change, edit the external file without needing to change the original SWF file. As long as the code is not broken by your changes, everything will still function perfectly.

Extending Flash is just as easy; you can use the `fsCommand` and Flash Player methods. The `fsCommand` action can be passed to a JavaScript function in an HTML file that opens a new window.

You can also use Flash components over and over again. They are possibly the single most dramatic development in Flash MX for sharing and reusing elements.

⇨ *For more information about components, see Chapter 22, "Components," page 511.*

TROUBLESHOOTING

I placed a file into a shared library, but it does not appear there. What should I do?

This is a common problem. You should check that the linkage information in both the source and destination files is the same.

When I use Flash Remoting, should I declare that my Java methods throw exceptions?

No, not at all. Typically, you throw exceptions when you care about propagating application exceptions to your Flash client, but as the gateway itself doesn't handle checked exceptions, declaring them is not necessary.

What are the two Local connection object handlers?

`LocalConnection.allowDomain` is invoked whenever the receiving local connection object receives a request to invoke a method from a sending local connection object. `LocalConnection.onStatus` is invoked after a sending local connection object tries to send a command to a receiving local connection object.

Why do I get the Resolve Library Conflict dialog box?

This dialog box is displayed when you try to import or copy a Library item into a movie that already has an asset with the same name. To resolve the conflict, you can click Don't Replace Existing Items to preserve the existing assets in the destination movie. Alternatively, you can click Replace Existing Items to replace the existing assets and their instances with the new items of the same name.

FLASH AT WORK: THE LOCALCONNECTION FEATURE

As you will discover throughout this book, Flash MX has many new powerful and exciting features, and one of them is the `LocalConnection` class. In simple terms, this class has methods that enable you to send data from one movie to another. In Flash MX, you can do this without needing to use JavaScript or the `FSCommand`.

`LocalConection` has the power to send strings and complete objects (including properties) from one movie to another; this can even be done across different browsers.

Creating a Local Connection

The `LocalConnection` class has four methods: `send()`, `connect()`, `close()`, and `domain()`. In this example, we will look only at the `send()` and `connect()` methods, which are required to pass information between two movies on the same domain.

Start by creating the movie to receive the message using the following steps:

1. Create a new movie in Flash. Name the file **receiving.fla**.

2. In the file, create a dynamic text field. Name the instance **MessSent**.

3. Place all the following code for the receiving movie in the Actions panel in frame 1:

```
receiving_lc = new LocalConnection();
receiving_lc.methodToExecute = function (param) {
    MessSent.text = param;
}
receiving_lc.connect("lc_test");
```

4. This code first creates the `LocalConnection` object using a variable name and the correct constructor for the `LocalConnection` class.

5. The method to be called when the receiving movie receives information from the sending movie is then defined. Here, the `MessSent` is populated with a string sent by the sending movie.

6. Use the `connect()` method to connect to the local object named `lc_test`.

7. Save your work.

Now create the movie to send information:

1. Create a new movie in Flash. Name the file **sending.fla**.

2. In the file, create a text field. Name the instance **MessSending**.

3. Place a button in the movie and name the instance **sendButton**.

4. As with the receiving file, place all the following code in the Actions panel for frame 1:

```
sendButton.onRelease = function() {
    sending_lc = new LocalConnection();
    sending_lc.send("lc_test", "methodToExecute", userMessage.text);
```

```
        delete sending_lc;
    };
```

5. After you save your work, embed both movies in the same HTML page and test them within a Flash 6 Player–enabled browser.

6. Type a message in the first text box, click the button, and the text should appear in the second text box, as shown in Figure 24.4.

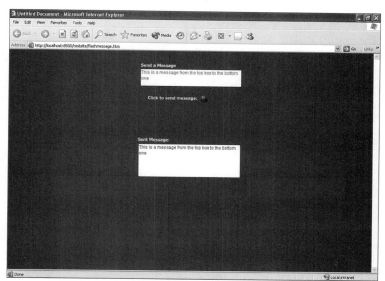

Figure 24.4
Sending messages between movies on the same domain is simple; just click the button and it appears.

24

As you have seen, setting up this connection is very straightforward and simple. These text boxes appear in the same page; however, it would work just as well if they were on two pages. It also works as long as they reside on the same domain.

Sending Messages Between Domains

You can even send messages between domains; however, setting up this connection is more complicated and also presents various security issues that you must consider.

The main difference in communicating across domains is the need to define the connectionName parameter in both movies to ensure that Flash does not add the current subdomain. You can achieve this by adding an _ (underscore) at the beginning of the connectionName parameter in both movies:

```
receiving_lc = new LocalConnection();
receiving_lc.aMethod = function(param) {
 trace(param);
}
receiving_lc.allowDomain = function(senderDomain){
 return (senderDomain == "allowedDomain.com");
}
receiving_lc.connect("_lc_test");
```

A LocalConnection in a sending movie from a different domain can then use the send() method to send messages to the destination movie:

```
sending_lc = new LocalConnection();
sending_lc.send("myDomain:_lc_test", "aMethod", "This is a string parameter");
delete sending_lc;
```

TESTING, DEBUGGING, AND TROUBLESHOOTING

IN THIS CHAPTER

AVOIDING COMMON PROBLEMS

The whole concept of troubleshooting is more a case of common sense than it is a deep technical knowledge, yet still people run into problems that they could have avoided by simply applying good business practices. Avoidance is always better than cure. In practice, good planning and early testing of scenes and movies will always make troubleshooting less painful and considerably easier than leaving everything until the end of a project.

Some standard rules should apply to work in progress, whether you're creating a small Flash movie or a huge development project. In this chapter, you'll look at these rules and how to solve problems when they actually occur.

In most cases, problems with your movies can be broken down into one of three categories: the movie doesn't work, the movie doesn't work on the system, or the software doesn't work.

The first category is usually caused by errors that you make; changing variables, misnaming variables in an instance, or assigning actions incorrectly can all lead to problems in your files. Testing and saving as you go will help to quickly identify and eliminate these kinds of problems.

System-related problems are often harder to trace in terms of the cause. If a particular file is causing a crash, try testing the file on a different system. Look at any new applications that you have installed and see whether they could be causing problems. Also check display settings; if they have been changed, this can lead to problems.

The software not working or behaving as expected may indicate that there is a configuration problem on your system. If you have a new or upgraded installation, are you sure that your system meets requirements? Again, see whether the problem appears on another machine. If it does, the fault may lie with the software; if not, more than likely it is your system.

From a planning perspective, make sure that your project planning allows time for testing and any required debugging. A broken movie is no use to anyone, and will certainly not enhance your reputation as a designer or developer. Rushing a project due to bad planning will lead to errors, and no testing time will almost inevitably lead to an unhappy client and no further business.

Building in testing time should be part of the planning process for all your Flash projects, no matter what they are or how many people are involved. The process of testing and problem solving during each stage of development gives you control over minor issues before you add the next stage of the project and suddenly create a huge problem that could have occurred a long time ago.

When you're handling multiple movies that need to work together, always make sure they work in a standalone capacity before linking them. Again, taking this step ensures that you can narrow down, identify, and solve the root of a problem as soon as possible.

If you have multiple scenes, test each scene individually; try to isolate the exact place and cause of the fault.

If you're moving to MX from an older version of Flash, make sure that you are using the correct syntax in code and expressions.

⇨ *To learn how to use the current version of ActionScript correctly, see Chapter 11, "Getting Started with ActionScript," page 169.*

Save your projects regularly with different filenames and in different locations. Having a previous version that worked perfectly allows you to work backward through the development cycle, if necessary, to find the exact point at which a project falls apart or to identify changes that were made to the script that seemingly stop functioning for no reason.

Let me be totally brutal: Flash files do not just fail or suddenly stop working without any user input. Somewhere in your workflow or development cycle, someone somewhere (maybe even you) has changed or added something. Making sure that you can find the error makes fixing it much easier and certainly far less time consuming.

Using a well-documented plan of work will also enable you to back-track through the process in a seamless manner. However mundane these ideas sound, good practice from the planning stage onward will lead to a far more successful overall project.

Multiple Platform Testing

Unless you are developing a project for a controlled audience, chances are that your completed movies will be seen by different users on different platforms on all types of machines. For this reason, ensuring that your movies will work the way you intended is vital.

You might think I'm jumping backward here, but ensuring that your movie is accessible to the intended audience should be part of the planning process. In a solid project, the planning should be as painstaking and exact as the development itself.

After you decide the minimum system requirements for your project, you should test on that platform and specification regularly.

Testing on multiple machines is always the best policy, but not always immediately possible. Not everyone has access to an array of machines of different operating systems and quality; however, you cannot assume that a project that works perfectly on a Windows 2000 machine will even load on a Macintosh running an older operating system.

Problems caused by operating systems have no reflection on your design or development skills but are equally important in terms of resolution.

Making sure that you are aware of the possible drawbacks and planning a workaround if a total solution is not available will ensure that the completed project is as usable as possible to the target audience. Waiting until you finish the perfect movie and then finding that only 10 percent of users can view it will mean a total rethink and redesign. This is obviously unacceptable, even to the most inexperienced of Flash designers and developers.

In simple terms, the better you plan the project, the better the result.

25

Effective Testing Procedures

Having used common sense and taken reasonable precautions to ensure that you have at least a minimum of troubleshooting skills, you can use the following list to get the best from your testing. These tips can be used as a handy guide to effective testing.

- Always use the Control, Test Movie function to test your creations. Unlike other options that offer only limited facilities, this route allows you to best simulate the finished movie. Links, sounds, and navigation should all be in full working order. Using this function is an ideal way to spot problems quickly and easily.

- If you find a problem, try extracting the problem area of the movie to a standalone file and then see whether the problem still exists. This test will help greatly in identifying whether the problem relates to the specific area of the movie or is tied into other areas of the project.

- Test the whole movie on a different computer. This test will tell you if the problem relates to the hardware you're using, or possibly even a problem with the actual installation of Flash that you have been working with.

- Test the file on a server. If you discover a problem on one server, try it on another. This test will tell you if the problem relates to the original server or servers in general.

- For server-related problems, ensure that the problem server has the correct MIME types associated with the .swf extension. Refer to the Macromedia Web site at http://www.macromedia.com for more information on this issue.

- If the problem movie or project has ActionScript included, before panicking about trying to fix it, check for inaccurate spelling, naming problems, or punctuation errors. All these errors can cause seemingly massive problems that actually require a minimum of effort to resolve.

Optimization

Although optimizing your files will not specifically solve problems, you certainly need to include this approach in this area of problem avoidance. As I said already, avoidance is better than cure. Certain optimization techniques are common-sense based but can save a lot of time and heartache later.

Flash does not need you to do everything because the built-in publishing functions automatically remove duplicate shapes and add them into the final playback a single time. Check out Chapter 30, "Publishing, Exporting, and Optimizing Files," for information about how to compress files during the process to help reduce file and download size.

For more information on optimizing your movies, see Chapter 30, "Optimizing, Publishing, and Exporting Movies," page 643.

Testing Download Performance

Testing your movie's download performance helps to ensure that the movie is viewed the way you intended. There is nothing worse than finding out the movie you planned and built so carefully is constantly pausing when the player can't meet the frame rate you set.

You can use the Bandwidth profiler to generate a graphical report so that you can see the amount of data sent per frame. This is done based on the connection speeds you specify. You should test the movie on as many different machines and connection speeds as possible; however, where that is not possible, Flash will attempt to simulate the performance for you.

You can test your download performance with the following steps:

1. From the Control menu, choose either Test Movie or Test Scene.

2. From the Debug menu, choose the connection speed that you want to test against. You can specify your own settings by opening the Custom Modem settings dialog box (Debug, Customize).

3. From the View menu, choose Bandwidth to see the graphical representation of your settings.

You can change how the Profiler shows your information by changing your selections on the View menu. The menu options are as follows:

- **Show Streaming**—Toggles the playback between having a simulated Web connection or not. Changing this setting while the playback is in operation causes the movie to start over.

- **Streaming Graph**—Shows you which (if any) of your frames will cause the playback to be paused. The frame blocks are shown in alternating colors. Normally, the first frame is larger than the others because it contains more information. Clicking on any frame in the graph displays the frame information on the left panel.

- **Frame by Frame Graph**—Shows any frames that will lead to pauses in the playback. A red line like the one located at 100B in Figure 25.1 is a guide. Any frames that go above this line cause a pause while the rest of the frame loads.

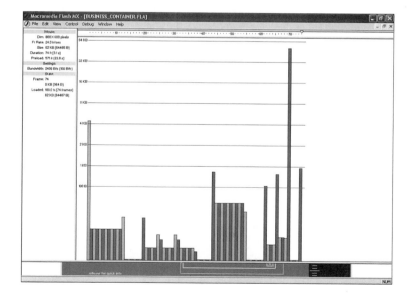

Figure 25.1
The Bandwidth profiler allows you to identify problem areas in your movie files.

Flash allows you to create a text file with a frame-by-frame breakdown of the data in the final file. From the File menu, choose Publish Settings and then select Generate Size Report. Flash generates a .txt file with the same name as the .fla file. For example, movie1 would become movie1 report.txt.

Troubleshooting ActionScript

Like any scripting language, ActionScript can and does go wrong from time to time. The more careful you are with your scripting, the more problems you can avoid. It doesn't matter how experienced you are using ActionScript; certain actions are still common sense and great at avoiding pitfalls. The following tips should help you work in a logical manner and stop problems before they start:

- Comment your ActionScript with good notation about how it should work. Comments help team members to not mess with your carefully crafted code and, on a large project, help you remember why you created it a certain way.

- Name your elements in a logical fashion. A simple word like `button` is meaningless when you have 15 or 20 different ones! `SmallDepressedButton` at least tells you something about the element as well. Start new words in your element names with capital letters to make them more legible.

- Make sure that the names mean something to you, especially when you're working with variables. Again, putting useful information into the variable name will help if you need to troubleshoot. A variable that contains e-mail information is much better named `EmailForm01` than simply `email`.

Remember that to see all your ActionScript and other movie elements, you can use the Movie Explorer.

⇨ *For more detailed information on troubleshooting your ActionScript, see Chapter 11, "Getting Started with ActionScript," page 169.*

USING THE DEBUGGER

Okay, so you've tried all reasonable means to ensure that things work correctly the first time around, but somehow something has still gone wrong. It's time to move to the tools that Flash offers you to find and fix problems that go beyond your common sense.

The Debugger in Flash MX has a much better performance record than the one in Flash 5 and is therefore a much more powerful tool.

My favorite feature of the Debugger is the facility to work with local- or server-based files. Opening the Debugger (Control, Test Movie) not only automatically opens the Debugger itself, but also loads the current movie in test mode. Figure 25.2 breaks down the debugging screen for you.

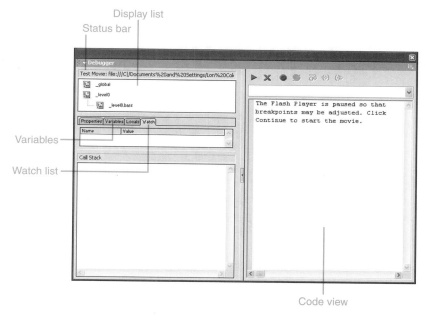

Display list

Status bar

Variables

Watch list

Code view

Figure 25.2
The Debugger allows you to step through the movie to find and fix errors.

Breakpoints and Step Through

Breakpoints control your movie as it plays in the Flash Player. Breakpoints allow you to test scripts that are causing problems, make edits, and then test again. For example, you might have a series of statements in your code; you know there is an error but are not sure where. By adding breakpoints before each statement, you can step through them in turn and see where the error occurs.

Stepping through the code breakpoint by breakpoint ensures that you are able to stop the code-fix problems and move on to the next potential problem area.

You can set breakpoints that remain part of the .fla file and use them over and over, or you can add them within the Debugger itself. When you use the Debugger to set your breakpoints, they remain only for the current session and are then removed.

Setting and Removing Breakpoints

To use the Debugger for setting or removing your breakpoints, find the line of code into which you want to add a breakpoint in the Script pane of the Actions panel. This is likely to be at the start of a series of statements, such as if-else statements that are not working as expected. Then drop down the Debug Options menu and choose the appropriate menu option.

To set or remove breakpoints in the Debugger, these steps are required:

1. Locate the line of code to which you want to either add or remove a breakpoint.

2. Click either the Toggle Breakpoint or Remove All Breakpoints button located above code view.

   Alternatively, use the options menu and then choose the option that suits your needs.

3. When the Player stops at your breakpoint, use the control buttons shown in Figure 25.3 to step through your code.

Figure 25.3
Use the control buttons to control the movie in the Debugger.

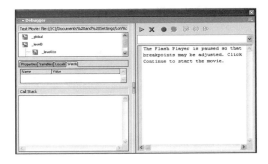

Stepping Through Your Code

The process of moving through your code breakpoint by breakpoint is called *stepping through*. When you commence a debugging session, the Flash Player automatically pauses to give you control over the session. For breakpoints that are set within the Actions panel, click the Play button. The movie proceeds until it reaches your first breakpoint.

If you set the breakpoints inside the debugging environment, use the control buttons to move to the first breakpoint.

When you move through the code, the display in the Debugger changes. The watch list, variables, locals, and properties change to display the current information from the code. In the code view pane, a yellow arrow indicates the point where the code is stopped.

The panel above the code view, shown in Figure 25.3, gives you control over the debugging process, which performs as follows:

- **Step In**—This button works only with user-defined functions. When the Step In button is clicked, the Debugger moves or steps into a function.

- **Step Out**—This button works only when you have already stepped into a function.

- **Step Over**—This button moves the Debugger forward by a single line of code regardless of functions.

- **Continue**—This button continues the movie from its present location to your next breakpoint.

- **Stop Debugging**—When you click this button, the movie carries on playing in the Flash Player, but the Debugger stops functioning.

The Output Window

The Output window (displayed by clicking Window, Output) has been designed specifically to help you solve problems within your movies. Problems such as syntax errors are shown in the Output window automatically; however, by using commands such as List Objects and List Variables, you can expand on the information displayed, thus giving you greater abilities to find and fix problems.

Using List Objects is a simple way to find target paths and instance names. When you're working in text mode, the output automatically displays any syntax errors in your code, giving you the chance to fix them and continue testing. You can use the Trace Action to send particular information to the Output window while the movie is actually playing. This option is discussed in more detail later in this chapter.

You can work with the information in the Output window by using the options menu located at the top left of the window.

The options in this menu allow you to perform the following commands:

- **Copy**—Takes the contents of the window and adds it to the Clipboard

- **Clear**—Clears the Output window

- **Save to File**—Allows you to save the contents of the Output window into a text file for further troubleshooting

- **Print**—Prints the contents of the Output window

- **Find**—Allows you to search for a text string

- **Find Again**—Repeats the previous search

Working with Variables in the Output Window

You can use the List Variables command when testing a movie to send a list of the current variables to the Output window. The main difference between using this command and the Debugger generally is that the list is not updated unless you use such a command. Each time you want the display updated, you must choose the List Variables command.

Figure 25.4 shows the variables listed from a movie. Note that global variables are displayed at the top of the List variables output. All global variables are given the prefix `_global`.

Figure 25.4

The List variables output displays the variables in your movie, along with associated properties.

The List variables output also shows any properties that are created with the `Object.addproperty` method and that invoke `set` or `get` methods. These properties are displayed alongside any other properties of the object, but you can easily identify them by the presence of a `[getter/setter]` string. Evaluating the `get` function of the property causes the value of `[getter/setter]` to be displayed.

> One of the most important points at this early stage is that the debugging is not backward or forward compatible.

Using the Trace Action

Using the trace action in a script allows you to send information from the movie being tested into the Output window. The most common use for the trace action is to test whether a function is called successfully. The most common reason for having a Flash movie that does not perform as expected is an incorrect path to a movie clip, variable, object, or function. Even something seemingly as simple as this can lead to variables having the wrong values, functions being called incorrectly, or not even being called at all. The trace action allows you to test this.

In scripting terms, the trace action is similar to the JavaScript `alert` statement. You can use it to send specific information or programming notes for display; then the frame is played in test mode.

To use the trace action, you use expressions as parameters. It is the value of the expression that is displayed in the Output window.

Remote Debugging Facilities

Although you can debug your movies from any of the three types of Flash Player (standalone, plug-in, or ActiveX), the preparation for doing so must take place when you publish the file rather than later.

If you don't enable debugging within the Publish Settings dialog box, you cannot activate the debugging screen remotely.

To set the properties for remote debugging, take the following steps:

1. Choose File, Publish Settings to open the Publish Settings dialog box, as shown in Figure 25.5.

Figure 25.5
To enable remote debugging, you must first enable the option in the Publish Settings dialog box.

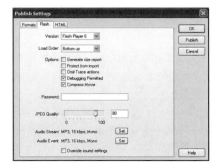

2. Select the Flash tab at the top of the dialog box, and enable the Debugging Permitted check box.

3. Add a password in the Password field. This password will ensure that only you or those you work with can access the debugging screen.

   You are now ready to publish the movie to your server.

4. Upload the newly created .swd file to the same location as your .swf file on the server.

5. Within Flash, choose Window, Debugger; then from the Panel drop-down menu, select Enable Remote Debugging.

   You are now ready to debug your movie remotely.

> After you complete the preceding steps, Flash creates a new file with the same name as your .swf file. This file has the file extension .swd, and is vital to the remote debugging of your files.

Activating the Debugger Remotely

Assuming that you have correctly uploaded the .swd file to the same server location as the .swf file, the remote debugging should work perfectly. If the .swd file is not found, although the debugging window will open, functionality such as stepping through code is immediately lost.

Even though you're working with a remote file, you need to open Flash MX before you start:

1. Use your browser window (or Flash Player) to open the .swf file from its remote location. Note that this is the .swf file, not an .fla file.

2. The Remote Debug dialog box is displayed. If the dialog box is not visible, the .swd file was not located in the expected place. In this case, you need to open the Context menu in the movie and then choose Debugger from the options.

3. In the Remote Debug dialog box, select the appropriate option depending on whether your Debug Player and Flash authoring tools are on the same machine. If they are not, enter the IP address of the other machine.

   Click OK to continue and wait for a connection to be made to the .swf file. When prompted, enter the password you attached to the movie earlier in the "Remote Debugging Facilities" section.

   You should see the display list for the movie in the debug window.

Still Having Problems?

This chapter has taken you through the built-in functions for testing and debugging your Flash files. If this chapter and the troubleshooting tips at the ends of the other chapters in the book have still not helped, other options are available to you.

Start by heading out to the Macromedia Web site (www.macromedia.com). The Flash Support Center is a great resource not only for helpful hints and tips, but also for tech notes that deal with specific problems. You can join in the Flash Forums to ask and find answers to specific problems that you have been unable to solve.

25

The forums and other types of support for Flash are located within the support section of the site. If you want to go straight there, simply go to http://www.macromedia.com/support/flash/.

The Macromedia Web site also lists external sites that offer help and advice to Flash designers and developers. Regardless of your Flash skill level, chances are that any problem you are having has happened before to someone else.

One of the great things about Flash and other Macromedia products is that, in general, the people who use them are happy to share information and help solve problems.

25

EXTERNAL COMMUNICATION
WITH FLASH

IN THIS PART

COMMUNICATING LOCALLY

IN THIS CHAPTER

CONTROLLING THE BROWSER

Your Macromedia Flash movies can run in one of several environments. The most common environment is a Flash Player in a Web browser. You can also run a Flash movie as a standalone projector or inside a Macromedia Director movie. In all these cases, the movie can communicate with the environment in a number of ways. In this chapter, you'll look at each environment and how the movie can communicate with it.

Flash movies can work just like the HTML <A HREF> tag when viewed in a Web browser, acting as a navigation control for the browser and changing the page being shown in the browser. They can also affect the page being shown in other browser windows and frames.

Using getURL

The main tool for controlling the browser is the getURL command. This command sends a message to the browser to tell it to load a new page from a specified URL. Executing the getURL command is just like a user clicking a link in an <A HREF> tag in the browser.

The following button script uses the getURL command to load a page named newpage.html:

```
on (release) {
    getURL("newpage.html");
}
```

An URL is a Uniform Resource Locator. It is the one required parameter of the getURL command.

There are two types of URLs: relative URLs and absolute URLs. A relative URL can be a local file, such as the newpage.html file in the previous example. It can also be a relative path to a file or directory.

An example of a relative URL that specifies a file in a directory below the current one is myfolder/newpage.html. This example specifies the file newpage.html, which is found in the folder named myfolder.

An absolute URL is a complete path to a file or directory on a server. An example of an absolute URL is http://www.mysite.com/newpage.html.

You can use getURL with a relative URL to load a page on the same server as the current Web page. You can also use a relative URL to load a page on your local hard drive when the page is on the hard drive or when the movie is running as a projector.

You can use an absolute URL in getURL only if you have an Internet connection because it usually calls out to a site on a Web server, not a page on your local machine.

Because the power of getURL is not in Flash, but rather in the Web browser, you can use anything as a parameter that the browser will understand as an address. For instance, if you want to make the browser list the files on an FTP server, you can use an URL such as ftp://ftp.myserver.com/. The browser will list the files there, as long as the browser supports FTP and the FTP site exists.

Remember that the Flash Player does not perform the actual page loading. It sends a message to the browser. It is then up to the browser to do the work.

Targeting Windows and Frames

A second parameter that you can give getURL is a target. This target can be a browser window, a browser frame, or a special command.

All Web browsers can have multiple windows open, each showing a different URL. These windows can be different sizes and have different toolbars, depending on how they were opened and how the user has adjusted them. You can also have multiple URLs visible in the same browser window by dividing it into frames. This is done at the HTML level with special HTML tags. Each frame in the window holds a separate URL and can be altered without affecting the other frames. Most browsers can also accept special commands in their address fields as alternatives to URLs. These commands change the browser's behavior or get information about the browser.

To give getURL a window or frame name, you first must name your browser frames and windows. Naming them takes some planning when you create your HTML pages.

Suppose you have a two-frame page with a small navigation bar on the left and a large content frame on the right. The content frame can be named contentFrame. The navigation frame can have a Flash movie in it with navigation buttons. One of these buttons can direct the contentFrame to go to a new page like this:

```
on (release) {
  getURL("newpage.html","contentFrame");
}
```

Targeting a frame is as simple as that. The same command would even allow one browser window with a Flash movie to control the URL shown in another window. You could have a movie in the main browser window that controls a smaller pop-up window.

Creating New Browser Windows

If you use getURL with a target that doesn't exist, the browser will create a new window to hold the content. For instance, if you target newWindow, and no window has that name, a new window named newWindow will open.

Once this window exists, you can continue to address it by this name. So you can use newWindow as a target over and over again. The first time you use newWindow, the browser will create the window. Each time after that, you will just change the content in the window. So a new window can be created, and you can also change its content later by using the same name. You can show HTML content to the user by creating and reusing the same window.

Using Special Targets

In addition to using your own names for targets, you can also use one of four special targets. Their names all begin with an underscore character. Here is a list of these special targets:

- _self—This target is the same as using no target parameter at all. It will target the current window or frame.

- _parent—This target refers to the frame one level up from the current page.

26

> ■ `_top`—This target refers to the window where the current frame or page is located.

> ■ `_blank`—This target creates a new window. Using this target is the only way to guarantee that a new window will open, regardless of what any current windows are named.

To open a new window with a button, you could use a script such as this:

```
on (release) {
    getURL("newpage.html","_blank");
}
```

CALLING JAVASCRIPT FUNCTIONS

Although `getURL` allows you to load new pages with your Flash movie, you can take almost complete control of the browser by using `fscommand`. Using this command, you can send messages to JavaScript in the browser. In addition, your Flash movie can receive messages from JavaScript on the Web page as well.

Problems with JavaScript

Before you start to learn about Flash-to-JavaScript communication, you should know about JavaScript's shortcomings. Mainly, it doesn't work in several browser variations.

To communicate between Flash and JavaScript, you need to have a piece of software that facilitates this communication. For Internet Explorer on Windows, this piece of software is called ActiveX. For older versions of Netscape Communicator, this piece of software is called LiveConnect. Both of these pieces of software are part of their respective browsers.

Although ActiveX is a part of Internet Explorer in Windows, it is not a part of Internet Explorer for the Mac. LiveConnect is a part of Netscape browser versions 4.7 and earlier, but it is not a part of Netscape 6 on either Mac or Windows. This leaves quite a few variations where the `fscommand` will not work: Windows users with Netscape and most Mac users. You can assume that any other browser, such as iCab or Opera, will also not support this communication. For this reason alone, most developers avoid Flash-to-JavaScript communication.

Altering the OBJECT/EMBED Tag

For Flash and JavaScript to communicate, you must first alter the `OBJECT/EMBED` tag on the Web page to properly set up the Flash movie. The easiest approach is to use Publish Settings, found in the File menu. You can select the HTML template's Flash with FSCommand. Selecting this option automatically places the correct information in your `OBJECT/EMBED` tag.

> ⇨ *For information about Publish Settings, see Chapter 30, "Optimizing, Publishing, and Exporting Movies," page 643.*

If you decide to use `fscommand`, put a warning on your site for Mac and Netscape users so they understand the movie will not work completely with their browsers.

Most developers, however, need to understand exactly what they must add to the tags because they want to place the Flash movie in their own pages, not in Macromedia's templates.

Both the OBJECT and EMBED tags need to include an ID parameter. For each tag, it is merely a parameter in the main part of the tag. For instance, if the movie is communicationtests.fla, the compressed Flash file will be communicationtests.swf. Thus, the ID parameter needs to be set to communicationtests. The following is a complete example of an OBJECT/EMBED tag with ID parameters:

```
<OBJECT classid="clsid:D27CDB6E-AE6D-11cf-96B8-444553540000"
codebase="http://download.macromedia.com/pub/shockwave/cabs/flash/
➥swflash.cab#version=6,0,0,0"
ID="communicationtests" WIDTH="550" HEIGHT="400" ALIGN="">
<PARAM NAME=movie VALUE="communicationtests.swf">
<PARAM NAME=quality VALUE=high>
<PARAM NAME=bgcolor VALUE=#FFFFFF>
<EMBED src="communicationtests.swf" quality=high bgcolor=#FFFFFF
WIDTH="550" HEIGHT="400" swLiveConnect=true
ID="communicationtests" NAME="communicationtests" ALIGN=""
TYPE="application/x-shockwave-flash"
PLUGINSPAGE="http://www.macromedia.com/go/getflashplayer">
</EMBED>
</OBJECT>
```

Adding ID parameters is not the only change. For the EMBED tag, you also need to add an swLiveConnect=true statement, which you can see in the preceding example.

Adding the JavaScript Hooks

Changing the OBJECT/EMBED tag is only the first step. You also need to put some basic JavaScript code on the page for it to get messages from the Flash movie. These Javascript hooks act as a bridge between Flash and JavaScript.

All Flash messages go to a JavaScript function called DoFSCommand. However, the exact name of the function depends on the name of your movie. For instance, if your movie is communicationtests, the JavaScript function should be called communicationtests_DoFSCommand.

So the most basic script you will need is something similar to this:

```
<SCRIPT LANGUAGE=JavaScript>
function communicationtests_DoFSCommand(command, args) {
    // Code goes here
}
</SCRIPT>
```

However, this script will work only for Netscape 3.x and 4.x browsers. It will not work on Internet Explorer because IE cannot facilitate communication between Flash and JavaScript. However, Flash can communicate with VBScript, a proprietary scripting language found in Internet Explorer. In turn, VBScript can communicate with JavaScript. So you need to set up a system in which Flash sends a message to VBScript and VBScript sends a message to JavaScript.

26

Such a system will make the code much more complex. First, you need to test whether the user is on Internet Explorer. If she is, she needs to add a VBScript function. You use `document.write` commands to add this function to the page:

```
if (navigator.appName && navigator.appName.indexOf("Microsoft") != -1 &&
      navigator.userAgent.indexOf("Windows") != -1 &&
      navigator.userAgent.indexOf("Windows 3.1") == -1) {
   document.write('<SCRIPT LANGUAGE=VBScript\> \n');
   document.write('on error resume next \n');
   document.write('Sub communicationtests_FSCommand(ByVal command, ByVal args)\n');
   document.write('  call communicationtests_DoFSCommand(command, args)\n');
   document.write('end sub\n');
   document.write('</SCRIPT\> \n');
}
```

Setting Up JavaScript to Flash Communication

Now you have everything you need to begin communication from Flash to JavaScript. However, to send information back to Flash, you need to know the location of the address. You've already specified the ID of the movie in both the `OBJECT` and `EMBED` tags, but unfortunately the Netscape and Microsoft browsers use these IDs differently.

The Netscape browsers will refer to the Flash movie as part of the *document*, so you need to address the movie as `document.communicationtests`. On the other hand, Internet Explorer will just use the ID, such as `communicationtests`.

To make things easier, the default Flash HTML template will set a new variable, `communicationtestsObj`, to one of these two references. It uses the following code to do so:

```
var InternetExplorer = navigator.appName.indexOf("Microsoft") != -1;
var communicationtestsObj =
  InternetExplorer ? communicationtests : document.communicationtests;
```

This way, the function can return information to `communicationtestsObj` regardless of which browser the user has. The use of this kind of JavaScript syntax is not very common, so the following alternative method does exactly the same thing but is easier to read if you're a JavaScript novice:

```
if (navigator.appName.indexOf("Microsoft") != -1) {
   var communicationtestsObj = communicationtests;
} else {
   var communicationtestsObj = document.communicationtests;
}
```

From Flash to the Browser

To send a message from the movie to the browser, you need to use the `fscommand` function. The following button script gives an example:

```
on (release) {
  fscommand ("alert", inputText);
}
```

The fscommand function passes two parameters to JavaScript. The first is the command, and the other is the data. In the earlier example of the JavaScript function communicationtests_DoFSCommand, you can see that these parameters would be received as command and args.

Neither parameter means anything to JavaScript until you write some code to handle it. For instance, this function handles the alert command by creating a JavaScript alert box with the contents of the args parameter:

```
function communicationtests_DoFSCommand(command, args) {
    if (command == "alert") {
        window.alert(args);
    }
}
```

Of course, this code will work in Internet Explorer only if the VBScript code from earlier in this chapter is included.

You can see an example of this code in the sample movie communicationtests.fla. An HTML file named communicationtests.html includes all the necessary JavaScript code. Run the movie using the HTML page in your browser. Fill in the field at the top of the movie and then click the red button. The text you enter will be sent to the JavaScript function, which will then show the user an alert box.

For instance, if you enter the text **"Hello World!"** you should see a dialog box that looks similar to Figure 26.1.

Figure 26.1
This alert dialog box was created by a Flash movie communicating with Internet Explorer for Windows version 6.0.

26

From the Browser to Flash

Although only one ActionScript command is associated with sending information from Flash to JavaScript, many commands send information from JavaScript to Flash. The most basic is the SetVariable command. The following function will send the browser name string to a variable named fromJavaScript in the movie:

```
<SCRIPT LANGUAGE=JavaScript>
function sendToFlash(args){
    window.document.communicationtests.SetVariable("fromJavaScript",
➥ navigator.appName);
}
</SCRIPT>
```

The result of this script is that the variable fromJavaScript in the movie named communicationtests will now contain the value of the JavaScript constant navigator.appName. This requires that the ID parameters of the movie's OBJECT/EMBED tag be set to communicationtests.

You can also see the result of running this script in the movie communicationtests.fla. The HTML page includes a simple button that calls the `sendToFlash` JavaScript function. In turn, this function sends the value of `navigator.appName` to the Flash movie, where it will be displayed in the dynamic text field linked to the variable `fromJavaScript`.

`SetVariable` is only one of many functions that you can call in JavaScript that will affect the Flash movie. Here is a list of all the others:

- `GetVariable(variableName)` — Gets the value of the variable at the movie's root level.

- `GotoFrame(frameNumber)` — Moves the movie to the frame number you specify. See also `TGotoFrame`.

- `IsPlaying()` — Returns `true` if the movie is playing at that moment.

- `LoadMovie(layerNumber, movieURL)` — Loads a new movie at the layer you indicate.

- `Pan(x, y, mode)` — After a movie is zoomed in (see also `Zoom`), you can pan around by using the *x* and *y* values in this command. If *mode* is `0`, then *x* and *y* are pixels. If *mode* is `1`, then *x* and *y* are percentages.

- `PercentLoaded()` — Returns a value from `0` to `100` to tell JavaScript how much of the movie has been loaded.

- `Play()` — Same as issuing a `play` command at the root level of the Flash movie. See also `TPlay`.

- `Rewind()` — Sends the movie's root level back to frame 1.

- `SetVariable(variableName, value)` — Sets a variable at the movie's root level to *value*.

- `SetZoomRect(left, top, right, bottom)` — An alternative to `Zoom`. Zooms the movie so that the rectangle fits into the current movie area.

- `StopPlay()` — Same as issuing a `stop` command at the root level of the Flash movie. See also `TStopPlay`.

- `TCallFrame(target, frameNumber)` — Executes the entire script (except functions) that exists at the frame you indicate. Can be at the root level or with a movie clip. See also `TCallLabel`.

- `TCallLabel(target, frameLabel)` — Same as `TCallFrame`, but uses a label rather than a number.

- `TCurrentFrame(target)` — Returns the number of the current frame in the movie clip.

- `TCurrentLabel(target)` — Returns the name of the current frame in a movie clip.

- `TGetProperty(target, propertySymbol)` — Returns the value of a movie clip's property. This value will be a string. See the list of property symbols in Table 26.1. See also `TGetPropertyAsNumber`.

- `TGetPropertyAsNumber(target, propertySymbol)` — Same as `TGetProperty`, but returns a number value.

26

- TGotoFrame(*target*, *frameNumber*)— Sends the movie clip to a specific frame number. See also TGotoLabel.

- TGotoLabel(*target*, *frameLabel*)— Sends the movie clip to a specific frame label. See also TGotoFrame.

- TPlay(*target*)— The same as issuing a play command in ActionScript to the movie clip. See also Play.

- TSetProperty(*target*, *propertySymbol*, *value*)— Sets a property in a movie clip. See the list of property symbols in Table 26.1. See also TGetPropertyAsNumber.

- TStopPlay(*target*)— The same as issuing a stop command in ActionScript directed at the movie clip. See also StopPlay.

- TotalFrames()— Returns the total number of frames in the movie.

- Zoom(*percentage*)— Zooms the movie by a specified amount. See also SetZoomRect and Pan.

Several of these commands and functions use a target parameter. Those commands and functions that do not will always work on the root level of the movie. But a target parameter allows you to specify a movie clip in the movie instead.

The value "/" for a target indicates the root level of the movie. If you want to specify a movie clip named myMovieClip, you could use the target "/myMovieClip". If you want to specify a movie clip named myOtherClip that is inside myMovieClip, you could use "/myMovieClip/myOtherClip". So myMovie.TPlay("/") and myMovie.Play() perform exactly the same task.

The TGetProperty function and TSetProperty command both take a *propertySymbol* parameter. It would be nice to be able to use ActionScript syntax such as _x and _alpha for these two. Unfortunately, this is not the case. Instead, you must use a special set of symbols that map to ActionScript properties. Table 26.1 shows a complete list.

Table 26.1 Getting ActionScript Properties with JavaScript

ActionScript Property	JavaScript Symbol
_x	X_POS
_y	Y_POS
_xscale	X_SCALE
_yscale	Y_SCALE
_currentFrame	CURRENT_FRAME
_totalFrames	TOTAL_FRAMES
_alpha	ALPHA
_visible	VISIBLE
_width	WIDTH
_height	HEIGHT

Table 26.1 Continued

ActionScript Property	JavaScript Symbol
_rotation	ROTATE
_framesLoaded	FRAMES_LOADED
_name	NAME
_dropTarget	DROP_TARGET
_url	URL

In addition to all these commands and functions, a Flash movie triggers two events automatically. The OnProgress event sends the percentage of the movie downloaded to JavaScript as the movie streams. Likewise, the OnReadyStateChange event goes from 0 to 4, representing loading, uninitialized, loaded, interactive, and complete stages.

Round-Trip

Often you'll want to ask the browser for information from your Flash movie. Such an operation involves two steps. The movie sends a message to JavaScript. This message then triggers JavaScript to send information back to the movie.

Suppose that you want the browser to send the browser name to your movie. You start with an fscommand in your movie. Something similar to this would do it:

```
fscommand ("sendMeInfo", "appName");
```

Next, on the Web page, you need all the standard options mentioned earlier: ID parameters, the swLiveConnect parameter, the myMovie_DoFSCommand JavaScript function, and the VBScript bridge.

This function accepts the message from the movie and also sends back a message. Here's an example:

```
function myMovie_DoFSCommand(command, args) {
  var myMovieObj = InternetExplorer ? myMovie : document.myMovie;

  if (command == "sendMeInfo") {
    if (args == "appName") {
      myMovieObj.SetVariable("returnValue", navigator.appName);
    }
  }
}
```

When the movie sends an fscommand to the page, the page then runs the previous function. It checks the command and args variables. If they are sendMeInfo and appName, the JavaScript property navigator.appName is sent to the movie, where it appears as the value of the variable returnValue.

Alternative Techniques

Another way to communicate from Flash to the browser relies on the fact that most browsers accept JavaScript commands in the Address field at the top of the window. You can use this technique to get around the Mac and Netscape limitations for standard JavaScript communication as mentioned earlier in the chapter.

For instance, you can open your browser and type **javascript: window.alert('Hello!');**. When you press Return (Mac) or Enter (Windows), the JavaScript after the colon should run. This results in an alert box.

When Flash sends a `getURL` command, it is really just sending a string to the Address field in the browser. So, by using `javascript:` plus some JavaScript, you should be able to trigger the browser to do just about anything.

You can issue JavaScript commands or even call JavaScript functions that have been defined on the page. This technique works in most browsers, including more recent versions of Netscape on Windows and Internet Explorer on Mac. You can quickly test any browser by using a `javascript:` command in the Address field.

Although this technique is a good way to send messages from Flash to the browser, it won't help you send messages from the browser to Flash. It also has other drawbacks, such as it frequently replaces the contents of the current browser window with the results of the JavaScript function you called.

Asking Questions with JavaScript

JavaScript allows you to perform simple input tasks very easily. For instance, you can ask a quick question with only one command. Using the JavaScript `confirm` command, you get a small dialog box with a message and OK and Cancel buttons. If you click OK, `true` is returned.

You can access this JavaScript function by using an `fscommand`. The following button uses this command:

```
on (release) {
    fscommand("askYesOrNo", "Do you really wish to continue to the next frame?");
}
```

Then, on your Web page, you can place the following script. Remember to include all the other necessary elements such as the ID and `swLiveConnect` tags and the VBScript bridge. This code assumes that the movie ID is askquestion.swf:

```
function askquestion_DoFSCommand(command, args) {
  var askquestionObj = InternetExplorer ? askquestion : document.askquestion;
  if (command == "askYesOrNo") {
      if (confirm(args)) {
          askquestionObj.play();
      }
  }
}
```

26

Figure 26.2 shows the confirmation dialog box that is created. This box may look slightly different with a different browser version.

Figure 26.2

This confirmation dialog box was created by a Flash movie communicating with Internet Explorer 6.0 for Windows.

You can also use the JavaScript `prompt` command to ask for a short string.

Creating Custom Windows

The most common need for Flash-to-JavaScript communication is to open a new browser window. Although you can open one with `getURL`, you can't control the window's size or appearance. You need JavaScript to do that.

The sample movie openwindow.fla allows you to test opening custom windows. You can change just about every aspect of a window and then use the buttons at the bottom to open the window.

The ActionScript code is nothing special. It combines the various window settings into one long "features" variable. JavaScript expects an URL, a window name, and a list of features.

The ActionScript code sends these values to JavaScript using a single string, with the URL, name, and features divided by semicolons. Because only one argument can be passed between Flash and JavaScript, you combine the three arguments into one long string, as in the following:

```
on (release) {
    features  = "left="+x;
    features += ", screenX="+x;
    features += ", top="+y;
    features += ", screenY="+y;
    features += ", width="+width;
    features += ", height="+height;
    features += ", toolbar="+toolbar;
    features += ", resizable="+resizable;
    features += ", directories="+directories;
    features += ", status="+status;
    features += ", location="+location;
    features += ", menubar="+menubar;
    features += ", scrollbars="+scrollbars;

    fscommand("openwindow", url+";"+name+";"+features);
}
```

Consider reading a good JavaScript reference, such as Que's *Special Edition Using JavaScript* by Paul McFedries (ISBN: 0789725762) if you plan to do Flash-to-JavaScript communication.

Learning More About window.open

Most of the feature parameters for the window.open command show or hide elements such as the Address field, the toolbar, scroll bars, and so on. Netscape browsers require *screenX* and *screenY*, whereas Microsoft browsers require *left* and *top*. For a complete description of the JavaScript window.open command, see a JavaScript reference such as a book or a Web site.

On the other end, JavaScript uses a split command to break the string back into three parts. It then uses window.open to create the window from these parts:

```
function openwindow_DoFSCommand(command, args) {
  var openwindowObj = InternetExplorer ? openwindow : document.openwindow;
  if (command == "openwindow") {
      var argsArray = args.split(";");
      window.open(argsArray[0],argsArray[1],argsArray[2]);
  }
}
```

Another method would be to forget about standard ActionScript-to-JavaScript communication and use the javascript: command with getURL. You don't need anything on the Web page. Just change the last line of the button script from fscommand to this:

```
getURL("javascript: var myWindow = window.open('"+url+"','"+name+"',
➥'"+features+"');");
```

You need to make the line look as though it is setting a variable. Otherwise, the result of the window.open command will be placed in the current browser window. This means your Flash movie will be replaced with "[Object]".

If you're up for an advanced technique, send a test message to JavaScript when the movie starts. Then have JavaScript send a message back to the movie, such as setting the variable jsCommunication to true. If the user has a browser that works with ActionScript-to-JavaScript communication, jsCommunication will be true and you can send more messages and expect to receive messages. If not, you can use an alternative technique. For instance, if you want to open a browser window, you can use a javascript: call, or you can try to open a plain window with a target in getURL.

CONTROLLING THE PROJECTOR

fscommand has a completely different functionality if you're running inside a Flash projector. In that case, you're sending messages to the projector player, which will accept a limited, but useful, set of commands. For instance, you can force the projector to resize itself or quit when the user presses a button.

Modifying the Window

When using `fscommand` in a projector, you still give it two parameters: `command` and `arguments`. The commands, however, are hard-coded into the projector, so you need to choose from a small set.

The `fullscreen` command enlarges the projector to the full size of the user's monitor. It stretches the contents of the Flash movie to fit this new window size. The result is that the movie takes over the whole screen. There aren't even any window borders or a title bar left.

To enlarge the projector to full screen, use this command:

```
fscommand("fullscreen", true);
```

To return the projector to its original size, use this one:

```
fscommand("fullscreen", false);
```

You can also adjust whether the movie inside the window scales. To turn off scaling, use the following:

```
fscommand("allowscale", false);
```

Then, when the projector is full screen, the movie will remain its original size, centered in the window. This is also true when the user clicks and drags the window corner to enlarge or shrink the window. You can turn scaling back on by using the following command:

```
fscommand("allowscale", true);
```

Hiding the Context Menu

In a projector, a user can Cmd-click (Mac) or right-click (Windows) to bring up a context menu. This menu allows the user to pause the movie or change the volume. You can disable this feature in a projector by using this command:

```
fscommand("showmenu", false);
```

You should disable this menu if you don't want the user controlling different aspects of your movie. You can turn it back on by using this command:

```
fscommand("showmenu", true);
```

Note that turning off this feature does not turn off the context menu completely. The user can still access Settings and About categories, but he cannot control the movie.

If you want to turn off these context menus when the movie is playing in the browser, you can turn off the Display Menu option in the HTML Publish Settings. This inserts a `menu` parameter with a value of `false` in the `OBJECT` and `EMBED` tags. Or you can insert these tags in the HTML yourself.

Other Commands

The `quit` command simply exits a projector. Although it doesn't need a second parameter, `fscommand` insists on a second parameter, so you can give it anything:

```
fscommand("quit", "");
```

You can also launch external applications with `fscommand`. All you need to do is feed the command `"exec"`, plus the path to the application:

```
fscommand("exec", "C:\notepad.exe ");
```

Definitely use this command with caution. At the time of this writing, I was not able to get it to work on my computer. You may have better luck.

COMMUNICATING WITH DIRECTOR

One of the most powerful aspects of Flash is that you can embed movies into Macromedia Director as cast members. It can also be said that this is one of the most powerful aspects of Director.

When a Flash movie is in Director, you can send messages back and forth between ActionScript and Lingo, the programming language inside Director.

Macromedia Director 8.5 can have Flash 5 movies embedded in it. This includes all the communication methods mentioned in this section. By the time you read this, Director may have been upgraded to include Flash MX support, which could include new communication methods as well.

Flash-to-Director Communication

You can send a message to Lingo in two ways. They both use the `getURL` command. The first method sends the message to a predetermined Lingo handler. Lingo handlers are Director's equivalent to Flash functions. The following ActionScript button will send this message:

```
on (release) {
    getURL("lingo: this is a test");
}
```

In Director, you need to place a script, sometimes called a *behavior*, on the sprite that contains the Flash movie. It needs to have an `on getURL` handler, as shown in the following example.

```
on getURL me, stringFromFlash
    alert stringFromFlash
end
```

The `me` parameter is Lingo's way of linking the handler to the sprite object. The second parameter is the string passed in from Flash—in this case, everything after `lingo:`.

You can pass in any string you want, such as the name of a frame that the Director movie should jump to or a value to set a text field to. This Lingo handler will jump to the frame named by the Flash call:

```
on getURL me, frameToJumpTo
    go to frame frameToJumpTo
end
```

You can find out more about using Macromedia Director in *Special Edition Using Macromedia Director 8.5* by Gary Rosenzweig (ISBN: 078972667X).

26

Another, more advanced way to call from Flash to Director is to use `event:` rather than `lingo:`. Using this approach, you can direct your message at a specific handler attached to the sprite. For instance, this code in the Flash movie will call the handler `myHandler`:

```
getURL("event: myHandler");
```

On the Director side, you could have the following:

```
on myHandler me
    -- do something
end
```

If you want to pass parameters into the Lingo handler, you can add them to your `getURL` string:

```
getURL("event: myHandler 7");
```

If you want to use quotation marks, you need to put a backslash before them so that ActionScript passes the quotation marks on instead of interpreting them:

```
getURL("event: myHandler \"jump\", \"frame name\"");
```

By using `event:`, you can customize the behavior placed on the sprite to have several different functions, each defined by its own handler.

Director-to-Flash Communication

Sending information from Lingo to a Flash movie embedded inside a cast member is similar to sending information from a Web page. You use a similar set of commands.

This section explains the commands that you can use to determine how much of the Flash member is ready to be played. When the Flash member is embedded in the Director movie, chances are that the entire member is available at once. However, you also can use Director to create a Flash member that is a link to an external Flash file. In that case, the Flash movie will stream in just as it does by itself on a Web page.

You can use the `percentStreamed` property of the member to determine whether the Flash movie is ready to play:

```
if member("my flash movie").percentStreamed = 100 then
```

You can also use `frameReady()` to determine whether a specific frame has been loaded. The `frameCount` property of the member will tell you how many total frames are in the movie.

For more detailed information about what is taking place while a Flash member is being loaded, you can use the `state` property of the member. The following is a list of possible values:

- 0—Not loaded
- 1—Header is loading
- 2—Header is finished loading
- 3—Media are loading

■ 4—Media are finished loading

■ -1—Error

After the movie is loaded, you can use frameRate to get the frame rate of your Flash movie. Director's Property Inspector allows you to select Flash members and sprites, and change how their frame rate matches the frame rate of the Director movie. Check the Director documentation for more details.

Speeding Up Flash Image Display

Many Director developers use Flash movies as a substitute for bitmaps. In these cases, the Flash movie is just a still image, not an animation. You can set the static property of either the member or sprite to false to speed up the Director movie because the Flash member's contents will not be updated every frame.

You can use Lingo to control the Flash movie in a variety of ways. The play() and stop() commands work on a sprite and do the same thing as play and stop in Flash. The following Director button script will trigger a Flash movie in sprite 7 to play:

```
on mouseUp me
    sprite(7).play()
end
```

You can also issue a rewind() command to move the Flash member back to frame 1. To find out which frame the movie is currently on, use the frame property. You can use the getFrameLabel() function to convert any frame number to a name. The opposite function is findLabel(), which will return the number of the frame that contains the label you specify. You can use the playing property to determine whether the movie is currently playing.

To control the playback of the movie, use goToFrame(). This function jumps the Flash movie to the frame number or label you specify. In addition, you can set the frame property of the sprite to a frame number.

If you want to find out the value of a property in the Flash movie, use getProperty(). This function takes both a target and a special property symbol. For instance, to find out the _x property of the movie clip named myMovieClip, you could do this:

```
x = sprite(7).getFlashProperty("myMovieClip",#posX)
```

Table 26.1 showed the special property name for each major movie clip property. Unfortunately, you need to use a different set of property names in Lingo. It is pretty obvious which Lingo symbol links to which property: #posX, #posY, #scaleX, #scaleY, #visible, #rotate, #alpha, #name, #width, #height, #target, #url, #dropTarget, #totalFrames, #currentFrame, and #lastframeLoaded.

As you can guess, you can use the setFlashProperty() function to change any movie clip property. For instance, to set the _alpha property of a movie clip, you could do this:

```
sprite(7).setFlashProperty("myMovieClip",#alpha,50)
```

26

You can also get and set your own variables with Lingo. Unfortunately, this technique works only with variables at the root level. For instance, to get a variable, you might use this command:

```
sprite(7).getVariable("myVariable")
```

To set a variable at the root level, you can use this command:

```
sprite(7).setVariable("myVariable",42)
```

The most powerful Director Flash command is `callFrame`. This command runs the ActionScript on a frame of the Flash movie at the root level. For instance, you can run the ActionScript on frame 5 of the Flash movie by using this line:

```
sprite(7).callFrame(5)
```

Any commands in the frame will execute as if the Flash movie had just arrived on that frame. So functions will not run unless they are specifically called in the frame.

If you used Flash 4, you will recognize this type of functionality. Flash 4 didn't have functions. Instead, you placed code into different frames of the Flash movie and used `callFrame` to run the code in those frames.

By combining `setVariable` and `call`, you can trigger just about anything in a Flash member. For instance, if you want to call an ActionScript function with the parameters `hello` and `79`, you can use `setVariable` to set the variables `param1` and `param2` to `hello` and `79`. Then you can use `callFrame` call the script on frame X. This frame would simply take the value of `param1` and `param2` and send it into the function you want to run:

```
myFunction(param1,param2);
```

Lingo can also trigger ActionScript's `print` and `printAsBitmap` functions by sending messages of the same names to the Flash sprite. These functions work exactly the same as if you were to print using ActionScript:

```
sprite(7).print("myMovieClip",#bframe)
```

One last interesting piece of functionality in Director is the capability to retarget any of the Flash messaging commands to a specific movie clip. You do this by first issuing a `tellTarget` command. You also need to end the sequence of messages with an `endTellTarget` command. So, to call the ActionScript in frame 5 of the movie clip named myMovieClip, you can use the following:

```
sprite(7).tellTarget("myMovieClip")
sprite(7).setVariable("myVariable",99)
sprite(7).callFrame(5)
sprite(7).endTellTarget()
```

You can tell the movie clip to go to a frame like this:

```
sprite(7).tellTarget("myMovieClip")
sprite(7).goToFrame(10)
sprite(7).endTellTarget()
```

As mentioned, version 8.5.1 handles only Flash 5 movies. However, when a new version of Director that handles Flash MX movies is released, it may be able to call functions directly.

Lingo Commands

The following Director Lingo commands send messages or get information about a Flash movie member. I've left out any Flash sprite properties that affect the appearance of the sprite or member. Lingo programmers can find them easily enough in Director's Property Inspector.

- `endTellTarget()`—See `tellTarget`.

- `findLabel(`*`frameLabel`*`)` —This function returns the frame number associated with the frame label.

- `frame`—This property represents the current frame number of the Flash movie. It can be both tested and set.

- `frameCount`—This property returns the total number of frames in the Flash Timeline.

- `frameRate`—This property returns the frame rate of the Flash movie.

- `frameReady(`*`frameNumber`*`)`— This function returns `true` if the specified frame of the Flash movie has been loaded.

- `getFlashProperty(`*`target, property`*`)`— This function gets the value of a movie clip or root property. Use one of these symbols to specify the property: `#posX`, `#posY`, `#scaleX`, `#scaleY`, `#visible`, `#rotate`, `#alpha`, `#name`, `#width`, `#height`, `#target`, `#url`, `#dropTarget`, `#totalFrames`, `#currentFrame`, and `#lastframeLoaded`.

- `getFrameLabel(`*`frameNumber`*`)`— This function returns the frame label of the frame.

- `getVariable(`*`variableName`*`)`— This function returns the value of the variable from the current level, usually root. See also `tellTarget`.

- `goToFrame(`*`frame`*`)`— This function jumps the current Timeline to the frame number or label. See also `tellTarget`.

- `percentStreamed`— This property returns a value from `0` to `100` telling you how much of the movie is ready to play.

- `play()`— This command starts the Flash movie playing. See also `tellTarget`.

- `playing`— This property is `true` if the Flash movie is playing.

- `rewind()`— This command returns the Flash movie to frame 1.

- `setFlashProperty(`*`target, property, value`*`)`— This command sets the value of a movie clip's property. See `getFlashProperty` for a list of symbols to use as properties.

- `setVariable(`*`variableName, value`*`)`— This command sets the value of a variable at the current level. See also `tellTarget`.

- `state`— This property returns a value from `0` to `4` or a `-1`. See the list in the "Director-to-Flash Communication" section.

- `stop()`— This command stops the current Timeline from playing. See also `tellTarget`.

26

- `tellTarget(target)`—This command makes all future Flash calls target a specific movie clip in the movie. It is particularly useful for `play`, `stop`, `goToFrame`, `setVariable`, and `getVariable`. Use `endTellTarget` to once again direct calls to the root level.

STORING INFORMATION LOCALLY

One of the most talked-about techniques for Flash 4 and 5 ActionScript developers was the way to communicate with JavaScript to set cookies on the user's machine. This technique allowed movies to store information such as the user's name or a best score for a game. However, because it used JavaScript, this technique didn't work on all browsers.

Flash MX has a built-in way of storing small pieces of information on the user's machine. This feature, called a *local shared object,* is similar to a JavaScript cookie but totally built into Flash.

Creating a local shared object takes a few lines of code but is relatively easy. You first need to create the object. Then you can set a property of the object to the value you want. Finally, you need to force Flash to save the value to the user's hard drive. Here is an example:

```
mySO = SharedObject.getLocal("mySharedObject");
mySO.data.username = "Gary";
mySO.flush();
```

The first line of code here does one of two things. First, it tries to access a shared object named `mySharedObject` on the user's hard drive. If the object is there, the code sets up `mySO` as a reference to this object. If it is not there, the code creates this new object.

Each shared object has an all-important `data` property. This is the place where you store any or all information. To create a new property of `data`, just assign it a value, as I did in the second line.

The last line issues a `flush` command, which is needed to tell Flash that you're done altering the shared object for now, and it should update the file on the user's hard drive.

When you first use a `flush` command with a shared object, the user will see the Macromedia Flash Player Settings dialog box, shown in Figure 26.3, that asks for her permission to store the data on her hard drive.

Figure 26.3

The Macromedia Flash Player Settings dialog box appears inside your Flash movie when you first attempt to save a shared object.

You don't need to do anything in your code to enable this feature. You cannot disable it. The user can refuse the request or set a size limit on your data. If the data is not written for one of these reasons, `flush` will return `false`. If the user is prompted for her permission, you will get the result `pending`.

You can specify a minimum file size with the `flush` command to reserve a certain amount of space, pending the user's approval, for the shared object. Only if the size of the object grows past that amount will the dialog box appear again asking the user for permission to store more data.

Getting information from a shared object is just as easy as setting it. If you have not yet assigned the shared object to a global in your movie, you must start with that step. You can then access the property as follows:

```
mySO = SharedObject.getLocal("mySharedObject");
thisUsername = mySO.data.username;
```

If the shared object does not exist yet, or if there is no username property, you will get a value of undefined.

Each time you create a new shared object, it is put in a place where only movies from the same Web site can access them. By default, only requests from the same movie can access the shared object. However, by including a full path to the shared object, you can have other movies from the same site access the information.

For instance, if your Flash movie is on your site at the location http://www.mysite.com/cool/stuff/, the path to the shared object on the user's hard drive is /cool/stuff/. You could access it by using the following:

```
mySO = SharedObject.getLocal("mySharedObject", "/cool/stuff/mymovie.swf/");
```

This code line allows you to have your movies share information across a user session or when the user returns.

COMMUNICATING BETWEEN FLASH MOVIES

One last method of location communication you should know about is movie-to-movie communication between two movies running in the same browser.

To communicate this way, the movie receiving the message must first set itself up for incoming messages. It does so by setting up a new local connection object. Then it uses the connect command to prepare for incoming messages:

```
myLC = new LocalConnection();
myLC.connect("myconnection");
```

Next, you must create functions to handle incoming messages:

```
myLC.onMessage = function(myString) {
    // do something with myString
}
```

The movie that sends the message will create a local connection object and use the send command to send the message. The first parameter is the receiving movie connection's name. The second parameter is the message name that corresponds to the function that will be called. The last parameter is the data to be sent, as you can see here:

You can communicate between two movies only if they are on the same site.

```
myLC = new LocalConnection();
myLC.send("myconnection", "onMessage", "Hello World!");
```

If you plan on sending just one quick message, you will probably want to use a `close` command to close the connection:

```
myLC.close();
```

TROUBLESHOOTING

Caution

As of this writing, local shared objects are barely used by developers in real-world situations. Check Macromedia's technotes and developer sites for the latest techniques and pitfalls.

Why can't I get ActionScript-to-JavaScript communication to work?

You need to complete several steps before this communication will work: Set the ID parameters of both the OBJECT and EMBED tags, set the swLiveConnect parameter of the EMBED tag, and include a JavaScript function to get the message and a VBScript function to pass the message from VBScript to JavaScript. If any one of these elements is missing or contains a mistake, the communication will not work. Also, check to make sure your browser supports this communication.

I can get ActionScript-to-JavaScript communication to work on my machine, but it doesn't work for others.

Chances are the users are using browsers that do not support this type of communication. They also could have simply turned off JavaScript or ActiveX in their browsers. Some organizations have this feature turned off by default in all their browsers for security reasons.

Some users report that my local shared object is not working for them.

Some computers, like ones in schools and libraries, are set up to not allow browsers or Flash to save local information.

When I use Flash movies in Director, the Director movie really slows down.

Director operates at about 40 times the speed of Flash. So adding a Flash movie to Director can really bring down the speed of your Director movie. When possible, do as much data processing as you can in Lingo and as little as you can in your Flash member. Also remember to set the `static` property of any Flash member that is not animating.

COMMUNICATING WITH THE SERVER

LOADING TEXT DATA

You can choose from many methods for passing data back and forth between a Macromedia Flash movie and the server. Movies can read simple text files or data from an HTML page. This data doesn't have to come from a static source, either. Your movies can load updated information from CGI programs and databases. You can even send data back to the server.

Flash MX features a new way to load data from the server. It's called the `LoadVars` object. This object takes the place of the old `LoadVariables` function and its variations.

Loading Information with `LoadVars`

To get a piece of information from the server, you simply need to create the `LoadVars` object and then issue a `load` command as follows:

```
var myLoadVars = new LoadVars();
myLoadVars.load("data.txt");
```

The preceding code uses data.txt as an example of the filename to be loaded. This text file should have a special format: *propertyName=propertyValue*&. The two special characters here are the equals sign and the ampersand. The equals sign divides the property name and its value. The ampersand ends the value. You can place as many property/value pairs in the text file as you like. The following is an example:

```
a=7&b=42.8&c=Hello World!&
```

You don't need to put quotation marks around strings. In addition, you can have line breaks inside strings, and they will be included in the property value, as in the following example:

```
a=7&myString=This is a test
of a multi-line variable
passed to Flash&
```

When this data is loaded, the properties are added to the `LoadVars` object. For instance, in the previous examples, the property a is added with the value 7. You can get it like this:

```
trace(myLoadVars.a);
```

⇨ *For more information about strings, see Chapter 12, "Managing Variables, Data, and Datatypes," page 187.*

Completing `LoadVars`

When you use the `load` command, you don't see the results instantly. First, Flash requests the file from the server; then it must wait until the file arrives. Only then can it read the information within. This process could take a fraction of a second or several seconds.

So how do you know when the `load` is complete? There are two ways.

You could just check to see whether the `loaded` property of the `LoadVars` object is true, but doing so requires you to loop and check the `loaded` property over and over again. Instead, you could use the `onLoad` event of the `LoadVars` object to create a function to execute when the loading is done. Here is an example:

```
myLoadVars = new loadVars();
myLoadVars.onLoad = function() {
    results = myLoadVars.toString();
}
myLoadVars.load("loaddata.txt");
```

This code segment, which you can find in the button in the sample movie named load.fla on the CD, will set the value of the variable `results` to the result of the `toString` function. This function, when used with a `LoadVars` object, will show you the properties of the object in one long string. The result is as follows:

```
c=Hello%20World%21&b=42%2E8&a=7&onLoad=%5Btype%20Function%5D
```

The file loaddata.txt contains the following:

```
a=7&b=42.8&c=Hello World!&
```

The order of the variables here is backward. Also, the characters are converted to use escape characters similar to what you find when working with Internet data. For instance, `%20` stands for hexadecimal number 20, which is the decimal number 32, which is the character code for a space.

MIME Types

Technically, any data should be stored on the server as MIME type `application/x-www-urlform-encoded`. MIME types on servers define what type of data files contain. A typical text file is `text/html`. Flash movies seem to be able to handle both types of files correctly but have had some trouble with `text/html` files in previous versions. Talk to your Webmaster about these MIME types if you have any questions.

While you're waiting for a large data file to load, you can use ActionScript to track its progress. The `LoadVars` object includes `getBytesTotal` and `getBytesLoaded` properties. You can use them to create a progress display. However, in most cases, the data file will be too small to need such a display.

Security Issues

Flash can read information only from the same server where the Flash movie is located. This is not true when you're testing a movie in Flash MX or using a standalone projector, but this restriction is enforced when you're viewing the movie over the Internet. So you cannot use Flash to load information from one site to the other for security reasons.

The Old Method of Loading Variables

It is worth mentioning the old LoadVariables method of getting information from the server. Many developers who have learned to program in earlier versions of Flash will continue to use LoadVariables for years to come because they are used to it, so you might run into it.

LoadVariables is similar to the LoadVars object, but instead of storing the data it receives inside its own object, it creates and populates variables of the movie clip it is in, or the root level if it is at the root level. It looks like this:

```
this.LoadVariables("data.txt");
```

If the data.txt file is the same as in the previous example, variables a, b, and c will be created and populated.

You'll discover two major disadvantages to using LoadVariables. The data is scattered into variables at the current level, rather than stored neatly inside the LoadVars object. The other disadvantage is that no event like onLoad can be used to deal with the variables when they have been loaded. Instead, you must use onClipEvent(*data*) to capture this event, which is not always convenient.

An even more serious problem with LoadVariables is that when you use it to send data (with an optional second parameter of POST or GET), it sends all the variables at the current level. This means you usually must create a special movie clip to hold only the data that LoadVariables should send. LoadVars is much easier to deal with in such situations. You'll learn how to use LoadVars to send information back to the server later in this chapter.

EMBEDDING DATA ON THE HTML PAGE

Perhaps the most reliable and efficient way to send information from the server to your movie is to embed the information in the Web page in a place where your movie can get to it. You can do so by placing information in the src/movie parameters of both the OBJECT and EMBED tags on the Web page. For instance, a typical OBJECT movie parameter would look like this:

```
<PARAM NAME=movie VALUE="frompage.swf">
```

You also can place a question mark and a list of variable definitions after the name of the movie like this:

```
<PARAM NAME=movie VALUE="frompage.swf?pageVar1=7&pageVar2=42.8&pageVar3=Hello
➥World!&">
```

The result is that those three variables, starting with pageVar1, are set to their respective values. This happens immediately after the movie is loaded, so you can expect these values to be present when your scripts begin. All the variables will be at the root level.

27

Including Variables with loadMovie

The technique of placing variables after the movie filename also works in loadMovie commands. You can tell your Flash movie to load a new movie in its place and include a question mark and then variable declarations. The new movie will load with these variables set. Here is an example:

```
loadMovie("mynewmovie.swf?a=7b=42.8&");
```

You will also need to include the same information after the `src` parameter of the EMBED tag. Otherwise, only Windows users who have Internet Explorer will get the variables. The following is a complete OBJECT/EMBED tag with the variables set for both parts of the tag:

```
<OBJECT classid="clsid:D27CDB6E-AE6D-11cf-96B8-444553540000"
codebase="http://download.macromedia.com/pub/
shockwave/cabs/flash/swflash.cab#version=6,0,0,0"
WIDTH="550" HEIGHT="400" id="frompage">

<PARAM NAME=movie
VALUE="frompage.swf?pageVar1=7&pageVar2=42.8&pageVar3=Hello World!&">

<PARAM NAME=quality VALUE=high>
<PARAM NAME=bgcolor VALUE=#FFFFFF>

<EMBED
src="frompage.swf?pageVar1=7&pageVar2=42.8&pageVar3=Hello World!&"

quality=high bgcolor=#FFFFFF
WIDTH="550" HEIGHT="400" NAME="frompage" ALIGN=""
TYPE="application/x-shockwave-flash"
PLUGINSPAGE="http://www.macromedia.com/go/getflashplayer">
</EMBED>
</OBJECT>
```

You can see this HTML page in action by using the Frompage.html and Frompage.fla sample files.

This technique is already powerful without any server-side support. For instance, you could make a Flash title movie for your Web site. Inside the movie, you could have a place to display the title of the page where the movie appears. This dynamic text field can be linked to a variable that is set on the Web page. So on one page, `titleText` could be My Home Page, and on another page `titleText` could be My Links. Both pages use the same Flash movie, but with a different value for `titleText` set in the `src`/`movie` parameters. You could run the same title movie on all your Web pages.

You could also send dynamic data to your movie by using this technique. A simple example is to send the current time to a movie. The `Date` object relies on the user's computer's time, which is usually set correctly but can easily be changed to anything. If you have a popular Web site, chances are good that people with incorrect dates and times will access your site every day. Even those site visitors with correct times may live in different time zones. What if you need to display the accurate date and time as it stands on your server?

You can display the correct time with a server-side include. A server-side include is a little tag that is put inside a Web page to add a bit of information, or a complete file, before it is sent to the user. The user gets a complete page that doesn't appear to be any different from a normal Web page, but the HTML on your site is specially coded so that the server knows what to include and where.

27

To use server-side includes to send the time to Flash, you need to alter the `src`/`movie` parameter to look like this:

```
timefrompage.swf?timeVar=<!--#echo var='DATE_LOCAL' -->&
```

The server-side include is the `<!--#echo var='DATE_LOCAL' -->&` part. If the server is correctly parsing the file for server-side includes, it will see this and replace it with the date and time. The result might look similar to `Sunday, 24-Feb-2002 10:18:19 MST`.

The change is made before the page is sent to the user. If you view the source of the page, you will see the actual date and time, and no hint that a server-side include tag actually appears there on the real HTML page.

The sample files Timefrompage.shtml and Timefrompage.fla will not work if you run them from your hard drive or the accompanying CD-ROM because you are not passing them through a Web server. Upload the .shtml and .swf files to a test directory on your site to see them in action. If you don't see a date and time in the dynamic text field in the movie but instead see the `echo` tag, you know that server-side includes have not been turned on.

Using server-side includes is probably the least sophisticated way to add dynamic information to your Web pages. Other systems are very popular now—for example, Active Server Pages (ASP), Java Server Pages (JSP), Personal Home Pages (PHP), WebObjects, and ColdFusion. You could use any one of these examples to generate dynamic Web pages that include custom variables to be passed in to the Flash movie.

The main disadvantages of sending information to your movie with the `src`/`movie` tags is that the information typically needs to be short and that any user can see it if she simply views the source of the Web page she is visiting.

LOADING DYNAMIC DATA

27

Using dynamically generated Web pages is one way to feed your movies with dynamic data. However, you can also use the `LoadVars` object to get data from a dynamically generated source. To use this object, you must write server-side programs, also called Common Gateway Interface scripts, or CGI scripts. CGI scripts are written with a variety of languages, such as Perl, C, and Java. Because teaching you any of these languages is beyond the scope of this book, I'll try to keep the examples as simple as possible. I'll use Perl because it is widely available and easy to understand.

Consider the example of getting the current server time. A Perl program to get the current server time and return it looks like this:

```
#!/usr/bin/perl
print "Content-type: text/html\n\n";
```

```
$time = localtime();
print "$time\n";
exit 0;
```

If you want to try this Perl program on your server, you need to take several steps. You can find this script, named Time.pl, on the CD-ROM. Upload it to your Web server. If your server allows CGI scripts to work only in a special cgi-bin directory, you must place it there. You must then set the permissions of the file to allow it to execute.

Creating a CGI Program

If you are already lost, it probably means that you have never made a CGI program. I strongly recommend that you get help from your Web administrator or someone with CGI program experience. The slightest variation in your server configuration could make this an impossible task if you don't have the help of someone with experience.

Now point your browser to the Web location of the CGI program. You should see a page that looks something like this:

```
Sun Feb 24 12:13:02 2002
```

If you see an error message, either your server is not configured to run CGI programs or you have not set the permissions properly. There are also other minor reasons why the Perl program might not work: Perl is not installed on the server, it is at a different location than /usr/bin/perl, the Time.pl file was not uploaded as text, and so on. Finding someone who has used such programs before is the best way to solve these problems.

Now that you have a Perl program that generates a simple Web page that a browser can use, you can alter it so that Flash can use it.

The first step is to use the proper MIME type for the returned information. This is the second line of the code. Right now it is `text/html`, but you want it to be `application/x-www-urlform-encoded`.

The next step is to format the output in the `propertyName=propertyValue&` format. Assume that the movie is looking for the variable `currentTime`. Here is the resulting program:

```
#!/usr/bin/perl
print "Content-type: application/x-www-urlform-encoded\n\n";

$time = localtime();
print "currentTime=$time&";
exit 0;
```

For your Flash movie to read this data, use a `LoadVars` object. Your new script will be similar to the script at the beginning of this chapter:

```
on (release) {
    myLoadVars = new loadVars();
    myLoadVars.onLoad = function() {
```

```
        currentTime = myLoadVars.currentTime;
    }
    myLoadVars.load("flashtime.pl");
}
```

You can see this code in the sample movie Flashtime.fla. When the user presses the button shown to them, the movie calls out to Flashtime.pl and gets the value it returns. The result should be something like `currentTime=Sun Feb 24 12:13:02 2002&`.

Then the `myLoadVars` property `currentTime` is copied to the root-level variable `currentTime`. This variable is linked to the dynamic text field, so you can see the result.

To get this movie working on your server, you need to upload the Flashtime.pl file, set its permissions, and upload the Flashtime.html and Flashtime.swf files. They should all be placed in the same directory.

The important point to realize here is that the time displayed in the Flash movie will be a reflection of the real time on the server. So the time will be different each time you run the movie. Your Flash movie is truly loading dynamic information now.

Setting the time is the simplest example of using dynamic information. From here, using such information all depends on your ability as a server-side programmer (or your connections with one). You can replace this simple Perl program with one that reads from a database and returns some complex data. For instance, it could return a random set of trivia questions or the latest stock quotes.

SENDING DATA

Sending information back to the server from Flash is similar to sending it back to the server from an HTML page. If you have ever sent information this way before, you know that a CGI program must be at the other end to accept and record the information sent. You should also know that two protocols are used: GET and POST.

The GET method is the simplest. You can see it clearly in the Address field of your browser when it's in use. For example, this field might contain a URL that uses GET to send information to the server:

```
http://myserver.com/myscript.cgi?name=Gary&age=32&
```

The preceding sends two pieces of information to the script named Myscript.cgi. It is up to that script to do something with the data.

The following example is such a script. This Perl script will grab the GET input string and write it to a file named Collect.txt. It will also return the text Success! to the browser.

```
#!/usr/bin/perl

$input_data = $ENV{'QUERY_STRING'};

open(OUTFILE,">>collect.txt");
print OUTFILE "$input_data\n";
close(OUTFILE);

print "Content-type: text/html\n\n";
print "Success!";
```

The original URL could come from something that the user hand-typed, from a standard HTML link, or from an HTML form using the GET method.

The data is taken from the portion of the URL after the question mark, also called the *query string*. The open command opens the file named Collect.txt with a >> option, which means that new data will be appended to the existing data in the file. The information is then written out, followed by a newline character. After the file is closed, the word Success! is written out. This message replaces the current Web page in the browser. It gives you an indication that the CGI program did its job.

To get this script working on your server, you need to upload the Collect.pl file and the empty text file Collect.txt. You need to set permissions for both. You can then test them in your browser by entering different text after the question mark in the URL. Whatever you put there should be recorded in the file.

You can write to this file with Flash by using a LoadVars object. In addition to a load command, LoadVars also includes a send command. The following button collects three variable values in a LoadVars object and sends them to the CGI script:

```
on (release) {
    myLoadVars = new loadVars();
    myLoadVars.name = username;
    myLoadVars.age = userage;
    myLoadVars.comment = usercomment;
    myLoadVars.send("collect.pl","_self","GET");
}
```

The first parameter of the send command is the location of the CGI program. The second parameter is the target window, which will hold the results printed by the CGI program. In this case, "_self" indicates that the results should replace the current page, including the Flash movie. The third parameter is either a "GET" or a "POST", depending on the method expected by the CGI program.

Suppose you don't want to replace the page and Flash movie with the results. Instead, suppose you want the Flash movie to continue. You would then use sendAndLoad instead of send. The sendAndLoad command's second parameter is not a browser target, but another LoadVars object.

The initial LoadVars object holds the variables to be sent, while the second object contains the returned information. Here is an example:

```
on (release) {
    myLoadVars = new loadVars();
    myLoadVarsReceive = new loadVars();
    myLoadVars.id = userid;
    myLoadVars.password = userpassword;
    myLoadVars.onLoad = function() {
        // do something with information here
    }
    myLoadVars.sendAndLoad("collect.pl", myLoadVarsReceive, "GET");
}
```

27

You can also use the POST method for sending variable values to the server. As a matter of fact, this approach is preferable because POST allows you to send long strings. The GET method limits string sizes depending on the browser and server.

To read POST information in the Perl program, you should replace the line where $input_data is set with the following line:

```
read (STDIN, $input_data, $ENV{'CONTENT_LENGTH'});
```

Now the Perl program will read the data from the standard input stream, which is where the POST data will come from. Other than that, no change is needed in the program. Of course, in your Flash movie, you will need to change load, send, or sendAndLoad to use POST instead of GET.

TROUBLESHOOTING

I can't get Perl scripts to run on my server. What am I doing wrong?

It is important to realize that CGI programming is a different skill than Flash programming. If an electrician needs to have some water pipes moved to be able to run some wires, he would usually call a plumber to do the job rather than move them himself. Some Flash programmers can take on the extra skill of CGI programming, whereas others find it difficult to learn. If you're having trouble, you will definitely want to team up with someone else to get the job done.

When I run a movie in Flash MX, it can contact the server fine. But when I upload it to the Web, it doesn't work anymore.

Make sure that the LoadVars object is trying to get the data from the same server. If the Flash movie tries to contact a file or script at another domain, it will quietly fail. However, Flash MX and projectors can contact any server.

I am including variables in the OBJECT movie parameter. They work fine in Internet Explorer for Windows, but other browsers don't get them.

You probably forgot to add the variables to the src parameter of the EMBED tag, or there is a typo in the EMBED tag but not the OBJECT tag. Internet Explorer for Windows uses the OBJECT tag and ignores the EMBED tag, whereas Netscape and other browsers use the EMBED tag but ignore the OBJECT tag.

I'm sure that my CGI program is done right and should work, but I still can't get Flash to load data from it.

You can and should always test your CGI programs from your browser with HTML. For GET method programs, you can add the variables to the browser's address line. For POST method programs, you can create a simple HTML page with a form that calls the CGI program just as you would expect the Flash movie to do. The only change to the CGI program would be to have it set the MIME type to text/html. If you test the CGI program this way, you can determine whether the problem lies with the CGI program or your Flash movie.

27

FLASH AT WORK: SENDING E-MAIL FROM FLASH

A common task often requested by Flash developers is to have e-mail sent directly from a Flash movie. E-mail is typically sent by a full-fledged e-mail program on the user's machine, such as Microsoft Outlook. However, Flash runs in a browser, not an e-mail program. Browsers don't typically have any e-mail–sending capabilities at all.

To make your movie send e-mail, you will have to make it go through a server. The movie will actually just send the information to the server. It is the server that will do the work.

The program Email.fla on the CD-ROM includes a few text fields and a Submit button. The button, which contains the following script, will gather some information from text fields and send it to a CGI program named Email.pl. It will use the `sendAndLoad` command so that properties will be read back from the server. The only property will be `result`, which should contain the string OK if the e-mail was sent.

```
on (release) {
    // set up variables to send
    myLoadVars = new loadVars();
    myLoadVars.name = username;
    myLoadVars.email = email;
    myLoadVars.subject = subject;
    myLoadVars.message = message;

    // set up object to receive
    myLoadVarsReceive = new loadVars();
    myLoadVarsReceive.onLoad = function() {
        // go to frame depending on message returned
        if (myLoadVarsReceive.result == "OK") {
            gotoAndStop("done");
        } else {
            gotoAndStop("error");
        }
    }

    // send email
    myLoadVars.sendAndLoad("email.pl", myLoadVarsReceive, "POST");
}
```

On the server, the Email.pl program will establish a link to the server's sendmail program. This little program allows CGI programs to send e-mail from the server.

I don't want to teach too much Perl here, but the following code is commented so that you can see what each part does. Some of it even looks similar to ActionScript.

```
#!/usr/local/bin/perl

# location of server's mail program
$mailprog = '/usr/lib/sendmail';
```

> **Caution**
>
> The sendmail program is not installed on all servers. It can also be present on the server but in a slightly different location. Have your server administrator help if you are not sure.

27

```
# email address to send mail to
$mailto = 'myemail\@myserver.com';

# header for sending result back to Flash
print "Content-type: application/x-www-form-urlencoded\n\n";

# get POST data
read (STDIN,$input_data,$ENV{CONTENT_LENGTH});

# split post data into an array
# also remove escape character encoding
@data_array = split('&',$input_data);
foreach $data_item (@data_array) {
    ($tag,$val) = split('=',$data_item,2);
    $val =~ s/\+/ /g;
    $val =~ s/%([\da-f]{1,2})/pack(C,hex($1))/eig;
    $tags{$tag} = $val;
}

# link to server mail program
open (MAIL, "|$mailprog $mailto") || die "result=Can't open $mailprog!&";

# write out message
print MAIL "From: $tags{'username'} ($tags{'email'})\n";
print MAIL "Subject: $tags{'subject'}\n\n";
print MAIL "$tags{'message'}\n";
close (MAIL);

# report back to Flash
print "result=OK&";
exit 0;
```

You might want to think about whether sending e-mail is really what you or your client wants. For instance, if you make a game and want winners to be able to enter a sweepstakes, you can easily have the user's name and e-mail address sent via e-mail with this method. However, you might want to create a database instead and just have the names recorded there.

XML DATA

INTRODUCTION TO XML

XML has been a hot topic among computer developers for the past few years. But few people really know what XML is or how to use it.

Macromedia Flash MX includes an extensive set of functions that allow you to import, export, and process XML data. It is one of the most powerful, yet least utilized, features of Flash.

XML, which stands for Extensible Markup Language, is a simple way of storing a database of information. The data is stored in a simple text file. Tags are used to describe the data, much as they are used to describe the information in an HTML page.

XML looks like HTML. Looking at XML in this light is a good way to quickly understand what XML is about, but you also need to know that XML and HTML are different in many ways. HTML is used to describe a Web page. XML can be used to describe anything at all. HTML has a predefined set of tags such as <P>, <IMG>, and <A>, whereas XML does not have any predefined tags.

Now consider this simple XML example. The following is the inventory of a produce store that has five apples, seven oranges, and two peaches:

```
<inventory>
    <fruit>
        <apples>5</apples>
        <oranges>7</oranges>
        <peaches>2</peaches>
    </fruit>
</inventory>
```

The tag surrounding the entire document has the name `inventory`. The entire document could have more than one top-level tag. For instance, in addition to `inventory`, there could be `cash`, `supplies`, and `employees`. As it turns out, this XML document is presently only concerned with `inventory`, so it is the only top-level node.

Nodes are called *elements* of an XML document. The `inventory` tag is a node. It has one child node, `fruit`. `fruit` has three child nodes: `apples`, `oranges`, and `peaches`. Even the numbers 5, 7, and 2 are nodes. They are children of `apples`, `oranges`, and `peaches`, respectively.

Nodes like `inventory`, `fruit`, and `apples` are called *XML nodes*. Nodes like 5, 7, and 2 are called *text nodes*. An XML node has a node name but no value. Instead of a value, it usually has more child nodes. A text node, on the other hand, has no name, but it does have a value.

Figure 28.1 shows a graphical representation of the sample XML document. Each box represents a node. When a box is inside another box, the one inside is a child of the larger box.

Figure 28.1
A graphical representation of the produce store XML document.

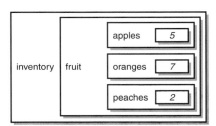

The first step toward using XML documents is understanding how to navigate inside one. For instance, `inventory` is the primary node. `fruit` is the only child of that node. `fruit` has three children, the first of which is `apples`. `apples` has one child, a text node with the value 5 in it.

So the 5 is the first child of `apples`, which is the first child of `fruit`, which is the first child of `inventory`, which is the first child of the document. Another way to say it is that 5 is the first child of the first child of the first child of the first child.

This description sounds wordy, so you may think that dealing with XML documents means that you'll have to deal with long associations like this. However, there is a way to shorten it. A fundamental rule of XML turns complex documents into simple ones: All XML nodes are, in fact, smaller XML documents.

So think of the `apples` node as its own document. The primary node is `apples`, and the child of that node is the text node with 5 in it. You'll use this technique to dissect XML data throughout the rest of the chapter.

Fundamentals of XML

One of the most important aspects of XML is that it is readable by both computers and humans. This makes it different from other database-like files, which are either in binary code or arranged in an unreadable fashion.

So you can easily generate and edit simple XML documents all by yourself, using just a text editor such as Notepad or SimpleText. But most of the time, XML documents will be created by other programs. Many server-side database programs can send XML data. Some database applications that you run on your local machine have an Export to XML function.

For Flash to be able to read an XML document, it should be *well-formed*. This means it needs to follow a certain set of rules, some of which are obvious.

All tags in an XML document must have matching closing tags. So `<apples>` needs `</apples>`. Plus, these tags need to be in the right order. So `<fruit><apples>2</apples></fruit>` is right, but `<fruit><apples>2</fruit></apples>` will cause an error and the document will not be parsed correctly.

You can place your entire XML document in one line, with no tabs or line breaks. However, using just one line can make a document that is unreadable by humans. So Flash MX has the capability to ignore whitespace such as tabs and line breaks. In Flash 5, you had to write special code to get rid of whitespace.

Tags in XML can have not only values or child nodes, but also attributes. For instance, if you want to specify more information than just `apples` in the tag, you can use an attribute to get more specific:

```
<apples type='green'>5</apples>
```

Flash likes single quotation marks for attributes, not double quotation marks or no quotation marks at all.

Using XML in Flash

You use XML in Flash for two reasons. The first reason is that you can communicate with other systems easily. For instance, if your movie is to get data from a medical database, chances are that the person in charge of that database is not familiar with Flash but does know about XML. You can agree on an XML format for the data and then use XML to transfer information. In many cases, the database or communications network that you want Flash to access already uses XML.

The other reason to use XML in Flash is that the XML functionality is more suited for large and complex data handling than other parts of Flash.

For instance, if you want to read in an array of data, how would you do it without XML? You could use `LoadVars` to read in a large string and then `split` to break it into an array. But this approach is super-slow. Even writing your own alternative to `split` is slow. Or you could read in dozens or hundreds of variables, but this approach would be harder to create outside Flash and organize inside Flash.

With the XML object, you can read in large amounts of data quickly and access it quickly. This approach is ideal for getting database information and displaying it. For instance, you could use it to read in a set of trivia questions for a game or display user information in a user database. Doing these things with normal variables and arrays would be much more difficult and much slower.

PARSING XML DATA

So how do you get XML data into Flash? To do that, a text XML document must be brought into Flash and converted to an XML object that ActionScript can use. Converting text to another format like this is usually called *parsing*. The following sections describe the basic XML object functions and how to use them to get and read XML data.

Converting Text into XML

The easiest way to make an XML object is to convert a small piece of properly formatted text into XML. You can do this just by creating a new XML object and feeding it the text:

```
myText = "<inventory><fruit><apples>5</apples><oranges>7</oranges>";
myText += "<peaches>2</peaches></fruit></inventory>";
myXML = new XML(myText);
```

You can also use the `parseXML` command to do the same thing:

```
myText = "<inventory><fruit><apples>5</apples><oranges>7</oranges>";
myText += "<peaches>2</peaches></fruit></inventory>";
myXML = new XML();
myXML.parseXML(myText);
```

Although creating XML from text already inside the Flash movie has limited use, this approach is very good for learning about XML. Later in this chapter, you'll learn how to import larger XML documents from external files and programs.

Examining XML Data

Notice in the previous function that the `trace` command is going to output the node name of the first child of the document. Because Produce.xml contains the produce store example shown earlier in this chapter and in Figure 28.1, you can predict that the output should be `inventory`. The `inventory` node is the first child of the XML object, and its name is `inventory`.

The `firstChild` property returns the first child node of the XML document. You can get any child node by using the array-like property `childNodes`. So `firstChild` and `childNodes[0]` are exactly the same thing.

Remember that a node of an XML object is another XML object. Nodes can be either XML nodes with a name and more children, or text nodes with no name or children, but a value.

> When discussing XML, be aware that many terms mean the same thing. For example, an *XML document* and an *XML object* are the same thing in Flash. A *node* of an XML object is another *XML object*.

You can use the `nodeName` property to get the name of an XML node and the `nodeValue` property to get the value of a text node.

The following is a list of all the different XML properties that you can use to get children, names, and information from XML objects:

- `firstChild`—Returns the first child of a node. This is the same as using `childNodes[0]`.

- `hasChildNodes`— Returns `true` if the node has children.

- `lastChild`— Returns the last child of a node. You can get the number of children by using `childNodes.length`.

- `nextSibling`— Returns the next node, if any.

- `nodeName`— Returns the tag name of an XML node or `null` if it is a text node.

- `nodeType`— Returns 1 if the node is an XML node or 3 if it is a text node.

- `nodeValue`— Returns the value of a text node or `null` if it is an XML node.

- `parentNode`— Returns the parent node of a node.

- `previousSibling`— Returns the previous node, if any.

- `attributes`— Returns a variable object containing the attributes, if any, or a node.

- `childNodes`— Returns an array-like structure of child nodes. You can use `length` to get the total number of nodes and square brackets to specify a specific node.

Although simple examples, like the previous one, use `firstNode`, it is more common to use `childNodes` in all cases to navigate through an XML document. So the following few examples will help you understand how to use `childNodes` to get the information that you need. Follow along with Figure 28.1 or the text that precedes it.

This line will return `inventory`:

```
myXML.childNodes[0].nodeName
```

This line will return `null` because the first node is an XML node that has a name and contains children, but has no value itself:

```
myXML.childNodes[0].nodeValue
```

This line will return `fruit`:

```
myXML.childNodes[0].childNodes[0].nodeName
```

This line will return `apples`:

```
myXML.childNodes[0].childNodes[0].childNodes[0].nodeName
```

This line will return `null` because the `apples` node is still an XML node and has no value, only a name and children:

```
myXML.childNodes[0].childNodes[0].childNodes[0].nodeValue
```

To get the 5 contained in the `apples` node, you need to look at its child, which is a text node. This line will return 5:

```
myXML.childNodes[0].childNodes[0].childNodes[0].childNodes[0].nodeValue
```

Because text nodes have no name, you will get a `null` when trying to get the name of a text node:

```
myXML.childNodes[0].childNodes[0].childNodes[0].childNodes[0].nodeName
```

The `fruit` node contains three children. You can determine this by examining the `length` property of `childNodes`. This line will return 3 because there are three children of the `fruit` node:

```
myXML.childNodes[0].childNodes[0].childNodes.length
```

You can get the name of the second node of the fruit node, which is `oranges`, like this:

```
myXML.childNodes[0].childNodes[0].childNodes[1].nodeName
```

If you want to determine if a node is an XML node or a text node, you can use `nodeType`. For instance, the `apples` node is an XML node. It will return 1:

```
myXML.childNodes[0].childNodes[0].childNodes[0].nodeType
```

On the other hand, the node with the 5 in it is a text node and will return 3:

```
myXML.childNodes[0].childNodes[0].childNodes[0].childNodes[0].nodeType
```

Making XML References Easier

Some of the lines in the previous examples get to be quite long. And this is a *simple* XML document. Imagine if the document contained a few more levels. You would have lines with half a dozen `childNodes` references. All these references could make for code that is quite long and confusing.

Fortunately, there is a simpler way to dig down to get the information you need. For example, suppose you want to get the number of apples in the store. Here's some code that could get that number:

```
inventory = myXML.childNodes[0];
fruit = inventory.childNodes[0];
apples = fruit.childNodes[0];
appleCount = apples.childNodes[0];
numApples = appleCount.nodeValue;
```

Although this code isn't really any shorter than a long string of `childNodes` references, it is much easier to understand. Plus, if you want to get the number of oranges next, you already have the `fruit` variable ready to go.

Referencing Attributes

In addition to having children, XML nodes can also have attributes. For instance, the following XML document has an attribute named `type` that has a value 4:

```
<test type='4'>123</test>
```

To get the value of an attribute, you need to know its name. The following is a piece of code that references the attribute in the previous example:

```
myXML.childNodes[0].attributes.type
```

The `attributes` property actually returns a variable object. This is a list of property names and values. If you want to see all the property names and values of an attribute listed, you could use code like this:

```
myAttributes = myXML.childNodes[0].attributes;
for(attribute in myAttributes) {
    trace(attribute+": "+myAttributes[attribute]);
}
```

BUILDING XML DATA

ActionScript also enables you to build an XML document from scratch or alter an existing document. After creating an empty object, you can use a variety of commands to add nodes.

But the process for making an XML object is a little confusing. Start with a simple example and create this small XML document that will look like this:

```
<test>123</test>
```

First, you must create the XML object, as follows:

```
myXML = new XML();
```

Next, you must add the node named `test`. You need to do this in two steps. The first step is to create the node:

```
testNode = myXML.createElement("test");
```

This step creates a node named `test`. Even though this node is part of `myXML`, it is sort of hanging out in the middle of nowhere. You have to attach it to a node. Because this is a new, empty XML object, you have only the object itself as a node:

```
myXML.appendChild(testNode);
```

To create the text node that will be a child of the `test` node, you need to use a slightly different command:

```
textNode = myXML.createTextNode("123");
```

28

Now, you have to add it as a child of the `test`. Fortunately, you still have the variable `testNode` to use to reference that node:

```
testNode.appendChild(textNode);
```

To test your series of commands, you can use the `toString()` function to send the XML document to the Output window:

```
trace(myXML.toString());
```

Check out the sample movie Build.fla, which builds the fruit stand example using only ActionScript.

The following are other commands that you can use to modify an XML object:

- `appendChild(node)`—Adds a node that has been created with `createElement` or `createTextNode`.
- `cloneNode(deep)`— Creates a copy of a node. If *deep* is `true`, it also copies all its children and descendants.
- `createElement(nodeName)`— Makes a new XML node. This node is not part of the document until you use `appendChild` or `insertBefore`.
- `createTextNode(nodeValue)`— Makes a new text node. This node is not part of the document until you use `appendChild` or `insertBefore`.
- `insertBefore(node, nodeNum)`— Inserts a node that has been created with `createElement` or `createTextNode`.
- `removeNode(nodeNum)`— Deletes a child node.

Creating and Modifying Attributes

What seems to be left out of the XML modification commands is a way to add or modify attributes. Modifying attributes is beyond simple. All you need to do is assign a value to a node to create or modify one. For instance:

```
myXML.childNodes[0].attributes.myAttribute  = 42;
```

To create a simple XML object with attributes, like `<test type="4">7</test>`, you could use the following:

```
myXML = new XML();

testNode = myXML.createElement("test");

testNode.attributes.type = 4;
myXML.appendChild(testNode);

text = myXML.createTextNode("7");
testNode.appendChild(text) ;
```

IMPORTING XML DOCUMENTS

Most of the time you will be using XML documents you will actually be importing them from outside the Flash movie. XML documents can be text files sitting on your server, or they can be generated by server-side CGI programs.

The XML object, in some ways, is like the LoadVars object. It can use load to load in data from an external file or program.

However, instead of the file using the property=value& format, it should be in XML format. If it is a proper XML document, it will be immediately parsed into the XML object as data.

Now consider this example. This code, placed in the first frame of a movie, will create a new XML object and load it in. Between these two commands, I set the ignoreWhite property to true. This means that the tabs and line breaks in the document will be ignored. If you didn't set this property, you would have to write the XML document with no whitespace at all, or you would have all sorts of unwanted text nodes in the XML object.

```
myXML = new XML();
myXML.ignoreWhite = true;
myXML.load("produce.xml")
```

The load command does not finish its task immediately. You have to wait for it to download the text file and parse it. Even if the files are all on your local hard drive, it will not happen fast enough for the next line to be able to access the data.

The XML object has an onLoad event just like the LoadVars object. You can define a function that will run as soon as loading is complete. Here's an example:

```
myXML = new XML();
myXML.ignoreWhite = true;
myXML.load("produce.xml")
myXML.onLoad = function() {
    trace(myXML.firstChild.nodeName);
}
```

Another way to tell if the XML file has been loaded is to use the loaded property of the XML object. It will return true only after the import is complete.

In addition, you can use several commands to monitor the progress of loading a large XML document. Here is a complete list:

- getBytesLoaded—Gives you the total number of bytes loaded so far.

- getBytesTotal— Gives you the total number of bytes in the XML file.

- loaded— Returns true only after the entire document has been loaded.

- status— Returns 0 if the load was successful. Other possible values are shown in Table 28.1.

28

Table 28.1 XML.status Return Values

Code	What It Means
0	Parse completed without errors.
-2	A CDATA tag not completed.
-3	XML tag not completed.
-4	DOCTYPE tag not completed.
-5	A component was not completed.
-6	Malformed XML element.
-7	Out of memory.
-8	Attribute parameter not completed.
-9	No end tag to match a start tag.
-10	End tag found without a start tag

The onLoad event occurs after two things happen. The first is that the text file with the XML in it is fully downloaded. The second is that the XML document is parsed into the XML object.

However, you can intercept the XML text before it is parsed. To do this, use the onData event. This event allows you to capture the data before it gets *parsed*. You can then parse the data yourself, perhaps performing some custom functions on it beforehand. Here's an example:

```
myXML.onData = function(xmlText) {
    myXML.parseXML(xmlText);
}
```

This example doesn't do anything that a normal load wouldn't do. However, you can see how you might be able to perform some unusual tasks. For instance, if your server-side program returns an XML document with an extra line at the beginning, you could trim that line from the xmlText parameter before passing it into parseXML.

After an XML document is parsed, either by load or parseXML, you can get some miscellaneous information from it by using one of these two properties:

- xmlDecl—If you're using XML standards, every XML document should have an XML tag at the beginning. This property gives you a string that contains that tag.

- docTypeDecl— Another standard tag for XML documents is the !DOCTYPE tag. This property will return a string with the value of that tag.

SENDING XML DOCUMENTS TO THE SERVER

After building an XML document with ActionScript, you may want to send it back to a server-side program for storage or processing. You can do this with the send and sendAndLoad commands.

These two commands work just as they do for the `LoadVars` object. The `send` command sends a complete XML object back to a server address. If you use an alternate second parameter, as in the following example, the server's returned text will be sent to another browser frame or window:

```
myXML.send("http://www.myserver.com/getxml.cgi",
➥"_self");
```

> If you need to send your XML data to the server using a specific MIME type, you can set the `contentType` property of the XML object to that MIME type before using send or sendAndLoad.

The preceding line uses `"_self"` as the return target, which means that the entire Web page will be replaced by whatever the server program returns. If you simply leave out the second parameter, the operation is silent and the Flash movie continues.

➡ For information about the LoadVars object, see Chapter 27, "Communicating with the Server," page 599.

Using the `sendAndLoad` command means that the second parameter should be another XML object. This new object will receive the returned XML from the server just as if it had been used in a `load` command.

```
returnXML = new XML();
myXML.send("http://www.myserver.com/getxml.cgi, returnXML);
```

If you want to monitor the progress of the load into `returnXML`, you must use `onData` and `onLoad` of the `returnXML` object, not the `myXML` object.

XML SOCKETS

XML sockets are a topic related to the XML object only in that they both use XML-formatted data. However, the XML Socket object does not use `load` and `send` commands to get and share its data. Instead, it uses `connect` to connect to a server program.

A socket server program is unlike a CGI program in that it is always running, not just when it is called. This means that your server must be sitting there waiting for incoming connections all the time. The Flash movie then uses `connect` to make a connection. After a connection is established, XML data can be sent back and forth in real-time. The server can actually send data to the movie even if the movie hasn't requested it. This is also known as *push* technology.

Most of what you need to know to use XML Sockets is not part of Flash or ActionScript. You'll have to write a server-side program, usually with Java or C++. You also need to be fairly knowledgeable about how servers and sockets work. For this reason, I will not go into any more detail about XML Sockets.

If you're using a third-party Flash-to-Sockets program, that third-party software provider should give you documentation on how to use XML Sockets to communicate with its product.

28

TROUBLESHOOTING

After importing an XML document, I can't find the nodes that I expect to be there. Is there a way to verify that the import worked?

There are many ways to verify a document after import. The easiest is to use the `toString()` function with `trace` to send the XML object to the Output window. You can also check the `status` property of the object. If either shows problems, your XML document must have errors in it. You can go through it line-by-line to find the missing or misspelled tag, or you can use a third-party XML creation tool.

After importing an XML document, I end up with a lot of blank text nodes. Why is that?

Any whitespace in your document, such as returns or tabs, will be converted to little useless text nodes unless you set the `ignoreWhite` property to `false` before parsing.

I can get the name of a node, but I can't seem to get the value of that same node. Why not?

Nodes don't have names *and* values; they have names *or* values. Chances are that the value you seek is actually the text node that is a child of the node with the name.

FLASH AT WORK: A SIMPLE XML APPLICATION

XML is mostly thought of as a database technology. Flash is rarely thought of when it comes to databases, but with its XML capabilities, it can certainly be used for them.

For this example, you'll build a simple database program. This program will allow the user to enter new database records, list the records in a database, and edit the records. In addition, a complete database can be loaded from an external file.

The sample movie Books.fla contains the finished product. Let's go through it frame-by-frame to examine the code.

The first frame contains two lines that initialize the database. The first will create an empty XML object. The second will set a global variable, `numToEdit`, to `0`. This variable will be used to keep track of which record the user is editing.

```
database = new XML();
numToEdit = 0;
```

The second frame contains four buttons: Load Books, List Books, New Book, and Edit Book. It also has a `stop()` command on the frame.

A dynamic text field is linked to the variable `total`. The following two lines on the frame will put the total number of records in the XML object into this field:

```
t = database.childNodes.length;
total = "Total Number of Books: "+t;
```

Each of the four buttons contains a simple on (`release`) handler with a `gotoAndStop` command in it. The buttons will go to the appropriate frame: load, list, new, or edit.

The `load` frame contains a simple script to load the XML document from a file named books.xml. This file should be stored in the same directory as the Flash movie. On the CD-ROM, you can find the sample file named Books.xml.

```
database = new XML();
database.ignoreWhite = true;
database.load("books.xml");
database.onLoad = function() {
    gotoAndStop("menu");
}
```

After the file is loaded and parsed, the movie will return to the menu frame. If you want to write a more robust version of this code, you can check for the `status` property of the database. If it is anything other than 0, you can use the return values listed in Table 28.1 to report to the user what went wrong.

So what does a record in this database look like? The books.xml file includes three records. Here is the first one:

```
<book isbn='0441142109'>
    <title>Deathworld</title>
    <author>Harry Harrison</author>
    <copies>1</copies>
    <price>5.00</price>
</book>
```

The main node is named `book`. It has a single attribute named `isbn`. There are four child nodes: `title`, `author`, `copies`, and `price`. Each has a single text node child.

The file can contain many of these records. Each `book` node is read in as a child of the XML document.

The new frame doesn't have much code in it. This frame is a collection of input text fields that will accept data entered by the user. The code simply clears these fields of previous values by setting the variables to which they are linked to empty strings:

```
isbn = "";
title = "";
author = "";
copies = "";
price = "";
```

Figure 28.2 shows the new frame. You can see the fields that the user can enter for a record.

Figure 28.2
The new frame allows the user to add a record to the database.

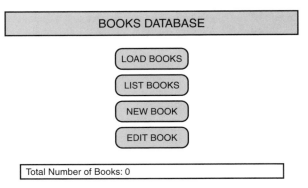

The new frame has two buttons at the bottom. The first will cancel the action by ignoring the data entered and returning to the menu frame. The second button, however, will create the XML nodes needed to add the record to the database. Here is the complete code for that button. Follow along to see how each element is created and added.

```
on (release) {
    // create book with isbn attribute
    book = database.createElement("book");
    book.attributes.isbn = isbn;

    // add title to book
    node = database.createElement("title");
    book.appendChild(node);
    text = database.createTextNode(title);
    node.appendChild(text);

    // add author to book
    node = database.createElement("author");
    book.appendChild(node);
    text = database.createTextNode(author);
    node.appendChild(text);

    // add num copies to book
    node = database.createElement("copies");
    book.appendChild(node);
    text = database.createTextNode(copies);
    node.appendChild(text);

    // add price to book
    node = database.createElement("price");
    book.appendChild(node);
    text = database.createTextNode(price);
    node.appendChild(text);
```

```
    // add book to XML
    database.appendChild(book);

    gotoAndStop("menu");
}
```

The next frame is the list frame. It contains a large dynamic text field linked to the variable booklist. It is set to be a multiline, no wrap field so that it can display many lines, each representing a book.

The code in the frame will loop through all the XML records and get the value of the text child of the title node. It adds these values to booklist with a newline character after each book:

```
booklist = "";
for(var i=0;i<database.childNodes.length;i++) {
    book = database.childNodes[i];
    titleNode = book.childNodes[0];
    title = titleNode.firstChild.nodeValue;
    booklist += title + "\n";
}
```

You can alter this code to display more than just the title of a book. You can add the author's name to each line by getting the text child of the second (number 1) child of the book node. Or you can put the number of the book node at the start of the line so that the books are numbered. You can get the ISBN number of the book by looking at the isbn attribute of the book node. The complete syntax for the ISBN number would be book.attributes.isbn.

The last frame of the movie, the edit frame, looks like the new frame in that it has the same input text fields. But the fields will be prepopulated this time with a function in the frame. This gets the values of the record indicated by numToEdit and puts them in the variables linked to the fields:

```
function populateForEdit() {
    book = database.childNodes[numToEdit];
    isbn = book.attributes.isbn;
    title = book.childNodes[0].firstChild.nodeValue;
    author = book.childNodes[1].firstChild.nodeValue;
    copies = book.childNodes[2].firstChild.nodeValue;
    price = book.childNodes[3].firstChild.nodeValue;
}
```

The frame script ends by calling the populateForEdit() function once to set up the fields for the current record. But the user can use two of the buttons at the bottom of the screen to jump to the next or previous records. The script for the previous button is as follows:

```
on (release) {
    numToEdit--;
    if (numToEdit < 0) numToEdit = 0;
    populateForEdit();
}
```

28

Here is the script for the next button:

```
on (release) {
    numToEdit++;
    if (numToEdit > database.childNodes.length-1) {
        numToEdit = database.childNodes.length-1;
    }
    populateForEdit();
}
```

The apply button on the screen will take the values of the input fields and apply them back to the record in the XML database:

```
on (release) {
    book = database.childNodes[editNum];
    book.attributes.isbn = isbn;
    book.childNodes[0].firstChild.nodeValue  = title;
    book.childNodes[1].firstChild.nodeValue  = author;
    book.childNodes[2].firstChild.nodeValue = copies;
    book.childNodes[3].firstChild.nodeValue = price;
}
```

The done button on the screen will take the user back to the menu, ignoring any changes done to the input fields. Alternatively, you could have the done button both apply the changes and return to the menu. In that case, you will want to offer a cancel button as well.

That is the complete example. Notably missing is a way to save the data entered. You can easily load data into Flash, but saving it back out is difficult. One option would be to save the data to a local shared object. But then the data would be available only to that specific Flash movie. This result may be okay if it's what you're going for.

➪ *For a discussion on local shared objects, see Chapter 26, "Communicating Locally," page 577.*

Another method for saving the XML database involves a server-side program that would receive the XML object from a send or sendAndLoad command. If you are skilled at writing such server-side programs, writing this method will be easy. Otherwise, you will want to team up with a server programmer to get this job done.

28

OUTPUT OPTIONS FOR FLASH

IN THIS PART

PRINTING A FLASH MOVIE

29

PRINTING FLASH CONTENT

Printing may seem the antithesis of many kinds of Macromedia Flash content, such as animation, video, and audio effects. How do you freeze and effectively capture multimedia content on paper? However, you cannot escape the fact that users will want and, in some cases, need to print portions of your Flash sites. Order confirmations, instructions, lengthy articles or text, and form data are all types of content that users may need to print.

With the diverse types of content that can be delivered in Flash sites, it is especially important to control the option to print. As with accessibility and general usability, the onus is on the Flash designer and developer to provide the means to print critical pieces of Flash sites.

Printing any Web-delivered content can produce unexpected and undesirable results. After all, Web content is designed for Web presentation, not for printing. This is especially true of Flash content. The nested nature of much Flash content can make printing far from straightforward. Therefore, it is imperative that Flash content, at least parts of it, is prepared for printing.

PREPARING FILES FOR PRINTING

Flash content can be printed from the Flash Player in two ways: from the context window within the Flash Player or from a print action—typically a button—within the Flash movie. The context menu, shown in Figure 29.1, is accessed by Ctrl-clicking (Mac) or right+clicking (Windows) a Flash movie within a browser.

Figure 29.1
One way to print a Flash movie is to select Print from the Flash Player context menu.

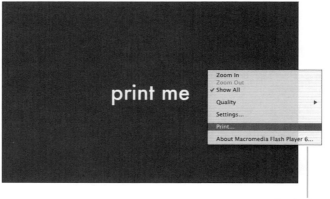

Context menu

Printing from the context menu provides limited printing options. Only frames in the Main Timeline can be printed. Nested movie clips will not be printed, and transparency and color effects will not be printed. You should rely on this printing option only if your movie has a single timeline—or the content you want to let users print is exclusively in the Main Timeline—and there are no color effects.

For best printing results, try to plan for printed content as you design the layout for your movies. If you plan to enable printing of specific content, be sure your layout can be printed as you intend onto standard 8.5- by 11-inch paper stock. You can control print settings for dimension, scale, and alignment in the HTML settings when you publish a movie.

➯ *For more information about using the Publish Settings, see Chapter 30, "Optimizing, Publishing, and Exporting Movies," page 643.*

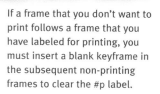

If a frame that you don't want to print follows a frame that you have labeled for printing, you must insert a blank keyframe in the subsequent non-printing frames to clear the #p label.

Assigning Frame Labels

Flash allows you to control which frames of your movies are printed. By default, all frames in the Main Timeline are printed. However, you can limit which frames can be printed by assigning frame labels to just those frames you want to be printable. This way, you can protect some content from being printed. This capability can also be used to make the printing process more user-friendly. If your movie contains multimedia content in addition to more conventional static content, you can designate that only the static content will print. There is no reason to frustrate users by allowing them to print content that will not print well.

To designate selected frames that can be printed, follow these steps:

1. Click within the Main Timeline of a movie to select a frame that you want to make printable.

2. With the frame selected, click in the Frame label field in the Property Inspector and enter **#p**, as shown in Figure 29.2.

Figure 29.2
Printable frames are designated by assigning #p as the frame label.

Disabling Printing

You can also disable printing of a movie from the context menu, although there is no way to disable printing using the browser's Print button. This task is also accomplished with frame labels. Follow these steps to prevent a movie from being printed:

1. Select a frame within the Main Timeline.

2. With the frame selected, click in the Frame label field in the Property Inspector and enter **!#p**.

3. Test your movie, and you'll find that the Print command is dimmed within the context menu, as shown in Figure 29.3.

Figure 29.3
To disable printing, assign !#p as a frame label. This label disables the Print option in the Flash Player context menu.

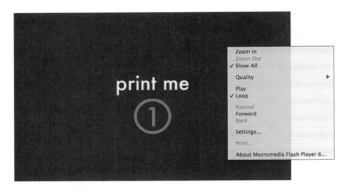

You can also disable printing in the Publish Settings by specifying not to display the Flash Player context menu. Choose File, Publish Settings to open the Publish Settings dialog box and then click the HTML tab. Within the Playback options, deselect Display Menu, as shown in Figure 29.4. Deselecting this option, however, removes the entire Flash Player context menu.

Figure 29.4
Deselect Display Menu within the Publish Settings to publish a movie without a Flash Player context menu.

Changing the Printed Background Color

The Flash Player will print the background color selected in the Document Properties dialog box. However, if you make a limited number of frames in a movie printable and want those frames to print with a different background color than is displayed for the other movie frames, you can. To change the printed background color, follow these steps:

1. Create a new layer below all other layers in a document that has had selected frames labeled for printing. Name it **background color**.

2. In the background color layer, insert a keyframe in a frame that is labeled for printing.

3. Select the Rectangle tool in the Toolbox and a desired fill color that will be the printed background color. In the background color layer, draw a shape that is larger than the Stage, as shown in Figure 29.5.

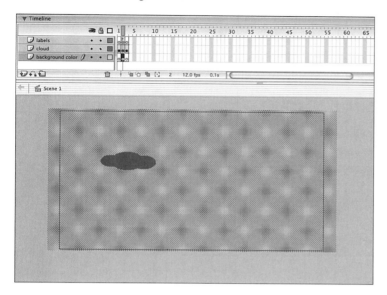

29

Figure 29.5
To change the print background color, draw a filled shape in the desired color that covers the stage.

4. If subsequent frames are not labeled for printing, be sure to insert blank keyframes in those frames within the background color layer. Otherwise, the background color from the printing frames will appear.

Determining the Print Area

Flash also allows you to specify a print area within a movie. By default, the boundaries of the Stage define the print area, or bounding box. But you can also specify three alternative print areas:

- A single bounding box for any printable frames defined by designating a shape in one frame as the bounding box by assigning a frame label of #b

- A composite bounding box for all printable frames defined by assigning the Max argument to a print action

- A bounding box for each frame defined by assigning the Frame parameter to a print action

To designate a bounding box, follow these steps:

1. Open a new file and draw a simple shape to one side of the Stage, as shown in Figure 29.6.

   If you were to publish the movie at this point and print it, the print area would equal the dimensions of the Stage or movie, as shown in Figure 29.7.

29

Figure 29.6
To designate a bounding box, begin by placing content in printable frames.

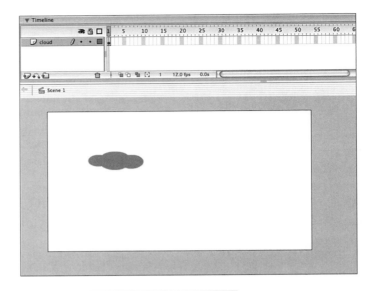

Figure 29.7
With no bounding box specified, the print area is the dimension of the Stage or movie.

2. Add two layers above the current layer to your movie by clicking Insert Layer at the bottom of the layers list.

3. Name the middle layer **border**. Select the Rectangle tool in the Toolbox and draw a rectangle with a stroke but no fill to frame the shape in your original layer, as shown in Figure 29.8.

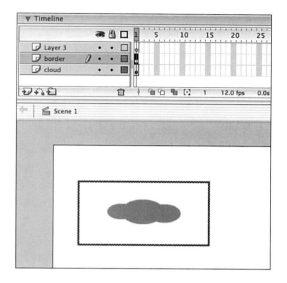

Figure 29.8
A shape within a frame can be designated as the bounding box for the print area.

4. Name the top layer **labels**. Assign **#b** as the frame label in the Property Inspector, as shown in Figure 29.9.

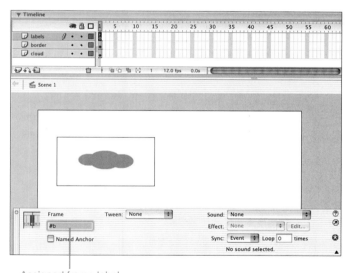

Figure 29.9
Assign a frame label of #b to a frame to create a bounding box for printing.

Assigned frame label

5. Save your file as **bounding1.fla** and test your movie. Open the SWF in a browser and select Print from the Flash Player context menu to test printing. Your frame should scale so that the border you created fills the print area, as shown in Figure 29.10.

Figure 29.10
When a frame is designated as a bounding box, the frame contents scale to fill the print area.

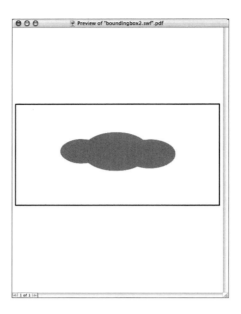

To create a composite bounding box, which uses objects in all printable layers to determine a collective bounding box, follow these steps:

1. Open bounding1.fla. Ctrl-click (Mac) or right+click (Windows) in the border layer next to its name and select Delete Layer from the context menu. For this example, you will use ActionScript to designate a bounding box.

2. Select frame 3 across both remaining layers and insert frames by pressing F5.

3. Click in frame 2 of the layer containing your shape and Shift+click in frame 3 to select frames 2 and 3. Ctrl-click (Mac) or right+click (Windows) and select Convert to Keyframes from the context menu, as shown in Figure 29.11.

4. Select frame 2 in your shape layer. Move the shape across the stage. Repeat this step in frame 3, moving the shape to different positions, as shown in Figure 29.12.

5. Save your movie as **bounding2.fla**.

To complete the composite bounding box, you need to create a print button.

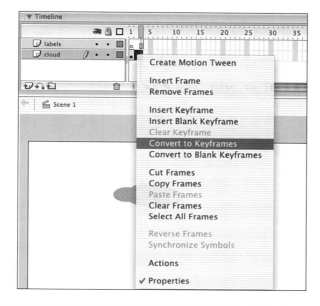

Figure 29.11
Shift-select a span of frames,
Ctrl-click (Mac) or right+click
(Windows) to open the context
menu, and then select Convert to
Keyframes.

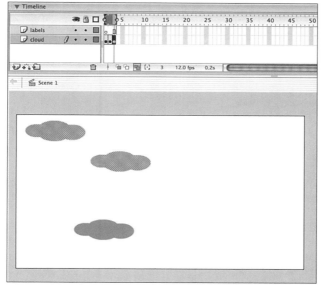

Figure 29.12
A composite bounding box will
encompass objects in different
positions in printable layers.

CREATING A PRINT BUTTON

Creating a print button with an attached Print action allows the greatest control over printing a movie. A Print action enables printing of frames in multiple timelines. Each Print action applies to a single timeline, but multiple print buttons can be used. Color effects will print, and there is the added capability to print frames as vectors or bitmaps.

To add a Print action to a movie and, in this case, to complete the composite bounding box, follow these steps:

1. Open bounding2.fla.

2. Insert a new layer by clicking the Add Layer button at the bottom of the layers list. Name it **button**.

3. Select frame 1 of the button layer—it must be a printable keyframe if you are not printing every frame—and create a button for printing, as shown in Figure 29.13.

Figure 29.13
Create a print button to which you can attach a Print action.

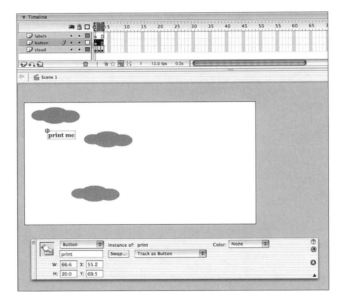

↪ *For more information about buttons, see Chapter 6, "Symbols, Instances, and Library Assets," page 89.*

4. Select the button instance, and choose Window, Actions or press F9 to launch the ActionScript Editor. Select Normal mode from the ActionScript pop-up menu in the upper right of the Actions panel.

5. On the left side of the Actions panel, click Actions, Printing, and double-click Print to send a Print action to the editor, as shown in Figure 29.14.

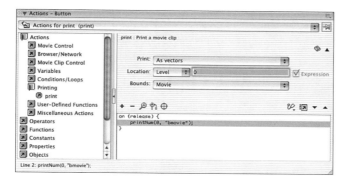

Figure 29.14
Select Actions, Printing to access the Print actions within the ActionScript Editor.

6. From the Print pop-up menu (on the right side of the Actions panel), select As Vectors. Printing as vectors prints at a higher quality but does not print transparency or color effects. The alternative is to select As Bitmap, which prints color effects and transparency, but may pixelate if the frame is allowed to scale.

7. Specify which timeline to print in the Location pop-up. Select Target and click in the field next to Target. Type in **this** and click to select the Expression check box. The alternative is to select Level, which is used to specify the level number of the Main Timeline or of a loaded clip. A level number for the desired clip is entered in the Location field. Either location designation—Level or Target—can be evaluated as an expression by checking the Expression check box.

8. Select Max from the Bounds pop-up. Figure 29.15 shows the completed script. The Bounds parameter—Movie, Max, or Frame—specifies a bounding box for printed frames. Movie uses the bounding box of an object in a frame labeled #b as the print area for all frames. Max uses the placement of all objects in printable frames to determine a composite bounding box to encompass the placement of all objects. Frame creates individual bounding boxes for objects in each printable frame and scales the objects within each frame to fit the print area, as defined in the Dimensions Publish Setting.

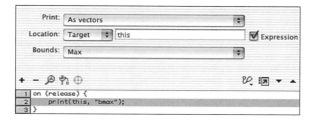

Figure 29.15
The completed Print action to create a composite bounding box.

9. Select frame 3 in the labels layer. Press F6 to insert a keyframe. Open the ActionScript Editor by pressing F9 and insert a `stop();` action.

10. Save your movie as **bounding3.fla** and test it. Open the SWF in a browser and click the Print button. Notice that each page prints within an area defined in a small portion of the screen, where the buttons were clustered across the frames, as shown in Figure 29.16.

For more information about loading movie clips and levels, see Chapter 17, "Unlocking the Power of Movie Clips," page 331. To learn more details about writing scripts, see Chapter 11, "Getting Started with ActionScript," page 169.

Figure 29.16
Printing from a composite bounding box results in a print area that spans the placement of content in each frame.

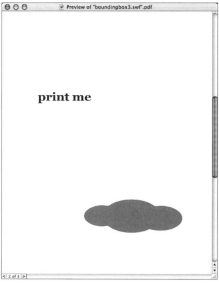

TROUBLESHOOTING

Why is Flash ignoring a bounding box I set within a frame label? Pages are printing with a much larger print area than I specified.

Check your ActionScript to be sure that you haven't also chosen Max or Frame within a Print action. Choosing either Max or Frame will override any bounding box set with a frame label.

A few users have indicated that they are unable to print from my site. I can't reproduce the error.

Users with Flash Player versions prior to 4.0.20 (Macintosh) and 4.0.25 (Windows) will not be able to print. If you suspect that users may have older Player versions, you can add a Player detection script to your movie.

 *To learn how to create a detection script, see the "Flash at Work" section of Chapter 12, "Managing Variables, Data, and Datatypes," page 263.*

FLASH AT WORK: INVISIBLE INK

29

The Flash Print action even enables printing of movie clips with visibility set to `false`, that is, movie clips that exist within a movie but are invisible during playback. All that is required is the targeting of a movie clip's location within the Print action. The beauty of this solution is that it is possible to preserve precious screen real estate and still provide printable content.

OPTIMIZING, PUBLISHING, AND EXPORTING MOVIES

TESTING MOVIES

After you complete the design and development of a Macromedia Flash movie, it's important to test the movie as users will see it. If you are not sensitive to the user's experience, the user can become frustrated to the point of leaving your site without accessing the content. Then all of your hard work has gone to waste. Fortunately, Flash makes it easy to simulate the user experience and identify potential problem areas.

30 Using the Bandwidth Profiler

The Bandwidth Profiler allows you to test-drive a movie, simulating streaming of content as it would occur over the Internet. This feature enables you to pinpoint bottlenecks and identify content that needs to be optimized. The goal is the highest quality at the smallest file size.

To access the Bandwidth Profiler, follow these steps:

1. Test your movie by choosing Control, Test Movie or by pressing Cmd-Return (Mac) or Ctrl+Enter (Windows). This creates an SWF file that is opened in a new window.

2. Select View, Bandwidth Profiler, as shown in Figure 30.1.

Figure 30.1

Test a movie and select View, Bandwidth Profiler to simulate streaming of a Flash movie.

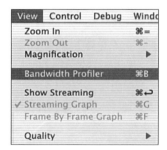

The Bandwidth Profiler appears above your SWF, as shown in Figure 30.2. The left side of the Bandwidth Profiler displays information about your movie, such as dimensions, frame rate, size, and how long it will take to preload the first frame, as well as the modem speed that is being displayed. The right side of the Bandwidth Profiler is a graph that displays a bar for each frame of the movie. The height of the bar represents the file size of each frame. A red line, the horizontal line at 400B in the graph in Figure 30.2, represents the point at which content will stream in real-time at the selected modem speed, so any frame with a bar that extends above that line will pause for its content to download.

To change the modem speed displayed in the Bandwidth Profiler, choose Debug, and select a modem speed, as shown in Figure 30.3. Today, the minimum connection speed for most users is 56K.

You can also preview a movie as it would stream, with content appearing as it downloads. To show streaming, choose View, Show Streaming. The movie plays as it would over a modem of the speed you've selected in the Debug menu. The left side of the Bandwidth Profiler indicates the percentage downloaded, and a green bar appears over the graph to show the loading progress.

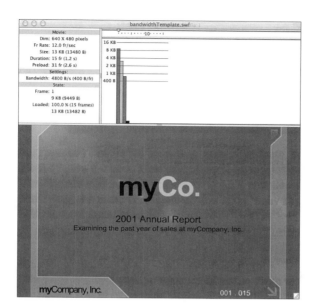

Figure 30.2
The Bandwidth Profiler simulates the streaming of content at varying modem speeds.

Figure 30.3
Use the Debug menu to select a modem speed to profile.

Take note of frames where streaming spikes, as indicated by taller bars in the Bandwidth Profiler graph. You'll want to re-examine the content in these frames to determine whether you can further optimize it to reduce the amount of streaming required. Click a bar in the graph to display the frame contents below the Bandwidth Profiler. If there are many spikes, especially in concurrent frames near the beginning of your movie, you'll need to create a preloader to indicate to your users that content is being downloaded.

Using the Size Report to Optimize Files

Another way to examine the size of movie elements is to generate a Size Report. A Size Report is a text file that can be created when you publish a movie; it breaks down the file size of your movie by frame, scene, symbol, and embedded font, as shown in Figure 30.4.

To generate a Size Report, choose the Generate Size Report option within the Flash Publish Settings. When you publish a movie, a text file is generated and saved to the same directory as your FLA and SWF files, and given the name of your SWF, as shown in Figure 30.5.

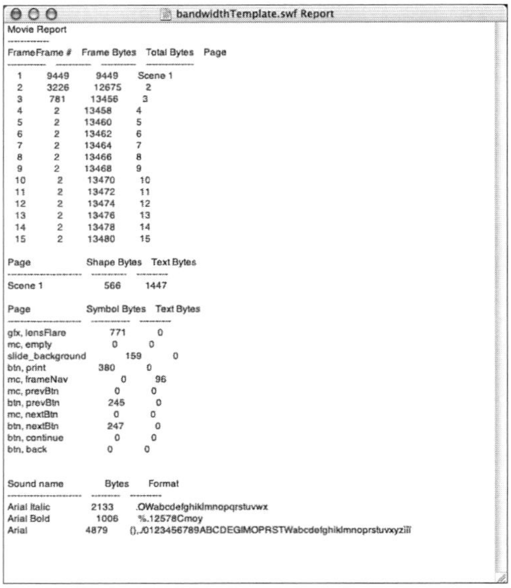

Figure 30.4
A Size Report lists the file size for individual elements within a movie.

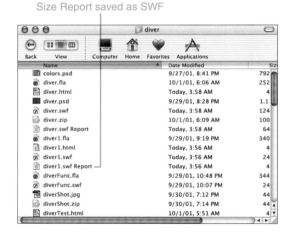

Size Report saved as SWF

Figure 30.5
A Size Report is generated during publishing and saved to the same directory as your SWF.

⇨ *For more information about using the Publish Settings, see "Specifying Publish Settings," later in this chapter, page 647.*

OPTIMIZING MOVIES

After you identify bulky elements in your movies, go back to your FLA files and try to optimize them. Elements that inflate file size the most are bitmaps, sounds, and video.

To optimize bitmaps, be sure that you've imported them at the size they will be used. Even if you scale a bitmap to a smaller size within Flash, the file size remains the same as when imported. If necessary, you can crop an image in an external image-editing program and swap the bitmap in your movie.

Animation techniques used with bitmaps increase file size dramatically. Try to minimize the use of large bitmaps, particularly in animations, and limit alpha effects. If you trace a bitmap, be sure to choose Modify, Curves, Optimize to simplify tracings and reduce file size.

➪ *For more information about importing and optimizing bitmaps, see Chapter 4, "Using Bitmaps in Flash," page 55.*

Using symbols keeps file size down, so make sure that any movie element that is reused is converted to a symbol. When animating, separate static and animated elements into different layers. Within keyframes, confine the action to as small an area of the Stage as possible. And, where possible, use tweened animation because it creates smaller file sizes than frame-by-frame animation consisting of consecutive keyframes.

With vector graphics, try to avoid broken line strokes and avoid strokes altogether if the stroke is the same color as the fill. Gradient and bitmap fills increase file size, so use them sparingly.

Limit the number of fonts and font styles you use. Each embedded character and font adds to the overall file size of a movie. Embed only the characters that are necessary.

To optimize sounds, edit them to the desired length before importing. Maximize a sound by reusing it when possible. Try to use MP3 compression, which produces the smallest file sizes.

➪ *For more information about optimizing animation, see Chapter 7, "Animating in Flash," page 109. For more details on optimizing text, see Chapter 5, "Working with Text," page 69. For more details on sound optimization, see Chapter 8, "Using Sound," page 129.*

SPECIFYING PUBLISH SETTINGS

After you complete and optimize a movie, you are ready to publish it. Publishing allows you to create multiple formats for your movie, in addition to creating an SWF file and an HTML file with the necessary code to embed your movie for display over the Internet.

To access the Publish Settings, choose File, Publish Settings, as shown in Figure 30.6.

The Publish Settings dialog box has three tabs: Formats, Flash, and HTML. On the Formats tab, you can specify alternative file formats in addition to the default SWF and HTML, as shown in Figure 30.7.

To select different formats, click in the check box next to a format. The options are Flash, HTML, GIF, JPEG, PNG, Windows Projector, Macintosh Projector, and QuickTime. Files are generated in the selected formats and are given the name of the FLA file plus the selected format extension by default. To name files individually, deselect Use Default Names and enter new ones in the appropriate fields. When a format is selected—with the exception of the projectors—a tab that you can click to specify options appears in the Publish Settings.

30

Figure 30.6
To access the Publish Settings dialog box, choose File, Publish Settings.

Figure 30.7
Alternative formats of your Flash movie can be created when the movie is published.

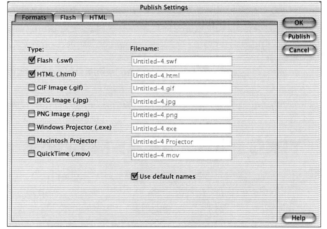

Flash

Selecting the Flash format, which is chosen by default, exports an SWF file. If you want to view the SWF on the Web, your browser must have the Flash Player installed. The Flash options, as shown in Figure 30.8, allow you to select a Player version. You can select a previous Player version, but some functionality will be lost. If your movie contains content that is not supported in previous Player versions, an alert message will appear.

The next option, Load Order, determines the order in which layers in each frame load—either Top Down or Bottom Up. This capability can be important when large files are viewed over slow modems, so you should examine your layer structure to determine which load order is best for each movie.

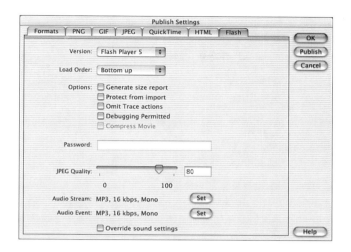

Figure 30.8
Publishing in Flash format creates an SWF.

Selecting the Generate Size Report option creates a report that details the file size of the individual elements within a movie. The Protect from Import option prevents users from downloading a movie and importing it into Flash as an editable FLA. The Omit Trace Actions option removes any trace actions in your ActionScript when a movie is published. Trace actions appear in the output window and are used for debugging.

The Debugging Permitted option enables remote debugging of Flash movies. To protect your movie, if you permit debugging, you can—and should—require a password to debug. To create and require a password, enter a password in the Password field.

If the Flash 6 Player is selected in the Version drop-down, you can choose the Compress Movie option to compress the movie. This option is selected by default when the Flash 6 Player is specified. Flash 6 compression is quite powerful and can dramatically reduce file size, especially if files are text- and script-heavy.

The JPEG Quality slider specifies compression for bitmaps. Higher settings result in higher quality but also higher file sizes. Experiment to find the best compromise between quality and file size.

For more information about compressing bitmaps, see Chapter 4, "Using Bitmaps in Flash," page 55.

To set global compression for streamed or event sounds, click the Set button next to Audio Stream or Audio Event to specify compression, bit rate, and quality. To use these settings and override any individual compression settings made in the Property Inspector for sounds, select the Override Sound Settings option.

For more details on sound compression, see Chapter 8, "Using Sound," page 129.

HTML

Flash movies must be embedded in HTML documents to be displayed within a browser. The HTML options, as shown in Figure 30.9, allow you to specify how an SWF is displayed in a browser.

30

Figure 30.9

The HTML options generate an HTML file during publishing that specifies how a movie is displayed in a browser.

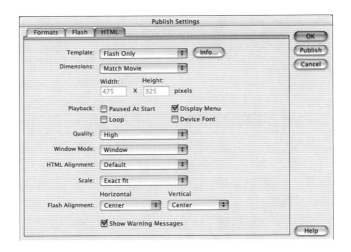

Flash creates an HTML document from a template. You can choose the template from the Template pop-up menu, as shown in Figure 30.10. The templates include detection for different versions of Flash, devices, and the inclusion of named anchors, which allow the browser Forward and Back buttons to jump to different specified frames within a movie.

Figure 30.10

Flash creates an HTML document from one of several templates.

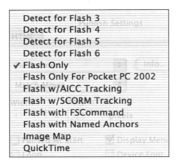

The Dimensions option specifies amounts assigned to the width and height tags that are placed within the HTML document. Match Movie matches the movie dimensions and does not allow you to manually enter amounts in the Width and Height fields. Choosing Pixels or Percentage allows you to enter numbers in the Width and Height fields, modifying the dimensions.

The Playback options control the movie's features and how it plays. By default, a movie will begin to play as soon as it downloads. Choosing Paused at Start prevents the movie from playing until the user clicks a button within the movie or chooses Play from the Player context menu. This option is deselected by default.

Loop moves the playhead back to frame 1 when the movie is finished so that it repeats. Looping is enabled by default. Choosing Device Font substitutes an antialiased system font for any fonts not installed on the user's system in blocks of static text that have been specified as a device font.

The Quality drop-down menu determines a priority for either playback or appearance. Typically, it should be left at High, which is the default. Choosing Low gives precedence to playback at the expense of quality, and turns off antialiasing. Auto Low is similar but some attempt is made to improve appearance; for example, antialiasing may be turned on if Flash determines that the user's processor can handle it. Medium applies some antialiasing but does not smooth bitmaps. Best favors appearance without factoring in playback. All text is antialiased and all bitmaps are smoothed.

For the Windows version of Internet Explorer 4.0 with Flash ActiveX control, you can select the Window mode option to specify transparency, positioning, and layering. Choose Window to display a Flash movie in its own rectangular window for the fastest animation. Opaque Windowless takes the movie out of its rectangular window and moves any HTML page elements that may be positioned behind the Flash window to prevent them from showing through any transparent areas of a Flash movie. Transparent Windowless shows any background HTML element through transparent areas of a Flash movie. This can slow animation.

HTML Alignment specifies the alignment of a movie within the browser window. Default centers the movie in the browser window and crops the movie if the browser window is smaller than the movie. Left, Right, Top, and Bottom options align the movie along the selected edge of the browser window.

Scale positions the movie within a selected area in the browser window. Default displays the movie within the designated area of the HTML document, maintaining the proportions of the movie without distortion. No Border forces the movie to fill the designated area, scaling and cropping it if necessary but maintaining the original proportions of the movie. Exact Fit forces the movie to fit the designated area, with no regard for the original proportions. No Scale prevents the movie from scaling when the browser window is resized.

Flash Alignment determines how the movie is aligned within the movie window. Use the pop-up menu beneath Horizontal to align to the left, center, or right, and the Vertical pop-up menu to align to the top, center, or bottom.

The Show Warning Messages option displays alerts if HTML tags conflict. It is selected by default.

GIF

In addition to the standard Flash and HTML formats, movies can be saved as static or animated GIFs. The GIF options are shown in Figure 30.11.

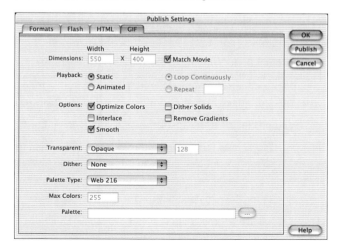

Figure 30.11
Flash movies can be saved as static or animated GIFs.

Enter dimensions in the Width and Height fields to specify dimensions for the GIF, or choose Match Movie to exactly match the movie dimensions.

Select Static or Animated for playback. If you select Static, Flash will save the first frame of the movie as a GIF. You can specify a different frame to be exported as a static GIF by assigning a frame label of #Static within the FLA.

If you select animated playback, there is an additional option to loop continuously or to specify a number of times to repeat. By default, Flash exports every frame in a movie to an animated GIF. Alternatively, you can specify a starting and ending frame for an animated GIF by assigning frame labels (#First and #Last) within the FLA.

GIFs compress images by limiting the palette of colors that are used. There are several appearance options for GIFs:

- Optimize Colors removes any unused colors from the GIF color table. This option is selected by default.

- Interlace displays a GIF incrementally in a browser as it downloads. Do not select this option for animated GIFs.

- Smooth applies antialiasing to the image. This feature can improve the appearance of an image but can also create a gray halo effect around the image if it is placed on a colored background. Smoothing also increases file size. This option is selected by default.

- Dither Solids simulates colors that are outside the GIF color table by scattering available colors.

- Remove Gradients converts any gradients to the first solid color that occurs in a gradient to reduce file size. Gradients can also display poorly in GIFs. If you select this option, be sure to choose the first gradient color carefully.

GIFs can display transparency:

- Select Opaque to display the background of a movie as a solid color.

- Choose Transparent to make the background transparent.

- Select Alpha to display partial transparency where alpha values have been specified within the movie. Enter a Threshold value between 0 and 255 to determine the degree of transparency. Lower values yield greater transparency, and 128 results in 50% transparency.

Dither options determine how colors outside the color table are represented:

- None prevents dithering and displays the nearest match within the color table for colors that aren't represented within the palette. Colors may shift dramatically, but file sizes are smaller.

- Ordered produces some dithering but restricts the scattering of colors to keep file size down.

- Diffusion produces the best dithering results by freely scattering colors to best simulate missing hues. Diffusion creates larger file sizes and can also increase processing time. It works only with the Web 216 color palette.

Palette type determines the color palette for the exported GIF:

- Web 216 uses the Web-safe color palette to create the GIF and produces the fastest processing of the image from the server.

- Adaptive analyzes the colors within the image and creates a custom palette. This option creates the most accurate colors but also the largest file size.

- Web-snap Adaptive is the same as Adaptive, except that it uses the Web-safe palette for any colors that are similar to that range.

- Custom allows you to create your own palette. Because the colors are prespecified, GIF images created from custom palettes load as quickly as those from the Web 216. You must, however, be experienced with creating color palettes to effectively use this option.

Finally, if you select an Adaptive or Web-snap Adaptive palette, you can specify the number of colors by entering a number in the Max Colors field. Specifying the number will keep file size down but can also degrade the colors in the image if the number is too low.

JPEG

Flash movies can also be saved in JPEG format as 24-bit bitmaps. This format is best for continuous-tone images such as photographs or gradients. The JPEG options are shown in Figure 30.12.

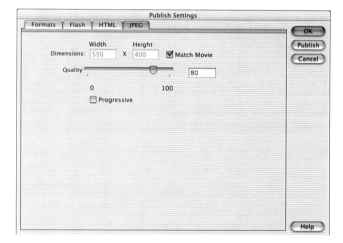

Figure 30.12
A Flash movie can be saved as a static JPEG.

As with the GIF format, the first frame of a movie is exported as a JPEG unless another frame is given the frame label #Static. You can set dimensions for the image to match the movie or can modify them by entering numbers in the Width and Height fields.

JPEG quality is set between 0 and 100, with 80 as the default. Drag the slider or type a number in the field to specify the quality. Bitmap quality can be set for individual bitmaps in the Bitmap Properties dialog box. The global setting within the Publish Settings is applied only if the individual bitmap properties are set to use default compression.

The progressive option displays JPEG images incrementally as they load.

PNG

PNG, or Portable Network Graphic, is the native file format for Macromedia Fireworks and the only cross-platform bitmap format that supports transparency. PNG options are similar to GIF options, and are shown in Figure 30.13.

Figure 30.13

Flash movies can be saved as PNGs.

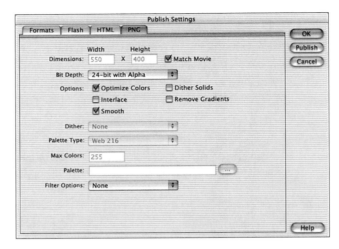

You can enter dimensions in the Width and Height fields to specify dimensions for the PNG or choose Match Movie to exactly match the movie dimensions.

PNGs compress images by limiting the color information that is mapped to images. Choose a bit depth to specify the amount of color information included per pixel:

- 8-bit to display 256 colors

- 24-bit to display thousands of colors

- 24-bit with Alpha to display thousands of colors plus transparency

The more color information that is included, the higher the file size.

PNGs have several appearance options:

- Optimize Colors removes any unused colors from the PNG color table. This option has no effect if an adaptive palette is selected.

- Interlace displays a PNG incrementally in a browser as it downloads.

- Smooth applies antialiasing and, as with GIFs, can create a halo effect against background colors when used with transparency. Smoothing also increases file size.

- Dither Solids simulates colors that are outside the PNG color table by scattering available colors.

- Remove Gradients converts any gradients to the first solid color that occurs in a gradient to reduce file size. Gradients increase file size and can display poorly in PNGs. If you select this option, be sure to choose the first gradient color carefully.

If 8-bit depth is selected, the Dither options are available to specify how colors outside the limited color table are simulated:

- None prevents dithering and displays the nearest match within the color table for colors that aren't represented within the palette. Colors may shift dramatically, but file sizes are smaller.

- Ordered produces some dithering but restricts the scattering of colors to keep file size down.

- Diffusion produces the best dithering results by freely scattering colors to best simulate missing hues. Diffusion creates larger file sizes and can also increase processing time. It works only with the Web 216 color palette.

The Palette Type defines the color palette for the exported PNG image:

- Web 216 uses the Web-safe color palette to create the PNG and produces the fastest processing of the image from the server.

- Adaptive analyzes the colors within the image and creates a custom palette. This is the best option for displaying millions of colors, or 24-bit depth. This option creates the most accurate colors but also the largest file size.

- Web-snap Adaptive is the same as Adaptive, except that it uses the Web-safe palette for any colors that are similar to that range. This is a good option for displaying colors in a 256-color system, or 8-bit depth.

- Custom allows you to create your own palette. You must, however, be experienced with creating color palettes to effectively use this option. Click the Ellipsis button to the right of the Palette box to specify a file containing a custom palette.

If you select an Adaptive or Web-snap Adaptive palette, you can specify the number of colors by entering a number in the Max Colors field. Specifying the number will keep file size down but can also degrade the colors in the image if the number is too low.

Filter Options allow you to select a filtering method to better compress the exported PNG. Filtering analyzes color information line by line:

- None turns off filtering.

- Sub transmits the difference between bytes plus the value of the corresponding byte of the previous pixel.

- Up transmits the difference between bytes plus the corresponding byte of the pixel immediately above.

- Average compares neighboring pixels to predict the value of a pixel.

- Path computes a function of neighboring pixels to predict the value of a pixel.

- Adaptive analyzes the colors within the image and creates a custom palette. This option is best used with 24-bit color, displaying thousands of colors.

Experiment with different filter settings to find the most effective compression for a particular image.

QuickTime

Flash movies can also be saved in QuickTime 4 format. All the interactivity is preserved, and Flash movies appear within QuickTime as they do within the Flash Player. Flash movies are copied to a separate QuickTime track and can be layered with other QuickTime content. The QuickTime options are shown in Figure 30.14.

Figure 30.14
Flash movies can be saved in QuickTime 4 format.

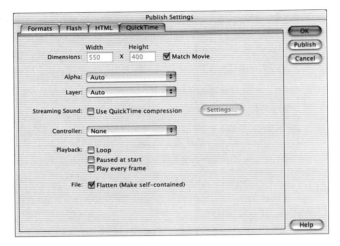

As with GIFs and JPEGs, you must specify dimensions. Select Match Movie or enter new dimensions in the Width and Height fields.

The Alpha option controls the transparency of the Flash track within QuickTime and does not affect transparency within the Flash movie:

■ Alpha-transparent makes the Flash track transparent, revealing content in tracks behind the Flash track.

■ Copy makes the Flash track opaque, obscuring any tracks that are behind it.

■ Auto sets the Flash track's transparency depending on its place in the stacking order. If it is on top of other tracks, it is transparent. If the Flash track is on the bottom of the stack or is the only track, it is opaque.

The Layer option specifies where the Flash track is placed in the stacking order: Top, Bottom, or Auto. Top places the Flash track on top of any other tracks. Bottom keeps the Flash track below any other tracks. Auto places the Flash track according to the placement of Flash objects in relation to video elements within the Flash movie. If Flash objects are on top of video elements, Auto places the Flash track on top. If Flash objects are behind video elements, Auto places the Flash track at the bottom.

The Streaming Sound option exports all streaming sounds from the Flash movie to a QuickTime sound track, recompressing them to the standard QuickTime compression settings. Click the Settings button to tweak the default QuickTime audio compression settings.

The Controller option specifies how the user can control the QuickTime movie. The options are None, Standard, and QuickTime VR.

The Playback options control how a movie is played. Loop replays the movie continuously. Paused at Start prevents the movie from playing until the user initiates play by clicking a button. Play Every Frame ensures that no frames are dropped during playback and disables sound.

The File option, which is selected by default, combines Flash content and imported video into a single QuickTime movie. This ensures that the exported QuickTime movie is self-contained and does not depend on linkage to external files.

EXPORTING DIFFERENT FILE FORMATS

The Export command allows you to create content in Flash that can be edited in other applications. To export content, choose File, Export Movie or File, Export Image, as shown in Figure 30.15.

Figure 30.15
Flash content can be exported as movies or images.

Designate a filename; then choose a file format and a destination to save to in the Export dialog box, as shown in Figure 30.16.

Figure 30.16
Flash can export to multiple file formats.

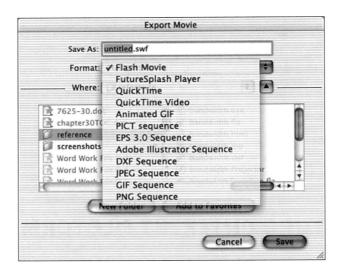

Movies are exported as sequences, and images are exported as individual files. Flash files can be exported in the following formats:

- Adobe Illustrator (.ai) is ideal for moving editable vector graphics between drawing applications. The Illustrator format preserves precise Bezier curves, lines, and fills. The import and export of Illustrator 3.0, 5.0, 6.0, and 8.0 are supported.

- The GIF (.gif) format includes animated GIFs and GIF sequences. GIF formats support images and sequences, and are best used with vector graphics and short animations.

- Bitmap (.bmp) is a Windows-only format for exporting bitmaps that can be used in other applications.

- DXF Sequence and AutoCAD DXF Image (.dfx) export vector elements that can be brought into DFX applications.

- Enhanced MetaFile (.emf) is a newer graphic format that supports vector and bitmap information in Windows 95 and Windows NT.

- EPS (.eps) enables the export of the current frame for placement in layout applications, such as Quark Express, Adobe PageMaker, and Microsoft Word.

- Flash Movie (.swf) allows the export of the entire movie for placement in applications such as Dreamweaver.

- FutureSplash Player (.spl) is the original format—and name—for Flash before it was acquired by Macromedia. The export options match the Publish Settings within Flash.

- JPEG Sequence and JPEG Image (.jpg) export bitmaps for use in other programs. See the Publish Settings described in the "JPEG" section earlier in this chapter.

- PICT (.pct) is the standard Macintosh graphics format, which supports vector and bitmap information.

- PNG Sequence and PNG Image (.png) are the only cross-platform bitmap formats that support transparency. It is also the native file format of FireWorks.

- QuickTime (.mov) can combine interactive Flash content and multimedia content of QuickTime into a single QuickTime movie that can be viewed in QuickTime 4.

- QuickTime Video (.mov) for the Macintosh converts a Flash movie into a series of bitmaps that are embedded into a QuickTime track. Interactivity is sacrificed. This option allows you to edit Flash movies in video-editing applications.

- WAV Audio (.wav) for Windows exports sound files into a single WAV audio file.

- Windows AVI (.avi) exports a movie as a Windows video. This option discards any interactivity. It is equivalent to QuickTime Video (Macintosh) but for Windows.

- Windows MetaFile (.wmf) is the standard Windows graphics format.

TROUBLESHOOTING

What's the difference between exporting a movie using the Export command and exporting a movie by testing it?

An SWF file is exported each time you test your movie (by choosing Control, Test Movie) as well as when you invoke the Export command. However, as you've just seen, the Export command is much more powerful because it supports multiple formats in addition to SWF. You will want to test a movie repeatedly during production, but will likely export to other formats only once—if at all— when a movie is complete.

Why do bitmaps and bitmap fonts look blurry when I view my SWF in a browser?

Check the Scale option within the HTML publishing settings. Be sure to specify No Scale. Allowing your SWF to scale will resize bitmaps, including bitmap fonts, and make them appear blurry. Also, be sure that you've selected High or Best for the Quality option in the HTML settings.

FLASH AT WORK: USING NAMED ANCHORS

Named anchors allow users to employ a browser's Back and Forward buttons to navigate to designated areas of a movie. Browser navigation functions as a backup to navigation systems within Flash movies. Ideally, the navigation you've designed within a movie allows users to traverse your content as needed to accomplish goals. However, named anchors enable you to bookmark frames or scenes so that the browser buttons provide some control over movie playback.

Named anchors are assigned in keyframes. To specify named anchors to a movie, follow these steps:

1. Open a completed movie.
2. Select a keyframe within the Timeline that you want to use as a named anchor.
3. Open the Property Inspector, if it isn't already open, by choosing Window, Properties or pressing Cmd-F3 (Mac) or Ctrl+F3 (Windows). Type a name in the Frame Label field.
4. Select the Named Anchor option beneath the Frame Label field in the Property Inspector, as shown in Figure 30.17.

Figure 30.17
Select the Named Anchor option in the Property Inspector to make a keyframe a named anchor.

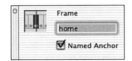

5. A named anchor icon appears in the keyframe in the Timeline, as shown in Figure 30.18. Named anchors must be selected in the publish settings to be functional. Choose File, Publish Settings and click the HTML tab. Choose the Flash with Named Anchors option in the Template pop-up menu.

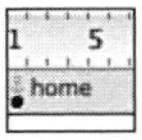

Figure 30.18
A named anchor icon designates keyframes that are named anchors.

Caution

Named anchors work only in browsers with `fscommand` support: IE on Windows and Netscape 4.

APPENDIX

MAKING FLASH ACCESSIBLE

ACCESSIBILITY GUIDELINES

Until the release of Macromedia Flash MX, Flash content had been woefully inaccessible to users who required screen readers or were hearing impaired. Now the Flash Player 6 can communicate with screen reader software and other assistive devices to convey visual content.

Screen reader software allows people with visual disabilities to use the Internet. Screen readers speak or read text, but cannot convey images or animations. Because much Flash content is inaccessible to screen readers, it's essential to make the most of the new Flash MX accessibility options.

The following five objects are defined as accessible within Flash and are passed from the Flash Player to screen reader software:

- Text
- Input text fields
- Buttons (including button movie clips)
- Movie clips
- Entire movies

Individual graphics, however, are not exposed to the screen reader. This is especially important to note with text. Any graphical text—text that has been broken apart into shapes—is not accessible, which can mean that entire navigation systems are inaccessible.

Keep this fact in mind as you design layouts and ensure that essential menu text is created with text, not shapes.

For each of the five accessible objects, Flash allows you to provide additional text descriptions—much like ALT tags in HTML—which make your content more useful and available to screen readers. The most powerful of these is the Name property, which can be assigned to objects and which will be read aloud by screen readers. You can also specify which of the Flash objects are exposed to screen readers.

To specify accessibility options for Flash objects, follow these steps:

1. Select a Flash object on the Stage.

2. In the Property Inspector, click the Accessibility button, as shown in Figure A.1, to open the Accessibility panel.

   Alternatively, you can press Opt-F2 (Mac) or Alt+F2 (Windows) to open the Accessibility panel.

Figure A.1
The Accessibility button within the Property Inspector launches the Accessibility panel.

3. Be sure that Make Object Accessible is checked and then assign a name and description within the Accessibility panel, as shown in Figure A.2.

Figure A.2
You can assign names, descriptions, and keyboard shortcuts for Flash objects within the Accessibility panel.

You can even assign a keyboard shortcut within the Accessibility panel to trigger buttons or input text fields. To do so, spell out key name abbreviations, such as Alt or Ctrl, and use a plus sign with no spaces to combine key names.

Be sure to provide names for any accessible objects. Even if an object contains content that is purely visual—such as an animated special effect—it is essential to provide an indication of the content to screen readers. If you do not, users employing assistive devices may be entirely unaware of important content or, in the case of a purely visual effect, may think they are missing vital content.

Screen reader software is currently available only on the Windows platform. Keep this fact in mind when you're creating shortcuts, and do not use Mac-specific keys such as Cmd.

When a Flash movie is complete, you must define accessibility for the entire movie for the objects you have made accessible to be exposed to the screen reader. To define accessibility for an entire movie, follow these steps:

1. When a movie is complete and ready to publish, deselect any items on the Stage and then access the Accessibility panel by clicking the Accessibility button in the Property Inspector or by choosing Window, Accessibility.

2. Select Make Movie Accessible, which is selected by default, as shown in Figure A.3. If you want to hide the movie from screen readers, deselect this option.

Figure A.3
A Flash movie must be made accessible for accessible objects to be exposed to screen readers.

3. Select Make Child Objects Accessible to expose accessible objects within the movie to screen readers.

4. Select Auto Label to use text objects as automatic labels for accessible buttons and input text fields. This option is selected by default.

5. Enter a brief, descriptive title in the Name field.

6. Enter a longer description in the Description field. Imagine that you cannot see the movie, and provide a description that will convey your content without relying upon any visual references.

Although Flash MX attempts to make content more accessible, designers and developers have to ensure that essential content can be conveyed. Take the initiative and do all that you can to make your content available for as wide an audience as possible.

INDEX

Camera.get() method, 470

capitalization
identifiers, 195
readability, code, 176-178

Cartesian coordinate systems, 92

cartoon animations, 124-125

Case Sensitive check box, 543

categories
Miscellaneous Actions, 558
variables, 190

Category Items list, 535

ceil method (Math core object), 427

center points, creating (circles), 370

centralizing code, 181, 189-190

CGI (Common Gateway Interface) scripts, 604, 608

channels, alpha channels (resizing bitmaps), 60

Character Options, button or dialog box, 80

characters
attributes, text, 73-75
blocks, distributing, 82
codes, 234
delimiter characters, array elements, 401
embedded fonts, 80
position, character attributes, 75
sets, 198
spacing (kerning), 74

charCodeAt() function, 234

Check Box component (Multiple Choice), 545

check boxes
Always Update Before Publishing, 554
Auto Label, 665
Case Sensitive, 543
Code Hints, 172

Correct, 543
Debugging Permitted, 572
Exact Match, 543
Export for ActionScript, 138, 525
Export for Runtime Sharing, 553
Export in First Frame, 138
Expression, 639
Feedback, 546
Flash (Publish Settings dialog box), 648-649
GIF (Publish Settings dialog box), 651-653
HTML (Publish Settings dialog box), 649-651
Import Audio (Import Video Settings dialog box), 160
JPEG (Publish Settings dialog box), 653
Knowledge Track, 547
Maintain Text as Blocks, 35
Make Child Objects Accessible, 665
Make Movie Accessible, 665
Make Object Accessible, 664
Number of Video Frames to Encode Per Number of Macromedia Flash Frames, 160
PNG (Publish Settings dialog box), 654-655
QuickTime (Publish Settings dialog box), 656-657
Randomize, 536
Remember, 470
Responses, 543
Show Results Page, 537
Show Tooltips, 172
Snap to Start, 541
Synchronize Video to Macromedia Flash Document Frame Rate (Import Video Settings dialog box), 160
Use Imported JPEG Data, 67

CheckBox component, 152, 514-515

child nodes, XML, 615

childNodes property (XML), 615

children
invisible children, reducing misses (movie clip overlap), 356
movie clips (tab ordering), 339

Circle class, properties, 377

circles
center points, creating, 370
drawing, 39, 376

class hierarchies
abstraction/specialization, 507-508
creating (_proto_ property), 502-506

class operand, 243

classes. *See also* movie classes; subclasses
ActionScript classes, Flash Remoting, 556
Button class (event handlers), 308
Circle class, properties, 377
Color class, transform objects, 449
components, defining, 520-523
custom classes, movie clips, 352
drawing organization, 370
information, storing, 290
inheritance, 285
init objects, 351
Java classes, Flash Remoting, 556
LocalConnection class, 560-562
methods, assigning, 282-285
MovieClip class, 308, 370
objects, 243

createElement(nodeName) command (XML), 618

createEmptyMovieClip() method, 332-333, 341

creategatewayConnection function, 557

createTextField method, 333, 461

createTextNode(nodeValue) command (XML), 618

cubic Bezier curves, 375

currentFps property (NetStream movie object), 479

_currentframe property (MovieClip property), 175, 335

cursors, mouse cursors, 452

curve points, converting, 42

Curved Fit (Trace Bitmap dialog box), 63

curves
Bezier curves, curveTo() method, 375
control handles, 42
drawing, 39-40, 374-378
modifying, 42
optimizing, 44, 64
smoothing, 44
trigonometric functions, 375

Curves, Optimize command (Modify menu), 647

curveTo drawing method, 369

curveTo() method, 374-375

Custom button, 46

custom classes, movie clips, 352

custom functions, 270, 415

custom gradients, creating, 48

custom interfaces, components, 528-530

Custom Modem Settings dialog box, 567

custom mouse pointers, creating, 319

custom objects
class hierarchies, creating, 502-506
constructor property, 499-502
event handlers, 307
inherited properties (overriding), 495-497
local properties, 490-492
OOP, 490
prototype property, 492-495
shared properties, 491
superclasses, accessing, 497-499
troubleshooting, 509-510
variables, declaring, 193

Custom option
GIF check box, 653
Palette Type, 655

custom tab ordering, 336, 339

custom windows, creating (JavaScript functions), 588-589

Customize command (Debug menu), 567

customizing
keyboard shortcuts, 30
panel layouts, 19

D

data
array literals, 210-211
constructor functions, 289
dynamic data, 603-606
embedding, HTML pages (server communications), 602-604
null value, 211
numbers and strings, versus literals, 210
object literals, 210-211
operators, 196
organizing, movie clips (reachability), 181
retrieving (get functions), 421
sending (server communications), 606-608
storing, 176, 601, 612
text data, loading, 600-602
undefined value, 211
XML data, 614-620

data containers, array core objects, 396

data conversion, 204-209

data elements, Knowledge Track, 547

data load event (sequencing), 327

data movie clip event, 320

data primitives, objects, 175

data properties, local shared objects, 596

data structures, objects, 175

DataGlue.as file, ActionScript class, 557

datatypes
ActionScript interpreters, 204
array datatype, 201, 242
Boolean datatype, 199-200
composite, 195
conversions, automatic, 234-236
function datatype, 202-203
movieclip datatype, 202
null datatype, 201
number datatype, 196-197
object datatype, 200-201, 242
primitive, 195, 500-501
string datatype, 197-199
undefined datatype, 203-204
variables, 195

external images, scripting improvements, 13

external MP3, sound (loading), 453

external sound, scripting improvements, 13

eye icon, 21

Eyedropper tool, 27

F

factoring properties, 507

fade-ins, transparency (movie clips), 447

fade-outs, transparency (movie clips), 447

false value, Boolean datatype, 199

family lines, 346-348

Fast command (View menu), 64

Fast Forward button, 163-165

Faucet modifier (Eraser tool), 27

Feedback, 546

fields. *See also* text fields
Address field, JavaScript functions, 587
Default Value, 514
dynamic text fields, troubleshooting, 85
Font field, 73
Frame Rate, 19, 113
Identifier, 138, 553
Input Text, 77, 528
Instance Name field, 104
Loop, 136
Maximum Characters field, text fields, 79
text input fields, screen reader software, 663

file extensions, .fla, 182

file formats
exporting, 657-659
imported bitmaps, 56
imported sound, 132
imported video, 158

File menu commands
Export Movie or File, Export Image, 657
File menu, 159
Import, 12, 53, 57, 163
Import to Library, 57, 132, 161
New, 113
New from Template, 535
Publish Settings, 325, 459, 572, 580, 632, 647
Publish Settings, Generate Size Report, 568

File option (QuickTime check box), 657

files
components (adding), 512
DataGlue.as file, ActionScript class, 557
existing files (Timeline), 540
importing, 53
NetDebug.as file, ActionScript class, 557
NetServices.as file, ActionScript class, 556
size, traced bitmaps, 63
sound files, size, 131
structuring (timelines), 150
SWF (ActionScript), 170
XML files, 524, 613, 619-621

Fill box, 28, 39, 47

Fill Color box, 27, 48, 448

Fill icon, 48-49

Fill in the Blank, configuring, 543

Fill Transform tool, 27

fills, 38
bitmap fills, 49
color, 39
deleting, 50

gradient fills, 48, 380-386
modifying, 47
selecting, 47
solid fills, 47-48, 379-380
troubleshooting, 387

Filter Options (PNG check box), 655

findLabel() function, 593

findLabel(frameLabel) command (Lingo), 595

Fireworks 3 (keyboard shortcut set), 30

Fireworks 4 (keyboard shortcut set), 30

Fireworks icons, creating, 525

firing
data movie clip events, 320
event handlers (troubleshooting), 328
Key events, 319
load movie clip event, 320
mouse events, 319
onLoad movie clip event, 320

firstChild property (XML), 615

.fla, Flash file extension, 182

Flash 5, 14-15, 30

Flash ActionScript Dictionary, 244

Flash Alignment option, HTML check box, 651

Flash Movie (.swf), file formats, 658

Flash Remoting, 555-557

Flash tab, 572

Flash UI Components folder, 154, 518, 545

Flash with Named Anchors command (Template menu), 33

floats, 9, 197, 223

floor() method, 427-428

gradient fills, 380-386

Gradient pointers, 48

gradients, 48, 373

Gradients (Clipboard Preferences), 34

graphic symbols, 90

graphical reports, 567

graphics. *See also* bitmaps; vector graphics
exported movie clips, 658
external images, scripting improvements, 13
screen reader software, 663

grids, 50-51

Group command (Modify menu), 38

grouping
shapes, 38
operators, 219

Guide icon, 51

guide layers, 22, 51

guidelines, 50-51

guides, 50-51, 116-118

GUIs, dynamic masks, 362

H

Hand
icon, 19
tool, 28

hand cursors, button movie clips, 323, 340

handlers. *See also* event handlers
dynamic handlers, Key events, 318
functions, components, 512
Lingo, 591
Local connection object handlers, 559
on getURL, 591

handles
control handles, 41
curve handles, 40
Envelope handles (sound), 135
text blocks, 72, 77

hanging indents, paragraph attributes, 76

hard coding, explicit scoping, 293

has relationships, versus is relationships, 507

hasAccessibility property, System.capabilities movie object, 446

hasAudio property, System.capabilities movie object, 446

hasAudioEncoder property, System.capabilities movie object, 446

hasChildNodes property (XML), 615

hash arrays (associative arrays), 399-400

hasMP3 property, System.capabilities movie object, 446

hasOwnProperty method, 416, 420

hasVideoEncoder property, System.capabilities movie object, 446

headers, control blocks, 254

height, setting (Math core object), 433-435

Height option
GIF check box, 652
PNG check box, 654
QuickTime check box, 656

_height property
MovieClip property, 335
Stage movie object, 458
text field, 463
Video movie class, 471

hexadecimal (base 16) notation, 448

hexadecimal numbers, 208

hide() method, 452

hiding
Actions Toolbox, 174
code, 181
context menu (projector control), 590
layers, 21
panels, 19

hierarchies
class hierarchies, 502-508
inheritance hierarchies, local properties (custom objects), 490-492
level hierarchies, movie clips, 346
movie clips, 341, 345
multi-generation hierarchies, 287
parent-child hierarchies, levels (visual stacking), 346
symbols, cartoon animations, 125

Highlight Color Options (General Preferences), 33

highquality property (text field), 462

hit areas
button movie clip events, 323
movie clips, 338

Hit states, 146-147

hitArea property, 335, 338

hits
movie clips (illusions), 357
multiple hits, movie clip overlap, 358

hitTest() method, 334, 354-356, 364-365

hooks, JavaScript, 581-582

horizontal guidelines, 50-51

How can we make this index more useful? Email us at indexes@quepublishing.com

NaN (not a number)
arithmetic operators, 220
strings, converting (automatic datatype conversion), 234
value, number datatype, 197

navigating
XML, 613
Web content, 150

negative numbers, bits (shifting), 230

negative settings, kerning, 74

negative shapes, 38

nested arrays, 401, 404

nested movie clips, printing, 630

nested symbols, cartoon animations, 125

nesting
conditional statements, 257
symbols, 107

NetConnection movie object, 475-481

NetDebug.as file, ActionScript class, 557

Netscape, 45, 582

NetServices functions, 557

NetServices.as file, ActionScript class, 556

NetStream movie object, 475-481

NetStream.setBufferTime method (NetStream movie object), 479

NetStreamplay() method, parameters, 479

network streams, 475

New command (File menu), 113

New Document dialog box, 535

New Folder icon, 106

New from Template command (File menu), 535

new keyword, 280-281, 287-289

New Layer
command (Insert menu), 133
icon, 133

new MovieClip() statements, 332

new operator, 200, 242
array datatype, 201
constructor property (storage), 502
proto property, 503

new statement, 350

New Symbol command (Insert menu), 144

New Video command (Library options menu), 394

nextFrame method (MovieClip method), 334

nextSibling property (XML), 615

No Color button, 28

noBorder value (scaleMode property), 459

nodeName property (XML), 615

nodes
child nodes, XML, 615
text nodes, 612
XML, 612, 617, 622

nodeType property (XML), 615

nodeValue property (XML), 615

None option
Filter Options, 655
GIF check box, 652
Palette Type, 655
PNG check box, 655

Normal
mode (Actions panel), 172-174
view, 64

noScale value (scaleMode property), 459

NOT operator (!), 237

notations, hexadecimal (base 16) notation, 448

null
datatype, 201
event handlers (disabling), 314
value, 211

Number core object, 405-410

number datatype, 196-197

Number of Video Frames to Encode Per Number of Macromedia Flash Frames check box (Import Video Settings dialog box), 160

Number return values, toString() method, 417

Number() function, 204, 207

Number.MAX VALUE, 197, 406

Number.MIN VALUE, 197, 406

Number.NaN property (wrapper classes), 406

Number.NEGATIVE INFINITY property (wrapper classes), 406

Number.POSITIVE INFINITY property (wrapper classes), 406

Number.toString method (wrapper classes), 405

Number.valueOf method (wrapper classes), 406

numbered properties, arrays, 400

numbering. *See* depth numbering

Paint Fills modifier (Brush tool), 26

Paint Inside modifier (Brush tool), 26

Paint Selection (Brush tool), 26

painting, Brush tool, 43

pairing, dynamic masks, 362

Palette Type option (PNG check box), 655

palettes, Web-safe color palette, 45, 73

Pan(x, y, mode) function (JavaScript), 584

Panel drop-down menu commands, Enable Remote Debugging, 573

Panel Sets
    command (Window menu), 19
    Default Layout command (Window menu), 170
    Property Inspector, 18

panels, 18-19
    Accessibility, 14, 664-665
    Actions panel, 163, 170-174, 558, 638
    ActionScript Reference panel, 13
    Advanced Effect panel, 449
    Align panel, 51, 121
    Color Mixer, 39
    Component Parameters panel, 528, 536, 542-544
    Components panel, 11, 153, 512, 518, 525
    docking, 19
    hiding, 19
    Instructions panel, quiz template parameters, 536
    interface improvements, 8
    layouts, customizing, 19
    Learning Interactions, 540
    Library panel, 162, 518-519, 548, 552-554

Movie Explorer, 182
Swatches panel, 48
troubleshooting, 36

panes, Script, 173

panning, cartoon animations, 124

paragraphs, 75-77

parameters. *See also* properties
    arguments, 590
    called functions, 290
    command, 590
    components, 513
    Editable, 153
    JavaScript, 583
    length parameter, NetStreamplay() method, 479
    lineStyle() method, 371
    loadSound() method, 454
    me (Lingo), 591
    menu, 590
    movie communications, 597
    movie parameter, 602
    OBJECT parameter, troubleshooting, 608
    passing, 353-354, 592
    quiz templates, 536-537
    send command, 607
    sendAndLoad command, 607
    Square class, 374
    src, 602
    start parameter, NetStreamplay() method, 479
    startDrag() method, 360
    target parameters, 585
    Target TextField, 518
    TextFormat class, 467

parent methods, super operator, 498

parent properties, overriding (subclasses), 495

_parent property, 335, 463

_parent special target, 579

parent-child
    hierarchies, 345-348
    relationships, 285, 341

parentheses (), 219, 283

parentheses/function call operator, 245

parentNode property (XML), 615

parsefloat() function, 207

parseInt() function, 207

parsing, XML data, 614-617, 620

passing
    arguments, 273
    information (arguments), 272-278
    parameters, 353-354, 592

password property (text field), 463

Paste Keyframes command, 112

Path option (Filter Options), 655

paths
    curves, 41
    defined, 372
    lines, 40, 371
    sinuous, 437

pause method (NetStream movie object), 477

pausing movies, 590

Pen tool, 25, 39, 117
    anchor points (adjusting), 41
    curves (drawing), 40
    lines (drawing), 40
    segments (adjusting), 42-43

Pencil, 22, 25, 39

PercentLoaded() function (JavaScript), 584

percentStreamed command (Lingo), 595

percentStreamed property, 592

How can we make this index more useful? Email us at indexes@quepublishing.com

screenResolutionY property, System.capabilities movie object, 446

screens, results or welcome, 537

Script pane, 173

scripts
CGI (Common Gateway Interface), 604, 608
comments (adding), 177
improvements, 12-13
learning interactions, 547
Perl, troubleshooting, 608
trace action, 572

scroll property (text field), 464

Scrollbar, 152, 518

scrollbars, TextFormat movie class, 469-470

scrolling text boxes, 517

ScrollPane component, 152

scrubbing animations, 123

Seconds button, 136

sections, content sections (movies), 150

security, data text (loading), 601

seek method (NetStream movie object), 478

segments, adjusting, 42-43

Select Named Anchor on Scenes (General Preferences), 33

selectable property (text field), 464

Selectable Text button, 79

selecting
anchor points, 41
bitmaps, 25, 65
fills, 47
keyframes, 33
objects (Arrow tool), 24
text, 81

selection events, 324

Selection object, 324, 452-453

Selection Options (General Preferences), 32

_self special target, 579

semicolon (;), 218, 252

send command, 607, 620

send() method, 478, 481-482

sendAndLoad command, 607, 620

sending
data (server communications), 606-608
messages
browser to Flash, JavaScript functions, 583-586
browser to Flash to browser, JavaScript functions, 586
Director, 591
Flash to browser, JavaScript functions, 582-583
Lingo (Director), 591-592
Lingo to Flash (Director), 592-594
local connections, 561-562
XML documents, servers, 620-621

sendToFlash function (JavaScript), 584

separating, layers (text blocks), 82

sequencing
actions, 327
animations, 110
exported movie clips, 658

serif typeface, 80, 84

server modules, 475

Server-Inf directory, Java classes (Flash Remoting), 556

server-side includes, 603-604

servers
communications, 600-608
multiple platform testing (troubleshooting), 566
service calls, Flash Remoting, 557
variables, loading, 602
XML, 620-621

serverString property, System.capabilities movie object, 447

service calls, Flash Remoting, 557

service objects, service calls (Flash Remoting), 557

services, remote services (connecting), 555

set
functions, 421-423
methods, troubleshooting, 509
routines, defining classes (components), 522-523
statement, 188, 253

Set button, 524, 532, 649

setFlashProperty() function, 593

setFlashProperty(target, property, value) command (Lingo), 595

setGain method (Microphone movie class), 474

setInterval() global function (calling functions), 358-359

setKeyFrameInterval method (Camera movie class), 472

setLoopback method (Camera movie class), 472

setMask() method, 334, 362

setMode method (Camera movie class), 472

setMotionLevel method (Camera movie class), 472

How can we make this index more useful? Email us at indexes@quepublishing.com

How can we make this index more useful? Email us at indexes@quepublishing.com

How can we make this index more useful? Email us at indexes@quepublishing.com

MACINTOSH INSTALLATION INSTRUCTIONS

1. Insert the CD-ROM disc into your CD-ROM drive.

2. When an icon for the CD appears on your desktop, open the disc by double-clicking on its icon.

3. Double-click on the icon named Guide to the CD-ROM, and follow the directions that appear.

Technical Support from Pearson

We can't help you with Windows or Macintosh problems or software from third parties, but we can assist you if a problem arises with the CD-ROM itself.

WHAT'S ON THE DISC

The companion CD-ROM contains many useful third-party tools and utilities, plus the source code and JavaScript samples from the book.

If Windows 95 is installed on your computer, and you have the AutoPlay feature enabled, the START.EXE program starts automatically whenever you insert the disc into your CD-ROM drive.

WINDOWS 95 INSTALLATION INSTRUCTIONS

1. Insert the CD-ROM disc into your CD-ROM drive.

2. From the Windows 95 desktop, double-click on the My Computer icon.

3. Double-click on the icon representing your CD-ROM drive.

4. Double-click on the icon titled START.EXE to run the installation program.

WINDOWS NT INSTALLATION INSTRUCTIONS

1. Insert the CD-ROM disc into your CD-ROM drive.

2. From File Manager or Program Manager, choose Run from the File menu.

3. Type *<drive>*\START.EXE and press Enter, where *<drive>* corresponds to the drive letter of your CD-ROM. For example, if your CD-ROM is drive D:, type D:\START.EXE and press Enter.